THE SOUTH

in American History

SECOND EDITION

BY

WILLIAM B. HESSELTINE
Department of History
University of Wisconsin

AND

DAVID L. SMILEY
Department of History
Wake Forest College

❊ ❊ ❊ ❊ ❊

Englewood Cliffs, N.J.

PRENTICE-HALL, INC.

The South in American History
(Formerly *A History of the South*)

© 1936, 1943, 1960 by
PRENTICE-HALL, INC.
Englewood Cliffs, N.J.

Library of Congress Catalog Card No. 60-6880

Printed in the United States of America
8 2 3 8 1 - C

Fourth Printing.........March, 1966

To

ARTHUR CHARLES COLE

Preface

ORIGINALLY published as *A History of the South* in 1936, this book —designed as a synthesis of the South's role in American history and as a synopsis of developments in the Southern regions of the United States—was revised in 1943 under the present title. In the present edition, the authors have especially concentrated on reorganizing and expanding the treatment from the end of reconstruction to the middle decade of the Twentieth Century. The theme of the volume remains the same: the South is American, its problems have been the nation's, its social adjustments have been reflections of national society, its politics have found their orientation about the federal government, and its economics has been an integral part of the national economy.

The United States is a congeries of regions, in each of which men of different traditions, outlooks, ways of life, and interests have sometimes vied with each other, sometimes cooperated with one another to control their regions. The story of the Southern regions, and of the differing traditions of the men who have dwelt in them, is a vital part of the American story.

Much of the revision, and much of the drudgery of typing, proofreading, and indexing has fallen upon David L. Smiley, who has consented to appear as co-author and thus to share the responsibility for the errors of fact and interpretation which, despite the advice and admonition of friends and critics, still remain.

The two dozen years which have elapsed since this book first appeared have been marked—as some of the items in the final chapter indicate— by a tremendous resurgence in Southern scholarship and by fresh investigations into aspects of Southern history. The Southern Historical Association, *Journal of Southern History*, new vigor in state historical magazines, and the growth of strong university presses in the South have increased the bibliography of Southern history to unmanageable proportions. Partly because usable guides to Southern writings are readily available, and partly to save space for new matter, we have dispensed with the conventional "selected bibliographies" at the ends of chapters.

Friendly advice and helpful criticism on earlier revisions came from Fred H. Harrington, Kenneth M. Stampp, T. Harry Williams, George Winston Smith, Richard N. Current, E. Bruce Thompson, Frank Freidel, Charlton W. Tebeau, Frank W. Prescott, and Carl Wittke. In addition to these, the authors are indebted to Steven Ambrose, Clement L. Silvestro, Frank N. Byrne, Larry Gara, Horace S. Merrill, Richard D. Younger,

v

George R. Woolfolk, John F. Stover, William T. Hagan, William D. Miller, Philip J. Staudenraus, Clifford Griffin, Gordon Parks, Bruce Robinson, Mary Dearing, William F. Thompson, Roman J. Zorn, William Russell, and Jefferson D. Bragg, who have clarified their views on many points.

For assistance in obtaining photographs and permission to use them as illustrations, the authors are grateful to President F. P. Gaines of Washington and Lee University, Vice-Chancellor Alexander Guerry of the University of the South, Miss Josephine Cobb and Mr. C. J. Laughrin of the National Archives, Mr. George A. Grant of the National Parks Service, and Mr. Roy Stryker of the Photographic Division, Office of War Information, U. S. Tennessee Valley Authority, U. S. Atomic Energy Commission, and Esso Standard Oil Company (N. J.).

WILLIAM B. HESSELTINE

DAVID L. SMILEY

Contents

CHAPTER 1

Planting the Southern Colonies

1. The American South

IN Stephen Vincent Benét's epic poem, "John Brown's Body," a Connecticut boy ponders, in 1860, about the mysterious South. To him it was a languorous land where grinning Topsies and obsequious Uncle Toms stood beneath each honeysuckle vine; where every white man was a gentleman, born to the manor, and every white woman a lady. Fields of cotton covered the land; banjo-strumming darkies made music in the evenings; Spanish moss festooned the great oak trees; the rivers were all named Suwanee; and the sun really shone all the time. The men sipped incessantly at mint juleps, and the girls were paragons of beauty. All of the houses were mansions with white pillars.

Such a picture of the South is a part of American folklore, shared by Northerners and Southerners alike. Writers of fiction, publishers of popular songs, and venders of pancake mixes have combined to keep the picture fresh in the national imagination. The influence of such popular tradition cannot be gainsaid: it has permeated the national consciousness, causing Southerners to model their conduct and their conversation to conform to the traditional pattern, and causing Northerners to approach southern problems as if the South were the unified area which folklore has portrayed.

The existence of the tradition has led to a perennial search for a "central theme" of southern history. Some who have searched have believed that the answer lay in the plantation system, with its slave labor and its devotion to the staple crops. The South, said one writer, was a

1

great "fabric of cotton." Commentators of a more mystical trend of thought have contended that the soil and the pastoral life have permeated the southern character. In the Old South, they saw a happy land, peopled by simple, yet extremely wise, men and women. Possessed of souls made great by living close to Mother Earth, the southern people practiced a gracious way of life, cultivated good manners, and radiated individual honor and worth. Still other writers have felt that the unifying principle of southern history has been the Negro, whether slave or free, whose presence bound the whites of the South into a homogeneous whole. The determination of the white race to maintain its dominance united the Old South in the defense of slavery and unites the New South in a complex system which still reserves the land for the whites.

Although such explanations of the South contain large measures of truth, they oversimplify the problem by placing too much emphasis on the similarities in southern society and neglecting the differences. The South is a land of diversity. In the vast area between the Chesapeake and the Rio Grande, regions differed widely in cultural and social development, in political philosophy, and in economic activities. The differences between regions of old establishment and frontier regions, between regions of cotton and corn and regions of tobacco, or rice, or sugar, between city and country, between coastal plain and mountain, have been greater in the South than in any other part of the nation. In racial elements, the gap between Anglo-Saxon and African in the South was greater than the gap between the Puritan and the Irish in New England or between the English and the Dutch in colonial New York. In economic status, far less division existed between merchant princes and common laborers in the North than between the great planter and the slave in the South. The tradition that pictured the South as a homogeneous whole represented an ideal rather than a reality.

Yet, amid the diversity, certain characteristics of the South have united the area. The most important of these characteristics has been the predominance of agriculture. Climate, soil, and physical features long combined to make the southern regions centers of agriculture rather than of industry and commerce. The institutions of the South thus became adapted to an agricultural society; and even after commerce and industry came to absorb a large portion of attention, the social patterns of an agricultural world continued to shape the mind and to influence the development of the section. Geography, therefore, was the primary factor in producing the social and economic phenomena of the South.

Comprised in the South are a number of physiographic regions. Along the Atlantic Coast is the low, ofttimes marshy, pine-grown Tidewater. This region extends from 100 to 200 miles back to the fall line of the rivers. Parts of Virginia and Maryland and larger portions of the Carolinas and Georgia are in the Tidewater. Bays break the seacoast of the Tidewater, and harbors are plentiful. The wide rivers that traverse the region flow slowly and are navigable up to the fall line. The soil, although always thin, was rich when the first settlers came. In this region were planted the first settlements of the English colonies.

The Gulf Coast stretches northward from the Gulf of Mexico and is similar in character to the Tidewater region. Most of Alabama, Mississippi, and Louisiana are in the Gulf Coast region, while Florida, a peninsula dividing the Gulf from the Atlantic Ocean, possesses the same characteristics. The soil cannot compare with the richest soils of the Ohio Valley, but the rainfall and the temperature have especially adapted the region to the production of cotton.

West of the Tidewater region are the southern extensions of the Appalachian highlands. The eastern slope, which borders on the Tidewater, is known as the Piedmont Plateau. Higher than the Tidewater, its contour is more rolling, its numerous rivers and streams less navigable, and its soil much richer. The Piedmont was suited to become a land of diversified farming, where crops of wheat and corn might compete with the staple products that dominated the other areas.

Beyond the Piedmont are the Blue Ridge Mountains, whose peaks in North Carolina reach to 6,000 feet above sea level. Pine covered and comparatively infertile, the Blue Ridge acted as a barrier to cut off the Great Valley from the eastern part of the Atlantic states. The Great Valley lay between the Blue Ridge and the Allegheny Mountains. The Valley was, in fact, a series of valleys, known as the Shenandoah Valley, the Valley of Virginia, and the Tennessee Valley. The soil of the valleys was the richest in the South, and their crops of wheat and corn, of cattle and hogs, made them the granaries of the cotton and tobacco areas. West of the valleys were the Allegheny and the Cumberland Mountains, similar to the Blue Ridge but rich in minerals which were scarcely developed before the close of the Civil War. West of the mountains stretched the Cumberland Plateau, a counterpart of the Piedmont, broken only by the fertile basins of the Tennessee and the Kentucky Blue Grass regions. The Valley of the Mississippi lay beyond the plateau and merged with the Ohio Valley on the north and the Gulf Coast on the south.

Although the physical features of the South were diverse, many of the geographical characteristics were common. The soil was not of the best, but soil and climate together made possible the production of cotton, tobacco, rice, and sugar, the staple crops of the South. The annual rainfall was heavy, and the direct rays of the sun spared the whole region from the colder blasts of winter and gave Florida and the Gulf Coast a semitropical climate. Large forests of white and yellow pine produced tar, turpentine, and even masts and spars for ships in the colonial period. Wild game was plentiful, and furs and skins furnished a readily exploited natural resource in the first days of settlement.

Within these physiographic regions, southern society developed— a society that took its form from the geographic character of the land. Just as the good harbors and the barren soil of New England invited men to seek the sea, so the climate, the soil and the contours of the land invited those who settled the South into agriculture. Land ownership became the active force which divided southern society into classes, making "planter aristocrats" of those who possessed large tracts of the better lands and "yeomen farmers" and "poor whites" of those who owned or rented smaller portions of less productive soil. In a society where land was the criterion of social status, it was inevitable that the non-owning, laboring class should be dependent upon the owners. Social stratification in the South, from Jamestown to the Industrial Revolution, was based upon the ownership of land. By law the slave was excluded from possessing property; by definition the great planters were those who owned much land. In between were the masses of the yeomen and the poor whites whose position in society was primarily determined by the acreage they owned and tilled.

Southern society first assumed its basic characteristics along the Tidewater. By the close of the seventeenth century, the division of society into clearly defined classes had taken form. Thereafter, as the western movement pushed men out into the Piedmont, the Valley, the Cumberland Plateau, the Mississippi Delta, and even to the edge of the Texas plains, each new region recreated the social pattern of the old. In the end, the South was a series of physiographic regions, given over to agriculture, and occupied by a population stratified by land ownership.

2. THE GENESIS OF VIRGINIA

Southern society was the product of English traditions modified by American conditions. Although both Spaniards and French explored and planted settlements in the South, it was the English who eventually established their type of civilization in the southern regions. For a century after John Cabot sailed along the shores of North America and claimed the land, England gave little attention to the profits to be drained from colonies. Meanwhile, the Spaniards gathered to themselves the accumulated riches of the Incas and the Aztecs and flooded the Iberian peninsula with gold and silver from the Americas. Eventually English cupidity, properly cloaked in political and religious zeal, turned to the almost holy task of plundering the precious caravels of the Spanish Main. Captain John Hawkins, patriot and Protestant, varied the usual procedure by flaunting the Spanish trade laws and carrying cargoes of Guinea Negroes to sell in the Spanish colonies. Equally religious, equally unscrupulous, and even more patriotic was Sir Francis Drake, who plundered Spanish settlements as well as ships.

First interested in the possibilities of exploiting the New World by the adventures of these daring sea dogs, Englishmen soon turned their attention to less dangerous and more certain schemes of commercial development. Drake had envisioned the settlement of English colonies in America as rivals of the Spanish colonies, and the publication in England of Hakluyt's *Principall Navigations, Voyages, and Discoveries of the English Nation* popularized the idea. In 1583, Sir Humphrey Gilbert made an unsuccessful effort to establish a colony on the coast of Newfoundland, and the next year Sir Walter Raleigh obtained letters patent from Queen Elizabeth to establish colonies in the land already named Virginia. Discouraged by hardships and the failure to find treasure, Raleigh's first colony, which had settled on Roanoke Island, returned to England. In 1587 the undismayed Raleigh sent out another colony of 150 settlers to take up the work at Roanoke. The next year Spain, through its Invincible Armada, attempted an invasion of England and diverted the attention of all Englishmen. Roanoke was neglected until 1591, when another expedition, landing on the island, discovered that the settlers had disappeared without a trace. The single word "Croatan," the name of a neighboring tribe of Indians, carved into the bark of a tree, was the only clue to their end. Generations of romantic antiquarians have bemused themselves in futile speculations on the mysterious fate of the settlers.

Despite the failure of Raleigh's experiment, the dream of a colony in the New World soon reappeared among Englishmen. Conditions within the island kingdom contributed to colonial expansion. From the time of John Cabot to that of the Jamestown settlement, the basis of England's economic life had slowly shifted from feudalism to commercialism. The War of the Roses, followed by the semi-parliamentary rule of the Tudors, definitely broke the political hold of the feudal nobleman. In his place, as the controlling force of British politics, the the businessman of the middle class rose to power. The breakup of the monasteries under Henry VIII, the plundering of the Spanish under Elizabeth, and the policy of aiding the commercial classes pursued by all of the Tudors resulted in the accumulation of more fluid wealth. In Parliament, representatives of the merchant classes legislated for the benefit of commerce. In the towns, an increase of handmade goods supplied a surplus for an overseas market and inspired the merchants to carry British goods to the corners of the earth. In the country, the shift from the self-sufficient manor of medieval feudalism to the enclosure of great tracts of land for wool production marked an agricultural and social revolution. Capitalistic landlords supplanted the lords of the manor, and bleating sheep grazed over the fields once tilled by sturdy yeomen and serfs. Victims of the transition from feudal establishment to commercial chaos, these erstwhile tillers of the soil crowded into the cities, where they sank into a poverty cursed by vice and disease. The merchants, who were looking for new economic worlds to conquer, did not overlook this potential labor supply for their colonies. The promoters of American colonies were men of wealth who expected commercial monopolies and feudal estates to increase their wealth. They transferred to the New World their own aristocratic concepts and continued in America the class distinctions and much of the social strife of old England.

Fluid capital, brought into service by the new device of the joint-stock company, enabled the British merchants to expand. Building upon the foundation of the Merchant Adventurers, who had co-operated in trading expeditions, a number of joint-stock companies arose. The Muscovy Company, the Prussian Company, and the East India Company were prominent examples of trading companies that combined the advantages of limited liabilities and great profits. To encourage such companies, the government granted them extensive monopolies, trading privileges, and the power of local government over the non-Christian areas in which they traded.

3. VIRGINIA UNDER THE LONDON COMPANY

Such a company was the London Company, licensed by James I in 1606, "to make Habitation, Plantation, and to deduce a colony of sundry of our People into that Part of *America,* commonly called VIRGINIA. . . ." To the knights, gentlemen, merchants "and other Adventurers" of the company was given the right to establish a plantation between the thirty-fourth and forty-first parallels of north latitude, together with "all the Lands, Woods, Soil, Grounds, Havens, Ports, Rivers, Mines, Minerals, Marshes, Waters, Fishings, Commodities and Hereditaments . . . directly into the main land by the space of one hundred like English miles." Rights of government, however, were reserved by the crown, which set up in England a Council for Virginia with power to appoint local councils in the colony. To this local council the charter gave almost complete control over the settlers, a control limited solely by the provision that laws might not endanger life or limb or be contrary to the laws of England.

Although the founders of the London Company never formulated their full intentions, and although they talked much of building outposts of England to combat the Spaniards or to convert the Indians, neither the company nor the settlers of Jamestown contemplated a colony in the modern sense. Instead, all had in mind a trading post which, though it would be partly self-sufficient, would trade for the benefit of the company. Certainly the settlers themselves could have had little intention of making permanent homes in the Virginia wilderness. In the popular literature of the day, Virginia was a land "where gold and silver is more plentiful than copper is with us," where the sands of the shores were precious jewels and the mountains were of bright stones. Jealously his royal majesty, James I, reserved to himself his feudal right to one fifth of the precious metals that might be discovered. With the legends of the Spanish *conquistadores* in mind, the settlers at Jamestown did not expect to linger long at the fountainhead of their riches.

The company's instructions to the governors of the Jamestown plantation show that the company itself had little except riches in mind. The 120 colonists who left England in December, 1606, bore instructions to establish a single fortified post near the coast to be used as a base for expeditions to trade with the natives, to search for gold, and to find a northwest passage to the Pacific Ocean. In the meantime, the company expected the settlers to cultivate the soil and provide themselves with a livelihood. The absence of women in the first settlement indicated that the "colony" was no more than a trading post.

From the very beginning, the emigrants to Virginia suffered hardships. The long and dangerous ocean voyage took the lives of 16 of the original company, and only 104 men and boys landed in Virginia. Among the arrivals, one third bore the technical denomination "gentlemen," and the others were artisans and laborers. Of the leading men, no one had had experience with the management of far-off enterprises of a similar nature. However physically fit they may have been, ignorance and inexperience made them unprepared for an adventure in pioneering. Long before the three ships landed their passengers in the New World, violent factional quarrels had broken out between Captain John Smith and Edward Maria Wingfield.

National Park Service

HERE, AT JAMESTOWN, THEY LANDED. The land which lay before the settlers charmed them with its beauty. It was the spring of the year, and the flower-strewn forest was alive with color. "Heaven and earth," exclaimed Captain John Smith, "never agreed better to frame a place for man's habitation."

On April 26, 1607, four months after leaving England, Captain Christopher Newport's three ships arrived in Virginia. After they landed, Newport opened sealed instructions from the council in England which revealed that seven of the colonists were designated the "Council in Virginia." Responsible to the council in England for the government of the colony and to the London Company for the expected profits, the Virginia council's task was rendered no easier by the factional dissensions among them. A vote of the councilors made Wingfield president of the council, and John Smith, released from the irons in which he had been placed, took a seat among the governors of the plantation.

The land which lay before the settlers charmed them with its beauty. It was the spring of the year, and the flower-strewn forest was alive with color. Berries glistened invitingly from the bushes, and the streams ran crystal clear. "Heaven and earth," exclaimed Captain John Smith, "never agreed better to frame a place for man's habitation."

Deluded by the natural beauty of their surroundings, the council ignored the sound advice given by the London Company. The company had instructed the colonists to select some point upon a navigable river, not densely wooded, and on a high point, free from marshes and swamps. Instead, the council settled upon a peninsula thirty miles up the James River, in a densely wooded section near a mosquito-infested swamp.

Here at Jamestown, on May 14, they landed and immediately proceeded to work. Some set to building a triangular, stockaded fort, others to building houses and planting gardens, and still others to cutting clapboards in order that Newport might carry a merchantable commodity back to England. Newport himself set out on an exploring expedition up the James River. During his absence, the neighboring Indians, members of a confederacy of 34 tribes under the rule of Wahunsonacock, the Powhatan, attacked the post. Moreover, dissensions continued among the leading men of the colony, and when Newport sailed for England in June with his cargo of sassafras and clapboards, the colonists were on the verge of mutiny against Wingfield.

Added to dissension and the Indians, disease came to destroy the colonists. August brought malaria and famine to the little settlement, and death reaped a harvest. "There were never Englishmen left in a foreign country in such miserie as we were in this new discovered Virginia," bemoaned one of the sufferers. "If there were conscience in men it would make their hearts bleed to hear the pitiful murmurings and outcries of our sick men without reliefe, every night and daye for the space of six weekes: in the morning their bodies being trailed out of their cabines like Dogges, to be buried." After eight months of such existence, only 38 of the original 104 settlers were alive. In September the council deposed Wingfield, and plots and conspiracies marked the turbulent winter. Captain Smith became treasurer of the colony—a position which demanded that he furnish supplies to the settlers. Expeditions among the Indians resulted in a temporary peace and some supplies of corn. But starvation and malaria swept away one after another of the settlers. In January, 1608, Newport returned with the "first supply" from England and 70 more colonists to eat the scarce food and die from the unaccustomed malaria.

Newport's conduct made it apparent that the company still had no idea of establishing a colony in Virginia. During his stay, he diverted the labors of the men from raising food and providing shelter to another effort to collect a cargo for the English market. In the meantime Jamestown burned, and the labor spent in rebuilding it could ill be spared from the growing of foods. Soon after Newport left, another ship came from the company with 40 more mouths to feed upon the scanty supply, and in September Newport was back with a "second supply" and 70 passengers, who raised the total population of the death-ridden post to 120. The inadequate conception of the problem confronting them was evident in the new instructions which Newport carried. He was to find a gold mine, search for survivors of Raleigh's "lost colony," and locate the northwest passage to the South Sea! Months were diverted from useful employment on these futile undertakings.

That the colony of Virginia did not completely collapse was due in no small measure to the energy and ability of Captain John Smith. A soldier of fortune who had fought against the Turks, been enslaved by them, and escaped in a series of thrilling exploits which lost nothing in his recitation of them, Smith was the best-fitted man in the Virginia plantation to cope with the exigencies of pioneering. Thanks to his efforts, the Indians made peace and traded maize to the starving colony. Once, according to his own unsupported account, he was saved from violent death by the intercession of Pocahontas, daughter of the Powhatan. Whatever the facts of this story may be, there is no doubt that Smith, more than any other man in Virginia, grasped the problem of the settlement. When Newport returned to London after the "second supply" in December, 1608, he carried a cargo of pitch, tar, and iron ore for the company's coffers. In addition, he bore a report of Smith, new president of the council, to the company. "It were better," Smith told the London Company, "to give £500 a ton for pitch, tar, and the like in the settled countries of Russia, Sweden, and Denmark than send for them hither till more necessary things be provided . . . for, in overtaxing our weake and unskillful bodies to satisfie this desire of present profit, we can scarcely recover ourselves from one supply to another."

Smith's letter was not needed to convince the company that all was not well with Virginia. Various explanations were offered in England, the most common being that Jamestown had been settled by "idle spendthrifts" who could not be expected to work. But more generally it was thought that the government of the colony needed to be remedied. Were it brought more closely under the control of the company, difficulties might be overcome. Accordingly the company launched a campaign to obtain both a new charter and new subscriptions to its depleted capital stock. It published pamphlets setting forth its prospects in none too realistic colors, enlisted the forensic abilities of leading clergymen, and got under way an elaborate promotion campaign.

On May 23, 1609, the king yielded to pressure and issued a new charter to the "Treasurer and Company of Adventurers and Planters of the City of London for the first colony in Virginia."

By the new charter, the company received control over 200 miles of seacoast on either side of Old Point Comfort with the interior country "up into the land, throughout from sea to sea, west and northwest." By the charter, too, the government of the company should be transferred albeit gradually, into the hands of the company itself. A treasurer and a council were to preside over the company's destinies, and to "correct, punish, pardon, govern, and rule" the settlers in Virginia. By a modification of the charter in 1612, the stockholders, meeting in quarterly "courts," were given complete control over the company.

During the first years of the Virginia experiment the company had slowly come to perceive that Virginia would not be a success as a trading post, or as an exploring base, or as a mining camp. Under the new charter, the company combined the ideas of a plantation and a colony. Shares of stock sold for £12 10s., and clerks, knights, and nobles of London became members of the company. Emigrants to Virginia were accounted stockholders—"adventurers of the person" as distinct from "adventurers of the purse." These migrants were to labor for the company on its plan-tation for seven years, at the end of which time the "planters" were to become free and were to receive a dividend of one hundred acres of land. Thus the Jamestown plantation would become a colony, and the company would derive its profits both from its own "particular plantations," which it would continue to work with its servants, and from trade with the "planters." An annual quitrent of two shillings per one hundred acres would further swell the coffers of the confident London adventurers.

Still as a plantation—since the colony was postponed for seven years—the company went to work on the labor problem. New money gave fresh impetus to the task, and by June, 1609, nine ships with five hun-dred emigrants were ready to sail. Included in the number—and complete evidence of the change of intentions—were one hundred women and children. The number of emigrants, however, was more impressive than was their character. Not only did they share the Englishman's general ineptitude for the new conditions, but they were personally less desirable than the earlier settlers had been. "Unruly gallants" they were, said Smith, who were sent to Virginia to escape a worse fate at home.

With this "third supply" the company had sent Lord Delaware to act as governor of the colony. But Delaware delegated his authority to Sir Thomas Gates, who was shipwrecked on the Bermudas and was months in arriving at his destination. In the interval, the colony con-tained not one strong man, for Smith, injured by an explosion and weary of the constant bickerings of the councilors, had returned to England. His contributions had been made to the colony. He had kept the settle-ment in existence and had pointed out to the company the possibility of developing an agricultural colony from a trading post. In a sense, he was the father of the plantation system with its disciplined and regi-mented labor, its self-sufficiency, and its attention to the production of a marketable surplus. Back in England he added the work of historian to his other exploits and, in writing his *True Relation* and a later and larger *General H'story of Virginia*, earned for himself clear title to the claim of being the father of American history.

The colonists fared badly without Smith's guiding hand. The Indians, who had been kept under control by the shrewd captain, now became hostile and murdered wandering Englishmen or slaughtered and drove off their cattle and hogs. As the savages refused to trade, the colonists, who were too many to be supported by the scanty supply in the company's storehouses, faced starvation. The ensuing winter passed into Virginia annals as the "Starving Time," during which men ate their chickens, their dogs, and even snakes and rats. As the pangs of hunger drove them into the outstretched arms of death, one man cast his Bible into the flames, exclaiming in anguish, "There is no God!"

Meanwhile Gates, with the better element of the 1609 caravel, had gone aground on the abandoned coast of the Bermudas. Here wild fruits hung from the trees, and wild hogs ranged the islands. After a winter spent among scenes that contrasted strangely with those being enacted in Virginia, Gates set forth for Virginia in two newly built boats that were loaded with pork.

In May, 1610, Gates arrived to find a miserable handful of people still alive. Sixty dejected wretches staggered to the shore to fall greedily upon the provisions he had brought. Jamestown had fallen in ruins: the gates were off their hinges; the church was in ashes; the food in the storehouses would last but 16 days at starvation rations. Gates saw nothing to do but to abandon the place, and, loading the survivors on his ship, he left Virginia only a step ahead of the grim reaper. But as the colonists were sailing out of the mouth of the James, they met Delaware, with a fresh "supply," and, despite the hardships of the "Starving Time," they turned back.

As governor, Delaware organized a council, rebuilt the church, and erected new forts. The new governor established himself with pomp and ruled harshly, but he brought a degree of order to the plantation. In less than a year, however, he returned to England, leaving Sir Thomas Dale as "High Marshal" of Virginia.

To the task of governing the Jamestown plantation, Dale brought the experience and habits of mind of an army officer. Soon he established discipline among the turbulent colonists. Given full power over the lives of the company's laboring force, Dale administered the plantation with a harshness that proved valuable as a preparation for the future. Failure to attend church he punished by death, and he broke men on the wheel or hanged them for trivial infractions of his martial law. A blasphemer had a bodkin thrust through his tongue and was tied to a tree until he died. Dale regulated the lives of the laborers as he would have regulated an army camp.

In two respects, however, Dale brought about a better regime in the colony. Through craft and a display of force he overawed the Indians, and he kidnapped Pocahontas to make sure that the Powhatan would preserve the peace. Also, he modified the labor system of the colony, assigning to each of the settlers a plot of land upon which to raise his own provisions. Each settler paid to the company an annual rent and worked for the company one month in every year. The change was significant, for it was but a step from individual allotments of land to individual holdings in fee simple. But one other change was necessary before the trading post could become a colony. The development of a staple crop would solve the last difficulty.

Meanwhile, there was dissatisfaction in the company over the progress of Virginia. In 1612, a new charter gave the company control over the Bermudas and marked the complete abandonment of the trading-post idea which had impelled the stockholders of the original venture. A group in the company, headed by Sir Edwin Sandys, were political liberals who believed that there was a close connection between economic and political freedom and contended that the grant of economic freedom to the colonists would result in larger profits to the company. Gaining control of the company, Sandys's faction, known as the "country party," sent Sir George Yardley to govern Virginia.

The so-called "joint-stock" arrangement of the earlier charter should have expired in 1616, but under Yardley's predecessor, Argall, it had been continued while the governor himself had defrauded both settlers and company. The new group in control of the company ordered Yardley to abolish Dale's system of martial law. Moreover, since the "planters" in Virginia were coequal stockholders in the company, Yardley had instructions to call a representative assembly of the shareholders. Although the meeting was in essence only a branch meeting of the company court which met quarterly in London, it was significant for the political precedent that it set. On July 30, 1619, representatives from eleven plantations or boroughs met with the governor and his council in the Jamestown church. It was the first representative assembly held in America.

More than a stockholders' meeting, this first assembly proceeded to enact laws for their own governance. It confirmed the Church of England in its authority and required church attendance. It considered the education of the Indians and took the first steps toward founding a college. It prohibited extravagance in dress and fixed the price of tobacco, the weed being authorized as legal tender in the payment of taxes and fines. The assembly and its laws were final proof that Virginia had passed from plantation to colony.

Two cargoes which came to the wharf at Jamestown in this year of 1619 symbolized the change in Virginia. The first was a Dutch privateer which brought in 20 Negroes and sold them to the colonists. Although the beginning of an involuntary African migration to the English colonies, the Negroes were not slaves, but indentured servants. The story of their future has been lost. Possibly some of them died during the process of acclimatization, and the remainder were absorbed into the population after serving their terms of indenture. The market for the Negroes, however, bore evidence of the need for laborers in a colony that was rapidly growing into a land of plantations. Equally important was the arrival in the same year of 1,200 people who were coming to make homes in the colony. Among them were 90 maidens, "agreeable persons, young and incorrupt," who were sent by the company to find homes and husbands for themselves. Men married the maidens and paid for their transportation in tobacco. More such cargoes were sent—additional evidence that Virginia was becoming an established colony and a place of homes.

As the prospects for Virginia brightened, the prospects for the company in England rapidly grew darker. Sir Edwin Sandys belonged to the parliamentary opposition to the king, and this may or may not have had some effect on the attitude of James I toward the company. Within a year after Yardley had begun his governorship in Virginia, the king had determined upon the dissolution of the London Company. There were many reasons for this move. The company itself had proved its own inefficiency in dealing with the situation, and the mounting toll of deaths in the New World indicated derelictions in the duty of properly caring for the immigrants. Despite changes in the governmental structure of the colony, the population grew but slowly. In 1619, it was estimated that 1,000 people were in the colony, and within the next three years 3,500 more were added by immigration. Yet, in 1624 but 1,132 were alive. Some of them, it is true, had fled back to England; but the majority had lost their lives as a result of the malaria. In the meantime, the company had spent £200,000, and its treasury was exhausted.

In 1622, an Indian massacre supplemented the ravages of disease. Since 1614, when the marriage of the captive Pocahontas to Captain John Rolfe brought peace with the Indians, the colonists had gone their way unmolested. As they expanded, however, contacts between the races were inevitable. Although laws forbade whites to teach the Indians to use firearms, many of the natives acquired weapons and a skill in their use. In 1618, the old Powhatan died, and Opechancanough, his successor, determined to drive the Englishmen from the Indian's land. Secretly gathering his tribesmen, the chief awaited an opportunity to crush the invader. On March 22, the Indians fell upon the whites and, before they could be defeated, killed 347 persons.

Although the company minimized the reports and made efforts to repair the damage, they could not hide the extent of the disaster. Petitions to the king to investigate conditions in the colony were soon forthcoming, and a visiting governor of the Bermudas, Captain Nathaniel Butler, passing through Virginia, indicted the company's management in a pamphlet entitled *The Unmasking of Virginia*. Already the company had grievously offended the king. In 1619, actuated partly by a desire to raise revenue and partly by a dislike of the tobacco habit, the king had levied a tax of one shilling a pound on all tobacco imported into England. The company asked for and received a monopoly for its tobacco, but the next year a royal proclamation limited the production to some fifty thousand pounds. The company thereupon sent its entire crop to Holland, depriving the king of his revenue. The following year another proclamation ordered the company to bring its tobacco into England.

Inefficiency in management of the colony, the dispute with the king, and the objectionable political activities of some of the company's leading spirits combined to impel the king to proceed against the charter. In addition, the company was on the verge of bankruptcy. In November, 1623, the Privy Council appointed a commission to investigate the company, and the following June the courts voided the patent. Thus, in 1624, Virginia passed into the hands of the king. The dissolution of the company was perhaps fortunate for the Virginians, for the colony had outgrown the company's original plans. From a trading post it had become a plantation, and from a plantation, a colony of many plantations. Despite its inefficiency, the company had done a good work.

4. MARYLAND

Two elements entered into the settlement of the English colonies in the New World: the dying feudal system, and the commercial revolution which was supplanting the economic and political order of the

Middle Ages. A strange commingling of the remnants of feudalism and the embryo of a nascent commercialism was present in the Jamestown plantation. The feudal concept that the right to govern was one of the rights of land ownership had made the London Company, itself a product of the new economic order, ruler over its Virginia settlers. That government was a function of the state and might exist apart from, and superior to, the owning of land did not appear in practice until after the English colonies had been planted in the South. English colonies proceeded under the forms of feudalism even though the spirit was that of a newer commercialism. In Maryland, the adherence to the feudal prototype was clearly seen.

In 1632, King Charles I granted to Cecilius Calvert, second Lord Baltimore, a section of the Virginia colony's territory. George Calvert, the first Lord Baltimore, had been interested in the East India Company, the Virginia Company, and the Council for New England. Cecilius Calvert added a religious to an economic motive. As a Catholic, he looked upon his grant, which the king named Maryland, as a haven for his persecuted coreligionists.

The charter given to Baltimore made him a feudal lord over his colony. The Palatinate of Durham was specified as the model for the proprietor's powers. In the Palatinate, the accepted rule was, "Whatever power the King has in England, the Bishop has in Durham." As a recognition of the royal overlordship, the proprietor was required to deliver two Indian arrows to the king each year. In return for this symbolic obeisance, Baltimore received full rights of government. He might administer justice even to the point of inflicting the death penalty; he might make ordinances for government and appoint all officials. On the other hand, the proprietor might make laws only with the assent and advice of the freemen, and the laws must be reasonable and in harmony with the laws of England. Settlers were to have all the liberties of British subjects. The king was to receive no taxes nor did he reserve the right to veto the colony's laws.

Lord Baltimore lost no time in gathering the nucleus of a colony. In November, 1633, the *Ark* and the *Dove,* carrying two hundred passengers, including several Jesuits, set sail from England. The proprietor's brother, Leonard Calvert, accompanied the expedition as governor while Baltimore remained in England to save his colony from the protests that the Virginians were making. In March, 1634, the colonists settled at St. Mary's, on St. George's River.

The experience of the Jamestown colony was of practical benefit to all other English colonies. Profiting from that experience, the settlers chose a high bluff for their first town, made peace with the neighboring Indians and purchased the land from them, and hastened to plant crops. These settlers had come to found a colony rather than a trading post, and so they lost no time in futile searches for mythical northwest passages or elusive gold. As a result, there was no "starving time" in Maryland, and the enterprising colonists exported a shipload of corn at the end of their first season.

From the beginning, dissensions with the proprietor marked the political development of Maryland. Baltimore appointed the governor and all other officials. The governor had the right to veto acts of the assembly. At first the proprietor attempted to initiate legislation, sending his proposed laws to the assembly. But that body insisted upon its own right to initiate legislation and, by refusing to accept the proprietor's laws, secured its right in 1638. The assembly, however, could not agree with the proprietor over the taxation of the proprietary lands, and was almost constantly in conflict with the Baltimore family.

In the beginning, Baltimore, who had dreamed of creating a feudal state in Maryland, had offered large estates and extensive political rights to purchasers. In true feudal fashion, he planned to establish manors over which the lords of the manor would hold full sway; to import tenants who would attend his manorial court. This dream was never realized. A few manors were established, but tenants were unwilling to remain in subjection when land was cheap and the opportunity to become freemen beckoned. Instead of developing manors, Marylanders turned to Virginia for a model, and the plantation system with its slaves became the typical economic and social institution.

A quarrel with Virginia made turbulent the early days of the Maryland colony. Before Baltimore's grant was made, William Claiborne, a member of the Virginia Council, had established a trading post on Kent Island in Chesapeake Bay. Virginia incorporated the settlement, and its representatives sat in the Jamestown assembly. When Virginia became a royal colony, the king promised to respect the establishments of the planters. Relying on this promise, Claiborne refused to yield to Baltimore's authority. The Virginia councilors, resenting the loss of a portion of the colony's territory and being ardently Protestant, upheld their colleague against the Catholic interloper. When Governor Calvert attempted to assert jurisdiction, he was referred to the king, who recognized Baltimore's rights. Claiborne awaited an opportunity to obtain vengeance. His chance came at the time of the Puritan Revolution in England.

Baltimore's desire to found a refuge for Catholics led him to adopt a policy of religious toleration in Maryland. The policy was well calculated to attract settlers, but it failed to bring large numbers of Catholics. The harsh laws of England against adherents of Rome were honored more in the breach than in the observance, and the Catholics were faced with comparatively minor discomforts on account of their faith. Moreover, most of the English Catholics belonged to the upper classes, from whose ranks came few settlers. The Catholic population of Maryland, therefore, was always a minority, although birth, rank, education, and wealth made them the leaders of the colony. On the other hand, Baltimore's toleration attracted Puritans to Maryland. About 1645, a group of Puritans, driven out of Virginia by the conservative and Anglican Governor Berkeley, sought refuge in Maryland, where the governor gave them land in Ann Arundel County. Unappreciative of such kindness, the Puritans, who were accustomed to the English system of land ownership and resented quitrents, began to oppose the proprietor. As the Civil War approached in England, these Puritans formed a party in opposition to the Catholics. To forestall trouble, Baltimore appointed a Protestant governor, and when the king was executed, Baltimore accepted the new regime. But the Parliamentary Party classified Maryland as disloyal and appointed commissioners to assure its allegiance. One of the commissioners was Baltimore's old enemy, William Claiborne. As a result, Baltimore was deprived of all governmental power in Maryland. Claiborne then led a revolt of the Puritans against the proprietary governor. The governor resisted with arms and was captured by the rebels. Baltimore, however, obtained Cromwell's support and was restored to his rights, which he held until the Revolution of 1688. When news of this revolution arrived in the colony, the Puritans took up arms, seized the government, and proclaimed William and Mary. The monarchs accepted the revolution and made Maryland a royal colony. Baltimore retained his property rights, and in 1715 the fourth Lord Baltimore received back his political powers. Maryland remained a proprietary colony until the American Revolution.

5. The Carolinas

As in Maryland, the remnants of feudalism gave initial form to the government of the Carolina colonies. After the restoration of the king in 1660, Charles II paid his political debts to his supporters with a grant of land in America. In 1663, he gave eight courtiers a tract of land south of Virginia between the 36° 30' and the 29° parallels of latitude and westward "from sea to sea." These eight proprietors received full governmental power to establish courts, appoint officials, and make laws, with the consent of the freemen, not repugnant to the laws of England. Colonists were to enjoy the rights and privileges of Englishmen.

Before the proprietors received their grant, settlers from Virginia had moved into the region around Albemarle Sound. For the most part, these settlers were from the classes who were being pushed into the Virginia back country and who were anxious to escape the taxes and the laws of the older colony. Virginia's Governor Berkeley, however, as one of the proprietors of Carolina, sent a governor to collect quitrents. The governor was also to hold an assembly, which might make laws for the colony. In 1665, the first assembly met. Because of the inaccessibility of the region, and possibly because there was an established government, the Albemarle settlements grew slowly.

Unwilling to depend upon an overflow from Virginia to fill their colony, the proprietors sought settlers elsewhere. To encourage settlers and at the same time protect the rights of the owners, they employed John Locke, famous English philosopher and secretary to one of the proprietors, to draft a model government. The result was the curious Fundamental Constitutions, which demonstrated that a great philosopher knew nothing of American conditions. Locke dreamed of a feudal land, divided into counties, seigniories, baronies, precincts, and colonies possessed by a colonial nobility entitled *landgraves* and *caciques*. The proprietors and the nobility would retain two fifths of the land, and the rest would be granted to the common people. Manors, possessed by the nobles and manned by "leetmen," would be formed on the medieval model. The government of this unique system was to be in the hands of the proprietors, whose meetings were to be presided over by the eldest, denominated the "Palatine." A Carolina Parliament, consisting of the proprietors, the nobility, and the representatives of the people, was to be established.

The proprietors proclaimed these constitutions but made little effort to put them into effect, although the danger that they might be enforced troubled the actual government. Circumstances produced in the Carolinas a government which did not differ in essentials from that in other English colonies. The proprietors were more interested in attracting colonists than in making political experiments in the American wilderness. They encouraged groups to settle in their colony, welcoming Puritans from New England, French Huguenots, and Barbadian planters without discrimination. In northern Carolina, a short-lived colony of Puritans settled on the Cape Fear River. In 1690, Huguenots from Virginia received lands on the Pamlico River, and other groups of Europeans made settlements. At New Bern, settlements of Swiss and German Palatines, economic and religious refugees, found a haven until an Indian war decimated their ranks and scattered them over the colony.

The proprietors gave more personal attention to the southern than to the northern portion of their grant. They encouraged a migration from Barbados and themselves financed an expedition that sailed from England, gathered recruits in Barbados, and settled in Charleston Harbor in 1670. Soon these settlers moved to the present site of Charleston. After a brief period of hardships, the colony prospered and grew, and other groups came in. Huguenots began to arrive in Charleston about 1680, and Scottish colonists came in a few years later.

Although settlement was rapid in the first years, the Carolina colonies were subject to both external and domestic troubles. The Spanish in Florida, resenting the English settlement on lands claimed by Spain, attacked the outlying settlements and inspired Indian raids. This danger prevented the rapid growth of South Carolina. The internal troubles were centered in quarrels between the assembly, representing the settlers, and the proprietors. The two Carolinas were separately governed from the beginning and were formally separated in 1729. Both assemblies quarrelled with the governors over the initiative in legislation. In North Carolina, which the proprietors neglected, a succession of weak governors yielded to the people's representatives. The payment of quitrents and the enforcement of the navigation laws occasioned riots and revolts. The people deposed one governor, and disorders continued throughout the colonial period.

The settlers of South Carolina blamed the slow growth of their colony on the policies of the proprietors. The proprietors' eagerness for immediate profits led to general mismanagement. In 1681, the settlers deposed the governor and the proprietors acquiesced in their action. Troubles broke out anew in 1704, when the governor attempted to tax dissenters for the support of the Anglican Church. The settlers appealed to London, where the Board of Trade, determined to bring the colonies under royal control, failed to support the proprietors. This circumstance weakened proprietary power and encouraged the settlers. In 1716, the Commons House altered the system of elections by providing polling places in the various settlements rather than in Charleston. The governor vetoed the law, and the assembly sent an agent to England with a petition that South Carolina be made a royal colony. The Board of Trade approved, and South Carolina became a royal colony in 1719. In 1729 an act of Parliament removed the proprietors from both colonies but compensated them for their loss of property.

Life in the Tobacco Colonies

1. THE IMPORTANCE OF TOBACCO

IN each of the southern colonies, the nature of the colony, the development of the government, and the social life of the people were intimately bound up with the cultivation of staple crops. From tobacco, in Virginia and Maryland, and from rice, in the Carolinas and Georgia, the plantation system developed; from them stemmed most of the activities of southern life.

As the London Company recovered from its gilded hopes of a golden harvest from its Jamestown plantation, the company and the settlers looked for a marketable agricultural crop. In the early literature promoting the company, the enthusiastic "adventurers of the purse" pointed to the possibility of growing in America those products which England was obliged to import from foreign shores. Early in the development of Jamestown, the company sent over eight Polish and German artisans whom Captain John Smith immediately put to work preparing potash and naval stores. Some time later, the enterprising company sent vine dressers from France to experiment with the Virginia grapes. Although the vineyardists succeeded in improving the native fruit and producing a palatable wine, wine-making never passed the experimental stage. A similar result followed an attempt to introduce silk. Imported experts demonstrated that the silkworm thrived on the native mulberry trees, and the assembly made an effort to force every planter to set out and care for trees; but the colonists showed no interest in the development of a silk industry. What was needed in Virginia was a staple crop which could be produced with a minimum of expert care. Such a crop was developed in 1612, when John Rolfe perfected a method of curing tobacco.

From the days of Rolfe's experiments, the future of Virginia was assured. Immediately the Virginians set to raising tobacco, and when, a few years later, land was distributed to the planters, the culture of food-stuffs was neglected for the more profitable tobacco. So pronounced was this tendency that in 1616 Governor Dale forbade the planting of tobacco until each settler had planted two acres of corn. Yet the next year an arriving governor found even the streets and the marketplace of Jamestown planted with the leaf. King James I condemned the "black, stinking fume" and excoriated the habit of smoking, but the "weed" brought many shillings a pound in the English market, and the colonists ignored both royal diatribes and gubernatorial edicts. By 1627, the colonists were exporting 500,000 pounds annually and felt themselves on the way to riches. By 1639, Virginia and Maryland together produced 1,500,000 pounds, and before the close of the century, the crop exceeded 40,000,000 pounds. By the time of the Revolution, the annual crop was over 100,000,000 pounds.

As the annual production of tobacco increased, the price per pound decreased. From approximately 55 cents in 1619, the price declined to 4 cents a pound by the outbreak of the Revolution. Despite repeated efforts of the Virginia assembly to fix the price and to evaluate other commodities in terms of tobacco, the price varied annually with the size of the crop. In addition, the assembly made efforts to limit by law the number of plants which a planter could set out and also to limit the planting season. The government appointed inspectors to destroy poor grades of tobacco, and voluntary associations of growers co-operated, sometimes using violence, in destroying the surplus crop. Maryland planters did not co-operate generally, and the Virginians blamed their neighbors for the failure of their efforts to raise the price. The market for the colonial crop was limited, since the British navigation acts, while granting a monopoly to the colonial tobacco, forbade colonial products being carried to other than English ports.

The methods of planting tobacco did much to determine the nature of the land-holding systems in Virginia and Maryland. In general, when a planter had acquired land, whether by distribution from the company or under the lax laws of the royal colony, he first destroyed the trees by the Indian method of girdling. Then, among the dead trunks which were left standing, he put tobacco plants on little mounds about four feet apart. When the plants began to grow, they were worked with a hoe in order to keep them free from weeds. When the tobacco had obtained a required height, the plant was "suckered" by removing the top. This process produced the broad, full lower leaves which were most desired on the market. Late in the summer, the ripened plants were cut and hung in sheds to dry. When fully cured, sometimes with the use of slow-burning fires, the leaves were carefully sorted according to grade and packed in hogsheads for shipment. Altogether, this process extended over a long period, and it was common in the South to declare that the tobacco year had thirteen months. Usually a second crop was in the ground before the first was loaded on the wharves awaiting the ship that would carry it to England.

The constant work needed in the tobacco fields put practical difficulties in the way of large-scale production. Only a few acres could be worked by one man, and the necessity for constant supervision of hired, indentured, or slave labor made very large tobacco fields unusual. On the other hand, the crude methods used in cultivating tobacco soon exhausted the soil, and the deforestation of the Tidewater region for tobacco fields caused the topsoil to wash away rapidly. This condition made it necessary for the successful planter to hold more land than he actually cultivated. On any holding, only a few acres were in cultivation at any one time. The greater part was either virgin forest or abandoned fields.

Although tobacco dominated Virginia's economy and determined the outlines of its social system, it was not the only crop. The colonists produced hemp and flax, grew such garden vegetables as carrots, turnips, parsnips, and potatoes, and cultivated orchards of peach, pear, and apple trees. Virginians exported corn and wheat, peas and beans, beef and pork to other colonies and to England. An early Maryland law required farmers to plant two acres of corn for each acre of tobacco, and the western part of the colony produced wheat and flour for export. In both colonies cattle and hogs furnished wealth, and the fur trade with the Indians went on steadily.

Nor were the tobacco colonies completely devoid of industry. Flour mills, brick kilns, and even glass factories served local needs and left some surplus for export. In Virginia, the iron industry had promising beginnings and held out a constant hope. In 1608, the Jamestown settlement sent iron ore to England and soon established a forge. Almost a century later iron mining and manufacture received renewed stimulus from Governor Alexander Spotswood who began mining and smelting on a plantation at Germanna. In 1732, William Byrd found these mines in profitable operation, with large areas of wooded land available for charcoal and many acres under cultivation to provide food for men and animals. Although iron continued to attract some attention, the British Iron Act of 1750 prevented the expansion of the industry.

2. LANDHOLDING IN THE TOBACCO COLONIES

In both Virginia and Maryland, the colonial authorities regarded the land as primarily a means of attracting immigration. The London Company promised a dividend in land to any who would become an "adventurer of the person," and Lord Baltimore granted manorial estates to any who would import 50 persons to his colony. Some 60 such manors were established in Maryland, and in the course of Virginia's development royal favorites received a number of large grants. In both colonies, however, the principal method of acquiring land was through the head-right system.

In order to encourage immigration, the colonies allowed head-rights of from 50 to 150 acres to anyone importing a laborer who remained for three years. For this land, the grantee paid an annual quitrent of one shilling. In Maryland, the law provided that this land be given to the laborer and that the employer was to escort him, at the expiration of his indenture, to the court to receive his deed. In Virginia, the land went to the person importing, although the laborer frequently obtained an additional allotment for himself. In both colonies, extreme laxity characterized the administration of the laws. Officials frequently accepted false lists, and shipmasters received headrights on their crews on each trip to the colony. Sailors sometimes obtained headrights for themselves. Clerks in the office of the secretary of the colony often sold headrights without even the pretense of complying with the laws. As a result of these practices, land sold cheaply. By the close of the colonial period, the good lands were exhausted, and purchase had become the most common method of acquiring land.

Because of the headright system and the high cost of importing immigrants, the size of estates in the tobacco colonies remained small throughout the seventeenth century. The records of the Virginia patent office and the tax lists show that the average holding was 446 acres in the period 1634-1650, and 674 acres in the second half of the century. In the seventeenth century, Virginia was a land of comparatively small farms. In the eighteenth century, estates of more than 5,000 acres became common. The introduction of slavery overcame most of the impediments to expansion which the system of indentured servants entailed, and the exhaustion of the soil compelled men to obtain estates larger than they needed at the moment.

3. The Labor Supply

The labor system of the tobacco colonies grew directly out of the cultivation of their staple. The greatest need of these colonies was a supply of cheap labor. With a ready market in England for all that the colonies could produce, the only obstacle to wealth was the high price of free labor. In England, labor was cheap and unemployment was a desperate problem, but the cost of transportation to the colonies was so great that the surplus population of the mother country could not migrate. The system of indentured servitude solved the problem of bringing the labor force of England to the eager tobacco planters.

Indentured servants were of two classes—voluntary and involuntary. In the former class were numbered those English laborers who, in return for passage, entered into bonds of indenture with ship captains. Arriving in the colonies, the captains sold the indentures to planters for tobacco. In Virginia, the laborer could work out his passage, usually from six to ten pounds sterling, in four or five years. At the end of that period he could be a freeman in a country where land was cheap, wages high, and opportunity abundant. Involuntary indentured servants were criminals and paupers who, for minor crimes or for debt, were sentenced to terms in the colonies. Moreover, children were kidnapped in the English cities and consigned to the colonies. These involuntary servants were purchased by the planters in the same manner as were the voluntary servants. The system of indenture became the basis for the economic life of the tobacco colonies and furnished the overwhelming majority of the population.

Throughout the seventeenth century this type of immigration furnished the labor supply of the colonies. In the last two thirds of the century, from 1,500 to 2,000 men, women, and children came annually as indentured servants to Maryland and Virginia. This made between 100,-000 and 140,000 persons, most of whom sought to better their conditions by migrating to the New World. Since lands were cheap, they might easily acquire property and independence. Some of them rose to the highest ranks, becoming members of the House of Burgesses in Virginia; and at least one signer of the Declaration of Independence came to America under bonds of indenture.

The system of indentured service was more efficacious as a builder of population than as a solution to the labor problem. Despite the number of servants who migrated, there was always a shortage of labor in the colonies. In 1671, after the system had been in operation for more than half a century, Governor Berkeley reported that there were 6,000 servants—including 2,000 slaves—in Virginia's population of 45,000.

4. Virginia Society in the Seventeenth Century

In both Virginia and Maryland, the yeoman farmer was the backbone of society. Master of a few acres, working along with the members of his family and an occasional indentured servant, the yeoman was free and independent in a land of opportunity. In the election to the House of Burgesses, the yeomen selected men of ability to represent them and to resist the encroachment of the crown on colonial liberties.

Not all of southern society, however, was composed of the yeoman class. From the earliest years, large planters constituted an upper class and lived on a scale quite different from that of the poorer yeomen. Such a man was Samuel Mathews, who possessed a feudal domain upon which he raised his own household supplies of flax and hemp, employed weavers, kept shoemakers, and dressed his own leather from the dozens of beeves which he killed annually. From his beef and wheat, Mathews reaped a fortune selling supplies to incoming ships from England. In a similar manner, Colonel Robert Carter maintained a force of indentured servants which included carpenters, glaziers, tailors, blacksmiths, and brickmakers. Such a large plantation was a world in itself, producing its own food and converting the products of the land into articles of food and clothing. Among others who maintained such establishments were

Ralph Wormeley, George Menifie, Richard Kemp, John Banister, John Robbins, and Christopher Wormeley. All of these men were leaders in the society and the government of the Virginia colony. They served on the vestries of the churches, were justices of the peace by the appointment of the governor, and many of them were members of the council. They bore the title of "squire," and their mode of life and thought established one of the basic traditions of America.

Throughout the seventeenth century, a number of forces worked to break down the influence of the yeoman and, consequently, to exalt the position of the wealthy squires in Virginia society. First in importance was the position of the planters in the councils of the governors. Selected by the governor, the council soon became almost a self-perpetuating body, and the council members came to regard themselves as a colonial House of Lords. Inevitably they made use of their power to entrench themselves both economically and socially. In 1635, the council, already showing signs of a desire to manage the colony in its own interests, expelled the royal governor, Sir John Harvey, and sent him to England under arrest. In this action it had the wholehearted assistance and support of the House of Burgesses. Although the king was incensed at this act and returned Harvey to the colony, it was not long before a new governor arrived to attempt the delicate task of representing the king at the same time that he conciliated the colonists. Except during the commonwealth period, Governor William Berkeley remained in control of Virginia from 1642 until 1677. The governor himself soon became one of the leading planters in the colony, acquiring extensive acres and even becoming one of the proprietors of Carolina. Together with the leading members of the council, Berkeley was soon engaged in the fur and skin trade with the Indians, thus becoming identified with such prominent councilors as Robert Beverley and William Byrd. Thoroughly a royalist and an aristocrat, Berkeley used his position as head of the colony's church to attempt to take the appointment of clergy out of the hands of the relatively democratic vestries. In persecuting Puritans, also, he showed decidedly aristocratic tendencies. In Virginia the Puritans, some of them from New England, felt the heavy hand of the governor, and hundreds of them left the colony for the less intolerant colony of Maryland. In all relations with the colony, Berkeley supported the handful of squires against the wishes of the yeomen farmers.

When the Puritan revolution in England brought about the execution of the king and the proclamation of the English Commonwealth, the planter aristocracy, under Berkeley's leadership, proclaimed their loyalty to the aristocratic cause. The assembly, too, which by this time was becoming less representative of the yeomen, endorsed this position.

Parliament, however, would not tolerate the insubordination of a colony, and commissioners soon arrived to subdue Virginia. Over Berkeley's protests, the council and the burgesses made peace with the Parliament, and for a few years Virginia was a democratic and practically independent colony. The Puritans in Virginia got some measure of control. The people elected the governor and the councilors, and no taxes were levied without the consent of the people's representatives. Under this regime, Virginia prospered, but the prosperity did nothing to further the development of Puritanism or democracy. As yeomen rose to become planters, they took on the social philosophy of the squires and became supporters of Berkeley and the royal cause. Months before the collapse of the Commonwealth, the Virginia Assembly re-elected Berkeley governor.

During Governor Berkeley's second administration, he showed himself to be even more aristocratic and reactionary than his associates in the government. He continued to persecute adherents of democratic religions, again drove out the Puritans, and forced members of the new sect of Quakers, who held to equalitarian doctrines, to seek refuge in the back country of North Carolina. At the same time, the government rapidly became an oligarchy. The governor appointed members of the council and of the House of Burgesses to lucrative offices. The House of Burgesses sat continuously for the ten years 1666 to 1676 without a new election. In local government, the governor appointed the justices of the peace, who constituted the county courts, from among the wealthy planters; and before the close of Berkeley's rule, the vestries had become closed corporations with the privilege of filling vacancies in their own membership.

Although the legend of the "cavalier migration" to Virginia in the years of the Commonwealth and the Restoration is without basis, these years marked the rise of the lord of the manor on the plantations of Virginia. Many substantial members of the English middle class did migrate to America, bringing with them considerable capital to invest in tobacco lands or the fur trade. From 1640 to 1660 these people, as well as the older, established planters, benefited from free trade and increased their holdings. In addition, former indentured servants and others who had migrated freely to Virginia during the earlier years rapidly rose from the yeomen to the squire class. Berkeley himself stated that he could cite many cases of poor men rising to high estate, and the list of the Long Assembly contained thirteen persons who had had their passage to the colony paid by some other person. If there was no migration of the cavaliers, the period of Berkeley's administration found many a yeoman rising to the wealth, social position, and outlook on life of the cavalier planter.

While some of the more energetic or more fortunate were rising in social position and in possession of worldly goods, the yeomen of Virginia were falling upon evil days from other causes. Increasing taxes bore heavily upon the poorer groups. In 1673, an additional quitrent was imposed to buy off the claims of Lords Culpeper and Arlington, to whom the King had granted Virginia as a proprietary colony. The heavier taxes fell at a time when the people could ill afford them. During the Commonwealth, the colonists had built up a considerable trade with the Dutch, but the Dutch wars of 1664 and 1672 had robbed them of the market. Dutch vessels seized tobacco ships and ruined trade between England and the colonies. Immediately after the restoration of Charles II to the English throne, the British government enacted navigation acts by which the trade with the colonies could be monopolized by English shipmasters. Moreover, the government imposed a tax on colonial tobacco which ranged from 200 to 600 per cent of its value. The result was hardship for the tobacco growers in Virginia, and this hardship was increased by poor crops during several years about 1670. The average crop of Virginia's growers was about 1,200 pounds, which sold for half a penny a pound. When the grower had paid colonial and imperial taxes, he received approximately 50 shillings for his year's work. The result of this situation was that fewer and fewer indentured servants were able to enter into the ranks of the yeomen, and that therefore, at the close of their period of bondage, they migrated to the frontier or to Pennsylvania. Small farmers, too, weary of the lack of rewards, sold their lands to the large planters and moved to the frontier. In the end, the yeoman farmer class, earlier the backbone of the colony, tended to disappear from Virginia society. The more able rose to the planter class, while the less able were shunted into the back country to become the ancestors of the later "poor whites." In 1670, the right to vote was restricted to free holders, and the influence of the poorer classes in society rapidly declined.

5. BACON'S REBELLION

In 1676 the discontent of the lower classes with the hegemony of the planter aristocracy came to a head. In 1675, the Indians were restless and kept the frontier alarmed by occasional forays and murders. The frontiersmen petitioned the governor for protection, but Berkeley and the councilors, interested in the fur trade, hoped to maintain peace with the Indians. Instead of complying, therefore, the governor forbade his subjects to repeat their petition. Believing that Berkeley was concerned "that no bullits would pierce beaver skins," the people of the frontier counties decided to take matters into their own hands. A leader for the movement was found in Nathaniel Bacon.

Bacon had arrived in Virginia in 1674 and had taken up land near the frontier. His family connections in both England and Virginia were influential, and he had been in the colony only a short time when he was given a seat on the council. Although allied both socially and politically with the ruling oligarchy, Bacon owned lands on the frontier, and one of his overseers had been killed by the Indians. Incensed at Berkeley's failure to move, Bacon accepted the invitation of the people of Charles City County, placed himself at their head, and marched against the Indians.

Regarding Bacon's action as both unnecessary and insubordinate, Berkeley denounced him. But public pressure was such that the governor felt constrained to call for a new election for the assembly. The new assembly prepared to reform some of the greater abuses of government and proposed extending the suffrage and reducing taxes. When Bacon, suspended from the council, arrived in Jamestown to take his place in the new assembly, Berkeley had him arrested, but released him on his taking an oath of submission. As soon as he was released, Bacon returned to the frontier and gathered a force of five hundred men. With these, he marched on Jamestown and forced the assembly and the governor to give him a commission to proceed against the Indians. In order to get the armed mob out of the town, Berkeley complied; but as soon as Bacon had left, the governor repudiated the commission and again denounced Bacon as a traitor. Upon hearing this news, Bacon assembled his followers at Williamsburg, or Middle Plantation, where they took an oath to support their leader against both the governor and the crown. In September, 1676, Bacon turned against Berkeley in Jamestown, defeated the governor's hastily gathered troops, and seized and burned the city. In essence, Bacon's Rebellion was far from a social revolution directed against the wealthy planting oligarchy, although Bacon issued some proclamations and made some statements which indicated that he was looking to a thorough transformation of both government and society. But an attack of fever cut short the revolution, and a month after the burning of Jamestown, Bacon was dead. With no leader to take his place, the people soon submitted to Berkeley, who proceeded to stamp out the sparks of revolution by hanging twenty-three of the leaders. Berkeley's vengeance caused Charles II to exclaim, "That old fool hang'd more men in that naked Country than I have for the Murther of my Father." So saying, the king called Berkeley to give an account of his governorship.

One result of the rebellion was the strengthening of the position of the planter aristocracy. The king disallowed the reform laws of the new assembly, and under subsequent governors the suffrage was limited to freeholders. The most significant aftermath of the rebellion, however, was the decline of the indentured servant system and its supplanting by Negro slavery.

6. The Coming of Slavery

Although the indenture system supplied Virginia with population and labor, the evils of the situation were generally apparent. Many of the immigrants were criminals who returned to their past practices as soon as the restraint of their indentures had been removed. Among the women there were many who were immoral, and the percentage of those who were of low-grade intelligence, among both men and women, must have been large. With the decline of profits on tobacco, these classes tended to degenerate and to pull others down with them. The social defects of the indenture system were seen in the widespread poverty and the well-filled jails of the colony. In addition, there were economic defects. At best, the indenture system was expensive. The cost of transportation was great, and the need for laborers kept the time of service low. As a result, by the time a servant had learned the routine of the tobacco fields, he was free to become a competitor of the man who had taught him. After the experience of Bacon's Rebellion, the political effect of the addition of such numbers of people to the yeoman and poorer classes must have been apparent to the planter.

Since 1619, Negro slavery had been known in Virginia. During the early years of the colony, Negroes from Africa found a better market in the Spanish colonies to the south, and Dutch, Spanish, and Portuguese traders kept the English from engaging in the trade. At the same time, the cost of slaves was greater than that of indentured servants. The number of slaves in Virginia grew slowly, and in 1649 there were but 300 in the colony. Most of these were held by a few of the larger planters, one man having as many as 100. In 1662 the Royal African Company was chartered, and under the protection of the crown it was able to supply the American colonies. After 1680, the number of slaves in Virginia grew rapidly. In 1683, there were 3,000 slaves in the colony, and six years later the number had risen to 5,000. By 1705, there was an annual importation of 1,800 slaves and in 1715 there was a slave population of 23,000. By the time of the Revolution there were 206,000 Negroes in a population of 479,000 in the colonies of Virginia and Maryland.

Since English law did not formally regulate slavery, colonial law defined the slave's status. Essentially, the laws of the tobacco colonies were modifications, in the direction of greater security for the planter, of the same English apprentice laws which lay at the base of the system of indentures. Colonial slave codes aimed at two things: the protection of the property rights of the masters and the protection of society itself from the dangers inherent in the presence of a large population of an alien and savage race. The laws of slavery differed from the laws of indenture in that the slave had fewer rights than the indentured servant. Laws forbade Negroes to assemble, to wander without a permit from the master's plantation, or to own firearms. For the general protection of society, slaves were not permitted to testify in the courts except in cases where another slave was a party. A slave's crimes received different punishment from that accorded to freemen. For some crimes, notably those against society, the punishments were less severe. In every case, the fundamental consideration in the administration of the law was the protection of the property rights of the master. Colonial officials caught runaway slaves and housed them in the public jails. On the other hand, the rights of the slaves were modified in order to protect the master. If a master killed a slave in the process of administering a legal punishment, the act was declared by law a justifiable homicide. If the killing were willful and deliberate, the master received a punishment considerably less than that accorded the murderer of a freeman. Cases involving relations between master and slave were tried in special courts without juries. Justices of the peace, designated by the governor for such duty, sat with a selected group of planters of the community in administering justice. The members of these courts, themselves representative of the planter and slaveholding groups, were likely to be especially careful of the property rights of the owners.

Such a system of labor, protected by special legislation and by a special system of courts, was more to be desired by the planters than was indentured servitude. Economically, the planter concluded that slaves paid 20 per cent on the capital invested in them, and were cheaper to feed and more dependable than were white servants. Moreover, the social advantages were not overlooked. Protests against the British practice of dumping convicts on the colonies became frequent, the planter-controlled legislatures finally forbidding the landing of such shipments; and indentured servants were declared to be, "most of them, the very scum and offscouring of our nation, vagrants, or condemned persons, or such others as by the looseness and viciousness of their lives have disabled themselves to subsist any longer in the nation, and when they come hither know not how, or will not betake themselves to any sober, industrious course of living." Such condemnation of the indentured servants constituted the first chapter of a rising southern proslavery argument.

Slavery determined the social character of Virginia for the remainder of the colonial period. With its coming, the great planters increased the size of their holdings, while the yeoman farmer, finding himself unable to compete in the tobacco markets with the cheap produce of the plantations, retired into the back country. As it became possible to buy land, the planters purchased tracts along the navigable rivers, built their manor houses along the banks, and maintained their own wharves for the loading and unloading of the ships that sailed directly from England to their doorsteps. Many planters maintained storehouses from which they sold supplies to the farmers who had been shunted off into the back country and in which they stored the tobacco of the small producer. Economically, the small farmer became dependent on the planter; socially, he became inferior; and politically he found himself without representation in local or colonial government. While the planters grew in strength and importance, the once sturdy yeoman succumbed to adverse economic conditions, was forced into the back country, and gradually merged with the poorer and sometimes degenerate populace.

7. Society in the Eighteenth Century

As some of the yeomen of Virginia and Maryland sank into poverty, others rose to be planters. Their plantations became self-contained communities, and access to the rivers rendered unnecessary the rise of towns and cities. Upon the plantations were quarters for the slaves, storehouses, smokehouses, and tobacco barns. Surrounding the houses of the more pretentious planters were gardens and orchards. The houses themselves were of wood or Virginia-made brick. In their architecture, such houses were intelligent adaptations of the prevailing English styles. As the planters grew in wealth, they imported skilled artisans from England to direct the construction of pretentious homes. The first years of the eighteenth century saw the erection of the governor's palace in Williamsburg, a two story building, fifty-four by forty-eight feet, covered with slate. Quickly the palace, with its huge ballroom, its great stairs, its three dining rooms, and its surrounding formal gardens and box hedges, became the model for the mansions of the planter aristocrats. The palace influence was but temporary, for, by the middle of the century, the planters were adopting the popular Georgian style which remained dominant until after Thomas Jefferson inaugurated a classical revival.

As the profits from tobacco made it possible, the planters imported from London furnishings and equipment to adorn their mansions. Tables, chairs, and settees of carved mahogany replaced the cruder

National Park Service

THE GOVERNOR'S PALACE AT WILLIAMSBURG. The first years of the eighteenth century saw the erection of the governor's palace in Williamsburg, a two-story building, fifty-four by forty-eight feet, covered with slate. Quickly the palace, with its huge ballroom, its great stairs, its three dining rooms, and its surrounding formal gardens and box hedges, became the model for the mansions of the planter aristocrats.

products of home manufacture. Other articles, too, were imported. Candlesticks, clocks, and tapestry adorned the walls, and oak paneling, especially in the dining rooms, was common. The kitchens of the houses, still equipped with fireplaces in which spits and cradles for boiling pots were hung, were housed separately in order that the odors of cooking might be kept from the great house.

Food for the plantation was obtained on the estate itself. Since much of the land was uncultivated, the surrounding forests abounded in game; and the annual slaughter of cattle at the approach of winter kept the community supplied with beef. Vegetables were abundant, and beverages ranging from the homemade "hard" cider to imported wines and brandies graced the boards.

Gracious hospitality traditionally characterized these manor houses. To others who were to the manner born, the great houses were open, and a cordial welcome was accorded to the traveler who would bring news from distant places. Among the planters, entertainment and visiting occupied a prominent place. As amusements, the planters raced horses and rode to hounds in the best traditions of the English countryside. Cards and gambling, music and dancing stimulated social intercourse and made Virginia famed throughout the English colonies.

The workaday life of the plantation centered about the production of tobacco, although slaves, and occasionally indentured servants, were shoemakers, carpenters, or blacksmiths. Work in the tobacco fields began at sunrise and lasted until after sunset. For the noonday meal, the Negroes cooked "hoecakes," so named because they were made of a batter of meal and water and baked before a fire on the blades of the hoes. Customarily, the Negroes worked in gangs under the supervision of an overseer, although on some plantations the system of tasks was applied. Under this system, when the Negro had completed his daily "stint," he was free to follow his own devices for the remainder of the day.

The fear of punishment rather than the hope of reward kept the slave to his work. Occasionally there were revolts among the Negroes. In 1687, the slaves in the Northern Neck, and in 1710 those in Surry County, worked out elaborate plots to obtain their freedom. In 1722 a plot to kill the whites brought two hundred Negroes to a church near the mouth of the Rappahannock. None of these came to a point of violence, but eight years later the rumor that Governor Spotswood would free Christian Negroes produced slave riots in Williamsburg. In a slave society, planters frequently read evidence of plots into ordinary crimes of passion. Never was the slaveholder completely free from the fear of insurrection.

Yet, as a general rule, the plantation Negro was happy and reasonably contented with his lot. Frequently, especially on the smaller plantations, a bond of affection developed between master and slave which ofttimes led to the latter's emancipation for meritorious acts or upon the master's death. As was inevitable under a system in which one man owned another, whatever good relations between the races existed were mostly to the credit of the Negro. He made the adjustments demanded by the system. The very process of bringing the Negroes to America, however, selected those natives of Africa who were most likely to make the necessary adjustments. The Negroes were captured in Africa by other tribes of their own race, and it was inevitable that the least courageous should fall victims to the slave hunter. The long trek to the sea and the wait for the slave traders tested the Negroes for both endurance and good nature. The more fractious among them seldom reached the seacoast, while the weaklings succumbed to tropical diseases or to the bad treatment which they received. The horrors of the middle passage served further to select those whose physical equipment was rugged and whose mutinous tendencies were suppressed. Such Africans were the least capable of their race to preserve their native culture or to transplant it to the New World. The rigid discipline of the plantation prevented the development of qualities of leadership among them, making them far safer for the planter than were the maladjusted or ambitious indentured servants whom they displaced.

Despite the self-sufficiency of the plantation, the planter was not economically independent. Although he raised his own food, his main dependence for the luxuries of life was upon the tobacco trade. The English ships that came to his wharf to carry away his crop carried, on their return voyage the following year, the goods that he had ordered from London. The tobacco was consigned to commission merchants in England who sold the leaf in the market and purchased in turn—charging commissions for both transactions—the furniture, the tools, and even the women's clothing which the planter ordered. Seldom was there a surplus left to the planter's account; indeed, he usually found himself indebted to the factor. In addition to commissions, the planters paid heavy charges for insurance, freights, warehouse fees, and duties. In the beginning, the profits from tobacco had been so great that the planters had invested all their surplus in lands and slaves. When tobacco declined in value, the planters found that they possessed heavy fixed investments which could not be easily transferred to other pursuits. English merchants readily extended credit and granted new loans, but on condition that the planters should raise more tobacco. Slowly, throughout the first three quarters of the eighteenth century, these debts to the London merchants mounted, being inherited with the land by the planters' sons. The burden of these debts eventually led the planters to listen to the seductive words of revolutionary radicals who promised that with American independence would come freedom from the entangling commitments.

As the planters' debts to London mounted, they grew more tobacco, thus depressing the price and beginning a vicious circle. At the same time, the crude agricultural methods used in producing the tobacco caused a rapid depletion of the thin soil of the Tidewater region and forced the planters to acquire both more land and more slaves. Slowly the plantation system reached out toward the western part of the colony, and planters formed land companies, such as the Ohio Company, to petition the king for grants of lands in and beyond the mountains. The expansion of the plantation system, too, pushed the yeoman farmer farther into the back country, while the falling price of tobacco doomed him to an increasing poverty. The entire process aided in the economic dislocations that brought Virginia to the verge of revolution against England.

8. Religion in the Tobacco Colonies

In the planter-dominated society of the tobacco colonies, organized religion played little part. With the founding of the Virginia plantation, the Church of England was established, and throughout the seventeenth century it had a slow growth. In Maryland, the church was not established until the close of the century, and Baltimore made a real effort to maintain the toleration, in both letter and spirit, with which he had launched the colony. From the beginning, Virginia's Anglican church showed wide variations from the church in England. Democratic tendencies in the seventeenth century created divergences from the ritual and the governance of the church in the mother country. There was no bishop in America, and for years the Bishop of London, who was nominally at the head of the colonial churches, paid but little attention to this part of his diocese. In his place, the governor of the colony was the head of the church, charged with the maintenance of its creed, the employment of its ministers, and the preservation of its property. The governor, however, soon found that the churches refused to conform to his dictates. In the beginning the parishioners elected the vestries, and these managed the ecclesiastical life of the parishes without heeding the governor's wishes. Later, when the vestries became closed corporations and were themselves dominated by the established planters, they showed no greater inclination to yield to the authority of governor, king, or bishop.

The greatest conflict that occurred between the governor and the vestries was over the induction of ministers. The king instructed the governor to induct ministers into their holdings, and the governor ordered the vestries to present their clergy for induction. However, the vestries customarily refused to present their clergymen, and, without formal induction, the clergy were but hired servants of the vestries. In this position, without rights of their own and without tenure, the better classes of the clergy were not attracted to the colonies.

Although the "living" which the clergyman received in Virginia was probably superior to that he would have received in England, the colonial parishes were poorly served. Many of the priests were lazy or vicious, drunkenness was common among them, and few showed either inclination or aptitude for their duties.

Even those priests who were capable and energetic were handicapped by conditions. Always a large part of the parishes were without clergymen and all of the parishes were so large that a man had difficulty in visiting his parishioners. One Virginia parish was thirty miles wide by fifty miles long, and others were but slightly smaller. Water transport was the only feasible means of communication, for the few roads in the colonies were impassable during parts of the year. As a result, variations from the established practices of the church developed. In the seventeenth century, Virginia had laws compelling church attendance, but the difficulty of keeping priests and the distances from the churches produced a general indifference. Under canon law, marriages had to be performed in the churches, but distances demanded that the ceremonies be performed in homes. Funerals, too, were held in the homes because of the difficulty of entertaining guests and carrying corpses to the church-yards. Despite the protests of the clergy, private burial grounds became the rule. Moreover, there was a general laxity in other religious observ-ances. Laymen read the services in the absence of priests, communion was given to unconfirmed persons, and many parts of the church services fell into disuse.

For the masses of the people in the back country of Virginia, the established church had no meaning. Attendance at its services was seldom considered, and the church made little or no effort to meet the spiritual needs of the lower classes. At the same time, the back country was restive under the condition of subordination and actual oppression in which it found itself. Though supported by taxes upon the poorer classes, the church was intimately bound to the aristocracy and the oligarchic govern-ment. The people were without religious instruction—many of them never having read the Bible or heard it read—and were unfamiliar with the ordinances, rituals, and doctrines of the church. Religiously, there was need for a revival in Virginia, and such a revival would inevitably possess political and social aspects.

Two factors produced the revival. One of them was the coming of the Scotch-Irish and Germans to the frontier of the colony. These people settled in the Great Valley and brought with them the Presby-terianism and the pietism of their homelands. The second factor was the Great Awakening.

The Scotch-Irish and the Germans began to arrive in the Valley of Virginia in the decade after 1730. Migrating for the most part from Pennsylvania, these hardy pioneers were welcomed by the government of the colony although Tidewater land speculators who were expecting to push the plantation society beyond the mountains regarded with considerable suspicion the tendency of the Scotch-Irish to squat upon land without paying for it. These people were devout Presbyterians, militant in their faith, and rendered hardy by a long experience in social and economic subjection. The native leaders among them had not been drained off into planter society as had the leaders in the Tidewater regions, and they possessed a hard culture and a taste for theological scholarship. To the leaderless classes of the back country, then, the Scotch-Irish and the Germans offered both leaders and a spiritual and emotional stimulus to do battle with the planter aristocracy. Governor William Gooch, in encouraging the Scotch-Irish to settle in Virginia, adopted a liberal land policy, and, assuming that the mountains would prove an effective barrier against too close contact with Anglican Vir-ginia, had given them the right to maintain ministers of their own faith. Soon these ministers were crossing the mountains, carrying the gospel of Presbyterianism and of revolt against the Anglican church to the people of the back country.

In 1738, the House of Burgesses created the two counties of Frederick and Augusta west of the mountains, and divided each of the counties into parishes. For years no attempt was made to send Anglican ministers into the region, but the people chose vestries composed of dissenters who took the necessary oaths and then administered the parishes in accordance with their own ideas. Burgesses elected from these counties opposed both the established church and the Tidewater planters. The Scotch-Irish Presbyterians of the mountains and valley were affiliated with the "old side" synod who were not evangelical; but "New Light" ministers, ardently carrying the gospel of the Great Awakening, soon came among them.

The Great Awakening in America was a part of a revived world interest in a personal and emotional religion. In Europe, the twin phenomena of pietism in Germany and Methodism in England attracted widespread attention. Late in the second decade of the eighteenth century, seemingly spontaneous revivals sprang up in America. In Massachusetts, Jonathan Edwards began to preach the necessity of a personal religious experience, and John Wesley, founder of Methodism, himself visited Georgia. Following Wesley, George Whitefield came to America, and his fame soon spread into Virginia. In December, 1739, Whitefield preached in Williamsburg, and after he left the revival grew apace.

Before Whitefield had arrived in Virginia, another and apparently unconnected movement had lighted the fires of evangelism in Hanover County, Virginia. Under the leadership of one Samuel Morris, a group of back-country people had begun to assemble to read Luther's writings and Whitefield's sermons. The movement grew, and soon there were reading houses in a number of places. These people knew nothing of church services, of extemporaneous praying, or of religious music. When the activities of the reading houses caused a noticeable drop in church attendance, the law stepped in, and several persons were arrested for failure to attend church. When these people learned of the Act of Toleration, they declared themselves to be Protestant dissenters. Having been reading the writings of Luther, they declared themselves Lutherans and were allowed to depart in peace.

Not long after this experience, the Hanoverian reading houses, beginning to hear of the New Light Presbyterians, invited a traveling evangelist who preached the first sermon most of them had ever heard. The reading-house groups found themselves in accord with the teachings of the Presbyterians and received instructions in the conduct of worship. Henceforth, they called themselves Presbyterians. For several years they were visited by migratory preachers, until in 1748 Samuel Davies, later president of Princeton University, became their pastor.

Before Davies arrived, Governor Gooch instructed a grand jury to bring in an indictment against the preachers and worshipers on the grounds that they were vilifying the established church. The extent to which the movement was taking a hold on the people was seen in the failure of a petit jury to find the Hanover Presbyterians guilty.

The methods of the New Light preachers were described by one of the better educated of the Anglican clergy. "[They] strive with all their might, to raise in their hearers, what they call convictions, which is thus perform'd. They thunder out in awful words, and new coin'd phrases, what they call the terrors of the law, cursing & scolding, calling the old people, Grayheaded Devils, and all promiscuously, Dam'd double damn'd, whose [souls?] are in hell though they are alive on earth, Lumps of hellfire, incarnate devils, 1000 times worse than Devils & c, and all the while the Preacher exalts his voice puts himself into a violent agitation, stamping and beating his Desk unmercifully until the weaker sort of his hearers being scar'd, cry out, fall down, and work like people in convulsion fits, to the amazement of spectators, and if a few only are thus brought down, the Preacher gets into a violent passion again, calling out Will no more of you come to Christ? thundering out as before, till he has brought a quantum sufficit of his congregation to this condition, and these things are extoll'd by the Preacher as the mighty power of God's grace in their hearts, and they who thus cry out and fall down are caress'd and commended as the only penitent Souls who come to Christ, whilst they who don't are often condemn'd by the lump as hardened wretches almost beyond the reach of mercy in so much that some that are not so season'd, impute it to the hardness of their own hearts, and wish and pray to be in the like condition."

From Hanover, the revival spread over all of Virginia, and "New Light" Presbyterians even carried their work into the strongholds of the Old School Presbyterians in the Valley of Virginia. In their train, too, came Methodists and Baptists, adopting the same techniques and gaining converts throughout the back country. The members of the established church, confronted by the phenomena of this movement, were unable to combat it. Reforms were attempted in the Anglican church, but ridicule was deemed a more potent weapon than reform. Ridicule, however, only contributed to the sense of martyrdom which these converts felt, and the movement went steadily on despite the greater social prestige of the Episcopalians.

The political and social aspects of the Great Awakening were soon apparent. With the alliance of the Scotch-Irish and Germans in the valley, the representatives of these people began to attack the established church and the clergy. Patrick Henry came from Hanover Parish, and first won a name for himself in the Parson's Cause, in which he defended the vestries for failure to pay their ministers. Although the clergy were awarded a two-penny damage by the jury representing the people and acting on royal orders, Henry won a personal victory and was sent to the burgesses to represent not only the attack of the back country upon the power of the church but also the attack of the oppressed classes against the vested interest of the planters. The Great Awakening soon grew into a social revolution.

In the meantime, the planters were making a tentative alliance with the forces of the back country and the Scotch-Irish. At the height of the revival, the French and Indian War was brewing, and the revivalists urged on their converts the duty of killing Catholics and Indians. The colonial authorities therefore tolerated them. Originally, the Scotch-Irish had been admitted to the frontier in the hope that they would prove a buffer against the Indians. The alliance of the Scotch-Irish with the people of the back country, effected through the Great Awakening, proved of value to the planters in their war for the acquisition of the Ohio valley. The alliance was to continue until the Revolutionary War.

9. EDUCATION

Closely allied to the church and to the aristocratic nature of Virginia society was the system of education in vogue in the colonies. The settlers of Virginia and Maryland were accustomed to the educational practices that prevailed in England. Although Oxford and Cambridge were flourishing institutions, and although there were a number of smaller "public" schools in the mother country, the consensus of prevailing educational ideas was that education was for the upper classes and was no concern of the people. With the exception of the practice of binding out poor children as apprentices, the state itself paid no attention to the education of youth. The earliest settlers carried over these ideas to Virginia, and the school system of the South bore a close resemblance to that of England. Education was an individual matter and no concern of any public body except the church.

The Virginia Company, however, was interested in the education and civilization of the Indians, and with the support of the church it launched paper plans for the University of Henricus, which would train the Indian youth and return them to their people as missionaries. The scheme failed when the Indian massacre of 1622 convinced the Virginia settlers and the company that the Indians would not respond to attempts to spread white civilization.

With this exception, no effort was made to establish public schools in Virginia until near the end of the seventeenth century. In the meantime, planters established schools on their plantations for the younger members of the community and often took the children of neighbors and friends into their homes for the duration of the school session. These plantation schools were frequently taught by indentured servants, some of whom were highly educated men and others of whom had the poorest intellectual and social equipment. In addition to these schools were some "old field" schools, so-called because they were situated in abandoned fields. These schools were private schools, taught by independent masters or by the minister of the parish. Tuition was charged for the instruction. As for higher education, the planters hoped to send their sons to the great English universities, although an occasional youth sought Harvard, Yale, King's College, or Princeton in the northern colonies.

Although some of the plantation and field schools took the children of the yeomanry, education was generally held to be the privilege of the rich. In 1671, Governor Berkeley expressed an idea common among the limited planter group by declaring, "I thank God there are no free schools nor printing, and I hope we shall not have these hundred years, for learning has brought disobedience and heresy and sects into the world, and printing has divulged [them] and libels against the best government. God keep us from both." The statement was hardly accurate, but it was a good summary of the hopes of the reactionary governor and his class.

Following upon Bacon's Rebellion, the church made an effort to strengthen its position. To the colony, the Bishop of London sent a commissary, Dr. James Blair, who soon interested Governor Francis Nicholson in a proposition to establish a college. Nicholson contributed to the endowment for a college, and Blair went to England to obtain support. Although he met an official who, when told that the purpose of the college was to save souls, responded, "Damn your souls, make tobacco," Blair succeeded in getting gifts from a number of leading men and interesting the king and queen, who granted the college a charter, assigned to it the accumulated quitrents in the colonial treasury, and requested Sir Christopher Wren to design the building. The colony gave the college 20,000 acres of land, the right to appoint a colonial surveyor, and appropriated over a hundred pounds a year, to be raised by an export tax on furs and skins. The college, named "William and Mary" for its royal benefactors, was established at Williamsburg with Blair as president. Ministers of near-by parishes constituted the majority of the faculty. So that clergy might be trained for the established church, ministerial students were accorded free board and tuition. In 1693, a preparatory school was opened, and for several years the efforts of the faculty were devoted to training younger students. Indians were admitted to the institution and a few attended.

Despite the promising beginnings of William and Mary, the college did not prosper. In 1705 the building burned, and for some years its existence was hardly more than nominal. In 1724 one of the professors declared that it was "a college without a chapel, without a scholarship, and without a statute, having a library without books, comparatively speaking, and a president without a fixed salary till of late." As the century progressed, however, the college grew and was eventually an important molding influence on the intellectual life of the colony. Many of the Revolutionary leaders of Virginia received their training within its walls.

With the settlement of the back country by the Scotch-Irish, academies began to spring up in the western region. Most of these were taught by Presbyterian ministers. In all the schools, whether under the church or private management, the subjects of study were limited. Hebrew, Latin, and Greek constituted the backbone of the curriculum, but there was instruction as well in arithmetic, in mensuration, in geometry, in trigonometry, in handwriting, and in bookkeeping. Literary societies trained students for later activities in the pulpit or on the political stump.

Despite the paucity of schools, the tobacco colonies were not without a cultured society. The planters took pride in their acquaintance with classical literature, and the shelves of their libraries were filled with fine bound editions of Homer and Horace, Ovid and Virgil, Euripides and Sophocles. Volumes of law, works on architecture and agriculture, histories, and the best of contemporary English literature were also there, standing side by side upon the shelves with solemn treatises on theology. Many of the Virginia libraries were of respectable size, the largest on record being that of William Byrd II of Westover, with over 4,000 titles. In Maryland the commissary of the church, Dr. Thomas Bray, established libraries in nearly all the colony's thirty parishes.

The planter showed, too, an interest in art, adorning the walls of his home with engravings of famous paintings, and giving patronage to wandering portrait painters. Charles Willson Peale, of Maryland, studied painting in London and returned to paint the portraits of the leading personages of Virginia and Maryland. Music delighted the planter, and harpsichords, pianos, flutes, guitars, or organs were found in every mansion. Traveling dramatic troupes found ready welcome from appreciative audiences in Williamsburg and Annapolis. Although neither of the colonies supported a newspaper until near the end of the colonial period, literary activities were not unknown. William Byrd's *History of the Dividing Line* revealed keen insight, ready wit, and an urbane style.

Society in the Carolinas and Georgia

IN the seventeenth and eighteenth centuries, a society developed in the Carolinas and Georgia which, although having many differences, yet bore a fundamental resemblance to that in the tobacco colonies. In North Carolina, the production of tobacco and the character of the population created a colony which closely resembled the Virginia back country. Rice and indigo in South Carolina and Georgia, while producing a different mode of life, yet made for a basic similarity in social organization. In each colony the presence of an African labor force in the midst of a white population produced far-reaching social consequences. In each, a struggle between the dominant planters and the back country yeomen marked the course of the colony's development and prepared the way for the democratic concepts of the American Revolution.

1. NORTH CAROLINA'S DEVELOPMENT

The North Carolina region was first settled by an overflow from Virginia. Comparatively isolated from the sea, lacking as many broad tidewater rivers as did the northern colony, the North Carolina area merged into the Virginia back country. Long before Charles II created the colony of Carolina, migrants from Virginia had crossed the line into North Carolina. As early as 1653 a group of 100 men settled on the shores of Albemarle Sound. From the back country of Virginia, others came. Most of them were servants just released from their indentures, though some were fugitives from justice or labor in the older colony.

Virginia's Governor Berkeley took note of the settlement and, as a proprietor of Carolina, made the first effort to extend a government over the region.

The character of the population and their motives for settling in North Carolina were reflected in the colony's early legislation. In 1669 a law provided that no settler could be sued for any debt that had arisen before he came into the colony. Moreover, no action could be taken for five years against any settler for any judgment outside of the colony. In addition, the laws exempted newcomers from the payment of all taxes for one year after arriving in the settlement. Laws, too, reserved the Indian trade, in which many Virginians had grown wealthy, for residents. Soon Virginians, noting that their servants and dependents were escaping their jurisdiction, spoke contemptuously of "Rogue's Harbor." But the laws attracted settlers, the population grew, and even Quakers and Puritans, exiled by Virginia's harsh intolerance, found refuge in North Carolina.

From the beginning, North Carolinians had little respect for aristocracy and less for the authority of government. The grasping proprietors, hoping to encourage immigration, accepted the laws of the colony, and for a time made little effort to establish either law or justice in the region of Albemarle. When courts were established, they frequently sat in the taverns and, in lieu of keeping records, cried their decisions from the doors of the inn. Nor did organized religion lend a hand in preserving order in the "tranquil anarchy" which prevailed. In 1672 George Fox visited the Quaker settlements, and occasional traveling preachers of other denominations entered to preach and to leave. Not until after the turn of the century was there a clergyman resident in the colony, and churches were few in number as late as 1750. In 1729 William Byrd wrote of Edenton, "I believe this is the only metropolis in the Christian or Mohammedan world where there is neither church, chapel, mosque, synagogue, or any other place of public worship, of any sect or religion whatsoever."

The economic arrangements of the people of Albemarle paralleled their social life. Along the coast a row of islands and shifting sand bars prevented navigation, while pine barrens near the seacoast kept the people from settling near the ocean. Yet North Carolina possessed commodities to stimulate commerce. The pine trees furnished turpentine, tar was produced in large quantities, and a poor grade of lumber was available. The products encouraged the maritime New Englanders to risk treacherous shoals in order to trade. The coast was infested with pirates, who had generally the sympathy of the settlers and who rendered commerce extremely difficult.

Agriculture rather than commerce was the basic industry of the North Carolinians. Tobacco, similar to the poorer grades of Virginia, was the chief marketable crop, but the difficulties of getting it to market prevented the creation of a tobacco aristocracy in the colony. The crop had to be hauled long distances to the Virginia markets, and Virginia imposed taxes upon the importation. As a result, North Carolina remained a land of small farms, or even of clearings in the wilderness. Occasionally there was a large plantation, and an infrequent manor house might compare with the manor houses in the more prosperous colonies; but the owners did not control the governmental and social institutions of the colony. Instead, the land was dotted with small clearings, and subsistence farming was the rule. Both life and property were insecure, and wandering ruffians paid little attention to the ill-administered law. Altogether, there was little in the North Carolina situation to produce the class divisions that characterized her northern neighbor.

Virginians never learned to regard North Carolinians with any-thing but contempt. At the close of the first quarter of the eighteenth century, Colonel William Byrd, running the boundary line between Virginia and North Carolina, expressed the common disgust of the Virginia planters with the shiftless population of the Carolina back country. The men, he said, made their wives arise early in the morning while they lay abed "until the sun has run one third of his course and dispersed all the unwholesome damps. Then, after stretching and yawning for half an hour, they light their pipes, and under the protection of a cloud of smoke, venture out into the open air, though if it happens to be ever so little cold, they quickly return shivering into the chimney corner. When the weather is mild, they stand leaning with both arms upon the corn-field fence, and gravely consider whether they had best go and take a small heat at the hoe, but generally find reasons to put it off until another time. Thus they loiter away their lives, like Solomon's sluggard, with their arms across, and at the ending of the year scarcely have bread to eat."

Politically, the history of North Carolina from its settlement to the outbreak of the Revolution was a long story of conflict between the people and the proprietors. For the most part, the ruling officials opposed the turbulent frontier democracy. In 1673, the proprietors sent a governor with instructions to put the Fundamental Constitutions into effect; but the governor soon died, and it became apparent that Locke's dream state could not exist in the wilderness. The attempt to enforce the constitutions met resistance, and the attempt to enforce the navigation acts further stimulated the spirit of dissent in the colony. The enforcement of the acts would have stopped the New England traders from coming to exchange the lumber and cattle and tobacco of North Carolina for the goods of the world.

By 1676 the colony was at the point of rebellion. Bacon counted on help from the North Carolinians in his war against Berkeley. In the midst of troubles in Virginia and disaffection in Carolina, the proprietors sent as governor a North Carolinian who had been tried in Virginia for seditious utterings against Berkeley. Thomas Miller should have been acceptable to the people of North Carolina; but he soon attempted to enforce the navigation acts, and a mob under John Culpepper seized both governor and council, took possession of the official records and residences, and convened the assembly. The revolutionary assembly chose Culpepper governor, selected new judges, and seized £3,000 gathered by Miller in his capacity of customs collector. When invasion from Virginia threatened, Culpepper went to England to persuade the proprietors to approve his acts. But Miller arrived before him, and although Culpepper persuaded the proprietors that he was right, the king's officials arrested the popular governor for robbing the customhouse. When he returned to America, he went to Charleston, where he laid out the present site of the city.

Following Culpepper, one of the proprietors, Seth Sothel, came to North Carolina. Sothel had bought out the rights of one of the proprietors and was, under the Fundamental Constitutions, entitled to assume control whenever he visited the colony. For five years Sothel ruled Carolina as his personal possession, seizing the people's belongings, accepting bribes to save criminals from the gallows, and ignoring the laws. In 1688 there was a new revolution, and the people expelled the proprietor. Such disorders, however, served as no handicap to the settlement of North Carolina. "Theeves" and "pyrates," runaway servants and persecuted dissenters, came from Virginia to swell the turbulent population.

For a time after Sothel, there was peace in North Carolina, largely because the proprietors and their agents left the colony to its own devices. In 1704 a deputy governor, Robert Daniel, arrived with instructions to establish the Church of England, and trouble immediately followed. Up to this time no church had existed in the colony, although the Quakers were organized. When Daniel required an oath to be taken by all officials, the Quakers succeeded in getting another deputy-governor, Thomas Cary, appointed. But Cary proved disappointing, for he undertook to administer the oaths, and the Quakers sent an agent to England to present their case to the proprietors. These gentlemen, far more interested in profits from their colony than they were in the establishment of the church, removed Cary and took the government of North Carolina out of the hands of the governor of South Carolina. For a time after Cary's removal, North Carolina was governed by the president of the council, who was a member of the established church and who continued to attempt to administer oaths. In desperation the Quakers turned to Cary, and for a time both Cary and his opponent acted as governors, while the colony returned to anarchy. After three years, Edward Hyde arrived to act as governor and to challenge Cary's authority. Virginia's Governor Spotswood sent aid, and Cary fled to Virginia, where he was arrested and sent to England to stand trial for treason. Owing to a lack of evidence, he was acquitted.

Partly as a result of the weakened condition of the colony during this rebellion, and partly as a result of the pressure of settlement on their lands, the Tuscarora Indians along the frontier rose against the whites in 1711 and killed hundreds of settlers along the Neuse and Pamlico rivers. When these troubles broke out, Hyde called out the militia; but the militiamen refused to respond, and the governor had to get troops from South Carolina to drive the Indians out of the country.

Throughout these disorders, settlers continued to migrate to the colony. Huguenots driven from France found refuge there; Germans and Swiss, under the leadership of Baron de Graffenried, founded New Bern; and in the years to follow other European settlers came into the region. After about 1740 Germans and Scotch-Irish began to fill up the western portion, and Scottish Highlanders soon joined them. The coming of these new elements changed the character of the population. Thriftier than the original English settlers and bringing a deeper desire for culture and a better religious organization, they gave greater stability to the colony and at the same time added a new element to those who were discontented with the established church, the proprietors, and the colonial officialdom.

In 1719 a revolution against the proprietors gave the king control of South Carolina. But at the moment there was peace in North Carolina, the council was loyal to the proprietors, and the assembly was not in session. Since the councilors stated that they were "entirely easy and satisfied" under the government of the proprietors, the colony remained in proprietary hands until 1729. In that year the proprietors surrendered all their governmental powers to the king, and all but one sold to the crown their interest in the lands of North Carolina. For fifteen years, Lord Carteret retained his landed interest and then received almost one half of the colony in exchange for his claim.

Under royal rule the machinery of goverment in North Carolina was little changed, although the general spirit that actuated the rulers was altered. The proprietors had been primarily interested in profits and had tolerated loose and anarchical conditions in the hope of attracting settlers for their lands. Less interested in dividends than the proprietors had been, the royal government managed the colony in the interests or the empire as a whole. Less yielding than the proprietary governors and more able to exert pressure on the unruly colonists, the royal governors succeeded in ruling with considerable efficiency. In 1734 Gabriel Johnston became royal governor, and when disputes arose between him and the popular assembly, there was no yielding. Throughout the eighteen years of his rule he was in constant conflict with the people over the issuance of land patents and the collection of quitrents.

When Johnston assumed control of the colony, he found that former governors had given large blocks of land to certain favored planters. The patents had not passed the seal of the province, and Johnston withheld the grants. Since many of these grants had been made to members of the council and the assembly, an immediate opposition arose which eventually resulted in a victory for the claimants. Such a system of loose granting of lands had resulted in the development of the planter class in Virginia. By the end of Johnston's administration, a similar social order was taking form in North Carolina, modified, however, by the colony's long experience in democracy.

The struggle over the collection of quitrents kept alive North Carolina's tradition of turbulence. Johnston's opposition to the creation of large estates antagonized the large planters; his course on quitrents allied the small farmers and the masses of the back-country people with the councilors in opposing the governor. The quitrent was the major source of colonial income, and from it the salaries of the officials were paid. Under North Carolina law the quitrents, which were a permanent tax on the land, were payable in commodities. Johnston insisted that they should be paid in English or colonial money at a fixed rate of exchange. Morever, contention arose over the collection. The people insisted that the taxes should be collected at their doors, while the governor demanded that the commodities be brought to centrally located depots. Despite efforts to settle this dispute, it continued until the Revolution. In the process, the council agreed with the governor, and the lower house blocked his proposals.

The increase of population under the royal government led to still another struggle in North Carolina. Within a few years after the cessation of the proprietary government, North Carolina exceeded South Carolina in population. Johnston encouraged settlement, especially in the Cape Fear region, where he hoped to develop a port that would carry the colony's products to European markets. European immigrants came in to fill up the southern and middle portions of the colony at the same time that Scotch-Irish settled the western counties. Soon a situation similar to that in Virginia developed. The older regions had a disproportionate power in the assembly. The Albemarle settlements, home of the more wealthy people, had five representatives in the assembly for each county, while the other regions had two each. Since Johnston had encouraged the settlement of these newer regions, and since he was having troubles with the representatives from the older districts, he sympathized with the demand of the southern section for a more equitable representation. Accordingly, in 1746, he called the assembly to meet at Wilmington, largely in the hope that enough of the northern representatives would fail to attend to enable a new apportionment law to be passed. But the Albemarle representatives met this move by an agreement among themselves not to attend and therefore to prevent a quorum. Johnston recognized his Wilmington assembly and approved a law establishing New Bern as the provincial capital. In protest against this act, the people of the northern portion refused to pay taxes, and for a time North Carolina returned to its wonted state of anarchy. When the privy council vetoed the laws of the Wilmington assembly, the Albemarle sections regained their supremacy. However, within a few years the march of settlement brought a majority of new settlers into the colony, and the assembly reluctantly consented to the removal of the capital to New Bern. This conflict, leading the Carolina frontiersmen to regard the king with suspicion, combined with the quitrent controversy and the land struggle to bring North Carolina to the point where it would welcome an American revolution. The settlement of the West and the War of the Regulation completed the estrangement between the crown and the democratically inclined people of North Carolina.

While North Carolina developed politically until it was the most democratic of the southern colonies, its cultural and social development lagged. At the time of the Revolution, the colony had the largest proportion of whites of any of the southern communities, there being but 20,000 Negroes in a total population of 130,000. But this white dominance did not produce cultural development comparable to that of North Carolina's neighbors. Small farms and the scarcity of a landed and slaveholding aristocracy resulted in less time for leisure and for the cultivation of the arts. The colony had few libraries and no colleges, though Edenton and a few other places had schools. The sons of the few great planters went to Princeton or to English schools for their higher education.

2. South Carolina

Far different from the social order of North Carolina was that of South Carolina. While North Carolina became a land of small farms, of yeoman farmers, and a few slaves, South Carolina became a land of many Negroes and a fully developed plantation system. The plantation system that developed in South Carolina was quite different from the plantation society of Virginia, Maryland, and North Carolina.

Fundamentally, the difference between South Carolina and her northern neighbors was the difference between rice and tobacco. For the first few years the settlers, themselves representing an overflow from Barbados, sought for a crop that would enable them to duplicate the plantation system that they had known on their island home. A series of experiments came to an end in 1694 when the governor raised a crop of rice in his garden. Legend has it that a captain of a ship from Madagascar presented rice to the inhabitants. Whatever the truth of this story, the "Madagascar" variety of rice was found to be particularly suited to the colony's swamps, and immediately the colonists turned their energies to the production of the new crop. Soon population increased, and the introduction of Negro slavery solved the labor problem. In 1708, a little over a decade after the first rice was grown, the colony had a population of 3,500 whites, 4,100 Negroes, and 1,400 enslaved Indians. Of the whites, only 120 were indentured servants. In the next few years the number of Negroes increased, and the production of rice became almost the exclusive source of wealth of the colony. In 1718 the colony was producing 19,530 hundredweight of rice, and by 1724 about 4,000 tons of rice were being produced by 14,000 whites and 32,000 Negroes. Steadily throughout the eighteenth century the production of rice increased. In 1765, 32,000 tons of rice were produced by a population of 40,000 whites and 90,000 Negroes. A decade later, at the outbreak of the Revolution, the production of rice had increased to over 55,000 tons.

As in Virginia, the headright system of granting lands enabled the first settlers to obtain the best lands for the growing of the staple crop. Along the coast and beside the rivers, the available swamps became rice fields. After the Revolution, the system of flooding the fields came into general use and enabled the planter to expand the region where his crop was grown.

Because of the unhealthful and malarial conditions in the swamps, laborers soon succumbed to disease. Negroes, however, were cheap, and the planters, familiar with slavery in the West Indies, readily adapted the Africans to new duties. The plantation system, however, was more closely related to Jamaica than to Jamestown. The lands of South Carolina were held in large estates with large numbers of slaves. The rice planter's profits were large and immediate and he procured slaves rapidly.

Promoters of the colony were certain that great fortunes lay in rice culture, and one of the pamphlets of the time asserted that an Englishman with £100 could count upon a profit of 40 per cent from the beginning. In order to obtain this return, the planter was advised to buy English goods, which he could import into the colony and sell for 150 pounds. With this money he might invest in livestock, tools, provisions, and a couple of slaves at £45 a head. Assuming the cultivation of three acres for each laborer—two in rice and one in foodstuffs—the rice would yield for the market 1,000 pounds, which would sell for 15 shillings a hundredweight. After making allowances for the care of each slave, the farmer should realize a 40 per cent return on his investment the first year. The enthusiastic promoter did not explain why one should enter the cultivation of rice at 40 per cent when the trade in English goods would bring 50 per cent.

Although this prophecy was highly optimistic, the profits from rice brought a rapid growth in population and enabled the planter to enjoy luxuries and a cultural fulfillment impossible in Virginia. Part of this result was due to the system of slave management and part was due to Charleston's role as the center of colonial life. After 1742, indigo supplemented rice as a staple product of South Carolina. In 1748, Parliament gave a bounty of six pence a pound to the colonial producers of indigo. When the West Indian supply of dyestuff declined, the Carolina planters reaped a profit of from 33 to 50 per cent.

The existence of large plantations in South Carolina made the system of slave control different from that in the other colonies. Almost as soon as rice became a feasible crop, the number of Negroes in the colony exceeded the number of whites. Moreover, the planters of South Carolina did not live on their plantations, but left them to the management of overseers. The Negroes were thus deprived of the opportunity for personal service and for advancement in the affections of their masters that was possible on the smaller plantations of the northern colonies. South Carolinians were wont to complain that their Negroes were harder to manage than were those of the other colonies, and they attributed this fact to differences in the type and intelligence of the Negroes imported. While it is true that the system in vogue in South

Carolina required intelligent laborers, it is also true that the Negro had little contact with white civilization on the large plantations of the colony. Legally, this situation was reflected in the harsher slave code of the rice colonies.

The slave code of the tobacco colonies was based primarily upon the English laws of apprenticeship; but the South Carolinians, borrowing many of their institutions from the West Indies, based their code upon Spanish law. The Spanish system derived from Roman law, in which the slave was the absolute property of his master. In Virginia and Maryland the slave had rights which his master was bound to respect, but in South Carolina the owner had practically absolute authority over the lives of his chattels. In South Carolina the willful murder of a slave was punishable by a fine of £50 and three months' imprisonment. No restrictions were placed on the methods of treating the slaves, and cruel and unusual punishments were not unknown. Excessive punishment resulting in the death of a slave was not considered a criminal offense. Runaways were punished more severely than in the northern colonies, and overseers were required to whip all slaves found upon their plantations without permits from their masters.

The laws in South Carolina differed not only in words from those of the tobacco colonies, but also the different system produced variations in the spirit of the laws. Slavery was harsh at its best; but in the northern colonies the hardships were mitigated by the smallness of holdings and personal contacts between master and servant. In South Carolina such mitigating influences were absent, and the law's full rigor bore upon the slave. Overseers, more interested in the commissions that they were to receive from the year's crop than in the preservation of the capital invested in either land or labor, were likely to be unduly severe. The death rate of slaves in the rice fields was high, but Negroes were cheap and the system thrived.

The greater severity of the Carolina slave code was reflected in more serious slave outbreaks. In 1711 a number of escaped slaves, led by a Spanish Negro named Sebastian, established a base for marauding expeditions and terrorized the frontier until Sebastian's capture. In the next three decades five other uprisings matured beyond mere plots. In 1740 an insurrection under the leadership of one Cato resulted in the massacre of twenty or more whites and the plundering of a number of plantations. Drastic punishments followed the suppression of each of these plots. Under the circumstances, the number of such outbreaks was small—testifying to the efficiency of white control and to the lack of competent leadership among the blacks. But the masters lived under constant fear of slave insurrection.

While overseers controlled their slaves, Carolina's planters spent much of their time enjoying the cultural and social advantages of Charleston. The city was both the political capital and the center of commerce and society. Since it was free from the malarial conditions of the rice regions, the planters spent their summers there. Those of sufficient wealth, or with trustworthy overseers, remained for the winter season when the assembly met and balls and sports gave ample entertainment. So important was Charleston in the life of the colony that until 1719 it was the only polling place, and the city itself sent several representatives to the assembly. The only city of consequence in the colonial South, it boasted a public library, several newspapers, and a society in touch with the latest European fashions in dress and entertainment. Some of the best-known English actors performed in the theater, and imported musicians gave concerts.

The planters who migrated to Charleston for the social season maintained town houses. In contrast to the prevailing types of town planning and household architecture in the other English colonies, the houses of Charleston were built with their ends upon the street. High walls kept the enclosed gardens from the gaze of the curious passer-by. The houses that faced on the gardens were most notable for their two-storied porches, upon which the household spent much of its time. Unique in domestic architecture, Charleston was the most beautiful of the American cities and retained for generations something of the charm which characterized it in the colonial period.

Like her neighbor to the North, South Carolina had no college. The close connection between the colony and the mother country led the planters to send their sons to England for higher education. The colony possessed some lower schools, however, which were better supported than were those in the other colonies. In 1712 the legislature made an appropriation for a school in Charleston and provided for a schoolmaster in each parish of the colony. Public education, however, as in the other southern colonies, retained an atmosphere of charity. Libraries, mostly semipublic in nature, were established at Charleston. The proprietary charter established the Anglican church in South Carolina, but for a number of years no one made an effort to enforce observance of its services, and Charleston had the only church in operation. In 1704, Governor Johnston tried to secure a more effective establishment. A few years earlier the law had extended religious freedom to all but the Roman Catholics. The colony now taxed dissenters for the support of the church and restricted offices to Anglican communicants. Opposition to this move was immediate, as well as to the law that put church affairs in each parish under the direction of laymen who had the power to remove ministers. The dissenters appealed to England and secured a modification of the colonial law.

Politically, the story of South Carolina differs in few essential respects from that of the other southern colonies. If there was somewhat less dispute between the planter aristocracy and the upcountry democracy than was to be found in Virginia, there was greater trouble between the discontented and debt-ridden planters and the governors who attempted to carry out the will of the proprietors or to force the colonials to conform to the imperial policies of the British Board of Trade. During the first years of the colony, the proprietors made efforts to establish

Locke's Fundamental Constitutions, but the plan was so ill-designed for frontier conditions that even the distant proprietors perceived its impracticability. Instead of the complicated system devised by the philosopher's fertile imagination, government in South Carolina took on the form that it possessed in the other colonies. A governor, representing the proprietors, ruled over the colony with the advice and assistance of a grand council and an assembly representing the people. During the proprietary period there was constant wrangling between the governors and the people. Fundamentally, this division was due to the fact that the proprietors regarded their colony as a source of revenue, while the settlers were equally intent upon their own well-being. In the eighteenth century, a particular source of dispute was the extension of the suffrage to the large number of Huguenots who had settled in the colony. By 1700 the Huguenots had been admitted to the suffrage and had been granted religious freedom.

Constant danger assailed the colony from the Spanish settlers in near-by Florida, who made occasional raids upon Charleston and stirred up the Indians against the colonists. In 1715 a quickly won war with the Yemassee Indians was a source of long-continued troubles in the colony. In 1719, as a result of quarrels growing out of the war, the proprietors were forced to surrender their political rights.

As a royal province, South Carolina differed little from the other colonies. The assembly quarrelled with royal as it had with proprietary governors over the powers of the assembly and the right to issue paper money. The paper-money issue served to align the merchants of Charleston against the planters and the people of the colony. The dispute was finally settled by a law fixing the value of the outstanding currency and forbidding any addition to its volume.

Although this procedure settled the particular issue, the fundamental conflict between the merchants and the people was to continue in other forms. Especially virulent was the struggle between the council and the assembly over the right of the assembly to initiate money bills. From 1730 to 1739 the government was torn over this issue, until unsatisfactory compromise gave the council the right to amend appropriation measures which originated in the lower house. The council, however, seldom attempted to exercise its power, so that the practical victory was with the popular representatives.

The last years of the colonial period in South Carolina were marked by an absence of major disputes. Part of the reason for this peace was the prosperity of the colony dating from the introduction of indigo culture in 1741. For this new commodity, the colony was indebted to Eliza Lucas, nineteen-year-old daughter of the governor of Antigua, who imported plants and succeeded in extracting a high grade of dye. The profits from this new industry were increased by a bounty from the British government, and indigo joined rice as a staple crop. The colony also produced corn, pork, beef, and vegetables for export, and carried on various experiments with oranges, olives, and silk. Charleston was also the center of a large trade in deer skins.

3. The Development of Georgia

Georgia, the last of the English colonies to be established in America, was the only one formed as a result of deliberate planning by the British government. The purposes of the colony, at once military and philanthropic, had their origin in the fertile brain of James Oglethorpe. As a military man, General Oglethorpe realized that South Carolina was exposed to attacks by the neighboring Spaniards of Florida and was weakened by slavery and the plantation system. As a business-man with large interests in the Royal African Company, General Oglethorpe wished to retain and protect the rich market that his company had in the rice colony. But General Oglethorpe was also a philanthropist, and as a member of Parliament he had investigated conditions in Eng-land's debtors' prisons. The combination of these interests led Oglethorpe to conceive of a buffer colony between South Carolina and Florida, settled by the inmates of the debtors' prisons on condition that they render military service, and free from the weakening evils of slavery and rum. Parliament, perceiving both an opportunity to strengthen the English grip on the southern fur trade and a means of defending the frontier against Spain, authorized a group of philanthropists to establish the colony of Georgia. The proprietors were to act as trustees of the colony, supervise its settlement, rule over it in a patriarchal fashion, and turn it over to the crown at the end of twenty-one years. The profit motive was absent, for the trustees were not to hold land in the colony or to derive a revenue from it.

In the spring of 1733 Oglethorpe landed at the mouth of the Savannah River with one hundred and thirty men, women, and children who had been gathered from the poorest classes of London. The general immediately negotiated with the Indians and obtained from them a promise to abandon the French and the Spanish. He laid out the city of Savannah and be~an to encourage immigration. Soon Salzburger Lutherans arrived to found Old and New Ebenezer, Highland Scots came to New Inverness, and even pacifist Moravians found temporary refuge in the military colony. Nearly five thousand persons came to Georgia in the first half-dozen years of its existence. All were settled on the land under promise to render military service. Upon the approach of war, however, the settlers left for other colonies and Georgia was almost depopulated.

The trustees had no desire to establish the plantation system under which the poorer classes would have to compete with the large planters. They did not intend their colony to compete with rice and tobacco. Instead, they hoped that Georgia would grow silk and other commodities not already produced under the British flag. Accordingly, they established the settlers on fifty-acre tracts, which were to be held on the condition of the performance of military duties. These lands could not be sold, mortgaged, or divided by the holders. Partly because Negroes might aid the Spanish in case of war, Parliament forbade the importation or use of slaves in the colony. The trustees, however, furnished indentured servants who were to receive fifty acres of land from the colonial government upon the completion of their indentures. Independent settlers, paying their own way, might receive allotments of land not to exceed five hundred acres, but they were required to transport from six to ten servants. The trustees fixed the rate of wages for laborers and provided for loans to worthy settlers to enable them to acquire farms.

Almost from the beginning it was evident to the Georgia settlers that the policy of the trustees was unfeasible. "It's hard living here without a servant," complained a settler who found that the task of clearing the forest and building houses and fences prevented his planting a crop. Despite the effort of the trustees to supply indentured servants, their cost remained high and the people of Georgia complained against being deprived of slaves. Moreover, the colonists objected to the land ordinances which stayed the growth of a plantation system. Across the Savannah River they beheld with envy the mansions, wealth, and freedom of the South Carolinians. Some of the settlers moved across the line while others, hoping to bring about a modification of policy, petitioned the trustees for permission to import slaves. But Oglethorpe thought that slaves would weaken the colony for military defense, that they would flee to the surrounding Indians, and that the colony, instead of being a haven for the poor and the oppressed, would be overrun by slaveholders.

Soon after 1740 the Georgians began to ignore the law against possessing slaves. In England, the pressure of the slave traders on Parliament was sufficient to cause the trustees to close their eyes to the tacit violation of their decrees. In 1749 the trustees themselves asked Parliament for a repeal of the act excluding slaves. With this, the plantation system came to Georgia, and thereafter the economic structure of the colony was much like that of South Carolina. Rice and indigo came to dominate the colonists' attention, and by 1756 Georgia was exporting over a million pounds of the former and two and a half tons of the latter commodity. In addition, the colony exported corn, flour, beef, pork, and tobacco. The slow growth of population, however, continued, and most of the social problems of the plantation system remained in an embryonic stage until after the Revolution.

Under the trustees, the government of Georgia was solely in the hands of the trustees or the governor whom they sent to control the settlers. In 1751 the trustees turned over their rights to the crown, and until the Revolution Georgia was ruled as a royal colony. Under the first of the royal governors, there was friction between the king's agent and the colonial council; but later governors tactfully evaded questions of prerogative and power. On the eve of the Revolution, Georgia was the most loyal of the southern colonies.

CHAPTER 4

The Southern Frontier

1. THE FRONTIER REGION

WHILE plantation agriculture was producing a stratified society in the Tidewater regions of the southern colonies, an entirely different economic and social order was forming beyond the Blue Ridge Mountains. From an early date, settlers in the Tidewater had been interested in the western country and an occasional trader had ventured into the Piedmont, over the mountains and down into the Great Valley. In 1650 Captain Abraham Wood led a party through the mountains to the falls of the Roanoke River. Fur traders sought the Indian country and penetrated the Cherokee lands to the southwest. The fur trade enabled some of the Tidewater entrepreneurs to lay the basis of fortunes with which they founded plantations and stocked them with slaves. In 1671 Governor Berkeley, hearing Indian stories of a great western river, sent an expedition under Wood which reached the New River. Other exploring expeditions reached the Yadkin River and entered the Tennessee Valley. News of the western land stimulated a desire to secure grants in the Piedmont region. The assembly granted land on condition that it be settled and forts erected against the Indians.

Tidewater interest in the frontier gave impetus to Governor Alexander Spotswood's expedition to the Blue Ridge. In 1710 Spotswood became governor of Virginia and immediately undertook vigorous measures to develop the colony. He imported winemakers to inaugurate grape culture and formed a settlement of Germans at Germanna to smelt iron. In 1716 the energetic governor with a company of 50 "gentlemen," their horses shod with the newly made iron, crossed the Blue Ridge and proceeded into the Valley of Virginia. The land was formally claimed for the king, and Spotswood and his "Knights of the Golden Horseshoe" returned to Williamsburg to petition the crown for land in the fertile valley. The wasteful system of tobacco culture made the planters eager to desert their exhausted acres for new fields.

2. GERMANS AND SCOTCH-IRISH

While the Tidewater planters were obtaining grants for lands beyond the mountains, the Valley received population from another source. The settlement of Pennsylvania, beginning after 1685, had diverted the stream of indentured servants from the South to William Penn's new colony. Germans migrated to Pennsylvania in large numbers, and Quakers found there a refuge from religious and economic persecution. Some time before 1720, Scotch-Irish began to arrive in the New World, entering at ports from Boston to Savannah. To the Scotch-Irish, as to the Germans, the opportunities offered by Pennsylvania's proprietor were especially attractive. The eastern portion of Pennsylvania soon filled up and the newcomers were forced into the west. The contentious character of the Scotch-Irish led them to quarrel with the proprietors over the price of lands, dealings with Indians, and the payment of quitrents, and when the proprietors attempted to force them to pay for lands upon which they settled, they moved southward, along the Great Valley, into Maryland and Virginia. The southern frontier was thus filled by Pennsylvania's overflow population.

About 1726 the first settlers arrived in the Virginia Valley. Germans, English, and Scotch-Irish were inextricably mixed in this migration. The first groups settled near Martinsburg and Shepherdstown in present-day West Virginia and along the Opequon and Cacapon creeks in the vicinity of Winchester. The population of these regions grew so rapidly and spread so widely that in 1734 Virginia organized Orange County to extend government over the western regions. In 1738 the assembly organized two "districts," Frederick and Augusta, west of the Blue Ridge. In 1743 and 1745 these districts became counties. The remaining region, including the present states of West Virginia, Kentucky, Ohio, Indiana, Illinois, Michigan, and Wisconsin, was known as West Augusta. In 1754 the settlements along the South River were included in Hampshire County, the last county to be created in Virginia before the Revolution.

From Virginia, both Scotch-Irish and Germans spread into North Carolina. Between 1743 and 1762 the counties of Granville, Bladen, Anson, Orange, Rowan, and Mecklenburg were formed to incorporate the expanding population. In order to fill up her frontier, South Carolina made land grants and furnished livestock and provisions to prospective settlers. Georgia, too, furnished equipment to settlers. Lands in Virginia and Maryland sold cheaply, and Governor Gooch offered religious toleration to the Scotch-Irish Presbyterians who moved into the Valley of Virginia.

These frontier settlers differed greatly from the inhabitants of the Tidewater. Some of the Germans were members of pietist religious groups and settled in religious communities. Others were members of the Lutheran and Reformed churches. All were Protestants. The Scotch-Irish were a particularly hardy race inured to hardships by long years of bitter struggle against the forces of man and nature. Lowland Scots in origin, they had inhabited the frontier between England and Scotland through long generations when there was almost constant war between these sections. For a century before their migration to America these stern Presbyterians had acted as an outpost of Protestantism in fiercely Catholic Ireland. In Ireland they had found themselves discriminated against by the English and victims of economic measures to protect English landlords and industry. Seeking freedom, they had moved to America, bitterly resolving to brook no tyranny from landowners, lawmakers, or priests of the established church. They squatted on the land in Pennsylvania and the southern colonies, defiantly informing the Penn family that "it was against the laws of God and nature that so much land should be idle, while so many Christians wanted it to labor on and to raise their bread." In Virginia they quarrelled with Lord Fairfax over the ownership of land, and in North Carolina they refused to pay quitrents.

In religion, these frontiersmen were ardent Presbyterians and enemies of the established church. They were not without culture, and they established academies and "log colleges" as readily as they built churches. The distance from markets and the inaccessibility of the seacoast prevented tobacco culture from developing among them, and therefore slavery took no root. Their farms were small, and they produced wheat and corn, rather than marketable crops. Once established on the frontier, they demanded political rights, and through their religious leadership at the time of the Great Awakening they organized the back-country people of Tidewater and Piedmont in opposition to the planter aristocracy.

3. LAND SPECULATION

The settlement of the Valley by Scotch-Irish and Germans increased the Tidewater planters' desire to acquire western lands. Land-hungry Virginians petitioned the crown for large grants or patented lands in the colonial land office. In 1745 Lord Fairfax secured title to the Northern Neck between the Potomac and Rappahannock rivers and in 1748 employed young George Washington to survey his lands. A decade earlier, William Byrd II had received 100,000 acres on the Roanoke River. In 1748 a number of the leading families of Virginia, including the lieutenant governor, Robert Dinwiddie, several members of the Lee family, and Lawrence and Augustine Washington, half brothers of George Washington, formed the Ohio Land Company to petition the king for a grant of land. At the moment, the English were asserting claims to the Ohio Valley, and the company received 500,000 acres of land on the Ohio between the Monongahela and the Little Kanawha rivers. The company was given 200,000 acres on condition that it settle 100 families and build a fort to protect them against the Indians. When this settlement had been made, the company would receive the additional 300,000 acres.

In 1750 the Ohio Land Company employed Christopher Gist to survey its lands and to make peace with the Indians. Gist looked over the lands, reported to the company, and went back to join other British agents in a conference with the Indians at Logstown, a trading post on the Ohio River. The Virginia assembly offered inducements to settlers and began building a road and a fort on the company's lands.

Other land companies were formed after the model of the Ohio Company. In 1749 the Virginia assembly chartered the Loyal Land Company and granted it 800,000 acres along the North Carolina line. In the same year, the assembly gave the Greenbrier Company 100,000 acres in western Virginia. Land speculation, combined with the needs of the plantation system, was expanding the borders of colonial Virginia.

4. The French and Indian War

The land into which the Virginians pushed was claimed by the French. Owning both the St. Lawrence and the Mississippi rivers, the French wanted the Ohio Valley to connect Canada and Louisiana. Their relations with the Indians, other than the Iroquois, were friendly, and their fur traders rivaled the English in trade with the red man. In 1749, just after the Ohio Company's grant was confirmed, the French in Canada sent Céloron de Bienville down the Ohio River to plant lead plates upon which were written the claim of the King of France to the land. When Gist held council with the Indians, French traders made efforts to defeat his negotiations. As the Virginians began to build their road into the Ohio Company's lands, the French planned to construct a series of forts from Lake Erie to the mouth of the Mississippi. In 1753 they built the first fort on a branch of the Allegheny River.

The Virginians prepared to protest against this advance of the French. Governor Dinwiddie commissioned young George Washington to carry a message to the commander of the fort. Gist guided the messenger to the fort, where Washington formally notified the French that they were trespassing. The commander received the Virginian with courtesy but refused to leave. Washington returned to Williamsburg to recommend the use of force against the invader. The governor dispatched a party to build a fort at the forks of the Ohio and sent Washington forward with a force of 300 men. Approaching the region, Washington met a French force. In a skirmish the commander was killed. Pressed by the French, Washington hastily constructed a fort, which he named Fort Necessity, and prepared to meet the advance. The French approached, and June 3, 1754, forced Washington to surrender.

Upon the news of this defeat, Virginia prepared for war, and the English government determined to support its colony's claims. General

Courtesy Washington & Lee University

COLONEL GEORGE WASHINGTON OF THE VIRGINIA MILITIA. Governor Dinwiddie commissioned young George Washington to carry a message to the commander of the fort. Christopher Gist guided the messenger to the fort, where Washington formally notified the French that they were trespassing. The commander received the Virginian with courtesy but refused to leave. Washington returned to Williamsburg to recommend the use of force against the invader.

Edward Braddock arrived in Virginia with two regiments of regular troops. The general consulted the governor and prepared to march into the wilderness, accompanied by militia from the colonies. Following the trail which the Ohio Company had cut to their lands to Cumberland, Maryland, the red-coated soldiers struck out into the wilderness. Knowing nothing of Indian warfare, the British general built a road as he advanced and insisted upon maintaining an orderly march which was more suited to European than to American conditions. The colonial militia, enlisted for short terms, were disgusted with the slow progress and objected to cutting the road. Understanding full well that his regular soldiers would be worthless in such conditions, Braddock ignored Washington's advice to follow the frontier method of warfare. On July 9, 1755, French and Indians attacked the advancing columns. Braddock was wounded and died four days later, and the British and colonials fell back. In Virginia, terror and despair mingled with pride in a militia that had held off the enemy until retreat could be made. The assembly voted £40,000 to prosecute the war.

Under Washington's direction, the southern colonies constructed a line of frontier forts against the Indians. The British government sent 1,300 regular troops into the South, and the colonies furnished 5,000 men. Especial danger came from the Cherokees on the Carolina border. The forts in the Cherokee country, notably Fort Loudon, served to keep the Indians quiet and to protect Charleston. The Indians, too, prevented Louisiana from being active in the war, and corruption among the rulers of the French colony saved the southern colonials from attack. The result was that the French and Indian War was fought out in the northern colonies and in Canada. To the credit of Braddock it should be noted that the decisive movements of the war were fought by regular troops in campaigns conducted according to European methods. The colonial militia and their Indian allies were relatively unimportant in the war's more significant aspects.

5. WESTERN LANDS AND BRITISH POLICY

The Treaty of Paris, ending the war in 1763, gave the English Florida, Canada, and the Ohio Valley. Soon thereafter France transferred Louisiana to Spain and abandoned her colonial dreams in North America. Immediately Virginia's land speculators prepared to take possession of the Ohio Valley. Along the frontier, Scotch-Irish and Germans moved into the newly conquered regions, and Tidewater planters formed companies to develop the land.

The declining fortunes of France struck terror among the Indians. In 1760 the Cherokees rose in South Carolina and destroyed Fort Loudon. The next year an expedition from Charleston devastated the Cherokee territory and made peace, but the southern Indians remained hostile to the colonists. In the West, the Indians offered even stronger resistance. Abandoned by the French, and especially fearful of the "Long Knives" from Virginia, the Indians took courage from desperation. Led by Pontiac, chief of the Ottawa tribe, the western Indians united. In May, 1763, they captured the British forts from Mackinaw to Fort Pitt and laid waste the settlements along the whole frontier. British officials and colonial governments took immediate action. Virginia sent one thousand militiamen against the savages. From Fort Pitt, Colonel Henry Bouquet led a stronger force which defeated the red men. The experience convinced the British government that some more definite policy must be adopted for the American frontier.

Although the French and Indian War had been part of a worldwide conflict between France and England, the British government for the first time paid serious attention to the American scene. Experience showed the rulers that the colonial militia was inadequate and that the frontier attitude toward the Indians was fraught with danger to imperial well-being. Moreover, interested colonials gave the government conflicting advice. While Virginian land speculators clamored for virgin lands, Pennsylvania's fur traders advised the crown against encouraging the advance of agricultural settlement. The confused Board of Trade determined to delay a decision until it could formulate a policy for the West. Accordingly, in October, 1763, the king issued a proclamation suspending settlements in the West. The proclamation created the colonies of East and West Florida and the Province of Quebec and placed the West under their political jurisdiction. The management of Indian affairs was taken out of the hands of the several colonies and placed under the control of two Indian agents, Sir William Johnson for the North and John Stuart for the South, responsible to the crown. The land west of the Alleghenies was set aside as Indian territory from which all settlement should be excluded until the Indian title could be cleared. Only the crown's agents could negotiate with the Indians for the evacuation of the western lands.

Although Pontiac's Conspiracy proved the necessity for approaching western questions with caution, the land-hungry Virginians of both Tidewater and frontier were eager to move west. The war had prevented the Ohio Company from complying with the terms of its grant and its title had lapsed. The members of the company thought that the circumstances should be considered and that they should be given additional time for making settlements. The crown, however, had determined to substitute the principle of the king's proclamation for the earlier policy of encouraging settlements. In Virginia, the hopeful speculators believed that the proclamation was but temporary and that there would soon be a return to the older system. Leading Virginians, many of them members of the Ohio Company, formed a new company to petition the king for a grant along the Mississippi River in present-day Illinois and Kentucky. Anxious to obtain lands, Washington sent a surveyor across the mountains to mark out suitable lands which might be patented as soon as the proclamation line was erased. Moreover, Washington busied himself in organizing the militia officers who had been promised land bounties by Virginia. These officers, too, sent an agent to England to secure their claims. At the same time, Pennsylvanians and New Yorkers turned their attention from fur trade to land-jobbing. Sir William Johnson, the Indian agent; George Croghan, fur trader; the fur trading firm of Baynton, Wharton and Morgan; New Jersey's governor, William Franklin; Benjamin Franklin, and others prominent in colonial politics and business formed a company to petition for a new colony east of the Mississippi and north of the Ohio. This scheme was defeated by Lord Hillsborough, president of the Board of Trade. Undismayed by this setback, the company enlarged its membership to include important London bankers, made peace with the rival petitioners for land by incorporating the old Ohio Company's claims and those of the Virginia bounty-seekers in their own request, and changed their petition to one for a colony south of the Ohio and east of the Little Kanawha River.

Skillful lobbying by Benjamin Franklin, agent for Pennsylvania, and the London bankers succeeded in removing Lord Hillsborough, and the charter for the colony of Vandalia was drafted in 1772. Before the papers could be issued, however, the American Revolution began, and the proposed fourteenth colony was never launched.

Meanwhile, the Indian agents had been at work clearing the Indian title to the western lands. In 1768 Sir William Johnson made a treaty at Fort Stanwix by which the Iroquois gave up western New York and Pennsylvania. In the same year, Colonel John Stuart met the Cherokees at Hard Labour and negotiated a treaty which cleared the title to lands south of the Ohio. In 1770, by the treaty of Lochaber, the Cherokees gave up most of what is now West Virginia and Kentucky.

6. WESTERN SETTLEMENTS

To the people of the frontier, neither the dangers from the Indians nor the solemn pronouncements of imperial policy acted as a deterrent for settlement on the forbidden land. Germans and Scotch-Irish moved across the proclamation line as soon as Pontiac's conspiracy had been suppressed. Without title to their possessions, they marked off their boundaries with their tomahawks and defended their occupancy by concerted action against claim-jumpers and land speculators. Within a few years, western Virginia was dotted with settlements at Charleston, Morgantown, Buckhannon, and Wheeling, and the Kanawha and Greenbrier valleys were occupied.

Farther south another movement of population was taking place. The region of the Holston River had become known to Virginians about 1767, and in the following two years a number of settlers sought the fertile valley. From Augusta County in Virginia a party moved in under the belief that they were settling in Virginia. In the spring of 1770, seventeen North Carolina families under James Robertson joined the settlers in the Watauga country. Many of them were former "Regulators" fleeing from the royal officials of North Carolina. John Sevier joined the colony in 1772. About this time the settlers learned that they were not in Virginia and requested the North Carolina government to extend its protection. But the Carolina government delayed action, and the settlers, in true frontier spirit, formed themselves into the Watauga Association and drafted laws for their own government. They created a "Court" with full legislative, executive, and judicial powers and proceeded to negotiate with the surrounding Indians. In 1774 they leased lands from the Indians for ten years, and the next year succeeded in making a treaty giving them the lands permanently. In 1778 North Carolina organized the Watauga settlements as the "Washington District," and the frontier government disappeared.

Land speculation was not limited to Virginia and the northern colonies. The dream of acquiring fortunes from western settlements developed in North Carolina at the same time that the Virginia planters were petitioning the king and settlers were moving to western Virginia and the vicinity of the Holston. A few years before the French and Indian War, the back country of North Carolina received an influx of planters from Virginia. These men soon created a plantation society similar to that of the Virginia Tidewater. Among these planters, young Richard Henderson practiced law and looked beyond the mountains with hopes of acquiring a fortune. In the course of his legal activities, Henderson came into contact with young Daniel Boone, who had made hunting trips through Cumberland Gap into the "Dark and Bloody Ground" the Indians called Kentucky.

Before Boone, explorers had entered Kentucky. In 1752 John Findlay had traveled down the Ohio River to the falls and had learned of Cumberland Gap from the Indians. In 1761 a party of "Long Hunters" entered the region from Cumberland Gap, and other hunting parties followed them during the succeeding years. In 1765 George Croghan visited the region and penetrated as far as the Great Bone Licks. The Indians, however, resented the hunters, and about 1770 began to attack them.

The reports of the fertile blue grass and the beautiful forests of Kentucky stimulated Boone's characteristic wanderlust. In May, 1769, Boone set out for Kentucky, where he explored the region, was captured by the Indians, escaped, and returned to his hunting. After two years he made his way back with glowing accounts for all who would listen.

Among his hearers was Richard Henderson, who organized a land speculating company and employed Boone to return to Kentucky and make a detailed report on the land. Then Henderson received assurance from Indian agents that a purchase from the Indians would be legal. Armed with their opinion, in August, 1774, Henderson reorganized his company into the Louisa Company, to purchase lands from the Indians. Henderson then visited the Cherokee territory and made preliminary arrangements. Returning, he reorganized his company, in January, 1775, as the Transylvania Company. The company promised lands to actual settlers at a rate of 20 shillings for 100 acres. Early in the year Henderson, Sevier, Robertson, and Isaac Shelby met the Indians at the Watauga council grounds. The Indians offered to sell lands which had already been sold to Virginia but which had not been paid for. This the whites refused, and the Indians agreed to sell lands south of the Cumberland River. But the speculators were still dissatisfied, and on March 17 the "Great Grant" was made. By this the Indians sold all of Kentucky and part of Tennessee for goods valued at 10,000 pounds. The Watauga settlers also purchased a tract on the Holston River for 2,000 pounds and made several smaller purchases.

Before the Great Grant was made, Boone set forth with a party of axmen to clear the way into Kentucky. Henderson followed with a party of settlers. Despite raids by hostile Indians, the party reached Boonesborough and prepared to establish homes. The entire expedition, however, was assailed by enemies. In Virginia there was considerable resentment at the purchase by a North Carolinian of lands claimed by the northern colony. In both North Carolina and Virginia the governors issued proclamations condemning the Transylvania Company, and in Virginia leaders were greatly excited. Washington listened to talk of reducing the invaders to obedience, and Patrick Henry, who had earlier been refused permission to join the company, denounced Henderson.

Despite these objections, Henderson's colony went forward. Before Boonesborough was established, Harrodsburg had been founded, and settlers were present at St. Asaphs and in other places. Henderson planned to unite these settlements under one government. In May of 1775, delegates from four towns assembled at Harrodsburg, constituted themselves a legislature for Transylvania, and passed laws protecting game and encouraging the breeding of horses. The proprietors reserved the right to veto laws. The company opened a land office and a store. In September the Transylvania settlers petitioned the Continental Congress to admit them as the fourteenth American state. The congress, however, refused to recognize the new state. Virginia and North Carolina declared Henderson's purchase illegal, while the Kentucky settlers, resenting Henderson's assumption of authority, petitioned Virginia to extend protection. In 1776 Virginia incorporated the settlements in Kentucky County.

Other land-speculating movements in Virginia occurred almost simultaneously with the founding of Transylvania. Lord Dunmore, Virginia's royal governor, was as eager as any Tidewater planter for western lands. He looked with favor upon a scheme proposed by Dr. John Connolly to plant a colony on Virginia's lands south of the Ohio, and when the Vandalia project was launched, the governor protested that Virginia had charter rights to the region. The governor's legal advisor on land matters was Patrick Henry, himself interested in acquiring landed wealth. Henry assured Dunmore that individual purchases from the Indians were legal. In 1773, Dunmore joined the Wabash Company and took an immediate interest in westward expansion. This company was one of two formed by William Murray, who had bought two tracts in Illinois. Murray gave Dunmore a controlling interest in one company in order to enlist his support. The governor promptly commended the Illinois and the Wabash companies to the British colonial secretary.

Lord Dunmore's interest in the West made him intolerant of Indian efforts to protect their lands. As frontiersmen pushed into the Indian territory, repeated clashes occurred between the races. The stubborn and relentless Scotch-Irish showed no disposition to respect Indian rights. All over the West, frontiersmen adopted the Indian methods of conflict, and both races practiced the worst barbarities of savage warfare. Raids of Indians upon white settlements were met by retaliatory plunderings of Indian villages. The frontier was in ferment and the colonial officials in the West did nothing to discourage the excesses of savagery. In January of 1774 Dr. Connolly fired upon a party of Shawnees at Fort Pitt, and in April he issued a proclamation urging the frontiersmen to defend themselves. At the same time, Dunmore placed the militia under Connolly's command. Primarily, Dunmore was interested in quieting the Indians in order to make a treaty which would further his own land speculations.

The war came quickly. The frontiersmen interpreted Connolly's proclamation as an invitation to begin hostilities, and on April 30, 1774, frontier drunkards murdered the family of a friendly half-breed, Logan. The bereaved man immediately aroused his tribesmen, and Indians began to attack settlers from the Ohio to the Tennessee. Dunmore personally marched at the head of 1,200 men, and a second expedition under Andrew Lewis advanced upon the Great Kanawha. The governor reached the Indian villages near the mouth of the Hocking River while Lewis assailed the savages under Cornstalk at the mouth of the Great Kanawha. On October 10, 1774, Lewis fought Cornstalk at the battle of Point Pleasant. Although defeated in the battle, the Virginians obtained a treaty by which the Indians agreed to stay north of the Ohio. The war removed the Indian menace from Kentucky and Virginia's western settlements.

Lord Dunmore's War was the final act in colonial relations with the Indians before the Revolution. The war was not approved by the imperial authorities but was precipitated by Dunmore's own personal interests. Nevertheless, it resulted in preventing the Indians from giving effective aid to the British during the forthcoming Revolution.

7. TIDEWATER AND FRONTIER

The settlement of the western region brought a new element into southern society. Upon the lands between the seacoast and the mountains, planters exercised dominion over both the slaves who worked the land and the poorer whites of the back country. Supported by staple crops, controlling government through the county courts, parish vestries, and seats in the assembly and the council, and giving a nominal support to the Anglican church, the squires developed an ease and grace of living marked by annual convenings at Williamsburg or Charleston and the dilettante pursuit of culture.

In contrast with the Tidewater, the frontier regions were settled by a virile and hardy folk who had little respect for the gentler graces of planter culture. Faced with hostile nature and treacherous savages, and equal in their comparative poverty, the frontiersmen were predisposed to a practical democracy. Their agriculture was devoted to food crops and they supplemented their diet with the game of the forests. In religion they were dissenters, organized into democratic congregations which followed the tenets of Calvinism.

A more fundamental difference between the Tidewater and the frontier was based upon geography. The rivers of the Tidewater led down to the sea and to England. At the same time they acted as barriers to intercolonial co-operation. On the frontier, the Great Valley was a highway of communication which crossed the nebulous boundary lines of the separate colonies. The West had geographical unity and constituted a backbone to which were attached the separate ribs of the Tidewater colonies. In but one matter did the East and West see eye to eye. They were united in a desire for western expansion; on all other problems they were in almost constant conflict.

The political structure of the colonies was heavily weighted in favor of the Tidewater region. The Virginia House of Burgesses was composed of two members from each county, but there were many small counties in the Tidewater and only a few large ones in the West. In addition, three boroughs and the College of William and Mary, all in the East, had representatives. This inequity gave the control of the Assembly to the Tidewater. Taxes bore with greater weight on small farmers than on great planters. The right to vote was limited to those holding fifty unsettled acres or twenty-five acres and a house. The council was composed of the colony's richest aristocrats.

In North Carolina, each of the eastern counties sent five members to the assembly while the larger western counties had but two representatives each. The Westerners also complained of the assembly's dilatory reluctance to establish new counties. The members of the assembly were required to have one hundred acres of land. The council, as aristocratic as that in the neighboring colony, was completely subservient to the royal governor.

South Carolina's frontier had even less voice in its government. There were no upland counties, and the frontiersmen were incorporated in lowland parishes which extended westward to indefinite boundaries beyond the outermost settlements. The settlers of the West had to travel to the seacoast to courts or even to vote. The Commons House had forty-eight members elected every three years by property holders. A member had to own five hundred acres and ten slaves or have taxable property worth one thousand pounds. Upcountry settlers protested against these inequalities, but their only relief prior to the Revolution was the establishment of four judicial districts in the West. Even this reform was primarily designed to extend the power of the seacoast planters and conferred no right of participation in the government.

The conflicts between the regions of the southern colonies were generally confined to the assemblies or to electoral campaigns. In Virginia, the common interest of the planters and the frontiersmen in the western lands prevented conflicts from becoming serious, while the religious leadership which the frontier Presbyterians furnished the people of the back country enabled the frontiersmen successfully to challenge the planter control. In 1765 a scandal in the public treasury resulted in the election of frontiersmen to the burgesses and brought into power the democratic leaders who were to carry the colony into the Revolution.

Less easily resolved were the problems in the Carolinas. The corrupt administration of justice by Tidewater parish officials and the exaction of exorbitant fees caused the South Carolina upcountrymen to form associations. Calling themselves "Regulators," the associations defied the power of the colony and resorted to lynch law to break their oppression. The Regulator movement spread to North Carolina, where the sheriffs were especially oppressive. The court officials and tax collectors charged illegal rates and showed an intolerant efficiency in collecting quitrents. The result was an uprising of Regulators in 1766 which continued for several years. In 1770 rioters broke up the court at Hillsborough and prevented the judge from exercising his official duties. With the frontier in arms, Governor Tryon marched against the Regulators and defeated them in the battle of Alamance in 1771. The movement collapsed and a number of Regulators fled from the governor's vengeance to the Watauga settlements, but the frontier seethed in opposition to the governor and to the royal power.

CHAPTER 5

The Revolution in the South

1. British Colonial Policy

THREE thousand miles of salt water separated England from her colonies in America. The vessels which traversed that dangerous barrier were frail craft, dependent upon the wind and fearful alike of its deathlike calm and its stormy fury. Long weeks were required to carry the hopeful settler or the ambitious official from his native heath to his new home. Distance made communication difficult and made impossible a uniform development in mother country and colonies. Differences in conditions, however, were more significant than the ocean in causing the two lands to grow apart. The conquest of the wilderness, the defeat of the Indians, the production of new and strange crops, and the development of a new system of agricultural production occupied the attention of the southern colonists at the same time that England was turning from an agricultural into a commercial nation. During 150 years the southern colonies developed the plantation system, with its tobacco, rice, and indigo, with its Negro slavery and its planter aristocracy. Social stratification came as the planters filled the bottom lands and the later comers and the less acquisitive were crowded into the back country or pushed out to the frontier. Sectional divisions representing economic, social, and political diversity accentuated the rise of southern classes, but everywhere in the southern colonies civilization was based upon the ownership and exploitation of land.

While a landed aristocracy arose in the South, England witnessed the creation of a commercial aristocracy. The commercial company which had founded Virginia had many counterparts in seventeenth-century England. The economic device of the joint-stock company enabled men to extract huge profits from trade and stretched far the outer borders of the British Empire. The men who made the empire came to rule it, and Whig aristocrats, flaunting their purchased titles, took over the government. Wealth gave them control of local election districts, and they filled Parliament with their representatives. William and Mary yielded to the Whig politicians who had brought them to the throne and lent royal encouragement to the commercialists. The German Hanoverians gave little attention to their island kingdom and permitted the parliamentary majority to dictate a cabinet which assumed the real power of the crown.

These commercial lords were interested in the expansion of business and looked upon the colonies with eyes made astigmatic by long gazing on profits. Their economic and political philosophy was summed up in the creed of mercantilism, which had for its essence the search for gold. In the pragmatic philosophy of the mercantilists, each business transaction involved a winner and a loser. He was the winner who emerged from the market place with gold. Therefore, they reasoned, an individual should sell more than he bought in order to show a balance in money, and a nation should obtain a favorable balance of trade by exporting more than it imported. In this scheme of things, colonies played an important part, for they could produce the raw materials which the mother country needed and could purchase her manufactured surplus which other nations would not buy. Therefore, the colonies should be restricted in their manufacturing, prevented from competing in commerce, and limited in their trade so that the nation might be prosperous.

Pursuing this policy, the British government undertook to regulate American commerce. Beginning in 1651, when the government was in the hands of the rising Puritan business classes, Parliament passed the first of a series of navigation acts which limited the trade of the empire to British-owned ships. Designed to injure the Dutch carrying trade during a war, the principle was continued. In 1660 a new act "enumerated" certain colonial products which could not be exported outside the empire. Tobacco, the principal southern product on the enumerated list, bore an import duty from one to two and a half times the market value. This increased the price and decreased consumption. Maryland and Virginia planters overproduced, met declining prices, and blamed the government's policy. The navigation acts, however, gave colonial tobacco a monopoly in the empire which more than offset the loss of the continental market. Nevertheless, the planters criticized the government and resented the necessity of shipping their product at the higher protected rates of English-owned vessels. In 1705 rice was put on the enumerated list. South Carolina rice had already entered the markets of the Mediterranean countries but the enumeration so increased the cost that South Carolina lost her outlets until the law was modified. Later navigation acts proved more irritating than burdensome to the South, but the colonists learned their first lessons in opposing parliamentary control as they grumbled over restrictions. The New England colonies were much harder hit by the navigation acts, and the discontent of their neighbors occasionally echoed through the South. Merchants in Charleston, Savannah, and Norfolk complained of the acts, and since many planters were merchants on a smaller scale, they too complained of high costs and restricted markets.

In addition, the British government regulated colonial manufacturing both to prevent competition with home industry and to limit colonial production to raw materials. Although this policy placed little burden upon the staple-producing South, it deterred a diversification of economic activities. Early industrial enterprises, especially iron manufacture in Virginia, proved abortive, but the government's acts stopped any efforts to revive industry. In the interests of the English merchants, Parliament attempted to regulate the use of commodity money in the colonies and refused to permit the southern colonies to raise the value of their silver coins in relation to the English shilling. Northern colonies, from whom the English government received less revenue, were permitted to increase the exchange rate, and thereby drew coin from the South.

Other features of the colonial administration also proved distasteful to the South. Royal officials in the colonies received their instructions from the Board of Trade, which was more interested in English than in colonial problems. The officials seldom understood the viewpoint or the interests of the colonials, and constitutional squabbles between governors and assemblies resulted. In general, these disputes were over the payment of salaries, the control of the public treasury, the collection of quitrents, or the installation of the established clergy. Yet they were symptoms of a fundamental division between the commercial lords who ruled the empire and the agricultural masters of the colonies.

The French and Indian War marked a new advance in the efforts of the English government to make the colonies conform to an imperial pattern. At the close of the war, the government found itself with a greatly increased debt and with a growing realization of the necessity for adequate colonial administration. Wartime experience with the colonial militia showed that the undisciplined troops were but frail reeds, while new Indian outbreaks gave proof that a standing army in America was necessary. Moreover, the rising industrial classes of England became more insistent upon a control of colonial raw materials and a monopoly of the colonial markets. Statesmen of the empire sought to improve the colonial administration and to raise enough revenue in America to maintain a standing army. The first act in this direction was a new Sugar Act passed in 1764 to replace an older Molasses Act of 1733. Although the new act was less restrictive than the old, stricter enforcement caused objection from New England and southern merchants. On the other hand, a high tariff gave full protection to South Carolina indigo.

The revenues derived from this act were to be used for defending the colonies, and the ministry determined to station an army of ten thousand men in America. Since more money would be needed for their support than could be obtained from the Sugar Act, Parliament passed a Stamp Act. This measure provided that all business documents, newspapers, and legal documents should bear a revenue stamp. As a legitimate tax measure, the new law was well conceived. It constituted a tax upon special privileges and fell upon those best able to bear it. But while it was economically valid, it soon proved politically unwise. The newspaper editors and the lawyers, whose activities were thus singled out for taxation, were the most articulate groups in the colonies. Merchants, less articulate, were nevertheless both burdened and annoyed by the tax. Militia officers, who lacked the perspective of the English war office, were vain of their martial prowess and denied the necessity for an army in America. And at the moment, the Proclamation of 1763 rankled in the acquisitive hearts of land speculators. The result was widespread opposition to the Stamp Act.

In the hands of the lawyers, the colonial objections to taxation became discussions on the nature of the empire. For several years the younger lawyers of the country had been evolving a constitutional rationalization for colonial discontent. In 1761 James Otis in Massachusetts, arguing against writs of assistance, had declared that an act of Parliament was contrary to the English constitution. In 1763 Patrick Henry harangued a Virginia jury with a vitriolic denial of the right of the Privy Council to disallow a colonial law. The case was the "Parsons Cause," growing out of a law permitting vestries to pay ministers' salaries, usually provided for in tobacco, at two pence a pound in lieu of tobacco. The act was evidence that the control of Virginia had passed from the hands of the Anglican planters to the dissenting population of the back country and the frontier. The Privy Council disallowed the law, and the ministers brought suit. Henry declared the crown's action tyrannical and illegal, and the jury granted the ministers one penny in damages. From this time Henry was the leader of Virginia's radical element.

When news of the Stamp Act arrived in Virginia, Henry arose in the assembly to present resolutions embodying the colonial position. Two royal charters, declared the Virginia Resolves, had given the settlers of Virginia "all the liberties, privileges, franchises, and immunities, that have at any time been held, enjoyed, and possessed, by the people of Great Britain." The "distinguishing characteristic" of British freedom was the people's right to be taxed by their own representatives. The colony of Virginia had not yielded its right, and the sole authority to levy taxes in the colony was vested in the General Assembly. The people were not obliged to pay taxes levied by any other body, and tax collectors of the British government were to be considered enemies. Speaking on his resolutions, which were more extreme than those adopted, Henry verged upon treason when he exclaimed that Caesar had his Brutus, Charles the First his Cromwell, and some American might still arise to oppose George the Third. Rebuked by the speaker, Henry apologized to the house by attributing his intemperate remarks to his zeal for his country's dying liberty.

The Virginia Resolves were published in the newspapers and sent to the other colonial assemblies. The Massachusetts General Court proposed an intercolonial congress to formulate the American position, and the southern colonies elected delegates. Meantime, the first stamps arrived in America. Stamp collectors were hanged in effigy in Charleston, Wilmington, and Williamsburg, and a ship carrying a stamp agent was forced to leave the South Carolina port. Mobs attacked houses suspected of harboring stamp agents or containing stamps. As the day approached when the stamps were to go on sale, the South Carolina *Gazette* announced that most public business would cease and that the paper would suspend publication. In November, the South Carolina chief justice found his court without business and unable to proceed without stamps.

October 3, 1765, the Stamp Act Congress assembled in New York, but South Carolina and Maryland were the only southern colonies represented. In the congress, Christopher Gadsden, Charleston merchant and planter, declared that the colonial protest should be based upon the natural rights of man, including that of revolution. He opposed a petition to Parliament on the ground that Parliament was not the author of colonial rights. The Stamp Act Congress, however, passed resolutions basing its case upon the right of Englishmen not to be taxed without their consent. The congress advised bringing pressure on Parliament, and this soon had its effect. London merchants, faced with a loss of business, joined with the colonials in urging repeal of the Stamp Act. Early in 1766 the House of Commons yielded, but passed a Declaratory Act asserting the control of crown and Parliament over the colonies.

In the general rejoicing in America, this threat for the future was almost lost from sight; but in Charleston, Christopher Gadsden was fully aware of the continued danger. He organized and supported a group of artisans and skilled craftsmen, known as "mechanics," who kept up a continual agitation against the crown. In other colonies the Sons of Liberty, an outgrowth of the Stamp Act mobs, kept up their organization and united the lower classes against the royal governments and parliamentary authority.

During the discussion of the Stamp Act, the colonials had made a distinction between internal and external taxation and had admitted that Parliament possessed the right to levy "external" taxes to regulate imperial commerce. Basing their acts upon this nebulous distinction, a new ministry soon provided for a new series of taxes. These taxes (known as the Townshend Acts) were to be collected as customs duties and used not only to defray the expenses of the American army but also to pay the salaries of royal officials in the colonies. At the same time, Parliament suspended the New York assembly because it had not provided for quartering English troops.

Immediate reaction followed in all the colonies. Charles C. Pinckney and John Rutledge wrote against the new acts and denied that Parliament could lay any taxes upon the colonies. Early in 1768 the Massachusetts House of Representatives sent a circular letter to the other assemblies declaring their loyalty to the king but denying Parliament's constitutional right to levy a tax. The Virginia House of Burgesses adopted resolutions reaffirming the exclusive rights of the assemblies to tax the colonies. In a letter transmitting these resolutions to the other colonies, the Virginians protested their loyalty, but urged the colonies to unite in defense of their constitutional rights. When Massachusetts refused to rescind her letter at the demand of the British government, the recalcitrant members of the General Court were toasted on the streets of Charleston. A new election in South Carolina resulted in increasing strength for the mechanics, and the governor failed to prevent the new assembly from replying to the Massachusetts circular letter.

Colonial economic pressure again brought relief from taxation. Merchants and planters of Virginia and the Carolinas and importers of Maryland signed nonimportation agreements. Trade with England immediately declined, and in April, 1770, Parliament repealed the Townshend Acts with the exception of a tax on tea. The colonists objected to this measure, but there was relative quiet for several years. In the interval, the Sons of Liberty maintained their organization and radical agitators continued to oppose Great Britain. In 1773 Parliament, primarily for the benefit of the East India Company, remitted a re-exportation tax in England. The company planned to distribute its tea through local agents who were able to sell at a lower price than were the colonial merchants. The prospect seemed to American merchants only an entering wedge for a far-flung monopoly. When a ship bearing the tea entered Charleston harbor, a mass meeting of the citizens resolved that the tea should not be landed or sold. The governor, fearing the popular wrath, ordered the tea landed and stored under bond. In November, 1774, tea was dumped from a British vessel. At Annapolis a mob burned a ship that attempted to land tea.

More famous than these earlier acts, the "Boston Tea Party" served to bring upon the Colony of Massachusetts the full fury of British authority. Determined to force colonial compliance, Parliament passed a series of "Intolerable Acts" which closed the port of Boston, remodeled the Massachusetts Charter, and provided that crown appeals should be tried in England and that army officers might commandeer unoccupied buildings when needed for quartering troops. These acts aroused the indignation of southern colonists who felt their own local governments threatened. More mass meetings were held, more resolutions passed, and the Southerners prepared to co-operate in a Continental Congress to formulate the colonial position.

2. Overthrowing the Royal Governments

Throughout the American colonies, men's attitudes toward recent British policy followed social and economic lines. Conservatives favored remaining within the empire and submitting to parliamentary enactments, while radicals sought both the overthrow of the colonial aristocracy and independence from England. In the southern colonies, royal officials, a majority of the established clergy and many men of property were loyalists. In the ranks of the radicals were to be found many classes. The Scotch-Irish of the frontier and the people of the back country were opposed to the land policy of the crown, resented the imperial Indian policy, and were consistent opponents of the royal officials. They did not wish to pay quitrents or taxes for the support of the established church. They suffered from the lack of courts and the erratic administration of justice. At the same time, they resented their lack of political power, the property requirements for suffrage, and the inequities of representation in the assemblies. They were the natural enemies of the wealthy Tidewater and low-country planters.

Allied to these frontiersmen, who furnished the backbone of the patriot party in the South, were a number of other elements. The merchants of the southern ports, with the exception of some from Charleston, were one in feeling with the business interests of New England and the middle colonies, and co-operated, albeit half-heartedly, with the radicals. The ministers and congregations of dissenting churches were opposed to the established Church of England. Young lawyers, especially those from South Carolina who had been trained in England, were jealous of the crown officials and ambitious to take a prominent place in civil affairs. But the most important allies of the radical elements were the planters.

The southern planters were closely associated with the mother country. They imitated the landed gentry of England in their social customs, manners, and tastes. The sons of leading families were educated in England, and the fathers were communicants of the Anglican church. Yet, the planters were supporters of the Revolution.

Among the causes which contributed to planter disaffection was the long history of constitutional conflict between the crown officials, especially the royal governors, and the people. In each of the colonies the governor's exercise of a suspensory veto had led to clashes. In Virginia, the governor suspended seventy-five laws in the six years between 1767 and 1773, while in the entire period before that time less than sixty laws had been challenged. To the Virginia planters, this increased interference in their legislation was but part of a great plan to reduce the colonists to slavery. The tax on tea seemed but another step in the general direction of tyranny and caused the planters to give their sympathy and support to the merchants' objections. In North Carolina, the executive and the assembly were in almost constant conflict over quitrents, fees, and expenditures from the colonial treasury. Governor Alexander Martin refused to accept the repeal of excise and poll taxes in 1772, and the resulting conflict brought a deadlock that was not settled until Martin was in flight from his capital. Struggles also occurred over the control of the judiciary and representation in the legislature. In South Carolina, similar troubles kept the planters suspicious of the imperial agents.

In addition to constitutional considerations, two economic conditions separated the planters from the crown. Taxpaying planters objected to the management of public finance. Quitrents, poll taxes, and custom duties constituted the main sources of colonial revenue. In Virginia, the money from quitrents and customs was at the disposal of the governor, and any surplus went into the royal treasury. The assembly, relying mainly on the poll tax, had to devise new taxes to meet deficits. Moreover, the rapid payment of the debt and the contraction of paper currency following the French and Indian War brought hardship. At the same time, an adverse balance of trade drained bullion from the colony and aided in producing a depression. The planters joined with the back-country radicals in a demand for more paper money.

The bad condition of public finance was paralleled by an equally depressing situation in private business. Virginia planters were heavily indebted to Englishmen. Their debts were hereditary, being handed down from father to son "so that the planters were a species of property annexed to certain mercantile houses in London." Thomas Jefferson estimated that Virginia planters owed over two million pounds to British merchants. After the Revolution, a group of merchants claimed £2,304,408 from Southerners. The only hope for relief from the pressing burden of debts was complete repudiation. Before the actual outbreak of the Revolution, Jefferson and Henry proposed that all payments on debts to Britons should cease. Although the measure did not pass, the promise involved brought many debt-ridden planters to the patriot ranks. During the war, the assembly assumed the debts, permitting the planters to pay depreciated colonial currency into the state treasury. Much later, when Jefferson was president of the United States, these debts were assumed by the national government.

The depressing nature of public finance and the mounting volume of debts forced the Virginia planter to look to the West for escape. The exhausting agriculture of staple crops and the modifications of slave labor made expansion necessary. Virginia blood and money had saved the region from the French, and the planters could see no reason in the restrictive policy of the British government. They had resented the Proclamation Line but they had pinned their hopes upon the promises that it would be but a temporary expedient. While waiting a change of policy, they made treaties with the Indians, formed land companies, and petitioned the crown. In 1774, at the same time that the "Intolerable Acts" were passed, the "Quebec Act" added the territory north of the Ohio River and east of the Mississippi to the Province of Quebec. The French laws of Quebec extended to the new territory, and the Catholic Church was recognized and its clergy permitted to collect tithes. The act placed the government of the province in the hands of royal officials and made no provision for a popular assembly. Jury trial would not exist under French law. To the land-speculating planters, the Quebec Act was the death blow of their hopes. Settlement was out of the question in a region where the Catholic Church was strong and where participation in the government was prohibited. The planters lumped the Quebec Act with the "Intolerable Acts" and read therein a British determination to end colonial liberty.

With debts pressing and hopes of recuperation by land speculation fading, the planters joined the Revolutionary cause. "Men of fortune," moaned Lord Dunmore, "joined equally with the lowest and meanest." Only Georgia, which was still dependent upon British protection against the Indians, failed to send delegates to the First Continental Congress. In South Carolina a convention duly elected by the parishes but dominated by Charleston's radicals passed resolutions denying that taxes could be levied without the people's consent, condemning the alarming nature of the "Intolerable Acts," and declaring in favor of a congress. Five delegates were selected to attend the congress "to consent, agree to, and effectually prosecute such legal measures as . . . should be most likely to obtain a repeal of the late acts of Parliament and a redress of American Grievances." Although conservatives feared lest the congress should take action leading to independence, Virginia sent her radical leaders, Henry and Jefferson, together with Washington and Peyton Randolph, to Philadelphia.

In the First Continental Congress, Randolph was made president, and the Virginians joined the radical delegates of Massachusetts against the conservatism of many of the delegates. The congress adopted a petition to the king and drafted a nonintercourse agreement, called the Continental Association. The members agreed on behalf of their constituents not to import English goods after the following December. The members had no authority to bind their constituents, but the congress provided for local committees to obtain compliance. In fact, the association had the force of law, and committees of safety in the colonies enforced the law against reluctant importers. The enactment of a law and the creation of the machinery for its execution was the first act in the Revolution. The congress agreed to call a second congress to meet in May, 1775.

In the meantime, the royal governments in all of the colonies were coming to an end. The assemblies of the southern colonies were in the hands of the radicals, and all had had experience in conflicts with the governors. As early as 1769, the Virginia burgesses had met in a private house after being dissolved by the governor. In 1773, Governor Dunmore dissolved the assembly because it had appointed a committee of correspondence. The following May, when news of the Boston Port Act arrived in Williamsburg, Jefferson, Henry, and Richard Henry Lee persuaded the burgesses to proclaim a day of fasting and prayer. Lord Dunmore promptly dismissed the assembly. But the burgesses moved in a body to the Raleigh tavern, where they continued their session. Shortly after they adjourned, Speaker Peyton Randolph called a special session for August 1, 1774. This body constituted itself a provincial convention, and the Revolution in Virginia began.

In Maryland, revolutionary proceedings followed closely upon the arrival of news of the Boston Port Act. Mass meetings in Baltimore and Annapolis chose committees of correspondence. The Baltimore meeting called for a colonial congress from all of the counties, and ninety-two delegates organized a provincial convention at Annapolis on June 22, 1774.

In March, 1774, the governor of North Carolina dismissed the assembly in a quarrel over taxation and the judicial systems. When he announced that he would not recall them, the assemblymen asserted that the people would meet in convention. John Harvey, speaker of the house, and a few radicals called a provincial convention, which assembled at New Bern on August 25, 1774.

South Carolina's conservatives took part in the overthrow of its royal government, although the mechanics of Charleston had already perfected an organization. The conservatives controlled a "General Committee," which late in 1774 called for a general election. The country was divided into electoral districts in such a manner that the low country had control. The elections were so conducted that "gentlemen" controlled the provincial congress and Scotch-Irish and Germans were excluded. On January 11, 1775, the congress assembled and proceeded to set up a government for the colony. A "General Committee," controlled by Charlestonians, took charge of the colony and set up local committees to direct the parishes. The congress presented the people's grievances to Lieutenant-Governor William Bull, who refused to receive them.

Only Georgia, lagging far behind her sisters, was not aroused to action in 1774. There were but 17,000 whites in the colony, and there was little feeling of resentment against England. The planters received bounties for silk and indigo and were protected against the Indians on the frontier and the Spanish on the southern border. There were radicals in the colony, however, some of whom had been in the inevitable conflicts between the executive and the assembly. In July, 1774, these radicals called a meeting to denounce the Boston Port Bill, but chose no delegate to the Continental Congress. While the other colonies were taking steps toward revolution, Georgia was quiet.

Having effected revolutionary governments, the patriots completed their organization through the work of committees of safety. Such committees, acting sometimes as vigilance committees, seized control of local governments and forced compliance with the Continental Association. Moreover, the local committees organized and armed militia companies. Everywhere the royal authority was undermined and government passed into the hands of the committees of safety and the provincial conventions. The result of nonimportation was soon felt in England, and the colonists learned that this time there would be no yielding to colonial demands. Clashes of arms were inevitable, and Patrick Henry urged the creation of a colonial militia and preparations for war. Declaring that the next breeze that blew from the North would bring news of war, Henry expressed a fervid preference for liberty and death over chains and slavery. His prediction was soon confirmed. On April 19 the war began at Concord and Lexington, and by the time the Second Continental Congress assembled, actual war was in progress.

The day after the battle in Massachusetts, Lord Dunmore seized powder that had been stored in Williamsburg. Virginia's radicals were immediately aroused and the militia threatened to march on the capital. Early in May, Patrick Henry, at the head of several thousand men, forced Dunmore to pay for the powder. On June 1, the assembly met again and approved the acts of the provincial convention. Dunmore began to fear for his safety and took refuge on a British war vessel. In North Carolina Governor Martin called the assembly to meet at New Bern on March 29, 1775, and John Harvey called the provincial congress to meet at the same place on April 3. The membership of the two bodies was largely identical, and when both bodies organized on the same day, in the same room, Martin dissolved the assembly. The local vigilance committee stole the cannon that Martin had placed before his house, and the governor fled to Wilmington for safety. In the other colonies, the governors remained in their places until after Bunker Hill, but their authority was gone. The colonies had already begun to send troops to the Continental armies.

The Second Continental Congress, composed of delegates selected by these revolutionary bodies, found a war already begun. The current of events was moving the conservatives to act with the radicals. George Washington was chosen to command the Continental forces and left the congress to take charge of the war. The congress appealed to the colonies for arms, men, and money, and assumed the functions of government.

The overthrow of the governors in the other colonies produced a belated reaction in Georgia. The mass meeting of January, 1775, had resulted in the creation of a provincial congress, but there had been no support for the movement. When war began, however, Georgia's radicals took control. They seized powder from the royal magazine, began to enforce the Continental Association against the loud protests of the Savannah merchants, and called for a new provincial congress. The congress assembled July 4, 1775, and Georgia co-operated with the other colonies in the Revolution.

3. THE SOUTHERN STATES IN THE REVOLUTION

The provisional governments which had overthrown the older authorities ruled the southern colonies until the sentiment for complete independence matured. In all the colonies the committees of safety made adherence to the association the test of loyalty. In South Carolina, where conservatives still had a voice in the provincial congress, an effort was made to modify the enforcement of its rulings. But everywhere the activities of the patriot committees drove deeper the wedge between the parts of the empire and prepared the way for independence. The spirit of the radicals was shown in North Carolina by the Mecklenburg Resolves, drafted by the assembled militia at Charlotte on May 31, 1775, which declared that governmental powers had been transferred to the provincial congress. The militia recommended the formation of a new government, and the provincial congress drafted a temporary constitution. The colony was divided into six military districts, over each of which was to be a committee of thirteen. The provincial council was to supervise the work of the district committees. Similar organizations, bringing centralization of county activities and establishing executive committees, began work in the other colonies.

These early governments were drawn up in haste and revealed that the sponsors of the Revolution had not yet clarified their aims. Perhaps their most serious and far-reaching feature was their failure to provide for complete democracy or to remove the inequalities of representation. In the moment of stress, men had little time to formulate new systems of government, and they revealed a tendency to adapt older and well-known institutions to new needs. Thus, they retained the property qualifications for the suffrage and failed to give populous western counties proportional representation. In Virginia 24 acres, in Maryland 50 acres, and in North Carolina a settled freehold were required for the suffrage. South Carolina's provincial congress with 144 delegates from the more populous upcountry was somewhat more democratic.

Under these governments, the colonies progressed toward independence. The spread of the war from Boston to the South moved the southern colonies to break away from England. Virginia placed her militia under Patrick Henry's command, and Henry fought against Dunmore, who had established himself at Norfolk. At Great Bridge the Virginia militia won a victory. In Georgia the British attacked Savannah, and in the back country of the Carolinas the Tories were in arms. In February, 1776, the North Carolina patriots defeated loyalists at Moore's Creek. These military events set the stage for independence and convinced the doubting that England would not make peace without victory. The provincial congresses of Virginia and South Carolina asked the Continental Congress for instructions and were advised to form state constitutions. Before the Declaration of Independence was drafted, the states had begun to draw up permanent governments. Meantime, they instructed their delegates in Philadelphia to move for independence. In Congress, Virginia's Richard Henry Lee offered resolutions that the colonies "were and of right ought to be free and independent states." July 2, 1776, the Congress received a committee report drafted by the skilled hand of Thomas Jefferson. The Declaration of Independence placed all the colonies under the necessity of adopting permanent constitutions.

In the South, the constitutions were drawn up by the provincial conventions, usually after special elections had been held. Conservatives and radicals divided on the nature of the governments, and each side resorted to pamphlets. In Virginia, Lee, Henry, and Jefferson favored democracy while the aristocrats were in favor of a government with a popularly elected lower house, an upper house of twenty-four members chosen for life by the lower house, and full power of appointment of judges and military and civil officers in the hands of a governor.

The early constitutions contained many of the features of the colonial governments. In each there was a governor, a bicameral legislature, and a system of courts. Their difference lay in the allotment of power to these branches. In North Carolina, democracy went to an extreme and denied the annually elected governor all power except, in the words of one framer of the document, "to sign a receipt for his salary." He could not even call the legislature in special session. Judges were elected but retained office only during good behavior. Religious freedom was guaranteed, and any freeholder could vote for senators while all adult freemen could vote for members of the assembly. The property requirements for officeholding were low.

New York Historical Society

THOMAS JEFFERSON. The states instructed their delegates in Philadelphia to move for independence. July 2, 1776, the Congress received a committee report drafted by the skilled hand of Thomas Jefferson.

In Virginia a sharp fight between conservatives and radicals resulted in a constitution that gave the governor little power and surrounded him with a council. The legislature, consisting of two members from each county, was still elected by those who owned fifty acres. The senate was chosen by popular vote in twelve districts. The lower house had most power, with exclusive right to originate money bills and the right to choose judges and other civil officers.

In Maryland, the conservatives had control of the congresses which drafted the constitutions. Maryland's constitution provided for a system of indirect election for the senate—a provision that furnished the basis for the electoral college of the United States Constitution. Voters were required to have 30 pounds or 50 acres; senators had to have 1,000 pounds' worth of property, members of the house 500 pounds, and the governor 5,000 pounds.

South Carolina's constitution, adopted by the provincial congress in March, 1776, provided for a legislative council and a general assembly. The 202 members of the assembly were elected biennially from 28 districts, and the 13 members of the council were chosen from the membership of the lower house. The lower house had the right to initate money bills. There was no governor, but a president and a vice-president were elected by the legislature. A privy council composed of the vice-president and three members of each house advised the president.

The Virginia and North Carolina constitutions contained bills of rights, and only Virginia was without some religious test for officeholders. The great amount of power given to the legislatures caused some of the radicals to fear a popular tyranny. Jefferson declared that the Virginia legislators might become 173 despots, and Madison said that such a concentration of power "may justly be pronounced the very definition of tyranny." The greatest defect in the southern constitutions, however, was the unequal representation of the western regions. When the Revolutionary War was over, the old aristocracy of Tidewater and low-country planters was still in control. The new governments failed to accomplish the social revolution that the radicals of back country and frontier had desired.

Under these constitutions, the southern states conducted the Revolutionary War. In the midst of the war, the divisions between radicals and conservatives, between coastal plain and mountain appeared in local politics as harbingers of future troubles. In Maryland, the conservative senate was in almost constant conflict with the democratic house. They quarrelled when the senate refused to raise the pay of legislators and again when the senators opposed measures to punish Tories. The governors were as conservative as the senators, representing property rather than the populace, and were usually found to be in opposition to radical social reforms.

In Virginia the same division was equally pronounced, but the conservative forces did not have complete control of a single branch of the government. The radicals had a far-reaching social program, to which the aristocratic planters were heartily opposed. The leader of the radicals was Patrick Henry, who was elected governor in 1776, taking office the day after the Declaration of Independence was approved. Unfortunately for the radicals, the cares of office and his natural indolence prevented his carrying out the liberal program, and Jefferson assumed headship of the radicals. Jefferson preferred to remain in Virginia rather than to go to Congress, because he wished to adapt the whole Virginia system "to our republican form of government." His program contemplated a revision of the law and of the courts, the abolition of primogeniture and of entail, and the disestablishment of the church. The conservatives immediately rallied behind Edmund Pendleton, speaker of the house. Although he gained the enmity of the aristocrats and the clergy and was roundly castigated as an atheist and infidel, Jefferson succeeded in forcing the abandonment of entail and the suspension of church taxes. In 1779 Jefferson succeeded Henry as governor, and the reforms stopped, partly because Jefferson could no longer lead them through the assembly and partly because of the British invasion, which drove the government from Williamsburg to Charlottesville and finally to Staunton. Jefferson's successor, Thomas Nelson, was a conservative, and in 1782 Patrick Henry, now thoroughly alarmed at radical excesses, returned to the governorship.

In North Carolina the radicals were in control of the state. The two conservative sections of Edenton, just south of the Virginia line, and the Cape Fear region furnished a number of leaders, such as Samuel Johnston, James Iredell, William Hooper, and Archibald Maclaine, but they were unable to make headway against the western radicals. Thomas Person, John Penn, Willie Jones, and Thomas Burke led the democratic forces. They were more interested in low taxes and in freedom than in the effective prosecution of the war. The governor was destitute of power and could not even call the legislature in session to prepare for a British invasion. The legislature did little throughout the war either to promote the military or to insure the continuance of the social revolution which the new constitution had contemplated.

In contrast to her northern neighbor, South Carolina was controlled by the conservative planters and merchants. John Rutledge, aristocratic planter and businessman, was chosen the first "president." Opposing him was Christopher Gadsen, long a leader of the mechanics of Charleston and of the underprivileged classes of the upcountry. The radicals demanded revision of the state constitution and in 1778 forced a new document through the legislature. But the aristocrats retained control of the government. Then the British invaded the state, the legislature placed dictatorial power in Governor Rutledge's hands. The British took Charleston and practically stamped out rebellion in the state. Until the British withdrew, civil government was virtually suspended.

Georgia's conservatives and radicals followed a pattern like that followed in the other states. After Button Gwinnet, the second governor, was killed in a duel with a conservative, the radical strength grew. In 1778 Savannah fell to the British, and the government fled to Augusta. But the British drove them from the temporary capital. After the enemy abandoned Augusta, the conservatives attempted to seize control, and for a time the state had two governors. The patriot cause was reduced to a few guerilla bands until after the British marched northward into South Carolina.

In all of the southern states the Revolution caused extensive changes in the organization of society. The Anglican church was disestablished without difficulty in Maryland. In Virginia the movement against the church proceeded more slowly and succeeded only after a bitter fight. The dissenters were in the majority, but the Tidewater planters who controlled the legislature were Episcopalians. Jefferson's early efforts to break the establishment resulted only in a suspension of financial support. The churchmen attempted to have all churches supported by the state and were almost successful. Not until 1786 was Jefferson's Statute for Religious Freedom adopted by the legislature. In North Carolina, the establishment disappeared when the Tory clergy were driven from their parishes, but in South Carolina the church held on until the Constitution was modified in 1778. In 1777 the church lost state support in Georgia.

Other evidences of the radical desire for social reform appeared in the abolition of primogeniture and entail and in efforts to abolish slavery. Virginia's radical leaders were opposed to slavery, and the colony had attempted to abolish the slave trade before the Revolution. In 1778 Jefferson obtained an enactment to stop the importation of slaves. North Carolina imposed a tax on imported slaves, and temporary acts prohibiting importation were passed in South Carolina. Only Virginia, however, would consider the abolition of slavery, and even there, only the more extreme radicals countenanced such a proposal. The leading Virginians were convinced, however, that slavery was a dying institution, and many were willing to wait for time and economics to affect its extinction.

In their relations to the Continental Congress the southern states showed that they were more intent upon local than upon national problems. Although Patrick Henry had early proclaimed that colonial lines had disappeared and that he had been transformed from a Virginian into an American, the Southerners were not able to divest themselves of their provincialism. Henry's own Americanism was more oratorical than practical, and he rapidly lost sight on national interests as he devoted himself to local politics. This southern provincialism resulted in the crippling of the nation's finances and thereby prolonged the war. Congress made requisitions on the states, but the states seldom took steps to comply with the requests. Congress first issued paper money, which it asked the states to redeem; but the credit of the states was low, and the money quickly depreciated in value. Then Congress asked for direct gifts of money. Between 1779 and 1781 Congress received $278,000 from Virginia, $116,000 from Maryland, and $73,000 from North Carolina. According to Alexander Hamilton, all of the southern states contributed $3,751,252 to Congress while Congress paid to the states $3,775,049. Since this brought little benefit, Congress requested the states to furnish requisitions in kind. This system, being both cumbersome and extravagant, was abandoned. The states were also negligent in furnishing soldiers. Militiamen were frequently sent to Washington's army, but, since their terms were short, they were seldom of value. Georgia raised a total of 13,000 for the army and Virginia 51,000. The entire South raised 149,685 troops in the years from 1775 to 1783.

The finances of the southern states during the Revolution were chaotic. Paper money, forbidden by Parliament during the colonial period, was issued in floods. Maryland and South Carolina, where the conservatives were in a position to check radical excesses, issued $950,000 and $1,250,000, respectively, while radical Virginia turned $125,941,000 off the printing presses, and democratic North Carolina issued $34,575,000. Taxation supplemented these worthless issues. Virginia shifted from a poll tax to a land tax as her principal source of revenue but also taxed live-stock, slaves, licenses, and income. The other states imposed like taxes but collected few of them. Constant depreciation of the paper currency added to the confusion, and by the end of the war the southern states were practically bankrupt.

4. THE WAR IN THE SOUTH

While the southern states were working out their political organization, they were also the scenes of military activities. The South had many loyalists, and in some places they attempted to rise against the patriots. The British co-operated with the Tories of the Carolinas by sending ships to Wilmington and Charleston. The patriots, however, met the Tories at the battle of Moore's Creek, North Carolina, in February, 1776, before the British fleet arrived in near-by Wilmington. Realizing the hopelessness of victory in the northern colony, the British captain moved on to South Carolina, where the militia prevented his landing.

Along the frontier, more troubles arose. Under British influence, the Cherokees began raids against the Watauga settlements. Warned of their danger, the settlers held off the Indians until expeditions from Virginia and North and South Carolina arrived. Carolinians and Virginians pushed the war into the enemy country, destroyed the principal villages of the Cherokees, and brought the warriors to terms. The Watauga region was also raided by Indians from north of the Ohio.

The British governor, Henry Hamilton, the "Hair Buyer," encouraged Indians to overrun the Ohio Valley. In 1778 Patrick Henry commissioned George Rogers Clark to raise men and attack the British forts in the Illinois country. Raising his troops along the Virginia frontier, Clark set forth down the Ohio and made his way to the French town of Kaskaskia. Learning that France had joined the Americans against England, the inhabitants welcomed the Virginia forces. Soon after, Clark took Vincennes and guaranteed religious freedom to the French settlers. In December, Hamilton returned with a large force and recaptured Vincennes, but he soon sent his men away. Learning of this, Clark led his troops through swamps, flooded roads, and trackless wilderness to the attack. Although faced with starvation, Clark's 170 men plunged on until, on February 24, 1779, they invested the fort. Hamilton was captured and sent to Virginia. The expedition brought the region under Virginia's control and confirmed her old charter claims to possession of the West.

Late in the year 1778, the British changed the area of the war from the North to the South. The fortunes of war had given the Americans victory in campaigns in New England and the middle states, but the British expected aid from the back-country loyalists of the South. The plan of campaign contemplated a beginning in Georgia and a northward advance which would roll up the South.

Savannah was captured in December, 1778, and became a base for operations toward the interior. Before the summer the British were in possession of most of the state, while the patriot government, split into factions, was in hiding. Washington sent General Benjamin Lincoln to take control in the South. In October, Lincoln from the land and the French fleet from the sea failed to drive the British from Savannah. Quarrels between the French and the American commanders resulted in the withdrawal of Admiral d'Estaing from Savannah. General Sir Henry Clinton then came South with 7,000 men and besieged Lincoln in Charleston. In May, 1780, Lincoln surrendered and both South Carolina and Georgia were overrun by the British. After Colonel Banastre Tarleton cut to pieces and massacred the force of Colonel Abraham Buford at Waxhaws, only guerilla bands represented the American cause in South Carolina. Thomas Sumter, Francis Marion, Andrew Pickens, and other leaders plagued the invader, but had no appreciable effect on him. In June, 1780, Clinton turned the command over to Lord Cornwallis and went back to New York.

Against Cornwallis's 5,000 men, Congress sent, contrary to Washington's advice, General Horatio Gates with 3,000 men. In August Gates attacked Camden, South Carolina, and was badly defeated with a loss of 2,000 of his troops. Gates fled precipitously from the scene. In December he was replaced by General Nathanael Greene.

After the battle of Camden, Cornwallis advanced into North Carolina, stopping at Charlotte while Colonel Ferguson with a force of Tories raided the western part of the state. As the news of Ferguson's approach reached the Watauga country, the settlers banded together and marched eastward to meet him. Militia from North and South Carolina joined the frontiersmen and forced Ferguson to fall back toward Charlotte. On October 7, the Americans caught the retreating Tories at King's Mountain. In a sharp battle, Ferguson was killed and 700 of his troops were captured. The battle forced Cornwallis to fall back into South Carolina.

When Greene took command of the American forces, he had but 2,300 men. Six hundred of these he sent into the west to gather recruits while he held off Cornwallis. The British commander sent Tarleton after the recruiting squad and marched his own army between the divided Americans. At the battle of Cowpens, Tarleton was defeated, but Cornwallis was between the patriot forces. Both branches of the American army fell back into North Carolina, and Cornwallis moved forward in order to keep between them. A second battle at Cowpens enabled the western wing to escape and fall back toward the other wing. Rising rivers which slowed up Cornwallis enabled the Americans to unite at Guilford Court House, North Carolina. Joined by militia from North Carolina and Virginia, Greene attacked Cornwallis on March 15, 1781. Defeated in battle, Greene held his men together and Cornwallis marched toward Wilmington. Greene then turned to South Carolina and succeeded in clearing the state and driving the British back into Charleston. Meanwhile, a similar movement in Georgia resulted in cooping up the enemy in Savannah.

National Park Service

GUILFORD COURT HOUSE: STATUE OF NATHANAEL GREENE. Rising rivers which slowed up Cornwallis enabled the Americans to unite at Guilford Court House, North Carolina. Joined by militia from North Carolina and Virginia, Greene attacked Cornwallis on March 15, 1781. Defeated in battle, Greene held his men together and Cornwallis marched toward Wilmington.

While Greene was pushing the British back in South Carolina, Cornwallis led his army into Virginia where Benedict Arnold, using Portsmouth as a base of operations, had been raiding the Tidewater at will. The legislature and Governor Jefferson had retired from Richmond to Charlottesville. Cornwallis took command of Arnold's troops and sent Tarleton to drive the government from its retreat. Commanding in Virginia was the Marquis de Lafayette, who abandoned Richmond as Cornwallis approached. Tarleton almost succeeded in capturing Jefferson. After finding that Lafayette was elusive and would not fight, Cornwallis took his 7,000 troops to Yorktown.

In late summer the French admiral, Count De Grasse, offered his services to Washington. The American commander requested him to besiege Yorktown from the sea. Then, leaving a handful of men to guard Clinton in New York, Washington led 6,000 men to Virginia. French

troops numbering 7,800 joined the Americans and began a siege of Yorktown on September 2, 1781. On October 17, Cornwallis accepted Washington's terms for a surrender of his troops. With the largest British force
gone, the military phase of the Revolution ended. Wilmington was
abandoned by the British in January, Savannah in July, and Charleston
in December. In March the British government decided to make peace,
and by November English and American commissioners had negotiated
the Treaty of Paris, which recognized American independence.

CHAPTER 6

The South Under the Confederation

1. THE ARTICLES OF CONFEDERATION

IMMEDIATELY after the Continental Congress had adopted the Declaration of Independence, it began to discuss a structure of government for the new nation. In the years preceding the outbreak of war, many proposals for uniting the colonies had been made. Some of the plans had been drafted by conservatives and looked to a firmer union with England; others had reflected the governmental ideas of those who sought practical independence. When the war began and the Declaration of Independence was adopted, the radicals were in control. The government which they evolved was designed to give constitutional form to the philosophy of the Declaration of Independence.

The Declaration, drafted by Thomas Jefferson, was the expression of southern radicals. Its assertion that all men were created equal and endowed with natural rights to life, liberty, and the pursuit of happiness was a product of the democratic ideas of Virginia's back country and frontier. "To secure these rights, governments are instituted among men," declared Virginia's revolutionary philosopher, who had ousted "property" from its accustomed place beside "life" and "liberty" and enshrined "the pursuit of happiness" in his political trinity. The men who made the Articles of Confederation were more concerned with protecting equality and insuring freedom than they were with upholding wealth. In accordance with the radical concept that the best government was that which governed least, the Articles of Confederation limited the powers of the national government and interfered as little as possible with the independent states. Remembering, as the states had done, the obstructive course of the royal governors, the articles provided for no executive. Such power as was allotted to the central government was entrusted to the Congress, composed of representatives of the states. Each state, regardless of size, power, or wealth, was given a single vote. The members of Congress were to be less lawmakers than ambassadors of the states by whom they were appointed and paid and to whom they were responsible. The states, being close to the people, retained their powers, and Congress was allowed to deal only with such matters as might for convenience be safely delegated. Congress was given power over foreign affairs, might conduct war, and might control the postal service. It might regulate the value of coins, standardize weights and measures, and control Indian affairs. The consent of nine states was necessary to pass important measures, and unanimous consent was needed to amend the articles.

The Articles of Confederation were debated intermittently from June, 1776, to November, 1777. During the discussion, disputes which involved the South arose to trouble the congressmen. Congress was not authorized to levy taxes, but it might make requisitions on the states in proportion to their population. Southern members protested that slaves should not be counted as citizens in apportioning such demands. South Carolina delegates declared that slaves were comparable to land or livestock, while John Adams, of Massachusetts, held that slaves produced wealth and were therefore parts of the population. The final solution based requisitions on the occupied land in each state. South Carolina and Georgia delegates clashed upon granting Congress power to regulate trade with the Indians. Georgians had relied upon the British government for protection and now felt the need for a central control, while South Carolinians, safely removed from the danger of attacks, wanted a free hand in exploiting the savages. Congress received power to deal with the Indians, but each state retained a right to legislate on the subject.

With final approval by Congress, the Articles of Confederation went to the states for ratification. Immediately there was opposition from the states. Most serious was that which came from Maryland, where members of the old Illinois and Wabash Companies, now combined, saw an opportunity to prevent ratification until the company's land claims had been recognized. In Maryland's provincial convention in 1776, resolutions condemning Virginia's extensive claim to western lands were passed, and it was asserted that "if the dominion over these lands should be established by the blood and treasure of the United States, such lands should be considered common stock to be parcelled out at any time into convenient, free, and independent governments." Pursuant to this resolution, Maryland's legislature held out until the other states agreed to surrender their western lands into the hands of the Congress. New York, whose claims were tenuous, led the way; and finally Virginia, whose claims were sound and ancient and whose armies, under George Rogers Clark, had just confirmed them by conquest, surrendered her lands to

Congress. When this was done, early in 1781, Maryland ratified the articles.

From the standpoint of those who envisioned a government with power, the merely regulatory functions of Congress under the articles seemed woefully inadequate. The course of the war demonstrated the weakness of the government. Washington found that Congress was unable to raise and equip an army and without power to coerce the states into making contributions. Without the right to levy taxes, Congress had no money to wage war. Structurally, too, the government was weak. The lack of an executive, the equality of the states, and the necessity for unanimous consent to amendments were defects which hindered efficient action. The supremacy of the states led the ablest men to prefer service in legislatures to ineffectual discussions at the national forum. To the disgust of the conservatives, the quality of the personnel of Congress declined during the war. Yet tne radicals were content with a government that did not interfere with liberty in behalf of property, and twice defeated amendments that would have given Congress the power to raise a revenue by import duties.

Yet this government, structurally weak and without real power, was surprisingly successful. Despite inadequacies and weakness, it successfully prosecuted the war with England and negotiated the highly favorable Treaty of Paris. During the succeeding five years, it furnished a bond of union between the discordant and jealous states until it stepped aside with sufficient, if not enthusiastic, grace for the new Constitution. But the greatest success of the Confederation was its solution of the problem of the West. Paradoxically, the success of the Confederation produced its overthrow, for without the formula which it evolved for the western lands, the Constitution could not have been successful.

2. THE CONFEDERATION AND THE WEST

All during the Revolution the southern frontier had been extending farther into the West. Henderson's Transylvania colony was launched on the very eve of the war. In 1776 Virginia erected the Transylvania region into Kentucky County. In 1779, when the state recognized the validity of land titles acquired from the Cherokees and made arrangements for selling land, settlement increased rapidly. The next year, Kentucky was divided into Fayette, Lincoln, and Jefferson counties. In 1779, Henderson, the ubiquitous speculator, transferred his interest to Tennessee and made arrangements with James Robertson to lead settlers from the Watauga regions to Henderson's lands on the Cumberland River. In January, 1780, the site of Nashborough was settled, and thereafter throughout the Cumberland region the palisaded forts of the pioneers appeared. When the Revolution was over, settlers once more rushed into these two outposts of the South. Soldiers from the armies, militiamen who expected bounty lands, and back-country people seeking opportunity or relief from their debts followed the Wilderness Road and the Ohio River into Kentucky or sought out the trail which Robertson had blazed from Watauga to the Cumberland. Louisville, Lexington, Maysville, and Paris were settled in Kentucky. In two years, 1783 to 1785, Kentucky's population grew from 12,000 to 24,000, and the Virginia legislature created four more counties.

During the Revolution, North Carolina's legislature had passed liberal land laws, opened land offices in each county, and offered one hundred acres for sale at fifty shillings. To protect Henderson, the radical Willie Jones moved that Indian cessions should be recognized. At the moment, however, there was more interest in settlers than in speculators; but as soon as the war was over, the speculators renewed their ante-bellum activities. William Blount, associate of James Robertson in speculation, persuaded the legislature to reopen the land offices. Blount and Robertson laid out Knoxville and secured lands in Tennessee as a result of advance knowledge. Then, in order to have their lands protected and developed, they induced the legislature to cede the Tennessee lands to Congress.

As soon as this cession was made, a group of speculators formed the state of Franklin; but a rival group persuaded North Carolina to repeal the act of cession. The movement for an independent state went on in the Watauga country, however, and the people chose John Sevier, an ally of Blount, as their governor. Sevier worked with the conservatives in North Carolina for peace and concessions, while the rival group of speculators aligned themselves with the radicals to prevent another accommodation.

At the same time, a movement for separate statehood began in the Kentucky region. The settlers found the distance to Richmond too great and believed that they were being neglected. Difficulty in raising a militia to repel an Indian attack led to the first steps toward forming a new state. The Virginians were willing to grant statehood upon conditions, but the outbreak of an Indian war delayed action until after the Constitution had been adopted. Then Virginia consented to separation, and in 1792 Kentucky was admitted to the Union.

The delay in admitting the western regions to the Union and the inadequate protection afforded by Congress led the western settlers to listen to proposals for alliance with Spain. By the treaties which closed the war in 1783, the Spanish received both East and West Florida. This, with Louisiana, gave Spain control of the mouth of the Mississippi River as well as control of those rivers which flowed southward to the Gulf of Mexico. A provision in the Treaty of Paris gave the Americans the land as far as 31°, but Spain claimed that the boundaries of West Florida had reached the 32°28′ parallel under British rule. The Westerners were dependent upon the rivers that Spain held, and they wanted the right to navigate them to the sea. Spain had closed the rivers to American commerce. Moreover, the Indians of Florida raided the western settlers, and frontiersmen suspected that the border warfare was inspired by Spanish agents.

The Spanish made contact with General James Wilkinson, of the American Army, who accepted a commission and a salary from the Spanish king. Wilkinson intrigued to detach Kentuckians and Tennesseeans from the United States. The wily general was probably more interested in obtaining money for himself than in promoting Spain's ambition, but he held out to Kentuckians the prospect of creating a new nation in the West under Spain's protection. In Tennessee, Sevier and Blount engaged in dubious negotiations with the Spaniards in an effort to open up the Tombigbee River. The speculators hoped to effect, also, a cessation of Indian raids on their colonies.

Slowly the Congress of the Confederation awoke to the dangers involved in the western situation. In two significant movements, the Jay-Gardoqui Treaty and the Northwest Ordinance, the Confederation attempted to deal with western problems. In 1785 Congress instructed its secretary of foreign affairs, John Jay, to treat with the Spanish minister. Jay was a New York conservative whom the Spaniard characterized as weak and self-centered. His narrow view prevented him from perceiving the significance of the southern frontier, and he negotiated with Don Diego de Gardoqui a commercial treaty by which the United States agreed not to exercise its right to navigate the Mississippi for twenty-five years. Immediately the southern states became alarmed, and southern leaders accused Jay of dishonesty. James Monroe wrote Patrick Henry that it was one "of the most extraordinary transactions I have ever known, a minister negotiating expressly for the purpose of defeating the object of his instruction, and by a long train of intrigue and management seducing the representatives of the states to concur in it." A self-constituted "Committee of Correspondence" flooded Kentucky with handbills denouncing Jay's outrage. The organized opposition of the South and West defeated Jay's efforts, and the problem of the Mississippi remained unsettled.

The second effort of the Confederation Congress to deal with western problems resulted in the enactment of the Northwest Ordinance. The pressure of settlers on the frontier north of the Ohio River and the desire of the Congress to realize a revenue by the sale of western lands led Congress to appoint two committees to deal with the problems of government in the West and with the sale of lands. Thomas Jefferson was chairman of both committees. On March 1, 1784, he reported a proposal for organizing ten territories in the Northwest. When any one of them had a population as large as the smallest of the original states, it would be admitted to the union as a state with full equality. Jefferson proposed further that slavery should not exist in the new territory after 1800, but southern opposition defeated the provision. Jefferson's second report, in 1785, provided for the survey and sale of western lands. Both of Jefferson's reports were adopted, but no action was taken until, in 1787, the opportunity to wipe out outstanding debts by sales to land companies led to the drafting of a new Northwest Ordinance providing for a government for the region and holding out to prospective settlers the promise of eventual statehood. A clause of far-reaching significance in the ordinance provided that neither slavery nor involuntary servitude should exist in the region.

3. MOVEMENT FOR A STRONGER UNION

The Northwest Ordinance, with its promise of statehood, had the good result of quieting dissension in the Southwest. Henceforth there was little thought of joining with Spain or establishing a western confederacy under Spanish protection. Moreover, the ordinance had the significant result of bringing in a revenue and freeing the Congress, to some extent, from its dependence on the states. The greatest defect of the Articles of Confederation was their failure to provide the national government with an independent income. The more optimistic proponents of the Confederation hoped that the sales of western lands might pay off the debt, bring in a revenue, and enable the government to pursue an independent course.

Such a prospect, however, was not pleasant to many conservatives. The government, under the Articles of Confederation, was primarily designed to govern as little as possible, and practically all power was left in the hands of the states. The separate commonwealths themselves were torn by conflicts between radicals and conservatives, and there was no place where property could be considered safe. Radicals generally were more concerned with insuring an uninterrupted pursuit of happiness than they were in guaranteeing the rights of property and promoting the economic interests of ambitious entrepreneurs.

The period of the Confederation was one of economic depression. Business was stagnant; old markets were closed and new ones were not yet open. The burden of debt which rested upon the states was intensified by inadequate revenue systems and by large issues of paper money. Although many causes combined to produce this condition, the propertied and business groups blamed the weakness of the government for their troubles. If the government were strong, they thought, it could open up the British markets, force Spain to open her colonial ports to American trade, and take a firm hand with the English, who, in defiance of the Treaty of Paris, were still occupying the posts of the Northwest and excluding Americans from the fur trade. At the same time the states, each acting for itself, imposed tariffs, regulated commerce, and taxed business in a manner to lay grievous burdens upon trade. There was no way to restrain the states from enacting stay laws for the benefit of debtors or flooding the channels of commerce with paper currency. To the propertied classes, it appeared essential that a strong national government be created to limit the excesses of the radicals and insure protection to property. Some conservatives even rejoiced at the economic collapse. John Jay thought that "good will come out of evil; these discontents nourish federal ideas. As trade diminishes, agriculture must suffer; and hence it will happen that our yeomen will be as desirous of increasing the powers of Congress as our merchants now are."

Throughout the South, the years of the Confederation were marked by bitter struggles between radicals and conservatives. In Maryland the radicals opposed the conservative proposals for creating a college, for disfranchising those whose religion prevented them from taking oaths, and for appropriations to the Potomac Company, which planned to improve the river and make it navigable to the Great Falls. Radical farmers and artisans demanded paper money, but the conservative Senate prevented the radical House from granting the demand. In Virginia, the fight between radicals and conservatives made progress impossible. After Jefferson's unfortunate gubernatorial career, conservatives occupied the governor's chair and the legislature grew in conservatism. Immediately after the war, the radicals persecuted Tory refugees who sought to return to the state and refused to restore British property confiscated during the war. A proposal to allow British creditors to collect their old debts precipitated a violent struggle. Virginians asked, "If we are now to pay the debts due to the British merchants, what have we been fighting for all this while?" Patrick Henry defeated the measure. Tidewater planters who saw no benefit to their region opposed radical appropriations for internal improvements.

South Carolina's career during the Confederation was a repetition of the Maryland story of conservative control. When the British were driven out, the radicals assumed control, expelled loyalists from the state, and confiscated the property of British sympathizers. Conservatives immediately objected to these measures, and within a few years they so far succeeded in modifying the Confiscation Act that even the former royal governor was allowed to return. When the old merchants returned to their shops, Charleston radicals rioted and instituted a reign of terror against the Tories. Christopher Gadsden, grown conservative with age and new-made wealth, cried out against the democratic excesses. In his place as radical leader stood Alexander Gillon, an ex-privateer who had been a British prisoner. The conservatives, declared Gillon's "Whig Club," planned to destroy "the republican equality of citizenship, . . . for which the middling and poor had shed their blood in profusion, to introduce family influences into the government, and thereby establish in their own homes an odious aristocracy over their betters." In 1784 the conservatives obtained control of the assembly, and with the governorship in their hands they controlled the state. Yet even this was not enough to preserve the wealthy classes. As the post-war panic brought increasing distress, Gillon forced through the assembly laws increasing paper money and a stay law postponing the payments of debts.

North Carolina radicals were led by Willie Jones, one of the largest slaveholders in the state. As time went on, the conservatives, supported by the land speculators, gained control. In Georgia there was a radical persecution of Tories, a fight between radicals, and eventual victory for the conservatives. Everywhere in the South the conservatives favored a strong national government that would aid them in checking the economic and social program of the radicals. The large planters, the merchants, and the land speculators were willing to co-operate with the conservatives of the northern states in forming a new constitution.

The first steps that led to the formation of a new constitution were taken in Virginia. The leader in the movement was Washington, who had become impressed with the need for improving the navigation of the Potomac River. One of the largest landholders in the state, Washington had given his attention to his extensive properties as soon as he returned from the war. With large holdings and larger claims to lands beyond the mountains, Washington perceived the necessity of making those lands accessible from the East. Improvement of the Potomac would make communication easier. In a larger sense, Washington saw that easy communication with all parts of the West would tend to break up the Spanish intrigues and bind the frontiersmen to the eastern sections.

But the navigation of the Potomac was a joint problem of Virginia and Maryland. The Potomac Company, in which Washington was interested, received grants from both states, and each legislature appointed commissioners to deal with the problem. Washington invited the commissioners to meet at Mt. Vernon. In the spring of 1785 the commissioners met and immediately realized that any settlement of Potomac problems would involve Pennsylvania. The commissioners returned to their legislatures, and the Maryland body invited Virginia, Pennsylvania, and Delaware to send delegates to a new conference at Annapolis. Congress adopted the idea and invited the states to meet at Annapolis to consider the necessity for a uniform system of commercial regulations. In September, 1786, delegates from five states assembled in the Maryland capital. Other states had sent delegates, but some of them purposely delayed their journey in order that the meeting might fail. The conservatives had no desire to strengthen the Articles but desired a new constitution that would crush the radicalism of the states and aid business. The delegates who assembled were of the same mind and issued a call for the "united virtue and wisdom" of the states to assemble at Philadelphia in the following May to propose amendments to the articles.

4. THE SOUTH AT PHILADELPHIA

All of the southern states sent delegates to the Philadelphia convention, and most of the leaders of the convention were from the South. Virginia's delegation was headed by Washington and included James Madison, Edmund Randolph, George Mason, George Wythe, and John Blair. Washington and Mason were large landholders, Randolph was a conservative, and Wythe was the leading member of the Virginia bar. Patrick Henry had been appointed to the delegation, but he refused to attend. Only Madison lived outside of the Tidewater, and he had been born in it. Maryland's delegation was divided between conservatives and radicals: Daniel Carroll, Daniel of St. Thomas Jenifer, and James McHenry were conservatives, while V. F. Mercer and the brilliant but tiresome Luther Martin were radicals. South Carolina sent John Rutledge, Charles Cotesworth Pinckney, Charles Pinckney, and Pierce Butler, all representatives of the low country and all of whom had opposed the radical mechanics of Charleston. Radical North Carolina, torn by conflicts over land speculation, sent a conservative delegation headed by William

Blount and including other speculators. Willie Jones, like Patrick Henry, refused to attend the conservative gathering. Except for William Few, Georgia's delegation, too, was of conservative, low-country land speculators.

Late in May the delegates mustered a quorum and, with Washington in the chair, organized. Immediately the Virginia delegates, through Randolph, offered a plan for a new constitution. Early on the ground, the Virginians under Madison's direction had met frequently to discuss problems, had consulted arriving delegations, and had finally drafted a complete program of reorganization. Although appointed by their legislatures only to propose amendments to the articles, the delegates ignored their instructions and decided to form an instrument of government with legislative, executive, and judicial branches. The Virginia plan proposed a national legislature of two branches, the first chosen by the people of the states and the second selected by the first. The legislature was to have the powers of the old congress and other powers which the states could not exercise. An executive, either singular or plural, was projected, as well as a judiciary with limited powers. The Virginia plan became the basis for the debates in the convention, and the final Constitution followed the general form of this preliminary proposal. As soon as Randolph had presented his plan, Charles Pinckney presented a plan which closely resembled the one from Virginia. This proposal was not formally discussed, but the Pinckney plan was before the committee which finally drafted the Constitution, and many of the South Carolinian's phrases found their way into the completed document.

Since the Virginia plan reflected the national views of the larger states, the smaller states, some of which were still in the hands of radicals, rallied behind a plan presented by Paterson, of New Jersey. This plan provided for a single-chambered legislature, in which the states would be equally represented, and for a weaker executive and judiciary. In principle, the New Jersey plan was merely an amended and improved version of the Articles of Confederation. Its acceptance would, however, have effected many of the fundamental changes desired by the conservatives. The leaders were in general agreement on the changes that were necessary, and few disagreed on the economic ends to be obtained by the new Constitution. On the choice of political methods to obtain their ends, however, there were many opinions, and the convention occupied the greater part of its time in formulating compromises between opposing ideas. The members were willing enough to compromise on methods so long as the government was strengthened and the states deprived of power. The resulting Constitution contained compromises on the composition of the Senate and the House of Representatives, on the election of the president, and on innumerable minor points. Many of its phrases were purposely left indefinite in hope that later developments might clarify their ambiguity. Perhaps the greatest compromise of the Constitution was the Constitution itself. It was a compromise between the desires of the conservatives for a truly national government on the one hand and the radical concepts of the people on the other. The framers of the Con-

stitution kept constantly in mind the fact that their handiwork would
have to be submitted to the country.

Although they were in general agreement with the northern delegates on the major ends and the principal methods, the southern members had some interests to protect from their associates. Several of the
compromises of the convention were necessary because of the peculiar
interests of the South. On the question of apportioning representation
for the lower house, South Carolina and Georgia delegates united in demanding that slaves should be counted as population. The conservatives
advocated representation of slaves not on the grounds of the natural
rights of man but on the theory that population was an indication of
wealth. They were all convinced that wealth should be given power in
the new government. But there arose also the question of the apportionment of direct taxes. The slaveholders did not want their slaves counted
as men when taxes were apportioned on a basis of population. Upon
the motion of a North Carolina delegate, an agreement was made that
three fifths of the slaves should be counted for purposes of both taxation
and representation. This three-fifths compromise was to become one of
the most significant clauses in the Constitution and a sore spot for many
decades.

Slavery had its most ardent supporters in the two states of
the lower South. There it had not yet become the economic failure that
it was proving itself to be in the upper South and in the North. Washington, Madison, and Martin were convinced that slavery was unprofitable
and out of accord with revolutionary philosophy; but the South Carolinians, far more conservative, had never given adherence to radical
theories and were certain that slavery was necessary in the rice swamps.
Pierce Butler was so sure that slavery was right that he would tolerate
no compromises on the issue. He impetuously proclaimed on one occasion
that the interests of South and North were "as different as the interests of
Russia and Turkey." When the convention discussed giving Congress
power to regulate commerce, the proslavery delegates became alarmed
lest the northern states should prohibit the slave trade. Charles Pinckney
passionately declared that slavery was justified by history and that half
of mankind had always been slaves. Madison, Mason, and Martin combated the arguments of Carolinians and Georgians, but in the end the
issue was compromised. Congress received the right to regulate commerce, but with the proviso that no law should be passed to affect the
slave trade before 1808 and that no import duty on slaves should exceed
ten dollars a head. These controversies over slavery were harbingers of
long years of conflict between the sections.

5. THE CONSTITUTION IN THE SOUTH

The Constitution marked a complete revolution in American
political organization. Whereas the Articles of Confederation had embodied, albeit imperfectly, the governmental concepts of the Revolu-

tionary radicals, the new document was designed to meet the needs of the conservative classes. It created a government with more strength and a supreme court which might sit in judgment on the states. It limited the economic activities of the states, forbidding them to pass stay laws or to issue paper money. But the members of the Philadelphia convention knew that their Constitution could not obtain the unanimous consent necessary to confirm changes in the articles. Accordingly, in complete disregard of the express provision of their appointment, they provided for a new method of adopting their document. They sent the Constitution to the legislatures and instructed them to call conventions to decide upon its acceptance. The constitutional party counted on two things to bring a favorable result. The first was speed, and the second was the relatively high property qualifications, ranging from Georgia's ten pounds of taxable wealth to the fifty acres or thirty pounds of Maryland, for voting. Thanks to these limitations on the suffrage and the quick action taken, only a small percentage of the people voted for the conventions.

In spite of the effort to hasten action, sufficient time elapsed for the formation of a definite opposition party. Some of the members of the convention had refused to sign the Constitution and hastened home to defeat ratification. Radical leaders, suspicious of the movement from the beginning, were ready to pounce upon the conservative offering. In Maryland, Luther Martin fought against ratification; in Virginia, Patrick Henry and Richard Henry Lee, joined by Randolph and Mason, who had refused to sign, headed the Antifederalists. Willie Jones and Thomas Person opposed the Constitution in North Carolina, while South Carolina's upcountry dissenters were led by Rawlins Lowndes.

Antifederalists and Federalists carried their cause to the people in public speeches, newpaper columns, and pamphlets. Ablest of the documents on the Federalist side was a series of eighty-five letters written by Alexander Hamilton, John Jay, and James Madison, Madison being the author of at least fourteen and possibly twenty. These letters elaborated upon the alleged weakness of the articles and set forth the advantages of the new scheme. On the other side, Richard Henry Lee's *Letters from the Federal Farmer to the Republican* rivaled the *Federalist Papers* in completeness and penetrating analysis. Lee denied that the new Constitution was demanded by the whole people, denounced it as undemocratic, and asserted that it would be an agency for the suppression of the majority of the people.

With the arguments before them, the states began to act. First in the South and fourth in the nation to accept the Constitution was Georgia. The election for delegates was uncontested, and the twenty-six members of the state convention ratified the Constitution on January 2, 1788. The exposed position of the little state and the immediate danger of Indian wars caused the Georgians to see clearly the need for a strong government.

Maryland was the second southern state to ratify the new instrument. When the legislature met in November, 1787, Luther Martin appeared to condemn the Constitution. The new government, Martin said, tended toward consolidation, and liberty would be destroyed if the states were weakened. After this address, the legislature barely mustered a majority for calling a state convention. The campaign for the Constitution was bitterly fought, with the commercial city of Baltimore and conservative Annapolis in ardent support of the constitutional party. To Maryland Federalists it seemed that debtors and bankrupts comprised the rank and file of the Antifederalists. Less than one fourth of the people voted, but so overwhelming was the Federalist victory that the convention would not even listen to opposing arguments. The vote for ratification stood sixty-three to eleven. Maryland was the seventh state to accept the Constitution.

South Carolina, as much in the hands of the conservatives as Maryland, delayed calling a convention until May, 1788. In January, the legislature heard representatives of the upcountry allege that South Carolina would lose out to New England in the Union, that the slave trade should not be limited to twenty years, and that the government was too strong. Lowndes denounced the Constitution as an experiment, and predicted that the "sun of the Southern States would set" and that the restrictions on the slave trade would deprive the South Carolina legislature of all powers. Against Lowndes' argument that the states were independent, Charles Cotesworth Pinckney asserted that "the separate independence and individual sovereignty of the several states were never thought of by the enlightened band of patriots" who framed the Declaration of Independence. The legislature was in the hands of Charleston merchants and planters, who called the convention. The delegates were chosen on the same basis as were the legislators, and the low-country Federalists had an overwhelming majority. South Carolina accepted the Constitution by a convention vote of 149 to 73.

Before Virginia's convention met, nine states had accepted the Constitution. As part of the Philadelphia convention's contempt for the Articles of Confederation, it had provided that the new government should go into effect when ratified by nine states. But without Virginia and New York, the new union could not function. All eyes, therefore, centered on Virginia, where the contest rapidly became bitter. The western counties were already suspicious of a national government and were aroused over the question of the Mississippi. Patrick Henry suspected northern commercial interests, and his worst fears had been confirmed by the Jay-Gardoqui negotiations. Mason and Randolph, refusing to sign the Constitution, returned to Virginia to aid its opponents. Mason was a large landholder and owned many slaves. His interests in the West may have led to his action, for he had not hitherto given adherence to radical philosophy. Back of such leaders were possibly two thirds of the people of the state, but the Federalists had able men on their side. Washington, Madison, Wythe, and the young lawyer John Marshall—already showing the strength of a great mind—were a host in themselves. The elections for the convention were close, but the under-representation of the western counties gave a narrow Federalist majority.

The eighty-nine Federalists who carried the convention for the Constitution came from the Tidewater, the Shenandoah Valley, and from several western counties where speculators had control. The seventy-nine Antifederalists represented the Piedmont, the back country, and Kentucky.

In the convention, Henry brought to the fight the full power of his brilliant oratory. "What right had they to say 'We, the people' . . . who authorized them to speak the language of 'We, the people,' instead of 'We, the states'?" he demanded. The new government was consolidated; it would destroy the states and liberty. Henry demanded amendments that would guarantee the rights of the states. Mason objected to the limitations on the importation of slaves. The Antifederalists finally extracted a promise to submit twenty amendments, constituting a bill of rights, before they would vote. In the end, the character of Washington, Marshall, and Madison won out over Henry's oratory, and Virginia ratified the Constitution.

The Virginians' insistence that the people of the states be given guarantees against the aggressive tendencies of the national government won support in other states, and won promises from the Federalists that they would support amendments to the Constitution strictly limiting the national government. In the first Congress, amendments, largely framed by Virginia's Mason and supported by the Southerners, were offered and submitted to the states. Ten of the amendments received approval, and constituted a "Bill of Rights" which its supporters hoped would protect popular liberties and the rights of the states against the federal government. The so-called "Bill of Rights" was in effect the Constitution's last compromise.

Alone of the southern states, democratic North Carolina refused to ratify. The conservative delegates whom the state sent to Philadelphia did not represent the prevailing sentiment. The people of the state were poor and could not approve of federal taxation. The result of the election was to bring 184 Antifederalists and 84 Federalists to the convention at Hillsborough in July, 1788. The Federalists were unable to prevail against Willie Jones's oratory, and the radicals would not even consent to a conditional ratification. Since the Constitution had already been accepted by nine states, North Carolina was in fact and in law an independent state. The new government was inaugurated without her. In November, 1789, a new convention met. Already the Bill of Rights had been submitted to the country, and Federalist propaganda had won over many doubtful men. In the elections for the convention, Willie Jones was defeated, and the Federalists were able to point out that the United States surrounded the state and had already proposed to impose customs duties on her products. The new convention yielded to such arguments and accepted the Constitution by a vote of 195 to 77.

The ratification of the Constitution was not the end of the contest. The document itself was but the bare frame of government, and many of its provisions were vague or ambiguous. Much depended on the men who were first chosen to put it into operation. In the hands of the Federalists it might become the foundation of a strong nation; in the hands of the Antifederalists it might preserve the rights of the states and defeat the ends of the conservatives. Federalists watched anxiously the coming elections. Fortunately for their cause, Washington was unanimously chosen president and John Adams vice-president, and the House of Representatives was safely Federalist. As the states acted, it became apparent that the friends of the new government would control the Senate, too. South Carolina chose Pierce Butler and Ralph Izard, both lowland planters; Maryland sent Charles Carroll, of Carrollton, and John Henry, both conservatives; but the Virginia legislature, completely under the influence of Patrick Henry, selected Richard Henry Lee and William Grayson, active Antifederalists, for the national Senate.

CHAPTER 7

The Beginnings of Sectional Conflict

1. AMERICAN TRADITIONS

THE Constitution which had thus been ratified and implemented dealt only with political organization. It did not touch directly the underlying economic and social problems of the nation. In reality, the nation was composed of a series of regions which differed from one another both in their human inhabitants and their geographical characteristics. North of Mason and Dixon's line lay the valleys of the Susquehanna, the Delaware, the Mohawk, and the Hudson. There, too, were the seacoast and the back country of New England. South of the line were the Virginia Tidewater, the Virginia-Carolina Piedmont, the Great Valley, the Appalachian highlands, the low country and the upcountry of South Carolina and Georgia. The inhabitants of each region had a distinctive background, history, and culture and each region had separate and peculiar interests. Within each, conflicting groups struggled to control the region. The primary task of the new government was to bring harmony among these divergent groups and oft-conflicting regions.

The inhabitants of the various regions did not all adhere to the same social and political philosophy. Among the people of the United States there were at least four basic, and often conflicting traditions— attitudes of mind, and theories of government and of society which were commonly related to economic interests but were often reflected in cultural and in political organizations and institutions. The four traditions, finding their origin and development in the colonial period, profoundly affected the development of the United States.

Strong in New England and Northern regions, but by no means foreign to the South, was the trustee tradition which found much of its argument and rationale in Calvinist theology. The trustees believed, as did the Sage of Geneva, John Calvin, that those whom God had elected for salvation should rule society; should, in fact, so order society that the whole social fabric should "glorify God." The trustees were the Elect, the Stewards of the Lord, who possessed property because those whom the Almighty favored He prospered. They used their property—and more importantly, they used their position in society and in government—to make a good and a Godly society. The tradition was as old as the Puritan rulers of Massachusetts, as old as the first shipbuilders of Massachusetts Bay, and it found expression in the preachments of the New England clergy and in the teachings of Harvard College.

Men of the trustee tradition contemplated the control of all government, local, state, national, and even international, by the Elect. They favored a strong state which would, at one and the same time, better mankind and prosper the Elect. With a moral orientation, they were offended by corruption. They were reformers ready to use the power of the state to harry evil from the land. In their economic activities, men of the trustee-tradition tended to be merchants, industrialists, or financiers. In religion they tended to be Calvinists—Congregationalists or Presbyterians—and in politics they were Federalists. They had supported the American Revolution against British tyranny and corruption and they supported the Constitution in the hopes that a new society, dominated by the Stewards of the Lord, would set a moral example to the nations.

Paralleling the trustee tradition, and often in conflict with it, was the tradition of the squires. Perhaps the squires derived less of their moral justification from theology than did the trustees, but they were no less convinced they had a responsible role to play in social and political affairs. In religion the squires tended to be Episcopalians or Old School Presbyterians, and less concerned with organizing society for the glorification of God than with managing their personal affairs to meet Divine commands. The squire felt a personal responsibility for the lives, the well-being, and the moral conduct of his "people," be they slaves, employees, or less favored neighbors who looked to them for political and cultural guidance.

The squires were the heirs and the imitators of the landed gentry of England, and they sought to live as they knew or imagined their English counterparts lived. They built manor houses of Georgian or neoclassical design, surrounded them frequently with formal gardens, cultivated urbane manners, and entertained graciously. They imported Madeira wines or pressed their own grapes, and they cultivated the tastes of gourmets. They danced waltzes, played violins or spinets, travelled to watering places, to England, or to continental spas. They rode in carriages, they owned and read books. They took part in government because it was a gentleman's duty to participate in public affairs, and they brought culture, personal integrity, and a sense of personal responsibility to the consideration of affairs of state. In the tradition of the squires stood Dutch patroons of the Hudson and planters of Virginia, Maryland, and the Carolinas. In combination with men of the trustee tradition, the men of the squire tradition had made the Constitution of the United States.

Although in some regions of the United States the trustees or the squires constituted the dominant group, controlled politics, and guided the economic development of the area, there were other strong, even basic traditions in America at the beginning of independence. One fundamental tradition was that of the artisans—the men who made and manned the ships of commerce, built the houses of the cities, mined the ores, and tended the shops. There was an element of craftsmanship in the artisan tradition, of the pride of silversmiths and cabinet makers who signed their work. In the colonial period they proudly bore the name "mechanics," and it was upon their skills that much of colonial life depended.

For the most part they were dwellers in villages and towns, finding in association with their fellow mechanics something of the same social satisfactions that the trustees and the squires found in their churches and their societies. They needed no theological rhetoric to bolster their position or to justify their way of life. They were content in the knowledge that in their smithies, their forges, their tanneries, and their printing shops the foundations of America were laid. In the Revolution they had given their support to Christopher Gadsden in Charleston and to Samuel Adams in Boston. They expected the government under the Constitution to support their way of life, and to give benefit to honest, industrious men.

Larger in numbers, and perhaps more incoherent in social outlook than any other group were the men who adhered to still a fourth basic tradition in America. This was the tradition of the yeomen, or better, of the agrarians. From the beginning of English settlement in the New World, the majority of the people had been farmers. Back of them, in England and Scotland and in Germany, lay generations of men who had tilled the soil and who knew in their hearts that agriculture was the noblest employment in which men could engage. Although many a yeoman aspired to become a squire, and many succeeded, the tradition of the squires did not dominate the yeoman groups. They had, instead, a distinctive tradition of their own, a tradition of many phases and aspects.

In religion the yeomen were Protestant Evangelicals: Methodists or Baptists or New School Presbyterians, and they applied a moral touchstone to the conduct of non-agrarians. They danced, when their church permitted, square dances at play-parties. They preserved Elizabethan ballads and played folk-music on "fiddles." They went on picnics, attended political barbecues, tested the quickness of finger and accuracy of eye at shooting matches. They drank cider, apple jack, and corn whiskey. In occupations they were sometimes river raftsmen, occasionally cattle or slave drivers and plantation overseers, but always farmers. They were the producers of foodstuffs and raw materials and the primary processors of meat, meal, flour, and wool. Out of their way of life came their economic, social, and political concepts. They were democrats in their political views, and placed value—inevitably a moral value—on the use of land. The agrarian democrat knew that farming was the only occupation with a divine blessing, and that farmers should know no restraints upon their efforts to earn their bread by the sweat of their brows. He conceived of himself as democratic, hardy, virile, independent—and the backbone of the nation. To the agrarian every restriction upon the free use of land was a sin. He opposed quitrents, direct taxes, proclamation lines, and grants to speculators and land companies.

In the colonial period British and colonial governments, more concerned with mercantile interests than with colonial producers, levied taxes, fixed prices, managed Indian affairs, and restricted settlements with no regard to agrarian interests. As a result, embattled farmers stood at Lexington and Concord, or gathered from the mountains to hurl back the invader at Cowpens and King's Mountain. After the Revolution the yeomen pressed forward to the frontier, expecting the governments of the states to protect them in their liberties. Excluded by suffrage restrictions from a full voice in public decisions, they regarded the new Constitution with skepticism.

Within the regions of the United States, groups of men partook of these basic traditions. In some regions the trustees controlled the institutions of society; in others the squires were dominant. In the population centers, artisans sometimes controlled and set the tone of government; in frontier regions, the agrarian tradition colored the thinking of the leaders and gave form and program to governments. In bringing harmony between the groups in the several regions, the new government had to conduct itself within the concepts of these basic American traditions.

2. THE HAMILTONIAN PROGRAM

On April 30, 1789, George Washington, squire of Mt. Vernon, became president of the United States. Like him, a majority of the members of the new Congress were Federalists, partaking of the traditions either of the squires or of the trustees. Nearly all of them had been members of either the Philadelphia convention or the ratifying conventions of the states. They were thoroughly familiar with the new Constitution, and they were experienced politicians. Moreover, the majority belonged to the propertied classes who had framed the Constitution. Fully cognizant of the evils of the old confederation, and in complete agreement on the ends of government, the members of the new government lost little time in drafting laws to give effect to their ideas.

Four executive offices were provided by the early legislation and Washington quickly filled them, choosing Alexander Hamilton, of New York, for secretary of the treasury, Henry Knox, of Massachusetts, for secretary of war, Thomas Jefferson for secretary of state, and Edmund Randolph for attorney-general. That the first cabinet was evenly divided between the North and the South was accidental, but this arrangement was destined to have far-reaching effects.

It was not unnatural that Alexander Hamilton should have assumed the leadership in the new government. The problems of the nation were economic, and the new Congress turned to the secretary of the treasury to report on the financial needs of the government. In a series of four reports from January, 1790, to December, 1791, Hamilton proposed that the national debt be funded in new bond issues, that the Revolutionary debts of the states be assumed by the national government, that Congress impose an excise tax in order to impress the power of the government on the people, that a national bank be established, and that Congress undertake the protection of manufactures through a tariff.

Hamilton's program was designed for both financial and political ends. Financially, he desired to make the government strong and to redeem its credit. He believed that credit was needed for industrial development and for commercial prosperity. To a large extent, Hamilton shared the viewpoints inherent in the trustee tradition. He had little respect for either the intelligence or the honesty of the masses of the people, and contended that men generally were actuated by ambition and personal interests. "It will ever be the duty of a wise government to avail itself of those passions in order to make them subservient to the public good," he declared. He hoped, indeed, for balance between contending interests, and he looked upon the Constitution as a means of strengthening the conservative groups who had made it. His program would organize the conservatives into a strong party who would be bound to the government. Essentially, Hamilton was a politician rather than a financier.

Congress adopted each of Hamilton's recommendations except the one explicitly favoring the protection of manufactures. But the protective principle was implicit in the first tariff measure of the new Congress. Speculators reaped a rich harvest in new bonds which funded the national debt. Congress established a national bank in which the government was a large stockholder, and adopted an excise tax on whiskey which bore hard on western farmers. Each of these measures was of greater benefit to Northern than to Southern men. Massachusetts and New York with commercial and maritime interests profited from the system, and merchants welcomed a stable currency and good credit. Businessmen breathed a sigh of relief as the threat of paper money disappeared. Southern interests, however, were largely those of consumer-debtors, and did not find benefits so easily in the new order.

3. DEVELOPMENT OF A SOUTHERN PROTEST

As the Hamiltonian program developed, Southerners remembered the prophetic words of Patrick Henry in Virginia's ratifying convention: "A gentleman has said . . . that there is a contest for empire. There is also a contest for money. The states of the North wish to secure a superiority of interest and influence." By August 1789, South Carolina's Pierce Butler was begging North Carolina to ratify the Constitution in order to bolster up southern strength: "I came here full of hopes that the greatest liberality would be exercised; that the consideration of the *whole* and the general good, would take place in every object; but here I find men scrambling for partial advantages, state interests, and in short, a train of those narrow, impolitic measures that must, after a while, shake the Union to its very foundation."

Hardly had the new Congress begun when the first evidence of conflicting sectional interests appeared. Significantly, the issue was precipitated by petitions from Pennsylvania Quakers and the Pennsylvania Society for the Abolition of Slavery. The petitions, signed by the president of the society, Benjamin Franklin, asked Congress to go to the limit of its powers in suppressing slavery. Immediately some Southerners showed nervousness, and Aedanus Burke, of South Carolina, declared that the reference of the petitions to a committee would "blow the trumpet of sedition." Madison, however, insisted upon discussion and a reference. After considerable discussion, the Southerners persuaded the House of Representatives to adopt four resolutions asserting that Congress had no power to prohibit the importations of slaves before 1808 and no power to interfere with the institution in any state, but that it had powers over the interstate slave trade. The result was the passage of a fugitive slave act.

The Fugitive Slave Law of 1793 was passed, not at the demand of the slaveowners, but on complaint of the state of Pennsylvania that a free Negro had been kidnapped and that the governor's requisition for a rendition of the kidnappers had not been honored. The law which Congress passed at this time stayed in force until 1850. It provided that a white man claiming a Negro as a slave should prove his claim to the satisfaction of a state or federal magistrate, who would thereupon issue a certificate or warrant for the fugitive's arrest.

Relatively unimportant at the moment, this discussion served only to indicate a deep-seated division in sectional interests. Further evidence came in the dissensions over a tariff measure. Members from the North were in favor of levying import duties in such a manner as to protect nascent American industry, while Madison, with the support of others from the South, contended that the primary purpose of the tariff was revenues. The protectionist principle was evident in the first tariff measure.

As Hamilton's reports set the course of congressional legislation, James Madison, ably assisted by Virginia's William B. Giles, became the spokesman of the southern interests. A strong supporter of a strong government, active in the formation of the Constitution from the Mt. Vernon conference to Washington's inauguration, Madison was unable to adopt Hamilton's conservative theories or follow him in enriching the propertied interests at the expense of government and people. When Hamilton proposed funding the national debt, Madison objected to accepting Continental certificates of indebtedness at their face value. The certificates had depreciated to approximately twelve cents on the dollar and had passed into the hands of speculators. The Virginian saw no reason for giving such enormous profits to money lenders and even proposed that the difference between the face and the market values should be paid to the original holders. But since many members of Congress were speculators, they enacted Hamilton's schemes into laws.

Essentially the objection to the Hamiltonian program came from the agricultural regions. Western settlers in the middle states and frontiersmen who were pushing their way into the Ohio Valley were as opposed to the commercial classes as were the planters of the South. But city artisans too, long the enemies of merchants, feared Hamilton's social philosophy. This situation required that some leader should express the widespread discontent. Madison's thorough identification with the planters of the Virginia Tidewater and his record as a Federalist prevented his appealing to the masses of farmers and artisans.

The leader for the opposition was found in Thomas Jefferson, who returned from France to become secretary of state. Jefferson could speak the language of liberty and could present the cause of the agricultural classes in the terminology of Revolutionary radicalism and the Declaration of Independence. With Jefferson's assumption of leadership, there began an alliance of South and West which was to elevate the Virginian to the White House and give the South a momentary control of the nation. With it, too, began the constitutional arguments which were to cloud the basic economic issues of the sectional conflict.

As soon as Congress had accepted the funding measure, it turned to consider the assumption of the state debts. Some of the southern states had paid off large portions of the state debts, while Virginia and North Carolina had ceded to the federal government large sections of land that would go far toward paying the total national indebtedness. The additional taxation would benefit Northerners rather than Southerners and enrich the commercial classes at the expense of the planters and small farmers. On April 12, 1790, by mustering all their strength, the Southerners succeeded in defeating the assumption measure in the House. There was great rejoicing in the South. "Miss Assumption" was dead. "Her death was much lamented by her parents, who were from New England," wrote one politician. "Miss Direct Tax may rest more easily in Virginia as she will not be called into service to support the deceased Miss Assumption. But a motion to reconsider was made, and Miss Assumption was not as dead as she appeared."

At this juncture, Jefferson returned from Paris. His arrival was opportune—for Hamilton. With Jefferson perhaps not fully understanding the issues at stake, Hamilton besought him to influence the southern members. In a long conference, pacing the street before Washington's house, the New Yorker explained that the fate of the Constitution was at stake and that the creditor states were on the verge of secession.

Under this presentation of the case, Jefferson invited the leading southern politicians to dinner. In the discussion at the table he learned something of the significance of events, but, having committed himself, he went through with the plan. Compromise, however, was necessary. At the moment, the location of the capital was being much discussed, and Jefferson arranged that the capital should be situated on the banks of the Potomac in return for the votes of certain Southerners. "And so," said Jefferson, "the assumption was passed and twenty millions of stock divided among the favored states and thrown in as pabulum to the stock jobbing herd." Jefferson regretted his action, and soon put himself at the head of the movement against Hamilton.

Jefferson quickly learned his mistake. State legislatures passed resolutions denouncing the assumption. On January 13, 1791, James Monroe presented to the Senate the resolutions that Virginia, who had paid her debts, had passed against assumption. The law, said the Virginia legislature, was "repugnant to the Constitution of the United States as it goes to the exercise of a power not expressly granted to the general government." Hamilton, alarmed, wrote to Jay in prophetic mood, "this is the first symptom of a spirit which must either be killed or will kill the Constitution of the United States."

In addition to this resolution of the legislature, the Virginia House of Delegates also drew up a memorial to Congress. "In an agricultural country like this," said the House of Delegates, ". . . to erect and concentrate and perpetuate a large monied interest, is a measure which your memorialists apprehend must in the course of human events produce one or other of two evils, the prostration of agriculture at the feet of commerce, or a change in the extant form of federal government, fatal to the existence of American liberty. . . ." With this statement of the issues of the sectional conflict, the House of Delegates made a contribution to constitutional theory. It was the duty of the legislature to combat such class legislation. "During the whole discussion of the federal constitution by the convention in Virginia your memorialists were taught to believe that 'every power not granted was retained.' Under this impression and upon this positive condition, declared in the instrument of ratification, the said government was adopted by the people of this Commonwealth; but your memorialists can find no clause in the constitution authorizing Congress to assume the debts of the states. As the guardians then of the rights and interests of their constituents, as the sentinels placed by them over the ministers of the federal government, to shield it from their encroachments, or at least to sound the alarm when it is threatened with invasion, they can never reconcile it to their consciences silently to acquiesce in a measure which violates that hallowed maxim."

This was the doctrine of sentinelship and implied that the state legislature was the proper guardian of the liberties of the people and the proper agency for interpreting the acts of the federal government. It was the first expression of a constitutional doctrine which was to expand to uphold states' rights, nullification, and secession.

Hamilton's proposal to establish a national bank brought the next step in the developing constitutional theory. By that time the opposition was well organized, and Madison hastily denied that the Constitution gave the government power to establish a bank. When the bill came to the president, he called on his cabinet for opinions. Jefferson and Hamilton sharply clashed on the nature of federal powers. Jefferson held that the government was one of limited power, specifically granted, and Hamilton insisted that its powers were practically unlimited. Jefferson could find no specific grant of power to incorporate a national bank. Hamilton found the power in the clause which gave Congress the right to make all laws "necessary and proper" to levy taxes and emit bills of credit. Jefferson would interpret the Constitution in its strictest literal sense. The school of "strict construction" of the Constitution which the South was to support so vehemently was born in the discussion over the national bank.

Washington rejected Jefferson's arguments and approved the bank bill. In the next few years the administration faced a host of new problems growing out of foreign affairs. On these, as on domestic affairs, Hamilton and Jefferson disagreed sharply, and in general Washington sided with Hamilton. Gradually Jefferson placed himself at the head of the opposition, and eventually resigned from the cabinet. In 1796 his supporters made him their presidential candidate.

Throughout the intervening years, the Southerners continued to express their opposition. One Southerner opposed the "continued drain of specie which must take place to satisfy the appetites of speculators at the seat of government. . . . Connecticut manufactures a great deal. Georgia manufactures nothing and imports everything. Therefore, Georgia, although her population is not near so large, contributes more to the public treasury by impost." When the bank was before Congress, this same Georgian declared that it was a scheme to benefit the mercantile interests only. The farmer would get nothing. On the tariff bill, Lee, of Virginia, declared that the tariff would operate as "an oppressive though indirect tax upon agriculture." John Taylor, of Virginia, wrote two pamphlets denouncing the stockjobbers of Congress and gave the names of the members of Congress who were interested in government securities and in the bank. More and more the opponents of Hamilton found his plan unconstitutional, until that bitter Federalist, Fisher Ames, declared, "I scarce know a point which has not produced this cry, not excepting a motion for adjournment. . . . The fishery bill was unconstitutional; it was unconstitutional to receive plans of finance from the Secretary; to give bounties; to make the militia worth having; order is unconstitutional; credit is tenfold worse." Meanwhile, New England's Federalists fumed against the demagoguery of the Jacobin Jeffersonians. Timothy Dwight, president of Yale, was highly alarmed at the rabble that was gathering around Jefferson. "Shall our sons become the disciples of Voltaire and the dragoons of Marat; or our daughters the concubines of the Illuminati?" he asked with no respect for reason. Another New England preacher declared that the "atheistical, anarchial, and in other respects immoral principles of the French revolution" were actuating the Republicans. In the fires of this partisanship were born the hatreds that consumed the nation in the Civil War.

4. FORMULATION OF THE COMPACT THEORY

By 1796 Jefferson and Hamilton were both out of Washington's cabinet, but Hamilton was still a power behind the throne while Jefferson was devoting his energies to organizing his party of opposition. In 1792 Washington had been re-elected without opposition, but he signified his unwillingness to serve a third term. His retirement gave opportunity to the parties of Hamilton and Jefferson to wage a contest for the presidency. Quarrels within the Federalist ranks resulted in the selection of Massachusetts' John Adams as Jefferson's opponent, with Thomas Pinckney, a South Carolina planter, as the leading candidate for the vice-presidency. Aaron Burr, leader of Hamilton's opponents in New York, was the Jeffersonian choice for second place.

The South was a unit against the Federalist candidates. In South Carolina a bitter struggle had resulted in a victory for the upcountry elements and an overthrow of the Charleston planters. Federalism was strong in Charleston and remained a force for years, but in 1790 the radicals demanded a new constitution which should abolish primogeniture, give an increased—although not yet a fair—representation to the upcountry, and move the capital inland from the seacoast to Columbia. Hamilton's program unified all southern groups in support of Jefferson. Yet in the elections, Adams gained the presidency by the narrow vote of 71 to 68. Dissensions among the Federalists, however, resulted in Jefferson's being elected vice-president.

During all of Adams's administration, events played into the hands of the Jeffersonians. A quarrel between Hamilton and Adams weakened the Federalist party, while the Federalist solution for foreign problems reacted in favor of the Republicans. The French Revolution, which began just as the new government in the United States was being inaugurated, had progressed from the stage of enthusiastic equalitarianism to one of bourgeois corruption. At the head of the government was a directory of five members who, for their personal profit, ruled the country and dictated to the conquered European continent. In the last months of Washington's administration, James Monroe was recalled from France for making apologies to the Republic for the Jay Treaty. Adams sent a minister, who was not received, and then a commission to deal with the French. Agents of the directory met the American commissioners and offered to make a treaty if bribes were paid. Adams published the correspondence of these agents, and the American people rose in indignation. French seizures of American ships had already aroused Adams's home section, and the insulted Federalists prepared for war. In preparation for the conflict they increased the army and navy and authorized the president to call out the militia.

Taking advantage of popular excitement, the Federalists prepared to injure the Republican party. The commercial aristocracy of federalism resented the criticism the Jeffersonian rabble bestowed upon the government and its officers. Accordingly, Congress enacted a series of "Alien and Sedition Acts," which extended the period for nationalization and authorized the president to expel or imprison dangerous aliens. Since foreigners were usually attracted to the Republican ranks, these laws had an obvious political purpose. The Sedition Act was even more clearly designed to embarrass Jeffersonians. Any conspiracy against the officers of the government, or any malicious criticism of president or Congress, should render its author liable to fine or imprisonment. Under the Sedition Act a number of Republicans were brought to trial and convicted. Frequently the offenses they had committed were trivial, but Federalist judges enforced the law with excessive partisan zeal.

To the Republicans, successors of the Revolutionary radicals and the Antifederalists, such legislation confirmed their worst fears of tyranny and centralization. The Federalists, it appeared, had secured control of the government, ruled it to enrich themselves, and were now bent upon destroying all opposition. The courts were apparently becoming agencies of oppression, destroying the liberties of the people. The Republicans therefore turned to the states for protection.

The Southerners had already become alarmed at the states' loss of power. In 1792 Georgia had been summoned before the bar of the Federal Supreme Court to defend itself against a suit brought by a citizen of South Carolina. Georgia protested that the Supreme Court had no jurisdiction, but the Court, under Chief Justice John Jay, had declared that Georgia was liable to be hailed before it. Significantly, the only dissent came from North Carolina's James Iredell: "Every state in the Union in every instance where its sovereignty has not been delegated to the United States, I consider to be as completely sovereign as the United States are, in respect to the powers surrendered. The United States are sovereign as to all the powers of government actually surrendered; each state in the United States is sovereign as to all the powers reserved. It must necessarily be so, because the United States have no claim to any authority but such as the States have surrendered to them." In Georgia it was believed that submission to the jurisdiction of the Supreme Court would effectually destroy the sovereignty of the states and "render them but tributary corporations to the government of the United States." The lower house of the Georgia legislature proposed that any federal marshal serving a writ against the state should be hanged. Throughout the South there was an immediate objection to this assault upon a sovereign state. Virginia's representatives sponsored an amendment to the Constitution, and on March 5, 1794, Congress submitted the Eleventh Amendment for the approval of the state legislatures. In January, 1798, the amendment declaring that states could not be sued became part of the Constitution.

The action of the Supreme Court in the case of *Chisholm v. Georgia*, the increasing concentration of power in the hands of the government, and the Alien and Sedition Acts led many Southerners to favor a dissolution of the Union. Some of them proposed to Jefferson that Virginia and North Carolina secede and form a southern confederacy. Jefferson, however, was willing to rely upon popular reaction and political methods. "Let there be no violence, no open insurrection," he counseled, "and in the end public opinion will sweep from power the party responsible for these acts." Publicly, he declared that freedom of speech and republican institutions were in danger, and that if a protest were not made, the Federalists would make a monarch of the president and transform the Senate into a House of Lords.

Preferring to maintain the Union, Jefferson sought for a procedural control of the national government. The states, thought Jefferson, should have the power to protect the people from tyranny. This idea was not new. It bore a close resemblance to the concept of "checks and balances" that the framers had attempted to write into the Constitution. In the Philadelphia convention, Madison had asserted that the state legislatures would ever be ready to sound the alarm if the Congress should overstep its bounds. The Virginia House of Delegates expressed the same concept in the doctrine of sentinelship. To Jefferson fell the task of formulating the constitutional doctrines that would justify states in protecting the assailed liberties of the people.

With Madison's help, Jefferson drafted a set of resolutions to be presented to the legislatures of Kentucky and Virginia. The Kentucky Resolutions declared that "the several states composing the United States of America are not united on the principle of unlimited submission to their general government; but by a compact . . . they constituted a general government for special purposes, delegated to that government certain definite powers, reserving each state to itself, the residuary mass of right to their own self-government; and that whensoever the general government assumes undelegated powers, its acts are unauthoritative, void, and of no force." Each state acceded to the compact as a state, forming an agreement with the other states, and the general government which they formed "was not made the exclusive or final judge of the extent of the powers delegated to itself; since that would have made its discretion, and not the Constitution, the measure of its powers." The compact set up no common judge and each state was the judge of infractions of the Constitution "as well as of the mode and measure of redress." The Alien and Sedition Acts exceeded the powers granted to the government, and Kentucky was "determined, as it doubts not its co-states are, tamely to submit to undelegated and consequently unlimited powers in no man, or body of men, on earth." The state therefore instructed its senators and representatives to work for the repeal of the acts.

These resolutions brought forth varied replies from the other states, although only one state took notice of the compact theory upon which they were based. After the replies of the "co-states" had been received, Kentucky adopted a second set of resolutions, declaring that the states had the right to "nullify" an unconstitutional act of Congress. With these resolutions, the compact theory that had guided the Revolutionary patriots against England was given a new application; henceforth, it was the basic concept of those who held to the "states' rights" school of constitutional thought.

The resolutions were not primarily designed to embody a constitutional philosophy. Their immediate purpose was to formulate a political platform for the election of 1800. In the elections of that year, Jefferson and Burr defeated Adams and Pinckney. After a tie between the Republican candidates had been resolved by the House of Representatives, Jefferson was inaugurated. The southern protest against the Federalist regime had been successful and the South was in control. It remained to be seen how complete would be the political revolution. New England merchants and their conservative cohorts were convinced that the government had passed into the hands of the rabble. Actually, it had passed to groups whose social and political views stemmed from the traditions of the squires and of the yeomen.

CHAPTER 8

The Alliance of South
and West

1. THE COTTON KINGDOM

THE "revolution of 1800" gave control of the national government
to the agricultural party of Thomas Jefferson. At once, spokesmen
of the trustee tradition, and Federalists generally, gave voice to
fantastic forebodings of calamity. Theodore Dwight, speaking the fears
of the trustees, predicted such a leveling of society as would not only
snatch children from their mother's breasts but also, and far worse, would
take from property-holders the right to own material goods. As if to
confound the alarmists, however, Jefferson was to show by the acts of
his administration that the "revolution of 1800" was something less than
the social upheaval those words implied. He did handle affairs so as to
benefit the agricultural more than the commercial groups, and he introduced minor changes that brought a greater semblance of democracy
to governmental practice. But the Constitution stood, and he gave only
lip service to the principles of states' rights. Nevertheless, the New
Englanders were soon to have grounds for complaint against the administration, and under Jefferson the sectional conflict was to grow steadily
more intense.

The sectional alliance of South and West, though victorious for
the time being through Jefferson's election, could endure only so long
as the ties of common interest and common principle held firm; and the
strongest of these ties were the dependence of both Southerners and
Westerners upon agriculture and the belief of southern and western yeomen in the political theories of Jefferson. Now the wealthier planters

of the South, however critical they had been of Hamiltonian policies, could hardly stomach Jeffersonian doctrines, for these included a democratic assertion of the rights of the common man. Within the South, a conflict between the greater planters and the lesser farmers was to continue until eventually the squires should again secure the upper hand. Thereafter there would be little to hold the South and the West together, and the Westerners would ultimately transfer their support to a New England which had meanwhile undergone a metamorphosis.

Greatest of the forces leading to the eventual dominance of the planters was the coming of cotton to the lower South. At the time of the adoption of the Constitution, the southern social system was based upon the production of the two staple crops—rice and tobacco. Although slavery furnished the labor for these crops, the slave system was definitely on the decline. The upper South, under the influence of the frontier, was tending to become a land of small farmers. In the rice regions the pressure of the upcountry was threatening a social revolution, and, in any case, the areas where rice could be grown profitably were limited; the planter aristocrats of Charleston were fighting a losing battle with the forces of democracy. Cotton, however, changed the entire nature of South Carolina and Georgia and gave the planter gentry a new lease on life.

The Industrial Revolution had already transformed the English textile industry. In fact, a succession of inventions in spinning and weaving had so improved cotton manufacture that the potential capacity of the mills exceeded the supply of raw material. Experiments had shown that cotton could be raised in the South; but only the sea-island or long-staple variety was profitable, and it could be grown nowhere but along the coast. Short-staple cotton could be grown almost anywhere, but its seeds were matted in the fibers in such a way as to make cleaning so difficult that a skillful slave woman could clean no more than a pound a day. Everywhere, South Carolinians and Georgians sought a machine to perform this labor. The Georgia legislature finally offered a prize for an effective device, and meanwhile planters hopefully seeded acres to the new type of cotton. A market was waiting and a crop was ready for harvest, when Eli Whitney, a recent graduate of Yale University, came to Georgia to visit the widow of the late General Nathanael Greene. Learning of the legislative award and hearing much conversation about the expected "engine" or, for short, "gin," the ingenious Whitney in a short time brought forth a contrivance that actually worked. This comprised, first, a pair of toothed rollers that seized the fibers of the cotton boll and drew them through slats which excluded the clinging seeds and, second, a simple brush that removed the lint from the rollers. Whitney patented his invention, collected his award, and formed a partnership with Phineas Miller, Mrs. Greene's second husband, to market the gin. Unfortunately, Whitney had Yankee contentiousness as well as Yankee ingenuity, and lawsuits against rival gins soon reduced him to poverty.

But the South went on to a new prosperity. In 1791, eight bales of southern cotton were denied entry to England by an incredulous

Liverpool customs officer who did not believe that America could grow cotton; yet Whitney's gin, invented two years later, soon furnished practically all the fiber used in English mills. In 1800 the South exported 79,000 bales, and in 1810 over 124,000; by 1820 the total southern crop was over 484,000, and the exported part of it brought over $27,000,000 to southern growers. Within the South this new source of income had two effects: it created a demand for western expansion, and it made possible the rise of new recruits for the planter class.

The possibility of producing cotton in the Carolina upcountry freed the planters from dependence on the rice swamps, and, turning inland, they moved their slaves to newly acquired cotton plantations. At the same time, men of the upcountry abandoned the production of foodstuffs and their small beginnings in manufacturing and likewise turned to growing the new staple. The advantages of cotton were many. It required less cultivation than did rice and tobacco, was more easily prepared for the market, could be adapted to slave labor or to cultivation by unskilled white hands, and was just as profitable whether raised on one acre or on a thousand. Upcountry farmers found their profits increased by purchasing slaves. One such farmer, the father of John C. Calhoun, purchased a single slave whose presence changed the whole attitude of the Calhoun family. The father had been identified with the radicals of the Revolution, struggling with the Tories and with the reactionaries of Charleston; the son became the spokesman for the most conservative, propertied class in the nation. And the case of the Calhouns was typical. Cotton tied together the upcountry and the low country, spread slavery everywhere in the Cotton Kingdom, and induced men of the uplands to expand their acres, buy more slaves, and dream of rising into the planter class.

As the area of cotton culture widened, aspiring planters began to crave additional land; and at their insistence the federal government entered into a series of arrangements for opening the Gulf region to plantation settlement. Especially attractive to prospective cotton growers were the lands lying between the western boundary of Georgia and the Mississippi River; but four parties—Spain, the United States, Georgia, and South Carolina—possessed conflicting claims upon the territory, and large-scale migration in that direction had to wait until these conflicts had been resolved. In 1789 the Georgia legislature, some of its members having a personal interest in the enterprise, assumed the power to make extensive grants along the Yazoo River to four groups of land speculators, prominent among whom was the erstwhile patriot Patrick Henry. In 1802, seven years after Spain had relinquished her claim to the Mississippi country north of Florida, Georgia also ceded her interest in that territory to the United States. However, although her legislature had at one time canceled the grants to the so-called "Yazoo companies," Georgia stipulated in the act of cession that the federal government reimburse the Yazoo men for their claims. In his efforts to get an appropriation from the House of Representatives for this purpose, President Jefferson ran against the opposition of John Randolph, an eccentric Virginia planter who controlled the public purse as chairman of the Committee of Ways and Means. Randolph, his language picturesque, his accusing finger active, made it embarrassingly clear that the land speculators (most of them Northerners) had bribed the Georgia legislature, and he induced a considerable following of southern Republicans to join him in denouncing their party leader and the Yazoo frauds. Eventually Jefferson was able to secure the money he desired, but only after he had maneuvered Randolph out of the leadership of the House.

During the quarrel in Congress, migrants were already moving into the ceded area to the west of Georgia. The federal government extended its land system to the region, opened land offices, cleared the Indian titles in a series of treaties, and set up a territorial government for Mississippi Territory. Within its boundaries some 23,000 white people, taking with them 17,000 slaves, occupied over half a million acres by 1812. Georgia grew even more rapidly, almost doubling in population between 1800 and 1810. During the War of 1812, the Creek Indians rose against the white men in the Southwest, but Andrew Jackson effectually suppressed them, and further Indian cessions and a greatly increased migration followed the war. Consequently, the federal government divided the territory into two parts, Mississippi and Alabama, and then admitted Mississippi as a state in 1817 and Alabama in 1819.

While speculators and settlers were taking possession of the land east of the Mississippi, others passed over into the Louisiana country and there set in motion a similar process of state-making. In 1803, Jefferson, taking advantage of Napoleon's need, purchased the vast Louisiana tract from the French emperor. For such a gigantic deal in real estate there was no specific warrant in the Constitution, but, his party being devoted to agricultural expansion, Jefferson laid aside his constitutional scruples and took the territory. Out of it Congress created the Louisiana and Orleans Territories, and in 1812, when Orleans had over 75,000 inhabitants, admitted that part to the Union as the state of Louisiana. From the remainder, renamed Missouri Territory, Congress carved out the Territory of Arkansas in 1819.

Meanwhile, agrarian zeal for expansion also led the Republican administration to look toward the Floridas. The words of the Louisiana Purchase treaty being vague, Jefferson could allege that Napoleon had sold the Spanish territory of West Florida along with Louisiana. Soon enough, in 1810, following an American-inspired revolution in the region, Congress simply declared it part of the United States. Then East Florida became the goal of the expanding Southerners. They especially desired this Spanish colony because the Spaniards had never given up intriguing with its Indians, who now and again raided American settlements in Georgia and Alabama, and because slaves frequently escaped from southern plantations and fled to freedom among the Florida red men. The expansionists applauded when, in 1818, Jackson led his frontier militia against the Seminoles, pursued them into Florida, captured two Spanish forts, and hanged two British citizens for aiding the Indians.

Persuaded by this series of assaults on her territory, Spain agreed, the next year, to sell Florida to the United States. In 1821, Florida became a territory, and in 1845, a state.

2. THE AGRARIAN PROGRAM AND COMMERCIAL REACTION

Once they were ensconced in office, the Republicans made no drastic effort to reorganize the federal government in accordance with the principles they had laid down in the Kentucky and Virginia Resolutions. True, they secured the adoption of the Twelfth Amendment, altering the procedure of the electoral college by having each elector designate his separate choice for president and vice-president; but this was a simple adjustment made in response to a recognized need and embodied no serious change in the constitutional edifice. In fact, the Republicans were content with the existing form of government so long as they might direct it to their own ends.

The Republicans did intend, however, to prevent the judiciary from infringing upon popular rights. In 1789, as Antifederalists, they had objected to the creation of a federal hierarchy of courts, for they believed that state courts could function for minor cases, and they feared that federal judges, appointed for life, would be repositories of aristocratic power. Jealous of the rights of the states, they thought it undesirable to bring the force of the national government to bear so closely upon the people. They had intended in the Kentucky and Virginia Resolutions to suggest a method of checking the federal courts and protecting the states. They believed that only the latter could pass upon the constitutionality of acts of Congress. They feared that giving the justices this power, as Federalists proposed, would destroy the basic principles of checks and balances, so dear to the founding fathers. And yet, despite the protests of Republicans, the courts had gathered increasing strength throughout the period of Federalist rule.

When Jefferson came into office, he was particularly irate over a recent deed of Federalist aggression through the courts. The Federalists in the expiring Congress had provided for a number of new judicial offices, and in the last days of his term President Adams had busied himself filling them with faithful partisans. Although the executive and legislature might thereafter fall to the Republicans, the judiciary, at least, was to be made safe for Hamiltonian principles. The incoming Republicans immediately set themselves to repeal this Judiciary Act of 1801. When Federalists objected that removing judges by repealing the act was unconstitutional, Giles of Virginia thought it sufficient to reply that their program was in "direct hostility to the great principles of representative government" and would "produce a gradual demolition of the state courts."

The Republicans found proof of judicial usurpation when Chief Justice John Marshall, one of Adams's appointees, made bold to declare in the case of *Marbury v. Madison* that a part of the Judiciary Act of

1789 was unconstitutional. "It is emphatically the province and duty of the judicial department to say what the law is," Marshall insisted. Jefferson indignantly retorted that if this were true, the states had committed suicide when they adopted the Constitution. "For," he said, "intending to establish three departments, co-ordinate and independent, that they might check and balance one another, it has given, according to this opinion, to one of them alone the right to prescribe the rules for the government of the others, and to that one, too, which is unelected by and independent of the nation." Jefferson concluded: "The Constitution, on this hypothesis, is a mere thing of wax in the hands of the judiciary, which they may twist and shape into any form they please."

Already the Republicans had launched an attack on the courts and had attempted to remove some of the more obnoxious Federalist judges by impeachment; but the obvious partisanship of this assault prevented its success. As John Marshall continued to give opinion after opinion against the rights of states—*Fletcher v. Peck, Cohen v. Virginia, McCulloch v. Maryland*, and *Martin v. Hunter's Lessee*—Jefferson and the southern Republicans writhed in anger but found no satisfactory means of self-defense. The Virginia legislature denied the right of a federal court to hear appeals from the state's courts, and proposed suitable amendments to the Constitution. Judge Spencer Roane, Virginia jurist whom Jefferson would have made chief justice, wrote a series of articles for the Richmond *Enquirer* which were, in effect, dissenting opinions in Marshall's cases. He asserted that the federal government was the agent of the sovereign people, who, working through the states, might stop the excesses of a Supreme Court acting upon the principle that "itself is never in the wrong." With more philosophy but with no less vigor John Taylor of Caroline in *Construction Construed and Tyranny Unmasked* assailed Marshall's doctrines. Jefferson thought Marshall and his colleagues a "subtle corps of sappers and miners constantly working underground to undermine the foundations of our confederated fabric." Yet Jefferson, unable in his constitutional thinking to go beyond protest, did nothing effective to combat the Court. In 1821 Kentucky and Virginia congressmen unsuccessfully proposed an amendment to give jurisdiction to the Senate in cases of dispute between the nation and a state. It remained for John C. Calhoun to formulate a legal procedure whereby the states might check congressional laws and judicial decisions that they deemed unconstitutional.

If the Federalists retained control of the courts, the other branches of the government were safely in the hands of the agricultural allies from the South and the West. Both sections were growing so fast that New England and the commercial North and East had become the home of a minority. The sectional fires first lighted in the days of Hamiltonian supremacy burned more brightly than ever.

When Jefferson purchased Louisiana in the interests of the South and West, his critics foresaw the day when Westerners would rule the nation and New Englanders would have no influence in Washington. Said Uriah Tracy of Connecticut, "The relative strength which admission of states from Louisiana territory gives to a southern and western interest is contradictory to the principles of our original Union. This would be absorbing the northern states, and rendering them as insignificant in the Union as they ought to be, if by their consent the measure should be adopted." Students of Williams College declared the acquisition undesirable. Men who had thought nothing of Hamilton's funding schemes thought the price for Louisiana too high. Resorting to constitutional argument, some maintained that new states could be formed only from the territory of the original Union, that the federal government had no right, as one objector phrased it, to admit a foreign power into "co-partnership without the consent of the states." Republicans answered the Federalists by asserting that the right to acquire territory was an essential part of the sovereignty of any nation, and that the right to acquire implied the right to admit the new territory into the Union.

Yet it was evident that the Jeffersonians had for the nonce deserted their compact theory and their devotion to the individual states. Equal to Jefferson in their aptitude for inconsistency, the Federalists of New England took up the principles of the Kentucky and Virginia Resolutions and used these to justify their own stand.

In Massachusetts there was, indeed, a strong sentiment for secession. There, the legislature proposed an amendment to base representation in Congress on the number of free inhabitants of the states, so as to reduce the influence of the Southerners. Georgia immediately answered, branding the proposition as unjust and calculated to disorganize the Union. The replies of the other states were likewise unfavorable, but the idea remained alive in Massachusetts.

In 1811, when Louisiana was ready for statehood, the old antagonism flared up again. The erstwhile fear on the part of New Englanders that acquisition would mean new states now seemed fully justified. The Yankee spokesman Josiah Quincy declared: "It is my deliberate opinion that, if this bill passes, the bonds of this Union are virtually dissolved, that the states are free from their moral obligations, and it will be the right of all . . . to prepare for a separation, amicable if they can, violently if they must. . . ." Then he asked whether the proprietors of the "good old United States" should manage their "own affairs in their own way" or should permit the country to be turned over to foreigners. The people of the northern states, he said, would not allow "the representatives from the Red River and the Missouri to manage the affairs of the seaboard 1500 miles away."

That the inhabitants of the old Union were to be ruled in the interests of the newer states became evident in the foreign policies of the Republican administration. The Napoleonic wars were bringing welcome profits to New England merchants and shipowners, until both of the leading belligerents, England and France, began to place restrictions on American shipping. Jefferson, who was both an agriculturalist and a pacifist, could see no reason for going to war with either France or England over commercial rights. Believing that the warring nations could be brought to terms by the application of economic pressure, he persuaded Congress to pass an embargo which would forbid American ships to sail into the war zone. The result was a paralysis of business in the North and a great protest from the New England states. Massachusetts instructed her congressmen to work for the law's repeal. When, in 1809, the Republican Congress passed an act to enforce the embargo, the men of Massachusetts protested against it on the grounds of unconstitutionality, adopted Jefferson's old views of strict construction, and boldly talked of resisting the law. The legislature passed a memorial and resolve which proposed an amendment to the Constitution securing "commerce and navigation from a repetition of destructive and insidious theories" and another abolishing the three-fifths rule. Additional resolutions warned that some kind of understanding among the eastern states was necessary to preserve their influence in the national government. In Connecticut the governor called the representatives of the people into special session. "Indeed," he told them, "it would be useful for the general good if the state legislatures were often to cast a watchful eye toward the general government, with a view candidly to consider and judiciously discern, whether the powers delegated to the United States are not exceeded." He went on to advise the legislators, in terms close to those of the Virginia doctrine of sentinelship, that it was their duty to protect the people against the aggressions of the national government. Thanks to this New England opposition and to the fact that the farmers of the middle states were hurt by the loss of the European market, the embargo was eventually repealed. But New England was soon to have a new grievance against the South and West—the War of 1812.

War was precipitated by the arrival in Congress of a group of determined young men from the West. The reapportionment after the census of 1810 had given the newly settled regions many more representatives in the House. From Kentucky now came young Henry Clay and Richard M. Johnson; from Tennessee, Felix Grundy; from Georgia, William Crawford, from the upcountry of South Carolina, William Lowndes and John C. Calhoun. These men were eager to push back the American boundaries in ever-widening arcs. As patriots, they hated the English, the Spanish, and the Indians; as sharers of the agrarian traditions of the yeomen, they coveted the good lands of Florida and Canada. Before long, they forced the hand of Madison and pushed the United States into a war with England, which they confidently expected to end in the acquisition of territory. According to the slogans of the day, war was being fought to protect American seamen and American commerce, but the Federalists from the commercial states of the North, who ought in such a case to have shown the martial spirit, were wholly out of sympathy with the youthful "war hawks." As soon as war was declared, the Federalists in Congress issued an address disclaiming all responsibility for the deed and advocating the organization of a peace party to resist the policy of the government.

Throughout the duration of the war, Madison's administration had trouble with the discontented Yankees. Governors of New England states refused to furnish militia, quarreled with the president over the appointment of officers, and insisted, in the words of the chief executive of Connecticut, that the United States was a "confederation of states . . . a confederated and not a consolidated republic." New England bankers refused to loan money for the conduct of the war. When Congress passed a new embargo as a war measure, the states protested, and when Congress discussed a conscription bill, Massachusetts sent out the call for a convention of New Englanders, who finally assembled in Hartford. Revealing their jealousy of the South and the West, the delegates to the Hartford Convention agreed that new states should be admitted only upon a two-thirds vote of Congress and repeated the old proposal to eliminate the "three-fifths clause" of the Constitution, which gave partial representation to southern slaves. Although the Hartford Convention may have contemplated the ultimate secession of New England, the coming of peace forestalled such an attempt on the life of the Union. Ironically enough, as a result of the hated war, New England gained new industries and with them new economic interests which within a few years would enable the section to bid for an alliance with the West against the South.

The War of 1812 resulted in no settlement of the commercial issues, the technical casus belli, which had existed between the United States and Great Britain. The treaty of peace made no mention of the ostensible causes of the conflict, but did provide for a series of commissions that made lasting arrangements to preserve amity. From the war itself the South derived certain tangible gains. Andrew Jackson had led his Tennessee militia against the Creek Indians and destroyed their power to stop the advance of settlement. His victory over the British at New Orleans had filled the southwestern militia with pride. His march into Pensacola and his later assault upon Spanish sovereignty during the Seminole War had given the South the territory of Florida and security against Indian wars. All the territorial gains resulting from the war inured to the benefit of the South.

3. Nationalism and States' Rights

The War of 1812 at once intensified the struggle between North and South and marked the beginning of southern decline. During the Jeffersonian period, the farmers of the new West had followed the planters of the Old South in their attacks upon the commercial interests. But even while this battle was being won, the Westerners acquired leaders of their own who began to seek control of the Republican party for themselves. A sign of the changing times was Madison's feeble yielding to the insistent demands of the "war hawks." Meanwhile, the contrariety of interests between the two sections—the one democratic, small-farming, food-producing; the other aristocratic, planting, staple-producing —became increasingly apparent. The farmers of the Western regions made demands on the national government, such as "internal improvements" at federal expense, which the southern planter-statesmen were reluctant to grant. All in all, the Southerners found themselves growing more uncomfortable in their sectional alliance. At the same time, the politicians of Yankeedom and the middle states, where the war hastened the beginnings of an industrial revolution, were taking an interest in such a nationalistic policy as a protective tariff. In exchange for this they were willing to offer to the West the internal improvements that Southerners withheld. As East and West affiliated more closely in a common philosophy of nationalism, South and West were being wedged apart by the opposing interests of their sectionalism. The forces here involved were to break up the old Republican party of Thomas Jefferson and cause the northeastern Federalists to fish skillfully and patiently for a new alliance with the West.

The period following the War of 1812 was an era of intense nationalism. The war itself had freed the Americans from both intellectual and economic dependence upon Europe, and under the leadership of the new West the country was now launched upon a program of nationalistic legislation. Forgetting both the strict-construction doctrines of Thomas Jefferson and the dogma of states' rights, western Republicans supported a program which included an increase of the army and navy, a higher protective tariff, a national bank, and internal improvements. On each of these questions a fundamental division in interest between the South and the West gradually became apparent.

One of the first questions to engage national attention after the war was the problem of a national bank. The Constitution did not provide for such a financial organization, and Jefferson and Madison, realizing the need, had early suggested an appropriate amendment. When the charter of the Bank of the United States expired in 1811, the war had not yet taught other Republicans the necessity of centralized financial control, though Secretary of the Treasury Albert Gallatin advocated renewing the charter. In his message of 1815, Madison urged Congress to attend to the banking problem, and Calhoun again introduced a bill for rechartering the old bank. Using Hamiltonian arguments, the Republicans succeeded in passing the bill despite the determined opposition of the Federalists.

But the question was not yet settled. Investors in state banks opposed a national institution that would regulate their activities, and they supported proposals to limit the Bank of the United States to the District of Columbia. Some of the states made efforts to destroy the bank. Maryland, for example, required that the bank print notes on paper which the state sold, or pay a tax of $15,000 annually. McCulloch, cashier of the Baltimore branch, refused to pay the tax and was sued. The case came to the Supreme Court in 1819. Counsel for Maryland argued that Congress had no right to charter a bank or to give such a corporation the right to establish branches in the states; but in his decision Marshall upheld the bank. The people of the United States, he said, had made the Constitution the supreme law of the land. "Let the end be legitimate, let it be within the scope of the Constitution, and all means which are appropriate, which are plainly adapted to that end, which are not prohibited but consist with the letter and spirit of the Constitution are constitutional." If the Congress should exceed its power, he reminded, the Supreme Court would be obliged to declare the law unconstitutional. This opinion occasioned an outburst of protest. Madison publicly condemned "this latitude in expounding the Constitution." Jefferson thought that the banks would have to conform to state laws; otherwise, "we must shut their doors, and join the other states which deny the right of Congress to establish banks and solicit them to agree to some mode of settling this constitutional question." In Kentucky, where the bank was taxed $5,000 for each branch established in the state, an editor declared, on hearing of the decision in the Maryland case, that Kentucky might as well give up its constitution and return to the status of a territory.

In Ohio, also, an attempt was made to tax the bank. The Ohio case was carried to the Supreme Court and met a decision from Marshall like that in the Maryland case. The Ohio legislature protested, the Georgia legislature responded with resolutions of sympathy, and the Virginia legislature considered resolutions stating that the decision was calculated to "sap the foundations and rights of the state governments," and instructed its senators to seek an amendment to the constitution which would establish an impartial tribunal to pass upon cases of disputed jurisdiction.

The bank issue revealed the opposition of some of the southern states to the nationalism of the West, but the question of internal improvements showed even more clearly the division between the agrarian allies. Westerners, far from their markets and badly in need of means of communication, clamored for canals and highways and, unable to bear the burden of building such enterprises, looked to the national government for help. Southerners, on the other hand, did not need extensive improvements, for their rivers flowed to the sea and enabled them easily to float their cotton to the coast, where it could be transshipped to European markets. The end of the Napoleonic wars resulted in greater production of foodstuffs in Europe and consequent losses to western farmers but increased the demand for cotton and made the South prosperous. With navigable rivers and a good market, they were satisfied and were unwilling to be taxed for internal improvements. The Westerners, with poor means of transport and a falling market, wanted something done for them. At last the West and South came to a parting of their political ways.

The problem of internal improvements had long been before the country. When Jefferson came to the presidency, he proposed that Congress initiate a constitutional amendment giving the federal government the right to build certain highways; and Congress began to follow his advice, although more and more the Westerners were taking this power for granted. When Henry Clay arrived in Congress from Kentucky, one of his first acts was to provide for an appropriation for a bridge, and he had the support of most of the war hawks, Calhoun among them.

The War of 1812 showed the need for more military roads, and Madison favored doing what could be done within the limits of the Constitution. He, too, proposed an amendment giving the government specific power to build roads and canals. But the congressional leaders had no patience with the slow processes of amending the organic law, and under Calhoun's leadership they proceeded more directly by passing the Bonus Bill. This bill would distribute to the states the bonus paid by the newly rechartered bank, so as to aid them in building turnpikes and waterways. Madison considered the Bonus Bill unconstitutional and vetoed it. His successor, Monroe, also a representative of the southern interests, held similar views. Burdened at this time with no such theoretical scruples, Calhoun spoke again in favor of internal improvements, asserting that they clearly came within the rightful authority of Congress.

In 1817, a Virginia representative introduced an amendment which would give Congress the right to build roads but only with the consent of the states, the distribution of public funds to be in accordance with state population. A committee of Congress, headed by another Virginian, reported that Congress already possessed the right. The discussion caused considerable uproar in the South, where some Republican leaders saw a new attempt to increase the power of the national government at the expense of the states. Once again men called upon the theory of states' rights to protect southern property against national taxation.

4. THE MISSOURI COMPROMISE

In the midst of the postwar wave of ebullient nationalism, a conflict came which laid bare the underlying sectional division. The application of the Missouri Territory for admission as a state brought to a head New England's objection to the growing West and to the increased representation which slavery gave to the South. In the constitutional convention of 1787, conservatives had objected to the admission of new communities on equal terms with the original members of the Union; but the final draft of the Constitution evaded the question with a simple provision that Congress might admit additional states. Yet both the Ordinance of 1784 and the Northwest Ordinance had provided that new western states were to be equal to the original thirteen, and this proviso was inherent in the conditions under which the various states had ceded their western lands. When Kentucky and Vermont applied for admission, it appeared impossible to deprive them of full equality. Jefferson's Republicans, drawing strength from the West, continued to hold out the promise of complete statehood and incorporated in the Louisiana Purchase Treaty the assurance that people of the region would be entitled to full citizenship in the Union.

But in the creation of new southern states there lay a threat to the East's nascent industry. Men of the commercial regions, having tasted the spoils of office and enjoyed the beneficence of favorable legislation under Hamilton's brief regime, longed to return to the fleshpots of the national government. Southerners showed no will to legislate for the industrial regions. With clear instinct, they perceived that prosperous industry would give the manufacturing regions a preponderance of population. Hence, at the same time that they pushed the plantation system into new western areas, they determined to give no encouragement to manufactures.

Inevitably, the difference in economic systems meant a difference in population, for plantation regions supported fewer people than did industrial regions. Immigrants from Europe, seldom seeking southern shores, went instead to areas where labor was free, and many a yeoman farmer of Methodist or Baptist or Quaker proclivities left the South for the Northwest in silent protest against slavery. By 1819 it was plain to the intelligent Southerner that his institutions must expand if he was to maintain his influence in Washington. It was equally obvious to the New Englander that the power of the North would be increased if southern expansion could be stopped. Already the more rapid growth of the North had given the section control of the House of Representatives. Only in the Senate were the sections equal.

Missouri offered the Southerners a new slave state whose votes in the Senate would counterbalance the North's preponderance in the House. The territory had been settled by Southerners who had followed the course of the Missouri River and occupied its fertile valley. By 1817 the Missourians were ready to erect a state, but Congress disappointed them by taking no action. In 1818 they renewed their request, and on February 13, 1819, a committee of Congress reported an enabling act. On the same day James Tallmadge, a representative from New York, offered an amendment providing that the further introduction of slavery be prohibited, and that all slave children born in the state after admission should be freed at the age of twenty-five years. The Tallmadge amendment clearly raised the question of whether Congress could place restrictions on a member of the Union. Contending that the Union was made up of equal sovereign parts, Southerners hastened to deny any congressional power to limit a state's sovereignty. Rufus King, of New York, presenting the northern case, launched an attack on slavery. The balloting on the Tallmadge amendment showed a definite sectional cleavage, only one Southerner casting his vote for it. The original bill, without the obnoxious amendment, was finally passed by the Senate and sent to the House, but a majority of the representatives refused to accept it without the proviso against slaves.

At once, mass meetings throughout the country expressed popular opinion on the issues. In St. Louis business was stagnant while the bill was being discussed. In New York and Philadelphia, public gatherings asserted that Congress had the power to exclude a state or to impose conditions on its admission. In Boston, Webster spoke and Josiah Quincy sent resolutions to Congress affirming that opening a new territory to slavery was contrary both to the end sought by the Union and to the opinions of the early slave-state leaders themselves.

State legislatures took up the agitation when the next session of

Congress again debated the Missouri question. Above and below the Mason and Dixon line states took their appropriate stands. The Virginia House of Delegates resolved that Virginia would support Missouri in her rights. The Pennsylvania legislature declared that to admit Missouri as a slave state would impair the political relations of the states and mar the social happiness of present and future generations; it would perpetuate an odious stain, would be a covenant with crime, and would be contrary to duty, to God, and to the fathers of the Republic; it would "open a new and steady market for the lawless venders of human flesh." The Kentucky and Maryland legislatures protested against imposing conditions on a state. The New York legislature insisted that Congress had both the power and the duty to confine slavery to its existing bounds.

In the end, the Senate and the House agreed to a compromise. Massachusetts had given the Maine district permission to apply for admission as a separate state, and this application was before Congress. Early in the debates, a suggestion had been made to divide the Louisiana Purchase territory into free and slave areas. The final compromise combined these proposals. Missouri entered the Union with slavery, Maine without, and the remainder of the Louisiana Territory was divided along the line of 36° 30', slavery to be prohibited in new states north of that line and permitted in those south of it. On February 17, 1820, the Senate accepted this arrangement by a vote of 34 to 10, every northern senator except those from Indiana voting in favor of it. The House finally acceded in almost exactly the same ratio of ayes and nays, 134 to 42. Southerners were evenly divided, but the Virginians, holding strict-construction views of congressional power, were pretty solidly opposed.

Despite Congress's action, the future of Missouri remained uncertain. There was some question whether President Monroe, since many of his fellow Virginians favored a veto, would approve the compromise. In the midst of his indecision, he consulted his cabinet and found Calhoun, Crawford, and Wirt, all Southerners, agreeing that Congress had power to prohibit slavery in the territories, though Missouri might repudiate this stipulation after becoming a state. Desiring re-election, Monroe delayed putting his signature to the compromise bill until opinion in Virginia had shifted to its support.

Some doubt still existed whether the Missourians would accept the terms imposed upon them. When the Missouri convention met to frame a state constitution, the slaveholders were in control. To provide for the security of slavery, they forbade the legislature to manumit slaves without getting the consent of the owners and without giving adequate compensation, and they instructed the legislature to prevent free Negroes from entering the state. This flaunting of proslavery intransigeance aroused northern prejudices and set going another debate in Congress. For a time it seemed that Missouri would have to stay out in the cold; but congressmen finally tired of the discussion and decided to extract a promise from the Missourians that they would not discriminate against the citizens of any other state. The Missouri legislature gave surly acquiescence, and Monroe, anxious to be rid of a troublesome matter, accepted the arrangement.

In the Missouri conflict was involved a constitutional question—what was the proper relationship of the states to the Union? But beneath that question lay the deeper issue of the economic well-being of the respective sections. Looking upon the situation with the cynical eye of a professional politician, Thomas Jefferson declared that the Federalists had raised the Missouri question as a party trick. They had sought to divide the people geographically by taking advantage of the virtuous feeling of Northerners in regard to slavery. At the time, Rufus King, heir of the trustee tradition, frankly avowed that he was opposed to the extension of the political power of slavery, and John Quincy Adams believed that King had set on foot a concert of measures that would form the basis for a new sectional alignment of parties. Whether or not the trick helped the Federalists as a party, the slave problem was thereafter never entirely absent from national politics, as later generations of politicians learned to use this moral issue as a means of confounding the southern people and weakening their economic system.

By the Missouri Compromise the North won an apparent victory. She had secured the consent of the South to the exclusion of slavery from the greater part of the Louisiana Purchase. Although this exclusion was limited to the territorial period, it would also affect the period of statehood, for Southerners would not migrate to a region which was closed to slavery. The clash over Missouri marked the end of the alliance of South and West and drove the South to take refuge again in the old doctrines of states' rights. Jefferson said the quarrel had wakened him "like a fire bell in the night," and he predicted that the Union would eventually split over the question of slavery.

CHAPTER 9

Southern Reaction to Nationalism

1. Party Politics of the 'Twenties

FROM the time of the Missouri Compromise, politicians of the industrial centers, the strongholds of the old Federalist party, never lost sight of the possibility of injecting an ethical issue into American politics. Capitalizing on the strength of the trustee tradition, they sought through moral appeals to win the Northwest from its southern alliance. The Southerners had already shown a lack of sympathy with the internal-improvement program of their allies. The effort to create a new East-West political alignment, beginning with the Missouri agitation, continued through the careers of Webster and Clay until in the 1850's the union was finally consummated under the auspices of the Republican party. In the end, it was a combination of economic interests and moral enthusiasm that arrayed the northern sections against the South. The process of realignment was slow, however, and for a long time the momentum of early co-operation kept the agricultural sections nominally united in political fellowship.

Throughout the decades from 1820 to 1850, the South and West were developing separate and distinct institutions, social customs, and philosophies of life. The Northwest was a land where small farmers produced wheat, corn, cattle, and hogs, where from the beginning the Northwest Ordinance had prohibited slavery and prevented the development of large landed estates worked by laborers of fixed status, where high wages enabled the propertyless laborer to acquire a farm with comparative ease. There, villages and small towns developed as centers of trade and commerce to supply the needs of the surrounding farms. Merchants, lawyers, and physicians gathered in the towns, and small manufacturing plants and the rudiments of the service industries sprang up. The South, on the other hand, was a country where the plantation system supplied the necessary services, and slave handicraft sought to provide the manufactured goods needed in the slave community. Here, too, were yeoman farmers and a small professional class, but the plantation ways set the dominant pattern of society. In the Southwest ambitious men looked forward to acquiring a great estate, well stocked with slaves; in the Northwest they aspired to own a trading business or a manufactory. In the Northwest the farmers and merchants needed internal improvements, the common man demanded schools, the villages strove to become commercial towns and the towns to become industrial cities; but in the Southwest planters were content with a rural way of life. Such differences in economic and social organization underlay the increasing divergence in politics, as the Northwest gradually came to feel a closer affiliation with the industrial regions of the East than with its older agricultural ally to the South.

The divisive forces working beneath the surface were seldom apparent during the two administrations of James Monroe, who was the choice of Jefferson and Madison and the last of the "Virginia dynasty." Although Monroe was elected in 1816 by an overwhelming majority over his Federalist opponent and was re-elected without opposition in 1820, the Federalist party was not yet entirely dead. Jefferson feared that Federalism would come to life after the Missouri controversy. Indeed, eight of the members of Congress from Massachusetts claimed adherence to the dying party, half the delegation from Maryland, mostly commercial representatives from Baltimore, and six each from both Pennsylvania and New York. These made up a nucleus large enough to cause trouble in the future. The eight years of Monroe's administration were known as the "era of good feelings," but the good feelings were all on the surface.

Underlying the superficial harmony were the jealousies of sectional candidates for the succession to the White House. As the election of 1824 approached, each of the sections of the country had a presidential candidate who represented its interests and who was willing to make concessions to the other sections to obtain the presidency. New England had John Quincy Adams, the secretary of state, to offer; the South had both Crawford, the secretary of the treasury, and Calhoun, the secretary of war; the West presented Henry Clay, the Kentucky champion of frontier interests in Congress, and Andrew Jackson of Tennessee, the hero of the battle of New Orleans. The quarrel among these contenders intensified the growing sectional self-consciousness in the various parts of the nation.

John Quincy Adams, though perhaps not the best representative of New England interests, could boast an experience in public affairs far greater than that of any of his rivals. Although his foreign travels and diplomatic experience widened his outlook and leavened the rich culture of his native New England, and in spite of his great and obvious abilities, he was never in all his long career truly a popular man. He was too much the Puritan: rising at dawn and laboring until midnight; full of moral precepts and a stern sense of duty; seldom smiling wholeheartedly. He confessed in his diary that he was "a man of reserved, cold, austere and forbidding manners." Being such a man, the problem that John Quincy Adams faced in 1824 was a huge one: to conciliate the South, harmonize his enemies in New England, and gain support in the West.

Willam Crawford hailed from the Georgia frontier, had been a conservative and a Federalist, but had finally come to stand with Virginia's Madison and Monroe on most issues. In the Senate his native ability, handsome figure, and ready wit had made him a favorite among his colleagues. After two years as minister to France, he returned to become Madison's secretary of the treasury. Popular with congressmen, he could have had the Republican nomination in 1816, but he stepped aside for Monroe. Nevertheless, everyone understood that the affable Georgian was the heir apparent to the Virginia dynasty, and leading congressmen and Republican editors sang his praises. In general, he and his supporters stood for the doctrine of states' rights, though—with an eye for votes— they were willing to approve a moderate tariff and a national bank.

Unlike Crawford, who continued the traditions of the older South, John C. Calhoun represented the newer South that cotton had created as it united the uplands and the low country in the Carolinas and tied them in with the states of the planting frontier. Calhoun, a son of the Carolina upcountry, was soon to become the voice of the cotton capitalist everywhere. His forbears had followed the customary pathway of the Scotch-Irish frontiersmen from Pennsylvania southward, his grandmother had died in an Indian massacre, and his father had fought on the patriot side in the Revolution and had been identified with the radicals. In Calhoun's boyhood, cotton had come into the uplands, and the family had purchased a slave to work the cotton fields. They had added other slaves, one by one, so that, by the time the young man entered a Presbyterian "log college," the Calhouns were well on the way to becoming proud and prosperous planters. Calhoun went on to Yale and from there to Litchfield, Connecticut, to read law in the office of a Federalist, but the frontier was still so strong within him that he remained attached, if only verbally, to the principles of Thomas Jefferson. In time, his Presbyterianism, his training among the Federalists, and his identification of himself with the planters were to make him the peculiar advocate of property and slavery rather than the defender of Jeffersonian equalitarianism. When he married his cousin, Floride, the daughter of a low-country planter, he hastened the merger of his philosophy with that of the planters and the squires.

Calhoun had not yet found his distinctive role when, in 1811, he took his place in Congress among the war hawks. During his early years as a congressman, he was one of the more enthusiastic nationalists. He helped to loose the dogs of war in 1812; during the hostilities he labored valiantly to raise troops, supplies, and funds; ready in debate, he flung anathemas upon New England pacifists and obstructionists. He was, indeed, "the young Hercules who carried the war on his shoulders." After the war he warned against a "low, sordid, selfish and sectional spirit," as he pleaded for a vast program of nationwide internal improvements. "In a country so extensive," he proclaimed, "and so varied in its interests, what is necessary for the common good may apparently be opposed to the interests of particular sections. It must be submitted to as the condition of greatness." He asserted that the Constitution was broad enough for the whole nation, that it was not a fit subject for finespun theories about the limitations of its powers. Later, as secretary of war in Monroe's cabinet, he strengthened and improved the army as an instrument of national strength. Even to the carping diarist Adams, he now seemed to be a man "of fair and candid mind," "of enlarged philosophical views," "of ardent patriotism," and one who clearly stood "above all sectional and factious prejudices." Like Crawford and Adams, he hoped to get control of the South and at the same time to win support from the nationalistic West.

Photo by U. S. Army Signal Corps

HENRY CLAY. Virginia-born, Clay had migrated to Kentucky in 1797. Himself the embodiment of the impetuous and warm-hearted spirit of Kentucky, Clay quickly gained fame and fortune from the practice of law and began to gather political rewards. He had acquired a wide reputation as an ardent nationalist and a political compromiser, but his cup was not yet full. He had ambitions for the presidency and hoped to win it by making a new alliance of the East and the Northwest.

Both Henry Clay and Andrew Jackson came from beyond the mountains, from the lusty West that held the balance of power in the politics of the 'twenties. Virginia-born, Clay had migrated to Kentucky in 1797. His adopted state combined the characteristics of the upper South and the Ohio Valley, for, although Kentuckians held slaves and raised tobacco and hemp, they considered themselves equally well fitted for industrial and commercial development. Himself the embodiment of the impetuous and warm-hearted spirit of Kentucky, Clay quickly gained fame and fortune from the practice of law and began to gather political rewards. He became in succession a Kentucky legislator, a United States senator, speaker of the state House of Representatives, again United States senator, speaker of the national House of Representatives, and a member of the Peace Commission at Ghent in 1814. He had acquired a

New York Historical Society

ANDREW JACKSON. He wore a halo of heroism that aroused the emotions of the common man. Although personally he was one of the planter aristocracy, he became the popular idol of frontiersmen in the West and of city artisans and yeomen farmers in the older states.

wide reputation as an ardent nationalist and a political compromiser, but his cup was not yet full. He had ambitions for the presidency and hoped to win it by making a new alliance of the East and the Northwest.

Clay alone of the presidential aspirants offered a definite legislative program, his "American System," which he set forth in the debates on the tariff of 1820. He had been an apostle of internal improvements from his first days in Congress, and as New England and the middle states came to demand protective duties, he had extended his platform to incorporate their interests. In its developed form, the American System proposed a tariff high enough to protect the "infant" industries of the North and low enough to bring in revenues for building roads and canals ' in the West and improving the navigation of western rivers. These projects would enable Westerners to take their wool and hemp to eastern mills and carry the products of those factories back to western markets. The food-producing West would feed the manufacturing East. And, perhaps, the combined votes of the united regions would place the author of the "System" in the White House!

Andrew Jackson brought to the presidential contest no such intelligible program, but he wore a halo of heroism that aroused the emotions of the common man as much as Clay's system appealed to the property sense of the better born. His early life offered parallels to the lives of both Calhoun and Clay. He was born of Scotch-Irish parents in the Waxhaws district near the border line between North and South Carolina. As a boy, he helped fight Tories in the Revolution; he spent a riotous youth in the Carolinas; and in 1788 he migrated to Nashville, in Tennessee. There he practiced law and administered a crude frontier justice during a brief judicial term. During the last days of Washington's administration, he entered the United States Senate, but resigned to speculate in Tennessee lands and in the more turbulent phases of Tennessee politics. He commanded his state's militia in numerous Indian campaigns and emerged from the battle of New Orleans in 1815 as the only authentic military hero of the War of 1812. Although personally he was one of the planter aristocracy, he became the popular idol of frontiersmen in the West and of city artisans and yeomen farmers in the older states.

The names of Jackson, Clay, Calhoun, Crawford, and Adams remained before the country from about 1820 to 1824, and politics during the last half of the "era of good feeling" centered around them and the sectional interests they represented. The acquisition of Florida reacted in favor of both Jackson, who had dramatically invaded the province, and Adams, who as secretary of state had succeeded in persuading Spain to sell the territory. In the House of Representatives Clay, alarmed by the popularity of his western rival, denounced him and warned the country of the danger of a military dictatorship. In the Cabinet, Calhoun and Crawford proposed to court-martial Jackson for his flagrant disregard of international law. Again, the Missouri controversy affected the fortunes of the various contestants. By his efforts to compromise the question, Clay lost support in New England. Crawford had hoped to benefit from the reaction in the North, but New York and Pennsylvania broke away from the old Virginia alliance on the issue. Jackson, then Governor of Florida, profited from the distress of his rivals, for as a slaveholder he was not suspect in the South, as a military hero his popularity was undimmed in the West, and he safely avoided committing himself on Missouri. Calhoun, too, kept silent, but his silence availed him nothing. Adams, who

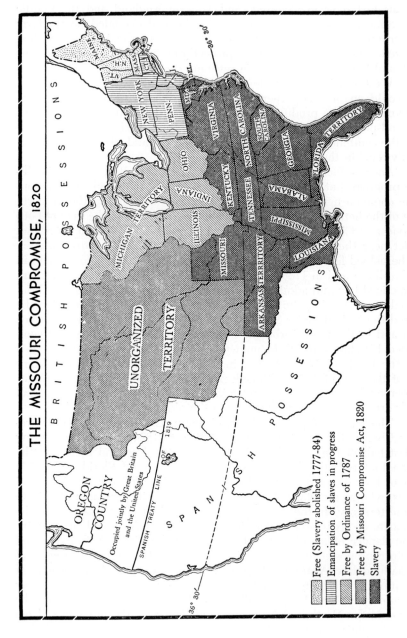

THE MISSOURI COMPROMISE, 1820

Free (Slavery abolished 1777-84)
Emancipation of slaves in progress
Free by Ordinance of 1787
Free by Missouri Compromise Act, 1820
Slavery

From *America's Road to Now*, by Charles H. Coleman and Edgar B. Wesley, by permission of D. C. Heath and Company.

saw as clearly as did Clay the possibility of aligning the West and the North, benefited from the break between Virginia, Pennsylvania, and New York.

After the election of 1824 none of the sectional candidates had a majority in the electoral college, Jackson receiving ninety-nine votes, Adams eighty-four, Crawford forty-one, and Clay thirty-seven. Calhoun, expecting Jackson to win, had agreed to aid the Jackson men in return for their support in 1828 and had dropped out of the presidential race to run for vice-president. Now he was safely elected to the lesser office. With the final choice of a president (from among the three leading candidates) devolving upon the House of Representatives, victory for Jackson was not yet assured, though his followers insisted that the House should carry out the popular will by electing their hero. Clay, the eliminated candidate, wielded great influence in the House. Personally and politically he was closer to Adams, the aristocratic New Englander, than to Jackson, the democratic rival from his own West. Clay and Adams had served together as American commissioners to negotiate the Treaty of Ghent after the War of 1812. They understood and respected each other though they were opposites in personality, and they both realized the political potentialities of the American System.

Though the Jackson men brought enticing offers of a cabinet appointment, Clay used his congressional influence in behalf of Adams and put him in the executive mansion. The new president, ignoring the cry of "bargain and corruption" that Jacksonians at once raised, gave Clay the position of secretary of state, an office which then seemed a sure steppingstone to the presidency.

The Adams administration, applying the teachings of Clay, soon aroused widespread opposition among those who feared a return to Hamiltonianism and the adoption of a nationalistic program benefiting the North and Northwest at the expense of the South. Capitalizing upon the popular suspicions of a corrupt bargain between Adams and Clay, the Jacksonians immediately began a belligerent campaign for the presidency in 1828. Everwhere opponents of the American System united with the Jackson men to wage war on the administration. Even the representatives of the southern planters, though they detested the rag-tag and bobtail of society who hailed Jackson as a hero, were willing to co-operate in efforts to embarrass Adams. The proud Calhoun was not above agreeing to give Jackson the presidency in 1828 on the condition that he himself be permitted to succeed Jackson in the White House. Throughout the South and the Southwest men watched the administration with growing distrust.

One element of the American System was a foreign policy in which both Adams and Clay were vitally interested. As Monroe's secretary of state, Adams had been largely responsible for the writing and issuance of the Monroe Doctrine, which was intended not to gain only the good will but also the trade of the Latin American nations. Clay wished, on the one hand, to preserve behind a tariff wall the independence of American producers from Europe and, on the other, to benefit both New Englanders and Western farmers by opening up markets in the American hemisphere. With these two ardent Pan-Americans in power, the government of the United States took a greater interest than ever before in Latin American affairs. In December, 1825, Adams and Clay presented to the Senate their plans for a congress of the American nations to consider the interests common to all.

Immediately protest came from the southern states. One of Adams's good-neighbor nations had been created by slaves who had risen against their white masters; and, unmoved by the considerations of New England commerce, Southerners shuddered at the thought of co-operating with revolutionary Negroes. John Randolph, of Virginia, declared that the South would have no dealings with a nation that made Negroes equal to white men and had an army commanded by mulatto generals. Robert Y. Hayne, of South Carolina, said: "With nothing connected with slavery can we consent to treat with other nations." An inter-American congress finally met in Panama, but the southern outcry delayed the sending of delegates from the United States until it was too late for them to attend.

Besides suggesting diplomatic dalliance with black men, Adams did other things to offend the sensibilities of the South. At the same time that he proposed sending delegates to the Panama congress, he also offered a grandiose plan of internal improvements—roads, canals, universities, observatories, all to be built at the expense of the general government. Again the South objected. The legislature of Virginia, and representatives of the agricultural classes generally, denied the existence of constitutional authority for such a far-reaching program. This southern opposition was largely responsible for the failure of Adams's high-minded schemes.

Over the perennial Indian question Adams had further trouble with the South, when, in the case of Georgia and the Cherokees, he seemed to show that his nationalistic administration had little respect for the wishes of the states. In 1802 Georgia had ceded her lands to the government on the condition that the United States remove the Creeks and the Cherokees as soon as possible. These civilized and peaceable Indian farmers, trusting for protection in their treaties with the federal government, refused either to sell their lands to greedy frontiersmen or to cede them back to the state of Georgia. Governor George M. Troup, voicing the desire of most Georgians, demanded that the United States expel the Indians and make way for the white men. It appeared that the Indians were beginning to yield when in 1825 McIntosh, the chief of the lower Creeks, signed a treaty of sale with federal commissioners. But his people alleged corruption in the making of the treaty, killed their chief, and rebelled. Adams then sent General Edmund P. Gaines to Georgia, and soon Gaines was quarrelling with Troup. Convinced that the McIntosh treaty was spurious, Adams negotiated a new one in which the Creeks ceded a large area, and this quieted the Georgians for a while. When they began to survey the region, however, there were further disorders, and at the request of the Indians Adams interposed again. Defying him, Governor Troup called out the state militia. In Congress, amid a furious debate, the Southerners as a group took the side of the governor against the president.

Neither Adams nor his Congress had the final word to say on the fate of the Creeks and Cherokees. Once Andrew Jackson was in the White House, however, he disposed of the problem in his own impulsive way. The old Indian fighter simply ordered that the red farmers be sent, bag and baggage, to a hunting-ground beyond the Mississippi; presumably too far away for them ever again to obstruct the westward course of empire.

2. THE SOUTH AND THE TARIFF

Southern opposition to the Neo-Federalism of Adams and Clay came to a head over the tariff. In 1816 John C. Calhoun and many other leaders of the South had been protectionists, for after the War of 1812 they cherished schemes for the development of industries of their own. The growth of the Southwest and the failure of some of their early industrial enterprises, however, caused most of these leaders to accept the theory that their section was suitable for agriculture alone. In 1820, partly as a result of their resentment against the North for having stirred up the Missouri controversy, the southern members of Congress cast but nine votes for a protective measure, and the bill was lost. Suffering from a decline in cotton prices, Southerners blamed their distress upon the existing duties rather than upon the increased cotton acreage opened in the Southwest. The planters of South Carolina, whose poorer lands suffered most from competition with the new cotton fields, were most outspoken against the agitation of northern industrialists for a higher protective barrier. Even in 1816 a discordant element in the state had condemned Calhoun and Lowndes for their part in enacting the tariff of that year. As the tariff advocates continued their demands, the South Carolinians grew more articulate and more determined. The politicans gave heed, Calhoun and George McDuffie abandoning their protectionist and nationalist views and becoming enthusiastic devotees of free trade and states' rights.

When Congress raised the general level of duties, in 1824, Governor John L. Wilson warned the South Carolina legislature against the dangerous tendency toward unlimited nationalism. "Every friend of our present Constitution in its original purity," he declared, "cannot but have witnessed the alarming extent to which the Federal Judiciary and Congress have gone toward establishing a great and consolidated government subversive of the rights of the States, and contravening the letter and spirit of the Constitution and of the Union. The act of the last session appropriating money to make surveys is but an entering wedge which will be followed, no doubt, by the expenditure of millions, unless the people apply the proper corrective. The day, I fear, is not far distant, when South Carolina shall be grievously assessed, to pay for the cutting of a canal across Cape Cod." The legislature condemned both internal improvements and the tariff, asserted that the people had an inalienable right to protect themselves against such unconstitutional abuses of power, and sent a formal protest to Congress. Later a mass meeting in Charleston adopted resolutions against a system "designed to elevate one interest in society to an undue influence and importance" and "intended to benefit one description of citizens at the expense of every other class."

The tariff of 1824 was not sufficiently high for northern protectionists, and in 1827 they introduced a bill raising still higher the duties on woolen goods. Representatives from the North and the West succeeded in putting the measure through the House, but a tie vote held it up in the Senate. Presiding over the Senate, Vice-President Calhoun was now in a position to determine the fate of the bill. Heretofore he had been able to avoid committing himself on the tariff since it had become a troublesome issue, though in 1825 he had made a speech that could be interpreted as protectionist. Subsequently Virginia and Georgia had joined South Carolina in condemning tariffs and internal improvements, and Calhoun had become convinced that the system he formerly thought of as beneficial to the whole nation was resulting in the aggrandizement of selfish groups in one particular section. With the eyes of the South upon him, he made his decision and cast the determining vote against the woolens bill.

The defeat of their project aroused the protectionists to take collective action. In the summer of 1827 they assembled in Harrisburg, Pennsylvania, and passed resolutions advocating a general increase in tariff rates and demanding congressional action. The next presidential election being only a year in the offing, the friends of Jackson saw an opportunity to gain the votes of the industrial states and destroy the sectional alliance based upon the American System of Adams and Clay. At the next meeting of Congress, the cunning Democrats sponsored a new tariff bill which they thought would injure Adams without losing them support in the South. This bill provided for high rates on raw materials—which New Englanders desired to keep as nearly duty-free as possible. The Jacksonians expected that the president would veto the measure in order to retain the support of his home section, and that they themselves would get credit for being friends of the tariff without having to meet the protectionist demands. Disgusted with these proceedings, John Randolph declared that no manufactures were concerned except "the manufacture of a President of the United States."

The scheming president-makers had better success with their tariff bill than they had intended. The southern congressmen, of course, were almost unanimously opposed to it. In the course of the debate, when told that the South should set up factories and gain like the North from a protectionist policy, Robert Y. Hayne, of South Carolina, replied that an industrial society could not be based upon the labor of slaves. George McDuffie, also of South Carolina, added that protective tariffs would bring to Washington the political debauchery of ancient Rome, subvert the liberties of the people, and in the end destroy the Republic itself. Speaking in more matter-of-fact terms, Thomas Hart Benton, of Missouri, pointed out that the tariff enabled the North to surpass the South in wealth and forced the South to borrow money from the North. On the other hand, most of the spokesmen for New England and the middle states were quite willing to accept the tariff bill despite the duties it would levy on the supplies that manufactures bought. Wealthy men of that section, who since the War of 1812 had been transferring their interests from seagoing ships to textile mills, were ready to support their representatives in this protectivist policy. These men could not have agreed with Randolph that the bill before Congress had reference only to one peculiar kind of manufacture. In the end the measure passed, and Adams signed it without fear of losing face at home.

In the South, however, men began to call the act of 1828 a tariff of abominations, and some whispered of disunion. The Charleston *Mercury* predicted that the people, exasperated beyond measure, would rejoice if the southern states should secede. Calhoun told Duff Green, editor of the *United States Telegraph,* that the rights of the southern states had been destroyed and must be restored—that the Union was in danger and must be saved. On the Fourth of July a South Carolinian offered a toast to the "hemp of Kentucky—better suited for cravats for the Kentuckians and tariffites than for the covering of South Carolina cotton." Dr. Thomas Cooper, president of South Carolina College, was eager for disunion; George McDuffie was ready for an appeal to arms; and Charles Cotesworth Pinckney proposed the toast, "Southern rights and northern avarice. When the Constitution is degraded to destroy one and support the other, resistance is a virtue."

Although the tariff controversy raged during the presidential campaign of 1828, the election did not turn solely upon that issue. Adams carried New England, but in the South and the West and parts of the North he made a poor showing against Jackson, the popular hero. In the frontier states the vote was usually given to every man who was free, white, and twenty-one, and the older states had likewise extended the suffrage, in an effort to prevent a drain of labor to the more liberal West. The common man, now the sovereign voter, frequently understood little and cared less about the intricate arguments over the American System. To him, the intellectual appeal of Adams seemed pale and weak beside the emotional appeal of his fiery, red-headed adversary. Thus it was that Jackson detached the West from its association with the East and united it again with the South. But within the Jacksonian democracy lurked the same divisive tendency that had begun to plague the Republican party in the days of Jefferson's rule. During the late campaign, Martin Van Buren had marshaled upstate farmers against the rich men of New York, and Jacksonian demagogues in other places had railed against aristocrats. It happened, however, that a considerable body of planters of the Tidewater country and the cotton-growing South belonged to the victorious party itself, and this group was sure to grow restive if Jackson in the White House should take his campaign orators at their word. The leader of this faction was John C. Calhoun, the man who had just been reelected vice-president.

3. THE NULLIFICATION CONTROVERSY

Both Jackson and Calhoun could claim to be political heirs of Thomas Jefferson, but their legacies were quite different. The new president, symbolizing the aspirations of frontiersmen of the West, came out of the agrarian tradition, and inherited the spirit of Jefferson's democratic teachings. The vice-president, embodying the hopes of Southern squires, inherited the letter of Jefferson's doctrine of states' rights. Calhoun took the principles of the Virginia and Kentucky Resolutions and transformed them into constitutional theories designed to protect southern planters in the possession of their acres and their slaves. To him was to go the distinction of turning the philosophy of Revolutionary patriots into a tool for cotton capitalists.

Since they possessed outlooks so divergent, it was inevitable, perhaps, that Jackson and Calhoun should fall to quarrelling. In appointing his Cabinet, the president tried to patch up the party differences by giving some of the places to adherents of Calhoun and the rest to friends of Van Buren, the leader of the Democrats in the middle states. Ambitious to displace Calhoun as Jackson's heir apparent, the wily New York politician awaited his opportunity to widen the differences between Calhoun and the president. The opportunity soon appeared, and Van Buren was ready to make the most of it.

Hardly had Jackson announced the membership of his Cabinet when a ludicrous but bitter contretemps upset the highest circles of Capital society. It happened that John H. Eaton, Jackson's secretary of war and one of his closest friends and political managers, had recently married a Mrs. Peggy Timberlake. She was then a vivacious young widow who, as Peggy O'Neal, the daughter of a Washington tavern keeper, had long been a favorite topic at the sessions of gossiping women. When the object of their gossip became a lady of the Cabinet, the other ladies of official Washington were properly scandalized. Now, Jackson being a widower, Mrs. Floride Calhoun, prominent in her own right in South Carolina society, looked upon herself as the first lady of the land. With her taking the lead, the wives of the Cabinet members determined to ignore and to ostracize Mrs. Eaton. Jackson, ever mindful of the gossip that had troubled his own recently deceased wife, gave his sympathies to the young bride. In the teapot tempest that ensued, the embarrassed husbands in the Cabinet, along with Calhoun, followed the social edicts of their irate wives and suffered the president's displeasure. Free from such uxorious entanglements, the widower Van Buren gained the favor of Jackson by paying ostentatious attention to his colleague's maligned mate.

Van Buren took advantage of the ill feelings growing out of the Peggy O'Neal affair to drive another wedge between Calhoun and the president. Slyly he revealed to Jackson the long-hidden fact that, in 1818, as secretary of war in Monroe's Cabinet, Calhoun had wished to censure the general for his unauthorized invasion of Florida. Jackson already knew that the Cabinet had discussed such a proposal, but Calhoun had allowed him to believe that Crawford had been responsible for the suggestion. Scrupulously honest himself, and unable to distinguish between personal enmity and political disagreement, Jackson concluded that Calhoun had been guilty of deliberate deception. Under Van Buren's tutelage, he decided to await a favorable moment for forcing a break with the vice-president.

In the meantime Calhoun, perceiving that the Jacksonians would never put him in the White House, assumed leadership of the South Carolina malcontents and made a bid for support from other disgruntled elements in the South. Already, during the summer of 1828, while a candidate for the vice-presidency on the Jacksonian ticket, he had consulted with the leaders of South Carolina politics and found them all strongly opposed to the late tariff. When a committee of the legislature called on him for advice, he wrote the "South Carolina Exposition and Protest," in which he gave anonymous expression to his ideas about the constitutional and economic aspects of protectionism.

The Exposition displayed the irresistible logic of a mind unexcelled, indeed unequalled, among the American intellects of the time. Proceeding in a clear and orderly way to expound his views on the nature of the Union, Calhoun refuted the muddled reasoning by which Marshall and the Federalists had spoken of a "divided sovereignty" and proved, to his own satisfaction at least, that the states had not abandoned their separate sovereignties when they accepted the Constitution. The Union was based on a compact between sovereign and equal states. They had created the federal government to act as an agent to carry out certain specifically delegated powers. The Constitution, instead of creating a sovereign nation, was but the body of instructions which these principals gave to their agent. And the people of the individual states—not Congress, not the president, not the Supreme Court, for these were but their agencies—must judge whether their directions were being carried out. Now, when the economic results were examined, it was plain that the federal government had gone beyond its original instructions when it enacted tariff laws. The southern staples constituted two thirds of the exports of the United States. "We export to import," Calhoun wrote. "The government is supported almost exclusively by a tax on this exchange." It followed that the southern states, composing one third of the Union, contributed two thirds of the expenses of the national government by paying duties on the foreign goods they bought.

So far in the Exposition, though his arguments were clearer and more detailed, Calhoun had not passed beyond the Kentucky and Virginia Resolutions of Jefferson. But the Virginian had failed to devise a process by which encroachments of the national government might be checked. Now, however, Calhoun found in the reserved rights of the states the machinery which Jefferson had sought in vain. He proposed that a convention, representing the full sovereign power of the people of a state, should assemble and suspend the operation of a questionable law. By declaring the act of Congress null and void within the state, the convention would "create a presumption against the constitutionality of the disputed power, exercised by the general government." The government would then either abandon the power it had assumed or submit to the states a constitutional amendment specifically conferring the authority. If three fourths of the states agreed to the amendment, "a disputed constructive power" would be converted into "a certain and express grant"; but if the required majority did not agree, its exercise would be inhibited and it would be of no effect. "And thus in either case," said Calhoun, "the controversy will be peaceably determined."

Although the legislature did not adopt the South Carolina Exposition, the friends of Calhoun, concealing his authorship, circulated it through the country in the weeks before Jackson came into office. Then they sat back and waited for an opportunity to gain converts, and thus unite the South and the West under a new formula of states' rights. They saw a chance to put forth their doctrines in a favorable light when, in January, 1830, Senator Samuel A. Foot, of Connecticut, expressing New England's jealousy of the growth of the West, introduced resolutions to stop the survey and sale of western lands. At once Thomas Hart Benton, of Missouri, took up the challenge and presented the western view that settlers should be encouraged with pre-emption rights. With eastern and western senators thus at odds, the southern friends of Calhoun could step in to suggest that the South and the West were equally victims of eastern policies, and that the West might adopt their program of nullification and set aside unpopular land laws. And so Robert Y. Hayne, a brilliant and graceful orator, the pride of South Carolina, arose to present the Calhoun theories. With force and skill he pointed out that they were the doctrines which had "saved the Constitution" at the time of the Alien and Sedition Acts, and they were adequate to save the Constitution again. Daniel Webster, of Massachusetts, replied on behalf of those with the nationalist point of view. In his powerful voice he declared that not the states but the people of the United States as a whole had created the national government. The union was older than the states. The framers of the Constitution had intended "to establish a Government that should not be obliged to act through State agency, or depend on State opinion and State discretion," and they had provided for a "suitable mode and tribunal for settling questions of constitutional law" when they made their document the "supreme law of the land." Nullification, therefore, was revolution. The Webster-Hayne debate clarified the constitutional issues, but both sides withdrew with claims of victory. It remained to be seen how the West would respond.

The response of the West would be pretty much the same as that of Andrew Jackson. The Calhounites, after trying to convince the president that their theories embodied the will of the party, planned to compel him to declare himself in their favor at a gathering of the party chieftains on Jefferson Day. They were shocked to hear the toast he offered at the banquet: "Our Federal Union—It must be preserved." He had accepted the constitutional theories of Daniel Webster, and the West would follow him. Soon after, he demanded that Calhoun explain his conduct at the time of the Seminole War. Dissatisfied with the evasive answer he got, the president severed personal relations with Calhoun and swept the latter's adherents out of federal office. He called Francis Preston Blair from Kentucky to edit the *Washington Globe* as the administration newspaper in place of the *Telegraph* of Duff Green, who remained loyal to Calhoun. Hereafter Van Buren was to be the heir apparent.

Welcoming this split in the Democratic ranks, Henry Clay now furbished his hopes of becoming president. With the idea of gathering votes, he sponsored a new tariff bill which he announced he would enact in spite of "the South, the Democratic Party, and the devil." This placed Jackson in the same dilemma in which his friends had hoped to put Adams four years before. Whatever he did, the president was bound to lose either Pennsylvania or part of the South, and so he signed the bill. No sooner had he done so than the South Carolina congressmen issued an address to their constituents declaring that "all hope for relief from Congress is irrecoverably gone."

In South Carolina the election of 1832 turned on the issue of the tariff, and those who favored nullification won an overwhelming majority in the legislature. When this body assembled in October, 1832, Governor James Hamilton proposed that it call a state convention. To this convention, too, the people sent a majority of nullificationists, and when they met, November 19-24, they lost no time in passing an ordinance to the effect that the tariff acts of 1828 and 1832 were "unauthorized by the Constitution of the United States and null and void, and no law, nor binding upon this State, its officers or citizens." The delegates went on to prohibit all state and federal officers from enforcing these laws and all persons from appealing to the state supreme court or to the federal courts. After the convention had adjourned, the legislature reassembled and passed acts carrying out the ordinance and providing for the defense of the state. Hayne resigned his seat in the Senate to become governor of South Carolina, and Calhoun left the vice-presidency to take Hayne's place and lead the nullification fight from the Senate floor.

In Washington, Jackson and Congress understood that South Carolina was willing to compromise. The president took precautions, however, by sending troops to Forts Moultrie and Sumter and preparing to send revenue vessels to Charleston Harbor. On December 10, he issued a proclamation condemning the theory of nullification and approving Webster's views on the nature of the Union. The South Carolina legislators replied that Jackson's opinions were "erroneous and dangerous" and that they would oppose force with force. Meanwhile they appealed to the neighboring states for support in their struggle against "centralization."

The replies from the states were not encouraging to the nullificationists. Although Georgia was sympathetic, the Georgians at the moment were primarily interested in getting rid of their Indians. The Supreme Court had upheld the right of the red men to their lands, but Jackson had nullified Marshall's decision and was proceeding with their removal. Profiting from this presidential endorsement of states' rights, Georgia was unwilling to co-operate with South Carolina. The states of the Southwest, where Jackson was permitting his political supporters to despoil the Indians of still more lands, followed Georgia. North Carolina and Tennessee also supported the president, and Kentucky was too much under Clay's influence to endorse the nullifiers. Virginia, with much sympathy for the objectives but none for the methods of South Carolina, proposed her good offices to compromise the issue and sent cautious advice to the Carolina legislature.

In the Senate, John Tyler, of Virginia, approached Clay with suggestions for a compromise. Clay agreed to bring in a new tariff bill providing for a gradual reduction of the existing rates until they should reach a level of 20 per cent in 1842. Thankful for a chance to end a situation that was getting out of hand, Calhoun accepted Clay's proposal and brought his followers in South Carolina, still enthusiastic nullifiers, reluctantly to agree to it. At the same time that the two Houses enacted the compromise tariff, they also passed a Force Act authorizing the president to use the full military and naval powers of the nation to compel obedience to all laws of Congress. Thereupon the South Carolina convention reassembled, solemnly nullified the Force Act, and reasserted its contention that the allegiance of Carolinians was due primarily to the state.

The nullification controversy had served to give the two opposing sections their philosophies of government. The Constitution according to Calhoun was to become the gospel of the South, and by recourse to his principles the southern states were to justify their eventual secession. In much the same way, the nationalistic interpretation of Webster and Jackson was to become the accepted doctrine in the North, and Lincoln was to echo their words in his homilies on the Union. After 1830 the South was a minority section in national politics, but it possessed a constitutional theory in terms of which it might protest against the tyranny of the majority. This was the first step in the creation of a southern nationalism; the second step was to be taken in the course of the slavery controversy.

CHAPTER 10

The Antislavery Crusade

1. Antecedents of the Slavery Controversy

BY 1830, after years of debating over tariffs, banks, and internal improvements, the politicians had formulated constitutional theories that served to emphasize the opposing interests of the North and the South. Then, during the decade of the 'thirties, in the course of a controversy over the abolition of slavery, the sectional leaders formulated social philosophies that had the effect of wedging the northern and southern peoples still further apart.

Opposition to slavery was doubtless as old as the institution itself. Even in the eighteenth century, when the system was first becoming well established in America, slaveowning colonists could have heard voices raised here and there in protest against its growing evils. The humbler folk of the Tidewater region, too poor to own slaves, and the settlers of the back country, where slavery did not pay, came to be especially outspoken in denouncing both the system and its beneficiaries. Voicing the opinion of people such as these, a character in an early novel observed that plantation masters, "accustomed to domineering over their slaves," were "haughtier" and "more aristocratic in temper" than were men where slavery did not exist. The churches that drew their support from the less favored groups—such as the Quaker, the Presbyterian, the Methodist, and the Baptist—became almost unanimous in believing it downright sinful to possess chattels in the form of human flesh. In 1746 the Quaker John Woolman published a pamphlet condemning the "keeping of Negroes," and thereafter the Society of Friends frequently testified with quiet vehemence against the practice. In 1796 the Kentucky Synod of the Presbyterians recorded its opposition to slavery. About twenty years later the general assembly of the Presbyterian Church recommended that bondsmen be educated in preparation for eventual freedom, and a few years after that the Synod of Pittsburgh (with jurisdiction over the western counties of Virginia) forbade its members to hold slaves. In 1804 a number of Baptist ministers, representing the third largest frontier church, issued an abolition address on behalf of the "friends of humanity." And in 1821 the general conference of the Methodists—having declared at other times that human bondage was not only injurious to society but contrary to the laws of man, nature, and God—prohibited the ordination of slaveowners as elders in any local church.

The frontiersmen, the churchmen, and the poor were not the only ones who criticized the "peculiar institution" of the South. Many planters in the Tidewater country recognized the shortcomings of their social system. They favored emancipation but feared its consequences, for they felt that numbers of free Negroes, hardly more than a generation away from savagery and untrained for the obligations of freedom, would constitute a danger to property and to an ordered society. Indeed, the existing body of "free persons of color" presented problems enough, and the planters would have liked to send all freedmen back to Africa. When in 1817 men of the trustee tradition formed the American Colonization Society to "colonize" Negroes in their homeland, Bushrod Washington became its first president, while John Marshall, Henry Clay, and many men whose sense of personal responsibility stemmed from the traditions of the squires united in an effort to solve the problem. The legislatures of Maryland and Virginia appropriated money to speed the work along. In 1822 the society launched the Free Republic of Liberia on Africa's western coast. During the next decade the colonizationists sent over a thousand Negroes to Liberia, but could not care for them properly, and left many of them to succumb to the unaccustomed hardships of pioneering in their ancestral home. Meanwhile, the colonizers met opposition both from reactionary slaveholders, who accused them of abolitionism, and from extreme abolitionists, who charged them with trying to strengthen slavery. The fact was that they were primarily interested in solving the problem of the unassimilable free Negro. Their society declined in importance as abolition societies rose to prominence.

The organized antislavery movement had its beginnings in the South. Within the first quarter of the nineteenth century, several abolitionist editors founded antislavery papers and published them at least intermittently. Among these journals were the *Emancipator* in Tennessee, the *Abolition Intelligencer* in Kentucky, and the *Genius of Universal Emancipation* in Baltimore. Each of these papers directed its appeal to the masses of southern whites rather than to the planter class. While they were spreading the propaganda of freedom, Charles Osborn founded the Tennessee Manumission Society. In east Tennessee the Reverend Samuel Doak, a Presbyterian divine and educator who taught Sam Houston his earliest lessons in democracy, emancipated his slaves in 1818 and began to instruct other slaveowners to do likewise.

Benjamin Lundy, the direct inspiration of William Lloyd Garrison, found a welcome among the mountain men of east Tennessee when he determined to make emancipation his life work. A New Jersey Quaker who had migrated to Ohio, Lundy saw slaves for the first time in coffles at Wheeling, Virginia, and learned to hate the slave power at the time of the Missouri controversy. The uncertainty of Missouri's status in 1819 had so deranged business in St. Louis that a raft-load of saddles which harness-maker Lundy had floated down the Ohio could find no market. Returning home bankrupt, he turned abolitionist, began the publication of the *Genius of Universal Emancipation,* and moved to Jonesboro, Tennessee, where he was received by an earlier abolition society. Afoot, he travelled the mountain counties of Tennessee and North Carolina founding abolition societies and gathering subscribers to his paper. Later he moved to Baltimore, and thence to Washington, Philadelphia, and Illinois, working as an organizer and journalist until his death in 1839.

In Lundy's time, the antislavery agitation was usually rather mild and cautious. This was certainly true of the organization that bore the rather involved name of "The American Convention for Promoting the Abolition of Slavery and Improving the Conditions of the African Race." Its members met frequently to hear reports on the progress of emancipation and to encourage writers, petition legislatures, and urge the education and conversion of Negroes. They advocated gradual emancipation, preparation of the Negroes for freedom, and the establishment of an economic system based on tenancy as a transition stage. At first, few slaveowners took alarm at activities such as these, for the methods used seemed ineffective and harmless enough, and, in any case, many planters were willing to agree in theory that something ought to be done for the slave.

The Missouri controversy, however, served to awaken them to the dangers inherent in the possibility of an alliance between Northerners and southern nonslaveholders. Thereafter the political leaders, preparing to consolidate their section against the North, bent every effort toward suppressing antislavery agitation in the South. They did not hesitate to use violence and coercion when necessary, and frequently the mob helped them whip dissenters into co-operation with the ruling class. It was true, of course, that in parts of the South antislavery sentiment had never made much headway. In 1790, South Carolinians and Georgians in Congress asserted that their states would never have joined the "Confederacy" if slave property had not been guaranteed by the Constitution. In 1807, Representative Early, of Virginia, declared that a majority of Southerners did not regard slavery as an evil or the slave trade as a crime. But in the years following the Missouri Compromise an increasing "irritability of the South" appeared whenever these subjects were brought up. In 1821 the *New York Commercial Advertiser* remarked that "sectional animosity" was one of the "evils which slavery is shedding upon our country." The Manumission Society of North Carolina noted in 1826 that "the gentlest attempt to agitate the question or the slightest hint at the work of emancipation" was sufficient to call forth the indignant resentment of slaveholders. When some citizens of Smithfield, Virginia, met to form an antislavery society in 1827, a local magistrate broke up their meeting, contending that since there was no statute authorizing such an assembly, it must be contrary to law. A young South Carolinian had already canceled his subscription to Lundy's *Genius* on the grounds that neither his health nor the successful prosecution of his profession would permit him to receive so unpopular a publication.

The leaders of southern thought had remarkable success in solidifying public opinion against the critics of slavery. In 1827 Lundy estimated that one hundred and thirty antislavery societies with 6,625 members existed in the United States. Of these, one hundred and six, with 5,150 members, were in the South. By 1837 not one of these one hundred and six societies was left.

Cotton, in a word, was the chief reason why slaveholders abandoned their early indifference to antislavery activities. The westward expansion of cotton had brought new areas under the plantation system. Throughout the lower South cotton dominated men's thoughts. To growers of the staple it became apparent that an attack on slavery was a threat to the very foundation of their prosperity. Since the abolitionists gained most of their followers in the western regions, the planters were especially eager both to stop the agitation and to win the political support of the frontier farmers.

2. Regional Conflict in Virginia

In Virginia, cotton culture had not spread far enough to unify the political and economic interests of the Piedmont and Tidewater counties in the east and the mountain counties in the west. The people of the western counties had many grievances. They demanded representation in the state legislature in proportion to their numbers, internal improvements at the expense of the state, reforms in local government to make it more democratic, and the extension of the voting privilege to every man who was free, white, and twenty-one. In 1828 the frontier representatives compelled the legislature to submit to the people the question of reforming the constitution of the state. The western Virginians voted overwhelmingly in favor of holding a constitutional convention and carried the day, though the men of the Tidewater country were able to resist their demands for a census and the apportionment of delegates on the basis of white population.

To the convention came such national figures as James Madison, James Monroe, and John Marshall; such local luminaries as William B. Giles, John Tyler, L. W. Tazewell, John Randolph, and P. P. Barbour; and such determined leaders of the west as Samuel McDowell Moore, Alexander Campbell, Thomas Jefferson Randolph (grandson of the third president), and Phillip Doddridge. At once the democratic Westerners presented their demand for equal representation and full white suffrage. The conservative Easterners, desiring to change the Constitution only to the extent of eliminating its Jeffersonian Bill of Rights, contended that these reforms would lead to the taxation of slave property for the building of roads and canals in the west. They were unimpressed and unconvinced when a western delegate sought to allay their fears by arguing that internal improvements would cause slavery to expand into the hitherto slaveless parts of the state. One of the Easterners replied that the frontiersmen were too strongly prejudiced against slaves. "There exists in a great portion of the West a rooted antipathy to this species of population," said the skeptical Easterner; "the habits of the people are strongly opposed to it. With them, personal industry, and a reliance on personal exertion, is the order of society. They know how little slave labor is worth; while their feelings as free men forbid them to work by the side of a slave. And besides, sir, their vicinity to nonslaveholding states must forever render this sort of property precarious and insecure." The Easterners were even more outraged at the proposal to give every white man the right to vote. Universal suffrage, said one delegate, was as great a plague as the Hessian fly, the influenza, or the smallpox—an epidemic that had arisen in the North and spread southward but hitherto had always kept above the fall line of the rivers. To slaveowners, agrarian democracy was a dangerous disease indeed.

The Virginia constitution as finally amended embodied few of the western demands. It set up no fair and just system of apportioning seats in the legislature but arbitrarily reassigned them so as to give more to the West. (The disproportion would soon again be evident as that section continued to gain population far more rapidly than the East.) It extended the suffrage, but under such conditions as to exclude some thirty thousand white men. It made no change in county government, assigning to the governor the privilege of appointing sheriffs and justices of the peace, as before. On learning that they had been thus ignored, the people of the counties beyond the mountains were incensed, few of them were willing to vote for ratification of the new document, and some even talked of seceding from the state. The adoption of the new constitution aggravated more than it assuaged the conflict among the counties in Virginia.

In 1831 the Nat Turner insurrection caused the legislature to resume the same sectional debate that had divided the constitutional convention. Nat Turner was a slave preacher of Southampton County, Virginia. Inflamed by religious fanaticism, he gathered a band of Negro followers one summer night, fell upon the sleeping white community, and massacred sixty-one persons, most of them women and children. Vengeful Virginians put a hundred or more Negroes to death, and Southerners everywhere felt a kindred terror of the potential enemy in their midst. During the following winter, legislatures throughout the South revised their slave codes so as to make them more severe, and in particular to prohibit Negroes from preaching or assembling for religious or any other purposes unless white men were present. Volunteers, mindful of the warning from Virginia, organized militia companies to patrol the roads at night.

When the Virginia legislature met, the problem of the Negro and slavery was uppermost in the minds of the members, but they could not agree on what to do about it. Public opinion divided between those who favored immediate emancipation and colonization and those who favored a more gradual process. In the legislature, the conservative Easterners attempted to avoid debate, but the Westerners insisted upon discussion. To the disgust of the slaveholders, Thomas Jefferson Randolph revived his grandfather's plan for gradual emancipation. In the ensuing debates, western members compared Virginia with the free states of the North to show that the economic salvation of their state depended upon freeing the slaves. "All of the chief glories of Virginia style have faded," lamented Thomas Marshall, one of the critics from the West. "Gone is the massive coach, with its stately attelage of four or six; shut is the beneficent hall door; . . . the watering-places no longer blaze with the rich but decent pomp of Virginians; and the cities rarely bear witness of her generous expanse." Marshall concluded: "Slavery is ruinous to the whites; it retards improvements, roots out an industrial population, banishes the yeomanry from the country, and deprives the spinner, the weaver, the smith, the shoemaker, and the carpenter of employment and support." The Tidewater representatives, however, vigorously denied that slavery was responsible for the depleted fields of the eastern part of the state. In the end, the legislature took no action on the slave question, but the bitterness of the debate was evidence of the deep sectional and social cleavage in the Old Dominion.

A fundamental reason for the eastern slaveholders' refusal to accord reform and suffrage to the West or to consider the demand for emancipation was their fear of Jacksonian democracy. In 1828 they had helped to elect Jackson as president, but they had done so reluctantly and without enthusiasm. With more foresight, John Randolph opposed the Jacksonian movement as the "tyranny of King Numbers," a tyranny that would menace the liberty of the planter. The people of the western counties, on the other hand, had given their wholehearted support to Jackson. The combination of democracy and abolition within their own state caused the planters of Virginia eventually to come out into the open and declare themselves against Jacksonianism.

That the antislavery movement did not resolve itself into a struggle between southern classes was due to two developments: the formulation of the proslavery argument, and the beginnings of militant abolitionism in the North. Thanks to these, the South became almost a unit in support of slavery.

Soon after the Southampton massacre and the debates in the Virginia legislature, a counter-revolution of the slaveholders began the formulation of both an ideology and an organization in defense of slavery. Thomas R. Dew, professor of political economy in William and Mary, published a Review of the Debates in the Virginia Legislature of 1831–32 which called the planters' attention to the tremendous economic investment at stake. Slavery, said Dew, was a positive good, both for the master and for the slave. Negroes could not live in the South except in bondage, and the institution was profitable for Virginia white men. The time had come to abandon the fallacious principles of the

Declaration of Independence. The fear of slave insurrection was great. "This is the evil, after all, let us say what we will, which really operates most powerfully . . . upon these sections where slaves constitute the principal property." Society was rapidly becoming stratified, and necessarily so, for it was essential that some men should be the masters of factories and plantations, and others laborers and slaves.

With the publication of Dew's book, which had a far-reaching influence on southern thought, the proslavery defense of property rights began. At the same time Calhoun, with one eye on the White House, was preparing to test his theory of nullification. When it failed, the South Carolina leader bent his efforts toward uniting all Southerners into a block for the defense of the plantation system. It was at this juncture, in 1831, that William Lloyd Garrison issued the first number of his *Liberator* in Boston. This radical antislavery paper came as a godsend to the builders of southern unity, who, taking advantage of Garrison's indiscriminate polemics against the South, appealed to nonslaveholders to rally to the defense of a white man's society. So effective was the appeal to race prejudice and provincialism that the organized antislavery movement disappeared from the South.

3. The Abolition Movement

William Lloyd Garrison, who came to the attention of Southerners in the midst of Virginia's quarrel over emancipation, partook of the Puritan traditions of Massachusetts; but the forces and factors that led him to take up the cause of the slave arose from the process of his own psychological development. Deserted by his father at the age of three, he spent a childhood in poverty. Having no opportunity for formal education, he spent brief and unsuccessful periods as a cobbler's and then as a cabinet-maker's apprentice until, at the age of thirteen, he got a job as a printer's helper. This was a career that fitted his talents, and at seventeen he was a patriotic adolescent, solemnly praising the liberties of the United States. Before he was twenty he was expounding Federalism, throwing his youthful weight into the scales against the Holy Alliance, thinking of joining the war for Greek independence against Turkish tyranny, and contemplating a military education at West Point. At twenty-one, safely past the early stages of adolescence, he undertook to edit his own newspaper, but failed after ten months and began to pass through a succession of printing jobs, none of which satisfied his consuming ambition. "If my life be spared," he defiantly informed a critic, "my name shall one day be known to the world—at least to such extent that common inquiry shall be unnecessary." At twenty-three he was for six months the editor of a temperance paper in Vermont and meanwhile was lending his pen to every popular reform movement of the day—not only temperance but also pacifism, women's rights, and Sabbatarianism. He was definitely a journalistic knight-errant in search of a crusade.

At this juncture Benjamin Lundy found Garrison, and Garrison found the antislavery movement. He worked for Lundy's *Genius* as a printer and editor, but the editorial policy of the gentle Quaker was too mild for the Yankee crusader, and within a few months Garrison was in jail for libel. When he emerged—thanks to the benevolence of Arthur Tappan—he had determined upon his crusading career. From his experience with Lundy he had acquired both a new idea and a knowledge of the potential market for it. The idea was "immediatism"; the market was the free colored population of the North.

Since 1817, the American Colonization Society had been growing in strength throughout the nation. Although planters had supported the society, colonization made an appeal not only to those who favored slavery but also to many who condemned it. So long as the antislavery movement was confined to the South, the antislavery men had been confronted with the problem of adjusting the Negroes, once they had been freed, to a new social and legal status. The Colonization Society proposed two methods of escape from this problem, but its practical solution of inaugurating a transition system based on tenancy received less support than its impractical proposal to send the Negroes back to Africa. The Colonization Society was all things to all men. To slaveholders, it was a means of ridding them of the presence of free Negroes; to nonslaveholders it promised both to hasten emancipation and to solve the social questions involved in a biracial society. The society gathered money from interested individuals and received appropriations from southern state legislatures.

The free Negroes of the North, alarmed by the activities of the society, found a champion in the *Liberator*. In the prospectus appearing in the first issue of his paper, January, 1831, Garrison struck a new note in the antislavery movement by announcing that he would not hold with the "pernicious doctrine of gradual abolition." Instead, he would contend for the immediate emancipation and enfranchisement of slaves. "I will be as harsh as truth, and as uncompromising as justice," he proclaimed in words often to be quoted afterward. "On this subject I do not wish to think, or speak, or write, with moderation. No! No! Tell a man whose house is on fire to give a moderate alarm; tell him to moderately rescue his wife from the hands of a ravisher; tell the mother to gradually extricate her babe from the fire into which it has fallen—but urge me not to use moderation in a cause like the present. I am in earnest—I will not equivocate—I will not excuse—I will not retreat a single inch—and I will be heard!"

In this first issue, Garrison presented statistics to show that Massachusetts was the home of seven thousand free Negroes; and these he candidly besought for their patronage. In his second issue he began a denunciation of the Colonization Society which mounted in vituperative intensity until it culminated, a year later, in a denunciatory volume of *Thoughts on Colonization*. He also opened his columns to the black men themselves, so that they might give their views on the subject. "This is our home, and this our country," declared a New York group, taking advantage of the opportunity to speak to the public through the *Liberator*. "Beneath its soil lie the bones of our fathers; for it some of them fought, bled, and died. Here we were born, and here we will die." In New York, Philadelphia, and Boston meetings of colored freemen pledged their support to the journal and passed resolutions of gratitude to its editor. It became the organ of the free Negroes, stirring them up against the Colonization Society and drawing from them its chief financial support. The ambitious printer had found his crusade, his banner, and his sponsors.

But Garrison did not neglect the possibilities inherent in the American passion for organizations. Within a year the *Liberator* was urging the formation of a national antislavery society. "No truth is more self-evident," said Garrison, "than that moral power, like physical, must be consolidated to be efficient. The world is to be reformed through the instrumentality of societies, which shall be actuated by the principles of universal benevolence, and open to the inspection of the people. What progress can be made . . . in the cause of abolition without the adoption of similar measures?" Within a few months after this query, Garrison organized the New England Anti-Slavery Society.

Other forces were at work, meanwhile, to launch a drive against slavery. One of these forces was the new spirit which the Reverend Charles Grandison Finney had brought to Calvinism. Finney's fiery evangelism taught that conversion must be accompanied by benevolence, and among his converts were men, rich in the world's goods, who sought philanthropic expression for their faith. The doctrine of benevolence fitted well into the trustee tradition, which held that all wealth was God's bounty to His Elect, and should be used for the advancement of the Heavenly Kingdom. The trustees, stewards for the Lord, were obligated to reform society. Notable among the men who were the heirs of this tradition were the brothers Arthur and Lewis Tappan, merchants of New York who contributed generously to temperance societies, societies for the redemption of fallen women, crusades against gas lights in churches, manual labor colleges—and abolition.

Throughout the Northwest were many Southerners who had repudiated the southern system and had carried their hatred of slavery to new homes in free territory. In a land where the people were already aroused by the evangelism of Finney, these transplanted Southerners found many to agree that slavery was not only a social evil but a national sin. At Western Reserve College in Ohio, the president, some professors, and the pastor of the college church, inspired by the *Liberator*, announced their conversion to abolitionism. Eager to begin an organization and a press, they looked to Arthur Tappan for aid. In Kentucky, a "Society for the Gradual Relief of Kentucky from Slavery" held an organization meeting and denounced the southern institution as a "moral and political evil" that could not "be justified, before God, the world, or our own conscience."

In December, 1833, delegates from these various groups met in Philadelphia to found the American Anti-Slavery Society. The movement thus organized was a hybrid, compounded of Garrison's invective, Finney's evangelism, frontier democracy, and philanthropic benevolence. Like a hybrid, it intensified the characteristics that had entered into it. The seeds that had been originally planted in the soil of the southern frontier found lush fields already plowed in the North. Soon the movement had sprouted hundreds of societies from Maine to Wisconsin and from the Great Lakes to Mason and Dixon's line.

Almost every northern community came to have its local antislavery organization, with a constitution that quoted liberally from the Declaration of Independence. The members assembled once a month to discuss the cause, listen to a lecturer, or contribute their pennies and dimes. The officers kept in touch with other groups and devoted themselves largely to the distribution of tracts, books, and papers. These societies supported a host of lecturers, organizers, and newspapers. Most of their propaganda was devoted to obtaining new members and founding new societies. In this work they were so successful that, by 1838, the American Anti-Slavery Society contained 1,346 local groups with a total membership of 107,680—an average of about 80 members to a society. Most of those listed lived in Vermont and Massachusetts.

Many of the early agents had been at one time students at the Lane Theological Seminary in Cincinnati. This institution, subsidized by Tappan's money, was designed to train young evangelists in the "new measures" which Finney had expounded. There, youths from Kentucky, Tennessee, and Alabama mingled with lads from the Middle West and, instead of sticking to theological subjects, discussed the moral implications of slavery. A leader among them was Theodore Weld, a Tappan protégé, who organized a series of debates to convert the seminary to abolition. When the president, trustees, and neighbors of Lane Seminary attempted to suppress this student organization, Weld led the majority of the student body to Oberlin College, which thereafter began to admit Negro students and to develop abolitionist agitators. From the ranks of the Lane rebels, Weld selected and trained a group of organizers who lighted the fires of abolitionism throughout the North and West. So largely were the agents drawn from "Finneyized" converts that the *Working Men's Advocate*, looking with critical eye, concluded: "Abolitionists are actuated by a spirit of fanaticism, and are desirous of freeing slaves, more for the purpose of adding them to a religious sect, than for any love of liberty or justice."

From the beginning, the purpose of the abolitionists had been to make an ethical appeal, and it was only with the passing years that they entered into the political arena. Originally, the antislavery societies devoted themselves to "moral suasion" which they directed at the "understandings and consciences" of slaveholders. They stoutly denied that they were engaged in encouraging servile insurrection. It was by "appeals to the conscience, the sense of honor and shame, the feeling of humanity, the religious principle, and the enlightened self-interest" of the masters themselves that slavery was to be conquered. The primary thesis of abolitionists was that slaveholding was a sin. "It is," said one, "falsehood in theory; tyranny in practice; a violation of God's law, and a parent of abominations . . . the Mark of Guilt is upon it. . . ." A corollary of this argument was that God and every angel were on the side of the crusaders, and the salvation of humanity depended on their efforts. "The Abolition of Slavery," ran one report, "we recognize as the great task assigned to this generation, in this country. We accept it as our appointed work, and are grateful that we are permitted to assist in the evolution of this magnificent event." On the other hand, the Southerner who held slaves was a sinner against God and humanity. "Slavery imbrutes and heathenizes its immediate victims. It hardens the heart and depraves the morals of those who wield and administer it."

To gather evidence for these crimes, the abolitionists combed both the South and their imaginations and filled their speeches and the columns of their papers with horrible descriptions of what they had found. They made much of the brutality of the masters, peddled through the land stories of Negroes being whipped to death, and exploited the sexual aspects of the master-slave relationship for the edification and delight of the repressed Puritans, who readily accepted the numbers of mulattoes as evidence of the lustful nature of southern slaveholders.

Into the ranks of the abolitionists came a host of able workers. Gerrit Smith added his philanthropies to those of the Tappan brothers. The Reverend Samuel Joseph May, Dr. William Ellery Channing, and Asa Mahan preached abolition doctrines. Angelina (who married Theodore Weld) and Sarah Grimké, slaveholding South Carolinians, abandoned their native state in protest against its harsh slave code. James G. Birney, Kentucky born, took his slaves to Ohio, emancipated them, and devoted his life to freedom's cause. From these earnest crusaders, aspiring politicians took a lesson, and soon legislative halls and political stumps were resounding to the fiery voices of Wendell Phillips, Charles Sumner, Henry Wilson, Ben Wade, Salmon P. Chase, and Joshua R. Giddings.

Too great a mixture of erratic genius, however, brought division to organized abolition. From the beginning, rivalry between Tappan and Garrison had produced tension. The American Anti-Slavery Society had never supported the *Liberator* or admitted the editor to its innermost councils. Agents of the society, themselves violent in denouncing sin, were embarrassed by Garrison's even more intemperate speech. The breach widened perceptibly when, about 1835, Garrison added women's rights to his abolitionism and moved on to anticlericalism and eventually to a denunciation of all government. Following out the logic of his new philosophy, he refused to participate in politics, proposed the secession of the free states, and damned both the Constitution and the Union. In the meantime, the American Anti-Slavery Society had begun to advocate political action. The differences between the Garrisonians and the anti-Garrisonians came to a head in 1840 over the question of admitting women to the society. When Garrison and his cohorts descended upon the annual convention and forced an enthusiastic endorsement of women's rights, the New York philanthropists and their western allies withdrew and organized the American and Foreign Anti-Slavery Society —strictly for men only!

4. ABOLITIONISM IN POLITICS

Although the rival antislavery societies continued to operate, the division greatly weakened the force of nonpolitical abolitionism, which thereafter degenerated into a kind of wild-eyed mysticism. The fight against slavery went on, but the center had already shifted to the political arena, where the Liberty, the Free-Soil, and the Republican parties successively took up the banner and the battle cry.

The defeat of the Adams-Clay combination in 1828 had left the opponents of Jackson utterly disorganized, and so the time was ripe for new alignments in politics. Many politicians of the defeated party looked upon the rising tide of antislavery sentiment with mingled alarm and hope, before they decided that the antimasonic agitation offered a safer platform to stand upon. First in New York and soon in other states they formed an Antimasonic party, theoretically to combat the sinister influence of Freemasonry but actually to fight the political power of Jacksonianism. The Antimasons declared themselves for Clay's familiar program of internal improvements and a protective tariff, but denounced Clay himself on the ground that he was a member of the hated lodge.

For a while it seemed as if the new organization might prove to be a worthy successor of the old Federalist party. When it failed to become such a successor, its leaders began one by one to turn to slavery as a possible political issue. In 1831 William H. Seward, the leader in New York, and Thaddeus Stevens, the leader in Pennsylvania, met at an Antimasonic convention and found that they possessed "an earnest sympathy of political views." Seward noted that, like himself, Stevens was an advocate of popular education, of American industry, and of internal improvements, abhorring slavery in every form and restless under the system of intrigue by which the Republican party of that day sought to maintain itself in power, bent on breaking up the combination between a "subservient party at the North and the slave power of the South." Stevens rapidly became more and more interested in the political possibilities of slavery agitation. An itinerant lecturer of the Weld school once told him: "If you can turn your Antimasons into abolitionists, you will have a party whose politics will not bleach out. The slaveholders will not possum like Freemasons, but will die game." Stevens gave the agent a handful of money and requested him to lecture in Adams County, Pennsylvania, saying, "If they Morganize you, we'll make a party of it." Throughout the decade of the 'thirties, this Pennsylvania politician experimented with mixing antislavery and Antimasonry, even going so far as to get Negroes to vote for the Antimasonic ticket.

Leaders of the party in some of the other northern states were following a parallel career.

Although early abolitionists disclaimed any interest in political action, they were soon petitioning Congress to abolish slavery in the District of Columbia and advocating the same move in their periodicals. It was inevitable that these activities, painful to Southerners with a growing sensitiveness about their peculiar institution, should bring slavery into national politics. Indeed, the first numbers of Garrison's *Liberator* aroused the South. Within a year, the Vigilance Committee of Columbia, South Carolina, offered a reward of $1,500 for the arrest and conviction of anyone caught distributing the paper, and the Georgia legislature placed a price of $5,000 on the editor's head. When Charleston citizens broke into the local post office and burned abolitionist propaganda in 1835, Postmaster-General Amos Kendall declared that he had no authority to prohibit the use of the mails to abolitionists but added that, though he could not sanction, he would not condemn the action of the Charlestonians. "We owe an obligation to the laws," he explained, "but a higher one to the communities in which we live." He advised postmasters to interpret these remarks as they would. Excitement ran high at public meetings in both the North and the South.

Some of the gatherings in the North, though condemning abolitionism, defended freedom of speech and of opinion. This gave the abolitionists their cue to make the issue appear to be an assault upon the Bill of Rights. Accordingly, the American Anti-Slavery Society published an address admitting that Congress had no power to abolish slavery in the states, but insisting that the people had the right to express themselves on any subject under the heavens. The society drew attention to the fact that no antislavery literature had been sent to slaves. In the fall of 1835, while many Southerners talked of boycotting the North, their legislatures passed resolutions calling on the northern states to pass penal laws for the suppression of "incendiary" speech and literature. In some of the more conservative states of the North, where Garrison's actions had met with criticism, there was approval of this course. Thus in New York and in Massachusetts the governors recommended that the legislators comply at once with the southern request. In general, however, the northern people did not take kindly to this "insolence" of the slaveholders.

When Congress met in December, Jackson asked for a law to stop incendiary publications from using the mails, and this proposal was referred to a committee of which Calhoun was chairman. Calhoun declared that such a law as Jackson asked would be an abridgment of the liberty of the press, which Congress was forbidden to restrict. However, said Calhoun, the states were permitted to control the freedom of speech, and so he introduced a bill providing that no postal official should receive or put into the mails any literature that was forbidden by the laws of the state to which it was consigned. In the debates that followed, Northerners pointed out that Calhoun's bill would make even the Declaration of Independence and the constitution of Massachusetts "incendiary" literature in the South and, moreover, would transfer the regulation of the mails to the states and give judicial functions to post-office employees. The bill failed of enactment.

A few months after this discussion, the House of Representatives took an action destined to add new fuel to the flames. Tired of the consideration of petitions from antislavery societies, the House, on May 26, 1836, adopted three resolutions which were expected to put the whole issue at rest. These declared that Congress had no constitutional authority to interfere with slavery in any state; that it ought not to abolish slavery in the District of Columbia; and that, therefore, petitions relating to slavery should be laid on the table, "and that no further action whatever shall be had thereon." This was the famous "gag rule."

The immediate effect of the gag rule was an increased protest from the North. John Quincy Adams, whose presidency had been made miserable by Southern opposition, had entered the House of Representatives after leaving the White House. Taking up the cudgels against his former enemies, Adams asserted that the gag rule deprived his constituents of their constitutional right to petition for a redress of grievances. Adams made himself the champion of the petitioners, and the abolitionists deluged him with petitions, which he attempted to introduce. The southern congressmen, outraged at this trifling with their dearest sentiments, voted to censure and even threatened to expel him, but he defied them and continued to call their tactics to the attention of the North.

Abolitionists quickly seized upon the gag rule as a propaganda device. Their petitions to Congress increased. State legislatures added their voices to the outcry. After widely publicized hearings which the abolitionists used as a sounding board, the Massachusetts legislature passed resolutions to the effect that "Congress, having exclusive legislation in the District of Columbia, possesses the right to abolish slavery in said district, and that its exercise should only be restricted by a regard for the public good." Vermont, the state with the largest number of abolition societies, issued a statement agreeing that Congress had full power to abolish slavery in the District of Columbia and adding that neither Congress nor the states could prohibit freedom of speech or interfere with the free passage of antislavery literature in the mails.

While the states were putting forth their views, the issue arose again in Congress. On December 20, 1837, Representative William Slade, of Vermont, proposed the abolition of slavery and the slave trade in the District of Columbia. The southern members greeted this suggestion with cries of indignation, and Henry A. Wise, of Virginia, called upon his colleagues to leave the hall. Robert Barnwell Rhett summoned the South Carolina congressmen to meet in a committee room, and another South Carolinian invited the members from the other slave states to meet with them. Only a hasty adjournment prevented violent disorder.

Rhett later explained that he had desired to get united southern agreement on a set of counter-resolutions declaring that the Constitution had failed to protect the South in the peaceful enjoyment of its rights and that, therefore, it was expedient that the Union be dissolved. "The purpose of these resolutions," said Rhett, "was to place before Congress and the people what, in my opinion, was the true issue upon this great and vital question, and to point out the course of policy by which it should be met by the southern States." The majority of the Southerners were unwilling to go to such lengths, but they supported a resolution from John M. Patton, of Virginia, "that all petitions, memorials, and papers touching the abolition of slavery or the buying, selling, or transferring of slaves, in any State, district, or territory of the United States, be laid on the table, without being debated, printed, read or referred, and that no further action whatever shall be had thereon." Patton ironically said that the resolution was a "concession" which the South was willing to make for the sake of peace, union, and harmony.

The popular excitement in the country and the growing animosities in Congress disturbed the conservative classes of the North. Merchants who had trade relations with the South, and politicians who looked to a southern alliance, were opposed to any probing of the sensitive subject. In Cincinnati a definite prosouthern movement existed, and in Boston the trading districts looked with disapproval upon the activities of the abolitionists. Almost everywhere, the lower classes of the northern whites, who had come into actual or potential competition with free Negroes, were opposed to the emancipation of a class of cheap laborers. Indeed, these workingmen had taken part in riots against both Negroes and abolitionists. In 1835, an irate mob had broken up a meeting of the Boston Female Anti-Slavery Society and had dragged Garrison with a rope around his neck through the streets. In 1837, another mob had killed the Reverend Elijah P. Lovejoy, editor of an abolitionist paper in Alton, Illinois. The abolitionists, alleging that the murder was the inevitable result of southern brutality, made Lovejoy a martyr.

After Lovejoy's death, opposition to the abolitionists declined in the North, and the section slowly became consolidated against slavery. At the same time, the Southerners became more unified as a result of the widespread alarm. By 1837, abolitionism, which had begun as a moral protest, was becoming definitely a political movement as well. In 1838 the American Anti-Slavery Society went on record as favoring the questioning of candidates as to their abolitionist sentiments. In that year, the antislavery groups contributed largely to the election of William H. Seward as governor of New York. In that year, too, the abolitionists claimed the balance of power in a number of congressional districts and, in Ohio, took credit for the election of the governor.

The Proslavery Argument

1. A Positive Good

POLITICAL abolitionists were not so much interested in persuading slaveholders to give up their chattels as they were in wresting control of the federal government from the planter class. Northerners desired higher and ever higher tariffs, the extension of federal turnpikes and canals, and the perpetuation of a national bank. Antislavery politicians strove to satisfy these needs. "The tariff is as much an antislavery measure as the rejection of Texas," declared Joshua R. Giddings. "So is the subject of internal improvements and the distribution of the proceeds of the public lands. The advocates of perpetual slavery oppose all of them; they regard them as opposed to the interest of slavery. That party holds it a cardinal principle that slavery must be maintained together or they will all go down together."

The out-and-out abolitionists themselves also showed the close parallelism between antislavery and industry. They had little sympathy for labor in its rising struggle with capital, and upheld the interests of the employing group. In the first issue of the *Liberator*, Garrison condemned the class-consciousness of Boston workingmen. He had been a Federalist in his youth and consistently favored the American System of Henry Clay. He wished to see "a manufactory by the side of every suitable stream" and felt a strong interest in the perpetuity of that system which "fosters and protects the industry of the American People." At the time of the panic of 1837, he asserted that the South's extravagance, intemperance, and general lightheadedness had provoked the disaster; that slavery was the ruin of the nation and that northern merchants ought to beware of trading with the South; that the United States Bank was "the sheet anchor of our national prosperity."

Many industrialists, too, were interested in abolition. The father of the Reverend S. J. May was a manufacturer of woolens. Moses Grant was the owner of a paper mill at Newton Falls. Amasa Walker was an agent of the Methuen Manufacturing Company, director of a bank, and promoter of western railroads; Neal Dow (who combined temperance with abolition) was a tanner, a bank director, and an investor in manufactures and railroads in Maine. To such men as these, it seemed evident that slavery was a curse which was blighting the South. With the abolition of slavery, they argued, the southern worker would become a customer for northern industry and would buy its hats, bonnets, shoes, clothing, paper, glass, and other gadgets and trinkets. Under the new order he would spend five dollars for each dollar he had spent under the old. As for the southern employer, if he did not invest money in slaves, he would have capital for additional land and would thus be able to cultivate more cotton. The result would be that the price of cotton would be depressed and the owners of northern textile mills would be benefited. Perhaps, moreover, the southern employer would cease his opposition to the tariff.

Men of the trustee tradition—the advocates of abolition, of temperance, of missionary endeavor, and of universal education—all justified their programs in economic terms. The men of the trustee tradition were, in fact, learning to voice their desire for a better world in a new, less theological vocabulary. Temperance lecturers, pointing to the wastefulness of drinking, declared that intemperance cost thousands of lives and billions in property and predicted that bank deposits would increase if the cup were withheld from the laborer. Horace Mann, the greatest prophet of the free school, championed book learning as a panacea for the evils of unbalanced wealth and poverty; for education would produce new machinery, diffuse the ownership of property, and entrench industry and capital against the wild flights of agrarianism. Proponents of women's rights were equally sure that giving women the vote would bring peace and stability to society. Antitobacconists condemned smoking and chewing because these habits took money that people might save for houses, farms, and the products of the New England mills. In other words, the reform movement, of which abolitionism was only one part, was a by-product of the northern transition to an industrial society. The reformers were trying to substitute the new ideals of an industrial capitalism for the old ideals of the frontier and the farm.

But the agricultural South, undergoing no such industrial transformation, clung to the older formulas, defended its rights in terms borrowed from Jefferson, and continued to create its own social ideology. The tradition of the squires, of the landed gentry, was strong in the Southern regions, and there publicist and politician elaborated a defense of the South which lauded the values of the plantation way of life, and calmly contended that the relation of master and slave, wherein the master bore a personal responsibility for the material and spiritual well-being of the servant, was, instead of being an evil, a "positive good."

In January, 1837, Calhoun presented the southern point of view when he spoke in the Senate on the growing rift between the sections.

"However sound the great body of the nonslaveholding States are at present, in the course of a few years they will be succeeded by those who will have been taught to hate the people and institutions of nearly one half of this Union with a hatred more deadly than one hostile nation ever entertained towards another." A Union was unthinkable wherein one half of the states regarded the other half as "sinful and odious in the sight of God and man." The southern institution of slavery was not sinful. "We of the South will not, cannot, surrender our institutions. To maintain the existing relations between the two races inhabiting that section of the Union is indispensable to the peace and happiness of both. It cannot be subverted without drenching the country in blood, and extirpating one or the other of the races. Be it good or bad, it has grown up with our society and institutions and is so interwoven with them that to destroy it would be to destroy us as a people. But let me not be misunderstood as admitting, even by implication, that the existing relation between the two races in the slaveholding states is an evil—far otherwise; I hold it to be a good, as it has thus far proved itself to be to both, and will continue to prove so if not disturbed by the fell spirit of abolition. . . . I hold that in the present state of civilization, where two races of different origin, and distinguished by color and other physical differences, as well as intellectual, are brought together, the relation now existing in the slaveholding states between the two is, instead of an evil, a good—a positive good. . . . I fearlessly assert that the existing relation between the two races in the South, against which these blind fanatics are waging war, forms the most solid and durable foundation on which to rear free and stable political institutions."

With this declaration Calhoun introduced resolutions affirming that the Constitution gave the states control over their domestic affairs. In the adoption of the Constitution, he said, the states had acted as free and independent communities, and each had retained control over its own arrangement of society. Intermeddling with the internal affairs of one by the citizens of another was dangerous to the common peace. The federal government, being obliged to provide for the general security, must protect the domestic institutions of each from attacks by the rest. Any threat to slavery in the District of Columbia, or any interference with slavery in the territories, should be considered an indirect assault upon the southern states. Only if slavery were protected would the Union be safe. This was "the only question of sufficient potency to divide the Union, and divide it it would, or drench the country in blood if not arrested."

After several days of debate Henry Clay came forward to conciliate the sections. "I have no apprehension . . . for the safety of the Union from any state of things now existing," he explained, but "I will not answer for the consequences which may ensue from indiscretion and rashness on the part of individuals or of Congress, here or elsewhere. We allow ourselves to speak too frequently, and with too much levity, of a separation of this Union. It is a terrible word, to which our ears should not be familiarized." With this, Clay proposed that Congress should declare that slavery was a domestic institution of the states with which Congress had no right to interfere. Petitions for the abolition of slavery in the states should be rejected as being beyond the scope of Congress. Its abolition in the District of Columbia would be a breach of faith with Virginia and Maryland, but petitions for that end should be referred to a committee. As for slavery in the territories, it existed only in Florida and the people there had not asked to be rid of it. Finally Clay's resolutions were accepted, with modifications which took away much of their force.

In this debate, however, Calhoun had formulated a brief for the South. Defying those who would industrialize the nation, Southerners thereafter took refuge in a doctrine of localism and depended upon the Constitution to protect their institutions from outside assault. They felt justified in standing firm because they believed slavery essential to the welfare of the southern community. Slavery was no sin. It was a positive good.

2. Personal Liberty

Southerners could not, by their appeals to local rights, settle the question of ethics which the abolitionists had raised. The reformist agitation did not diminish in the North. In November, 1838, Clay noted that "reflective men" felt the deepest solicitude about the subject, and he expressed a fear that "the contagion" might spread until it had gripped all the free states. The agitators were gaining converts not only through oral persuasion but also through propaganda of the deed. Eager for martyrs, they gathered many tales of suffering from the adventures of those who travelled the "Underground Railroad." In popular belief there existed a system of "conductors" who led fleeing Negroes across the Ohio River to safety in the North or in Canada, following dark routes from one "station" to another. Although no such well-organized system existed in fact, both abolitionists and pro-slaveryites—each for his own purposes—affected to believe that two thousand slaves annually took the railroad from slavery to freedom. Decades later, when slavery was gone and the old abolitionists had won social approbation, men proudly claimed that they had taken an active part in the organization and operation of the road. Levi Coffin of Cincinnati claimed to have been the "president" of the road. Actually, many people helped slaves to make good their escape, but most of the aid came from the unorganized and unsystematized efforts of free Negroes to aid their brethren in bondage.

Frequently southern masters pursued their escaping property and enlisted the aid of state and federal officials. Abolitionists, demanding legislation to insure the "personal liberty of free Negroes and fugitives," secured the passage of a number of state laws giving Negroes protection in the courts.

An incident occurring in New York in July, 1839, illustrated the conflicts inherent in the situation. A group of abolitionists took a Negro named Isaac, a fugitive from Virginia, off a schooner in New York Harbor and carried him out of New York. The governor of Virginia then de-manded that Governor Seward extradite certain other Negroes who had facilitated Isaac's escape. Seward, who owed his position to antislavery votes, refused on the ground that their act was not criminal under the laws of his state. His legislature upheld him by passing an act requiring jury trial in cases where alleged fugitives were involved. The Virginia legislature retaliated by making it a penal offense for a resident of New York to carry a Negro out of Virginia, compelling all New York vessels to be searched before leaving a Virginia port, and offering to repeal this legislation when New York repealed its law and surrendered the fugitives from southern justice. In 1842, when the Democrats got control of the New York legislature, they passed a resolution that "stealing of a slave within the jurisdiction of Virginia was theft within the meaning of the Constitution," and that, therefore, the governor should surrender the criminals. Seward, still in the governor's office, refused to transmit the resolution to Virginia. He believed that "beings possessed of the physical, moral, and intellectual faculties common to the human race cannot, by force of any constitution or laws, be goods or chattels or a thing; and that nothing but goods, chattels, and things can be the subject of larceny, stealing, or theft."

In the same year, the Supreme Court heard the case of *Prigg v. Pennsylvania.* Prigg had seized a fugitive slave in Pennsylvania and, without magisterial consent, had taken her across the line into Maryland. He was arrested for violation of a Pennsylvania law of 1826 designed to protect the free Negroes of the state from kidnappers. Justice Joseph Story, speaking for the Court, declared that the fugitive slave law of 1793 was constitutional and that the Pennsylvania law of 1826 was not. The owner of slaves, said the Court, had the right to recover his chattels anywhere, and a state had no power to interfere. The Court refused to say, however, that the enforcement of the federal law was obligatory on the officials of a state. The inference was that a state might forbid its officials to render aid in the enforcement of the federal law.

After this decision, a new crop of "personal liberty" laws appeared in the North. Vermont passed an "Act for the Protection of Personal Lib-erty" which provided that the courts could not take cognizance of any case arising under the Fugitive Slave Law, nor could sheriffs arrest fugi-tive slaves. Other states followed Vermont's example. Cases of state officers refusing to enforce the Fugitive Slave Law became more fre-quent, and the publicity attending them benefited abolitionists, for there was widespread popular sympathy with the escaping slaves. But South-erners, alarmed for the security of their property, began to realize that passive assertions of constitutional rights would avail them nothing.

3. JUSTIFYING SLAVERY

While abolition societies were arousing the northern people to the sinfulness of slavery and northern politicians were eyeing with more and more interest the rising tide of antislavery sentiment, the South was organizing in defense of its fundamental economic institution. Even before the northern abolitionists had begun their work, the southern planters had seen the need for defending their institution from yeoman attacks within their own states. After abolition became a sectional cause and was taken up by the industrialists, southern white men of all classes began to unite in support of the planter group. In the footsteps of Thomas R. Dew marched a host of writers, speakers, and agitators who succeeded in persuading the southern masses that slavery was good. Without the abolitionists, the controversy might have resolved itself into a struggle between regions and classes within the southern states. Thanks to Garrison and his cohorts, the South became consolidated in support of the institution.

One of the most noticeable effects of the antislavery agitation, whether coming from within or from without the South, was the enactment of more stringent slave codes. In most of the southern states the Nat Turner insurrection was followed by new laws prohibiting the slaves to assemble, even for worship, without the presence of a white man and providing penalties for anyone who would teach Negroes to read and write. Other laws placed restrictions on emancipation. In some states, a master desiring to free his slaves had to obtain permission from the legislature and give bond that the Negroes would be removed from the state. If freed Negroes returned, they were to be remanded to slavery. Militia laws were refurbished, planters joined in voluntary associations to patrol the roads and catch wandering Negroes, and the "patterroller" became a familiar figure to the slaves of the southern plantations.

More significant than the new black codes was the rising tide of proslavery literature, justifying the southern system and emphasizing from every angle that slavery was indeed "a good—a positive good." Politicians encouraged the movement, turning to their own advantage the antislavery sentiment in the North. An observant Kentuckian, writing in the Louisville *Examiner,* pointed out the relation between the abolition movement and this proslavery propaganda. He noted that the "Ultraism" of the abolitionists in the North was suppressing antislavery expression in the South. The object of men of the "Carolina School," he explained, had been "to deepen the pro-slavery excitement, so that they may band all the slave States in one political union, and thus win power and secure it; and, for this end, they appeal constantly and ably to the pride, passion, sectional prejudice, avarice, and fears of the Slave States." The result of this was, in turn, to drive the northern people to excess, "to madden them and make them as ultra on one side as these perpetualists are on the other. How, indeed, could they gain ascendency in the South, were it not for the creation and extension of fanaticism at the North?" It was a vicious circle.

The process did not escape the attention of James Madison, who perceived that in Virginia and elsewhere the turn of events tended to make a unit of southern opinion. "It is painful," he wrote to Clay in 1833, "to observe the unceasing efforts to alarm the South by imputations against the North of unconstitutional designs on the subject of slaves. You are right, I have no doubt, in believing that no such intermeddling disposition exists in the body of our northern brethren. Their good faith is sufficiently guaranteed by the interest they have as merchants, as ship-owners, and as manufacturers in preserving a union with the slaveholding states. On the other hand, what *madness* in the South to look for greater safety in disunion." Madison noticed at other times how aspiring popular leaders were inculcating the impression that a permanent incompatability existed between the interests of the southern and the northern peoples.

James Henry Hammond, for example, declared in a letter to a New York editor that "Northern fanatics" must expect resistance from South Carolina. Another Carolinian asserted in a public letter that slavery was a "blessing to both Master and Slave" and warned Northerners to keep their hands off. The Charleston meeting to protest against the acceptance of abolitionist literature by the local post office resolved: "We view with abhorrence and detestation the attempt to deluge our State with incendiary publications; and . . . we consider the authors of such attempts no more entitled to the protection of the laws than the ferocious monster and venomous reptile." Such expressions gave evidence that a large market existed for proslavery writings, and all over the South men took to their pens to examine the merits of slaveholding. In the ensuing discussion, they compared the economic aspects of chattel and wage labor, questioned the constitutional power of Congress over their system, and inquired into the moral relations of master and slave. Harriet Martineau and many others detected a tone of apology in the works of most of these southern authors.

At first, the southern authors justified the existence of slavery on the ground that its abolition was an impossibility, and exculpated the present generation of slaveholders because these men were not responsible for the situation. They discussed the insecurity that would result to the whites should slavery be abolished, and pointed with shudders to the situation in Haiti as proof that the Negroes, if free, would never permit their former masters to live. Many contended that freedom would not materially alter the condition of the slaves, for "talent, habit, and wealth" would still make the white man master. Thomas R. Dew emphasized the financial burden of emancipation—it would produce destitution throughout the South, the slave property in Virginia alone being worth one hundred million dollars. "It matters but little how you destroy it, whether by the slow process of the cautious practitioner or with the frightful despatch of the self-confident quack, when it is gone, no matter how, the deed will be done and Virginia will be a desert." Another writer insisted that if slavery were abolished, the ruin would extend to the free as well as the slaveholding states. Governor Hammond asked the abolitionists if any people were ever persuaded to give up two thousand million dollars' worth of property? Throughout all their writings, Southerners emphasized the sacredness of property rights in slaves.

Supporting the appeal for respect to private property, southern writers found justification for slavery in the Bible. Professor Dew, Chancellor Harper, William Gilmore Simms, and a host of others added to the store of Biblical arguments for human bondage. The Jews had kept bond servants under the very rule of Jehovah; Hagar was a slave, "and the angel of the Lord said unto her, return to thy mistress, and submit thyself under her hands." The Ten Commandments three times mentioned "servants." And, as the Mosaic law authorized the buying and holding of bondsmen and bondsmaids, God's chosen people were not only permitted but positively enjoined to possess slaves. Then there was the curse of Canaan. Noah had said, "Cursed be Canaan; a servant of servants shall he be unto his brethren. . . . God shall enlarge Japheth, and he shall dwell in the tents of Shem; and Canaan shall be his servant." Although suitable texts were more difficult to find in the New Testament, the defenders of slaveholding made much of Jesus' silence on the subject. As final and triumphant justification in the Holy Scripture, they found the instructions that the Apostle Paul had given the fugitive, Onesimus, to return to his master. Jefferson Davis in the Senate was to declare that slavery "was established by the decree of Almighty God" and that "through the portal of slavery alone has the descendant of the graceless son of Noah ever entered the temple of civilization." Hammond added the logical conclusion that the precepts of Scripture therefore condemned the abolitionists.

Closely akin to the theological defense was the argument based upon the parallels of history. Slavery had been familiar to all ancient peoples, gentile as well as Jew, Roman as well as Greek. Aristotle had approved it. Medieval peoples, English and continental, had known villenage or serfdom. Even the fathers of the medieval church had given their assent to the condition. John Locke had provided for slavery in the Fundamental Constitutions of the Carolinas. All great societies, as history would show, were formed on a basis of forced labor of one kind or another. Indeed, slavery was the foundation of civilization itself.

A third line of defense was a consideration of the natural order of things. Professor Dew, Chancellor Harper, Governor Hammond, and others boldly abandoned the equalitarian ideas of the Declaration of Independence. It had been the work of revolutionary radicals and, as such, had little place among those who were seeking to protect their property rights. The proposition that all men were created equal was asserted to be impossible of proof. "Taking the proposition literally," exclaimed Calhoun, "there is not a word of truth in it." He found it difficult to understand how so unreasonable an idea could ever have become current among reasonable men. Governor Hammond referred to it as the "much lauded but nowhere accredited dogma of Mr. Jefferson that all men are born equal." Simms declared the phrase a "finely sounding one, significant of that sentimental French philosophy then so current." Inequality was essential to human progress, for, as Calhoun said, there had been and must always be "a front and a rear rank in the onward march of humanity." It was the natural destiny of some men to be without property and to toil for those who possessed it. Said Dew: "The exclusive owners of property ever have been, ever will, and perhaps ever ought to be the virtual rulers of mankind. . . . It is the order of nature and of God that the being of superior power should control and dispose of those who are inferior. It is as much the order of nature that men should enslave each other as that other animals should prey upon each other." Chancellor Harper believed that slaves should be kept in ignorance, so that they might better take care of the menial tasks which someone had to do. "If there are sordid, servile, and laborious offices to be performed, is it not better that there should be sordid, servile, laborious beings to perform them?"

To all of these writers, the Negroes were obviously fitted only for the lowliest tasks. "The Creator," said one, "when he called these races into being, when he stamped upon them different colors, different formations of brain, et cetera, stamped upon the Negro at the same time intellectual inferiority which cannot be changed until his whole organism is changed." Science was thus invoked to prove the natural inferiority of the Negro, and one writer declared that "no moral or physical agencies can redeem them from their degradation . . . ; any attempt to improve their condition is warring against an immutable law of nature." Since the Negro could not be improved, it was the duty of the white man to care for him. "Providence," cried Hammond, "has placed him in our hands for his good, and has paid us from his labor for our guardianship."

With history, the Scriptures, and the law of nature on their side, the advocates of slavery next examined its economic effects. Here, too, they found justification for the system. Beginning with the assumption that only the Negro could work the southern fields, they concluded that black slaves were an economic necessity. Dew, for one, drew attention to the profitability of the slave trade that Virginia carried on with the states of the lower South, and he and others favorably compared the profits on investments in the South with those in the North. After the panic of 1857 they made much of the fact that the slaveholding South had been relatively untouched by the catastrophe. Here, they said, was a stable and very nearly self-sufficient economic order. Here were no conflicts between capital and labor, for the slave was both.

A fourth defense of slavery was based on the sociological argument that slavery was beneficial to whites, blacks, and society at large. The whites were benefited because, being freed from menial tasks, they had leisure for the acquisition of knowledge and culture, for the practice of the arts and the sciences, and for participation in government. Their manners and morals were improved through caring for their dependents; in other words, as master folk, they acquired a spirit of kindliness. As for the Negroes, taken from savagery, they had been brought into contact with civilization. They were thus far better off, economically, physically, and morally, than their ancestors had been in Africa. Dew and Harper agreed that the slave was the happiest of men. As for society as a whole, in the South it was established, peaceful, calm, and free from the eyesores of northern society. In the South, there was no prostitution, and the white woman was placed on a plane equal to that of the angels. There

were no almshouses, for the plantation system cared for the young and
the old. There were few jails, and what there were, were usually empty.
The poverty of the northern slums was unknown.

A final justification of slavery was that it was good for the nation.
Through it, the South was able to support northern industry. "Upon the
South," said one writer, "as upon the strong arm of a brother, so long
as Negro slavery exists, the North can rely; it will furnish materials for
its workshops, a market for its manufactures, wealth to its capitalists,
wages to the laborers." Moreover, the cotton of the South supported the
country by bringing in a supply of ready money for the enrichment of
the North.

4. EFFECTS OF SECTIONALIZATION

With the formulation of the antislavery propaganda and the proslavery argument, the two sections diverged, each clinging to a philosophy
that justified its own mode of existence. This crystallization of sectional
opinion led eventually to a division in the Methodist and Baptist churches.
Before the proslavery defense began, these churches had represented the
frontiersman's opposition to the economic and political power of the planters. But many members, thanks to the spread of the area of cotton, rose
to be slaveholders and to influence the councils of the church. Preachers
now hesitated to rebuke the keeper of slaves. Indeed, as they were converted to the proslavery philosophy, religious leaders not only ceased to
voice the radical demands of the back country but became dependable
allies of the planter groups.

Among Presbyterians in the South a similar process was going on,
and the church came officially to sympathize with the slaveholder against
the abolitionist. In 1844, spokesmen for the Presbytery of Southern Alabama informed their Massachusetts brethren that "immediate emancipation was not only dangerous to [the slaves] themselves, but doubly so to
the safety of the white population," and that the agitation of the abolitionists had the effect of combining every class of man in support of
slavery. "We who dwell in the midst of the slave population and who ought
to be as much respected for our piety and our opinions as those at a
distance, see the fatal results and mourn over them as they spread desolation over the spiritual and temporal welfare of the slave. We have
remonstrated and expostulated with our northern brethren, but our
expostulations have been unheeded and treated with contempt, or our own
motives resolved into mere cupidity and avarice. You have asked us to
advise you as to your relation and duty, and how the emancipation of
the slaves is to be effected. Our answer to your inquiry is, we exhort you
to let it alone . . . as every step you have already taken has only rendered the condition of the slave worse than it ever has been, and has
more firmly riveted the chains of bondage, and can never reach the object before you. . . ."

The national organization of the Presbyterian Church managed to hold together for the time being, but in 1844-1845 the Baptist and Methodist churches both fell apart. The Southern Baptist associations withdrew from the general Mission Board and set up a central organization of their own. There had been earlier schisms among the Methodists, when various abolitionist groups withdrew and formed separate sects. Enough antislavery people remained, however, to dominate, in 1844, the Methodist General Conference. In that year, the conference considered the case of Bishop James O. Andrew, of Georgia, who had been elected a bishop twelve years before. He was not a slaveholder himself, but he had recently married a woman who owned slaves. The conference voted to suspend him from his office. Southern members had already informed their northern brethren that such a vote would result in a division of the church. Now the Southerners withdrew, and in Louisville the next year they formed the Methodist Episcopal Church, South. They made an agreement with the Northern Church for a peaceable division of the common property and for mutually exclusive jurisdictions. Within the next few years, both branches of the denomination increased in membership. To men who watched the horizons, this division was alarming. Clay declared, "I would not say that such a separation would necessarily produce a dissolution of the political union of these States; but the example would be fraught with imminent danger, and, in co-operation with other causes unfortunately existing, its tendency on the stability of the confederacy would be perilous and alarming."

CHAPTER 12

The South in Politics, 1832-1848

1. REACTION TO JACKSONIAN DEMOCRACY

POLITICAL alignments and party politics immediately reflected the impact of the proslavery argument and the abolition crusade. Within the South, the planters looked with ill-concealed alarm upon both the growing spirit of nationalism and the northern assault upon the South's basic social and economic institution. Regardless of party labels, southern politicians in and out of Congress united in support of aggressive prosouthern doctrines.

Although their opposition to the Neo-Federalism of Clay and Adams brought the Southerners into the Jacksonian ranks, conservative planters grew restive under the democratic nationalism of "King Andrew's" reign. Only South Carolina dared take a belligerent stand for states' rights, but nullification had its partisans throughout the planting sections. Jackson's belligerent proclamation against the nullifiers and his proscription of Calhoun's supporters drove the great slaveholders into the ranks of his opponents. With the addition of a southern element, the National-Republican party, whose greatest cohesive force was opposition to the "Toryism" of Jackson, took the name "Whig" and lost some of its earlier devotion to the American System. Southern Whigs who co-operated with Clay's northern supporters came from many sources and represented a confusing variety of interests. Clay himself had a large personal following in the South, to which he added the hemp-growers of his home state. In Louisiana the sugar planters, who were also manufacturers, favored a tariff: while the commercial interests of Maryland, survivors of an older Federalism, gave support. In Virginia the commercial interests of the Tidewater towns gave adherence to nationalistic policies, while the western counties, desirous of internal improvements and industrial development, were torn between their economic interests and their emotional enthusiasm for Jacksonian democracy. The western regions of North Carolina favored a national bank but rejected Clay's protective tariff, while in neighboring east Tennessee an opposition to the cotton planters and a hope for internal improvements alike drove the inhabitants into the Whig ranks. The southern Whig party was a creature of convenience, bound together by a common conservatism rather than an adherence to a definite, positive program. Many of its members had little in common except their disgust with Jackson's personal rule and arbitrary actions. While Jackson scorned "these antipodes in politics," Clay and Calhoun drew together to enact the compromise tariff of 1833.

Jackson's war against the Bank of the United States brought more supporters to the Whig party. Many Southerners were stockholders in the assailed bank; and planters, who had learned the advantage of a stable credit structure, favored a system which facilitated moving their crops to market. The bank had loaned money at low interest rates to Richmond newspapers, to George McDuffie, to Tennessee's David Crockett, and to other southern leaders. When Jackson removed deposits from the Bank of the United States and distributed the federal money to "pet" banks, southern conservatives declared his plan unconstitutional. The Virginia, Kentucky, and Louisiana legislatures denounced Jackson's action, and Virginia's John Tyler joined with Clay, Webster, and Calhoun in passing resolutions censuring the president. In closing up its business, the bank called in loans, thus producing distress in the South, and supporters of the bank joined with nullifiers and states'-rights men in the Whig party.

In the presidential election of 1836 the heterogeneous elements in the Whig party could not unite upon a single candidate. Unable to find any one person who could attract more votes than Van Buren from the country as a whole, the Whigs ran three tickets in the hope of appealing to disaffected groups in each section and throwing the election into the House of Representatives. In New England they offered Daniel Webster to the voters; in the Northwest and the middle states, William Henry Harrison; and in the South, Hugh Lawson White, a Tennessean who had quarreled with Jackson over Van Buren. They formed no national platform, but left each candidate to present the issues that would be most helpful in his particular section. Their strategy was unsuccessful, and Martin Van Buren was elected, though his majority of the popular vote was less than thirty thousand. In the South, White carried Georgia and Tennessee, and Harrison carried Kentucky and Maryland. South Carolina, still under the influence of Calhoun and the nullifiers, gave its votes to Willie P. Mangum, of North Carolina. In the other states the planters, believing Van Buren less radical than Jackson, voted for the Democratic nominee.

Less able than Jackson to appeal to the masses, Van Buren was forced to resort to politician's devices to heal the breach in his party. Although he announced that he would "follow in the footsteps" of his "illustrious predecessor," his administration was marked by a real effort to conciliate the South. In his earlier career he had opposed slavery, but now he momentarily dropped his antagonism and sought conservative support. Calhoun accepted his overtures and returned to the Democratic fold, for the late election had taught the Carolinian that he could never obtain the presidency through a party which stood for internal improvements, a tariff, and a national bank. In South Carolina he gained undisputed control of the party and even punished former nullifiers who refused to leave the Whigs. Many leaders in other states—such as John A. Quitman in Mississippi and R. M. T. Hunter, W. F. Gordon, and L. W. Tazewell in Virginia—perceived likewise that they had little in common with the nationalistic Whigs and followed Calhoun's example by going back to their Democratic organization, where they were received like prodigal sons and rewarded with political offices. The continuance of social divisions in the South, however, led many a planter to prefer the aristocracy of the Whigs to popular democracy, and the Whig party remained a force in southern politics.

2. The South under Van Buren

The greatest problems of Van Buren's administration grew out of the panic of 1837. During the last months of Jackson's term in office there had been an orgy of canal building and land speculation, but no sooner was Van Buren settled in the White House than the inevitable catastrophe came. It hit the country as a whole but fell with a peculiar force upon the South. The states from Maryland to Louisiana found themselves burdened with debt. Planters picked more than the usual amount of cotton, and its price fell rapidly to ten cents a pound. Commission merchants, upon whom the growers depended, went bankrupt. Bales of cotton remained unsold in warehouse and gin.

Panic and distress had repercussions in the congressional elections of 1838. The outstanding issue at the time was Van Buren's proposal for an independent treasury, which was to serve as a substitute for the defunct Bank of the United States. Since the independent treasury would act only as a government depository, the Whigs alleged that it would do nothing to stabilize credit in the nation and would reduce the money supply at a time when cheap money was badly needed. Southern conservatives supported the Whig contentions, and in the elections Whigs gained control of the Virginia and North Carolina legislatures; while Georgia and Louisiana returned solid Whig delegations to Congress. The Democrats were able to maintain a precarious hold on Alabama and South Carolina.

In the Congress elected in 1838 a majority opposed the administration. Hence, though he was an able politician, Van Buren could make no appreciable headway on his own program. Calhoun came to his support and made an alliance with Missouri's Thomas Hart Benton, the leading champion of the Democratic elements in the West. Together they supported the independent treasury, and Benton's pet bills permitting squatters pre-emption rights and a gradual price reduction for public lands. Here was, in effect, a new tentative alliance of the South and West, and it bore promise of future success. In June, 1840, just on the eve of the presidential campaign, the allies pushed the independent treasury bill through Congress.

Their hopes renewed by the returns in 1838, the Whig leaders, Clay, Webster, and Adams looked forward to the campaign of 1840. Clay, perceiving a chance to gain southern support, intimated that he was ready to abandon the American System and to allow the compromise tariff of 1833 to remain permanently. Many Southern leaders endorsed his candidacy and suggested John Tyler as a suitable running mate.

In 1840 the Democrats renominated Van Buren without dissent. Their platform endorsed states' rights, favored divorcing the government and the banks, and opposed internal improvements and the protective tariff. Although it asserted that the Declaration of Independence was a cardinal article of democratic faith, it was equally emphatic in declaring that Congress had no power to interfere with slavery in the states. Disliking these resolutions, which revealed the southern influence in the party, the Westerners were to voice their displeasure at the November polls.

The Whigs rejected both of their outstanding contenders, Clay and Webster, and nominated William Henry Harrison. His opinions, so far as they were known, hardly made him a good Whig, for he favored states' rights, opposed a high tariff, and was more Jeffersonian than Federalist on the issue of a bank. On the question of slavery, he had pleased the Southerners by his conciliatory statements. Even less a true and honest Whig was John Tyler, the vice-presidential candidate. His opposition to a bank, tariffs, and internal improvements would have made him a Democrat had he not opposed Jackson's dictatorial methods. The election was not to be won or lost, however, on the substantial issues of the day. Having learned something from the Jacksonians, the Whigs focused attention upon the personality of their candidate and tried to make him appear both a military hero and an agrarian yeoman. They presented Harrison as a man of the people, humbly willing to live in a log cabin and drink the beverage of the common man—hard cider. They pictured Van Buren, by contrast, as a gentleman of aristocratic leanings who dined from gold plate in the luxurious surroundings of the White House. In the South the poorer elements hurrahed for Harrison, much as they had once cheered for Jackson. Believing that the Whig candidate was the embodiment of Jeffersonian democracy, the people gave him the electoral votes of Kentucky, North Carolina, Maryland, Georgia, Louisiana, Mississippi, and even Jackson's own state of Tennessee. Virginia (by the narrow margin of a thousand votes), South Carolina, Alabama, and Missouri were for Van Buren.

In the campaign of 1840, the first definitely abolitionist party had appeared. In April a convention in Albany, New York, launched the Liberty Party and nominated James G. Birney for the presidency. The Liberty men, ignoring such basic issues as banks and tariffs, stood forth strongly against slavery. In truth, their candidate was their platform. Birney's father had been one of the richest slave-holders of Kentucky. The son, however, early became interested in the movement for colonizing free blacks. He persuaded the Alabama constitutional convention to prohibit the introduction of slaves for sale in the new state. In 1834 he emancipated his own slaves and later set free those he inherited from his father. An easy convert for Theodore Weld, he became a militant abolitionist, moved to Ohio, and began to publish *The Philanthropist*. In his campaign he denounced both Democrats and Whigs and urged political action on his fellow abolitionists. Violently opposing Garrison, he helped to change the abolition movement from moral protest to a political force. In 1840 the party which he led polled only 7,000 votes, but it had perfected an organization and formed a significant cloud upon the political horizon.

3. TYLER'S ADMINISTRATION

Although Harrison was president, Henry Clay expected to play the leading role in the new administration. The Whig party had no definite program: Westerners in the party had voted for internal improvements which Southerners opposed, and Easterners favored a tariff which Southerners believed had been abandoned. Clay still clung to his American System, however, and prepared to enact its features into law. Under Clay's influence, Harrison selected a Cabinet of nationalists and called Congress into special session.

Before Congress met, Harrison was dead, and John Tyler was president of the United States. A representative of the Tidewater planters, Tyler had no sympathy with Clay's program. When, in Congress, Clay assailed the independent treasury, Tyler accepted a bill destroying Van Buren's pet. But when Clay sent him a bill creating a new national bank, the president promptly returned it with a veto. The rejected bill contained a provision, framed to meet Calhoun's objections, that the bank could not establish branches in states that forbade their operation, and Clay considered this a sufficient concession to Tyler's prejudices. After the veto, Clay made further alterations, changing the name from "bank" to "fiscal corporation" and reducing the proposed capitalization; but to Tyler a bank by any other name was still a bank, and so he also rejected the new bill.

After this second veto, Clay consulted Tyler's Cabinet. At his suggestion, all agreed to resign in protest, except Webster, the secretary of state, who was carrying on negotiations, in which New England was vitally interested, with the British ambassador. Then the Whig congressmen met in caucus and, despite protests from the southern element, issued a declaration that Tyler had been in "free communion" with those who were trying to defeat Whig aims. "We have reason to believe that he has permitted himself to be approached, counseled, and influenced by those who have manifested least interest in the success of Whig measures." The caucus therefore repudiated the president and disclaimed responsibility for his actions.

Tyler immediately selected a Cabinet that more closely reflected his own ideas. Three Southerners, Abel P. Upshur of Virginia, Hugh S. Legare of South Carolina, and C. A. Wickcliffe of Kentucky, accepted positions, and most of the rest were also conservatives who would not offend the South. Tyler, however, was politically isolated for the rest of his administration.

When Congress met in December, 1841, Clay offered a new tariff bill. The compromise tariff of 1833 was about to expire, and northern Whigs were in no mood to conciliate the South. Tyler, who had been largely responsible for the compromise measure, declared in a message to Congress that he approved discriminating duties in favor of American industry but hoped that it would not be necessary to raise the rates to more than 25 per cent. The secretary of the treasury called attention to the fact that the "great principle" of the act of 1833 "was moderation and conciliation, and this should never be lost sight of." He proposed a 20 per cent tariff. On August 30, 1842, after twice vetoing obnoxious bills which came from Congress, Tyler accepted a revised tariff. The rates of the new tariff were slightly higher than those of 1833 but still fell far short of those demanded by northern industrialists. On the issue of the tariff, the Whigs and Democrats prepared to enter the campaign of 1844.

Among the Whigs it was widely believed that Tyler had opposed the tariff and the bank through a desire to conciliate Calhoun. Partly because he was convinced of this, and partly because he thought he could organize his followers from the outside better than from the inside, Clay retired from the Senate. In doing so he offered a "farewell" address in which he reviewed his record for the years that he had been in the service of the government. At the close of his address, Calhoun, for the first time in years, took him by the hand. Calhoun, too, gave notice that this was the last Congress in which he would serve. But the two men were not bidding farewell to public life altogether, for both had presidential aspirations. Eight years later they were both to be back in the Senate.

When Clay parted from the president, Whigs in the South were faced with the dilemma of which of their two leaders to follow. Prevented by the lines of social cleavage from entering the democratic party of the masses, the Whig leaders had to make their choice between Clay, representing the old principles, and Tyler, the states'-rights opponent of Clay's nationalism. Largely on the basis of local social differences, Whigs decided to support the Kentuckian.

Other forces contributed to Clay's following. In Mississippi the

Whigs, coming into power after the people had disapproved of a repudiation of the state debt, announced themselves to be the defenders of honesty. In Georgia the Whigs were opposed to lending state money to individuals. Throughout the South the party stood for honesty in government and charged the Democrats with supporting irregular methods of local finance and an unsound currency. Thus, in places where their opponents had been in power for some time, the Whigs were able to present themselves as reformers. These circumstances benefited Clay rather than Tyler, who had shown himself to be too close to the democratic position. Prominent leaders in many parts of the South had always been faithful to Clay, and now these rallied their followers to his cause. The earlier predilections of a large number of northern-born men in the South had been toward the American System. The Whig press in the South, having many northern connections and usually favoring a closer association between northern and southern Whiggery, was almost a unit in supporting Clay. And so, when the split between Clay and the president came, Tyler was able to count upon only a few adherents within his party, even in Virginia.

At the moment, another factor was working to the advantage of the Whig party in the South. Opinions were about to change on the issues between the sections. Tyler's attack on the bank was resented by many in the South who had been taught by adversity that the bank might confer benefits. At the same time, there was renewed talk of cotton manufacturing, and the promoters of industrial schemes desired protection for their infant industries. Cotton planters, thinking of the possibilities of manufacturing their own cotton, kept an eye on experiments in growing cotton in various parts of the British Empire. English competition in the production of the staple would make necessary vigorous competition for the textile market.

Democrats rejoiced at the division between Tyler and Clay. The editor of the Charleston *Mercury,* for example, exulted to Calhoun: "That the Democracy will come into power once more scarcely admits doubt. Neither Tyler nor Clay are now to be feared. No opposition is to be feared if the parties are true to the position in which South Carolina has placed them."

Calhoun's chief task in these years was to keep the Democrats aligned with the principles of states' rights and southern demands that South Carolina had long advocated. The Carolina leader had contacts with the leading politicians of every state in the Union and kept in close touch with every local development. To his supporters in the South he wrote frequent letters urging them to support a strict construction of the Constitution, states' rights, and the rights of the South. "The combinations in Christendom against the slaveholding interest," wrote R. M. T. Hunter, "the course of English diplomacy abroad, the state of northern feeling at home, and the present necessity for maintaining the balance of power between the free and the slaveholding states constitute a crisis which gives an importance to this question and also the election of a southern president, which I think our papers and speakers might turn to good account." And, indeed, southern newspapers began to advocate a southern president.

While Calhoun was staunchly defending the interests of his section, the southern Whigs were vigorously asserting that they, not he, were the true protectors of slavery and the South. Three fourths of the owners of slaves in the South voted the Whig ticket, and the Whig vote was largest in counties that had the greatest number of Negroes. Southern Whigs, demanding that abolitionists cease their agitation, seriously threatened to stop commercial intercourse with the North. In 1836 they presented White as a slaveholding candidate for the presidency, and in the next year they were among the more ardent supporters of Calhoun's famous resolutions. Yet, at the same time, the northern branch of the Whig party was becoming the political home of most of the abolitionists. The clash between northern and southern Whigs effectively prevented the party's becoming the controlling force in the nation, and the final collapse of this political organization broke one of the last ties that held the Union together.

During the summer of 1842 Clay made an effort to win the southern Whigs over to his cause and to present himself as a compromise candidate. At Richmond, Indiana, a Quaker presented him with a petition calling on him to emancipate his own slaves. Clay replied by condemning slavery and expressing the wish that every slave in the United States were back in Africa. But, although admitting the evils of slavery, he professed to fear that greater evils would result from its immediate abolition—a "contest between the two races, civil war, carnage, conflagration, devastation, and the ultimate extermination or expulsion of the Blacks." He said he preferred a gradual freeing of the slaves, a process which, he said, the abolitionist had set back by half a century. As for his own slaves, he could not set them free, however much he might like to do so, for there were among them the aged and infirm who needed his care. Turning to the Quaker who had presented the petition, Clay asked if he and the other signers would contribute $15,000 to provide for the wants of the slaves after they had been emancipated. The orator's skill in evading the issue of abolition lost him few votes in the South, although the extremists in the section saw that Clay could not be trusted to protect their rights.

4. THE TEXAS QUESTION

Cutting athwart the ambitions of candidates for the presidency in these years came the question of Texas annexation. The migration of Southerners into Texas had begun while Texas was still a part of the Spanish province of Mexico. The western movement of the cotton frontier brought the Southerners first to the limits of Louisiana. After the Louisiana Purchase, Americans claimed the Rio Grande as their western boundary; but in the Florida Purchase Treaty of 1819, John Quincy Adams, reluctantly abandoning claims on Texas, had contented himself with Florida, and had drawn the western boundary of the United States along the Sabine River. Southerners claimed that Adams had ignored their interests, and Jackson, Clay, and Benton denounced the treaty.

But international agreements could not stop either the expanding planter or the aspiring land speculator. Two years after the Florida treaty, Moses Austin received a grant of Texas lands from the Spanish government. Late in 1822, Stephen Austin received a confirmation of his father's concession from the newly created government of Mexico. The grant permitted Austin to bring in three hundred families, each of whom would receive over four thousand acres. The colonists were to take oaths of allegiance to Mexico and to join the Roman Catholic Church. Austin had little difficulty in finding settlers, although few of them were willing to subscribe in good faith to either the religious or the political requirements. A few years later, the Mexican government made provision for more such colonies.

Within a decade, over 20,000 Americans migrated to Texas, and the Mexican authorities became alarmed at the success of their project. The Americans refused to mix with the Mexican people, retained their religion, and continued the social customs of the South. A revolt among the Americans led the Mexican authorities to reverse their policy, to forbid further migration into Texas, and to suspend all unoccupied land grants. The Texans protested, and when their protests were ignored and further restrictions—including the prohibition of more slave importations —were placed upon them, they demanded self-government. Discontent soon led to armed revolt. In 1836, Texans raised the flag of rebellion and declared their independence. Sam Houston, a friend of President Jackson, led the Texan armies to victory over the Mexican general, Santa Anna.

The Lone Star Republic, having no desire to pursue an independent existence, immediately voted for annexation to the United States. President Jackson favored the acquisition but advised delay until after the election of 1836. The question excited an outbreak of sectional animosities in Congress. In the House of Representatives, John Quincy Adams not only opposed the annexation of more slave territory but even objected to recognizing the new nation. Other Northerners agreed that either recognition or annexation would lead to war with Mexico. Calhoun and his cohorts, on the other hand, demanded that Texas be admitted to the Union at once. Jackson delayed recognition until after England had received a Texan mission and then handed the problem of annexation over to his successor.

In 1837 and again in 1838 the Texans renewed their request to join the United States, but Van Buren was unwilling to take any action. He refused to reward Calhoun and his friends by adding another slave state to the Union, no matter how assiduously they supported his subtreasury schemes. To the request of the Texan minister, the president replied that the proposition "necessarily involved the question of war." After this decision, Van Buren's popularity declined rapidly in the South, and Calhoun assumed the leadership of those Southerners who desired annexation.

With Tyler's accession, the South brought renewed pressure for acquiring Texas. For a time the presence of Webster in the State Department prevented action; but in 1843, after having negotiated the Webster-Ashburton Treaty with England, he left the Cabinet. In his place Tyler promoted Abel P. Upshur, a Virginian who was anxious to take up the Texas question. Upshur consulted the southern leaders and found most of them equally eager for expansion. R. M. T. Hunter wrote to Calhoun that the president was "a little doubtful" of pressing annexation but that, "should he concur with Upshur, and should the question itself be vigorously discussed in the papers," the South must unite. "Perhaps also the West or a portion of it will join us. . . . I have been writing to our Richmond committee to write to our orators to take the stump. . . . This Texas question might be urged by them with great effect."

One powerful motive causing the South to favor the acquisition of Texas was the recent loss of representation in the national legislature. By the apportionment of 1841, South Carolina's delegation in the House of Representatives declined from nine to seven, while Virginia lost five members. At the same time, North Carolina, Kentucky, Tennessee, and Georgia made such slight gains in population that they barely kept their former delegations. Despite the three-fifths clause, the South was losing out in the race for population, for the slight gain in the Southwest was more than counterbalanced by the increased growth of the Northwest. With an area large enough to be divided into a number of states, Texas would enable the South to maintain her parity in the Senate and to approach equality in the House.

With this situation confronting them, politicians of Virginia and South Carolina united to force the Texas question to a conclusion. Ex-Governor Gilmer, of Virginia, became a leader of the movement to secure in Texas a "Gibraltar for the South." Henry A. Wise, contending that the South needed "more weight to her end of the lever," joined in the southern demand. Throughout the South newspapers added that annexation would afford "a permanent guaranty of protection" to slavery, and insisted that it must be accomplished "now or never."

Allies for the Southerners came, as expected, from the West, where there was considerable interest in the acquisition of Oregon. Since 1818 this region had been under the joint occupation of Great Britain and the United States. Almost from the beginning of this arrangement, Thomas Hart Benton had insisted that the United States denounce joint occupancy and assume exclusive control. Many throughout the North, hearing the laudatory reports of their missionaries in Oregon, came to accept Benton's point of view. The Southerners now saw their chance to obtain the votes of the West for Texas if they, in turn, would promise their support for Oregon. "I am sure it is our policy to unite the two questions together," wrote F. W. Pickens to Calhoun, "and thus separate the nonslaveholding northwest states from the northern states."

As the Southerners pressed the Texas issue, ambitious politicians were forced to take sides. Calhoun—eager for the Democratic nomination—and his friends scanned the political skies throughout 1843 in the hope that state elections would indicate a stronger support for him than for Van Buren. In the winter of 1843 a Baltimore paper printed a letter in which T. W. Gilmer asserted that annexation of all territory to the Pacific Ocean was inevitable. This letter was designed to force Van Buren out of the running. Jackson had endorsed it, but the enemies of Van Buren concealed this fact for the time being. They hoped to read Jackson's statement at the opportune moment in the Democratic convention and so prevent the nomination of Van Buren, who was no such expansionist as was the author of the Gilmer letter.

Meanwhile, the opponents of annexation rallied behind the anti-slavery delegation in Congress. Convinced of a southern conspiracy to annex Texas, John Quincy Adams, Joshua R. Giddings, and eleven other members of the House signed an address to the people just as Congress ended in March, 1843, in which they warned against the plot to bring additional slave territory into the Union. This plot, they said, was an "attempt to eternize an institution and a power of nature so unjust in themselves, so injurious to the interests and abhorrent to the feelings of the people of the free states, as in our opinion not only inevitably to result in a dissolution of the Union, but fully to justify it; and we not only assert that the people of the free states ought not to submit to it, but we say with confidence that they will not submit to it."

Other interests than southern expansion were involved in the Texas question. The finances of the Texan Republic had been muddled from the revolution of 1836. Its treasury receipts were less than a third of its annual expenditures, and it had met the deficit by the sale of bonds. So poor was the credit of the country that the value of the bonds declined rapidly, until some were selling at a few cents on the dollar. These, with principal and interest in arrears, were in the hands of American speculators. Americans had also bought large amounts of Texas land scrip, issued by companies with tenuous claims to large grants. The bondholders and the holders of scrip were as willing as the southern planters to see Texas become a state—provided that the federal government would assume its debts.

In 1843 a new development darkened the creditors' hopes of payment. Through the good offices of the British and French ministers in Mexico, the Texans effected a truce with their estranged mother country and so lost some of their eagerness for immediate annexation. President Sam Houston of Texas, though himself an annexationist, now looked to England for protection and told his minister in Washington to inform the United States that Texas would no longer consider entering the Union. Southern planters were alarmed lest England encourage Texas to remain independent. They feared that they would, in such a case, eventually lose their chief market, as the cotton fields of Texas began exclusively to supply the English mills. They heard rumors, moreover, that England was ready to offer Texas her protection and a loan if the republic would emancipate its slaves. In return for this loan, Texas was to adopt the free trade principles of Great Britain, so as to become both a source of supply for English factories and a market for English goods.

As the administration became convinced of this British plot, Secretary Upshur made new overtures to the Texas government. Although the Mexican minister warned the United States that the union of the two countries would be tantamount to a declaration of war on Mexico, Upshur went ahead with his negotiations and the Tyler government promised the Texans protection in case Mexico should attack them while the treaty was pending. In the midst of his negotiations, Upshur was suddenly killed by an explosion of a cannon on a naval vessel. Tyler then

Photo by U. S. Army Signal Corps

PRESIDENT SAM HOUSTON OF TEXAS. Houston commanded the Texas troops at the Battle of San Jacinto, April 21, 1836, which won independence for the Lone Star Republic. Born in Virginia, at the age of 13 he moved to the Tennessee frontier. He lived for several years with the Cherokee, who adopted him and gave him the name "The Raven." He was a military officer in the War of 1812, Congressman and Governor of Tennessee, and Senator and Governor of Texas. Lifelong friend of Andrew Jackson, Houston inherited "Old Hickory's" expansionism and nationalism.

called Calhoun to the State Department. Calhoun finished making the treaty, and on April 12, 1844, Tyler signed it. By its provisions, Texas was to be annexed as a territory, her public lands were to be surrendered, and the United States was to assume ten million dollars of the Texan debt. Calhoun explained to the British minister that the treaty was "made necessary in order to preserve domestic institutions, placed under the guaranty of the Constitutions of the United States and Texas." Slavery was "essential to the peace, safety, and prosperity" of those states in which it existed. The Mexican minister for Foreign Affairs protested to the American State Department: "In order to sustain slavery and avoid its disappearance from Texas and from other points, recourse is had to the arbitrary act of depriving Mexico of an integral part of her possessions."

With Mexico threatening war, many Americans took alarm. While the Senate was considering the treaty, they held public meetings in North and South in order to impress their conflicting views upon the senators. In the North, the people felt that annexation would be followed by war; but in the South they were convinced that Mexico would not fight and that, in any event, annexation was a necessity. W. H. Seward of New York expressed the feeling of the abolition extremists when he declared: "To increase the slaveholding power is to subvert the Constitution, to give a fearful preponderance which may and probably will be speedily followed by demands to which the democratic free-labor states cannot yield and the denial of which will be made the ground of secession, nullification, and disunion." With such protests from the North, the annexationists failed to rally the necessary two-thirds majority to ratify the treaty.

5. THE ELECTION OF 1844

While the Texas treaty languished, the presidential campaign of 1844 got under way. Despite Calhoun's efforts, Van Buren received the endorsement of more than a majority of the delegates elected to the coming Democratic convention. Among the Whigs, the nomination of Clay was a foregone conclusion. Neither of the potential candidates wished to campaign on the issue of the extension of slavery. In the spring, Van Buren, on his way to visit Jackson at Nashville, called on Clay at Lexington, Kentucky, and soon thereafter the two aspirants defined their positions in public letters. Both advised against discussing the Texas question in the elections, both stated that they were in favor of annexation if it could be accomplished without war, but both declared that such a war would be both impolitic and unjust.

The letters provoked wide discussion. Clay's did not especially injure him in the North. Van Buren's hurt him in the South, however. There, men prepared to go into the convention to defeat his nomination. "I would to God I had been at Mr. V. B.'s elbow when he closed his letter," exclaimed Andrew Jackson. "I would have brought to his view the proper conclusion. We are all in sackcloth and ashes." Clay, also injured in the South, wrote additional letters attempting to show that he was not personally opposed to the annexation of Texas and that he would favor it if it could be done without war and without dishonor, and with the consent of the states. Such temporizing cost him many votes.

Three days after the publication of his letter the Whigs, assembled in Baltimore, nominated Clay. Their platform made few concessions to the South but declared for internal improvements, tariffs, distribution of the proceeds of the sales of public lands, and hostility to executive usurpation. Later in the month, the Democrats also assembled in Baltimore, but they did not intend to nominate Van Buren. The Calhoun forces, taking a cue from a letter of Mississippi's Senator Robert J. Walker, had offered the West "reoccupation of Oregon" in return for western support of the "reannexation of Texas." In the convention, Walker succeeded in getting the two-thirds rule reaffirmed, and, since more than a third of the delegates came from the South, Van Buren could hope for little. After adopting a platform that demanded both Texas and Oregon, the delegates proceeded with the task of selecting a candidate. They balloted eight times, and none of the nominees received the necessary two-thirds majority. Then an adjournment gave the Southerners opportunity to rally around James K. Polk, of Tennessee, who had been portrayed as a friend of Jackson. On the ninth ballot, the Democrats nominated Polk.

"Who is James K. Polk?" asked the Whigs in ridicule. Since their candidate lacked an appealing personality, the Democrats centered attention on the issues of protection and annexation. The party was pledged to reduce the tariff of 1842. On the question of expansion it adopted the slogan, "The reannexation of Texas and the reoccupation of Oregon." In the South, the old Whigs tried to maintain the line for Clay, but their task was difficult. Many of them attempted to find southern arguments to support a candidate opposed to expansion. Waddy Thompson declared that annexation would weaken slavery by expanding and scattering it. Others, insisting that the Union was in danger, made a futile effort to present the Whig as the true "Union" party. Having no opportunity to repeat the "log cabin" campaign of 1840, the Whigs lost votes in all parts of the South.

At the same time, Clay lost the votes of northern extremists. The Liberty party again offered James G. Birney on a platform condemning slavery in no uncertain terms, and abolitionists in New York, reacting against Clay's attempts to ingratiate himself with the South, voted for the Liberty party's candidate. Sufficient numbers took this course to insure Clay's defeat, for it was New York's vote that elected Polk. Inadvertently the abolitionists thus put a southern slaveholder in the White House, but Birney rationalized their conduct by saying that Polk was a man of little ability and was therefore less dangerous than Clay.

Although the Senate had rejected the Texas treaty, Tyler interpreted the outcome of the election as a popular mandate for annexation. Having no chance of getting a new treaty ratified, he and Calhoun prepared to achieve their object by other means. When Congress met in December, the president recommended to both Houses that they annex Texas by joint resolution. Congress, after debating a month, passed a resolution to admit Texas to the Union, with the proviso that it be divided into as many as four states and that the terms of the Missouri Compromise be specifically extended over the area. Tyler hastened messengers to Texas to advise that annexation under the resolution be accepted. On the last day of his administration he was able to announce that Texas had accepted and was now a state in the Union. He left the consequences of his act to President Polk.

6. THE MEXICAN WAR

Birney's estimate of Polk as a man of little ability was but partly correct. The new president was active, and came into office with a positive program. He had much of the arbitrary temperament of Andrew Jackson, but was less acute in his political judgments. His advisors, too, were less able than Jackson's, and many of Polk's aggressive actions

Photo by U. S. Army Signal Corps

JAMES K. POLK. "Who is James K. Polk?" asked the Whigs, when in 1844 the Democrats nominated the Tennessean. But Polk was not a political unknown. He had been on the political scene for more than a score of years, as a Congressman for 14 years, four of which he was Speaker of the House during a time of bitter partisan divisions; and as Governor of Tennessee. The new president was active, and came into office with a positive program. He had much of the arbitrary temperament of Jackson, but was less acute in his political judgments

proved to have serious political consequences. When he took office, Polk was prepared to acquire Oregon, annex California and New Mexico, and to reform the tariff. Before he left the White House he had completed much of this ambitious program, but in doing so he had disrupted his party and had contributed more than a little to the eventual disruption of the Union.

In his inaugural address, the new president announced his intention of claiming all of Oregon, and at his suggestion Congress passed resolutions ending the joint occupancy which England and the United States had held since 1818. The British ministry showing a willingness to negotiate, Polk, in 1846, signed a treaty with England which agreed to a division of the territory. The long debates in Congress over Oregon emphasized the desire of Westerners for all of Oregon. "Fifty-Four Forty or Fight" symbolized Western demands and indicated Western displeasure with the long-continued Southern dominance of the Democratic Party and the government. Polk's failure to conciliate the West drove in deeper the wedge which was splitting the old West-South alliance.

In his first annual message, Polk recommended new legislation on the subject in which Southerners were vitally interested, namely, tariff reform. His secretary of the treasury, Robert J. Walker, of Mississippi, denounced the protective principle and proposed duties for revenue only, which should be "so imposed as to operate as equally as possible throughout the Union, discriminating neither for nor against any class or section." At once a swarm of manufacturers descended on Washington to lobby against the Walker bill. So effective were the arguments for protection that the Senate vote was tied, and the vice-president had to make the decision. He voted for the bill. Southern Whigs remained loyal to their party and supported the old tariff, yet the new law was pleasing to the South.

At the same time that he pushed the tariff and the Oregon settlement, Polk took steps to acquire California from Mexico. As soon as the joint resolution annexing Texas passed Congress, the Mexican minister left Washington. Polk, undismayed by the Mexican protest, blithely appointed Louisiana's John Slidell as minister to Mexico and instructed him to settle the disputed boundary between Mexico and Texas and to adjust the claims that American citizens had against the Mexican government. In annexing Texas, United States had annexed a boundary controversy as well. Texas claimed the Rio Grande as her southern boundary, and Mexico alleged that the Nueces River was the proper line; but, since Mexico had never recognized Texan independence, the Sabine River was technically the correct border. The claims which Slidell was to adjust amounted to $2,000,000 and had been agreed upon by a convention; but Mexican payments were in arrears, and Slidell had instructions to offer to assume these obligations and to pay $25,000,000 for California and New Mexico.

To Mexicans who were expecting an apology from the United States for the annexation of Texas, Slidell's efforts to acquire more territory seemed a gross insult. Their government refused to accept the American minister, and the Mexican people demanded war. While the martial spirit raged in Mexico, Polk determined to recommend a war on the ground that Mexico had refused to receive Slidell and adjust the unpaid claims. In preparation for this, the president ordered General Taylor to occupy the right bank of the Rio Grande. On April 24, a clash between American and Mexican skirmishing parties resulted in bloodshed. The news of this encounter gave Polk a better reason for recommending war, and on May 11, 1846, he advised Congress: "Mexico has passed the boundary of the United States, has invaded our territory, and shed American blood upon American soil." Congress immediately recognized the existence of a state of war with Mexico.

Congressional abolitionists, with Adams and Giddings in the lead, were quick to declare that the war was being fought for the extension and preservation of slavery. In the Northeast there was little enthusiasm for the conflict. A congressman from Illinois named Abraham Lincoln, voicing the general disapprobation of the Northern Whigs, offered a series of "Spot Resolutions" calling on Polk to name the "spot" on American soil upon which American blood had been shed. In the West, however, many people welcomed the war. Volunteers rushed to the hastily organized militia commands; in fact, more than half of the total number of volunteers came from the West. Western Democrats were most insistent in demanding the annexation of *all* of Mexico. In the South, opinions were divided. Honestly believing that armed conflict was avoidable, that it was not an inevitable sequel of his work in acquiring Texas, Calhoun refused to vote for the declaration of war. Southern Whigs, although they joined their northern co-partisans in voting for military bills, never ceased their denunciation of the warmongering president.

Northern Democrats, stung by abolitionist charges that the war was being fought to increase the area of slavery, sought an opportunity to give the lie to their detractors. When a bill to appropriate money for peace negotiations was under debate, David Wilmot, a Democratic representative from Pennsylvania, moved an amendment to the effect that slavery should not exist in any territory acquired as a result of the war. Southerners immediately objected to this Wilmot Proviso, and those of all parties united to defeat the scheme. As the war progressed, they came to the conclusion that slavery could not exist in California and New Mexico, and many of them began strongly to oppose the acquisition of these territories. At the same time, the injection of the antislavery proviso into congressional debates increased the desire of Northerners for these lands. Before the war was over, there existed a definite northern group of expansionists and a southern group opposed to new acquisitions, both of them convinced that slavery could not exist in Mexican territory. The southern opposition was largely responsible for the failure of a movement to annex all of Mexico. And so, by the Treaty of Guadalupe Hidalgo, the United States took only the land lying north of the Rio Grande and stretching westward to the Pacific.

The military campaigns of the Mexican War were notable for three things: the ease of American victories, the political jealousies aroused, and the number of later Civil War officers who gained their first martial experience on the battlefields of Mexico. General Taylor led the American advance against the armies of Santa Anna, fighting battles at Palo Alto, Resaca de la Palma, Monterrey, and Buena Vista. In Taylor, the Whigs hoped to have a new military hero for a presidential candidate, and so Polk sought a Democratic general with whom to divide the glory. For the first time in American history, a president attempted to assume the positive functions of his position as Commander-in-Chief, but Polk's military commands were based upon political considerations. He rejected the idea of putting Senator Thomas Hart Benton at the head of the armies, and failing to find a competent commander in the ranks of his partisans, the president sent General Winfield Scott, a rival Whig, to lead an expedition from Vera Cruz to Mexico City. In the armies of these generals, a number of men served who were to be military leaders of the Confederacy in the Civil War. Jefferson Davis, of Mississippi, resigned a recently acquired seat in the House to lead a regiment of Mississippi Rifles with Taylor's armies. At Buena Vista, he arranged his men in a V-shape to meet and repel Santa Anna's charge, and thereafter claimed credit for the victory. Robert E. Lee served on Scott's staff. Albert Sidney Johnston, Joseph E. Johnston, P. G. T. Beauregard, and many others saw service and gained valuable training.

The immediate political result of the Mexican War was the election of Zachary Taylor as president of the United States in 1848. General Taylor was a Southerner and a slaveholder. The Southern Whigs, devoted to states' rights and eager to challenge the antislavery sentiment in the party's northern wing, early launched a movement to nominate the general. When the Whig convention met in Philadelphia, he was selected on the fourth ballot. Millard Fillmore, long an opponent of the abolitionist William H. Seward in New York politics, was chosen for the vice-presidency. Taylor proved strong in the South, where many planters preferred a slaveholder to Michigan's Lewis Cass, the Democratic nominee. Cass had proposed leaving the question of slavery in the newly acquired territories to the settlers, and Southerners feared this program would result in the exclusion of the plantation system. In November, as Taylor carried Kentucky, Tennessee, Maryland, North Carolina, Georgia, Florida, and Louisiana, Southerners breathed more easily in the belief that the abolitionist principle of the Wilmot Proviso had been scotched. It was not long before they discovered that Taylor's silence during the campaign had deceived them. The new president was to prove no friend of the South.

The Southern System, 1830-1860

1. THE PLANTATION

WHILE Calhoun was uniting the South behind a definite southern policy in politics, and the newly inspired proslavery advocates were consolidating the social philosophy of the section, the whole organization of southern life was becoming fixed. In the North, by contrast, the period from Andrew Jackson to James Buchanan was marked by social chaos in which a variety of reform movements, ranging from an extension of the suffrage to highly emotional temperance agitation, kept pace with the transition from an agricultural to an industrial way of life. The factory system, beginning in Washington's administration with the small textile mills of Morris Brown and Samuel Slater, had spread over all of New England, most of the middle states, and parts of the West. By 1860 the northern section possessed factories valued at $1,884,861,000 and employing over a million men, women, and children. Mining, commerce, and banking had increased with the growth of manufacturing. Agriculture, stimulated by the markets of the rising industrial cities, had grown until its annual output far exceeded in value the total production of cotton, rice, sugar, and tobacco in the slaveholding states. In the midst of this wealth, industrial capitalists, great merchants, and bankers reigned supreme over a population of laborers, many of whom were crushed by poverty into squalid tenements, and small farmers whose total output, large as it was, seldom sufficed to give freedom from debt or opportunity for culture.

Quite different from the restless ways of the industrial North was the relatively placid social and economic life of the agricultural South. The

Kingdom of Cotton, bordered on its sides by the allied provinces of tobacco, rice, and sugar, stretched from the Potomac to the Rio Grande. In an area of almost a half million square miles, the production of cotton occupied the major part of the attention of all of the people. By the end of the period the South was producing almost 4,000,000 bales annually, which constituted nearly 60 per cent of the country's exports and brought $191,000,000 in the markets of Europe. In Louisiana and in portions of the bordering states, sugar demanded a capitalization of $100,000,000 and produced 280,000 hogsheads. The production of tobacco was 434,000,000

National Park Service

An Ante-bellum House at Fredericksburg, Virginia. Typical of the best planta-tion life in the Southeast, the "big house," set upon the top of a hill and surrounded by giant oaks, was both a beautiful and a comfortable dwelling. Tall white pillars across the wide veranda became popularized in nostalgia and imagination as the classic home of the southern planter.

pounds. Rice added $2,000,000 annually to southern wealth. Hemp, corn, wheat, oats, and livestock were also produced in scattered sections. But in all the South there was little else than agriculture to create wealth.

Within the Cotton Kingdom towns were few, and cities, with the exception of Richmond, Charleston, and New Orleans, were non-existent. The planters came into these metropolises for a winter season of balls and politics; but the center of southern life was the plantation. Although fiction has pictured the South as a land of great plantations, and nostalgic post-war generations have given credence to the legend, the Old South was in reality a land of small farms. Except in a few localities, the plantation was comparatively rare and small holdings were the rule. The large estates supported less than one tenth of the total population.

Plantations varied from a few hundred to several thousand acres, the average being about one thousand acres. The great landholders of the South, such as Wade Hampton, the Hairston family, and William B. Goulden, owned extensive areas, but seldom were their holdings in one place. Nathaniel Heyward, of South Carolina, for example, possessed fifteen separate plantations devoted to rice and cotton. Goulden, owner of a thousand slaves, had to purchase a new estate annually in order to provide for their natural increase. From sixty to a hundred Negroes were considered the most profitable agricultural unit, and these could best work an area of a thousand acres.

The plantation itself sometimes took on the general outlines of those plantations pictured in the popular legend. The "big house," set upon the top of a hill, surrounded by giant oaks which hid from view the rows of Negro cabins in the background, was both a beautiful and a comfortable dwelling. Large, high-ceilinged rooms furnished ample space for dancing and festivities and induced the coolness which the warm climate made desirable. A long, shady veranda aided in the quest for comfort and was used during the torrid months as the living room of the planter's family. Walls about the lawns not only protected them from wandering livestock but also served to preserve the illusion of grandeur with which many of the planters tried to surround themselves.

Life within the manor houses of the great planters had much of elegance and refinement. Hill Carter's "Shirley," on the James River, in Virginia, was a mansion of many rooms, cared for by many servants, and presided over by a hospitable master and a gracious mistress. When Henry Barnard visited Shirley in 1833, he found every facility provided for his entertainment. Before he awoke in the morning a servant had brushed his clothes, blackened his boots, and built a fire in his bedroom. After a breakfast of cold ham, hot bread, and coffee, the visitor rode about the 800-acre plantation, watching more than a hundred slaves working in the tobacco, corn, and wheat which Carter ground for the Richmond market. Dinner was served at three o'clock and lasted until late afternoon. Ham, beef, turkey, with the inevitable sweet potatoes and hominy, formed the main course of a typical meal. In the evening there were music—the piano was tuned once a year—and dancing, conversation among the elders, and courtship among the younger folk. Shirley, luxurious in its equipment, had possessed a bathtub since 1818. In the barns, threshing machines, reapers, and horse rakes had appeared almost as soon as they were invented. The Carters took pride in their progress.

Other Virginia plantations had similar features. In 1829 Westover, ancestral home of the Byrds, passed into the capable hands of John Selden, a student of agricultural improvements. Like Shirley Hall, Westover was at once a show place and an experiment in luxurious living. Further west was Bolling Hall, owned and managed—with two other plantations—by William Bolling. Vestryman, gentleman planter, master of hunting and riding horses, Bolling took especial pride in his orchards and vineyards. Tobacco and wheat were his main crops, but he also raised sheep and hogs. At the foot of the Blue Ridge lay the estates of Thomas Manu who, ignoring tobacco, grew wheat and apples. Such plantations as these rep-

HOME IN NATCHEZ, MISSISSIPPI. In the southwest the Spanish tradition, intermingled with festoons of Spanish moss, produced variations in the typical plantation home. White pillars and broad verandas remained the fashion, but ceilings were likely to be higher because of the heat, and white exteriors sometimes replaced the rich red brick of the southeastern style.

resented the ideal and were objects of imitation throughout the South.

Back of the manor house on such plantations were the cabins of the slaves—sometimes a neat row of whitewashed cottages—smoke houses, laundry, cooper's or carpenter's shop, barns, stables, and tobacco sheds. The slave quarters were surrounded by garden plots wherein the Negroes raised their own vegetables. Sometimes, too, the master provided a pig pen and a chicken house for the slaves, so as to dissuade them from seeking the delicacies of fried chicken and pork chops among his own possessions.

If their resources were small, the master and his family themselves managed the estate. If the master owned more than one plantation, he hired an overseer to direct the work of the slaves and, though rarely, a steward to direct the work of the overseers. The planter gave the overseers detailed instructions in slave-management, his first consideration usually being to maintain his chattels in efficient working order. Since the hired managers frequently received a share of the crop for their services, however, they were often more concerned in driving the slaves to produce a bumper crop than in preserving the health of property in which they had no permanent investment. They made daily, weekly, or monthly reports to the master. The owner frequently had to settle difficulties between overseers and slaves, and the hardest part of his responsibility was to find a good overseer. In general, the sons of the small planters were best fitted for the job; those who came from the poorer whites experienced difficulty in maintaining discipline among Negroes.

Under the overseer were foremen, drivers, or gang bosses recruited from the ranks of the more able or influential slaves. Frequently these Negroes enjoyed the power of punishing their fellows and were exempt from ordinary work. The use of Negro foremen was seldom satisfactory, for the drivers were almost as fertile a source of anxiety to the master as were the overseers. Occasionally, a planter tried the experiment of a Negro overseer, but slaves of sufficient tact, energy, and personality were rare.

Instead of this "gang" system, some planters used a "task" system of work. In the former system, the slaves were herded into the fields with drivers to keep them at their duties; in the latter, each slave received a daily "stint" to perform, after which he was free to follow his own desires. Neither system, however, was especially efficient. No matter how their work was organized, the productivity of slaves was far below that of free laborers in northern factories or on northern farms. The Negroes, after all, set their own standards. The "stints" could not be too difficult, for some free time had to be allowed as a reward, and the "gangs" were held back by the slowest member. The urge to work was lacking, for the coercion of the seldom-used whip was less potent than was the threat of dismissal in a northern factory. The capital investment in the Negroes restrained masters from inflicting punishments that would injure the slave as a worker. Frequently, the master threatened to sell the recalcitrant or lazy Negro to some other master or "down the ribber" to some mystic land of harsh treatment. Thus, tobacco slaves were told of the bad conditions in the cotton fields, and cotton slaves, of the terrible life on the sugar plantations. Sometimes these stories inspired the slave to spasmodic bursts of energy. He was taught, too, that the Yankee was a "debbil wit horns," largely to inhibit any latent desire to seek freedom. The ignorant credulity of the slaves was as potent a factor as the overseer's whip in maintaining discipline and productivity on the plantation. It is not surprising that southern laws forbade teaching Negroes to read.

2. CLASSES IN SOUTHERN SOCIETY

The plantation of large size, it should be emphasized, was the exception in the South. Of a total population of 8,000,000 whites in 1860, 2,700 were planters with more than 100 slaves, and fewer than 200,000 owned between 10 and 100 Negroes each. Almost 80,000 whites had but one slave, and 300,000 owned between one and ten slaves each. Almost three fourths of the southern white population possessed no slaves and no immediate economic interest in the maintenance of legal slavery or the plantation system of production. Despite this, the ideal of the plantation set the pattern for southern society; and the planter, through his ownership of wealth, his control of local county government, and the dependence

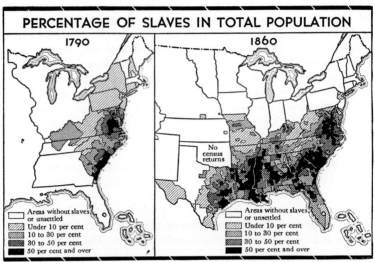

PERCENTAGE OF SLAVES IN TOTAL POPULATION

1790

1860

No census returns

Areas without slaves, or unsettled
Under 10 per cent
10 to 30 per cent
30 to 50 per cent
50 per cent and over

Areas without slaves, or unsettled
Under 10 per cent
10 to 30 per cent
30 to 50 per cent
50 per cent and over

From America's Road to Now, by Charles H. Coleman and Edgar B. Wesley, by permission of D. C. Heath & Co.

of legislators and congressmen upon him, was able to dominate the economic, political, and social life of the section.

Below the planter gentry in the social scale were the lesser plantation owners, the middle-class merchants, and the professional men. More numerous than the great planters, the lesser owners gave a larger portion of their time and acres to general farming and were less dependent upon the great staples for their support. In social outlook, however, they accepted the ideals of the squire tradition, feeling a sense of personal responsibility for the moral and spiritual welfare of their slaves and dependents. They cherished the ambition of becoming masters of many slaves and of many acres, and they voted and thought as did their richer neighbors. Success in business or in the professions was signalized by the purchase of a tract of land and the establishment of a manorial estate. Most of the defenders and exponents of the southern way of life came not from the gentry itself but from the more articulate groups immediately below in the social scale.

Third place in the stratified society of the South was held by the yeoman farmers and the skilled mechanics and smaller tradesmen of the towns. One of the wealthier of this group might own a slave, at whose side he worked in the field, but the majority were too poor to afford such a luxury. In general, the yeomanry of the South resembled the pioneering small farmers who filled up the states of the Northwest. Devoted to democracy, they applauded the doctrines of Thomas Jefferson and voted for Andrew Jackson. They made up the membership of the democratic Methodist, Baptist, and Presbyterian churches and scorned the alleged irreligion of the Episcopalian planters. From the farms of these yeomen came most of the cotton and tobacco and nearly all of the corn, wheat, and oats produced in the South. In the mountain regions, and along the frontiers of settlement, they were primarily herdsmen. Their cattle and swine fed on the open lands, and furnished most of the South's beef and pork. They were, in the last analysis, the backbone of southern society. Their votes determined in the end the attitude of the state and national legislators, and the fact that they usually supported the planters' ideas was a tribute to the ability of the politicians to present the planters' cause in such terms that it appeared to serve the yeomen's interest. They had, essentially, more in common with the squires of the land than with either the heirs of the trustee or the artisan traditions which furnished rationalizations for the industrial order of the North. The more ambitious of them, of course, expected to become planters; but in general they were content to till their fields. They had no especial desire to rise in the social scale and certainly had little thought of overturning the existing economic system.

Perhaps no factor was more potent in keeping these three classes united in support of the southern cause than the ease by which a man might rise from the yeomanry to the ranks of the aristocracy. The planter aristocracy was, so to speak, a democratic caste, for anyone who had sufficient cotton and slaves might be received into the homes and admitted to the social life of the squires themselves. Having acquired wealth, the newcomers, at least in the second generation, could easily enough acquire the manners of polite society. The rise of the family of Jefferson Davis illustrated the course by which a man, especially in the newer regions of the Southwest, might rise into the highest ranks. Sam Davis, the father of Jefferson, was definitely of the yeoman class in his Kentucky home. Joseph Davis, Jefferson's older brother, settled in Mississippi and became the owner of a plantation, where he established his family upon a higher scale. When Jefferson resigned from the army, Joseph set him up as a planter on an adjoining plantation. The two brothers grew in wealth and devoted their leisure to study and to the cultivation of their minds. When Varina Howell, daughter of a neighboring Whig planter and later Jefferson Davis's second wife, visited the Davis brothers, she was surprised to find that they were gentlemen, although both were Democrats and Baptists. Circumstances prevented Jefferson Davis from becoming a Whig as he climbed the social ladder, but he did join the Episcopal Church during the Civil War. In the Tidewater regions of Virginia and in Charleston, the aristocracy was more rigid in its entrance requirements; but in the newer regions of the South the planter class was paradoxically democratic. In the decade before the Civil War, however, a noticeable tendency prevailed everywhere to close the ranks of the highest class.

Not all of the southern whites, however, could be classed in these three groups. Below the yeoman farmer and separated from him by a wide gap were the poor whites, especially numerous in the sandy regions of the low country and in the infertile parts of the Appalachian highlands. Descendants, presumably, of the worst class of colonial indentured servants, these people eked out a miserable existence upon the poorest submarginal lands of the South. Though fishing and hunting supplemented the produce of their fields, malaria, scurvy, and hookworm kept

their physical vitality at a low ebb and deprived them of ambition. Sometimes irreligious, immoral, and even degenerate, they drank poor whiskey
of their own manufacture and chewed tobacco, snuff, or even resin and
clay. Their white neighbors despised them and called them "clay eaters,"
"red necks," "wool hats," or "hill billies." They in turn regarded the Negroes
with an enmity which they did not dare show their superiors. On the
whole, they were, in the words of Fanny Kemble, "the most degraded race
of human beings claiming an Anglo-Saxon origin" that could be found on
the face of the earth.

Occupying a still lower rung in the social ladder were the free
Negroes. With only the rarest exception, these people were slaves who had
been freed (or were descendants of slaves who had been freed) through
humanitarian zeal or as a result of some meritorious effort. Many of course
were merely "ownerless" whose former masters had wandered away or
who cared so little for them that they had, in substance, abandoned them.
Planters ofttimes gave their more energetic servants the opportunity to
accumulate enough property to purchase their freedom. Other planters
manumitted their slaves by wills. The number of free Negro women in
Charleston and New Orleans bore testimony to one reason for manumission. Presumably those servants who stood closest to the white owners
were most likely to obtain their freedom as the result of benevolence or
sentiment. Yet the implication that the free Negroes were the best of their
race was not borne out by the lowly position which they were forced to
occupy.

In 1860, more than a quarter of a million free Negroes were present
in the South, almost 200,000 of them residing in the states of Maryland,
Virginia, and North Carolina. Within their ranks were great variations in
social, economic, and cultural achievement. A few Negroes were slaveholders with such possessions that they ranked, in wealth at least, with the
middle-class planters. One free Negro held a pew in Charleston's most
aristocratic church. Some claimed ownership only of members of their
families, in order to keep them out of the insecure status of the free person
of color, but others possessed slaves whom they worked as did their white
neighbors. In the cities and towns free blacks were artisans, often carpenters or cabinet makers. Negroes served also as schoolteachers who
taught the children of the whites, or as preachers of piety and zeal who
ministered to their fellows in slavery with the full approval of the lords of
the manors. They had established huge churches in Washington and New
Orleans. In 1860, free Negroes owned property which, altogether, had
a value of $25,000,000.

But the great majority of the black people outside of slavery were
the degraded and often degenerate victims of a society that found no place
for them. They were essentially dangerous to the planters who dominated
the South. The slaveowner distrusted them and hesitated to hire them for
agricultural work lest they corrupt his slaves with notions of freedom.
Living outside the plantation system, they were not amenable to the discipline of the master and his overseer. Deprived of economic opportunity,
they drifted into petty crime and vice in order to maintain their unhappy

existence. In lieu of the discipline of the plantation, they were subjected to the discipline of the law. Most states required them to register with the county courts, to carry certificates of freedom, and sometimes to wear badges bearing their names and registration numbers. They were compelled to have licenses for peddling, and they could not enter at all certain types of employment. From their numbers came the great majority of the inmates of southern penitentiaries and jails. Their legal status differed little from that of the slave, for though they were technically free and entitled to hold property, they were limited in the protection afforded by the courts. Sometimes they were kidnapped and sold into slavery. Occasionally, in desperation, a freeman voluntarily surrendered his liberty. More frequently the courts remanded a free Negro to slavery as a punishment for crime.

At the bottom of the social structure were the slaves. In 1860 these numbered 3,838,765, and they were owned by approximately 400,000 masters. Among the Negroes there were definite grades—based upon racial origin and individual character and intelligence—ranging from the blackest and least cultured tribes of Africa to those with a more generous sprinkling of white blood. Although the system by which they were brought from their homeland seemed to select those with the weakest imaginations and the strongest physiques, better individuals had opportunities to prove their merit within the bounds of the plantation system. The highest places in the ranks of labor were those of the house servants and personal attendants of the master and his family—such as the coachman, the butler, and the body servant or valet, who were the aristocrats of the slave cabins. The masses of the slaves were field hands, working at the direction of the overseer.

Aside from their labors, the Negroes in slavery had a life of their own. They were deprived by law from contracting marriage and by the plantation system from assuming the responsibilities of a home, and so family ties rested lightly upon them. Hilarious revelry made possible a mental escape from the rigors of plantation labor. The camp meeting and the revival, offering even more acceptable diversions, were frequently the occasion for remarkable outbursts of religious enthusiasm. The plaintive music of the spirituals—adaptations of the music of evangelical sects—heard both at religious meetings and in the cabins, came to constitute the Negro's greatest contribution to culture and America's greatest contribution to musical art. Until the time of the Nat Turner uprising, slaves were usually allowed their own preachers and meetings. Thereafter, separate gatherings were forbidden, and the slave attended his master's church. There, seated in the gallery, he was likely to hear a pastoral exhortation from the text "Servants, obey your masters."

The religion of the slave played a part in the control which the master exercised. The planter also had other methods. He could use kindness, and he employed it more often and more effectively than he did punishment. He strove to balance a patriarchal benevolence with a strict justice. For petty offenses he might wield the whip or lay on some milder form of chastisement, so as to keep the slave in the path of right conduct and prevent the overcrowding of jails and expenses to the tax-payer. In more serious matters, however, the law came to the aid of the master. Designed primarily to protect the master's property rights in his slave and secondarily to protect society from insurrection, the law for-bade Negroes to wander from their homes or to bear arms. Theft, arson, assault, rape, and conspiracy were punished with the greatest severity. The roads of many southern states were regularly patrolled by the planters in order to apprehend runaways and to prevent gatherings which might lead to revolutions. Lynching occasionally punished the Negroes' more heinous crimes against society. But it was the disciplined control which the master could exercise on his plantation that maintained the social stability of which defenders of the South were so proud.

In comparison with the wage laborer of a northern factory, the slave was in many ways well off. He was cared for in sickness, in child-hood, and in old age. Yet he had grievances. He was always regarded with suspicion and frequently punished for crimes that he did not commit. He was powerless to resist the brutality of a cruel master or a bestial overseer. His only recourse was to flee. Runaways were frequent enough, though not nearly so common as polemical writers, both southern and northern, gave the public to believe. Often the fugitive slave was a fugitive from labor rather than from mistreatment, and returned to his master's plantation when the cotton-picking season was over.

Socially considered, there were serious defects in the plantation system and in chattel slavery. The abolitionists contended, though they did not prove, that the holding of men in bondage brutalized the masters. Certainly, the system did create a gap in society that had a tendency to make white men less receptive to the teachings of democracy. The most serious shortcoming of the system, however, was its failure to educate the Negro in anything beyond the merest rudiments of agri-culture. When freedom came, neither white men nor black men were prepared for the responsibilities of a free and democratic society.

3. Southern Economics

Whatever the social weaknesses of slavery, its opponents also brought economic arguments against it. Slave labor was unprofitable to the owners, they charged, because it deprived workers of the benefi-cent motive of personal gain and it encouraged slipshod work. It re-stricted southern economic endeavor to the simplest level, they said, because slaves were incapable of mastering more complex processes. Cassius M. Clay of Kentucky, an emancipationist who became Lincoln's Minister to Russia, was one who made a persistent economic attack upon slavery. It contributed to the depressed land values in the South, he declared, and it worked an economic hardship upon the white mechanics of the South. "We are *provincial*, an agricultural people, with-out division of labor and without capital, and must remain so while slavery lasts," he complained. "Slavery is destructive of mechanical excellence. The free states build ships and steam cars for the nations of the world; the slave states import the handles for their axes." Years before Hinton R. Helper of North Carolina was to make use of such materials, Clay used census statistics as evidence of the economic blight of slavery.

Despite these arguments, the slave system persisted and expanded because it was economically profitable both to the individual masters and to the community. Of course, not all slaveowners remained solvent, but usually the failures indicated a lack of managerial skill or the unpredictable fates of planting rather than any fundamental difficulty with slavery. The "peculiar institution" was innocent of many of the economic charges which abolitionists brought against it. Slavery contributed to, but was not primarily responsible for the alleged decline in fertility of the South's farm lands, nor of their reduced values. It did not materially prevent the adoption of improved methods of tillage, for what agricultural experiments were made were the work of slave-owning planters. Nor did the presence of slaves shackle a one-crop system upon southern plantations. Slavery did not in itself preclude either industrialization or the diversification of labor. Many masters successfully utilized slave labor in factories, mills, printing shops, and as skilled artisans such as carpenters and smiths. If industrialization was not generally accepted in the southern regions it was more the result of the prevailing traditions of the squires and of the yeomen than of any inherent shortcomings in the labor supply.

Indeed, the exploitation of slave labor held economic advantages over hired labor. In general, it was cheaper to buy the slave's labor for a lifetime than it was to hire free labor for wages. The maintenance costs for a slave remained constant at about $35.00 per year, and his total cost amortized over an average work-life was less than the value he added in production. Bookkeeping profits from slavery were debatable depending upon the manner in which cost items were entered into account, but there was evidence that slave labor was more economical than free labor. In addition, slave labor was more certain, and there were no strikes for higher wages or a better contract. Too, the slave-owner could utilize the labor of women and children, and he could exact a longer work-day.

But the question of dollars-and-cents profits from slavery ignored the basic difference between slave and free labor. The slave was both capital and labor. He represented capital investment from which interest could be drawn, while the cost of his labor was bound up in the capital investment itself. He represented stored, readily-available labor in whatever quantities were required. Slavery did not freeze southern capital to prevent investments in other things such as factories or tools, therefore; slavery was capital itself. Slaves provided the basis of southern credit, and were the principal capital instruments in the South. A Negro was fluid capital, readily negotiable. No investment was more secure than that made in slave property. Instead of depreciating, as did other forms of capital, slave values appreciated. The prices of prime field hands increased steadily to a peak at 1860. At the same time the number of slaves grew by natural increase. Therefore the owner enjoyed a double gain on his investment. As a pool of capital and as a source of credit, slavery was a form of capitalism with which finance capital could not readily compete. The resulting conflict between "money-in-the-bank" capitalism and "labor-in-the-bank" capitalism contributed to civil war.

Throughout the South slave labor was basic to the economic system, but it was not the only labor used. Free labor competed with slaves, especially in the towns and in the trades. Whatever the social status of the individual, however, the people were primarily concerned with the production of staple crops—tobacco, rice, sugar cane, and cotton. From these crops sprang the social and economic organization of the section.

The culture of tobacco, perfected in the colonial period, varied little throughout the decades before the Civil War. Because of the constant and somewhat skilled care necessary to produce the crop, the tobacco regions never developed the plantation system. An acre of tobacco required the full-time labor of one worker, and the gang system so much in vogue in the cotton and cane fields could not be efficiently used. The small farm with a few slaves was the most economical unit.

At the close of the colonial period, tobacco was the most valuable of the southern crops. After the turn of the century, however, this supremacy was challenged by the rising cotton culture. The War of 1812, with its disastrous effects on American commerce, cost the South its markets, and Europeans drew their supplies from Cuba and Latin America. Until 1840 the area of tobacco cultivation and the size of the annual crop remained about the same as they had been at the beginning of the century. New methods of curing tobacco and the introduction of the lemon-colored leaf in 1852 aided the tobacco planters to regain some of their markets. From 1850 to 1860, tobacco production increased 115 per cent. In the latter year the crop totaled 434,000,000 pounds.

The area of tobacco production was limited to the regions where the growing season was short. Only Maryland, Virginia, Kentucky, and parts of North Carolina and east Tennessee possessed a suitable climate.

Geographical conditions also limited the area of rice culture. At first rice was grown only on the swamplands of the Carolinas and Georgia, but after the Civil War, planters opened up new fields in Louisiana and Arkansas. Before the end of the colonial period, growers began to use irrigation, and during the first half of the nineteenth century they made a number of improvements, notably the introduction of the "golden seed." Confined mainly to regions where there were abnormal hazards of malaria, storms, and hurricanes, rice culture was declining some time before the Civil War. As in the case of tobacco, the nature of the crop determined the unit of production. Just as tobacco was not profitable when grown on a large scale, so rice was not profitable when grown on a small scale, for its efficient production required the use of many slaves.

Sugar cane resembled rice in its requirement of large investments and many laborers, and climatic considerations limited sugar production to a small, semitropical area along the Gulf Coast. Most complicated of the southern crops, sugar demanded both an agricultural and a manufacturing technique. Cane fields were planted with stalks which, when covered with soil, sprouted at the joints. Constant cultivation was necessary until the threat of frost ended this phase of the operations. The cane was then cut, stripped of its leaves, and carried to a mill, where the succulent juice was pressed out. Boiling was then necessary to reduce the juice to crude sugar or the far-famed New Orleans molasses. The investment in land, slaves, and machinery for sugar production was so large that small units could not exist.

In contrast with tobacco, rice, and sugar cane, cotton production was practically unlimited in the warm lands of the South. Profitable on any scale of production, cotton growing required a minimum of expert care. In spring the seed was sown in rows, and the plants were thinned when they began to grow. Throughout the long, dry summer months, from North Carolina to the Texas plains, gangs of Negroes hoed the growing crops. Late in August or September, the fleecy bolls began to burst, and the slaves went into the fields to pick the cotton. The number of acres which any planter could plant was limited by the number of Negroes he could muster for picking. Picking machines were never developed; because the bolls did not all ripen at the same time, they were impracticable. Ginning and pressing the cotton into bales completed the process.

The baled cotton was taken, invariably, down the most convenient rivers to the markets at Charleston, Savannah, Mobile, or New Orleans. There it was stored to await shipment to the mills of old or New England. At this stage in production, if not before, the cotton passed out of the hands of the planter and into those of the commission merchant. Small farmers in the southern upcountry, who could not afford to hold on to their cotton, or who had no means of getting it to the ports, sold their crop, usually before it was harvested, to local merchants or to larger planters. But even the local merchant consigned his cotton to the commission merchant, who customarily charged 2.5 per cent for his services. Upon his account with this factor the planter might draw drafts. Frequently he overdrew his account, and the factor became his banker, receiving from 8 to 12 per cent interest for the advances that he made. In this manner the planter was kept in debt to the large merchant in much the same fashion that the pre-Revolutionary Virginia planter had been indebted to the English commission house. The price of cotton, all too frequently, was set by the commission merchant. Small wonder that the cotton planter regarded commerce and banking with suspicion and, in words that smacked of Thomas Jefferson, asserted the moral superiority of agricultural production.

In addition to the staples, the South produced large amounts of other crops. The ideal plantation was a self-sufficing economic unit, and most planters made a conscientious effort to produce the foodstuffs needed by their family and their dependents. Both planters and slaves kept gardens. The smaller farmers devoted but a minor portion of their time to the staple crops. Indeed, in 1850, the South produced half the corn crop of the nation and a large part of the wheat, oats, barley, and rye. In many areas of the South farmers raised fruits and vegetables, mostly apples and sweet potatoes; in Virginia and North Carolina, pea-nuts; in central Kentucky, hemp as well as tobacco; in the Blue Grass region, livestock; in the mountains of Virginia, Kentucky, North Carolina, and Tennessee, hogs and mules for the ready market in the plantation areas; and in east Tennessee (the "hog and hominy" section of the South), corn and pork. The South as a whole had a greater per capita produc-tion of corn and hogs than did the North, but the demand for these items of the slave's menu was so large that the South annually imported much that it used. In most of the ordinary farm crops the poorer lands of the South were unable to compete successfully with the fertile fields of the West. People who inhabited the less fertile lands turned to other pursuits. In the sand hills of North Carolina, where only the pine tree grew readily, the natives turned to naval stores and extracted turpentine, tar, and pitch from the forests along the Weldon-Wilmington railway, and up the Tar and Neuse Rivers.

The system of labor and the nature of the crops produced in the South inevitably led to an exhaustion of the soil. With land cheaper than labor, the Southerner invested in slaves and ignored the care of his fields. The planter put in the same crops year after year and abandoned the depleted sections to the poor whites while he took his slaves to the fresh soils of the Southwest. For this reason, the population of the Tide-water and the Piedmont sections declined both in numbers and quality. The leadership that had once been found in Virginia passed to Missis-sippi, Alabama, and Georgia, and the lands which had once grown rice and tobacco were given over to scrub pines and the miserable clearings of the poor whites.

4. REFORM MOVEMENTS

Realizing the evil effects of this tendency, the more intelligent planters urged a reform in the system. In Virginia Edmund Ruffin and John Taylor, in South Carolina James H. Hammond, and in Mississippi Dr. Martin W. Philips joined with the farsighted in other states in urg-ing agricultural reform. Ruffin, the exponent of the use of lime as a fertilizer, devoted the pages of his *Farmer's Register* to teaching the lessons of scientific farming. Others urged improvements in the breeds of cattle and in the strains of cotton. Thanks to Ruffin's work, agricul-tural societies were founded in several states and the general newspapers gave increasing attention to the necessity of soil improvement. The total effect was negligible, but Maryland and Virginia witnessed a revival of agriculture, and truck farming developed in the region around Norfolk. For the most part, the Southerner showed the same conservatism about adopting new agricultural methods that he showed in other aspects of social and political life.

A movement for the introduction of industry in the South paralleled the movement for agricultural reform. Conscious of their industrial inferiority, and showing a growing tendency to resent their economic dependence on the North, Southerners talked much of the development of southern factories. There had been such talk in the period of the War of 1812, and it had accounted in part for Calhoun's support of the tariff of 1816. But, since then, cotton had absorbed the energies of the Southerners. Within a decade after the war, they were opposing tariffs even to the point of nullification.

The idea that the South might become industrialized, however, had never been abandoned. Cotton manufacturing ought to have prospered in the South, for the poor whites constituted a potential labor force, and water power was readily available. Yet the population was widely scattered because of the plantation system, and the influential factors in southern towns threw their weight against economic diversification. English influences, too, were in favor of a staple-crop economy for the South.

Only a few southern leaders were willing to encourage manufacturing at home. In 1827 the Georgians and the Georgia legislature considered proposals to encourage industries, and within the next few years several yarn factories began operation. In 1840 the low price of cotton along the seaboard induced some planters to consider working their slaves in factories. A leading propagandist for cotton mills was William Gregg, a South Carolina merchant. In numerous articles for southern periodicals he combated the prevalent idea that manufacturing could not prosper in the South. He dismissed the experiences of several unsuccessful undertakings as due to poor planning or bad management. In the end, he convinced a number of Charleston capitalists to experiment again.

In 1846, at Graniteville, Gregg began construction of a cotton mill which was to make sheetings and other heavy cloths. The mill housed 9,000 spindles and 300 looms, and its operatives were whites drawn from the surrounding region. Following Gregg's example other mills were erected at Columbia, Charleston, New Orleans, Mobile, Petersburg, Richmond, Augusta, Columbus, Huntsville, and Florence. Georgia, having in 1840 exempted new factories from taxation, was soon leading the South in cotton manufacturing. Before 1860 several states boasted cotton mills, Richmond had flour mills, and rudimentary iron works dotted the Appalachian highlands. Profits from some of these industries were enormous, and yet the conservatism of the Southerners prevented any rapid shift of capital into industrial enterprises.

Thoughtful Southerners continued to resent their dependence upon northern industry and credit facilities. Yankee ships carried the products of southern farms to New England mills, and Yankee merchants sold the finished goods back to the South. Thomas P. Kettell in his *Southern Wealth and Northern Profits* showed with an array of impressive, if inaccurate, figures that the North took out of the South an annual profit of $232,500,000. Southern journalists and politicians used his account to secure sectional unity against the northern states. Robert Barnwell Rhett, for one, proclaimed: "The South is . . . the very best colony to the North any people ever possessed."

In order to free the section from its economic bondage, southern extremists proposed that the people should boycott northern goods and that the states should impose a heavy tax on northern products in southern markets. Half of the New England population, said the governor of Alabama in 1856, would be paupers if the South stopped its trade. Southern commercial conventions, meeting frequently during the 'forties and 'fifties, sponsored proposals for southern economic independence. One such proposal would have established southern steamship lines for direct trade with Europe. Forty million dollars, estimated Thomas P. Kettell, was paid in annual tribute to northern shippers. Before the Civil War, a few lines of sailing packets were established between southern and European ports, but northern steamship lines developed rapidly and continued to carry the southern crops to market.

A second plan of those who would have broken southern dependence on the North was for a system of southern railroads which would link the coast with the cotton lands of the interior and even

U. S. Travel Bureau

THE ATLANTIC LOCOMOTIVE, BUILT FOR THE BALTIMORE & OHIO RAILROAD IN 1832. Southern merchants and community leaders were avid railroad planners in the period before the Panic of 1837. In the 'forties and 'fifties, though beset by financial problems and the opposition of men in the river cities of New Orleans and Memphis, southerners continued to draft plans for railroads to link the coast with the cotton lands in the interior. Southern railroad schemes were more ambitious in scope than was general in the North. Promoters envisioned long, interstate lines connecting Richmond, Charleston, and Mobile to the Tennessee and Mississippi Rivers, and looked to the establishment of an all-southern transcontinental railroad—a dream that had far-reaching significance in the politics of the 'fifties.

stretch westward to tap the wealth of the new territories acquired by the Mexican War. The achievements in railroad building far surpassed those in shipbuilding, though at the end of the period the North's railroad mileage was much greater. A railroad line running from Richmond to Chattanooga and connecting there with lines that tapped South Carolina on the one side and Tennessee on the other was the most important single system. The Mobile and Ohio Railroad, paralleling the Mississippi River, joined the Gulf Coast and the Middle West at Chicago. An east-and-west line connected Vicksburg and Montgomery. These through routes, combined with smaller lines, gave the South over 10,000 miles of railroad in 1860. But uppermost in the minds of the Southerners was the hope of an all-Southern transcontinental railroad—a dream that had far-reaching significance in the politics of the 'fifties.

After 1852 the southern commercial conventions, which sponsored these projects for sectional independence, met annually and mingled political debate with glowing plans for economic renaissance. Politicians came into the meetings of these businessmen, planters, and journalists to urge a united southern front against northern political aggression, and orators of provincialism proclaimed the necessity of cultural and commercial unity. As time went on, the gatherings lost their commercial character and became annual forums for the more extreme fire-eating opinions. In this final stage, the commercial conventions launched a movement for the reopening of the African slave trade.

Looming large in abolitionist writings and attracting the attention of publicists, both before and since the Civil War, the domestic slave trade has been accorded a greater importance than it actually bore in southern economics. The legal closing of the African trade in 1808 increased the importance of the interstate traffic in laborers. Throughout the period from 1808 to 1860, so much smuggling occurred that the number of Negroes illegally imported into the country perhaps totaled as many as 270,000. But the labor needs of the expanding cotton and sugar fields were supplied chiefly from the border slave states. As Maryland and Virginia soil deteriorated, the planters of the Tidewater and the farmers of the Piedmont turned to breeding slaves for the southern market. Established companies carried on the trading business and maintained their own auction houses, slave pens, and coastwise sailing vessels. Among the larger and more famous firms were those of Armfield and Franklin at Alexandria, Clark and Grubb at Atlanta, and Thomas Foster at New Orleans. Such companies usually maintained two depots: one in the East and the other in the Southwest. Individuals, too, went into business as slave traders and drove gangs of Negroes purchased in the upper South into the cotton regions. Some dealers gave the impression of being planters, bringing in gangs to work temporarily on their plantations while they awaited prospective buyers. Virginia exported 10,000 blacks a year in the interstate traffic.

The total annual turnover of slaves was possibly as great as seventy thousand. Masters sold those slaves who were the least amenable to discipline, the lazy or the rebellious being the first to go. Dealers, of course, preferred healthy chattels of meek demeanor. Mulatto men, being most likely to resent their lot, were less valuable than were pure-blooded Africans, but mulatto women—prized as "fancy girls"—were more expensive than their darker-skinned sisters. The prices of Negroes varied directly in proportion to the price of cotton. When cotton was high, slaves were much in demand; when cotton declined, slaves found a less ready market and masters culled the least desirable from their gangs. In 1837, cotton sold for thirteen cents, and field hands fresh from Virginia brought as much as $1,100. In 1845, cotton was selling for five cents a pound and slaves for $500. After the Walker Tariff, the rise in prices and the general prosperity of the country caused a rapid increase in slave values, and as late as 1859 field hands sold at $1,600 and $1,700.

Despite the fact that the slave trade was essential to the economic life of the South, the slave trader suffered a social ostracism that ill fitted his importance in the southern scheme. The poor character of the men engaged in this business was both a cause and a result of the social disapprobation with which they were regarded. One Alabaman described the slavemonger as "a coarse, ill-bred person, provincial in speech and manner, with a cross-looking phiz, a whiskey-tinctured nose, cold, hard-looking eyes, a dirty, tobacco-stained mouth, and shabby dress." Although he separated families, he suffered no pangs of conscience, declared this writer. Perhaps part, at least, of the condemnation of the slave dealer was due to the fact that he was a convenient scapegoat upon whom society imposed its own horror at the ugliest feature of the southern system.

The high prices of slaves had unfortunate effects upon southern society. Nothing had been more important in keeping the South a unit than the opportunity afforded by cheap land and available labor for ambitious overseers and yeoman farmers to enter the ranks of the planter aristocrats. The rise of slave prices and the exclusion of the slaveholders' property from the territories reacted to produce a stratified and static society. Realizing that slaves must be within the reach of all, the southern commercial conventions and the more rabid fire eaters proposed reopening of the foreign slave trade. Such a development would bring new lands into cultivation, obtain the support of the yeomen farmers, and, by increasing the number of slaves, aid in preventing the poor whites from an attempt to overthrow the existing regime. Just on the verge of the Civil War, William L. Yancey and J. D. B. DeBow, fire eater and economist, respectively, formed the African Labor Supply Association to agitate for reopening the foreign trade. The movement received the unqualified endorsement of the Vicksburg meeting of the Southern Commercial Convention.

CHAPTER 14

Southern Life

1. City and Country: A Contrast

THE plantation system ruled the South, but not all the South was plantation. Far more typical of the countryside, in fact, were the numerous small farms, where there were few slaves or none, and where not only cotton but also wheat and beef and pork were produced. For the plantations and farms, villages and towns served as commercial and cultural centers. Capitals like Richmond, Columbia, and Nashville ambitiously hoped to develop into industrial metropolises, and river ports like Louisville and Memphis were growing into thriving cities. Two seaports, Charleston and New Orleans, combined the culture of the South with just enough of the flavor of Europe to produce a distinctive civilization. No visitor from the North or from the old world carried away a complete picture of the southern way of life who had not seen and marveled at these urban communities.

Charleston—located precisely "where the Ashley and the Cooper Rivers mingled their mighty waters to form the Atlantic Ocean"— was a place of only 40,000 people. Although small in comparison with Northern cities, its unique characteristics gave it a distinction out of proportion to its size. At the tip of the peninsula was Battery Park, overlooking an excellent harbor which was guarded by the never-finished Fort Sumter. Hereabout, the planters of the rice region built their homes—great wooden mansions set with sides to the street and facing luxuriant gardens, walled off from curious eyes, where grew exotic plants, vines, shrubs, and the romantic magnolia tree. Ships from every nation crowded the harbor, unloading bananas, coconuts, coffee, and manufactures from old and New England in exchange for the bales of cotton and bags of rice piled high on the wharves.

The origins of Charleston society were diverse. To the original planters from Barbados, the years had added some Huguenots, royal officials, and factors of English commission houses. When slaves of Santo Domingo mistook the egalitarian slogans of the French Revolution as entitling them to freedom, white refugees from the island fled to Charleston. The City Council and private charity cared for them until they found places for themselves in the city. Some became cooks, bakers, and dressmakers; others, merchants and doctors; still others, talented painters and musicians. Many soon acquired new plantations, but they retained from their experiences in Santo Domingo a deep-seated suspicion of their slaves.

During half the year or more, from May to November, when the Carolina lowlands were flooded for growing rice, the planters spent most of the time at their Charleston homes. They remained in the country during the fall, until after Christmas; and then took their families back to the city before the end of January, in time for the St. Cecilia and the Jockey Club balls. In January they also had to make an annual settling of accounts with their factors, before they and their wives and sons and daughters settled down, in February, to a gala season of races, dinners, and elaborate balls.

For those who had a taste for them, other diversions were available. The great families worshiped in St. Michaels or St. Philip's churches; and lesser men, Methodists and Baptists, attended church in edifices of almost equal distinction. A literary circle comprised some of the state's ablest men. The public library, one of the oldest in the nation, housed collections of some importance, and the Apprentice Library, designed for mechanics and tradesmen, offered wide reading facilities. In the room above this library, Charlestonians might hear lectures by eminent scholars or see exhibitions of paintings and sculpture. The city possessed a theater which attracted able thespians from colonial days to the Civil War. Here Jenny Lind sang; here Fanny Essler danced; here even grand opera companies performed for the elite.

Charleston's Negroes—house servants and dock hands, workers in from the rice swamps, and sailors, bond or free, from the ships in the harbor—made up a third of the population. In 1822, a Negro insurrection, nipped in the bud, led to the enactment of strict laws and ordinances, for the Charleston slaveholder kept Santo Domingo ever in mind. Negroes might not appear on the streets after sundown, and those who had gone North might not return to the city. Since free Negro sailors could help fugitive slaves, able seamen were relegated to the city's jails while their ships were in port.

City life had a bad effect on both the morals and the religion of the Negroes. The law forbade teaching them to read and deprived them of religious leaders of their own race. This void was filled only in part by the missionary activities of such white men as Bishop William Capers. Son of a low-country planter, Capers became a Methodist minister and devoted much of his life to mission work among the Negroes of Charleston and the adjacent rice fields. With the support of the planters, he built over fifty churches along the seaboard and enrolled perhaps 30,000 colored people in his flock. But his work was not enough to elevate all the blacks.

Unlike Charleston—unlike anything on the American continent, in fact—was New Orleans, lying in a crescent-shaped bend more than a hundred miles above the mouth of the Mississippi. French engineers had originally designed the city, with streets uniformly forty feet wide and crossing each other at right angles. In early days it had been surrounded by a palisade with guarded gates that were closed at night. In the center of the town was a park faced by the Cabildo, the Cathedral, and the Ursuline Convent. American occupation and immigration had broadened the city's area, torn down the enclosing walls, and varied the architecture, without submerging the original French pattern of life. By 1860 New Orleans, fifth city in the nation, had a population of 168,675.

The street level of the Crescent City was lower than the Mississippi. Levees kept most of the river water out, but the unpaved streets were always muddy and drainage and sanitation were bad. The houses, built in solid front along the street, enclosed courts filled with flowers and shrubs. Balconies with elaborate iron grilles hung over the streets. The shuttered windows were protected with iron bars. Most of the buildings were of brick, covered with stucco, but some were of wood and adobe.

The port of New Orleans was the gateway to the Mississippi Valley. Through it passed the largest tonnage of any port in the land. Even in 1802 it had handled exports to the value of two million and imports worth two and a half million dollars. Down the river came flatboats, bringing the procedure of inland farms and fields. As many as fifteen hundred of these rude craft with their equally rude crews could be seen along the docks at any time. Among them, hundreds of larger, ocean-going vessels loaded from the long wooden platforms along the levees. Cotton from the valleys of the Red and the Arkansas Rivers, molasses and sugar from the Louisiana cane fields, and miscellaneous products from elsewhere were piled high upon the banks. Within the city, the French inhabitants patronized the local markets, where they could buy fresh fruits and vegetables the year around.

The population, resident and transient, was a strange mixture. Frenchmen and Yankees, Creoles and Louisiana planters, English factors and buyers from New England, sailors from the whole world, Negroes, mulattoes, Italians, Portuguese, Germans, and Irish mingled together in the market place and along the waterfront.

Commerce dominated New Orleans. Cosmopolitan in its population, commercial in its outlook, the city wasted but little of its time on cultural things. The opera and an active theater brought some contact with the arts, and the French and Creole inhabitants gave some attention to literature. The city's reputation was greater for entertainment, however, than for culture.

Early New Orleans also gained a reputation for vice. Here sailors sought and found recreation after the manner of their kind. Here rough river boatman fought in the waterfront saloons or in gambling houses fitted to every degree of taste. Here lived seductive quadroons and octa-roons, women of mixed blood but frequently of education and refinement, whom everyone knew to be mistresses of youths of the wealthier classes. On Sundays the whole city was a place of gaiety; shops were open, coffee houses crowded with revelers. In the spring, the festival of Mardi Gras brought streams of visitors to participate in balls, parades, and general merrymaking. Although there was wickedness aplenty in unrestrained New Orleans, puritanical visitors from New England or other parts of the more sedate hinterland saw perhaps more than actually existed.

The Negro population of New Orleans enjoyed a larger degree of freedom than did their fellows in other cities, for the French in-habitants did not share the Anglo-Saxon's aversion to people of color. From the time of its acquisition by the United States, New Orleans had many free Negroes, some of them men of wealth and culture. In 1860 more than 18,000 lived in Louisiana, most of these in the Crescent City. The people enjoyed opportunities for obtaining an education, since an educated Negro did not meet with social disapproval in New Orleans. Few public restrictions were placed even on the slaves of the city dwellers. The slaves made fair use of their opportunities, so that, by the close of the Civil War, more Negroes were ready for the respon-sibilities of freedom in Louisiana than in any other state.

The folkways of the mountain regions and the back country were quite different from the ways of life in the cities or on the great plantations. Journeying in the 1850's through the seaboard slave states and the back country, Frederick Law Olmsted observed southern life with as much thoughtfulness and fairness as could have been expected from a New Englander so far from home. He lodged in plantation mansions, in frontier cabins, in homes of overseers, and everywhere questioned his hosts and recorded their observations on the problems of their society.

In western North Carolina Olmsted spent one night with a family who worked a thousand acres of rich farm land and owned two other farms, an extensive cattle pasture, and a grist mill. The head of the family, his wife, one son, and several daughters, all lived together in a one-room cabin, though they cooked their meals and ate in a near-by kitchen hut. These people were good-natured and intelligent, but none of them could read. They grew no cotton, and their chief marketable crop was cattle. They, like most of their neighbors, who held few slaves, were pretty much opposed to slavery.

In east Tennessee, Olmsted discovered another area where there were few slaves or Negroes of any kind. In one slaveholder's home, the Yankee visitor was disgusted by dirt and squalor, poor food, and bad cooking, and women who were negligent and slovenly in their attire. In the same neighborhood he was pleased to find a poorer family of nonslaveholders who were neat, orderly, and pious, their food abundant, well-cooked, and tasty. The members of this family worked together on their acres. They disliked slavery, but their fear of Negro barbarity made them abhor abolitionists. In middle Tennessee, Olmsted stayed overnight with another well-to-do slaveholder who not only had considerable holdings of land but money invested in banks, railroads, and mines. His large white house was surrounded by Negro shanties. His family and guests ate in the cook cabin, where his daughters prepared the meal. He showed the visitor to the common bedroom equipped with four large bedsteads, each with a straw mattress.

In Mississippi, the inquisitive Yankee found mingled ignorance and crudity. In one single-roomed cabin the furniture consisted only of two bedsteads, three chairs with deerskin seats, a packing case used as a bureau, and a Connecticut clock. A crying baby lay on the floor. The mother sat tilted back in her chair while a little girl fried slices of fat pork and warmed up cornbread and coffee before the open fireplace. After supper the mother nursed the baby and the girl piled dirty quilts on the floor, dropped off her shoes, and retired. The mother then threw off her single piece of clothing and went to bed. The father, before retiring, merely removed his shoes. Next morning while the family ate breakfast—consisting of the same warmed-over bacon, cornpone, and coffee—rain leaked in through the roof, put out the fire, and dripped upon the table.

Throughout northern Mississippi, Olmsted found much poverty among a friendly but ignorant people. In the central part of the state he spent a day with an overseer of a plantation, several square miles in extent, with about 1,400 acres under cultivation. Among the 135 slaves were mechanics, seamstresses, cooks, a hogtender, a cattle tender, a teamster, a housekeeper, and a nurse. The field forces were organized under Negro foremen. The hoe gang for the cotton field was made up mostly of women and children, though there was a nursery to care for the smallest of the young ones. Except on Saturday and Sunday, the Negroes worked from daylight to dark. At nine o'clock, curfew was sounded upon a horn, and at ten an inspector checked up on all of the slaves. Each Negro received a weekly ration of a peck of corn and four pounds of pork, had his own garden, gathered his firewood from the swamp, and received about ten dollars at Christmas. The great house of the estate was closed. The overseer lived with his family in a cluttered and illkept cabin, hardly better than the cabins of the slaves.

In general, Olmsted's observations of southern country life would have applied to most parts of rural America. The farms of the upper Mississippi Valley would have shown the same general characteristics that the Yankee traveler saw in the South. Charleston and New Orleans were distinctive, but only slavery made variations in the pattern of American rural life.

2. Churches and Schools

Not only in southern politics and economics, but in every phase of southern life, the interests of the plantation system and the planters were predominant. In religion and education the southern people were as much subjected to the ideas of the dominant groups as they were in government.

The religious development of the United States before the Civil War reflected the changes in society. In the North there was a breaking down of the rigors of Puritanism and a rise of movements such as Unitarianism, which destroyed the hold of the traditional Calvinist philosophy on the minds of the people. In the 'fifties, the slow acceptance of the Darwinian theory precipitated a conflict between fundamentalists and modernists. In the South, on the other hand, the tendencies in religion were in the opposite direction. Instead of keeping pace with the ecclesiastical changes which characterized the North, the South became a land of religious conservatism. Deists like Washington and Jefferson disappeared, their places being taken by those who would interpret the Word in support of the southern system.

In the early national period, the frontier churches—Methodist, Baptist, and Presbyterian—reflected the economic outlook of their communicants, and preachers seldom hesitated to denounce slavery. Presbyterian evangelists condemned the institution, and Methodist conferences in the frontier regions went so far as to forbid their ministers to hold slaves. A profound change was wrought in the attitudes of these bodies, however, as their members became wealthier and rose into the ranks of the slaveholders. The churches ceased officially to oppose slavery. In Virginia, the Presbyterians criticized an "atheistic" professor of the University—Jefferson's shrine to freedom of thought—and compelled him to resign. In Kentucky, the Presbyterians drove the Unitarian Horace Holley from the presidency of Transylvania University and wrecked the school in the process. In South Carolina, the outraged fundamentalists forced President Cooper to resign the headship of the State College because he questioned the inspiration of the Pentateuch. There was, in a slaveholding society, little room for religious dissent.

As members grew wealthy and even clergymen acquired slaves, the churches began to contribute theological chapters to the proslavery argument. Pulpits became forums for expounding the Biblical justification of keeping one's fellow men in bondage. The divergence between the churches of the North and those of the South was both a cause and a result of the widening rift in politics. Yet, the evangelical congregations of the South remained similar to their northern counterparts in one respect. For both, the emotional revival was an annual event. In summer the camp meeting, remarkable for its frenzied excesses, had universal popularity. Its orgiastic rites drew the white population of the South into the churches, where ministers, themselves thoroughly identified with the prevailing social order, howled down abolitionists as agents of the devil and praised slavery as a divine institution.

Less potent than religion but equally significant of the prevailing order was southern education. The district school, which had been established in the southern colonies, maintained its existence in the more populous regions of the border states, supported by subscriptions. On the larger plantations the children of the planter and of plantation employees sometimes attended classes taught by a private tutor. But for most of the poorer classes of the rural regions educational opportunities were almost completely lacking. Although schools for the poor existed in the towns, the stigma of charity was attached to them, and few attended. When the movement for free public schools began in the North, faint flickerings of interest arose in the South. In Alabama, William L. Yancey made a futile effort to follow the example of Horace Mann in Massachusetts. In Maryland, the office of state superintendent of schools was established in 1826 but was abolished two years later. In Louisiana and Tennessee, the supervision of schools was a function of the secretary of state.

The experience of Kentucky in creating a public-school system, though different in detail, was typical of the experience of other states in the South. As early as 1798 the legislature granted public land to academies in six counties. Later the grant was extended, until, by 1820, fifty-nine county academies had each received 6,000 acres. Unfortunately, this gesture failed to produce a satisfactory system, and in 1821 the legislature put profits derived from the Bank of Kentucky into a "literary fund" which was to support the common schools without burdening the taxpayer. But this fund was never actually applied to the schools. In 1837 the state received one and a half million from the surplus in the federal treasury and set aside $850,000 for the fund. At this time, half the children of the state had never attended a class, and a third of the population was illiterate. When panic and depression followed the distribution of the surplus, the education program was temporarily halted. Not until 1847, when the Rev. R. J. Breckinridge became superintendent, did the Kentucky system begin to function. In 1849, Breckinridge persuaded a constitutional convention to provide for the support of public schools in the organic law of the state. The following year he induced the legislature to make the educational fund a first charge upon any money in the treasury. Through the 1850's schools flourished. By 1860 each county had one or more, and the literary fund exceeded $2,000,000.

Throughout the South the two decades before the Civil War witnessed the beginnings of an educational renaissance. In 1850 the southern states had 29,041 schools with 21,353 teachers and 583,292 pupils, and were spending $2,734,000 for education. This was a poor showing as compared with the North's 62,450 schools, 70,647 teachers, 2,777,381 pupils, and $6,857,527 annual budget. In 1850 the Southern literacy rate lagged behind the other sections of the country: only 1.89 per cent of New Englanders over twenty years of age were illiterate, while the Northwest had 5.03 per cent and the South 8.27 per cent of the white population.

As in the North, the youth received their secondary instruction, if any, in privately owned institutions. These academies, however, generally received some type of local public support. In curricula they not only offered a practical training in such subjects as mathematics and surveying, but also imparted the rudiments of Latin and Greek in preparing students for colleges. Tennessee and Kentucky granted subsidies for the establishment of an academy in each county. In other states, local subscriptions or occasional taxes supplemented the tuition charges.

Separate "female" academies cared for the education of women. In other private boarding or day schools young ladies of the better classes received rudimentary instruction in the art of writing and in sundry "accomplishments" such as elocution, poetry, painting, and plain and fancy needlework. Piano and singing lessons and a smattering of French—counted as "extra" subjects in the curriculum—rounded out an education more designed for ornament than for practical use. The age-old skills of getting and managing a husband and supervising a household or plantation were too vital to be relegated entirely to the schools. These the women learned in the laboratory of experience, under their mothers' tutelage.

In higher learning, the South compared more favorably with the North. Shortly after the Revolution, several states chartered colleges and gave them some state support. The University of North Carolina, established in 1787, came under complete state control after three decades. In 1785 the University of Georgia received its charter and with it a mandate to supervise all the public schools of the state. In 1798 the Kentucky legislature chartered Transylvania College but left it under the control of the Presbyterian denomination. Hardly had Louisiana come under the American flag when the territorial legislature established the University of New Orleans. With John Marshall's decision in the Dartmouth College Case, the establishment of both private and state colleges was stimulated. In 1819, the year of Marshall's decision, Jefferson secured a charter for the University of Virginia and devoted the remainder of his life to planning its buildings and its program and to selecting its first distinguished faculty. Alabama's first constitution provided for a state university which opened its doors in 1831. Missouri chartered its University in 1839, and Mississippi in 1844.

More important than the state universities were the denominational colleges. Methodists vied with Presbyterians and Baptists in establishing colleges for the training of ministers and the indoctrination of laymen. In 1858, for example, Alabama had twelve sectarian institutions with a total enrollment of 1,450. In the single town of Tuskegee the Methodists, the Baptists, and the Masons each had a college. In 1850, the South boasted 120 colleges and universities with 722 professors and over 12,000 students. Many southern youths went to northern schools. In the North there were 111 institutions of higher learning, with 879 professors and over 15,000 students. The proportion was in favor of the South.

Perhaps southern schools had lower standards than northern ones, and perhaps their curricula were poorer. Certainly the southern communities limited thought on social and economic problems. The church colleges confined themselves to the classics, ancient languages and ancient history, moral philosophy, and theology until the coming of academies, with their wide range of practical subjects, forced the colleges to broaden their offering. The state universities, somewhat less limited by ecclesiasticism, early began courses in law and in technical subjects. In 1799, Transylvania had a law school and a chair of medicine. The

University of Maryland established a law school in 1812, and Virginia opened its law course in 1826. In 1833 the University of Virginia had a series of lectures on civil engineering and mathematics, and three years later offered a full course in the subject. Science and technology were further cared for in special schools. In 1839 Virginia established the Virginia Military Institute, and in 1842 South Carolina set up its military academy. Numerous private schools of law and medicine, mostly short-lived, furnished a rudimentary training to practitioners of these arts.

Although the South had more colleges than the North, the Southern institutions regarded disinterested scholarship with suspicion. From 1835 to 1856 Francis Lieber, a German who produced the first systematic works on political science in America, was professor of history and political economy at South Carolina College. During that time he wrote his *Political Ethics, Legal and Political Hermeneutics,* and *Civil Liberty and Self Government,* and received acclaim from leading thinkers in the North and in Europe. Yet Lieber, finding no intellectual companionship in Columbia, hurried each summer to Boston or New York to mingle with kindred spirits. Genial, witty, and beloved by his northern companions, he was regarded with skepticism by his southern neighbors. Although he was a slaveholder, South Carolinians believed him sympathetic with abolitionism. Within two years after he resigned, John and Joseph Le Conte, sons of a Georgia planter, joined the faculty of South Carolina College. As professors of physics and geology, respectively, they were less suspect than was the German social scientist, but their very worth-while attainments passed comparatively unnoticed. It was not until after the war—and after their migration to the University of California—that they received the recognition that their work deserved.

In the 'fifties, the southern nationalists, who were urging self-sufficiency, made efforts to employ only southern teachers in the colleges and to use only textbooks published in the South. The Southern Commercial Convention, meeting in Savannah in 1856, appointed a committee to prepare a list of books "from the earliest primer to the highest grade of literature and science" suitable for southern schools. The movement resulted in increasing the attendance at southern institutions and in the establishment of professorships of commerce and of agriculture in a number of colleges. It culminated in an ambitious scheme, just at the outbreak of the Civil War, to establish at Sewanee, Tennessee, the "University of the South" under the auspices of the Episcopal Church.

The ambitious plans of this university called for the creation of thirty-two "schools," ranging from Greek language to mining, and including scientific agriculture, banking, insurance, bookkeeping, law, medicine, and theology. Within a few months Bishop Leonidas Polk of Louisiana and Bishop Stephen Elliott of Georgia raised half a million dollars in endowment. "At no time in all the past," declared Bishop Polk in inaugurating the movement, "have we been so threatened with the spread of the wildest opinions in religion and government; and at no period, therefore, has there been so great a call to . . . multiply agencies, whose high conservatism shall furnish us with the means of

CARNEGIE SCIENCE HALL, UNIVERSITY OF THE SOUTH, SEWANNEE, TENNESSEE. In the 'fifties, the southern nationalists, who were urging self-sufficiency, made efforts to employ only southern teachers in the colleges and to use only textbooks published in the South. The movement culminated in an ambitious scheme, just at the outbreak of the Civil War, to establish at Sewanee, Tennessee, the "University of the South" under the auspices of the Episcopal Church. On October 10, 1860, Bishop Leonidas Polk laid the cornerstone of the main building.

making fast the foundations of the State, securing a sound and healthy feeling in the social condition, and preserving . . . our holy religion." On October 10, 1860, Bishop Polk laid the cornerstone of the main building. Within eight months he was major-general in the Confederate army, laboring in another field to preserve the southern tradition.

3. SOUTHERN LITERATURE

In less formal fields of education, the Southerner was circumscribed by the peculiar conditions attendant upon the southern system. The South had but 24 of the 345 publishing houses in the country, and the products of their presses were seldom of a high order of literary merit. In 1850 the South published 721 periodicals of all kinds, religious, agricultural, scientific, and political. The planters gave little support to literary publications, however, and therefore few survived. The *Southern Literary Messenger* was remarkable for both its intrinsic excellence and its ability to survive the neglect which was accorded it.

Southern newspapers, on the other hand, ranked with the best in the country. Political journals of the most intense partisanship were potent forces in promoting southern unity. Such papers as the *United States Telegraph,* edited in Washington by Calhoun's ardent supporter, Duff Green; the Richmond *Whig* and *Enquirer;* the Charleston *Mercury,* edited by Robert Barnwell Rhett; the Columbus *Register;* the *Bee* and the *Picayune* of New Orleans; the Louisville *Journal;* the Nashville *Republican Banner;* and "Parson" Brownlow's *Knoxville Whig* were journals of great importance. However much they might differ as to methods, they were united in their expressions of devotion to the South and the southern way of life.

The Southerner's preoccupation with defenses of his peculiar social and economic order was reflected in his own reading and writing. The educated planter found in a study of the classics an intellectual justification for the slave system. In his perusal of ancient history he learned that the brilliant society of Athens and the power of Rome had been based upon human slavery. The literate Southerner also read the romantic historical novels of Sir Walter Scott and saw in the southern system a modern counterpart of the idealized feudal society of the Middle Ages. So far-reaching was the fad for Scott that the tournament became a regular feature of public gatherings in the South, and the more ardent enthusiasts proclaimed themselves the modern representatives of the knightly ideal of chivalry. Such writers as Dickens, who painted the horrors of the contemporary scene, found no place in the planter's library. When the Southerner read of modern subjects, he preferred constitutional law and elaborations of the doctrines of states' rights. His reading served to impress upon his mind the essential propriety of the southern ideal.

Although the South supported its writers but poorly, a number of them equaled or surpassed the more widely known writers and poets of the North. Conservative in their outlook, the Southerners saw little genius in such northern writers as Walt Whitman, poet of a mystic democracy. Rather, as the sectional lines became more tense, they gave ear only to those who praised the southern system. Such a one was Beverley Tucker, a Virginia romanticist, who followed the doctrines of Calhoun and deplored the leveling effects of Jacksonian democracy. His *The Partisan Leader* portrayed the devastation that was to follow Jackson. Van Buren, in the presidency, would convert the office into a dictatorship. As the story opened, the Red Fox had already been elected for a third term and was plotting a fourth. A bureaucratic crowd of followers held control of the public offices and formed an invincible political machine. But South Carolina and the lower South had seceded, and, freed from democratic tyranny and northern exploitation, were enjoying free trade with England. The moral was obvious. In time, Virginia would be enslaved by northern tariffs: prosperity was only possible if the Old Dominion followed Calhoun's doctrines. Not as a work of art, which it was not, but as a political polemic, Tucker's work had significance. His concept of a North given over to a democratic rabble with abolitionist leanings, mercenary and selfish, fitted well into the developing southern ideology.

Less violent than Tucker was William A. Caruthers, whose *Ken-*

tuckians in New York and *The Cavaliers of Virginia,* surveyed northern
civilization and the system in the deep South. Caruthers' sympathies
were with the democratic elements of the newer West, and he found
virtue in the vigorous spirit of Kentucky and the frontier. Caruthers had
none of Tucker's fear of democracy, though he recognized the difficulties
involved in abolitionism. In the end he concluded that the race relation-
ships of Virginia and Kentucky offered the best solution for the social
problem of the South. But among Southerners this endorsement of democracy found no favor. The works of Caruthers were ignored and his
name forgotten.

More suited to the southern mental climate were the gentle literary flowers that John Pendleton Kennedy planted about the old Virginia plantation. A dabbler in Whig politics, a Henry Clay protectionist, a romantic who believed in the doctrine of progress, Kennedy limned
the Virginia plantation in lines which the South took immediately to
heart. The graceful, placid life, the charming eccentricities of the local
gentry, the simple hospitality of the manor house, made a lovely picture
indeed. In *Swallow Barn,* published in 1832, slavery appeared in its most
attractive garb. The planter-hero believed slavery to be a southern problem, disowned interfering abolitionists, and thought that colonization or
a modified serfdom might mitigate its tolerable evils. In *Quod libet,* Kennedy assailed Jacksonian democracy with satire, voicing again the
planter's fears of the rabble.

Virginia plantations, populated by the high-minded aristocrats
created by Kennedy and Tucker, became standard ideals in southern literature. Standard, too, became literary assaults upon the democratic
masses. A. B. Longstreet's *Georgia Scenes* picturing robust, roistering
frontiersmen were acceptable as implying a contrast between the plantation ideal and democratic crudities. When Longstreet entered the proslavery defense and found Biblical justification for slavery against abolitionist ranters, the South showered rewards upon him. Successively he
was judge, Methodist ecclesiastic, and president of two colleges and of
two state universities.

Rewards came, too, to the prolific William Gilmore Simms. A
drug clerk of lowly origin, Simms battered down the exclusive walls of
Charleston society with his quill pen. Proclaiming aloud his complete
devotion to southern ideals, giving complete verbal adherence to Calhoun's political and social doctrines, Simms' endless stream of novels
were each cast in the prevailing literary form. High life and low life,
noble and commoner, the gentle and the crude passed in succession
through the pages of the contemporary novel. It was a pattern set by Sir
Walter Scott, whose romances so well fitted the southern taste. Simms
knew the lowly, and drew them with a master's hand. His upper classes,
however, appeared stilted, unreal, and vague. Simms saw the frontier
better than any other American writer of his generation, and he wrote of
it with gusto. He wrote honestly, even sympathetically, of rough and
robust men. Unlike those of many southern writers, his books were read,

and his income from them—and his marriage to a planter's daughter—gave him a plantation of his own.

As the slavery controversy took a deeper hold on southern thought, writers who offered supporting arguments for slavery alone were accepted. Such a writer was William J. Grayson, whose *Hireling and Slave*, a long disquisition in heroic couplets, compared the hard lot of the northern wage slave with the happy life of the southern Negro. With its condemnation for abolitionists, disgust for sentimentalists, and suspicion for reformers, Grayson's sociological poetry was mere metric propaganda. Other southern poets, such as Paul Hamilton Hayne, Edward Pinckney, Richard Wilde, and Henry Timrod struck their lyres in praise of the South. Less characteristic of the South—and completely rejected by it—was Edgar Allan Poe, the one indisputable genius of southern letters.

Through the history of southern letters runs the constant complaint that the Southerners gave no support to literature. Simms complained that "the South don't care a damn for Literature or Art" even while he persevered in writing over 100 volumes of poetry and prose. Paul Hayne, editor of *Russell's Magazine*, made futile efforts to attract subscribers and obtain support. Poe died in poverty, his erratic genius unnoticed by southern readers. Perhaps cultural unity might have strengthened the bonds which the political and economic systems were welding. Perhaps more tolerance for genius and less concentration on defense of the peculiar institution would have encouraged a better literature. As it was, southern writers found no support unless they warped their gifts to condemn abolitionism, defend slavery, and idealize the plantations. In literature, as in religion and education, the South was completely under the control of the ruling classes.

The Compromise of 1850

1. The Movement for Southern Unity

BEFORE Taylor came into office to face the problems of a rapidly dividing nation, the Southerners had begun to strike a new note in the constitutional defense of slavery. The occasion came amid debates over a territorial government for recently acquired Oregon. The joint resolution annexing Texas had provided that the Missouri Compromise line should be extended and that Texas might be divided into four or five slave states. Presumably, this re-enactment of the Missouri Compromise implied that the line of 36° 30′ should be extended over all of American territory, and in August, 1846, Stephen A. Douglas, chairman of the House Committee on Territories, proposed that the prohibition of the Northwest Ordinance extend over Oregon.

In the course of ensuing debates, Calhoun perceived an opportunity to make a new pronouncement upon the Constitution and slavery. In June, 1848, the southern champion offered a series of resolutions developing the theory that neither Congress nor a territorial legislature had the right to exclude slavery from a territory. Although neither Calhoun nor his supporters believed that slavery could exist in Oregon, they nevertheless asserted that the territory was common property and open to settlement by the citizens of all states. "If the existence of the Slave as property be admitted," asked Jefferson Davis, "what power has Congress to interfere with it? . . . Entering a territory with his property, the citizen has a right to its protection." Slavery could be excluded only by the citizens of a territory when they formed a state constitution. As for the congressional power to make rules and regulations for the possessions of the United States, Calhoun alleged that this was limited to the regulations of the public lands. As in 1837, Calhoun's theories were based upon the equality of the states and the constitutional recognition of slave property.

In supporting these resolutions, Calhoun pointed out that the free states were antagonizing the slave states. In the Senate, there was momentary equality between the sections, but Iowa and Wisconsin were ready for admission, while twelve more states might be carved out of the existing territory north of the Missouri line. In the House, the equality of the sections had long since been broken, and the North had 138 votes to the South's 90. In the electoral college, the figures were 168 to 118 in favor of the North. Soon there would be enough free states to give the North a two-thirds majority. But speeches and resolutions could no longer hold up the organization of Oregon. On August 14, 1848, President Polk signed the bill with slavery excluded. The majority of the Southerners, like Polk, were unwilling to follow Calhoun and the extremists.

In signing the Oregon bill, Polk expressed his regret that Congress had taken no action on the territory acquired by the Treaty of Guadalupe Hidalgo. In July, 1848, an effort had been made in Congress to solve this problem. Senator Clayton, of Delaware, had headed a special committee which had reported in favor of organizing the territories of Oregon, California, and New Mexico. The question of slavery in the region was to be left out of consideration. Oregon's territorial legislature might deal with slavery, but New Mexico and California were to be given territorial government corresponding to the first stage of the old Northwest plan. Clayton's committee believed that this solution would turn slavery over to the courts, with the result that the Supreme Court, a majority of whose members were from the South, would have the final decision on the question of slavery in the territories. Georgia's Alexander H. Stephens, however, had no hope of a favorable decision from the Court. The Court would hold that the municipal law of Mexico would remain in force in the region. Stephens also denied that the Constitution carried slavery into the territory. The Clayton compromise bill failed of passage, and the question of slavery in the new territory went over to Taylor's administration.

The discussions on Oregon and the Clayton compromise enabled men to formulate their opinions on the issues. At one extreme were the supporters of the Wilmot Proviso, whose position received its best expression in the Buffalo convention of the Free-Soilers. The abolitionist party recognized that slavery within the states depended on state laws, and asserted its willingness to refrain from interference with slavery in the states. But for the territories, "the true and in the judgment of this convention the only safe means of preventing the extension of slavery into territory now free is to prohibit its existence in all such territory by an act of Congress. . . . We accept the issue which the slave power has forced upon us, and to their demand for more slave states and more slave territory, our calm but final answer is no more slave states and no more slave territory. . . . We inscribe on our banner, 'Free Soil, Free Speech, Free Labor and Free Men,' and under it we will fight on, and fight ever, until a triumphant victory shall reward our exertions."

At the opposite pole was the position taken by Calhoun that neither Congress nor a territory could exclude slavery. During the Mexican War, the Virginia House of Delegates denied Congress' authority over slavery and asserted that Virginia would not accept an unconstitutional law which excluded the "peculiar institution." In the Democratic convention of 1848, William L. Yancey declared that noninterference by Congress in the rights of property was the traditional democratic doctrine. Throughout the South, many endorsed these principles.

Between such extremes stood the moderates. Even within the South many conservative slaveholders opposed territorial expansion. Moderates inclined to accept one of two possible solutions. One was the suggestion of such practical politicians as Polk and Buchanan that the Missouri Compromise line be extended to the Pacific. The other suggestion was Lewis Cass's doctrine of popular sovereignty. In a letter to A. O. P. Nicholson, Tennessee's leading democratic editor, just before the campaign of 1848, the Michigan aspirant for the Democratic nomination declared that local institutions should be left to local governments, while the power of Congress should be "limited to the creation of proper governments for new countries, acquired or settled, and to the necessary provisions for their eventual admission into the Union, leaving, in the meantime, to the people inhabiting them, to regulate their internal concerns in their own way. They are just as capable of doing so as the people of the states, and they can do so, at any rate, as soon as their political independence is recognized by admission into the Union." In the Senate, New York's conservative Daniel S. Dickinson submitted a resolution that all questions of domestic policy in the territories should be left to the people when they organized a territorial government.

Neither Zachary Taylor nor his party expressed any opinion on slavery in the territories. To ardent Southerners the silence seemed ominous, and many predicted that the new president would be no friend of the South. He might not even veto a bill with the hated Wilmot Proviso attached! The Southerners watched for a chance to unite in warning the new chief magistrate. The opportunity came when the House of Representatives passed a resolution to prohibit the slave trade in the District of Columbia. Immediately Henry S. Foote of Mississippi and Robert M. T. Hunter of Virginia called a caucus of all southern congressmen to discuss the situation.

To the southern caucus came both Democrats and Whigs: the former to define the rights of the South, the latter to prevent statements that might embarrass their incoming president. Despite Whig efforts, the caucus issued an address to the people of the United States. The address elaborated upon the difficulties which Southerners experienced in recovering fugitive slaves, protested against abolitionist agitation, prophesied that freed Negro voters would unite with Northerners to hold Southern whites in subjection, and demanded protection of the slaveholder's property in the territories. Only slightly more than half of the eighty members who attended the caucus signed the address, yet the movement for southern unity was definitely launched.

Simultaneously with the caucus, Virginia and North Carolina moved to express the southern demands. In North Carolina, Whig dissidents succeeded in getting a declaration of devotion to the Union, but in Virginia the extremists were in control. The resolutions of the legislature declared that the passage of the Wilmot Proviso would leave the people of the state the alternatives of "submission to oppression and outrage" or "determined resistance at all hazards and to the last extremity." The abolition of the slave trade in the District of Columbia would be regarded as a direct assault on the institution.

Other states followed Virginia's lead. The Missouri legislature instructed the state's representatives in Congress to vote against the Proviso. The Tennessee State Central Democratic Committee declared, "the encroachments of our Northern brethren have reached a point where forbearance on our part ceases to be a virtue." During the summer of 1849, the movement came to a head. In October a Mississippi state convention canvassed the situation and invited other states to send delegates to an all-southern convention at Nashville on June 3, 1850. The meeting would define the rights of the South and would recommend united action.

2. President Taylor

While southern arguments and organization proceeded, President-elect Taylor remained silent. For a moment after his inauguration, Southerners breathed easier. His Cabinet contained three Southerners and no representative of his party's abolitionist wing. Only for partisan purposes did Democratic extremists continue to warn that Taylor would accept the Wilmot Proviso if Congress passed it. Confident that Taylor would be under southern influence, southern Whigs remained unperturbed. Not until summer did they take alarm. Then they noted that the New York abolitionist, William H. Seward, had access to the White House. They had expected Millard Fillmore, the "Cotton Whig" vice-president, to control the New York patronage. Suddenly they found that Seward had won the president's favor.

During this summer, Taylor took an action which, had it been known, would have cost him his southern support. In the preceding year, gold had been discovered in California, and an ensuing "gold rush" filled the new territory with turbulent "forty-niners" who soon sorely taxed the inadequate military government. Vigilance committees of the more law-abiding citizens dealt summary justice to the worst robbers, claim jumpers, and horse thieves among them; but the situation demanded an organized government with adequate power and authority. With no hope that Congress would pass a territorial bill, Taylor essayed to cut the knot by secretly sending agents into both California and New Mexico to promise presidential support if the people organized state governments. Californians immediately acted on the suggestion and assembled a convention to draft a state constitution. Since the majority of the migrants were from the northern states, the convention had little difficulty in putting a prohibition of slavery into the constitution.

When Congress met in December, 1849, sectional feeling was intense. During the summer, elections in the southern states had revealed a deep-seated suspicion of Taylor and of Seward's influence on him. In the Whig caucus, Georgia's Robert Toombs attempted to commit the party against the Wilmot Proviso. When this failed, a group of Southerners withdrew from the caucus and refused to support the party's nominee for speaker of the House. In the House there was an equal division between Whigs and Democrats, with a handful of northern free-soilers holding the balance of power. After ballotting for three weeks, the recalcitrant southern Whigs threw the speakership to Howell Cobb, a Georgia democrat. Cobb signalized his election by giving the important committee positions to Southerners.

When the House had organized, Taylor sent his first message, stating, with something less than complete candor, that he had reason to believe that California would soon present itself for admission as a state. He recommended that Congress take favorable action on the application. New Mexico, he thought likely, would follow California's example. Until it did, he proposed it continue under the rule then in operation. The president did not mention the Wilmot Proviso, but he declared that dissolution of the Union "would be the greatest of calamities. . . . Whatever dangers may threaten it, I shall stand by it and maintain it in its integrity to the full extent of the obligations imposed and the power conferred upon me by the Constitution." Privately the president asserted his determination to admit California as a free state, even if he had to use the army to do it.

To many Southerners it seemed that Taylor's action in leaving matters to the people of California and New Mexico was but the Wilmot Proviso in a new form. Taylor's proposals would have effectively kept slavery out of all the territory acquired by the war. Although the president suggested that by this means the sectional issue might be avoided, southern extremists prepared to resist the proposal. Moderate southern Whigs, on the other hand, were ready to support the president. Henry Clay, who had returned to the Senate in the crisis, was unwilling to follow Taylor's leadership. On January 21, Taylor reported to the House that the people of California had formed a state constitution and recommended its approval. Doubtless the president preferred to have California come in as a Whig state rather than remain in a territorial position. But Henry Clay asserted his leadership over Congress and worked against Taylor to effect a compromise. Unwilling to ignore the other sectional questions, he introduced, on January 29, a series of resolutions designed to solve the nation's major problems.

3. Clay's Resolutions

Clay's resolutions provided for the admission of California under the free constitution and for territorial governments, without mention of slavery, in New Mexico and Utah. A boundary dispute between Texas and New Mexico should be settled adversely to Texas, but the Texan public debt was to be assumed by the United States. As for the constantly recurring question of slavery in the District of Columbia, he proposed a declaration that it was inexpedient to abolish slavery there without the consent of Maryland and of the people of the District and without compensating the slave owners, but that the slave trade should be prohibited. In addition, Clay suggested a more effective fugitive slave law. He ended with a proposal that Congress declare that it had no power to interfere with the slave trade between the states.

Speaking upon these resolutions a few days later, Clay pleaded for concessions from each section of the country. The state legislatures were, he said, "twenty odd furnaces in full blast emitting heat and passion and intemperance and diffusing them throughout the extent of this broad land." The North was receiving California and New Mexico. "You have got what is worth a thousand Wilmot Provisos. You have got nature itself on your side." For the South, Clay pointed to the benefits of an effective fugitive slave law.

When, later in the month, senators from California appeared with a petition that they be recognized as entitled to seats, southern opposition to either Clay's or Taylor's plans increased. Jefferson Davis expressed the extremist viewpoint by accepting the Calhoun doctrine that slavery was not a local institution but followed the flag. It could not be kept out of the territories by the act of either the people or Congress. On the other hand, Senator Benton, the old Jacksonian democrat from the Missouri borderland, held that the municipal law of Mexico remained in force in the acquired regions until it had been repealed by Congress.

On March 4, the dying Calhoun was carried into the Senate chamber where, too weak to stand, he lay while a fellow senator read his prepared address on Clay's resolution. The situation was packed with drama, and Senate and galleries listened to the old statesman's plea for the South. The sections had been equal in the original Union, but from the Northwest Ordinance to the California question the North had grown at the expense of the South. The Union, proclaimed the Carolinian, was being dissolved by northern acts. Even equal opportunities for the South in the territories, an effective fugitive slave law, and a cessation of abolitionist agitation would go but part way to prevent this from happening. In addition, the North would have to consent to a constitutional amendment which would "restore to the South, in substance, the power she possessed of protecting herself before the equilibrium between the two sections was destroyed by the action of this government." The admission of California as a free state would indicate that the North would do nothing to restore the lost equilibrium. A posthumous essay showed that Calhoun was preparing to suggest a dual presidency, with one president from each section having a veto over congressional acts.

Much of the attitude of the northern Whigs depended upon Daniel Webster, who had remained silent while Clay and Calhoun marshaled their followers. On March 7, he addressed the Senate in favor of the Clay compromise. Deploring a dissolution of the Union and denying that peaceable secession was possible, Webster made an impassioned plea for northern concessions. He earned for himself the hatred of the abolitionists, but his influence was great in securing the eventual enactment of the compromise measures.

Clay's resolutions were embodied in an "Omnibus Bill" which became the focal point for succeeding discussions. Two obstacles, however, stood in the way of their acceptance: the attitude of President Taylor and the fact that the bill contained too many controversial issues to obtain a majority. Taylor resented Clay's attempt to settle the issues through compromise, and there was general suspicion that he would reject any bill that embodied anything more than the admission of California. Obtaining no satisfaction when they tried to persuade the president to accept the measure, southern Whigs became convinced that Taylor would insist on the admission of New Mexico as well as California. On the floor of the Senate, Seward declared his opposition to tying California to a compromise of the slavery issue. The moral convictions of the North, said Seward, were opposed to the enforcement of the fugitive slave law. Although he admitted that the territories were held by Congress in stewardship for the citizens of the states, he proclaimed, "There is a higher law than the Constitution. . . . The territory is a part . . . of the common heritage of mankind, bestowed upon them by the Creator of the universe. We are his stewards," and therefore should exclude slavery. Many southern Whigs feared that these were Taylor's opinions too and prepared to oppose the administration and support the Compromise.

In July, 1850, Taylor's sudden illness and death cut short his effort to force Congress to admit New Mexico. The new president, Millard Fillmore, had long been a rival of Seward in New York politics and a friend of the Southerners in the Whig party. The change of presidents removed one obstacle to the enactment of Clay's measures. In Fillmore's Cabinet Webster became the Secretary of State, and Clay's influence was great.

Before Taylor's death it had become apparent that the Omnibus Bill could not pass. Amendments to the original measure finally reduced it to a bill creating a territorial government for Utah, without prohibiting slavery; and on July 31 it passed Congress as the first of the measures making up the "Compromise" of 1850.

Thereafter, the work of implementing the Compromise of 1850 devolved upon Illinois' Congressman, Stephen A. Douglas. Even before Clay's resolutions, Douglas had brought into the Committee on Territories a series of bills for the admission of California, a territorial government for New Mexico, and adjustments of the Texas boundary. Clay added his prestige and personal influence, but Douglas did the actual work of putting the various compromise measures through Congress. A fugitive slave law, and a bill for the abolition of the slave trade in the District of Columbia, added to the territorial adjustments to complete the full program as Clay had presented it. From August 9 to September 16 Congress enacted these measures and Fillmore gave his ready approval.

Southern extremists consistently opposed the passage of the compromise measures. California's admission destroyed the balance of free and slave states in the Senate, and Southerners refused to regard the other measures as a concession. In fact, the Fugitive Slave Law, which was the only concession in which the South was interested, was poor compensation for the loss of equality in the Senate. The Senate vote upon the various bills showed the Southerners dividing evenly on the Texas boundary bill. They unanimously favored the Fugitive Slave Law even though many believed it ridiculously framed and probably unworkable. They were willing to accept New Mexico without slavery. The Utah bill had but one southern vote against it—the abolition of the slave trade in the District of Columbia had but one Southerner in its favor; and only two southern Whigs were willing to accept California.

4. THE NASHVILLE CONVENTION AND THE SOUTHERN REACTION

While Congress debated the so-called compromise measures, the southern state legislatures gave heated attention to federal relations. The admission of California would destroy the South's equality in the Senate, and the southern fire-eaters had a field day. All eyes looked to Nashville where a southern convention might voice the authentic sentiment of the South. The Georgia legislature prepared to call a state convention and determined to send delegates to Nashville. Alabama's William L. Yancey cried loudly for action, and his state selected Nashville delegates.

Meanwhile, southern Whigs became lukewarm toward united action. In Virginia they succeeded in getting the selection of delegates referred to local conventions, and in Tennessee, Kentucky, and Maryland they prevented action. In general, the Whigs wished to avoid embarrassing Taylor's administration. Moreover, in the months before the Nashville convention, the Washington atmosphere cleared, and it became evident that the masses of southern people would not approve disunion. The Whig press marshaled sentiment against Nashville. When the convention assembled, it no longer fairly represented the South. Kentucky, North Carolina, Maryland, Delaware, and Missouri were unrepresented. One hundred Tennesseans, chosen by local meetings, attended, but only 75 came from other southern states.

Instead of announcing the southern position in stentorian tones, the convention soon fell into the hands of moderates who opposed any radical statement. Judge W. L. Sharkey, a Mississippi Whig and a Unionist, presided, while the leadership of the extremists fell to Robert Barnwell Rhett. Rhett possessed the fearlessness, the determination, and the ultraism of Calhoun but had neither the intellectual power nor the political acumen that had enabled the great senator to dominate and persuade his associates.

The convention's 28 resolutions reasserted Calhoun's doctrines that the territories belonged to the states and that Congress could not exclude slavery from them. However, the convention suggested that, if this principle were not acceptable, the South would be content with a division along the line of 36° 30'. In addition, the convention issued an address which followed the customary form of such documents. It began by re-counting the growing estrangement of the sections, placed the blame upon the abolitionists, and showed that Congress was a tool, in aboli-tionist hands, to ruin the South. If the South yielded now, within fifty years the North would have the two-thirds majority of Congress and three fourths of the states necessary to abolish slavery by constitutional amendment. The convention adjourned to meet again in November to determine upon further action.

The adjourned session of the convention attracted little interest in the South. Southern leaders such as Robert Toombs, Howell Cobb, and A. H. Stephens had accepted the Compromise. Attendance was small, the Whigs absented themselves, and the fiery resolutions condemning the Compromise were not the authentic voice of the South. The Nashville movement, however, was not without significance. From it the extremists learned that the time required to hold an all-southern convention gave unionists an opportunity to organize. A decade later, the extremists adopted a more successful technique.

During the congressional debates on the measures comprising the Compromise of 1850, many southern Whigs declared themselves in fa-vor of the various proposals. Taylor's death removed a vigorous person-ality who irritated the Southerners, and Whigs united to support Clay's program. On the other hand, southern Democrats declared that the ad-mission of California would be both an insult to, and a fraud upon, the South and would justify a dissolution of the Union. During the following year, the issue of accepting the Compromise or dividing the Union was fought out in elections.

Georgia was the first state to act. Its legislature, in the heat of controversy, had declared that California's admission would be an act of northern aggression. With the passage of the California bill, the gov-ernor called a state convention. In the elections, the Whigs, led by Ste-phens and Toombs, disguised themselves as the "Union and Southern Rights Party" in order to catch the votes of moderate Democrats, and urged acceptance of the Compromise. The convention had a majority of moderates pledged to maintain the Union. With little debate, the con-vention adopted the "Georgia Platform," declaring that the Union was "secondary in importance only to the rights and principles it was de-signed to perpetuate," but counseling moderation in order to preserve its blessings. The convention, however, thought that the state would be jus-tified in contemplating secession if Congress should abolish slavery in the District of Columbia, stop the interstate slave trade, refuse to admit a state because it had slavery, or modify the Fugitive Slave Law.

This platform was both an acceptance and a warning. Upon it Toombs attempted to organize a Southern Rights party in other states. In Mississippi, elections for a convention to consider the situation resulted in a Unionist victory, and the convention condemned the legislature for calling it into existence. Jefferson Davis and H. S. Foote, who resigned their Senate seats to appeal to the people, presented the respective causes of states' rights and unionism to the voters. By a majority of but a thousand, the voters decided in favor of Foote and the Union. Davis retired to his plantation to await a favorable chance to resume his political career. In South Carolina, the sentiment in favor of secession was too strong to be resisted by a Unionist party, and the state elections were held on the issue of immediate secession or of waiting for the co-operation of the other states. The voters repudiated the radical advice of Rhett and took sides with the "Co-operationists." In Tennessee, Virginia, Kentucky, and North Carolina the people accepted the Compromise, and the legislatures accorded it a reluctant acquiescence.

CHAPTER 16

Slavery and the Territories

1. Accepting the Compromise

THE struggle over the Compromise of 1850 disorganized southern political parties. For the moment, the Whig party had abandoned its organization in order to co-operate with Democratic Unionists in silencing threats of secession. With the success of the Union movements, Democrats began to entice their members back to their accustomed political fold. Whigs, on the other hand, feeling that devotion to the Union had given them a new and potent issue, sought to remain as a Union party. Many states'-rights Whigs preferred to remain in the Democratic party rather than to co-operate with the abolitionists of the northern Whig party. "The general rule of Whig affinity North is *abolitionward*," proclaimed one southern editor, as he explained that "we in the South never had any immediate interest in the establishment of the protective system."

On the other hand, for personal or social reasons numerous Whigs could not co-operate with the Democrats. Large slaveholders and urban merchants, allied with the small farmers of the mountains who thought their region ripe for industrial development, constituted the party's membership. Despite the divergences among the various Whig groups, they were held together by a conservative temper. For this reason, the southern Whigs who remained in the party after 1851 adopted the preservation of the Union and the acceptance of the Compromise as their major issues.

Among the Democrats, reasons for accepting the Compromise were equally strong. The state elections of 1851 had shown that a majority of the southern people were opposed to radical action, while the comparative freedom of northern Democrats from abolition heresies made co-operation with the national party easy. Although the South had gained little from the Compromise of 1850, the blessings of the Union seemed for the moment to overshadow the promises of secession. Only a handful of fire-eating extremists were inclined to continue agitating for southern rights and southern nationalism.

Within the Whig party were three leading aspirants for the presidency: President Fillmore, Daniel Webster, and General Winfield Scott. Fillmore's long opposition to the abolitionist Seward and his support of the Compromise measures, and Webster's conciliatory 7th-of-March speech made either of them acceptable to the Southerners. Scott, however, was less favored because he had support from the antislavery northern wing of the party. Whigs therefore prepared to go into their nominating convention with a demand for Fillmore or Webster on a platform asserting the full acceptance of the Compromise of 1850 as a final settlement of the slavery controversy.

In Congress the Southerners soon saw that northern Whigs were thoroughly tainted with "higher law" doctrines. In April, 1852, southern Whigs went into the party caucus determined to force acceptance of the "finality" of the Compromise. Failing to convince the Northerners, most of the southern members withdrew in disgust. In the South, Whig state conventions followed the congressmen's lead and instructed delegates to the nominating convention to demand acceptance of the Compromise in the platform and to select a nominee who would support it. Friends of the general quieted opposition to Scott by assurances that he was sound on the Compromise.

Relatively free from internal dissensions over the slavery issue, the Democrats found little difficulty in adopting a platform favoring all of the Compromise measures and giving specific assurances of support to the Fugitive Slave Law. This done, they struggled over the candidate. Lewis Cass of Michigan, Marcy of New York, Pennsylvania's Buchanan, and Stephen A. Douglas of Illinois were all acceptable to the South, but none could gain the necessary two-thirds vote. After a three-day deadlock, Franklin Pierce, of New Hampshire, a man whom few knew but who was not likely to depart from the conservatism of his party, was nominated. The vice-presidential nomination went to Alabama's William R. D. King, a unionist, an expansionist, and an avowed supporter of the Compromise.

On June 16 the Whigs convened in Baltimore. The southern members came determined to force acceptance of the Compromise upon the party. Overriding an abolitionist minority, the Southerners carried the Compromise planks and enough of them gave a half-reluctant support to Scott to insure his nomination. The general accepted the nomination "with the resolutions annexed." This careful avoidance of a definite statement disgusted Stephens and Toombs, who feared that Seward would influence Scott as he had President Taylor. Gathering a number of like-minded Whigs, these irate Southerners issued a card declaring that no known incident of Scott's career showed him to be in favor of the principles of Compromise.

Disapproval of Scott was widespread, especially in the lower

South. Even those who supported the ticket did so without enthusiasm, and in November only Tennessee and Kentucky voted for the Whig candidate. Lethargy characterized the election, and nearly a hundred thousand voters stayed away from the polls. Since these absentees were from both parties, Pierce's majority was not large. In Delaware the Democratic majority was 25 and in North Carolina but 700. In the entire country Pierce had a popular majority of but 50,000 votes. Throughout the country the people were losing interest in the slavery controversy.

John P. Hale, the abolitionist candidate, was completely ignored. In fact, the Whig party's inconsistent elements contributed to its defeat. Politics, in general, was regarded as an old man's game, and "fossilized Whig" was a common epithet. Younger men were turning their attention to economic enterprise, and they saw political maneuvering only as a means to further some particular economic end.

2. PIERCE'S ADMINISTRATION

In his inaugural address, the new president declared he believed that "involuntary servitude . . . is recognized by the Constitution" and that the Compromise measures of 1850 were "strictly constitutional and to be unhesitatingly carried into effect." But he devoted the major portion of his address to the necessity for the acquisition of "certain possessions" not under American jurisdiction. "The policy of my Administration," asserted Pierce, "will not be controlled by any timid forebodings of evil from expansion." The Cabinet, all but two of whose members were in favor of the South, were as devoted as the president to the dreams of expansion. William L. Marcy became secretary of state, James Guthrie of Kentucky was secretary of the treasury, Jefferson Davis headed the War Department, and James C. Dobbin of North Carolina was secretary of the navy. Caleb Cushing, of Massachusetts, who took the attorney-general's office, allied himself with Marcy and the Southerners in dominating the policies of the administration. Foreign missions, which would be important in a regime of expansion, were also given to Southerners or to "Doughfaces," as northern men with southern principles were contemptuously designated. James Buchanan of Pennsylvania went to England, John Y. Mason of Virginia to France, and Pierre Soulé of Louisiana to Spain. James Gadsden of South Carolina became minister to Mexico and an Arkansan represented the United States in Central America.

Pierce and his sectional Cabinet contemplated expansion southward. Southerners who felt, like Davis, that the Compromise of 1850 had deprived the South of its equality in the Union, wished to redress the balance by acquiring more territory to be made into slave states. Already the South was becoming interested in the Caribbean region. In January, 1852, a commercial convention in New Orleans had proposed a canal or a railroad across the Isthmus of Tehuantepec. In succeeding years, similar conventions advocated trade expansion into Central America. There was even talk of steamship lines from southern to South American ports.

The movement of American capital into the Caribbean area and Central America antedated Pierce's administration. In the years following the Mexican War, companies of Americans, many of them chartered in the South, were interested in one of the three possible routes across Central America to the Pacific. In behalf of a New Orleans company, Webster negotiated with Mexico for a concession for a canal and railroad route across Tehuantepec. Opposition to this scheme came from Cornelius Vanderbilt, himself interested in a railroad across Nicaragua. Political intrigue in Mexico resulted in the concession's being taken from the New Orleans company and given to a group formed in New York. The Tehuantepec project soon disappeared from rivalry, but in 1854 there appeared in Nicaragua the figure of the great freebooter, William Walker. Walker was a Tennessean who combined a love of daring adventure with at least a verbal devotion to the South. Earlier he had gathered a motley group in California and planned a filibustering expedition against Mexico with the avowed purpose of securing Lower California as a slave state. In Nicaragua, Walker's handful of followers succeeded in setting up a "Liberal" president of the country. As dictator, Walker was successful and received much applause from the South. In 1856 he proclaimed himself president, re-established slavery in Nicaragua, invited American capital to enter, and talked vaguely about annexing his slaveholding country to the Union. Pierce recognized Walker's government; but Vanderbilt, who had lost his railroad concession, inspired a counter-revolution which drove Walker from the country.

While Nicaragua and Central America interested the Pierce administration, the hopes of the Southerners were more often centered in Cuba. Since the Mexican War, the Southerners had regarded Cuba as a potential slave state, and had enthusiastically supported the futile efforts of Narcisco Lopez to launch filibustering expeditions against the island. A southern jury which triumphantly acquitted the adventurer brought to naught efforts under President Taylor to stop Lopez's expeditions. A federal grand jury indicted General John Henderson of Louisiana and Governor John A. Quitman of Mississippi for complicity. But no southern jury would convict for a crime which had such universal approval. Henderson was acquitted upon trial, and the charges against Quitman, who had valiantly asserted his immunity as the governor of a sovereign state, were dismissed. When Lopez was finally captured and killed by the Spanish authorities in Cuba, a New Orleans mob wrecked the Spanish consulate, defaced a picture of the queen, and destroyed the property of Spanish residents.

Because of the aroused sensitiveness of the Spanish, Secretary Marcy instructed Minister Soulé to proceed cautiously in raising the question of Cuban annexation. But Soulé was an ardent expansionist and soon took advantage of the capture of the *Black Warrior,* an American vessel seized for violating Cuban customs regulations. Soulé threw caution to the winds and sent a brusque demand for reparations within 48 hours. The Spanish refused to consider so high-handed a demand, and Marcy failed to support his minister. Instead, the secretary of state instructed Soulé to consult with Mason in France and Buchanan in England on the United States' policy in regard to Cuba.

The three ministers met at Ostend in Belgium in the summer of 1854. If Marcy expected that the conference would cool Soulé's ardor, he was doomed to disappointment. Sharing fully Soulé's expansionist sentiments, the three ministers drew up a manifesto declaring that Spain ought to sell Cuba to the United States. Cuba, the ministers explained, was necessary for the safety of slavery in the South, and if Spain should refuse to sell and the Union should be endangered through her obstinacy, "by every law human and Divine, we shall be justified in wresting it from Spain, if we possess the power." Soulé suggested to Marcy that the Crimean War, by occupying England and France, furnished an opportune time for declaring war on Spain. Marcy, however, failed to act on the suggestion or to support his jingoist minister. Public sentiment in the North condemned the Ostend Manifesto while the South applauded its authors.

Out of all the expansionist dreams of the southern-dominated Pierce administration, only one project materialized. Before the Mexican War, southern plans had been made for a railroad to run from California to the South. In 1845, the Memphis commercial convention had heard James Gadsden, president of the South Carolina Railroad Company, propose such a road which would connect with his own line. The settlement at the close of the Mexican War left the only feasible route for the road in Mexico's possession. But Pierce sent Gadsden to Mexico as minister, and Jefferson Davis became the principal sponsor of the southern route in the Cabinet. Marcy instructed Gadsden to obtain a cession of the desired territory. Taking advantage of Santa Anna's need for money, Gadsden purchased sufficient territory south of the Gila River to make the railroad project possible. Davis contributed the facilities of the War Department to survey the route.

3. Railroads and the Kansas-Nebraska Act

Unfortunately for Davis's plans for a southern railroad to the Pacific, rival schemes for a road to follow a northern route existed. Both Chicago and St. Louis demanded a transcontinental railroad which would connect, through these cities, with consolidated systems into the East. Ambitious Chicagoans wanted a road that would run due west from their city, while speculators of St. Louis desired a road direct to San Francisco. Two difficulties lay in the way of realizing these dreams: the lack of capital and the presence of wild Indians in the unorganized Indian territory known as Nebraska. The solution to the first difficulty lay in a government subsidy; to the second, in the establishment of a territorial government in Nebraska. The second problem was the more pressing, for the experience of the railroads in obtaining subsidies from states and counties gave confidence that government aid would be forthcoming. The first necessity was to clear the route.

Because the region lay north of the line of 36° 30' and was therefore not open to slavery, the southern members of Congress had long resisted any efforts to organize it into a territory. Indians, removed from the eastern states, roamed at will over the country, held in their boundaries by a scattered system of frontier army posts.

In the bordering state of Missouri, two groups had interests in Nebraska. The rich lands of the Missouri River invited agricultural expansion, and land-hungry Missourians would welcome the opening of the territory were slavery not prohibited. Already the free state of Iowa to the north tempted slaves to run away; a free state to the west would make slavery impossible in Missouri. Suppressing their desire for the fertile fields of Nebraska, these men followed the lead of Senator David R. Atchison, who proclaimed that Nebraska should never be organized as a free territory. Opposed to Atchison and the proslavery people were ex-Senator Benton and the St. Louis businessmen, who cared less about slavery than about a transcontinental railroad with its eastern terminus in their city. While Jefferson Davis was pushing his project for a southern road, Benton and Atchison contended for the control of Missouri. In the end Benton won, and Atchison decided to support a plan to organize the Nebraska territory.

At the same time, Chicago interests were ready to push a proposal to organize Nebraska. Stephen A. Douglas, himself holder of extensive lands in the city which might be sold to any newly created railroad, was in a strategic position as chairman of the Senate Committee on Territories. Knowing that Atchison would introduce such a bill, Douglas hastened to draft a measure establishing a territorial government for Nebraska. But Douglas realized that Southerners would oppose the measure, and he prepared to forestall them by providing that the people of the territory should have the right to determine its domestic institutions.

The idea of "popular sovereignty" was not new. In 1847 Lewis Cass had suggested it and had elaborated upon it in 1848 while a candidate for the presidency. The scheme had been derided as "squatter sovereignty." Southerners had long contended that the people of a territory, at the time that they drew up a state constitution, could legislate about slavery. Popular sovereignty was but the extension of this right to the people of the territory at the time they elected a territorial legislature. Douglas added the spurious rationalization that the principles of the Compromise of 1850 had superseded those of the Missouri Compromise, and that the prospective settlers of Nebraska should be accorded the same privilege as had the inhabitants of Utah and New Mexico.

In addition to ingenious argument, Douglas tried political means to get southern support. For many reasons it seemed advisable to divide the Nebraska country into two territories, one to bear the original name and the other to be called Kansas. The latter, lying directly west of Missouri, would normally be settled from the older state and would be slave, while Nebraska, settled from Iowa, would be free. With his bill in this form, Douglas approached Davis, and under Davis's influence, Pierce committed himself to support the project. Thereafter, the administration stood staunchly back of the Kansas-Nebraska Bill, even though it became apparent shortly that it was a grave mistake. Had Davis refused to support Douglas's scheme, the southern railroad of which he dreamed might have become a reality; and had he bargained with Douglas, he might have secured support in the Northwest for annexations in Central America and the Caribbean. Instead, Davis and the administration grasped hurriedly at the lure of a new slave state and the repeal of the oppressive Missouri Compromise. Douglas stood ready to obtain all the benefits of Davis's mistake: the administration was to share the obloquy which resulted.

Early in January, 1854, after having received Pierce's commitment, Douglas presented the Kansas-Nebraska Bill. Opposition was immediate. In a few days Charles Sumner, Salmon P. Chase, J. R. Giddings, and other congressional abolitionists published an "appeal of the Independent Democrats in Congress to the People of the United States." The Missouri Compromise, declared these Free-Soil spokesmen, had been regarded as sacred and inviolable. The Kansas-Nebraska Bill was a "bold scheme against American liberty worthy of an accomplished architect of ruin." It was a "falsification of the truth of history." The signers appealed to the people to "protest, earnestly and emphatically by correspondence, through the press, by memorials, by resolutions of public meetings and legislative bodies, and in whatever other mode may seem expedient, against this enormous crime." Throughout the North, press, pulpit, and public forum denounced Douglas and the Pierce administration. Petitions from the North deluged Congress when the debate opened.

Against the bill, Chase, Sumner, Wade, and William H. Seward raised indignant voices to deny that the principles of 1850 were intended to supersede those of 1820. The fires of sectional hatred burned furiously as Democrats and Southerners answered. Long ago Calhoun had contended that the Missouri Compromise was unconstitutional. Southern Democrats echoed his constitutional precepts, and southern Whigs welcomed a new area for slave expansion. Late in May, 1854, with southern Whigs supporting, the bill passed the Senate, and administration pressure and Douglas's persuasion brought the measure before the House. Northern Democrats, under the patronage lash, came to the aid of southern Democrats and Whigs to pass the bill. Yet two southern Democrats and seven southern Whigs, doubting that the South would benefit from the act, voted against it.

In the South there was widespread rejoicing, although Sam Houston's raven croak was heard declaring that "the people of the South care nothing for it. It is the worst thing for the South that has ever transpired since the Union was first formed."

4. The Struggle for Kansas

The Kansas-Nebraska Act turned Pierce's administration away from its expansionist program. Thereafter, it was primarily concerned with the effort to carry slavery into the newly created territories. As soon as Pierce signed the bill, parties of Missourians, anxiously awaiting the day, crossed over into Kansas to stake out homesteads along the Missouri and Kansas Rivers. Here they established the towns of Leavenworth, Kickapoo, and Atchison. But others were also interested in the possibilities of the fertile lands of Kansas. During the first summer, settlers came from New England, sent under the auspices of the New England Emigrant Aid Society.

The guiding spirit of the New England Emigrant Aid Society was Eli Thayer of Worcester, Massachusetts. Originally the company was designed to send Massachusetts' surplus population to Kansas. Thayer expected to assist the immigrants in establishing themselves by loaning them money to found local industries. Profits impelled Thayer, but almost from the beginning he capitalized upon the antislavery sentiment of his section. His company, he proclaimed, would keep Kansas in the ranks of the free states. To aid in this purpose, or to share in the expected profits, Charles Francis Adams, Amos Lawrence, and a number of New England's wealthy and influential citizens subscribed to the company. The first settlers, arriving in Kansas in the summer of 1854, founded the town of Lawrence and remained aloof from the settlements of the Missourians. With them came many other settlers from the free states of the Old Northwest.

To the inhabitants of Missouri, who interpreted the Kansas-Nebraska Act as a promise that Kansas should be slave, this migration appeared an invasion. Without penetrating the economic motives of the New England Emigrant Aid Society, the proslavery advocates accepted Thayer's verbose prospectus literally and took alarm at being deprived of the right to carry their slaves into Kansas. Immediately they appealed to the South for assistance. Southern congressmen, approached for their opinions, approved the idea of a counter movement but were unable to finance it. The lack of capital for such a purpose handicapped the South in the struggle for Kansas and forced the Missourians to appeal for a voluntary migration of Southerners who would save Kansas for slavery.

But if the South lacked capital for sending immigrants into Kansas, the proslavery forces could count upon the support of the Pierce administration, which was interested in saving Kansas not only for slavery but also for the Democratic party. In October, 1854, Andrew H. Reeder, of Pennsylvania, arrived in Kansas as territorial governor. After touring the settlements, Reeder announced November 9 as the date for the election of a territorial delegate. On election day some 1,600 armed men from the border counties of Missouri descended upon the polling places, and, amid much disorder and fraud, selected a Southerner to represent the territory in Washington. To this violence Reeder made no objection, and Congress, meeting a few days later, accepted the delegate.

During the winter of 1854-1855, it became apparent that the Missourians could expect little aid from the South in holding Kansas. Forced to rely upon their own efforts and inspired by their success in the first election, the residents of western Missouri formed secret societies to repress the northern settlers. In the spring, these "Blue Lodges" were ready to intervene in the election of a territorial legislature. Kansas had 2,905 qualified electors, but 6,307 votes were cast—over 80 per cent being cast by the visiting "border ruffians." The free-state settlers desired Reeder to invalidate the election; but the governor, surrounded by Missourians, seated but seven free-state representatives, while the proslavery men numbered twenty-eight. In the South, the violence and fraud were condoned as justifiable tactics to combat the northern invasion.

Governor Reeder, however, soon revealed his astonishment at the results of his complacent actions. En route to Washington to lay the situation before President Pierce, Reeder told a Pennsylvania audience the full story of Kansas' election disorders. Pierce was angered and asked Reeder's resignation, but the governor refused to resign unless Pierce should give him a written approval of his acts. Instead of resigning, he returned to Kansas to deal with the irate territorial legislature.

Reeder failed both to co-operate with the Missourians and to protect the free-state settlers. Perhaps his speculations in Kansas lands explained his vacillating course. The proslavery faction alleged that the governor's ownership of lots at Pawnee impelled him to assemble the legislature there. When they met, the proslavery majority immediately expelled the free-state members and moved the capital to Shawnee Mission on the Missouri border. Then they adopted a code of laws for the territory. Most significant was the adoption of Missouri's slave code. When Governor Reeder refused to sign these laws, the legislature appealed to Washington for his dismissal. Pierce immediately complied, and Reeder went home to denounce the president and the proslavery men.

The squabble between Reeder and his legislature was paralleled by violence in Kansas. Men of each party were driven out of the other party's settlements, and clashes between the members of the opposing factions were common. As the North's indignation grew, the South smiled approval on Kansas' legislators. The Democrats of Georgia formally expressed their strong sympathy with the "manly efforts" of their "southern brethren" in defeating the "paid adventurers and Jesuitical horde of northern abolitionism."

But while the South rejoiced, the free-state people of the territory took matters into their own hands. Under the leadership of Dr. Charles Robinson, who had witnessed the creation of a state government in California, free-state inhabitants began a movement to repudiate the territorial legislature and to adopt a free-state constitution. Mass meetings among the northern settlers sent delegates to a constitutional convention at Topeka in October. The resulting "Topeka Constitution" prohibited slavery, and gave the people an opportunity to vote on an ordinance excluding all Negroes from the territory. In an election for a territorial delegate, the free-state people chose ex-Governor Reeder to go to Washington to contest the seat of the proslavery delegate. This development inspired the South to renewed activity. Senator Brown, of Mississippi, proposed that his state should send 300 young men with an equal number of slaves, purchased by the state, into Kansas. In Georgia, the legislature considered a bill to raise $50,000 to be expended in Kansas. In the course of the discussion it was revealed that the Muskogee Emigrant Aid Company, planned to combat the work of Thayer's organization, had been able to raise but $950 for the great crusade. Moreover, cautious men feared that the youths who would be sent into Kansas would join with the free-state people. In other states the legislatures considered going to the aid of the embattled Missourians, but the only significant expedition was a private one led by Major Jefferson Buford, of Eufaula, Alabama. Private subscriptions raised $14,000 and Buford sold his own slaves to obtain the $24,000 which he spent to lead some 300 men into Kansas. Armed only with Bibles supplied by a Montgomery church, the band arrived in Kansas in April, 1856. The men scattered after a time, and Buford left Kansas after a year of futile effort to raise money.

While the southern states were discussing means of saving Kansas, the question was agitating the administration and Congress. To Congress, Pierce admitted that "acts prejudicial to good order" had occurred in Kansas but he alleged that they were not of sufficient seriousness to warrant interference. On January 24, the president sent a special message condemning the New England Emigrant Aid Society and the Topeka Constitution. The first was an "extraordinary measure of propagandist colonization," and the second "revolutionary." On February 11 he issued a proclamation ordering both the border ruffians and the free-state people to refrain from violence and warning citizens of other states against "unauthorized intermeddling" in Kansas.

Congressional discussion of Kansas problems began on March 12 with a report of Douglas's Committee on Territories. Douglas, too, named the New England Emigrant Aid Society as author of all the troubles. Proceeding from this premise, Douglas found the territorial legislature legally constituted and the Topeka government illegal. Later in the month, Douglas proposed calling a constitutional convention when the territory should have 93,420 inhabitants. The debates soon involved the entire question of slavery and called for the best oratorical efforts of such abolitionists as John P. Hale, William H. Seward, Benjamin F. Wade, Lyman Trumbull of Illinois, and Henry Wilson of Massachusetts. But the most powerful speech was delivered on May 19 and 20 by Charles Sumner, who declared beforehand that he would "pronounce the most thorough philippic ever uttered in a legislative body."

Sumner's speech, entitled *The Crime Against Kansas*, fulfilled its maker's promise. Filled with denunciations of the Southerners, the senator passed from generalities to personalities. Douglas was likened to a skunk, and South Carolina's Senator Andrew P. Butler was roundly excoriated. Douglas made immediate reply, pointing out that the "libels, the gross insults, which we have heard here today have been conned over, written with a cool, deliberate malignity . . ." and were not the result of sudden passion. Sumner, said Douglas, was a perjurer who had taken an oath to support the Constitution yet publicly announced that he would disobey the Fugitive Slave Law.

Two days later, Senator Butler's nephew, Preston S. Brooks, representative from South Carolina, avenged the insult to his uncle. Entering the Senate chamber after adjournment, Brooks found Sumner seated alone at his desk. Raising his cane, the irate South Carolinian rained blows upon Sumner's head until the cane was broken and the unconscious and bleeding senator lay upon the floor. Two southern senators gazed complacently upon the fray, but more than a few in the South condemned the Carolina knight-errant. The widening sectional gap was dramatically displayed in the reactions of North and South to the assault. Massachusetts left its martyr's seat vacant for three years until he had recovered sufficiently to resume it, while Brooks, resigning his place in the House, returned to it after triumphal vindication. While condemnation for Brooks filled newspapers and pulpits of the North, many southerners showered praises upon him and presented him with more canes with which to club abolitionists. One such cane, from South Carolina, was inscribed, "Use knock-down arguments." Sober men in the South, however, warned that Brooks' impetuous act was only new fuel to the fires of northern fanaticism.

While Congress and the country watched these scenes of verbal and physical violence, the situation in Kansas had rapidly grown worse. Reeder's successor as governor was Wilson Shannon, an Ohio Democrat as devoted to the Democrats and to slavery as Reeder had originally been. When he arrived in the territory, he gave immediate indication that he planned to support the proslavery forces in the legislature against the free-state settlers. He gave his approval to the organization of a "Law and Order Party" composed of the proslavery forces. The free-state communities, however, persisted in ignoring the governor and legislature, and clashes between the factions increased in frequency.

In November, 1855, occurred an incident which might have precipitated open civil war. A free-state mob rescued a prisoner from a proslavery sheriff and carried the culprit into Lawrence. The sheriff immediately appealed to the border ruffians, and 1,500 crossed the line to join the "Law and Order" militia in a march on Lawrence. Approaching the town, however, they found it guarded by earthworks and manned by men with rifles. While the sheriff's posse contemplated this unexpected development, Governor Shannon arrived on the scene and persuaded the two sides to make peace. Although this "Wakarusa War" resulted in no bloodshed, it was a portent of the violence that might occur.

A few days later, the free-state people went to the polls to adopt the Topeka Constitution and accept the ordinance excluding Negroes from the state. The governor and a legislature they elected wisely refrained from attempting legislation.

The winter of 1855-1856 was severe and enforced a truce between the ardent antagonists in Kansas. With spring, new settlers came from both North and South, and violence broke out anew. When a sheriff was shot by a free-state man, the chief justice of the territory instructed the grand jury that resistance to the laws of the territorial legislature was treason to the United States. The jury returned indictments of treason against Reeder, Robinson, and Jim Lane, who had presided over the Topeka convention, and presented a newspaper and a hotel of Lawrence as nuisances. Reeder resisted arrest and fled in disguise; Robinson escaped but was arrested in Missouri. On May 11, the United States marshal declared that residents of Lawrence had resisted the laws and called for a posse to march on the town. With the border ruffians, Buford's band, and the "Law and Order" militia, he proceeded to Lawrence, where the citizens protested that they had resisted no laws and appealed to Governor Shannon for protection. The governor failed to send aid, and the posse, dragging five cannon with them, invaded Lawrence. They destroyed the obnoxious newspaper, burned the hotel, and confiscated the cannon in the possession of the New England Emigrant Aid Society. Then the invaders sacked the town. Five lives were lost.

The excited state of the entire country was revealed in the incidents of a few weeks. On the day after the sack of Lawrence, Brooks assaulted Sumner. Two days after that came the avenging act of John Brown, an abolitionist religious fanatic who gathered a small band of men and murdered in cold blood five proslavery men. Brown's victims were all personal enemies who had only recently accused him of stealing horses. In fact, in the ensuing disorders in Kansas, squabbles over horse-stealing and claim-jumping were inextricably confused with the conflict between slavery and freedom. Armed bands, giving adherence to one or the other conflicting principle, roved the territory wreaking personal vengeance until, on June 4, Governor Shannon ordered them all to disperse. Marauding continued, however, and perhaps 200 men lost their lives in the guerilla warfare of the next few months.

In the rest of the country no one doubted that massacres and battles on a grand scale were taking place in Kansas. From the beginning of the "Kansas Question" energetic Northern newspapers had kept their readers informed about "atrocities" as they developed. A vigorous squad of newspaper correspondents representing Horace Greeley's *Tribune*, New York's *Herald, Times,* and *Post,* Boston's *Traveller,* and the Chicago *Tribune* became active adherents of the free-state cause and supplied their journals with an unceasing stream of horror stories. Eventually their reiterated pleas for aid brought response from both sides.

Early in July, 1856, a meeting at Buffalo formed a Kansas Central Committee whose avowed purposes were to organize the northern people and to send arms to the free-state men in the territory. The campaign went into the churches, and Henry Ward Beecher, speaking in New Haven, pleaded for subscriptions to buy Sharp's rifles for new companies of immigrants. Armed with these "Beecher's Bibles,"—a wry joke on the method by which the Brooklyn preacher planned to "convert" pro-slavery Kansans—reinforcements hastened to Kansas to add to the accumulating disorders.

In the South, newspapers and orators declared—to use Rhett's words in the Charleston *Mercury*—"Upon the proposition that safety of the institution of slavery in South Carolina is dependent upon its establishment in Kansas, there can be no rational doubt. He, therefore, who does not contribute largely in money now, proves himself criminally indifferent, if not hostile, to the institution upon which the prosperity of the South and of this State depends." Rhett proposed that "secret measures," carried out by a vigilance committee of the "Kansas Association" would encourage subscriptions. In Missouri, such vigilance committees seized vessels coming up the Missouri River, confiscated the merchandise of the free-state traders, and took arms away from arriving immigrants whom the Emigrant Aid Society had sent.

Violence might have continued in Kansas had not the necessities of the campaign of 1856 compelled Pierce to replace the drunken Governor Shannon with J. W. Geary, another Pennsylvanian and the ablest of the Kansas governors. Geary immediately announced that he would use the federal troops to suppress the guerilla bands of both sides, and the announcement brought peace in the territory until after the election.

5. KNOW-NOTHINGS AND REPUBLICANS

The struggle for Kansas had far-reaching effects on political parties. The Kansas-Nebraska Bill dealt the final blow to the feeble Whig party. In the South, the Whig party was composed of two groups: the nationalists, who would prefer to continue in association with the northern wing of the party, and the "Southern Rights" element, who placed the interest of their section before party unity. Whigs of the latter class had endorsed the Nebraska Bill in a separate caucus and had voted for it in Congress. The northern Whigs had been unanimously opposed to it. It was obvious that the Whigs of the South could no longer co-operate with their northern allies. On the other hand, social considerations and a long history of political opposition made it difficult for them to join the Democrats. Many sought for a third party. A. H. Stephens believed that the Southerners might unite with the Fillmore faction of New York and the "Cotton Whigs" of the other northern states in a new national party dedicated to the Compromise of 1850. But instead of forming such a party, the southern Whigs entered the Know-Nothing party.

The Know-Nothing party was essentially a new movement in

politics. Directed against the political influence of the foreigner and the Catholic, it expressed the growing fear that the influx of Irish and Germans would seriously undermine American standards and *mores*. In the North, workingmen disliked the competition which immigrants with low living standards produced. In the border states of the South similar feelings helped Know-Nothingism, while in the lower South the new party attracted Whigs who could not co-operate with the Democrats. Since the name, the principles, or the wardheelers of the Democratic party usually attracted the newly arrived immigrant, a party opposed to foreigners inevitably became an anti-Democratic movement.

Beginning in New York, the Know-Nothing movement spread rapidly to Maryland. In June, 1854, after successes in local elections in various states, representatives of Maryland, Virginia, Alabama, and Georgia formed a "Grand Council for the United States." With this beginning, the southern members immediately prepared to force a statement on the sectional issues. In November, 1854, the national council met in Cincinnati where a southern delegate demanded that the organization should "discourage and denounce any attempt coming from any quarter to destroy or weaken the Union and to maintain and defend it against all encroachments under all circumstances, and to put under the hand of proscription any and all men who might be engaged in impairing its vigor or resisting its authority."

Although the adoption of this Union-saving declaration brought many southern Whigs into the Know-Nothing ranks, it convinced many Northerners that the party was unfitted to express their sentiments. In state elections of 1855 the Know-Nothings carried three New England states, and the party's leaders announced that they had a million sworn members who could carry every city in the land. In Virginia, however, the party met a setback. There, the Know-Nothings nominated Thomas S. Flournoy, a former Whig leader, for governor. The Democrats nominated Henry A. Wise, who made a brilliant and aggressive campaign in which he made the most of the intolerant and proscriptive character of the opposition. The American platform in Virginia, as in the rest of the South, had declared in favor of religious toleration. In the Catholic parishes of Louisiana, in fact, the "American" movement was strong. But in his enthusiasm for the new principles, Flournoy declared that he opposed any Catholic's holding office in the state. The outcome was a Democratic victory of ten thousand votes.

In other southern states, the Know-Nothing movement met failure. In Georgia, Toombs and Stephens worked with the Democratic party. Stephens announced himself an independent candidate for Congress, but the Democrats adopted him and insured his election. In the fall elections, the Know-Nothings polled 43,222 votes, but the Democratic gubernatorial candidate had 53,478. Tennessee re-elected Andrew Johnson governor, although the Know-Nothings had a slight majority in the legislature and, thanks to east Tennessee, returned a majority of congressmen who adhered to the American platform. Maryland, Kentucky, and Texas elected Know-Nothings to office.

When the national council of the American party met in June, 1855, the southern delegates were prepared to commit the party to the principles of the southern Whigs. The Massachusetts Know-Nothings, on the other hand, had thoroughly identified themselves with abolitionism; and the Southerners attempted to keep Henry Wilson and the state's delegation out of the convention. Failing in this, they proceeded to make slavery the chief topic of discussion. They supported a platform denying Congress the power to legislate for slavery in the District of Columbia or the territories, and insisting upon the enforcement of the Fugitive Slave Law. Upon the adoption of these resolutions, a number of northern delegates followed Wilson out of the convention. From this time it was evident that the Know-Nothing party was but the Whig party under another name, and its northern adherents sought political refuge in the rising Republican party. The American party, its effectiveness limited to the South, continued with dwindling membership until the eve of secession.

A more permanent political outgrowth of the Kansas-Nebraska Bill was the Republican party. When congressional opponents of the bill issued a call for a new party, a ready response came from western states, where Whiggery, always weak, had just collapsed before a series of Democratic victories. In July mass meetings in Michigan, Wisconsin, Ohio, and Indiana, brought together disgruntled Democrats, ambitious Free-Soilers, and politically homeless Whigs. The Michigan and Wisconsin meetings denominated themselves "Republicans"; in the other states, "People's" or "Independent" parties carried the common banner of opposition to the Kansas-Nebraska Act, to the extension of slavery, to the Fugitive Slave Law and to the southern aristocracy. The meetings put state and congressional tickets in the field, and the movement spread to other states. In the elections of 1854, Republicans vied with Know-Nothings to lead the anti-Democratic forces. In the states, the successful candidates bore Republican or Know-Nothing labels, and in Congress the administration lost sixty-two seats. During the winter of 1855, opposition legislatures sent new members to the Senate. Amid the confusion of many party tags, Douglas proclaimed that the anti-Nebraska campaign had proved abortive; but it was evident that the electorate had rebuked the administration and the Democracy.

In 1855 the Know-Nothings made more progress in capitalizing upon the Democratic defeat than did the Republicans. Although the year brought no victories, the Republicans took hope as the party suffered defeats in the southern states and lost its northern members through its adherence to the Fugitive Slave Law. The Democrats regained their lost ground by carrying five southern states. When Congress met in the winter of 1855, there was chaos among the parties. In the House, Democrats had fallen from 159 to 75 and the Know-Nothings had 117, with 40 Republicans and a number of independents completing the membership. The division between the northern and southern "Americans" resulted in a delay of two months in electing a speaker. The final choice was N. P. Banks, a Know-

Nothing who was in the process of transferring his allegiance to the Republican party.

6. THE ELECTION OF 1856

The Know-Nothings went into the campaign of 1856 with a weakened party. The national council, meeting on February 18, modified the earlier declaration in favor of congressional noninterference with slavery to a statement that the people of a territory should be allowed to "regulate their domestic and social affairs in their own mode." Yet they condemned the Pierce administration for repealing the Missouri Compromise. Such absurd straddling availed them nothing. On Washington's Birthday, the party's national convention assembled with delegates present from all the southern states except South Carolina and Georgia. Debate immediately began on a resolution to repudiate the council's statement on slavery in the territories. A substitute resolution favored re-establishing the Missouri Compromise line. The party rejected the motion, and the delegates from New England and Ohio and some from other northern states withdrew from their convention. Millard Fillmore, a candidate most likely to be accepted by the South, and A. J. Donelson, nephew of Andrew Jackson, were nominated for president and vice-president. The seceding members called a convention to meet in June. It was evident that the Know-Nothings would be of little importance in the campaign and that the Republican party would draw the non-Democratic votes of the North.

The Democratic national convention met in June at Cincinnati. The party had profited by the elections of the preceding year and could expect the votes of its opponents to be divided between Know-Nothings and Republicans. On the other hand, the party had suffered seriously from the unpopularity of the Kansas-Nebraska Bill. The primary task of the convention was to select a candidate who would draw the North's wavering voters. Both Pierce and Douglas, each of whom hoped for the nomination, were too closely connected with Kansas to be considered. Passing over them, the party nominated James Buchanan and John C. Breckinridge. Buchanan had been in England during the Kansas struggle and had cautiously kept silent on the issue. As a conservative from highly conservative Pennsylvania, he could appeal to moderate men both South and North. As one of the authors of the Ostend Manifesto, he was acceptable to the southern expansionists. Backed by John Slidell of Louisiana, Buchanan could count on the support of the more crafty southern politicians. He had never, declared a Richmond paper, "uttered a word which could pain the most sensitive southern heart."

The Democratic platform was equally pleasing to the Southerners. The party declared "that Congress has no power under the Constitution to interfere with or control the domestic institutions of the several States, . . . that all efforts of the abolitionists or others made to induce Congress to interfere with questions of slavery, or to take incipient steps in relation

thereto, are calculated to lead to the most alarming and dangerous consequences." Moreover, the party declared itself in favor of the Compromise
measures of 1850, including the Fugitive Slave Law. As for the territories,
the Democrats repudiated "all sectional issues and platforms concerning
domestic slavery which seek to embroil the States and incite to treason
and armed resistance to law in the Territories." Therefore, "the American
Democracy recognize and adopt the principles contained in the organic
laws establishing the territories of Nebraska and Kansas as embodying the
only sound and safe solution of the slavery question." Popular sovereignty, in the form in which Douglas had presented it, was endorsed by
the party.

With two parties in the field with platforms and candidates acceptable to the South, the Republican party gathered to itself all opponents of
the South and of slavery. The first Republican nominating convention was
a mass convention with little attention given to the apportionment of delegates among the states. All of the northern states, together with Kentucky
and Maryland, had delegations of various sizes. Despite the appearance
of popular spontaneity, experienced politicians managed the party from
the beginning. Although the party was sectional in its nature and possessed
coherence only through its opposition to slavery, the politicians passed
over the leaders of the antislavery cause—Chase, Wade, Seward, and Banks
—and selected instead John C. Frémont. The candidate was an army officer
with a record of daring adventure as an explorer of the West and was the
son-in-law of Missouri's Senator Benton. As Seward had explained the year
before, the party's banner was "untorn in former battles and unsullied by
past errors." In the same spirit, a new and unknown man was made the
nominee. The platform showed similar youthful vigor. It declared its opposition to the repeal of the Missouri Compromise, to the policy of the
Pierce administration, and to slavery in the territories. It favored the admission of Kansas as a free state and incorporated the principles of the
Declaration of Independence in the platform. "We deny" asserted the Republicans, "the authority of Congress, of a Territorial legislature, of any
individual or association of individuals, to give legal existence to slavery
in any Territory of the United States." Instead, the party asserted "that the
Constitution confers upon Congress sovereign power over the Territories
. . . for their government, and that in the exercise of this power it is both
the right and the duty of Congress to prohibit in the Territories those twin
relics of barbarism,—polygamy and slavery." In addition, the party declared its adherence to an economic program that was as offensive to the
South as were its moral and constitutional declarations. A Pacific railroad
and congressional appropriations for internal improvements received the
hearty endorsement of the new party.

The nomination of an abolitionist candidate by a sectional party on
a platform which directly attacked the South and its institutions struck
terror in the South and among conservatives in the North. In the South,
old Whigs and Americans tended to go over to the Democrats in order to
defeat the Republican menace. In Georgia, the leading Know-Nothings
left the party asserting that Fillmore had no chance of election and a vote

for Buchanan was a vote to preserve the rights of the South. Throughout the South the idea spread that a vote for Fillmore was a vote for Frémont. Late in the campaign the remnants of the southern Whigs held a convention to endorse Fillmore, but the move did nothing to bolster the declining fortunes of the Americans. Everywhere were heard threats that the election of a Republican president on an antisouthern platform would constitute grounds for secession. The threat brought more southern Unionists into the Democratic ranks.

Even to northern conservatives the danger was apparent. Rufus Choate of Massachusetts understood the southern attitude. "I fear the consequences" of a Republican victory, he declared. "To the fifteen States of the South that government will appear a hostile government. It will represent to their eye a vast region of states organized upon antislavery, flushed by triumph, cheered onward by the voice of the pulpit, tribune and press; its mission, to inaugurate freedom and to put down oligarchy; its constitution, the glittering and sounding generalities of natural right which make up the Declaration of Independence." On election day, Buchanan polled the votes of all the southern states except Maryland, which went for Fillmore. New Jersey, Pennsylvania, Indiana, and Illinois were also Democratic, and Buchanan had 174 electoral votes to 114 for Frémont. A plurality of but 500,000 in the popular vote showed the South that there was still much to fear.

CHAPTER 17

A House Divided

1. LAST STAGES OF THE SLAVERY CONTROVERSY

WHILE political parties were in chaos over the extension of slavery, the slavery controversy entered a new phase. The most potent factor in the newer aspects was the operation of the Fugitive Slave Law. In the Georgia platform, the Democrats of that state had declared, "it is the deliberate opinion of this convention that upon the faithful execution of the Fugitive Slave Law by the proper authorities depends the preservation of our much-loved Union." But to Northerners the law was the most objectionable feature of the Compromise; and since its execution must necessarily involve some suffering, the abolitionists made the most of their new opportunity to stir up sympathy for runaway slaves.

Hardly had the year 1851 opened when the northern people were made aware of the presence of the slave hunter and the kidnapper in their midst. Abolitionists welcomed their presence and received a new stimulus from their activities. One rescue after another furnished fuel for abolitionist fires. A Baltimore sheriff shot William Smith, a Negro who had lived peacefully and happily in Philadelphia with his wife and two children. A Marylander laid claim to a Pennsylvania girl whose neighbors knew her to be free. When her employer proved her free status, he was hanged while returning home from the court. A woman was hastily sent out of Philadelphia in order that her expected child would not be born in a free state. William and Ellen Craft escaped from Georgia to the protection of the leading abolitionists of Boston, who resisted any efforts to arrest them and had their pursuers driven from the city. In Syracuse, a mob rescued one Jerry McHenry from the court of the federal commissioner and took him into Canada. A similar rescue in Pennsylvania resulted in the calling out of the marines from the Philadelphia naval yard to assist the marshal.

The rescue of a Negro named Shadrack was hailed by Theodore Parker as "the most noble deed done in Boston since the destruction of the tea in 1773." In April, the return of one Thomas Sims to slavery resulted in mass meetings and mobs in Boston which could not avail to prevent the federal authorities from placing the fugitive aboard a vessel bound for Savannah. These cases made it evident to the Southerners that the North would not give support to the law of Congress. There was no doubt that Emerson spoke the feeling of the northern people when he declared that the Fugitive Slave Law was "a law which no man can obey, or abet in obeying, without loss of self-respect and forfeiture of the name of gentleman."

This northern agitation against the Fugitive Slave Law mounted in intensity at the same time that the South was declaring its acceptance of the Compromise of 1850 and a renewed Union movement was turning the southern states from the ultrasectional views of the preceding years. In the same year that saw the election of Free-Soilers Benjamin F. Wade and Charles Sumner to the Senate, the Southerners were defeating their more rabid disunionists, retiring Jefferson Davis and other secessionists, and sending Unionists to Congress. Thereafter the Southerners labored in their political parties to commit their northern allies to accept the Compromise as a finality.

Even after both Whigs and Democrats had accepted the Compromise, continued agitation in Congress kept the question alive. Sumner lost no opportunity to condemn the Fugitive Slave Law. On August 26, 1852, he declared that the law lacked "essential support in the public conscience of the States where it is to be enforced." William Cullen Bryant declared that "we must make it odious and prevent it from being enforced." The constitutionality of the Fugitive Slave Law was also the subject of much agitation. In 1854 the Wisconsin Supreme Court declared the law unconstitutional on the ground that a jury trial was not provided for the fugitives and that the commissioners created by the law were illegally endowed with judicial functions. In 1858 the Supreme Court overruled the Wisconsin decision and upheld the constitutionality of the Fugitive Slave Law.

Contributing to the general agitation of the slavery question in the North came a renewed literary movement. Writers, varying in merit from forgotten abolitionist poets to New England's literary great, turned to penning indictments of the slave system. Richard Hildreth, the historian, laid aside his history of the United States to write *The White Slave*, a fictional account of the slave pen. Slave songs were popular in the North, among them such metrical lamentations as "Darling Nellie Gray," playing especially upon the anguished plight of the lover who had escaped from the system which had sent his dusky sweetheart from Kentucky to Louisiana's sugar plantations.

Most potent of all the fictional accounts of slavery was Harriet Beecher Stowe's *Uncle Tom's Cabin*. Actuated by high moral purpose and written in a style that appealed to plain people, Mrs. Stowe's work was doubtless intended to be an honest portrayal of the multifarious aspects of slavery. In presenting southern character, Mrs. Stowe pictured both weakness and strength, while she chose for the villain's role a New England migrant to the South. Culture, refinement, and peace were strangely mingled with murder, cruelty, and violence in pages which ran the gamut of human emotions from hilarious comedy to tragic tears. Measured by its influence and by the permanence of its appeal, *Uncle Tom's Cabin,* as a book or in its various stage versions, must be accounted the greatest literary work of an American writer. According to legend, Lincoln greeted Mrs. Stowe as "the little woman who wrote the book that made this great war." The soldiers who fought under Grant and Sherman had read the book, and by a strange and tragic substitution had identified Simon Legree as the typical Southerner.

To the Southerner, this refusal of the North to accept either the spirit or the letter of the Compromise was a distinct betrayal of confidence. Southerners took refuge in the contention that the Fugitive Slave Law was an integral part of a sacred compromise and assumed the role of defenders of the Constitution and the laws against northern disunionism. Although no accurate knowledge of the number of slaves who escaped from the South in the decade after the passage of the Fugitive Slave Law was possible, Southerners read with full credence a pamphlet of 1850 which declared that 46,000 escaped slaves were living in seven northern states. The average loss to the South for the preceding 40 years was $550,000, and the number of runaways was increasing rapidly. Alarmed by this property loss and by the statements of the abolitionists, the Southerners turned to a new defense of slavery.

Already fully convinced that slavery was justified on moral, biblical, historical, and economic grounds, the Southerners listened to the new rationalization which came from the pen of George Fitzhugh of Virginia. With the publication of *Sociology for the South, or the Failure of Free Society* (1854) and *Cannibals All, or Slaves Without Masters* (1857), the defense of slavery turned into an attack upon free society. Slavery was the natural lot of man, according to Fitzhugh, and God and nature had intended men to be slaves. The system of northern society, a new thing in the history of the world, was highly individualistic, primarily devoted to the acquisition of profits, wherein the weak were exploited for the benefit of the strong. "Free society asserts the right of a few to the earth— slavery maintains that it belongs, in different degrees, to all." Slavery was the only system that took for its primary task the satisfaction of the needs of all, and especially of the weak. To Fitzhugh, liberty was a fiction, for man could not exist without society, and the great need of man was to be cared for. The Declaration of Independence was founded upon falsehood, for nature had made men slaves to society. "All that law and government can do is to regulate, modify, and mitigate their slavery." In 1857, Fitzhugh carried this doctrine into the North and preached it to potential capitalists in the student bodies of Harvard and Yale. Nor did Fitzhugh fail to point out to the rising captains of industry that the adoption of slavery would prevent inevitable social revolution.

Science, as well as sociology, supported slavery and gave arguments to those who contended that the Negro was an inferior being. In 1854 Dr. Josiah C. Nott, a Mobile physician and briefly Professor of Anatomy in the University of Louisville, and George R. Glidden, elaborated in *Types of Mankind* a conclusion which Dr. Nott had been proclaiming for a decade. Nott declared, using evidence from his medical practice, that the Negro was a separate species, created apart, and demonstrably inferior. Thomas R. R. Cobb took up the argument, showing that the Negro's arched leg and receding heel were made for strength, and his nervous system fitted him for labor in hot climates. His mental capacity, limited by his cranial conformation, unfitted him for constructive social organization. Other respected scientific observers declared that the Negro had membranous eyelids—in addition to those in the Caucasian—which enabled him to look straight into the sun. Slavery and manual labor, said science, were the natural lot of the species.

Fitzhugh's aggressive doctrines were given a wide circulation in the southern press, from which they were copied by the Illinois State Journal and found their way into Abraham Lincoln's scrapbook to give a double meaning to his "house divided" speech. Southern advocates of slavery invaded the North, and Tennessee's "Fighting Parson," W. G. Brownlow, went into oratorical combat with the Reverend Abram Prynne, of Philadelphia, to defend and commend slavery. The Brownlow-Prynne debates, coming at the end of the era, summarized in a convenient textbook all the arguments that Southerners and abolitionists had been developing since the days of Dew and Harper.

The new spirit of southern aggressiveness manifested itself in two different fields: in a continued agitation for expansion southward, and in an agitation to reopen the slave trade. Perceiving that the North was growing rapidly and that the western territories would soon be converted into free states, the Southerners turned their eyes to Cuba. Quitman of Mississippi constantly raised his voice in favor of Cuban annexation, warning Southerners that "if slave institutions perish there they will perish here."

Less warmly supported by Southerners but ardently advocated by a handful of the leaders was the proposal to reopen the African slave trade. The scheme's proponents glibly pointed out that the great resources of the South could not be developed without an adequate labor supply, that the area of cultivation might be increased, and that if the price of slaves were lowered, the increased demand for land would raise the price and compensate the planters for the losses on slaves. Moreover, "it would admit the poor white man to the advantages of our social system; it would give him clearer interests in the country he loves now only from simple patriotism; . . . it would strengthen the peculiar institution." In addition, an increase in slaves would increase the South's representation in Congress. So attractive were these arguments that committees of the Louisiana and South Carolina legislatures favored reopening the trade, and the Southern Commercial Convention in 1859 announced its approval. Meanwhile, with such sentiment binding the hands of the officials, smuggling went on with impunity. Hundreds of Negroes were imported from Africa or Latin

America and southern juries refused to convict masters of slave ships. In 1859 the *Wanderer* landed over 300 Negroes in Georgia, but no efforts were made to stop the illegal traffic.

2. THE DRED SCOTT DECISION

In the midst of the agitation in the North over the Fugitive Slave Law and the actual hostilities in blood-flecked Kansas, the Supreme Court delivered its opinions in the case of *Dred Scott v. Sandford*. Dred Scott was the slave of an army surgeon, Dr. John Emerson, who in 1833 took Scott into Illinois and, a few years later, into Wisconsin Territory. Slavery was forbidden in Illinois by the Northwest Ordinance, and the Wisconsin territory was free under the Missouri Compromise. However, in both places Scott was held as a slave. In 1836 Emerson purchased a female slave whom Scott married and who gave birth to one child north of the Missouri Compromise line. In 1838 Emerson took his family of slaves back to Missouri. Four years later Emerson died, leaving Scott and his family to his widow, who married, some time later, C. C. Chaffee, an abolitionist congressman from Massachusetts. Scott remained in Missouri, where he was hired out at five dollars a month. Because he was incompetent, he was frequently without a master and depended upon the charity of Henry Taylor Blow, an opponent of slavery. Since the Negro would be less of a burden if he were able to keep his meager earnings, Blow brought suit for Scott's freedom. There were ample precedents in Missouri court decisions for giving freedom to slaves who had returned to the state after residence in a free state. In the first trial a decision was given against Scott, but after a rehearing the court decided that he was free. The case was then carried to the Supreme Court, where it took on a political aspect.

At the moment, Senator Thomas Hart Benton was waging a political battle in Missouri against the extreme southern viewpoints of some of the politicians. In 1847 Benton had challenged Calhoun's resolutions on slavery in the territories and had become anathema to the proslavery men of his own party. The Whig candidate for Benton's seat in the Senate made a bid for proslavery Democratic support by denying that Congress possessed power to legislate on slavery in the territories. Two judges of the Missouri supreme court agreed with this view and planned to co-operate in the movement by delivering an adverse opinion on Scott's case. However, the expected situation did not develop, and the case was not decided until 1852. Then the court declared that the laws of Illinois and of the territories had no force within Missouri and that Scott was a slave. In giving such a decision the court overruled the precedent already set in eight similar cases.

With this decision, Scott's friends decided to bring suit in the federal courts. To avoid endangering Chaffee's political career, Mrs. Chaffee transferred the ownership of Scott to her brother, John F. A. Sanford, whose name was misspelled "Sandford" in the printed report of the case. On the grounds that he was a citizen of Missouri, Scott brought suit in the federal courts against Sanford as a citizen of New York. In the circuit court, Sanford pleaded that the court had no jurisdiction, since Scott was a Negro and could not be a citizen of Missouri. The court accepted jurisdiction, and found that Scott was a slave, since his status was fixed by the laws of Missouri and the decision of the Missouri court. The case was then appealed to the Supreme Court.

It had been the hope of some of the Southerners that the question of slavery in the territories might be eventually resolved by court action. In 1859, Vice-President Breckinridge declared that the Kansas-Nebraska Act had "contained the provision that any question in reference to Slavery should be referred to the Supreme Court of the United States, and the understanding was, that whatever the judicial decision should be, it would be binding upon all parties." Soon after the Kansas-Nebraska Act was passed, Montgomery Blair took Scott's case, and in February, 1856, he appeared before the United States Supreme Court. In May the justices considered the case but were unable to decide whether the federal courts had jurisdiction. Accordingly, the case was re-argued in December, when a majority of the court agreed to dismiss the action on the ground that Scott was not a citizen of Missouri. However, it soon became apparent that Justices McLean and Curtis, the one for political and the other possibly for financial reasons, would present dissenting opinions covering the question of slavery in the territories. Chief Justice Taney was then instructed to prepare the opinion of the majority of the court.

As it turned out, each of the justices wrote opinions. The ablest was the product of Justice Nelson, who had first been instructed to write the majority decision. In his opinion, the status of a slave who had returned to a slave state was determined by the courts of the state. Since Scott had been declared a slave by the Missouri supreme court, the judgment of the lower federal court should be upheld. This opinion, however, attracted no notice, and public attention was directed to Taney's opinion, which was generally accepted as the decision of the Court. Taney, a Marylander who was personally opposed to slavery, began his argument with an attempt to prove that a Negro could not be a citizen of the United States. In doing so, he made a distinction between state and federal citizenship. Then the chief justice passed to a discussion of the power of Congress over the territories. Having earlier declared that Scott was not a citizen, he had practically declared that the Court had no jurisdiction. The latter part of his decision was, therefore, *obiter dicta*. The power of Congress to acquire territory, said Taney, carried with it the right to govern the territory. But this power must be exercised within the limits of a Constitution which forbade Congress to take property without due process of law. Since the prohibition against carrying slaves into the territories deprived the slaveholder of his property rights, the Missouri Compromise was unconstitutional.

In opposition to Taney, Justice Curtis wrote the ablest opinion. He destroyed Taney's contention that Negroes could not be citizens by

pointing out that they had been citizens of several states at the time
the Constitution was adopted. As for the power of Congress over the
territories, Curtis found no limitations upon what the lawmaking body
could do. Other opinions agreed with Taney on the question of Scott,
but not on the constitutionality of the Missouri Compromise. The only
opinion for which a majority could be counted was that a slave's status
was to be determined by the state of his residence.

No decision of the Supreme Court was more far-reaching in its
effects than the refusal to give Dred Scott his liberty. Contrary to expectations, the northern people did not respond to Buchanan's advice and
acquiesce in the judicial pronouncement. Instead, the Republicans, glad
to obtain an issue, hastened to attack the Court, and soon Seward
warned that the Court would be changed in order to obtain a reversal
of opinion. On the other hand, the southern adherents of slavery extension found the decision preferable to "popular sovereignty" and eagerly
embraced a doctrine that would guarantee them the right to carry their
property into the territories. To Douglas, the decision was a political
calamity. Whereas the people of his constituency would support popular
sovereignty, they would not endorse the Dred Scott decision. Douglas
faced the dilemma of abandoning his Illinois constituents in the hope
of Southern support for the presidency or clinging to his state and losing
the South.

3. The Panic of 1857

Simultaneous with Fitzhugh's sociological arguments in advocacy
of slavery, the economic justification of the institution seemed to receive new proof in the panic of 1857. The settlement of the controversial
issues in 1850 seemed to give a new impetus to the spirit of speculation,
and new gold from the Far West poured into the channels of trade,
while in the first half of the decade the settlement of the Midwest went
on with renewed vigor. Unhampered by restrictions, banking brought
unprecedented profits; prices mounted rapidly; and speculation in railroads, in city lots, and in new industrial projects encouraged the belief
that unending prosperity had arrived. Suddenly there came a reversal
of public hope: in August, 1857, the Ohio Life Insurance Company of
Cincinnati failed, carrying with it a number of banks in the surrounding
territory. In New York banks closed their doors to prevent runs. The panic
spread to Philadelphia, and soon most of the eastern banks suspended
specie payments. Railroads became bankrupt; mercantile houses withdrew their credit from retailers and went down with their customers.
With the approach of winter, unemployment grew serious; breadlines
appeared in the cities, and ominous warnings of disorders were perceived
in marching bands of men demanding various social reforms. Agitators
with socialistic or anarchistic panaceas found attentive audiences among
the urban unemployed.

Primarily a panic of the cities, the 1857 disturbance little affected the rural regions. The South, founded upon an agricultural economy, suffered less than did any other section. The banks of Kentucky and of New Orleans, thanks to better local regulations, did not close with the banks of the rest of the country. Moreover, the cotton crop for the year was better than usual and the foreign market remained good. Prices of cotton continued high, and Negroes sold for more than ever before.

To the Southerners, all this was proof of the superiority of their economic system. "The wealth of the South is permanent and real," proclaimed J. D. B. DeBow, "that of the North fugitive and fictitious." Boastfully the Southerners alleged that the money received for cotton had been the salvation of the North. The entire situation clinched the economic arguments for slavery and offered conclusive proof of Fitzhugh's contentions. When the Supreme Court gave judicial sanction to the inviolability of slave property, the fabric of the proslavery argument was complete.

4. The End of the Kansas Struggle

The Dred Scott case gave the Republican party a new issue. The party entered local contests in 1857 only to lose ground before the conservative Democrats and Know-Nothings. But their insistence upon the unholy character of the court's decision kept them alive until renewed troubles in Kansas stirred the country against Buchanan and gave a new lease on life to the northern sectional party.

Buchanan entered office with the Kansas question momentarily quieted by the belated firmness of Pierce and Geary. The Democratic party pledged itself in its 1856 platform to hold an impartial election in the territory, while the enabling act sponsored by Toombs in the previous July had provided for an election. Although Seward admitted that the Republicans were opposed to a fair election—"I recognize no equality in moral right or political expediency between slavery and freedom. . . . I do not think it wise, just, or necessary to give the people of a territory . . . the privilege of choosing"—the people of the country had approved the Democratic promises of an impartial election. The appointment of a fair-minded governor and the holding of a free and honest election would have satisfied the people. Unfortunately, Buchanan did not fulfill his promises of fairness.

The new president's first action in regard to Kansas was to replace Geary with ex-Secretary Robert J. Walker. The new governor was thoroughly honest and was committed to the policy of an impartial application of the principles of popular sovereignty. Before he arrived in Kansas, however, the territorial legislature had fixed the date for the election to a constitutional convention and the territorial secretary had apportioned the delegates so that the proslavery regions would dominate the convention. Accepting the situation, Walker appealed to the free-state men to participate in the election, but the northern settlers refused to vote. As a result, all the delegates to the convention were proslavery.

Only after this election were the free-state men convinced of Walker's impartiality. They then took part in a territorial election and succeeded in gaining control of the territorial legislature. This result caused Southerners to denounce Walker as a traitor to the South, and newspapers proposed that the forthcoming constitution should be declared in effect without submitting it to a popular vote.

The constitutional convention assembled in Lecompton lost little time in drafting a patchwork constitution for the proposed state. Knowing that a free submission of the slavery question would be defeated by the free-state majority, the convention resorted to subterfuge to establish slavery. The constitution was to be submitted to the people, who were to be allowed to vote "For the Constitution with Slavery," or "For the Constitution without Slavery." The slavery provisions were embodied in a special article which might, therefore, be rejected by the people. Even if the vote should be "For the Constitution without Slavery," however, other clauses in the document would protect slave property already in the territory. In either case, Kansas would become a slave state.

Even aside from the chicanery of this proposition, North and South were divided over the methods by which the constitution should be adopted. While Northerners were accustomed to having their state constitutions submitted to a popular vote, Southerners, who held that a constituent convention was itself the sovereign state, were familiar with the practice of declaring new constitutions in effect without popular ratification. The difference in constitutional practice intensified the attacks which Southerners in and out of Kansas leveled against the constitution. To Northerners the method, involving both a trick and denial of democracy, was doubly odious.

Walker himself deplored the actions of the convention and hastened to Washington to persuade Buchanan to repudiate the fraud. But Buchanan had filled his Cabinet with Southerners, and these, with the support of southern leaders in Congress, persuaded the president to accept the Lecompton constitution. In a message submitting the constitution to Congress, the president declared, "Kansas at this time is as much a slave state as Georgia and South Carolina." The rejection of the constitution would be "keenly felt by the Southern States." With this development, Douglas separated from the administration. Fully devoted to the principles of popular sovereignty, the Illinois senator saw its principles denied in the Lecompton constitution. Calling at the White House to protest, Douglas learned that his opposition would bring the enmity of the administration. "Mr. Douglas," said President Buchanan, "I wish you to remember that no Democrat ever differed from an administration of his own choice without being crushed." Indignantly Douglas replied, "Mr. President, I wish you to remember that General Jackson is dead."

In the Senate, the Committee on Territories brought in three reports. A majority report, signed by the Democratic members, declared that the free-state men did not have a majority of the people. Free-Soilers on the committee condemned the "border ruffians" and denied that a legal territorial government existed in Kansas. Douglas brought in a separate report declaring that the Lecompton constitution was not the work of the people or an expression of their will. In the debates that followed, Toombs declared, "this question involves the honor, rights, and safety of fifteen States, to whom the principle involved is of higher value than the Union itself." The power of the administration was sufficient to get the bill through the Senate, but the House failed to pass it. Eventually a conference committee agreed upon a bill presented by William H. English which offered the Kansans public lands if they would accept the constitution, but provided that the people should wait for statehood until they had sufficient population to elect a representative to Congress if they rejected the constitution. The constitution was to be submitted to a vote which would allow a negative vote on the entire document.

When the Lecompton constitution was submitted to the people of Kansas, on December 21, 1858, the free-state men refused to vote. The returns showed 6,226 for the constitution with slavery and but 569 for the constitution without slavery. Over 2,700 of the majority votes were fraudulent. There was little doubt that those participating in the election were a minority of the people. In January, the free-state men, acting under a law of the territorial legislature, went to the polls to cast 138 votes for the constitution with slavery, 24 for the constitution without slavery, and 10,226 against the constitution. The combined vote showed a majority against the constitution. The following August, the question was resubmitted with the English Bill dangling before the territory's land speculators. The vote showed that 1,926 were in favor of accepting the constitution and the bribe while 11,812 were opposed. The returns brought the Kansas struggle to an end, but the question had already served to upset political parties, to ruin the political ambitions of many men, and to intensify hostility between the sections.

5. THE LINCOLN-DOUGLAS DEBATES

The most significant political effect of the Lecompton question was Senator Douglas's opposition to the administration. During the congressional debates, Southerners used every effort to discredit the "Little Giant" before the country. At the same time, he lost his patronage, and his supporters, both in Illinois and in other states, lost their places. Douglas himself bore the brunt of the fight against the Lecompton "swindle." Republicans, who saw Douglas fighting their battle, gave him little help. Eastern Republicans such as Horace Greeley and Henry Wilson, however, regarded Douglas as a potential convert for their party and advised the Illinois Republicans not to contest Douglas's re-election in 1858. But the Republicans of the West saw clearly that Douglas was still struggling for popular sovereignty and was still a Democrat on all important issues. Although he might quarrel with Buchanan, he was none the less an opponent of the Republican party. Accordingly, they prepared to enter the campaign against him, hoping that the schism in the Democratic ranks would give them the victory.

Despite the opposition of the administration and the wholesale removal of Douglas's officeholders, the senator had sufficient influence over the Illinois Democracy to secure his renomination. Southerners denounced his actions and declared that Douglas was a traitor to the party. Administration supporters organized anti-Douglas tickets to divide the vote. But even with the Democrats split, no Republican cared to enter the lists against the redoubtable orator. Finally, Abraham Lincoln was chosen for the doubtful honor of running in a race that gave every promise of defeat.

Public interest centered in Illinois during the congressional elections of 1858, and Democrats and Republicans hung on the words of Lincoln and Douglas as the campaign progressed. In accepting the nomination, Lincoln declared his opposition to slavery and its extension. "A house divided against itself cannot stand," he announced. "I believe this government cannot endure permanently half slave and half free. I do not expect the Union to be dissolved—I do not expect the house to fall—but I do expect that it will cease to be divided. It will become all one thing or all the other. Either the opponents of slavery will arrest the further spread of it and place it where the public mind shall rest in the belief that it is in the course of ultimate extinction; or its advocates will push it forward till it shall become alike lawful in all the States, old as well as new—North as well as South." Carefully Lincoln had prepared the people of Illinois for this contingency. He had read Fitzhugh's arguments for the spread of slavery and he had diligently culled southern newspapers for aggressive statements on slavery extension. Reprinted in the Illinois State Journal, these items had made his audience aware of the real danger that "we shall awake to the reality . . . that the Supreme Court has made Illinois a slave State."

Against this viewpoint Douglas made laughing attack. "Mr. Lincoln," said Douglas, ". . . invites all the nonslaveholding States to band together, organize as one body, and make war upon slavery in Kentucky . . . upon slavery in all of the slaveholding States in this Union. . . . He then notifies the slaveholding States to stand together as a unit and make an aggressive war upon the free States of this Union with a view of establishing slavery in them all. . . . In other words, Mr. Lincoln advocates boldly and clearly a war of sections, a war of the North against the South."

After this opening declaration of principles, the two candidates began a tour of the state. Well supplied with money and supported by the railroads, Douglas waged a campaign of dramatic effectiveness. A special car was hitched to the trains for his convenience, and a small cannon mounted on a flat car heralded his arrival in a town. Lincoln's campaign was hampered by a lack of funds, his traveling arrangements were modest, and he was seldom able to attract the crowds which listened to his rival. However, the Republican press carried long accounts of his speeches and insistently demanded that Douglas answer questions which Lincoln propounded. Eventually, Douglas was constrained to accept Lincoln's challenge to a series of seven joint debates.

In the second of the debates, at Freeport, Lincoln proposed four questions to Douglas, the most important being: "Can the people of a United States Territory, in any lawful way, against the wish of any citizen of the United States, exclude Slavery from its limits prior to the formation of a State Constitution?" Douglas was faced by this question with an acceptance of the Dred Scott decision. Unable to repudiate Taney's opinion, lest he should lose the South, or to accept it for fear of losing support among Illinois adherents of popular sovereignty, Douglas replied in words which, while doing credit to his own realism, were also an effort to hold both groups of possible adherents: "I answer emphatically as Mr. Lincoln has heard me answer a hundred times from every stump in Illinois, that in my opinion the people of a Territory can, by lawful means, exclude slavery from their limits prior to the formation of a State Constitution. Mr. Lincoln knew that I had answered that question over and over again. . . . It matters not which way the Supreme Court may hereafter decide . . . the people have the lawful means to introduce it or exclude it as they please, for the reason that slavery cannot exist a day or an hour anywhere, unless it is supported by local police regulations. Those police regulations can only be established by the local legislature; and if people are opposed to slavery, they will elect representatives to that body who will by unfriendly legislation effectually prevent the introduction of it into their midst." The enunciation of the "Freeport Doctrine" saved Douglas in Illinois. The legislature elected in 1858 was Democratic and sent him back to the Senate. But the South preferred the Dred Scott decision to popular sovereignty as Douglas interpreted it and prepared to defeat the presidential aspirations of the "Little Giant."

Outside of Illinois, the elections of 1858 went against the Democrats. The Lecompton constitution and the Dred Scott decision had been widely condemned. New England went Republican; and in Ohio, Indiana, Michigan, and Iowa the party gained ground. In New York the governor and three fourths of the congressmen were of the new party. In Pennsylvania, the Republicans, Know-Nothings, and anti-Lecompton Democrats entered into a fusion that placed the tariff by the side of slavery as a campaign issue. The iron industry suffered heavily in the Panic of 1857, and iron manufacturers blamed the Democratic tariff. The fusion majority of 20,000 sealed the tariff as a cardinal Republican doctrine.

6. JOHN BROWN AND H. R. HELPER

The short session of Congress which followed the elections of 1858 constituted a sounding board for the sectional partisans. Republicans would control the next Congress and had more than an even chance of gaining the presidency in 1860. In spite of the aid which popular sovereignty and the Dred Scott decision had given them, the aggressive efforts of the Southerners to expand slavery had failed. With the coming of the Republicans to power, the Southerners would lose control of the government. Henceforth, the South faced the desperate alternative of secession or of remaining in a subordinate position in the Union. Preferring secession, Southerners defeated a bill to appropriate money for a Pacific railroad. "I am unwilling to vote so much land and so much money to build a railroad to the Pacific, which, in my judgment, will be created outside of a Southern Confederacy," explained a Georgian who believed that the southern states would soon "be compelled in vindication of their rights, interests and honor, to separate from the Free States." A homestead bill, long anathema to the Southerners, was rejected in the Senate, where the members turned to a proposal to appropriate $30,000,000 to purchase Cuba.

A new outbreak of the territorial question arose when an abolitionist proposed to repeal the English Bill and admit Kansas. Southerners revealed that they were prepared to demand a congressional slave code for the territories if one of them, in accordance with the Freeport doctrine, should pass "unfriendly legislation" against slavery. Douglas ignored southern support to reaffirm his adherence to popular sovereignty. Jefferson Davis informed Douglas that Mississippi would never vote for him, for the Freeport doctrine was offensive to the laws of the United States and destructive of sectional peace.

Before the Republican Thirty-Sixth Congress assembled in the winter of 1859, the country had been aroused to the highest pitch of excitement by the abortive raid of John Brown on Harpers Ferry, Virginia. The unsettled condition of Kansas had prevented Brown's arrest for the murders of Pottawatomie, and he had wandered freely about the northern states. In many respects, Brown was the embodiment of the most fantastic ideas of the northern abolitionists. Deeply religious, he had concocted a scheme so bizarre as to cast doubts on its author's sanity, yet he enlisted the moral support of many abolitionists and obtained money from such men as Samuel G. Howe, George L. Stearns, and F. D. Sanborn. In 1858 Brown made a raid into Missouri, where he rescued 11 slaves and stole a number of horses. In May, 1858, he gathered several of his followers into a "constitutional convention" at Chatham, Canada, where they adopted a "Provisional Constitution and Ordinance for the United States of America" and parceled out the national offices among the handful of disciples. In June of 1859, equipped with funds supplied by his New England backers, Brown leased a farm near Harpers Ferry, which he stocked with arms for his coming expedition. Seemingly his scheme was to seize Harpers Ferry and hold it as a base of refuge for the slaves of the surrounding region, who were expected to murder their masters and hasten to this new-found haven.

On October 16, Brown led the army of his new republic against the hill-encircled town. With 18 men he descended on the sleeping village and seized the railroad bridge and the United States arsenal. With his 30 prisoners, he established himself in the arsenal while a portion of his followers went into the country to arouse the slaves. One group was especially instructed to bring General Washington's sword from the near-by estate of Bushrod Washington, nephew of the first president. The raiding groups soon met failure. There were few slaves in the mountainous country near Harpers Ferry, which was far removed from the plantation area. No Negroes joined Brown, although some, notably those belonging to Bushrod Washington, were brought to Harpers Ferry by force.

The end of this fiasco came on October 18, when Colonel Robert E. Lee and Lieutenant J. E. B. Stuart arrived from Washington with a detachment of marines and besieged Brown in the arsenal. After a battle in which two of Brown's sons were killed, the raiders surrendered. On October 25 a grand jury indicted Brown for treason and waging war against the commonwealth of Virginia. Conviction quickly followed, and an alarmed judge sentenced the raider to death by hanging.

If it had not been for the excitement that these events inspired in North and South, John Brown's raid would have been merely a comic-opera war. In the weeks that followed, Brown himself seemed the calmest man in the nation. Convinced of the righteousness of his actions, welcoming the martyrdom that came to him, Brown bore himself with dignity while the nation engaged in a riot of extravagance. To aboli-tionists who could see no harm in an attempt to rescue slaves and who could even condone incidental murder, Brown was a martyr in a holy cause. To Emerson, Brown's gallows seemed comparable to the cross of Christ; and the Massachusetts legislature proclaimed the day of the martyr's death a day of prayer.

In the South, equal excitement prevailed. Governor Henry A. Wise of Virginia was panic-stricken, calling out the militia and the cadets of the Virginia Military Institute to protect the state. No one seriously thought of consigning Brown to an asylum for the insane, and Southern-ers trembled in the belief that Brown was but the advance guard of armies that would come in to "excite insurrection—apply the midnight torch—rob and murder." The lesson that the slaves would not arise at the behest of incendiaries was lost upon a people who shivered at the fear of being murdered in their sleep. Sanity was at a premium in both North and South, and the northern approval of Brown's murderous attempt gave impetus to the secessionists of the South.

The aroused sectional spirit found immediate expression in the Congress that assembled just as John Brown was going to the gallows. Resorting to strategy to prevent the Republicans from organizing the House, the Southerners raised the sectional issue. A Missouri member brought in a resolution that no man could be speaker who had endorsed Hinton Rowan Helper's *Impending Crisis of the South, and How to Meet It*. Since John Sherman, of Ohio, the leading Republican candidate, had endorsed a "Compendium" of this book, he was defeated for the office, while a debate over the slavery question prevented the election of a speaker until February 1, when a moderate Republican of New Jersey was selected. The debates gave new opportunity for the expression of violent southern sentiments and for renewed threats of a dissolution of the Union.

The book that was used as the occasion for this debate was written by a member of the yeoman class of North Carolina. Intended not as an indictment of slavery but as a condemnation of Negro labor, Helper attempted to show that the presence of the Negro in the South prevented the section from keeping pace with the rest of the nation. The material for Helper's arguments was found in the census of 1850, from which he drew startling comparisons between North and South. Taking states in pairs—New York and Virginia, Massachusetts and North Carolina, Pennsylvania and South Carolina—the author showed that whereas these states had had approximately equal wealth and population in 1790, in each case the northern state had surpassed the southern. Although part of Helper's effectiveness was due to the care with which he selected his pairs, the force of his argument was great. Especially striking were his statistics to show that the hay crop of the North exceeded in value the total returns of southern cotton, tobacco, and rice. To meet this situation, Helper proposed the gradual elimination of Negro slavery in favor of free white labor. In addition, he declared that the slaveholder owed the poorer whites the sum that slavery had cost the section.

Perhaps it was Helper's defense of the poor whites rather than his attacks on the Negroes that disturbed the southern leaders. Unable to gainsay figures—the census of 1850 had been compiled under the direction of J. D. B. DeBow—the Southerners took advantage of the use which Republicans had made of the book in the pending campaign to discomfit their enemies. Yet there were valid arguments against Helper's statistics. Since 1850 the price of cotton and of slaves had risen in the South, and the section had survived the Panic of 1857 so much better than the North that few of Helper's statements still had validity. The use of the book as a campaign document, however, the Southerners rightly regarded as another attack on the South. Of more significance politically than as an economic study, Helper's *Impending Crisis* did much to hasten the sectional conflict.

CHAPTER 18

The End of the Union

1. SOUTHERN PREPARATIONS

THROUGHOUT the congressional session of 1859-1860, nothing was accomplished beyond a clearer drawing of the sectional lines. All eyes were upon the approaching presidential election. A decade before, political parties with memberships from all sections had served to keep the Union together, but the Whig party had disappeared and a sectional party had taken its place. Internal dissensions rent the Democratic party along sectional lines, and the struggle between southern and northern men for control promised to break the last political tie holding the Union together. In Congress and in the states, southern leaders busily prepared to commit the Democratic party to a southern program.

Buchanan's quarrel with Douglas gave the machinery of the Democratic party to Southerners and their "doughface" allies. Secure in their hold on the organization, the southern Democrats prepared to drive Douglas from the party. On February 2 and March 1, 1860, Jefferson Davis introduced resolutions demanding a congressional slave code for the territories. Beginning with a reiteration of the southern theory of state sovereignty, Davis declared Congress must resist any discrimination in the territories against the people and property of any state. He denied the validity of the Freeport doctrine and announced that Congress should furnish a remedy for any unfriendly legislation by a territorial legislature. Only when the inhabitants of a territory formed a state constitution could they exclude slavery. These resolutions embodied the position of the southern extremists who warned Douglas that he must accept them or lose the votes of the South. On May 24, as the congressional session was drawing to an end, the Senate adopted Davis's resolutions.

While Democrats in Congress were formulating their demands, their party colleagues in the South were organizing for the coming election. "Southern rights" men controlled the party machinery in the states. In Alabama, William L. Yancey had control of the party. For a number of years Yancey had been agitating for an aggressive southern program. In 1847, extremists had forced the Democratic party of the state to demand congressional protection for slavery in the territories, and they had never lost their hold on the party organization. In 1858, Yancey formed the League of United Southerners, designed to work in all parties for the rights of the South. Although this league never had more than 75 members and was accounted a failure as an organization, the spirit that it represented continued to grow.

In South Carolina, too, the more ardent "southern rights" men controlled the state. In December, 1859, the South Carolina legislature proposed a convention of the slave states in order to formulate a united program. C. G. Memminger, who had long been accounted a conservative, introduced the resolutions. Memminger himself went to Virginia to induce the Old Dominion to co-operate. Addressing the legislature on January 17, he pointed out that in 1851 Virginia had urged acceptance of the Compromise of 1850 and that South Carolina had reluctantly followed her advice. But the Compromise had failed to secure the rights of the South, and a new movement, following South Carolina's program, was necessary. The elections of 1859 in Virginia preceding John Brown's raid had resulted in the election of John Letcher in a contest involving the extreme southern view. Letcher was from the Valley; he had formerly been an opponent of slavery and his support was drawn from the western counties, which also controlled the legislature. The Virginians were not ready to participate in a southern movement, and, although the legislature adopted resolutions declaring that sixteen northern states were united in a conspiracy against southern institutions, recommending an increase of the militia, and suggesting commercial nonintercourse with the North, the state sent no delegates to the proposed conferences.

Mississippi agreed with South Carolina and called a conference to meet at Atlanta, but the other states followed Virginia's example of fiery resolutions and inaction. In Alabama, however, the southern extremists were taking action. Governor A. B. Moore told his legislature that in the event of the election of a Republican in November he would call a state convention. In the Democratic convention, Yancey succeeded in getting his views endorsed. The Alabama platform, which the state's delegates were ordered to insist upon at Charleston, demanded protection for slavery in the territories, declared it the duty of Congress to open the territories to slaveholders, denied that a territorial legislature could exclude slavery, and endorsed the Dred Scott decision. In addition, the platform asserted the compact theory of the Constitution. Should these resolutions not be acceptable to the national convention, Alabama ordered her delegates to withdraw from the meeting. South Carolina, Louisiana, Mississippi, Florida, Texas, and Arkansas immediately endorsed the Alabama platform and their delegates prepared to follow Yancey.

2. THE DEMOCRATIC DIVISION

On April 23, the Democratic national convention met in Charleston. The selection of the place was itself a tribute to the strength of the party's southern elements, but a sufficient number of Douglas supporters were present in the convention to control its action and to prevent the nomination of anyone not acceptable to the Illinois senator. The fact that the nucleus of the Douglas support came from the states that gave every promise of voting Republican in November did not prevent Douglas's attempt to force his will on the party. His supporters were as willing as the Southerners to sacrifice the party's chances in the election, and they were determined to drive the Southerners out. A contest between two groups of New York Democrats, one representing the Douglas wing and the other the Buchanan officeholders, was settled in favor of the Douglas men. An attack on the unit rule resulted in a modification which the Southerners regarded as a trick to give Douglas more votes.

The platform committee, reporting on April 27, showed a hopelessly divided party. Unable to agree in committee, they reported three platforms. The majority platform, with the support of the slaveholding states, declared that Congress was obligated to protect slavery in the territories, while the principal minority report repeated the evasion of the Cincinnati platform of 1856 by declaring that "all questions in regard to the rights of property in states or territories . . . are judicial in their character" and pledging the party to adhere to a decision of the Supreme Court. The third report, signed only by Massachusetts' Benjamin F. Butler, endorsed the Cincinnati platform without comment. To the Southerners, the minority report was a dishonest subterfuge, for the Supreme Court had already acted and the time had come for congressional action. On the other hand, it was evident that while the Douglas platform might make headway, the southern platform could not carry the North. Southerners were therefore reduced to the position of asking northern Democrats to give up their chance of success at the polls for an abstraction. "Ours is the property invaded, ours are the institutions which are at stake," declared Yancey as he pleaded for a recognition of southern rights. But the convention adopted the minority platform.

As soon as the vote was taken, Yancey led Alabama's delegates from the convention. Then the delegations from Mississippi, Louisiana, South Carolina, Florida, and Texas withdrew, and part of the Arkansas and Delaware delegates followed them. Georgia withdrew the following day. After the withdrawals, the convention attempted to make a nomination, under the chairman's ruling that two thirds of the original membership was necessary for a choice. After fifty-seven futile ballots, the convention adjourned, May 3, to meet in Baltimore on June 18. Meantime the states were asked to fill their delegations.

The seceding members of the Charleston convention assembled to determine a program of their own. Upon the adjournment of the regular convention, these bolters called a meeting for June 11 in Richmond. They too prepared to appeal to the party in their states.

Within the seven states whose members had seceded from the convention, the Democrats faced the problem of taking action. There was still a possibility that the Baltimore meeting would accept the so-called "Tennessee Resolution," which expressly confirmed the Dred Scott decision. If this were done and a candidate selected who would give a southern interpretation to the platform, the South would have no need for a separate party. In Alabama, over Yancey's protest, the Democrats sent their delegation back to Baltimore, while the Douglas men effected an organization and sent a contesting delegation. Louisiana also sent a contesting delegation, representing Pierre Soulé's faction of the party, although the regular party reaffirmed the action taken at Charleston and a mass meeting of the businessmen of New Orleans endorsed the "Southern Rights" program. Texas, Arkansas, and Georgia returned their delegates to Baltimore, while South Carolina instructed her delegation to attend the Richmond meeting.

The Richmond meeting on June 11 accomplished nothing. Only South Carolina's delegates were officially accredited to it, and after two futile days the convention dissolved with all the delegates except South Carolina's going on to Baltimore. The possibility that the Tennessee resolutions, with a southern interpretation, would be adopted had disappeared when Douglas had announced his uncompromising adherence to popular sovereignty. Douglas's supporters had given a further blow to hopes of reuniting the party by declaring that the seceders from Charleston would not be restored to their seats. Douglas's supporters controlled the convention and they gave short shrift to the Charleston bolters, who, in most cases, were denied seats in favor of the contesting delegations. Upon this action, Virginia delegates withdrew from the convention, followed by those from North Carolina and Tennessee. Other delegations and individual members withdrew, until only thirteen states were left with full delegations. The remaining members were all enthusiastic for Douglas, but they represented less than two thirds of the original membership. A trick solved the problem of how to nominate Douglas without the customary democratic majority. By counting delegates who had withdrawn but who were still in the hall as voting for Douglas, the convention succeeded in obtaining a two-thirds majority for the Little Giant. Hershel V. Johnson, a Georgia Unionist, was nominated for vice-president.

On June 23, the delegates who had withdrawn from the convention, together with those who had been refused seats, held a meeting in Baltimore. Caleb Cushing, of Massachusetts, who had presided over the Charleston and Baltimore meetings until his own withdrawal, was made chairman of this new convention. Declaring themselves the true representatives of the Democratic party—and outnumbering those who had nominated Douglas—they proceeded to make nominations. The platform adopted was the rejected majority platform of Charleston. Vice-President John C. Breckinridge of Kentucky and Joseph Lane of Oregon were offered to the country in opposition to Douglas and Johnson.

3. CONSTITUTIONAL UNIONISTS AND REPUBLICANS

In the interval between the Charleston and the Baltimore meetings of the Democrats, two other conventions assembled. On May 9, the Constitutional Union convention met in Baltimore and on May 16, the Republicans assembled in Chicago. The Constitutional Union party was composed mostly of old southern Whigs who were still devoted to the Union-saving program of their defunct party and such elements of the Know-Nothing party as were unable to unite with the Republicans. The opening speaker struck the keynote of the convention as he pronounced slavery in the territories a "miserable abstraction." The assembled delegates from twenty-four states were intent upon continuing the old Whig practice of refusing to face the slavery issue. The platform was summarized in a slogan: "The Constitution of the country, the Union of the States, and the enforcement of the laws." Yet it contended for the rights of the states in a manner acceptable to the South. Although the leaders of the party did not deny the ultimate right of secession, they opposed the disunion tendencies which were everywhere apparent. For president they nominated John Bell of Tennessee, and they chose Massachusetts' gifted orator, Edward Everett, for their vice-presidential candidate. This ticket offered southern Unionists a political program and appealed to the patriotic sentiments of all men who were not intent upon dissolving the Union for partisan reasons.

When the Republicans assembled in Chicago, it seemed evident that the Democrats would heal their quarrels and nominate Douglas. That prospect made the candidacy of Abraham Lincoln more potent than any of the rival aspirants for the nomination had thought. Unlike the Democrats, the Republicans were united in purpose and had a large number of candidates who could well represent the unified sentiment of a sectional party. The meetings, held in a specially constructed "Wigwam," were crowded with enthusiastic Illinois spectators, who almost outnumbered the accredited delegates. Without dissent, the convention adopted a platform announcing the adherence of the party to the equalitarian principles of the Declaration of Independence, its devotion to the Union, and its observance of the rights of the states. It condemned the disunionists among the Democrats, opposed the "lawless invasion by armed force of the soil of any State or Territory," and excoriated the Buchanan administration for its course on Kansas. The "new dogma" that the Constitution carried slavery into the territories was pronounced "a dangerous political heresy," and the convention declared "that the normal

condition of all the territory of the United States is that of freedom."
It therefore denied "the authority of Congress, of a territorial legislature,
or of any individuals, to give legal existence to Slavery in any Territory
of the United States." Moreover, the convention favored a protective
tariff, a homestead policy, liberal naturalization laws, and appropriations
for rivers and harbors and a Pacific railroad.

Such a platform represented the interests not only of the ardent
abolitionists, but also of the small farmers of the West and the industrialists of Pennsylvania. In every respect, it was a northern platform in
opposition to all of the things for which the South had stood since the
formation of the Constitution. Willing to run on so violent an antisouthern platform were at least a dozen prominent northern politicians,
including Seward, Chase, Frémont, Sumner, and a host of favorite sons.
Seward was the leading contender, but the first ballot showed surprising strength for Lincoln. Upon the third ballot, Lincoln was nominated,
with Hannibal Hamlin of Maine as a running mate.

4. The Campaign of 1860

Abraham Lincoln was the least radical of the leading candidates
before the Republican convention. He was no abolitionist, and although
he was not in favor of the extension of slavery to the territories, he was
convinced that the national government had no power to interfere with
slavery in the states. He had, however, condemned slavery, and Southerners were inclined to read the worst interpretation into his remarks.
For political reasons, no southern orator could fail to point out the
inherent danger which a Republican success involved. Although the
Republicans pointedly condemned John Brown's raid and kept from
sight the harsher views of the abolitionists, Southerners regarded this
as an election trick. Fundamentally, the South was afraid that the election of a Republican would be only the first step in the abolition of
slavery. Helper's *Impending Crisis* made its reappearance as a campaign
document, accompanied by a brochure on *The Barbarism of Slavery* from
the vitriolic pen of Charles Sumner. Southerners were easily convinced
that these, rather than Lincoln's mild and conciliatory words, represented
the Republicans' real sentiments. With the elevation of the Republicans,
a process would begin by which no more slave states could enter the
Union. The multiplication of free states from the western territories
would eventually make possible a majority sufficient to amend the Constitution to abolish slavery. In the meantime, the failure of the government to enforce the Fugitive Slave Law would "abolitionize" the border
states and reduce the price of slaves in the lower South. Governors
of states, political leaders, and slave owners generally agreed that the
election of a Republican would be cause for dissolving the Union.

Deeper observers saw more than the abolition of slavery in Republican victory. The economic ideas of the Northerners—internal im-

provements, homesteads, and a protective tariff—were as obnoxious to the South as was abolitionism. Jefferson Davis had earlier charged the Free-Soilers with wanting to make the government into "an engine of northern aggrandizement," which "by an unjust system of legislation" would "promote the industry of the New England States, at the expense of the people of the South and their industry." His fellow Mississippian, Reuben Davis, saw that "there is not a pursuit in which man is engaged (agriculture excepted) which is not demanding legislative aid to enable it to enlarge its profits and all at the expense of the primary purpose of man—agriculture." From Pennsylvania came confirming echoes of a contest in which the Republicans were promising protection for industry, and from the West came the news of the vigorous campaign which Carl Schurz was making among the Germans who favored a homestead law.

There was, in fact, no unity among Republicans. Various state groups had coalesced upon a platform whose often ambiguous words held many contradictions. The common ground between the groups was an opposition to slavery's extension and to the continuance of Southern influence. State interests played a more important role than national issues in the Republican campaign, and the platform proclaimed the party's perpetual devotion to state rights. Yet Southerners ignored the conflict among Republicans, and saw only the doom of their section in Republican victory. Constitutional Unionists agreed with southern Democrats that the South should secede rather than submit to the "humiliation and degradation" of Lincoln's inauguration.

Although convinced that Republican success spelt doom to their section, the Southerners could not regard Douglas as preferable to Lincoln. Douglas's Freeport Doctrine and popular sovereignty would keep slavery out of the territories as effectively as would the Republican program. The supporters of the Illinois senator, however, charging that Breckinridge Democrats plotted to break up the Union, carried their fight into the South. They presented themselves as the only Union-saving party. Douglas himself came into the South to make a series of speeches pleading for Union and for peace. He denounced Breckinridge. Constitutional Unionists agreed with the Douglas Democrats on the charges of a Breckinridge conspiracy, but argued that only Bell's election could prevent disaster. Some observers hoped that the election might be thrown into the House of Representatives.

The election returns showed that the South was united against Lincoln. The Republican candidate polled but 3 per cent of the total vote of the South, and that in such disaffected sections as western Virginia and parts of the border states. Douglas had little southern support, receiving but 72,084 out of a total of 856,524 votes cast. Breckinridge received only a minority of the southern vote, and he lost the border states of Virginia, Kentucky, and Tennessee, which voted for Bell. Bell polled 34 per cent of the vote of the lower and 45 per cent of the upper South. The total vote against Breckinridge in the South revealed that a majority of Southerners opposed the extreme position that his party took. Of the South's electoral votes, Breckinridge received 72 and Bell 39.

In the country at large, Lincoln received 1,866,452 popular votes against 1,376,957 for Douglas, 849,781 for Breckinridge, and 588,879 for Bell. Although Lincoln had a minority in the popular vote, he received 180 electoral votes. These votes were so distributed that, had Douglas received all of Bell's and Breckinridge's votes, Lincoln would still have had a majority in the electoral college. While it was evident from the returns that the South preferred the Union to secession, it was also apparent that the majority of the northern people were unwilling to endorse the extreme proposals of the Republicans. In the House of Representatives, the Republicans would be in a minority of 21, and in the Senate their opponents had a narrow majority of 8 votes.

5. THE SOUTHERN REACTION

Lincoln's election shocked if it did not surprise the South. Throughout the campaign, southern leaders had freely asserted that his election would justify immediate secession. The nature of the situation had precluded the formulation of a positive program for action before the election. After it, there were several problems to face.

The first problem was to decide whether Lincoln's election was an attack upon southern institutions. Lincoln himself had taken pains to assure Southerners that he was no abolitionist and had asserted his willingness to guarantee slavery where it existed. Certainly, although it was possibly not known in the South, he had told his party colleagues that he favored the enforcement of the Fugitive Slave Law. Lincoln was only hostile to the extension of slavery in the territories. Moreover, moderate men and devoted Unionists pointed out that Lincoln's hands were effectually tied by a hostile Congress. With the Republicans in a minority in House and Senate, no element of the Republican legislative program could be enacted, and even the president's appointees need not be confirmed by the Senate. For at least two more years, no step could be taken against the South. After two years of presidential ineffectiveness, the people of the North would have lost confidence in a president who had, at best, but a minority vote in his favor. In addition, it was clear that Lincoln was not yet the leader of his party. State politics had nominated him, state issues had elected him, and state governors were —for the moment—more important leaders than the president-elect.

Despite these arguments, there was widespread agreement among southern political leaders that Lincoln's election was a threat to southern property. The Southerners were convinced that the North was contemplating an attack on the South's basic institution. Fundamentally, the Northerners were industrialists, foreseeing a society in which slavery would have no place. The victory of the Republicans, with tariffs for manufacturers and land for the landless, endangered the southern agricultural economy. The personal liberty laws, the failure to enforce the Fugitive Slave Law, the persistent propaganda of the abolitionists, and John Brown's raid were attacks upon the South, and the Republican party had been founded upon these assaults. Grown sensitive under a long series of attacks, the Southerners saw in Republican victory a menace to southern institutions which transcended in significance the personal opinions and yet undetermined influence of Abraham Lincoln.

Although the imminence of an attack upon slavery seemed obvious to extreme "Southern Rights" men, the leaders faced the problem of getting unified action from a section which was by no means an economic or social unit. The masses of the southern people were not slaveholders. Of the 8,039,000 white persons in the South, only 384,884 were slaveholders, and few of these had sufficient investment in slaves to be accounted members of the dominant planter class. Yeomen with but one or two slaves and the great mass of poor whites would not suffer great economic loss if slavery were eventually abolished. The life of the small farmer of the South differed little from that of the small farmer of the West. Yet these people were without organization and without a leadership from their own class. Dominated by the planter-politicians in politics and absorbing the planter's social philosophy in lieu of any other, they could be counted upon to follow the leaders in whom they had trusted so long. The poor whites were but little removed from the slaves, either economically or intellectually; and the threat of coming into immediate competition with emancipated blacks made them support a system which at least gave them a feeling of being socially superior, free persons. Ignorance of northern institutions and customs was a potent force in keeping these classes loyal to the South.

But the southern leaders themselves were not a unit for secession. The Bell and Douglas votes indicated that a majority of the people preferred the Union to disunion. Moreover, disagreement between economic interests and sectional groups made unified action difficult. The upper South feared that the cotton states would reopen the foreign slave trade and destroy the profits which the border slave states reaped from the traffic. The free-trade proclivities of cotton planters clashed with the protectionist desires of sugar growers. In New Orleans and other cities along the Mississippi, much of the commercial wealth came from trade with the Mississippi Valley. More articulate than the yeoman farmers, these moderating forces had prevented hasty action in 1850 and had generally thrown cold water upon the fire-eaters' ardent proposals.

To these moderate elements it seemed that Lincoln's election was not in itself an overt act against the South. Some of them favored co-operation among the southern states in order to obtain guarantees against further aggression; others favored waiting until assurances of foreign assistance could be obtained; still others feared that attacks upon slavery would be intensified if the South were to secede. All of them agreed that co-operation between the states should precede action.

The Secessionists resorted to haste to overcome the Unionists and "co-operationists." The lesson of 1850 was constantly in the minds of the leaders who favored secession. In 1850, co-operation had brought delay and compromise and had given Unionists an opportunity to organize and to render the Nashville convention ineffectual. In 1850, Whigs had controlled some of the states; but in 1860, fortunately for the secessionists, governors of all the states were Democrats and each had avowed his devotion to southern rights. Emerging from the campaign with organization intact, the Breckinridge Democrats were in a position to take quick action and present the Unionists with a *fait accompli*. On the other hand, the example of South Carolina's futile attempt to get other states to follow her in nullification had taught the lesson that unified action was imperative. The governors of Alabama and Mississippi solved the problem of how to get co-operation without a conference by appointing commissioners who visited neighboring legislatures in order to co-ordinate action between the states.

6. SECESSION OF THE LOWER SOUTH

South Carolina's peculiar electoral practice enabled her to take the lead in secession. The legislature, which had assembled to cast the state's electoral vote, stayed in session until it knew the results of the national election. When Lincoln's election was assured, the legislature called a state convention to consider "the dangers incident to the position of the State in the Federal Union." Mass meetings of aroused citizens chose delegates to the convention on December 17. Meanwhile, the other states were at work. Mississippi's governor convened the legislature, which called a convention for January 7, 1861. Alabama's Governor Moore, acting on earlier legislative instructions, ordered elections for a convention. Louisiana and Florida both acted quickly, but delays came in Georgia and Texas. In the latter state, Governor Samuel Houston bitterly opposed the movement for secession and refused to approve the call for a convention. In Georgia, the legislature assembled on November 8 and listened to a message from Governor Joseph E. Brown recommending retaliation against the northern states, an appropriation for the militia, and the calling of a convention. Georgia's Unionists, however, were especially active. Alexander H. Stephens, Linton Stephens, Benjamin Hill, and Hershel V. Johnson opposed secession, but Senator Toombs, T. R. R. Cobb, and Governor Brown favored immediate action. After listening to long and earnest debates between the two senators, the legislature called a convention to meet on January 16. It also appropriated a million dollars for military purposes.

When South Carolina's convention met, commissioners from Alabama and Mississippi came to promise co-operation. On December 20, the convention passed an "Ordinance of Secession," simply repealing the act by which the convention had ratified the Federal Constitution and the acts of the legislature ratifying the twelve amendments. "The Union now subsisting between South Carolina and other States, under the name of the United States of America is hereby dissolved." The convention appointed commissioners to visit the other states and propose a new Union on the basis of the old Constitution.

Photo by U. S. Army Signal Corps

HOWELL COBB. A Unionist in the crisis of 1850, a decade later Cobb resigned from Buchanan's cabinet to work for secession in Georgia. In 1861 Cobb presided over the Montgomery session which produced the provisional Confederate Constitution. He became an officer in the army, eventually a Major General commanding military districts in Florida and Georgia. He died in 1868, still resisting the national government.

Support for the secessionists came on December 6 from Secretary of the Treasury Howell Cobb, who published a letter to the people of Georgia declaring that each hour that Georgia remained in the Union after Lincoln's inauguration would "be an hour of degradation, to be followed by certain and speedy ruin." Cobb resigned from the Cabinet to hasten to Georgia to work for secession. A week later, thirty southern congressmen signed an address declaring that the Republicans would not compromise and that the South must secede. These addresses hastened action, and Florida and Alabama on January 9, Georgia on January 17, Louisiana on January 26, and Texas on January 31 seceded from the Union.

Despite the haste in which these conventions were called and the speed with which they acted, the Unionists were able to make some resistance. Unable to stop the wave of secession sentiment, Unionists took a stand for co-operation rather than for separate state action. South Carolina's action was unanimous, but in Florida 7 out of 69 members of the convention voted against secession. In Mississippi, 14 voted for the union and 84 for secession, while in Alabama's convention there were 45 co-operationists to 54 secessionists. The vote for the ordinance of secession in Georgia was 208 to 89 and in Louisiana 113 to 17. In Texas, where the ordinance was submitted to a popular vote, the 14,697 opposed to secession were overwhelmed by the 46,129 in favor of it. These votes, however, did not indicate the real Union strength in the South. The hastily called conventions and the lack of unity among the opponents of secession prevented Unionists from making a better showing. Many members of the conventions who had been elected as union or co-operation men found themselves unable or unwilling to resist the secession tide. Not the least considerable factor in this result was the failure of compromise proposals in Congress.

7. The Republicans and Efforts for Compromise

While the state conventions were being held in the lower South, Congress was considering proposals for compromise. Within Congress there were both moderates who were willing to make concessions to preserve the Union and extremists who were convinced that the time for compromise had passed. Among the former were the Bell and Everett men from the upper South and the Douglas men from the Northwest. Compromise would be a political advantage for the northern democracy. On the other hand, the secessionists from the lower South and the newly successful Republicans were opposed to compromise. Republicans could not afford to admit that their success in the elections had given the southern states justification for secession.

When Congress assembled, Buchanan offered his suggestion. The president had consulted his attorney-general, Jeremiah Sullivan Black, and had arrived at an interesting conclusion. He denied that the southern states had a right to secede, but he failed to find in the Constitution any power by which the federal government could coerce a state into remaining in the Union. In the dilemma, he proposed amendments to the Constitution which should recognize the right to hold slaves in the states where slavery existed, should give protection to slavery in the territories, and should write the Fugitive Slave Law into the Constitution.

In the House of Representatives, this part of the president's message was referred to a special committe of one member from each of the thirty-three states. In the Senate, it was placed in the hands of a special committee of thirteen. The House committee contained sixteen Republicans, some of whom had already indicated their opposition to compromise. While the committees were organizing, Congress considered two proposals which came from Andrew Johnson, of Tennessee, and John Crittenden of Kentucky. Johnson's suggestions for compromise struck at fundamentals and ignored such superficial remedies as Buchanan recommended. The Tennessee senator wanted constitutional amendments providing for the direct election of United States senators; the division of the country into electoral districts in presidential elections and a run-off election between the two highest candidates if no one received a majority vote; alternation of the president and vice-president between North and South every four years; and the division of the Supreme Court into three classes, one class to retire every four years and each class equally divided between free and slave states. Less drastic were Crittenden's proposals to extend the Missouri Compromise line to California and to protect slavery in the territories south of the line by a congressional slave code.

Johnson's suggestion received slight attention, but Crittenden's proposals were discussed in both Senate and House committees and were defeated by the Republican members of each committee. As Ohio's Ben Wade explained the Republican attitude, "It would be humiliating and dishonorable to us if we were to listen to a compromise by which he who has the verdict of the people in his pocket should make his way to the presidential chair." It was evident that the Republicans would not yield to the South or to the friends of the Union. Wade's speech was made on the day the South Carolina convention assembled and was generally accepted as an authentic statement of Republican intentions. Such speeches and the failure of Congress to agree on compromise proposals strengthened and hastened the secession movement.

As it became evident that Congress would frame no compromise, friends of the Union turned to a national convention which might represent the Union sentiment of the nation. Under a call from Virginia, delegates from twenty-one states assembled in Washington to consider making new efforts for compromise and to stop the drift toward secession and civil war. Already six states had seceded from the Union and, on the day the peace conference met, had assembled at Montgomery to form the Southern Confederacy. These states and Arkansas and Texas were not represented at the Washington peace conference, nor were the Republican-controlled states of Michigan, Wisconsin, Minnesota, California, and Oregon. The convention chose ex-President John Tyler as its presiding officer and immediately fell to discussing the bases of compromise. The sessions were secret, but on February 27 the convention adopted proposals differing only slightly from the Crittenden compromise. The amendment proposed by the convention would prohibit slavery north of 36° 30' but would not guarantee its existence against "unfriendly" legislation south of that line. Another amendment would require a three-fourths majority of the Senate to ratify a treaty acquiring additional territory, and the majority should include a majority of the senators from both the free and the slave states. A third amendment would guarantee slavery in the states and territories where it existed and in property under government control. A fourth proposal would prevent Congress from interfering with the surrender of fugitive slaves, would compensate owners for losses incurred by runaway slaves, and would prohibit the foreign slave trade.

In the convention, the border states supported these proposals while the New England states were in opposition to each of them. It seemed evident that the Republicans of the North would block any effort at compromise. Senator Zachariah Chandler wrote to the governor of Michigan that "no Republican State should have sent delegates, but they are here and cannot get away. Ohio, Indiana, and Rhode Island are caving in, and there is danger of Illinois; and now they beg us, for God's sake, to come to their rescue, and save the Republican party from rupture. I hope you will send *stiff-backed* men or none." In a postscript he added: "Some of the manufacturing states think that a fight would be awful. Without a little bloodletting the Union will not, in my estimation, be worth a rush."

The same opposition to compromise was expressed by Salmon P. Chase, who declared: "Mr. Lincoln was the candidate of the people opposed to the extension of slavery. We have elected him. After many years of earnest advocacy and sincere trial we have achieved the triumph of that principle. By fair and unquestioned majority we have secured that triumph. Do you think we who represent this majority will throw it away? Do you think the people would sustain us if we undertook to throw it away?

The peace conference submitted its recommendations to Congress, where Republicans prevented any action until the end of the session on March 4. This failure contributed to the secession of the states of the upper South. When Abraham Lincoln made no effort to compromise but showed instead a determination to enforce the laws in the seceded states, the upper Southern states followed the cotton states and entered into the Confederacy.

8. LINCOLN AND THE SOUTH

From the time of his election until his inauguration, Abraham Lincoln remained silent on the issues of the times. During the presidential campaign he had quite consistently told his friends that he was in favor of enforcing the Fugitive Slave Law, and he had expressed his willingness to guarantee slavery where it existed; but he was unalterably opposed to any extension of slave territory. In December, he declared privately that he was "sorry any Republican inclines to dally with Pop. Sov. of any sort. It acknowledges that slavery has equal rights with liberty and surrenders all we have contended for. Once fastened upon us as a settled policy, filibustering for all south of us and making slave states of it, follows in spite of us, with an early Supreme Court decision, holding our free-state Constitutions to be unconstitutional." This attitude, known to the leaders of the Republicans, strengthened them in opposition to compromise.

While the peace conference was in session, Lincoln left Springfield for a slow trip to Washington. He stopped to speak at numerous cities along the route, but for the most part his public utterances were in a trivial or a jovial mood. Yet he reiterated his belief that the Union should be preserved. In Philadelphia he declared that "the Government will not use force unless force is used against it," but he frequently asserted his intention of executing all the laws in all parts of the United States.

In his inaugural address, which was studied carefully in the slave states which had not seceded, the new president denied the right of secession and repeated his statements that he had no intention of interfering with slavery where it existed. Considering that the Union was unbroken, he would "take care, as the Constitution itself expressly enjoins upon me, that the laws of the Union be faithfully executed in all the states." In doing this no violence would be needed, yet he added the warning, "in your hands, my dissatisfied fellow-countrymen, and not in mine, is the momentous issue of civil war. The government will not assail you. You can have no conflict without being yourselves the aggressors. You have no oath registered in heaven to destroy the government, while I shall have the most solemn one to 'preserve, protect, and defend' it." The watchful people of the hesitating slave states found little satisfaction in these words. Unionist, co-operationist, and secessionist in the South agreed that states had the right to secede and that the federal government had no right to coerce a state. To all who had hoped for a program upon which the Union could be reconstructed, Lincoln's inaugural came as a disappointment.

Although Lincoln had announced that he would not be the aggressor, the possibilities of conflict were too great to be avoided. Most important was the question of the possession of federal property in the seceded states. As the states seceded, they occupied without difficulty most of the federal buildings on their borders. They took over post offices, mints, customs houses, and arsenals and garrisoned the harbor forts. In Texas, Brigadier General D. E. Twiggs surrendered the government property under his control to an irregular state militia.

The newest and strongest fort along the southern seaboard was Fort Sumter, nearing completion in Charleston Harbor. Just after South Carolina seceded, Major Robert Anderson moved his troops from the less defensible Fort Moultrie and Castle Pinckney to Sumter. The Carolinians immediately seized the abandoned forts and the secession convention appointed commissioners to arrange with the United States for Fort Sumter's surrender. Buchanan, however, declared that he had no authority to surrender the fort and referred the commissioners to Congress. With no intention of yielding to the southern demands, Buchanan reorganized his Cabinet with strong Unionists, and ordered reinforcements and supplies sent to Anderson in Sumter. As the steamship *Star of the West* approached the harbor, it was shelled from Castle Pinckney and Fort Moultrie. Since Anderson did not know the vessel's purpose, he made no attempt to protect her approach, and the ship returned to New York. Although this incident increased excitement on both sides, Buchanan failed to make the issue an excuse for war. By tacit agreement, the South Carolinians made no further demand for the surrender of the fort and the administration made no further effort to reinforce it. Buchanan thus turned

Photos by U. S. Army Signal Corps

JAMES MONROE, FROM A PAINTING BY WEIR (top). GEORGE McDUFFIE (bottom). While President James Monroe, tall and timid-looking, was remembered for the Doctrine which became the basis of United States diplomatic independence, South Carolina's George McDuffie was the champion of Nullification, the Doctrine which many in the South expected would become the basis for sectional independence through state sovereignty.

over to Lincoln the problem of protecting government property in the South.

As soon as Lincoln was inaugurated, commissioners from the Confederacy sought to make arrangements for the surrender of Fort Sumter. But Secretary of State Seward refused to receive either them or any communication from them. Finally, two justices of the Supreme Court attempted to act as intermediaries. Seward promised, on his own authority, to maintain the existing arrangements. Lincoln, however, was determined to make an issue of Fort Sumter and prepared, without Seward's knowledge, to send reinforcements to Major Anderson.

Meanwhile, the South made preparations to resist any effort to supply the fort. Brigadier General P. G. T. Beauregard supervised the placing of cannon along the shore and at Forts Moultrie and Pinckney. When the news arrived that Lincoln had sent supplies, Beauregard consulted Governor Pickens and asked the Confederate secretary of war for instructions. In Montgomery, the Confederate Cabinet considered the matter. The new government could not afford to have its authority defied by the relief expedition, and the Cabinet felt that action should be taken partly to vindicate the honor of the government and partly to hasten secession in Virginia and other southern states. President Davis instructed Beauregard to demand that Anderson evacuate Sumter.

On April 11, Beauregard made a formal demand for the surrender of the fort. Anderson refused but informed the messenger that he would have to abandon his place unless he received reinforcements. He did not know, as Beauregard did, that supplies were on the way. The Confederate general answered that he would open fire. Early in the morning of April 12—or so legend has it—the aged Edmund Ruffin, who had asked for the honor in recognition of his long agitation for southern independence, touched the match to the first cannon shot of the Civil War. All day, while the relieving squadron waited outside the harbor, the firing went on. On the evening of April 13, with food and ammunition exhausted, Anderson surrendered. There had been no loss of life on either side, though one of Anderson's men was killed by a bursting gun as a final salute was fired to the flag being lowered from the fort.

In North and South the bombardment caused great excitement. On April 15 Lincoln called for 75,000 militia to restore the authority of the Union.

9. SECESSION OF THE UPPER SOUTH

The immediate effect of this call for the militia was the secession of Virginia and other states of the upper South. On the day after the call, Governor Beriah Magoffin informed Lincoln, "Kentucky will furnish no troops for the wicked purpose of *subduing* her sister Southern states," and on April 18 Missouri's Governor Claiborne F. Jackson declared that the request was "illegal, unconstitutional, revolutionary, diabolical, and cannot be complied with."

Virginia's adherence to the southern cause was vital to its success. The division between the eastern and western counties, however, produced divided councils in the state. The planters of the Tidewater favored secession, while the western counties vigorously expressed devotion to the Union. As early as November 12, 1860, mass meetings proclaimed Union sentiments, denied the right of secession, and warned that the western counties would not follow the state into the Confederacy.

Governor John Letcher, who had been elected by the votes of the western section, found himself unable to resist the pressure of the politicians from the east and called the General Assembly to meet in extra session on January 7, 1861, "to take into consideration the condition of public affairs." Westerners opposed this action in fear that a convention would be called. The fear was soon realized, for on January 14 the assembly called a convention to meet on February 13. The call provided that any action taking the state out of the Union would have to be submitted to a popular vote. Westerners regarded this hasty action as an attempt to rush the state into secession.

The Virginia convention contained 152 members, 85 of whom were Bell men; 35, supporters of Douglas; and but 32, proponents of secession. From the elections it was estimated that a 50,000 majority was in favor of the Union. John Janney, a Unionist, was made president of the convention, which soon thanked Crittenden for his compromise efforts. Despite this Union majority, the secessionists in the convention succeeded in obtaining 14 of the 21 members of the Committee on Federal Relations. Commissioners from the states of the lower South appeared before the convention, holding out hopes for the state's prosperity in the Confederacy. Virginia would be the largest state in the Confederacy and would benefit from the trade of the cotton states. Such a lure was effective in causing Virginians to consider secession, and Unionists wavered in their devotion. Lincoln's inaugural met no favorable response in the convention, and five days later the Committee on Federal Relations made a report denying the fundamental principles of Lincoln's address and asserting the right of secession. The people of Virginia, declared the committee, would not allow the federal government to coerce the seceded states.

Slowly and insidiously the secessionists were leading the state from the Union. The convention recognized the independence of the Confederate States, and the secessionists prepared to take advantage of any development. When Sumter fell, a large crowd paraded before the governor's house, and almost immediately a mass meeting of residents of the surrounding counties began to assemble. The pressure of this volunteer convention soon forced wavering Unionists into the secession ranks. Under the excitement resulting from Lincoln's call for volunteers, the convention on April 17 voted 88 to 55 in favor of an ordinance of secession which should be submitted to the people for ratification on May 23.

Long before the vote was taken, Virginia had severed connections with the Union. Colonel Robert E. Lee, resigning from the United States

Photos by U. S. Army Signal Corps

ROBERT TOOMBS (*top*). PIERRE GUSTAVE TOUTANT BEAUREGARD (*bottom*). Toombs, a long-time southern rights leader, served the Confederate cause as Secretary of State and as a military official. Beauregard was a Louisiana general, popular among the troops as well as the southern populace, who commanded southern troops from Sumter to the siege of Petersburg.

Army, took command of the state's military forces. The state seized the arsenal at Harpers Ferry and the navy yard at Norfolk and made a military agreement with the Confederate government. It was generally understood that the capital of the Confederacy was to be moved to Richmond. On May 7, before the election was held, Virginia entered the Confederacy. The vote on May 23 was only a formal recognition of an accomplished fact. Secession was voted for by 126,000, and but 20,000 opposed it. The western counties, however, were not included in the totals. Already they had taken steps to secede from Virginia and form a separate state under the old flag.

Virginia's action was shortly followed by Arkansas and Tennessee. On January 16, the Arkansas legislature provided for a convention which assembled on March 4. Before that, Governor Henry M. Rector had obtained the surrender of the federal arsenal at Little Rock. The election, held on the question of "convention" or "no convention," resulted in a majority of 11,500 votes for holding a convention, but most of the delegates elected were avowed Unionists. Several propositions to pass ordinances of secession were defeated, and the convention adjourned on March 21 to reassemble five months later. However, the firing on Sumter and Lincoln's proclamation caused the convention to reassemble on May 6. On the afternoon of that day, by a majority of 65 to 5, it passed an ordinance of secession. Four days later Arkansas adhered to the Confederate States of America.

In Tennessee there had been but little secession sentiment before 1860. The popular leaders of the state were Whigs, and Bell carried the state by an overwhelming majority. Yet, largely owing to the energetic efforts of a handful of Democratic politicians, the Union strength of the state was broken down within six months following the presidential election. Lincoln's election, the failure of compromise efforts, and the gradual disaffection of such popular idols as John Bell weakened the Union cause, while Governor Isham G. Harris's indefatigable efforts for secession were eventually crowned with success.

On January 7, 1861, the Tennessee legislature met in special session. Governor Harris sent a message listing the outrages that the North had committed against the South and proposing a state convention. The legislature set February 9 for an election. Immediately a campaign began which revealed anew the deep-seated division among the sections of the state. The mountain counties of east Tennessee had few slaves, and the people were unsympathetic with the ambitions of the Confederates. The cotton-planting, slaveholding middle and western sections were in favor of southern rights. East Tennessee had been a Whig stronghold, but its Whiggery was that of Clay's American System rather than of the Black Belt aristocrats. Fully aware of the rich mineral deposits of their hills, eastern Tennesseans hoped for an industrial development which would never be possible in an agriculture-dominated Confederacy. Strong opposition to holding a convention developed in east Tennessee, and in the election the convention was defeated 68,282 to 59,449. At the same time, Unionist candidates for the convention, if one were held, received 91,803 votes to 24,794 for secessionists. This outcome gave the governor and his secessionist clique a temporary setback; but the failure of the peace conference, the firing on Sumter, and Lincoln's call for troops strengthened secession sentiment. Led by Bell, old Whig leaders issued a statement condemning Lincoln and approving Harris's course. To their mind, the solution lay in holding another conference. But the secessionists did not desire a conference. Harris called a special session of the legislature for April 25 and recommended to it an ordinance of secession and union with the Confederacy. Meanwhile John Bell pronounced in favor of secession and weakened the Union cause. The legislature passed an ordinance of secession to be submitted to the people in a popular election on June 8.

Without waiting for the election, the legislature received commissioners from the Confederacy and on May 7 approved a military league with Davis's government. For all practical purposes, Tennessee was a part of the Confederacy before the people had an opportunity to ratify the action. Preparations for the election went on, however, with east Tennessee again proclaiming Unionist sentiments. Congressman T. A. R. Nelson and Senator Andrew Johnson returned to campaign for the Union throughout the eastern counties. "Parson" W. G. Brownlow, who had only recently spoken the final word on the desirability of slavery, turned the vitriolic columns of his Knoxville *Whig* to a castigation of secessionists. "You may leave the vessel," he had told South Carolinians in November, 1860, ". . . you may go out in the rickety boats of your little state, and hoist your miserable *cabbage-leaf* of a palmetto flag; but depend upon it, men and brethren, you will be dashed to pieces on the rocks." He warned the people that the "vilest, most damnable, deep-laid, and treacherous conspiracy that was ever concocted in the busy brains of the most designing knave is being hatched to destroy [their] liberties by breaking up this government." Under such leadership, the east Tennessee counties held a convention at Knoxville before the election to declare that "the Constitution of the United States has done us no wrong. The Congress of the United States has passed no law to oppress us. The President of the United States has made no threat against the law-abiding people of Tennessee." The convention prepared for secession from the state if the election took Tennessee from the Union. On the eve of the election, Confederate troops arrived in the eastern counties and contributed by their presence to the results. The vote was 105,379 for the ordinance of secession and 47,233 against it. Of the minority, 30,000 votes came from east Tennessee. Andrew Johnson, alone of the southern senators, refused to resign his seat, and east Tennessee's Union congressmen remained in their places in Washington.

Last of the southern states to secede was North Carolina. There, too, the people of the western mountains were Unionists, but they were in a minority in the state convention. Small farmers were opposed to secession, and small manufacturers in the middle region preferred the Union. However, with her neighbors on all sides in the Confederacy, North Carolina was forced to yield to circumstances. On May 20, an ordinance of secession passed, and North Carolina joined the Confederacy.

Three southern states remained in the Union. In Maryland, Governor Thomas H. Hicks pursued a vacillating course but failed to assemble his legislature to take action. Riots broke out in Baltimore as the first troops answering Lincoln's call passed through the city. However, the Baltimore and Ohio Railroad was loyal to the Union, and federal troops soon suppressed the rioters. Lincoln authorized General Winfield Scott to suspend the writs of habeas corpus, and under martial law sufficient secessionist leaders were arbitrarily arrested to hold Maryland in the Union. Governor Magoffin proclaimed Kentucky's neutrality, which Lincoln respected until the state's secession was rendered improbable. In Missouri, Governor C. F. Jackson, hoping to take his state into the Confederacy, assembled the militia in St. Louis. However, the Blair family of Missouri had persuaded Lincoln to send Captain Nathaniel Lyon to command the federal arsenal. Lyon marched against the militia and forced their surrender. Although Jackson proclaimed Missouri's secession, he was driven from Jefferson City and the state remained in the Union.

Secession had come about through the better organization of those politicians who had feared the election of Lincoln. Quick action, the rejection of compromise by both the ultra-southerners and the Republicans, and the consequences of Fort Sumter brought secession. Many Union-saving forces in the South, however, might have prevented the action had they been given time to exercise a moderating influence. For the most part, the banks of the South were so dependent upon the preservation of the Union for their prosperity that they were opposed to secession. Commercial interests along the Ohio and Mississippi Rivers, whose business was intersectional in character, knew that they would be injured by secession. Moreover, there were sentimental reasons which might have operated against a dissolution of the Union. Many Northerners were resident in the South, such as Doctor George Junkin, president of Washington College at Lexington, Virginia, who devoted his time to teaching his senior class a northern interpretation of the Constitution. The mountain regions of Virginia, North Carolina, Tennessee, Alabama, and Georgia were potentially industrial regions that looked to the North rather than to the South. Religious connections in the Catholic, Episcopal, and Presbyterian Churches with the North contributed to the Union sentiment. In addition, numerous politicians, mostly old Whigs and Douglas Democrats, had been long dependent upon their northern connections. None of these forces was sufficiently articulate or well enough organized to prevent secession, but all of them remained to harass the days of the Confederacy and to hasten the eventual reunion of the United States.

C H A P T E R   1 9

The Confederate States of America

1. THE CONFEDERATE GOVERNMENT

ON February 4, 1861, just a month before Abraham Lincoln was inaugurated, representatives from six seceded states assembled at Montgomery, Alabama. Within four days the delegates, under the presidency of Howell Cobb, had adopted a provisional constitution for the Confederate States of America. The first of the fifty signers of the new instrument of government was South Carolina's Robert Barnwell Rhett.

The task before the framers of the Confederate Constitution was not difficult, for the South had few objections to the Constitution of the United States. Indeed, in southern theory, secession was a method of preserving the good features of the document of 1787 and of ridding themselves of obnoxious misinterpretations which had grown up. The new Constitution was therefore but a modification of the old, and was more notable for its resemblance to the familiar system of government than for its changes. Like the "fathers" at Philadelphia, the members of the Montgomery convention were more concerned with making a working system than with political experimentation. In the preamble of the Confederate Constitution the words "we the people of the Confederate States" appeared, but with the explanatory clause, "each state acting in its sovereign and independent character," added. Meeting a frequent criticism of the Federal Constitution, the preamble invoked "the favor and guidance of Almighty God" upon the new nation.

The Constitution incorporated the twelve amendments of the United States Constitution in the body of the document, eliminating the

285

clauses which had been supplanted. It conferred the same powers of taxation upon Congress but forbade appropriations for bounties or internal improvements and a protective tariff. It forbade the African slave trade, but permitted the importation of slaves from the slave states of the United States. The government was given the right to acquire territory in which slavery should "be recognized and protected by Congress and by the territorial government." Governors of the states must return fugitive slaves. The "federal-ratio" was continued in apportioning representatives among the states. The Confederate instrument also took care of states' rights. Although the "supreme law of the land" clause found its way into the new Constitution, and state officers must swear support, Confederate officials who operated solely within the limits of a state might be impeached by the state legislature.

More significant than perhaps the framers knew were other variations from the older frame of government. An executive budget was provided for; and the president, who was elected for six years but was ineligible for re-election, might veto separate items in an appropriation bill. The Cabinet might be invited to occupy seats, though not to cast votes, in the House and Senate. Before the end of the Confederacy, these provisions gave evidence of containing the germs of a modified parliamentary government.

Although this Constitution was provisional, its chief provisions carried over into the permanent one. The Montgomery convention also established a provisional government to take charge of the nation. After electing Jefferson Davis, of Mississippi, and Alexander H. Stephens, of Georgia, as provisional president and vice-president, the convention resolved itself into the Congress of the Confederate States. In choosing Davis and Stephens, the convention seems to have been actuated by a desire to select conservatives for the first places in the government. William L. Yancey, Robert Barnwell Rhett, Howell Cobb, and Robert Toombs were better known as secessionists, and would have appeared more appropriate choices. But the members of the convention were conservative; Yancey was not even a member, and Rhett was overshadowed by the moderate men in South Carolina's delegation. Georgia's leaders, Cobb and Toombs, neutralized each other, and the convention selected Stephens, who had vigorously opposed secession. Davis's military record in the Mexican War, his display of administrative ability as Pierce's secretary of war, and his senatorial career commended him to the conservative members of the convention.

Davis himself did not share the convention's estimate of his talents. Already appointed major-general of Mississippi's militia, he hoped to be made general-in-chief of the Confederate armies. He accepted the provisional presidency half hoping that the duties would be but temporary. Temperamentally, Davis was ill-fitted for the trying days before him. His health was bad and possibly clouded his judgment in crises. He knew little of the arts of politics, and his devotion to the strict letter of the Constitution was a liability in the head of a warring and revolutionary state.

Photo by U. S. Army Signal Corps

JEFFERSON DAVIS. Graduated from West Point in 1828, Davis resigned his commission in 1835 and became a Mississippi plantation owner. At Buena Vista, in the Mexican War, he commanded a militia regiment which "stood fast" against a charge of Mexican lancers, though Davis himself was severely wounded. In the crisis of 1850 he counselled moderation, and in 1853 he became Pierce's Secretary of War. Later he returned to the Senate as a proslavery leader. In 1861 he hoped to be made general-in-chief of the Confederate armies. Temperamentally, Davis was ill-fitted for the trying responsibilities as President of the Confederate States.

Never popular, he lacked the ability to dramatize the Confederate cause before the southern people.

On February 18, Davis was inducted into office. In his inaugural address he sought to define the Confederate position and to appeal to the North for peace. He hoped that the "beginning of our career in a Confederacy may not be obstructed by hostile opposition." As an agricultural country, "our future policy is peace"; but Davis warned the North and encouraged the South by stating that if "the integrity of our territory and jurisdiction be assailed, it will remain for us with firm resolve to appeal to arms and invoke the blessing of Providence on a just cause."

For his Cabinet, Davis selected Robert Toombs as secretary of state, C. G. Memminger of South Carolina as secretary of the treasury, L. P. Walker of Alabama as secretary of war, S. R. Mallory of Florida for the navy department, Judah P. Benjamin of Louisiana for attorney-general, and John H. Reagan of Texas for postmaster-general. It was a Cabinet of considerable ability, but it revealed Davis's lack of political insight. Only Toombs represented the ardent secessionists, and only Walker could be said to belong in the ranks of the planter aristocracy. Memminger was a Charleston lawyer who combined a devotion to sound currency with a taste for theological controversy. Mallory had served on the naval committees in the United States Congress, while Benjamin, a Jewish lawyer, possessed great ability but was highly unpopular. No member of the Cabinet brought political strength to the administration. The president made no effort to appeal to either the fire-eating secessionists or the devoted Unionists.

Confederate justice stemmed directly from the federal court system. Although no supreme court was ever established, district courts functioned without a hitch. In many places the same judges continued to preside over the courts and to apply the laws of the United States to new Confederate problems. The transition from Federal to Confederate justice was so simple that it was unnoticed. As time brought new problems, the Confederate Congress established courts of admiralty, territorial courts, and special courts for Indian troubles.

Hardly had the provisional government been launched when opposition raised its head. Rhett's Charleston *Mercury* began an opposition which was to continue with increasing bitterness during the Confederacy's existence. The Constitution's tariff provisions and its prohibition of the slave trade drew the *Mercury's* fire. Part of the discontent was due to Davis's having overlooked the Rhett faction in his Cabinet. More fundamental as a cause of opposition was the fact that the new Constitution neglected, and the new president ignored, states' rights. The secession of the southern states had been justified on constitutional grounds by appeals to the states'-rights philosophy. Although all Southerners talked in terms of these theories, to many, such theories were a convenient rationalization rather than a vital article of faith. In the newer states of the Southwest, which were less attached to the community, men thought in terms of southern nationalism; while in the older states, such as South Carolina, Georgia, and Virginia, local patriotism took precedence over loyalty to the Confederacy. The distinction was subtle but vital. Jefferson Davis was a southern nationalist, while Robert E. Lee, whose devotion to Virginia led him to resign his commission in the United States army and brought on him charges that he neglected the rest of the South, was the highest embodiment of the principles of states' rights. Some other adherents of Lee's constitutional views lacked his simple honesty and earnest devotion and cloaked a captious criticism of the administration in terms of pious jealousy for the liberties of their states. From the beginning, the Confederacy carried with it the germs of a paralyzing disease, and in the end it "died of states' rights."

Yet in essence the Southern Confederacy represented the principles, the precepts, the practices, and the defects of the old Federal Union established by the Fathers, and opposed the new ideas, the new concepts, and the revolutionary practices of the New Nation, which, under Abraham Lincoln's guiding hand, was taking form during the Civil War. To the Confederate supporters it seemed that revolutionary forces, seeking to alter the basic substance of America, had seized the apparatus of government and were attempting to effect far-reaching changes. The Confederates fought the ancient battle of conservatism against the forces of an alleged progress.

2. WAR PREPARATIONS

The Confederate States of America had no opportunity for a normal peacetime development. From the beginning, it faced a war, and the necessities of armed conflict distorted its civic evolution. Within six weeks after Abraham Lincoln's inauguration, the first shot at Sumter had lighted the holocaust that drove the border states into secession and forced the Davis government to devote its major efforts to military affairs. As soon as Virginia seceded, the Confederate capital was moved to Richmond, where President Davis was placed so close to the embattled armies that his vision of civil affairs was blinded by bayonets glistening in the southern sun.

The first task before the Confederate government was the organization of men and materials for the armies. The South received with joy the news of Sumter, and torch parades and fire-eating speeches marked the celebrations in many communities. In anticipation of the day, militia companies had organized, and during the 'fifties military training had appeared in southern colleges. States had purchased supplies of arms, and at the time of John Brown's raid Virginia had been put on a war footing. Yet the Confederacy's military resources were small compared with those of the North. The total population of the 11 Confederate States was but 9,000,000, over one third of whom were blacks; while the 23 states of the North contained 22,000,000 people. In terms of man power, these figures meant that the South had only a little over 1,000,000 men between the ages of 18 and 45 available for service, while the North had over 4,500,000 between these ages. The task of organizing an effective army to oppose such odds was Herculean, and the successful resistance that the Confederacy made to the overwhelming man power of the North was a tribute to both the genius of southern leaders and the morale of the men in the ranks.

The condition of material for the conduct of a war was even less favorable than the available man power. Federal arsenals in the South— which were immediately seized by the seceding states—contained 135,000 stands of arms, but only 10,000 of these were modern. The rest were smooth-bore muskets, many of which had to be altered from flintlock to percussion caps before they could be used. Among the southern people there were many arms, but these were so varied as to be almost useless for military purposes. Hastily Davis dispatched an agent to Europe to purchase 10,000 rifles. Five hundred thousand would have answered the need. Throughout the war the southern soldier was poorly armed and depended frequently on arms taken in battle. Sometimes deserters from the Union ranks who allowed themselves to be captured by the Confederates were sent home as prisoners awaiting exchange and were paid for the rifles they carried across the lines.

The South lacked both machinery and material for manufacturing munitions. Southern armories could make paper cartridges and caps for muskets, and women were organized in their counties to wrap cartridges for the armies. General Josiah Gorgas efficiently organized Confederate powder mills, and there seldom was a shortage of ammunition. The Tredegar Iron Works at Richmond, largest in the South, manufactured heavier ordnance, and smaller plants, notably at Selma, Alabama, and Atlanta, Georgia, turned their energies to the production of war material.

In wealth and resources the Confederacy was notably weak. The total taxable wealth was $4,220,755,834, of which $1,500,000,000 was in slaves and almost as much in real estate, $500,000,000 in loans and $94,000,000 in bank stock. The slave property was concentrated in few hands, and much of the real estate was burdened with debt. The railroads of the South could not compare with those of the North. One line of railroad ran from Charleston through Chattanooga to Memphis and the Mississippi, while another line, beginning at Chattanooga, ran at right angles to the first and terminated at Petersburg, near Richmond. On the military scene these roads were vital to the South, but the scarcity of material for their repair soon impaired their service. The Confederacy had no place where locomotives could be manufactured, and the concentration of the available iron works upon munitions prevented the construction of new lines of railroads or the repair of the old. Before the war was over, the rails were torn from vital lines to repair those of immediate necessity.

Two elements in the southern economic system were of value to the Confederacy and went far to make up for the deficiencies in other resources —the southern predominance in the world's cotton markets and the fact that the Confederate population was overwhelmingly agricultural. The cotton figured largely in Confederate diplomacy, while the agricultural resources of the South kept its armies in the field and fed them far longer than would have seemed possible.

In purely military matters, the southern nation had definite advantages at the beginning of the war. Southern men were more accustomed to handling arms than were those who entered the northern armies. Moreover, the South could build a complete military organization without being hampered by an existing army. The personnel of the southern military leadership was high. The officers had been trained in the army of the United States, and their resignations injured that army as much as they benefited the Confederacy. Because of the greater rewards which could be obtained from civil employment, many of the ablest graduates of West Point had left the army of the United States. Among those who remained, the most capable were from the South, where the military tradition was strong. Moreover, in recent years, the superintendents of West Point, the secretaries of war, and commanding officers of the army had been from the South. Not entirely without reason it was charged that General Winfield Scott had given the best appointments to Southerners. The result was that the tradition of the old army was southern. The Southerners had taken readily to army life and had given whatever social prestige there had been to army society.

At the outbreak of the war, the commanding general of the federal army was Major General Scott, a Virginian who remained true to the Union. Two of the brigadier generals were Southerners, while Scott's staff was composed largely of men with southern sympathies. Most promising of the officers of the army was Colonel Robert E. Lee, who had been superintendent of West Point and was at the moment attached to a western command. To Lee, Scott offered the actual command of the northern armies; but on the day after Virginia's secession, Lee resigned to follow his state. He was immediately made major general in command of Virginia's troops and began the task of reorganizing the Old Dominion's soldiers for the coming war. Like Lee, Albert Sidney Johnston, said to have been Scott's favorite subordinate; Joseph E. Johnston, quartermaster-general; and Samuel Cooper, New Jersey-born adjutant-general of the army, resigned their commissions to accept appointments from President Davis. Altogether, 387 out of 1,108 officers left the Federal for the Confederate service.

The higher ranks of the Confederate armies were well manned. The volunteers who came to answer Davis's call for 100,000 men came with their own arms in their hands and wearing their own uniforms. Occasionally a private, and frequently the officers, brought along their own personal servants. The men were familiar with weapons, and the officers, thanks to the experience of the plantation, had had some experience in handling men. The cavalry and the artillery were especially attractive to men of the upper social classes—possibly because of the chivalric ideal of the mounted knight—while the poorer classes, men from the sand hills and the pine barrens, had perforce to march in the infantry.

3. Disaffection in the Confederacy

While the state and Confederate governments were estimating their resources and marshaling the first of the "boys in gray," the new government faced disaffection in the vital Allegheny region. In western Virginia and eastern Tennessee the small farmers of the mountains and the valleys had little sympathy with their planting and slaveholding neighbors. The rich deposits of coal and iron in these regions were potentially valuable to the Confederacy, but the inhabitants had visions of industrial development and had long been adherents of Clay's American System. Their industrial potentialities would remain unrealized in a government dominated by the antitariff, anti-internal-improvements planters of the cotton

South. Nothing in their experience as parts of Virginia and Tennessee led them to expect prosperity in the Confederacy.

The secession of Virginia was accomplished without the approval of the delegates from the western counties. Before the secession ordinance had been ratified by a popular vote, the inhabitants, smarting under ancient grievances, made preparations to repudiate the action of the eastern Virginians. John S. Carlile headed a movement to make a separate and loyal state of West Virginia, while western delegates assembled in Richmond to covenant with each other to keep Virginia in the Union. Back in their districts, these men spoke against secession, and on April 22, 1861, a mass meeting at Clarksburg called for the election of delegates to a meeting at Wheeling.

The first Wheeling convention assembled on May 13 to listen to confused counsel and contented itself with an address advising the people to vote against the secession ordinance. However, it called for another convention to meet on June 11. On that date, 100 delegates from 34 counties assembled in the "Second Wheeling Convention" to denounce secession and form a loyal government for Virginia. Francis H. Pierpont was elected governor and the legislature was ordered to assemble. Secretly, it was understood, this "loyal" Virginia legislature would give permission, in the name of the Commonwealth, to the western counties to form themselves into a separate state. On July 1 the General Assembly met, elected senators for the vacant seats in the United States Senate, and filled other offices of the state government. With this they were content, but the Wheeling convention reassembled and ordered the election of delegates to a constitutional convention. The convention, meeting on November 26, adopted a constitution for the new state of "West Virginia." This constitution was ratified on April 3, 1862, and on May 14 the legislature gave its consent to the formation of the new state. In the following April, Congress admitted West Virginia to the Union.

From the beginning of this movement, the Virginia authorities attempted to prevent action. The Baltimore and Ohio Railroad, covering the northern part of West Virginia, was of strategic importance, while the disaffection of the western counties would complicate the state's military problems. Accordingly, Governor Letcher sent an expedition to protect the railroad. But the significance of both the western counties and the Baltimore and Ohio were apparent to the federal authorities. As soon as the disaffected in western Virginia began agitation, the governor of Ohio prepared to send General George B. McClellan across the Ohio River. On June 3, McClellan met the Virginian troops at Phillipi and defeated them. Following up the victory, the invader defeated Virginia's forces at Rich Mountain and at Carrick Ford. After these disasters, General Robert E. Lee, who had been busily engaged in organizing Virginia's army, marched into western Virginia at the head of 14,000 Confederates. Lee devoted his efforts to an attempt to get his subordinates to act together, but he failed both in this and in driving back the Federal forces. Behind the Federal lines the movement to organize the state of West Virginia went on, and by the end of the year Virginia's western counties were lost to the Confederacy.

Although actual secession from the state was prevented, the disaffection of east Tennessee was equally trying to the Confederacy. Before the state seceded, Confederate troops entered the eastern section. The railroad connections and the importance of the region for food production justified strenuous efforts to retain it. In May, Andrew Johnson and Horace Maynard appealed to Lincoln for aid, and organizations of armed men were formed. In August, the Confederates sent General Felix K. Zollicoffer into the section to secure it for the South. In October, Lincoln ordered Buell to advance from the Ohio into the region. At the same time, Unionists in east Tennessee burned five railroad bridges in order to co-operate with the advancing Federals. But Buell was still on the banks of the Ohio, and Confederate troops hunted down the east Tennessee conspirators. They hanged several and destroyed fiery "Parson" Brownlow's newspaper and arrested its editor. Determined to hold the section, the Confederates inaugurated a reign of terror. Soon Confederate vigilance committees and Unionist bushwackers skirmished among the mountains, and during the war neither life nor property was safe in the region. In August, 1861, in the Confederate congressional elections, Thomas A. R. Nelson and Horace Maynard, Unionists, were elected to the House of Representatives. Asserting that they had been elected to the United States Congress, they set out for Washington. Nelson was captured and forced to take an oath of allegiance to the Confederacy, but Maynard successfully got through the lines and took his seat in Congress in Washington. Martial law held east Tennessee in the Confederacy, but the disaffected region was a cancerous wound in the vitals of the South. Unionists co-operated with advancing Federal armies and aided refugees, Negroes, and prisoners escaping from Confederate prisons to make their way to the Union lines. Before the war was over, east Tennessee's mountains held many a deserter from Lee's armies.

4. The First Battle of Manassas

Faced with internal dissension and hampered by the lack of resources, the Confederacy was never able to launch an aggressive campaign during the war. In the North, Lincoln, who had the pragmatic approach necessary to a successful revolutionary leader, shrewdly manipulated political forces to obtain a degree of national unity which could never be equalled in the South. The conservative leader of the old order, Davis, lacked Lincoln's personality and could not harmonize the differences within the South by political means. Moreover, the southern dissent expressed itself in violence, which could be met only by force. The necessity for diverting part of its man power impeded the South's military activity. In addition, the whole philosophy upon which the Confederacy was based precluded a military invasion of the North. After Fort Sumter, the

Confederate Congress announced that the South would follow a defensive policy, insisting only on its right to follow peacefully its own course. In military terms, this insistence upon states' rights meant that the Confederacy would defend its frontiers but would not carry on a vigorous offensive.

Unfortunately for southern aims, the frontier of the Confederacy was too long to be successfully defended. Stretching from the Rio Grande to the Potomac, few places on the boundaries of the Confederate states were designed by nature for defense. West of the Potomac there were no natural frontiers. The Ohio River, a natural boundary, was beyond the neutral state of Kentucky. On the other hand, the Mississippi, the Cumberland, and the Tennessee Rivers were natural military highways into the heart of the South, and in the East the rivers of Virginia were broad avenues inviting northern invasion. The geography of the South bade the Confederacy to strike out into the North in order to obtain natural boundaries; the philosophy of the South forbade aggression. In the end, philosophy won, and the Confederacy became the victim of its geography.

To the people of the North, Abraham Lincoln presented the impending conflict as a war for the preservation of the Union. The troops for which he called were to protect the property of the United States. Nothing in his theory prevented an aggressive military movement; and as summer began, newspaper pundits and politicians insistently demanded that the volunteers who had been gathered at Washington be sent to capture Richmond. The terms of the ninety-day men were about to expire, and the newspapers clamored for action. When Congress assembled on July 4, the members added to the cry, "On to Richmond!" On July 16, General Irvin McDowell, commanding the forces about Washington, began the advance.

The Confederate troops in Virginia were at three important points: before Fortress Monroe between the York and the James Rivers, in the Shenandoah Valley, and near the junction of the railroads that ran to the interior of the state. In the valley was General Joseph E. Johnston with 11,000 men, and at the railroad junction at Manassas was General P. G. T. Beauregard with 20,000. Against Beauregard's force McDowell directed the Federal advance. General Robert Patterson, with 22,000 at Martinsburg, was instructed to keep Johnston engaged during McDowell's movement.

As soon as the movement was known in Richmond, the authorities ordered Johnston to join Beauregard. Making a feint at Patterson, Johnston so frightened the aged Federal commander that he withdrew ten miles from his former base. Leaving 2,300 men to guard Patterson, Johnston sent his army to Manassas. Moving with extreme caution, McDowell was before the Confederates on July 20 and the next morning began an attack on Beauregard's left flank. The Confederate army was drawn up along a small creek known as Bull Run. The Federal forces succeeded in turning the left and then attacked the right of the Confederate line. There General Thomas J. Jackson, a West Pointer who had been a professor of "Natural and Experimental Philosophy" at the

Virginia Military Institute, made such stubborn resistance that he gained the name of "Stonewall." But the wall gave way, and the Union forces took possession of Henry House Hill. Around this point the battle fluctuated, with the tide running toward the invaders until, in the middle of the afternoon, General Kirby Smith came up with the remnants of Johnston's valley army. With reinforcements, Beauregard pushed forward and drove the Federals from the field. Cannon shots falling among the retiring soldiers soon turned retreat into panic and riot. Mingling with sightseers who had brought picnic lunches with them from the capital, the Federal army lost all organization and ran to Washington, a frightened mob. The Confederates, who had lost 1,982 in dead and wounded, had killed 1,584 and captured 1,312 Federals.

Jefferson Davis arrived on the battlefield in time to send glowing reports of the victory back to Richmond, yet he ignored Stonewall Jackson's advice to pursue the retreating enemy. The mistake was costly. The victory inspired the South with confidence while it drove home to the North the lesson that the war was to be long and desperate. The next day the Federal Congress provided for a volunteer army of 500,000. In the South, the tactics of defense had won a deceptive victory.

5. CONFEDERATE FOREIGN RELATIONS

Weak in developed natural resources, troubled by violent internal dissension, and guarding a geometric rather than a geographic frontier, the South's chances of maintaining a separate national existence would have been slim had it not been for cotton. In Confederate thinking, cotton was king, and the possession of the fleecy staple overcame all other obstacles. As cotton had dominated men's thoughts before the war, it continued during the conflict to be the main reliance of the southern cause. In their diplomacy Confederates confidently believed that European nations would give their aid in order to open up the source of cotton.

As the echoes of the guns of Fort Sumter died away, Lincoln proclaimed a blockade of the Confederate ports. Although this was not immediately effective, the Confederates had already determined to ship no cotton to England in order to starve the British cotton mills the quicker. Unknown to the Southerners, Liverpool warehouses had large supplies of cotton, and there was no immediate prospect of famine. At the same time, the holders of the cotton, expecting a rise in price, could be counted on to oppose any governmental action looking toward breaking the blockade. Unaware of this situation, the Confederates complacently waited for economic necessity to force intervention. Perhaps a wiser policy than holding cotton in the South until the blockade was effective would have been to have stored it in British warehouses as a basis of credit. The resultant trade with the South might conceivably have produced more friends than the policy which was followed.

Lincoln's blockade, however, had one effect. Although the ruling classes of England were emotionally sympathetic with the South, they had no desire to enter the conflict. Alleging that Lincoln had technically recognized Confederate belligerency by proclaiming a blockade instead of simply closing the ports, Queen Victoria issued a proclamation of neutrality which recognized the belligerent status of the Confederacy and accorded southern vessels the same rights as Federal ships in British ports. The American minister, Charles Francis Adams, protested bitterly against the proclamation and saw an additional insult in the fact that it was issued just before he presented his credentials to the foreign office. The South was momentarily encouraged by the coincidence.

Yet the Confederacy could not remain content with merely a belligerent status. Recognition of independence was imperative and aid was greatly desired. Early in March, Davis had sent W. L. Yancey, P. A. Rost, and A. Dudley Mann to Europe to obtain recognition and make treaties. The commissioners met Lord Russell, the British foreign minister, but were able to extract no promises from him. Yancey's long defense of slavery made him particularly unacceptable to the English populace, and he soon came to appreciate the obstacles before the Confederacy. He asked permission to return, and Davis appointed James M. Mason to be Ambassador to England. At the same time the president commissioned John Slidell to seek recognition at the court of Napoleon III.

Mason and Slidell slipped through the blockade and made their way to Havana, where they took passage on a British mail steamer, the *Trent*. At that moment, Captain Charles Wilkes, commanding the American ship *San Jacinto*, was making his way back to the United States. Learning that Mason and Slidell were on the British steamer, Wilkes determined, without orders, to capture them. Consulting law books in his cabin, Wilkes decided that the commissioners were "embodied dispatches" and therefore subject to capture. On November 8, 1861, he overtook the *Trent* on the high seas and took the Confederates as prisoners to New York. On both sides of the ocean there was excitement. While Americans rejoiced, the English clamored for war. War was prevented, however, by the actions of two level-headed men. When the ministry submitted a fiery ultimatum to Queen Victoria, Albert, the Prince Consort, toned it down to less provocative terms. In Washington, Lincoln realized the illegality of Wilkes' action and prepared to surrender the prisoners. Although Secretary Seward wrote a vigorous defense of the American position, Mason and Slidell were restored to the deck of a British vessel and the war clouds disappeared.

Although recognition was not forthcoming, the Confederacy won a victory from the North on a point of international law. Although Lincoln proclaimed a blockade of the South, the official position of the United States was that secession was illegal and that the Confederates were insurrectionists and traitors. When Jefferson Davis replied to Lincoln's blockade with an offer to commission privateers, Lincoln announced that those accepting Confederate letters of marque would be treated as pirates. The issue was soon joined. In June, the Confederate schooner *Savannah* was captured and officers and crew were taken into a northern port to be tried for piracy. Davis protested, but his protest went unheeded until after the battle of Manassas. Then Congressman Ely, of New York, Colonel Corcoran, of a New York Irish regiment, and several others who had been captured at the battle of Bull Run were selected as hostages to meet the same fate as the Confederate privateers. Northern newspapers and the Irish population raised a cry against the government's position and demanded that the prisoners taken should be accorded the ordinary rights of prisoners of war. Fortunately, the jury of the *Savannah* case disagreed, and the government was relieved. Henceforth, captives were treated as prisoners of war, and exchanges of prisoners were carried on between commanders in the field. Practically, if not formally, the United States recognized the belligerent status of the Confederate States of America.

The War in 1862

1. CIVIL AFFAIRS

FROM the first meeting of the Confederate Congress, war preparations occupied its major attention. The first law of the new nation's
legislature, passed on February 9, 1861, provided that all laws of the
United States should be continued in the Confederacy. The second act,
February 14, continued Federal officials in their respective places during
the provisional government.

With such details attended to, the Congress turned to the all-
important subject of financing both the Confederate government and its
impending war. At no time did the Confederacy attempt to raise money
by drastic taxation; rather, it preferred to depend on loans. On February
28, Congress authorized a loan of $15,000,000, payable in ten years and
bearing 8 per cent interest. In order to meet the interest payments it
imposed an export tax on cotton. The operation of this loan quickly
absorbed the available cash in the banks of the southern states. In March
and May, the treasury issued notes, and in succeeding months more and
more such notes came forth, until by the end of 1863 it had issued over
$600,000,000. A few of these issues bore interest, payable in specie. In
May, 1861, a loan of $100,000,000 at 8 per cent was authorized which
could be subscribed in cotton, other produce, or manufactured articles.
Before the year was over, the Confederacy had on its hands over 400,000
bales of cotton and much other produce. Although foodstuffs could be
used for the armies, the blockade made the cotton a total loss. The reluctance of the people to bear the burden of taxation was shown in the War
Tax of August 19, 1861. This was a direct tax of one-half of one per cent,
apportioned, according to the Constitution, among the states upon all
property in the Confederacy. The law provided that any state might

assume its quota and receive a reduction of 10 per cent. Only in South Carolina, Mississippi, and Texas was the tax collected. The other states issued bonds and notes, thus transforming the tax into a loan.

In addition to providing for the financial needs of the country, the Congress made arrangements to supplant the provisional with a permanent government. On March 11, Congress proclaimed a permanent constitution and instructed the president to hold elections under it. In November, general elections resulted in the election of Davis and Stephens to the offices they held and returned most of the members of the Provisional Congress. February 22, 1862, was set as inauguration day for the new government.

By the time of the inauguration, military reverses had somewhat stilled the first enthusiasm, but Davis was able to point with pride to the year which had "been the most doubtful in the annals of this continent." A new government had been established, the Confederate states had grown to thirteen (he included Kentucky and Missouri), and the people had "rallied with unexampled unanimity to the support of the great principles of Constitutional government." A million men were in arms along a frontier thousands of miles in length. "Battles have been fought, sieges have been conducted, and although the contest is not ended and the tide for the moment is against us, the final result in our favor is not doubtful."

2. Disaster in the West

At the moment Davis made his inaugural address, the tide was indeed against the Confederate arms. Within a few days the news of disaster in the West could no longer be kept from the southern people. The Confederacy's long frontier was impressive only in distance. Already it had begun to crumble.

At the beginning of the conflict, Kentucky had refused either to secede or to respond to Lincoln's call for volunteers. The neutrality which Governor Magoffin proclaimed, however, could not withstand the pressure of military necessity. The United States actively recruited men in the state and furnished arms to the soldiers who volunteered. When Magoffin protested, Lincoln assured him that leading men of the state had asked for the government's action. Neutrality, for the moment, pleased Davis, who attempted to bolster the governor's stand. But in the meantime, fighting in Missouri made points on the Mississippi of great strategic value. Early in September, General Leonidas Polk, who had resigned his army commission after graduating from West Point to enter the Episcopal ministry and who had left the Bishopric of Louisiana to enter the Confederate service, learned of Federal plans to seize Columbus. To forestall such action, he crossed the line and took the city himself. This move gave Brigadier General U. S. Grant, commanding the Federal forces at

Cairo, an excuse for violating Kentucky's crumbling neutrality. Hastily throwing his army across the Ohio, he seized Paducah at the mouth of the Tennessee River and proclaimed his intention to save the state from invasion.

Before Kentucky was lost to the Confederacy, other troubles had effectually cut Missouri off from the South. After General Nathanael Lyon captured the militia encampment in St. Louis, General Sterling Price, commanding the state troops, withdrew to Jefferson City, where Governor Claiborne Jackson was attempting to take the state out of the Union. Lyon defeated Jackson's hastily gathered militia at Booneville, and Price retired to the Ozark Mountains in the southwestern portion of the state where he could be in touch with Confederates in Arkansas. Lyon established himself at Springfield, with control over the state. On August 10 the battle of Wilson's Creek, ten miles from Springfield, resulting in Lyon's death and a Federal defeat. Price then attempted to regain the state and in September captured 3,500 men at Lexington. However, the advance of General Frémont with 40,000 men forced Price to retire again to the safety of the Ozarks. Meanwhile a remnant of the Missouri legislature, meeting at Neosho, had formally seceded and joined the Confederacy. The gesture was an empty one, for less than 30,000 Missourians served with the Confederate armies, and no revenues were derived from the lost state.

While these events were under way, the Confederate lines in the West were being drawn. Under the command of General Albert Sidney Johnston, the Confederate line stretched from the east Tennessee mountains to the Mississippi. The frontier was political, not geographical, and the rivers that ran across it were open gateways for invasion. At the eastern end, facing the Unionist forces at Camp Dick Robinson in Kentucky, were Generals George B. Crittenden and Felix K. Zollicoffer. On the western end, General Polk held Columbus. Johnston's headquarters were at Bowling Green, in Kentucky, where he guarded railroads leading to Nashville and to Memphis. The Memphis line crossed the Cumberland and Tennessee Rivers, and the Confederates had constructed two forts, Donelson and Henry, on the rivers just below the Kentucky border.

Facing the Confederates were the Union forces scattered at vital points eastward from St. Louis. The western command was divided between General H. W. Halleck, who had succeeded Frémont in command of the Department of Missouri, and General Don Carlos Buell, who commanded the Department of the Ohio. Early in January, 1862, in a belated move to relieve the eastern Tennesseans, Buell ordered General George H. Thomas to advance against Crittenden and Zollicoffer was killed. Crittenden fell back into Tennessee. Jealous lest Buell obtain glory, and anxious for complete control in the West, Halleck gave orders for a movement against Forts Henry and Donelson, which Grant at Cairo and Commodore A. H. Foote, commander of the Federal gunboats, had long been urging. On February 6 the Federal gunboats came before Fort Henry on the Tennessee, from which General Lloyd Tilghman had hastily sent the garrison. The fort was indefensible and fell with little difficulty before the gunboats.

Fort Donelson, 12 miles away on the Cumberland, was better constructed than was Fort Henry. While Grant's army moved across to take up siege positions on land, Foote moved his gunboats around to the Tennessee River. On February 13 the attack began. Within the fort were 18,000 men commanded by General John B. Floyd, Buchanan's secretary of war. Under Floyd were Generals Gideon J. Pillow, veteran of the Mexican War, and Simon Bolivar Buckner, who had joined the Confederacy after Kentucky's neutrality had come to an end. At first, the fort held out against the gunboats, but Grant's troops soon invested it on all sides. By the night of February 14, a conference in the fort decided that it would have to be abandoned. The next morning an attempt was made to cut a path for escape through the besiegers, but Grant's line held. On the night of the 15th, the generals in the fort decided to surrender. Since Floyd was under indictment for embezzlement in the North, he turned the command over to Pillow, who hastily passed it on to Buckner. During the night Colonel N. B. Forrest, commanding the cavalry, led his men and Floyd's Virginia brigade out of the fort and along the river bank to safety. Buckner was left to surrender the fort with 14,000 men to U. S. Grant. Grant's fame and the Confederacy's downfall began on that day.

While Grant besieged Fort Donelson, Buell was pushing Johnston back into Nashville. With the river open, the Tennessee capital could not withstand the pressure, and on January 23 Buell's army took the town. Johnston fell back to Corinth, Mississippi, in order to protect the junction of the Memphis and Charleston and the Mobile and Ohio Railroads. Simultaneously, in the trans-Mississippi region, General Samuel R. Curtis pushed against the troops of Price, Ben McCulloch, and General Earl Van Dorn and defeated them at Elkhorn Tavern, Arkansas. Thereafter there was no serious opposition to the Union arms in Missouri.

Within the Confederacy, these western defeats brought severe criticism on General Johnston. At Corinth, the unpopular general gathered whatever troops were available. Meanwhile Grant began an advance upon Corinth. At Pittsburg Landing, on the Tennessee, he stopped his army to wait for Buell to join him from Nashville. This was Johnston's chance to defeat his enemy in sections, and he prepared to attack Grant before Buell could join him. On Sunday morning, April 6, Johnston's army of 40,000 men fell upon the surprised Federal encampment. So little prepared were the Union troops that Grant was seven miles down the river when he heard the opening shots. Throughout the day the battle raged about Shiloh Church, and by nightfall the Confederates were in possession of the Federal camp while Grant's men were forced against the river bank. But the Confederate success had been costly, for Johnston was killed. Beauregard succeeded to the command, but it was too late for victory. That night Buell's army came up to re-enforce Grant, but Van Dorn's troops from Arkansas, momentarily expected, did not appear. On the next day the hard-fought battle forced Beauregard from the field. He retired to Corinth. On the same day, Island No. 10 in the Mississippi fell before a Federal attack.

To the victorious Union army General Halleck came in person to command the advance. Having learned the lesson of Shiloh too well, he began a slow and cautious approach to Corinth. Each night the army encamped behind entrenchments. The delay was of priceless benefit to Beauregard, who removed all of the army and much of the private property from the doomed city. On June 1, Halleck occupied the empty shell. But the Confederacy had lost all of middle and west Tennessee, for Memphis could not stand after Island No. 10 and Corinth had fallen. Only disaffected east Tennessee remained in Confederate hands. Upper Mississippi was also gone, and Buell pushed a division as far south as Huntsville, Alabama, seizing the Memphis and Charleston Railroad.

3. Operations on the Water

While the West was rapidly slipping from Confederate hands, operations on the water were cutting off supplies from Europe and making costly inroads along the coast. At the beginning of the war, General Scott had advised Lincoln to inaugurate a policy of constriction by which the army and the navy would work together. The navy should blockade the coast, and its gunboats should co-operate with armies which could push up the southern rivers while other armies advanced southward on either side of the mountains. Thus the Confederacy would be pushed into the region of southern Alabama, where the combined Union armies could deal the final blow to the southern forces. Although never formally adopted, this "Anaconda Plan" embodied the natural strategy for the North, and in essence was the plan followed by the Union commanders.

The war on the water paralleled the conflict on land. Lincoln's blockade was proclaimed on April 19, 1861, although it did not become effective for some months. The Confederacy, with no navy, commissioned twenty privateers to prey on northern commerce. In August, 1861, came the first of the combined land and water attacks which were to prove so damaging to Confederate hopes for outside aid and supplies. Hatteras Inlet, at the mouth of Pamlico Sound, had two forts, Clark and Hatteras. On August 29 these surrendered to a bombardment of naval vessels and a siege of land troops commanded by General Benjamin F. Butler.

With this beginning, the Federal navy began a rapid conquest of the southern seacoast. On November 7, Port Royal in South Carolina fell and became a base for the blockading squadron before Savannah and Charleston. The conquest of the Atlantic coast was completed early in the next year. In February, Roanoke Island, between Pamlico and Albemarle Sounds, was taken, and the towns along the coast fell in rapid succession. With this accomplished, only Wilmington, North Carolina, at the mouth of the Cape Fear River, remained to the Confederacy. Fort Pulaski at the mouth of the Savannah River was taken in April, and the efforts of the Union naval forces were centered on the Gulf Coast.

Before the Gulf Coast campaign began, however, the Confederates definitely challenged—and lost—the control of the seas. When the Norfolk navy yard had been burned as Virginia seceded, the 40-gun frigate *Merrimac* had burned to the water's edge. Secretary Mallory, however, had sponsored a proposal to convert the hull into an ironclad vessel. Through the winter and spring of 1861-1862 work had gone on, and on March 8 the vessel was ready to take its part in the defenses of Chesapeake Bay. Barely rising from the water, the newly named *Virginia* mounted ten guns in a superstructure whose sloping sides gave the impression of a grotesque terrapin. Capable of a speed of only five knots, the vessel steamed out to meet Union vessels anchored off Newport News and Old Point Comfort. Before nightfall the *Virginia* rammed one Federal vessel and ran another aground. On the next day, as the *Virginia* steamed out to finish the destruction of the fleet, she was met by a craft as strange in appearance as herself. The Federal government also had been experimenting with ironclads, and had made ready the *Monitor* to meet the Confederate challenge. A "cheesebox on a raft," the Union defender was of lighter draft and of greater speed. The battle on March 9 was a harmless duel. Neither ship could injure the other, but the *Virginia's* threat to the northern navy was nullified. A few weeks later, the clumsy Confederate was run aground and burned.

On the Gulf Coast, Union operations began in September, 1861, with the capture of Ship Island, off the Mississippi coast, from which base the blockade of New Orleans could be made effective. In April, Captain David Farragut began an attack upon Fort Jackson and Fort St. Philip at the mouth of the Mississippi. Failing to reduce the forts, Farragut ran past them and pushed on to New Orleans. With little resistance he took the city, and on May 1 General Benjamin F. Butler landed to take over the military governorship of the South's greatest seaport. Farragut steamed on to take Baton Rouge, Louisiana, and Natchez, Mississippi, and then on to co-operate with the gunboats which were descending the Mississippi River. Only Vicksburg remained as a link to hold the almost dissevered Confederacy together.

In New Orleans, General Butler proceeded to bring order out of political, economic, and social chaos. His military career had hitherto been marked by aggressiveness, efficiency, and tactlessness. He had overawed Annapolis and captured Baltimore while leading his Massachusetts troops to answer Lincoln's first call for volunteers; he had commanded at the battle of Big Bethel and had taken Roanoke Island with efficient dispatch; he had contributed the word "contraband"—as applied to fugitive slaves—to the war's vocabulary; and he had neglected no opportunity to place himself in the limelight.

In New Orleans, Butler administered his new district with a dramatic instinct for publicity. When an overzealous citizen cut down the United States flag, Butler had him hanged. When the women of New Orleans refused to hide their dislike of Northerners and insulted soldiers in the streets, the general realized that arresting them would bring a rebellion. Seeking a method of dealing with the problem, the ingenious commander issued his infamous "woman order" declaring that any woman insulting a Federal soldier should be regarded "and held liable to be treated as a woman of the town plying her vocation." The order was effective in restraining the women, but it brought upon Butler's head the condemnation of the world. In England he was condemned, and President Davis issued a proclamation outlawing Butler and his officers, forbidding them the right to be treated as prisoners of war if captured.

Thereafter "Beast" Butler was anathema to the Southerners, but his dramatic career continued. He ordered an amended version of Andrew Jackson's Jefferson Day toast—"Our Federal Union, It must and shall be preserved"—inscribed on Jackson's monument, and he cleaned up the miasmic swamps which spread yellow fever over the city. Although Butler himself does not seem to have received money, his brother and some other speculators made fortunes out of cotton permits which the general issued. Persistent legend alleged that Butler—also known by the nickname "Spoon"—carried off the silverware of most of New Orleans' fine old mansions.

4. Declining Confidence

While disaster and defeat met the southern arms in the Mississippi Valley and along the seacoast, the "permanent" government of the Confederacy was meeting internal difficulties equally serious for southern success. Three factors entered into the situation to embarrass the southern government in the conduct of the war. One of them was the personality of Jefferson Davis, another was the secrecy which surrounded the government, and the third was the never-slumbering sense of states' rights.

President Davis never understood the necessity of molding southern opinion in support of the government. He made no effort to conciliate men and to reconcile opposing views. Unlike Lincoln, he was not a master of men. He understood the limitations of his position, but he was never able to marshal the morale of the people. Opposed by Rhett, of the Charleston *Mercury,* and Pollard, of the Richmond *Examiner*, at every step, he never made an effort to conciliate these articulate antagonists. Davis was a constitutionalist exercising his power in strict conformity to the fundamental law and ignoring the opportunities which the exigencies of the situation offered for personal aggrandizement. In addition to his unbending adherence to principles and his lack of dramatic appeal, the president was in poor health. Frequently his dyspepsia prevented either good judgment or good temper.

The Confederate government as a whole failed as signally as the president in rallying the people to the southern cause. While Lincoln's government was rationalizing the war in terms first of saving the Union and then of a war for democracy—"that government of the people, by the people, and for the people might not perish from the earth"—the Confederate propagandists contented themselves with arguments based on constitutional interpretations or in appeals to defend southern homes from invasion. The

Confederate government, in contrast with the Federal, never measured up to the psychological demands of the situation. Among a people noted for their individualism, the government made no effort to secure the voluntary co-operation of its constituents. Secrecy characterized its actions; and in the absence of news, rumors floated freely. Months after the beginning of the war, Davis was criticized for not having attempted to purchase supplies in Europe, although one of the president's first acts had been to dispatch purchasing agents abroad. The southern people waited impatiently for an advance after Manassas, all unknowing that the failure which was freely ascribed to cowardice was occasioned by a lack of supplies. Such things engendered a distrust that was strengthened by a strict censorship of the press. Southern newspapers did not print news of Donelson until after the inauguration of the permanent government, and the loss of Roanoke Island was suppressed for weeks. William L. Yancey, returning from Europe, went into the Confederate Senate to labor in vain for the abandonment of secret sessions. To all arguments for taking the people into its confidence, the government replied that such information would benefit the enemy.

With the government failing to inspire the people with faith, the adherents of states' rights took advantage of the growing distrust. In April, 1862, Davis recommended a conscription law to Congress. The enlistments of the twelve-month volunteers were about to expire, and the recent disasters were no encouragement to new enlistments. Conscription was an obvious necessity, and Congress hurriedly passed a conscription act. By the law, all male citizens between the ages of eighteen and thirty-five were liable to conscription for the duration of the war. The volunteers already in the ranks were kept in their organizations. This move met the approval of some of Davis's most captious critics, but the act itself carried the seeds of more discontent and distrust. Exemptions were allowed to newspaper editors, teachers, pharmacists, ministers, and owners or overseers of twenty slaves. These exemptions raised the suspicion that the conflict was to be "a rich man's war and a poor man's fight"—a suspicion that was fed by the provision that allowed substitutes for conscripted men.

The enactment of the conscription law gave states'-rights men an opportunity. Georgia's governor, Joseph E. Brown, proclaimed that a blow had been struck at constitutional liberty, and vice-president Stephens's younger brother stirred up his state's legislature to back their governor almost to the point of rebellion. Governor Zebulon B. Vance of North Carolina also raised objection to North Carolina soldiers serving under officers who were not natives of the state.

Although these factors were destined to destroy the Confederacy, they appeared but minor irritants in the summer of 1862. The concentration of attention upon military events in the eastern theater of the war caused both government and people to ignore internal disaffection as well as disaster in the West. This lack of perspective was the fatal defect of the Confederacy.

5. VICTORY IN THE EAST

While the western armies of the Confederacy were falling back before Grant's victorious army, and the seacoast was falling before the slowly strangling advance of the Federal navy, the war in the East was bringing momentary victory to the South. Throughout the winter of 1861-1862 the eastern armies had lain motionless. General George B. McClellan, called to Washington from western Virginia and placed in command of all the northern armies, had improved his time by bringing the troops before Washington to a high state of discipline. His apparent inaction annoyed Lincoln, however, and the president issued orders for all of the Federal armies to advance on February 22. Since the condition of the Virginia roads prevented action, Lincoln consented to a slight delay.

President Lincoln's lack of confidence in McClellan and his constant interference with the army was of definite benefit to the Confederacy. Upon studying the Virginia terrain, McClellan perceived that the land between Washington and Richmond was thickly covered with shrubs and second-growth timber. Moreover, the innumerable small streams and rivers, running approximately from west to east, would render difficult the overland advance of an army upon the Confederate capital. The country through which such an army must pass was admirably adapted for defense against an invader. Instead of taking this route, the Union commander proposed to establish a base at Fortress Monroe and advance upon Richmond up the peninsula between the York and the James Rivers. In this way, his line of supplies would be upon water and safe from Confederate raids.

Lincoln's comprehension of this military plan was inhibited by a fear that such a disposition of the forces would leave Washington exposed to Confederate attack. He gave McClellan permission to begin the peninsular campaign only on the condition that sufficient troops be left behind to protect the capital. Just as the general was starting his movement, the president took an additional 40,000 men from his command to man the city's defenses. At the same time Lincoln reorganized the armies and put the Federal troops in western Virginia and the Valley under separate commands. Unable to command the co-operation of these armies and weakened by the loss of troops, McClellan decided to approach Richmond by siege operations rather than in an aggressive campaign.

The Union general's fundamental weakness was his tendency to overestimate the number of his opponents. General Joseph Johnston could barely muster half of the invader's 90,000 men, and could throw only a fraction of his troops into the peninsula. McClellan's determination to adopt siege tactics enabled the Confederates to defeat his purpose. Early in April the Federal general began a cautious advance. General John B. Magruder's Confederate forces made a show of defending Yorktown, but, after taking a month of Federal time, abandoned the village and fell back to Williamsburg. This, too, they abandoned as the Union forces attacked. McClellan set up his headquarters at White House Landing, a colonial home on the Pamunky River twenty miles from Richmond. From this position the Union forces advanced to the Chickahominy River, which ran diagonally across the peninsula about ten miles from the Confederate capital. At the same time, Federal gunboats moved up the James River until they were stopped by the batteries at Drewry's Bluff. Had McClellan co-operated with this expedition, the defenses might have been taken; but the general clung to the banks of the York in order to unite with McDowell, who was expected to approach overland from Washington.

Although Lincoln had ordered McDowell to Fredericksburg in expectation that he would join McClellan, the sudden outbreak of activity in the Valley of Virginia brought a change of plans. At Staunton, in the lower end of the Valley, Stonewall Jackson commanded 19,000 men to oppose Frémont with 15,000 men in West Virginia and General N. P.

Courtesy Washington & Lee University

ROBERT E. LEE. "Marse Robert," as people of the South called him, was the son of Virginia's Revolutionary leader, "Light-Horse Harry" Lee. He was graduated from West Point in 1829, not having received a single demerit, and spent the remainder of his life in military service. He disagreed with most southerners about the right of secession; "I must say," he said in 1861, "that I am one of those dull creatures that cannot see the good of secession." And yet Lee became the symbol of the Lost Cause. He became commander of the Army of Northern Virginia in 1862, just before the Peninsula Campaign, and his tactical genius kept southern hopes bright.

Banks with 19,000 further down the Valley. At Harpers Ferry, at the other end of the Valley, there was a Union force of 7,000. Realizing that a diversion was necessary to save Richmond, Jackson began a sudden movement which paralyzed his opponents. First he turned to the west, where struck Frémont's advance under Robert H. Milroy, driving it back upon the main army. Then, hurrying into the Valley, he marched swiftly north to attack Banks at Strasburg. Banks had been weakened by having been compelled to send men to McDowell's army, and was unable to fight. He fell back to Winchester, where Jackson attacked him and drove his army in confusion to Harpers Ferry on the Potomac.

Consternation in Washington caused Lincoln to retract McDowell's orders to join McClellan. Instead, he was ordered to send troops into the Valley to co-operate in trapping Jackson. Before Frémont, coming from the west, could join Shields coming from the east at Strasburg, Jackson slipped between them. Then, with sharp fights at Cross Keys and Port Republic, he stopped each of his opponents and made secure his retirement to the upper end of the Valley. In a month's brilliant fighting he had disrupted McClellan's campaign and was safely back where he had started.

Before Richmond, McClellan continued his heavy-footed advance. His picket lines were in sight of Richmond, and his army was straddling the swollen Chickahominy, when on May 31 Johnston attacked two exposed corps at the Battle of Seven Pines and drove them from their position. During the battle, Johnston was severely wounded, and the next day as the Federals regained their losses, Robert E. Lee assumed command of the armies.

In General Lee the Confederacy had a master of tactics. Son of "Light Horse Harry" Lee of the Revolutionary War, he grew up in the best military traditions of the South. He married a great granddaughter of Martha Washington, and as master of Arlington, a plantation mansion that overlooked the Potomac opposite Washington, he was completely identified with the southern aristocracy. He had been graduated with honors from West Point, served in the Mexican War, been superintendent of West Point, and seen staff service in the War Department. Never concerned with politics, he had personally opposed both slavery and secession, but he had followed his state out of the Union, saying, as he resigned from the United States Army, that he hoped never again to draw his sword except in Virginia's defense. Even as commander of the southern armies, Lee's primary concern was his beloved state. In its defense he used his small armies to repel superior forces, proving himself on many a battlefield to be one of the world's greatest tacticians.

Less daring than Stonewall Jackson, less dramatic than Beauregard, less dashing than such admired cavalry leaders as J. E. B. Stuart and N. B. Forrest, Lee dominated the southern armies through the strength of his character. He embodied the best spirit of the South, and he inspired the southern armies to feats of magnificent heroism. Although bivouac and battlefield changed the men of the Confederate armies into soldiers, they remained civilians. Robert E. Lee was the ideal commander of civilian armies. He led rather than commanded; he maintained morale rather than discipline. Critics pointed out that Lee's gentle methods made him yield to subordinates and slowed action. They alleged that his devotion to Virginia prevented his perceiving the strategic importance of the war's western area. They criticized his subordination of the military to the civil branch of government. Yet, none questioned his character or the importance of his spirit in maintaining the morale of his soldiers. No other southern leader could have held the Confederate armies together so long.

Lee's first action was to entrench before Richmond, whereupon McClellan moved to destroy the Confederate line by artillery and siege tactics. Realizing that this attack might be successful, Lee planned an audacious counterattack. First he sent Colonel J. E. B. Stuart with 1,200 cavalry to scout McClellan's lines of supply. Stuart set forth and rode completely around the Federal army, crossing the peninsula and returning to Richmond. Then, with the information which Stuart brought, Lee called Jackson for a conference. Near Richmond, Lee held council of war with Jackson, James Longstreet, D. H. Hill, and A. P. Hill, unfolding to them a plan to drive the enemy from the peninsula. Jackson would slip from the Valley and strike the Union forces on the right flank while Hill's and Longstreet's divisions would follow up the attack.

Jackson eluded his enemies in the Valley without difficulty, but he was a day late in arriving on the battlefield. On June 26 A. P. Hill had moved against the Union lines at Mechanicsville but was beaten back. The next day Lee's four subordinates fell upon the Federals at Gaines's Mill and drove them from their position. McClellan might have pushed forward to Richmond, but instead he changed his base from the exposed White House to Harrison's Landing on the James River. Delaying a day, Lee pursued, fighting an indecisive battle at Savage's Station on June 29 and being stopped at Frayser's Farm on the 30th. Then Lee followed, and on July 1 attacked the Federals in strong position at Malvern Hill. The battle was a Union victory.

In these "Seven Days' Battles" Lee lost over 20,000 men while his opponent lost a little under 16,000. But the first assault on Richmond had been beaten off, and the northern government had lost confidence in its commander. As a result, Lincoln left McClellan with a handful of men at Fortress Monroe while he created a new army to march from Washington to Richmond.

This new Federal army was under the command of General John Pope, who had successfully taken Island No. 10 in the Mississippi. In July Pope, boasting that he had come from the West, where he had "always seen the backs of our enemies," marched his army of 50,000 past the old battlefield of Manassas to Culpeper. At Gordonsville, protecting the line of railroad which ran from Richmond into the upper Valley, Jackson had 24,000 men. Cutting around Pope's flank to Cedar Mountain, Jackson struck Banks, who was bringing 8,000 reinforcements for Pope. Lee hurried on to Gordonsville to strike Pope before the men from McClellan's army could be brought up the Potomac. But Pope captured

Stuart's dispatch book, learned of the plan, and fell back beyond the Rappahannock River.

With Lee's army momentarily equal to his opponent's, the Confederate leader planned to engage in battle. Jackson's fleet infantry, proud of the rapid movement which had earned them the name of "foot cavalry," marched off to cut in above Pope's rear. Pope's first knowledge of his danger came when Stuart's cavalry captured Bristow Station, near Manassas Junction, and destroyed the Federal line of supplies. Pope fell back toward Washington, preparing to crush Jackson at Manassas. But Jackson was not at Manassas, and as Pope marched out, the elusive Confederate fell upon him. The battle that day was indecisive, but Longstreet, with the rest of Lee's army, came on the field. Completely misinterpreting the situation, Pope believed that he was pursuing a small part of the Confederate forces. On August 30 he attacked again, part of the battle being fought over the field which had witnessed the Federal defeat the previous year. Decisive defeat again met the Federal armies, and during the night they retreated toward Washington. There was no rout, as after first Manassas, but the outcome was more decisive. With Richmond saved, Lee prepared to invade the North.

The moment was auspicious for aggressive action. In the western theater the Confederacy was making a new attempt to recover lost ground. After the Union advance, which had cleared middle and western Tennessee, the armies of Grant and Buell remained quiet. The interlude was used by the Confederates to rally men and to strengthen armies for counterattack. Along the Mississippi the armies of Price and Van Dorn raided Grant's district and caused Butler to abandon Baton Rouge. Farther to the east, Braxton Bragg assembled 35,000 men in the mountain fastness of Chattanooga, from which on August 28 he proceeded to march northward into Kentucky to threaten Buell's lines of supply. Buell was forced to fall back from Nashville to meet the threat.

With the western armies so well occupied with their own affairs, Pope's army disorganized, and Washington in such panic that government clerks were manning the city's ramparts, Lee's task seemed easy. Giving his soldiers a day's rest, he turned them toward the Potomac. His plan was to invade Maryland, advance to Hagerstown, and then threaten Harrisburg or Baltimore. On September 5 Jackson's corps crossed the river, and the next day they were in Frederick. Contrary to their hopes, the ragged and unshod soldiers inspired but few Marylanders to join the ranks. Then Lee ordered Jackson to turn west, take Harpers Ferry and Martinsburg, and open up a line of communications through the Valley. On September 15, the garrison at Harpers Ferry surrendered to Jackson.

In the meantime, Lincoln had recalled McClellan to command the army about Washington. With his accustomed slowness, McClellan pushed out toward Lee's army, reaching Frederick on September 12. Here he learned that Lee had divided his army. Planning to put himself between the parts, he moved cautiously to South Mountain. On the 14th there was fighting, and on the next day Jackson began to return to Lee. Had McClellan attacked on the 16th, he might have defeated Lee; but he delayed, and on the 17th Jackson's men were in line. Then McClellan attacked Lee's army near Sharpsburg, along Antietam Creek. Tactically the battle was indecisive. Lee lost 8,000 of his 40,000 men, while McClellan's army of 70,000 lost 12,000. But reinforcements came to the Federals, while Lee could hope for none. There was nothing for the Southerner to do but return to Virginia. Despite Lincoln's urgent pleas, McClellan allowed his adversary to recross the Potomac. The first Confederate invasion of the North was at an end.

In the meantime, Bragg's movement into Kentucky had met with disaster. A supporting movement of Kirby Smith's command had already pushed into Kentucky from Knoxville before Bragg left Chattanooga. Buell drew in his garrisons from the South, and both armies pushed on toward Louisville. Gathering his forces while the Confederates were wasting time inaugurating a governor for Kentucky, Buell returned to the attack. On October 8 the armies met at Perryville, where, with the fewer losses, Bragg drove Buell's forces from the field. The tactical victory was, however, a strategic defeat. Unable to hold the position, Bragg and Smith fell back into Tennessee.

In both East and West the failure of the Union commanders to follow up their victories brought their removal. In the East, Ambrose Burnside replaced McClellan, and W. S. Rosecrans took Buell's armies. Both were ordered to advance: Burnside to Richmond, and Rosecrans to east Tennessee.

After his retirement from Maryland, Lee remained at Fredericksburg. On December 13, Burnside attacked the Confederate position in the face of Confederate artillery. Charge after charge rolled against the Confederate entrenchments only to be driven back. Twelve thousand Union men were lost that day, while Lee's army lost but 5,000. Two days later, Burnside withdrew and handed in his resignation. In January he was removed and Joseph Hooker took command.

In the West, Rosecrans remained in Nashville while Bragg entrenched before Murfreesboro. On the day after Christmas the Federal army left Nashville. On December 31 it was in front of the Confederates at Stone's River. The fight that day seemed a Confederate victory, but Rosecrans did not abandon the field. On January 2 Bragg attacked, but he was defeated and forced to retire to Chattanooga. By the close of the year, central and west Tennessee were again in the hands of the Union armies.

6. DIPLOMATIC FAILURE

While the southern armies battled with varying success, the diplomatic representatives of the Confederacy were busy in a futile attempt to secure European aid. After their release by the northern government,

Mason and Slidell made their way to London and Paris to present the Confederate case.

In England the upper class had long felt a kinship with the South's landed aristocracy and were inclined to welcome Mason and to support his pleas for recognition. The cotton capitalists, upon whom the Confederacy pinned great hopes, were sympathetic but were in large part balanced by speculators who were holding the surplus cotton from the large crop of 1859 in British warehouses in expectation of a rise. The dealers in war supplies, too, had no desire to interfere with the profits that came to them through the continuance of the American conflict, while British shippers, picking up the business which fell from the hands of their Yankee competitors, were inclined to prefer profits to the hazards involved in recognizing the Confederacy. In international affairs, the constant suspicion with which Her Majesty's government regarded the second French Empire prevented the government from giving assistance to the Southerners, while the precarious political position of the coalition cabinet caused the ministry to pursue a hesitant policy. Mason found much sympathy but little assistance in England.

Soon after his arrival, Mason called privately on Lord John Russell. At this and subsequent interviews the Confederate exerted his best efforts to persuade the British foreign minister to declare the blockade ineffective. Secretary Benjamin kept his agents fully posted on the number and size of the vessels which ran the blockade to Confederate ports, but the British could never be persuaded to denounce it. Mason soon concluded that Russell was personally opposed to the Confederacy and would do nothing to extend aid. Seemingly, the British officials were fully determined upon an impartial neutrality, for at the same time Charles Francis Adams decided that the government's sympathies were all with the Confederacy.

Considerably more hopeful was the situation which Slidell found at the Court of Napoleon III. The emperor's personal sympathies were with the South, and he was willing to recognize the Confederacy or to denounce the blockade, but only in co-operation with England. In April, Napoleon declared that he was willing to join in sending a fleet to open up the Mississippi. Lord Russell, however, refused to receive this message because the emperor sent it through a member of Parliament rather than through the regular diplomatic channels. Napoleon explained to Slidell, whom he saw often, that a similar communication to Russell had earlier been sent to Lord Lyons in Washington and given to Secretary W. H. Seward. In July, however, Slidell persuaded the emperor to send Russell a formal request for joint action on recognition. Mason brought what pressure he could, but Russell pointed out that the United States had taken New Orleans and refused Mason an interview. Benjamin ordered Mason to make no more advances to the stubborn minister.

In the meantime, the government took no steps to prevent the Confederates from obtaining supplies from England and her possessions. At Nassau and other West Indian ports Confederate agents gathered stores of supplies to load upon the low, swift ships which were proving efficient runners of the Federal blockade. In March a cruiser built for Captain James D. Bulloch, the Confederate purchasing agent, sailed from Liverpool. Evading the letter of the British foreign enlistment act, the vessel sailed without armament but in the Bahamas picked up armament and crew. Renamed the *Florida*, it sailed the seven seas as a commerce destroyer. Before its career ended it captured over forty American merchant vessels. Meanwhile, another vessel, known on the ways of the Laird shipyards as "No. 290," was openly being built for Captain Bullock. Minister Adams and the American consul sedulously gathered information to prove that the ship was intended for the Confederacy, but late in July, before the law officers of the crown were able to make a report, the ship sailed forth on a trial voyage from which it never returned. In the Azores it was renamed the *Alabama* and armed and manned for a career which lasted two years, during which it destroyed fifty-seven vessels, released others for ransom, and did an estimated $6,750,000 damage to northern ships. As a result of its activities, rising insurance rates aided the work of driving American commerce from the seas.

The hope that the Confederate commissioners got from Adams's discomfiture in the *Alabama* case was raised still higher in September, when the question of recognition came up again. When the news of the second Manassas battle reached England, Palmerston, the Prime Minister, and Russell agreed that the time had come to offer mediation. A Cabinet meeting was called to consider action, and before it met, Gladstone, Chancellor of the Exchequer, speaking at New Castle, declared, "There is no doubt that Jefferson Davis and other leaders of the South have made an army; they are making, it appears, a navy; and they have made, what is more than either—they have made a nation."

Unfortunately, this speech stirred friends of the North to protest, and members of the Cabinet hesitated to adopt a more aggressive policy. Moreover, the news of Antietam was received before the Cabinet meeting and confirmed the desirability of remaining inactive. The Cabinet meeting decided to postpone action, and Slidell again besought Napoleon to make a new move. Late in October the emperor told Slidell that he could not trust England and suggested a joint offer of mediation by England, France, and Russia. Slidell feared that Russia's sympathies were with the United States, but Napoleon III made the suggestion to both courts. The Russian government declined the suggestion without discussion, but the English Cabinet considered the matter at length. Only Gladstone and Russell were in favor of the Confederacy, and the proposal was rejected.

Once again Slidell turned to the French Emperor, this time proposing that he should take the initiative in recognizing the Confederacy. It was certain, said the Confederate, that the other powers would follow his example. Napoleon formally offered mediation to the Lincoln government early in January, but the offer was refused. Fearing to go further without England, Napoleon dropped the matter.

7. EMANCIPATION OF THE SLAVES

Closely connected with these diplomatic maneuvers, and partly inspired by a desire to obtain foreign sympathies, was Lincoln's Emancipation Proclamation. At the beginning of the conflict the official position of the United States was that the war was for the purpose of saving the Union. Lincoln's first call for militia had specified that they were to be used to protect public property. Until the late summer of 1862, despite the efforts of abolitionists to insert the slavery issue, and despite the charge made by Democrats and Southerners that the Republican Party was waging war for the abolition of slavery, the preservation of the Union was the official dogma of the government.

In 1861 John C. Frémont, commanding in Missouri, issued a proclamation freeing the slaves of secession sympathizers in the region under his command. Fearful that Kentucky and Maryland would secede if slavery could be abolished by a military commander, Lincoln asked Frémont to recall his order. With an eye on the political support of the abolitionists, Frémont refused. Lincoln immediately recalled the order and removed Frémont from command. Henceforth, Frémont was the idol of the abolitionists, who were disgusted with Lincoln's timorous policy. A similar withdrawal of an order issued by General David Hunter in South Carolina convinced the abolitionists of his own party that they could not rely on Lincoln.

Just before Frémont's order, Congress passed the first confiscation act, which gave freedom to slaves who were employed in military activities and working on fortifications. General Butler, commanding at Fortress Monroe, used captured Negroes on his own works; and when a Confederate colonel appeared outside his lines asking for the return of fugitives, the ingenious Federal refused on the ground that such escaped slaves were "contraband of war." The legality of this definition was dubious, but the humor of it appealed to the northern people, who thereafter dubbed all escaped slaves "contrabands."

The pressure of the radical abolitionists, in addition to that of his own party, caused Lincoln to make gestures to appease the agitators who would change the purpose of the war. In March, 1862, he proposed that Congress compensate slave owners in the loyal states of Kentucky, Missouri, Maryland, Delaware, and the District of Columbia. He estimated the cost at $173,000,000. Although this suggestion was not satisfactory to the abolitionists and was opposed by the Democrats, Congress passed a bill for compensated emancipation in the District of Columbia.

In July, Congress passed a second confiscation act, which gave freedom to the slaves of those in the Confederate armies and provided for settling them on confiscated and abandoned lands in the possession of the army. At the same time, Lincoln faced the problem of what to do with the slaves in the event of their obtaining freedom. Knowing well, and perhaps reflecting in his own person, the attitude of the small farmers in the Middle West, Lincoln realized that the free Negro would not be received on terms of equality by the whites. He therefore proposed colonization outside of the United States, and several times considered sending the Negroes to various places that were suggested to him. The colonization schemes were as distasteful as compensated emancipation to the orthodox abolitionists.

Finally, coming to the conclusion that the war for the Union had little merit in international affairs, Lincoln decided to issue a proclamation freeing the slaves in the Confederate states. In July he read his Cabinet a proposed proclamation which received almost full approval. Secretary Seward, however, suggested that its issuance at a moment of defeat would be interpreted as an act of desperation and an invitation to slave insurrection. Convinced that the time was not auspicious, Lincoln decided to wait for a Union victory.

While waiting, the New York *Tribune* published a "Prayer of Twenty Millions" written by the editor, Horace Greeley. The editorial demanded immediate abolition. In reply, Lincoln assured the editor that he had but one purpose—"I would save the Union. . . . If there be those who would not save the Union unless they could at the same time *save* Slavery, I do not agree with them. If there be those who would not save the Union unless they could at the same time *destroy* Slavery, I do not agree with them. My paramount object in this struggle *is* to save the Union, and is *not* either to save or destroy Slavery. If I could save the Union without freeing *any* slave, I would do it; and if I could save it by freeing *all* the slaves, I would do it; and if I could save it by freeing some and leaving others alone, I would also do that. What I do about Slavery and the colored race, I do because I believe it helps to save the Union; and what I forbear, I forbear because I do *not* believe it would help save the Union. I shall do *less* whenever I shall believe what I am doing hurts the cause, and I shall do *more* whenever I shall believe doing more will help the cause. I shall try to correct errors when shown to be errors, and I shall adopt new views so fast as they shall appear to be true views."

Meantime, northern abolitionists began to organize to force the president's hand. Turning from Congress, they encouraged the governors to bring pressure on Lincoln. Massachusetts' Governor John A. Andrew almost threatened to withhold state troops unless the president permitted generals in the field to emancipate slaves and enlist them in the army. Other governors grumbled at Lincoln's policy which forced them to draft their constituents into the army but did not permit them to use Negroes who were willing to bear arms. A conference of governors assembled at Altoona, Pennsylvania, to consider the situation. More radical governors were prepared to propose that the state officials agree to raise no more men for Lincoln's forces but instead to enroll troops, white and black, and put them under the command of General Frémont. The impending conference, as well as the international situation, compelled Lincoln to act. He had already determined to wait for a Union victory. The battle of Sharpsburg was hardly decisive, but in the exigency it would have to do. Perhaps the failure of Maryland and Kentucky to receive the Confederate armies with enthusiasm reassured him. On September 23, just as the governors were assembling at Altoona, he issued a preliminary Emancipation Proclamation. After January 1, 1863, all slaves in states still in rebellion would be free.

The Proclamation was issued in the face of approaching elections, and the victory of the Democrats in November indicated that the northern people did not approve of the change in the purpose of the war. The unification of the Republican party, however, was obtained. Although the abolitionists were displeased by the failure to provide for Negro soldiers and by the limited nature of the emancipation, the Altoona Conference endorsed the Proclamation. In the South, Davis received the news of the Proclamation with scorn for a foeman who would appeal to slaves to rise against their masters. One immediate effect of the Proclamation was to produce more southern support for the Confederacy. Conservative men who had not been convinced by southern charges that the Republicans were an abolitionist party came out in support of the Confederacy. T. A. R. Nelson, east Tennessee's Unionist leader, for example, was henceforth as ardent as any original secessionist for the Confederate cause. Legalists were sure that the president had no right, even under a liberal interpretation of the war powers, to issue such a proclamation. Realists then and later pointed out that it freed no slaves; it did not apply within the regions held by the Federal army, and in other regions the Lincoln government had no jurisdiction. It was evident to all, however, that henceforth the North was waging a war for the abolition of slavery.

In Europe the first reaction to the preliminary Proclamation was similar to that of the South. Pointing out that Lincoln was not condemning slavery in the abstract but only when it was practiced by his enemies, the friends of the South ridiculed the futile gesture; but by the time of the final Proclamation, the friends of the North had aligned popular sentiment on Lincoln's side. Throughout the rest of the war, northern propagandists in Europe had an effective moral issue. In the next year, the psychological implications of Lincoln's move were to be seen in hundreds of mass meetings of Federal sympathizers.

The War in 1863

1. VICKSBURG

W HILE Lee was winning victories in Virginia and the center of the far-flung Confederate line was being pushed back to Chattanooga, the final phase of the Federal attack on the Mississippi River began. At Vicksburg and Port Hudson in Mississippi, General J. C. Pemberton had a little over 30,000 men to resist the advance. General Johnston, recovering from his wound, went to Chattanooga in November to take command in the West. He immediately ordered General T. C. Hindman, in Arkansas, to re-enforce Pemberton. But Hindman was defeated in a battle at Prairie Grove and could not assist, and Bragg's army was too weakened to help defend Vicksburg.

Vicksburg was situated on a bluff that commanded a bend of the Mississippi. On the northern and western sides were swamps crossed by many streams. Against this post General U. S. Grant planned to advance overland, with most of his army being transported by water. To support this movement, he established a base at Holly Springs, Mississippi. Late in December Van Dorn destroyed this base while General N. B. Forrest destroyed the railroad that led south from the Federal headquarters at Columbus, Kentucky. Grant's advance under W. T. Sherman met defeat when it tried to storm the heights above Vicksburg, and the expedition withdrew.

Prevented from approaching the Confederate citadel from the north, Grant decided to take his army below the city and advance on the high ground to the south. This involved getting his army past the bluffs. During the winter of 1862-1863 he kept busy digging a canal across the bend of the river which would turn the course of the river and permit the army to pass below the town. But the river would not go into the artificial channel, and a new scheme was needed. The naval officers on the river proposed running the batteries and establishing a base below the city. The army could be marched down the Louisiana side, crossed over to the Mississippi side below Vicksburg, and marched north to besiege Pemberton. In March, Farragut moved up from New Orleans to threaten Port Hudson, and on the night of April 16 the Federal gunboats ran the batteries. On April 30, Grant crossed the river with 20,000 men and almost immediately began to march against Vicksburg.

Johnston favored concentrating his army to defeat Grant, but President Davis interfered to forbid even the temporary abandonment of the river ports. Johnston went to Jackson, Mississippi, to take command, and ordered Pemberton to join him. But Pemberton delayed, and Grant struck at the Mississippi capital, which he took and destroyed. Grant then turned against Pemberton, defeated him at Champion's Hill, and drove him back into Vicksburg. Here there were ample defenses which the Federal commander was unable to take by direct assault, but he settled to siege tactics. With over 100,000 men he slowly advanced with pick and shovel against Pemberton's 30,000 defenders. The besieging army had ample supplies; the besieged only those that were in the city. Starvation worked on the side of the invaders, while Johnston struggled in vain to marshal an army to raise the siege. On July 3, Pemberton asked Grant for terms, and on the next day he surrendered the city. Five days later, the besieged garrison at Port Hudson, unable to hold out after Vicksburg was gone, surrendered. The Mississippi River was in Federal hands from source to mouth, and the Confederacy was cut in two.

2. Chancellorsville to Gettysburg

During the months that witnessed the Confederate failure in the West, the armies in Virginia won victories. After Fredericksburg, Joseph Hooker took command of the Federal armies in the East and decided on another effort to march overland from Washington to Richmond. His army, encamped in winter quarters along the Rappahannock, had grown to 130,000, while Lee at Fredericksburg had 60,000. Late in April, Hooker began his movement by crossing the river and sending one wing to threaten Lee's rear. But once he had made contact with Lee's army, Hooker began to doubt and withdrew his greatly superior army to Chancellorsville, where he waited attack. On May 2, Lee began a skillfully directed battle. By nightfall, Jackson had defeated one wing of Hooker's army. But that evening, as Jackson was returning from a reconnoitering expedition, he was shot by his own sentinels. With proper care his wounds should not have proved serious, but medical ineptitude completed the work of the blundering guards. On May 10, he died. His loss was one of the greatest catastrophes of a disastrous year. On May 3,

Photo by U. S. Army Signal Corps

THOMAS J. (STONEWALL) JACKSON. Left an orphan when very young, Jackson learned to shift for himself and got what education he could by working his own way. His ambition was rewarded by an appointment to the Military Academy, from which he was graduated in 1846. He distinguished himself in the Mexican War, after which he became a teacher in the Virginia Military Academy. In the Confederate Army his nickname arose from an incident in the first Battle of Bull Run, but he was chiefly noted for rapid flanking marches. He was killed in May, 1863, on the field at Chancellorsville, the victim of shots by his own troops. His death was a major catastrophe.

the battle was resumed, and the saddened Confederates drove the Federal army from the field. On the fourth, Lee completed the work of driving the Union forces back across the river.

With victory, the Confederate officials realized that aggressive action must be taken. At the moment, Grant was beginning his slow but sure movement against Vicksburg, Rosecrans was pressing against Bragg in Chattanooga, and the southern people were thoroughly aroused against the government. In foreign affairs there was also a crisis, while in the North there was a growing opposition to the conscription that was about to begin. From every standpoint it was desirable that the war be carried into the North, although there was a considerable sentiment for re-enforcing the armies in the West in order to force Grant to withdraw from Vicksburg. General Longstreet especially insisted that action be taken to relieve the West.

Both Lee and Davis preferred a northern invasion. On June 3, the first of Lee's army, under Longstreet, moved from Fredericksburg. The early part of the movement was hidden by a cavalry raid by General J. E. B. Stuart, which thoroughly alarmed Washington. But Stuart captured a wagon train near the Federal capital which he determined to bring back with him. This effort so delayed him that Lee's army was deprived of its cavalry and forced to march blindly into the enemy's country. Meanwhile, General R. S. Ewell had advanced across Maryland to Harrisburg, Pennsylvania, from which he was recalled by Lee, who had reached Chambersburg, further to the east. This concentration was made necessary by the unexpected speed which the Union army showed in moving to defend themselves. While panic reigned in Washington, Baltimore, and Philadelphia and draft riots brewed in New York, Hooker's army was hastily reorganized and placed under the command of General George Gordon Meade. On June 30, Meade led the army into Pennsylvania, and Lee immediately ordered his army to Gettysburg. On July 1, the Confederate advance met the van of the Union army, and there was hard fighting. The main body of each army hastened to the battlefield. On July 2 and 3, the Confederates strove in vain to dislodge the Federal forces from the hills about the village. Despite the grim heroism of the men of General George Pickett's division—who made the most gallant, dramatic, and futile charge of the war—the Confederates were defeated. Throughout July 4 the southern army lay stunned; on the morning of the 5th they began a retreat into Virginia. The second Confederate invasion of the North had been more disastrously defeated than the first. With Vicksburg falling simultaneously, the last hope of the Confederacy was gone. Thereafter they could only battle in desperate hope that the North might grow tired of the conflict.

3. CHICKAMAUGA AND CHATTANOOGA

After Gettysburg, the armies in the East remained inactive while all eyes in the South were directed to the series of events that were breaking the center of the Confederate line. After Stone's River, early in the year, Rosecrans held his army of 70,000 in Nashville, facing Bragg, who was protecting Chattanooga. Late in April a cavalry raid by Colonel A. D. Streight attempted to pass to the rear of the Confederate army, but Forrest pursued the Federals and fought a running fight until, near

Rome, Georgia, Streight surrendered. On June 23 Rosecrans began to advance, flanking Bragg out of his base at Tullahoma and forcing him back into Chattanooga. In August, Rosecrans moved his army across the Tennessee River at Bridgeport, Alabama, and marched toward the mountains to the south of the Confederate stronghold.

Chattanooga was located on the left bank of the Tennessee River at the point where the river, after flowing south from the vicinity of Knoxville, turns at Moccasin Bend to take a generally westward direction. On all sides, the town was surrounded by mountains. To the west, across the river, was Signal Mountain; to the north and east, on the left bank, was Missionary Ridge; to the south was Lookout Mountain, which ran far down into Georgia. Bragg expected an attack from the north, where Burnside had just occupied Knoxville. But Rosecrans came up from the south and determined to cross over Lookout Mountain far from the Confederates. This movement threatened Bragg's communications with Atlanta, and the Southerner was forced to move out of Chattanooga to give battle. As he moved out, a Federal corps moved in to occupy the town. Bragg, however, had delayed too long. Had he attacked earlier, he might have defeated Rosecrans' army while it was divided; but when he attacked Rosecrans on September 18 at Chickamauga Creek, the Federal forces were already concentrated against him.

In one of the few cases during the war, the Confederates outnumbered their opponents. Bragg's army had 66,000, while that of Rosecrans had 58,000. The maneuvers had resulted in putting the Federal army between Bragg and Chattanooga. The two days' fighting at Chickamauga were the bloodiest of the war. A mistake on the battlefield weakened the Union center, and Longstreet rushed into the breach. The Union lines were broken, and the routed army fled in confusion into Chattanooga. General George H. Thomas covered the retreat and drove back charge after charge which threatened his position at Rossville Gap. Unable to follow his enemy through the Gap, Bragg took up a position on Missionary Ridge, where he could watch the defeated army in the valley below. The Confederates also held Lookout Mountain, preventing supplies from coming in by the railroad or the river.

In Chattanooga the Federal army was in a state of siege. Supplies could come in only across the muddy mountain roads to the west. Perched vulture-like on the surrounding hills, the Confederates had only to wait for starvation to bring them success. Such a policy disgusted Forrest, who demanded that Bragg should follow up his victory. Other generals opposed Bragg's policy and petitioned Davis to remove their commander. Davis journeyed from Richmond, looked down into the camp of the starving enemy, reshuffled the corps commanders, and left the unpopular Bragg in charge. The intrepid Forrest, the untutored tactical genius of the Confederacy, was promoted to major general and authorized to raise a cavalry division in Mississippi. Longstreet was permitted to march away to Knoxville to besiege Burnside.

Meanwhile, in the Union ranks, Rosecrans was replaced by Thomas, and Grant, fresh from his victories in the West, was sent to take command. Arriving late in October, Grant found an army literally starving while the staff contemplated a fully developed plan for their relief. Ordering the plan put into operation, Grant sent a corps across the river to hold Brown's Ferry. This opened the river from the Union base at Bridgeport. The danger of starvation overcome, Grant brought Sherman's army up to a position opposite the end of Missionary Ridge. He planned to have Sherman cross the river and drive the Confederates down the Ridge while Hooker struck at the opposite end of the Ridge near Rossville Gap. On November 24, the movement began. The Confederates abandoned their outpost on Lookout Mountain to concentrate on the Ridge. Throughout the day, there was desultory fighting. Sherman crossed the river but was delayed in affecting a lodgment on the mountain, while Hooker's corps were slow in coming into action. In midafternoon, the order for a diversion in the center of the line facing the slopes of Missionary Ridge resulted in the Union soldiers charging up the steep sides of the mountain and sweeping the Confederates before them. The poor location of the guns on the top of the Ridge deprived the Confederates of the use of their artillery. The break in the center gave Sherman and Hooker the opportunity to press forward, and Bragg's army retreated to Dalton, Georgia. The spectacular battle had saved the Union army and deprived the Confederates of their last chance for an overwhelming victory.

4. DOMESTIC DIFFICULTIES

While its armies were meeting defeat in the field, the government of the Confederate states was experiencing comparable difficulties. The constitutional question of states' rights and the personality of Jefferson Davis combined to harass the government in its conduct of the war. In September, 1862, the issue of states' rights was raised by the action of the South Carolina convention, which instructed the state legislature to protect the citizens of the state from Confederate conscription. This convention was unique in the South. After passing the Ordinance of Secession, the convention, which alleged that it was the embodiment of the "sovereign" people of South Carolina, stayed in session to direct the course of the war. Eventually the people repudiated their self-constituted "sovereigns," but through most of the war the extraconstitutional convention arrogated to itself the right to give orders to the legislature.

Although continuing his opposition to Jefferson Davis, Rhett realized the necessity for conscription and denounced the attitude of his state. As South Carolina hesitated, however, Governor Brown protested to Davis in behalf of Georgia. The conscription act seemed to Brown contrary to the sovereignty of the states and in violation of the rights reserved to the states by the Constitution. Linton Stephens headed a faction in the Georgia legislature which held that conscription was both unnecessary and destructive of martial enthusiasm.

At the same time that the states were raising the specter of states' rights, the country was suffering from a shortage of supplies. The blockade was becoming efficient, there was a shortage of equipment for the army, and prices rose, to the consequent benefit of speculators. Denunciations of the "Richmond Jews" became increasingly common, and in the winter of 1862-1863 there were bread riots in the capital. The states attempted to fix prices, and the Florida delegation in Congress sponsored legislation for national price-fixing. In North Carolina, Governor Vance proposed calling a state convention, and Davis urged other governors to obtain legislation against speculative profits.

The spring of 1863 saw the Richmond government trying to solve its difficulties. To strengthen the government and supply the armies, Congress passed three measures. The first was the Impressment Act, passed in March, which authorized the president and the governors to appoint commissioners to fix the prices which the government would pay for commodities. The law immediately caused a drop in prices, although eventually it brought more troubles for the government.

The next month, Congress passed the Tax in Kind Act, which would enable the government to avoid being paid in its own depreciated paper money. The paper money of the government was as worthless to the government as it was to the people. To escape having this currency coming back into the Treasury in payment of taxes, the act provided that farmers should pay one tenth of their produce into local governmental warehouses. The law also provided for licensing a number of nonagricultural occupations and the imposition of a property tax and an income tax.

Opposition to both of these vital measures was stilled by a realization of the need for them. But a third measure, proposed by the government, brought down upon Davis's head the concentrated wrath of the states'-rights doctrinaires. In March a Mississippi congressman, a friend of Davis, introduced a measure to give the president power to suspend the writ of *habeas corpus* in any part of the Confederacy. Two previous acts, limited in time and area, had resulted in driving a lawless element of camp followers from Richmond and other cities. Nevertheless, the Charleston *Mercury* had raised the cry of despotism and had assailed the administration for its contemplated attack on southern liberties. In Congress the same H. S. Foote who had been Davis's nemesis in Mississippi a dozen years before led the opposition. Now a senator from Tennessee, Foote loudly bemoaned the assault on liberty and succeeded in defeating the measure. The opposition to Davis, thus brought to light, was never again concealed, and the president's days were thereafter harassed by a group who constantly suspected every executive action. The harmony which had marked the first enthusiastic days of the Confederacy was never again recaptured.

The opposition charged that the president was failing to take advantage of an opportunity to sue for peace. At the head of this movement was Vice-President Stephens, who was sure that Lincoln would be willing to make peace. At the moment, a serious quarrel was going on between the opposing armies over the exchange of prisoners. The cartel adopted in the previous summer had proved so disadvantageous to the northern government that Secretary of War Stanton had used disputes between the exchange officers as an excuse for ordering a cessation of exchanges. At this junction Stephens offered his services to proceed to Washington, ostensibly to settle this dispute, but in reality with the hope of securing peace with independence. On July 4, 1863, Stephens appeared in a flag-of-truce boat off Hampton Roads with a request that he be permitted to go to Washington. Delayed for a day, he was told that there was no need for such a visit. With the victories of Gettysburg and Vicksburg on the preceding day, it was small wonder that Lincoln was not interested in hearing propositions for Confederate independence.

As the congressional elections of the autumn approached, the attacks upon Davis became more vocal. Charges were freely made that the Gettysburg campaign had been a mistake and that troops should have been sent to relieve Vicksburg. The operation of the impressment law quickly produced a reaction. Farmers complained that the government prices were unjust, and manufacturers, deprived of excess profits, were equally indignant. In Georgia, Toombs warned that liberty was being lost. The tax in kind was also denounced as unjust, and the farmer who paid his tenth protested vigorously against bearing a disproportionate part of the burden. To the farmer it appeared that the rich man, whose slaves were not taxed, was escaping his just portion. Yet the income tax and the licensing provisions of the law served to set the wealthy classes and the professional men also against the administration.

Most serious was the opposition in North Carolina, where the small farmer of the western region had never been in sympathy with the ruling aristocracy. Mass meetings of farmers denounced the tax in kind, demanded peace, and pledged themselves to resist the government. W. W. Holden, editor of the Raleigh *Progress,* headed the movement and ran for governor against Z. B. Vance. Mobs terrorized the state, while deserters from the army joined in plundering the country.

In the elections, the southern people repudiated the Davis government and returned an opposition majority to Congress. Eight of North Carolina's ten congressmen were anti-Davis; nine of Georgia's ten congressmen were in opposition, while a majority of those from South Carolina were against the administration. Rhett had stood for the election, but he was defeated for local reasons. Henceforth Davis had a hostile Congress to hamper his efforts.

After the elections, Davis made a trip into the South, primarily to settle the disputes in Bragg's army but also to ascertain the political situation. He visited Mobile and returned through Charleston, where his reception deceived him into believing that the opposition had been exaggerated. But at that date it was too late to remedy the widespread lack of confidence in the government.

5. Failure Abroad

The year 1863 was as active and as disastrous in foreign as in domestic affairs. The year opened with the minister of Napoleon carrying a peace proposal to Lincoln, while in Paris Slidell was urging his daughter's father-in-law, Émile Erlanger, to launch a Confederate bond issue on the market. Erlanger was one of the largest bankers of France and close to the none-too-scrupulous group which surrounded the emperor. He conceived a scheme to grow rich on cotton speculations, and proposed, doubtless with Napoleon III's approval, that the Confederacy should issue through him bonds secured by cotton. The bonds, bearing 7 per cent interest, were to be issued to Erlanger at 77 and offered at 90, and the holder might redeem his bond in New Orleans middling cotton at 6 cents a pound. Since cotton was selling for over 40 cents in England, the purchaser might make a good profit if he could get his cotton out of the Confederacy. With some misgivings, the Confederate authorities issued the bonds, and Erlanger offered $15,000,000 in London, Frankfurt, Amsterdam, and Paris. For a time they sold higher than the bonds of the United States.

The purchasers of the bonds paid a first installment of 15 per cent. Before May 1, when the second installment was due, a change of opinion reduced the value of the bonds, and many were turned back on the market, thus depressing the price. In order to keep up the price, Erlanger, Mason, and Slidell spent over $6,000,000 in purchases. No appreciable effect on the market resulted, but the Confederacy lost much needed money and credit. The test gave final proof that King Cotton was a monarch of no power.

The real test of King Cotton's claims to supremacy came in England. Agents of both sides made valiant efforts to win British sympathy and support. Confederates, enlisting the aid of publicists and politicians, published as many books and pamphlets as their slender means permitted. Henry Hotze, who doubled as purchasing agent and propagandist, established the *Index* a special newspaper to furnish pro-Confederate information. The propagandists emphasized Confederate resources, proclaimed southern military superiority, and explained the reasons for secession. If slavery received little attention, the evils of Lincoln's government received much. With skill born of desperation, the Confederate propagandists pointed out that after independence they would trade no more with the North. The South's trade would all be with England!

Against these arguments the North made effective answer. Early in the war, Lincoln dispatched leading men of the North to Europe to present the American cause to the European peoples. Bishop C. P.

McIlvaine of the Episcopal diocese of Ohio, Thurlow Weed of New York, and the Catholic Archbishop of New York, John Hughes, were sent to influence whatever sections of the European populace they could. In their activities they received much help from such minor officials as John Bigelow, consul-general at London, and Henry Adams, son of the American ambassador. Later, Robert J. Walker of Mississippi, Polk's secretary of the treasury, went to England. Aside from personal influence, these men wrote and inspired others to write to the newspapers in behalf of the American cause. Walker was especially effective in persuading the British public that Jefferson Davis had been responsible for the repudiation of Mississippi bonds in the decade before the war. The Confederate propagandists, headed by Mason, tried in vain to show that it was really Walker who had been responsible for Mississippi's repudiation. The effect of such propaganda was seen in the fate of the Erlanger loan.

Particularly effective was the northern appeal to the working classes of England. The winter of 1862-1863 witnessed a cotton famine in England with a half-million operatives thrown out of work. Had cotton been king, the presence of these starving men might have forced English intervention. But the northern propagandists again circumvented the operation of economic laws. The Emancipation Proclamation had changed the American war into a crusade for human freedom, and English abolitionists took strong grounds in favor of the North. John Bright and other English humanitarians appealed to the workingmen to starve in support of a holy cause, and the workers in hundreds of mass meetings responded by passing resolutions in favor of the North. The northern government intelligently gave tangible co-operation in this movement by sending shiploads of wheat for distribution among the British unemployed.

Although a cotton famine on a lesser scale in France had a similar result, the French government, unlike the English, was eager to help the Confederacy. During an interview on southern problems, Napoleon suddenly asked why the Confederacy had not built a navy. When Slidell explained that the French neutrality laws prevented building such ships in France, the emperor blandly remarked that they could be built for some other purpose. A few days later, on January 7, M. Arman, a shipbuilder of Bordeaux and close friend of the Emperor, called on Slidell with an offer to build iron-clad ships for the Confederacy. The builder would accept cotton bonds and would obtain official sanction for the ships on the pretext that they were being constructed for use in the Pacific. Contracts were quickly signed.

Meanwhile in England the Laird shipyards were building two iron-clad rams for the Confederacy, and hopes were running high in the little southern group. In Parliament the most energetic supporter of the Confederacy was J. A. Roebuck, who watched for a chance to bring about recognition. As Lee advanced into Pennsylvania, Roebuck visited Napoleon and received assurances of support. Returning to London, Roebuck offered a resolution in the House of Commons instructing the government to co-operate with other powers in recognizing the Confederacy. Debate was held until July 13, but the news of Gettysburg turned the majority of the House against action. Moreover, Napoleon grew lukewarm as he heard of Gettysburg and Vicksburg. Roebuck withdrew his motion before it came to a vote, and a few weeks later Benjamin ordered Mason to withdraw from England.

The key to Napoleon's policy in these dealings lay in his attempts to put the Austrian archduke, Maximilian, on the throne of Mexico. Since such a violation of the Monroe Doctrine would be certain to incur the opposition of the United States, Napoleon needed an American ally. Unwilling to recognize the Confederacy without England's co-operation, the Emperor was obliged to follow English policy. The succession of Confederate military failures could serve only to prevent action by either England or France. In the summer of 1863, Minister Adams finally persuaded the British officials to prevent the completion of the Laird rams. Shortly thereafter, the nascent Confederate navy in M. Arman's yards was stopped when a clerk stole incriminating documents. These were sold to the American government, and an immediate protest followed. At the same time, Slidell rashly wrote to the emperor mentioning their former conversation and assuming that Napoleon was engaged in a plot to violate his own neutrality laws. In the circumstances, there was nothing for the emperor to do but forbid the completion of the ships. Henceforth, Napoleon gave no encouragement to the South.

A reflection of this changed attitude came in Mexico. In December, 1863, Davis had recommended sending a minister to the Imperial Mexican government. Congress approved, and Davis appointed General William Preston to the mission. Preston went to Mexico, where he was refused recognition. The one revolutionary government refused to prejudice its chances by recognizing the other.

After Napoleon's change of heart, the Confederacy's last chance for foreign aid was gone. In diplomacy, in politics, and on the battlefield the year 1863 was one of irreparable disaster.

C H A P T E R   2 2

Life in the Confederacy

1. SLAVERY IN THE CONFEDERACY

THE war between the states had the inevitable effect of throwing economic and social life out of its peace-time balance. The conflict gave momentum to some social forces while it diverted others from their normal courses. The gory hand of Mars reached into homes to snatch the South's youth from parents and friends and disturbed both the economic and the psychological balance of the people. The emotional groundwork for the war had been laid, on both sides, by the slavery controversy. The war's catastrophes brought distress and suffering, a loss of property, and the destruction of the Old South's economic system and its cultural heritage. After the war, the South was never to be the same.

The disruptive forces of war struck first and hardest at the Confederacy's most important economic institution. The problem of the slaves was one that involved not only the labor supply and the largest single investment of southern wealth, but that had, as well, military and social aspects. From the beginning, the Confederacy faced the task of diverting some portion of its agricultural labor into channels of military usefulness. Slaves might be used for servants, for work on fortifications, and even for garrison duty if they could be released from the plantations.

The first Congress of the Confederacy passed an act for the suppression of the African slave trade. The bill provided that the government should sell at auction the cargo of a captured ship. President Davis immediately perceived that this provision would permit the introduction of new slaves into the South and vetoed the act. His veto gave rise to much criticism, especially by those who pointed out that an increase in the slave population would help to release slaves for military purposes. The act would have been no help, but it was symbolic of the nation's problem.

The need for labor in military works and by the government led Davis to propose that he be given power to impress slaves. Slaveholders objected to the purchase of slaves by their government both because the government would thereby become a competitor and because of a fear of eventual emancipation. Opponents of Davis saw a real menace in a body of slaves under the exclusive control of the president. In 1862, however, Congress permitted the executive to impress slaves provided that the masters were given compensation. States also conscripted labor and permitted localities to do so, but in each case the rights of the owner were protected. Such use was rigidly restricted to military preparation, and the states prescribed the number of slaves whom Davis could conscript and the length of time they should serve.

In addition to the government's needs, there was the problem of directing the slaves in their accustomed work. The government's demand for the full man power of the South disrupted the plantation system. With the whites in the army, the slaves would be left without other direction than the women could give them. The social problems of slavery were always as important as were the economic ones, and there was real need for police control of the blacks. In the days before the war, the "pater-rollers" had watched the roads to curb migratory tendencies; but with the whites patroling the Potomac, the Negroes might go free. Accordingly, in the first conscription act, overseers on plantations having twenty slaves were exempted from the draft. Later laws modified this to one overseer for each fifteen slaves. This "fifteen nigger law" angered the poor man of the South who had left his women and younger children unprotected, and seemed to confirm his suspicion that the rich were allowing the poor to fight their battles. Since planters discharged overseers in order to take advantage of the law for themselves, the poorer men justified their own desertion and joined the opposition against Davis.

Although there were innumerable cases where the Negroes remained loyally at their tasks long after all coercion was removed, a large number of slaves took advantage of their first opportunity to escape from bondage. House servants, old family retainers, and the slaves of the smaller planters remained at their posts to defend their master's property and family long after the field hands had wandered away. Federal commanders in the South were constantly harassed by the Negroes who flocked to their camps. In order to care for these fugitives, the Federal government set up the Freedmen's Bureau with the object of settling the Negroes on the abandoned and confiscated lands of the Confederates.

2. WARTIME INDUSTRY

In industry as in labor, the dire need of the Confederate government disrupted the normal processes of development. In the decade before the war, southern industry had been growing, and the momentary stimulus which the war gave to manufacturing had effect in the later story of the South. Peacetime development would have taken place in textiles and lumbering, but the wartime diversion of capital from these natural channels was a distinct loss to the region.

The beginnings of industry, however, had been too recent to contribute much to the Confederacy. The government made strenuous efforts to stimulate production. With tremendous natural resources, the South found itself destitute of both technical ability and the tools of industry. It had thousands of bales of cotton but few cotton mills, little machinery, and no laborers who could be readily educated in the production of cloth. Wool was scarce, and woolen mills even scarcer. East Tennessee, north Alabama, and southwestern Virginia were regions rich in iron, yet few foundries and no equipment for establishing iron works existed. A nation designed to produce raw materials found itself utterly unable to produce manufactured goods for its military needs.

The situation had two results. First, both government and people bent every effort to produce the necessities. The government established medical laboratories to comb the South for herbs of medicinal values. Salt works were established at Wytheville, Virginia, in east Tennessee, and in the Kentucky mountains, and salt was boiled along the coast. Richmond's Tredegar Iron Works and the foundries of Selma, Alabama, worked to the limit. Iron was mined in Alabama and gunpowder was produced by the Niter and Mining Bureau. Every encouragement was given to manufacturing, and the government encouraged the blockade runners who brought supplies from the outside world. Even trade with the enemy was tolerated.

But all of these efforts were unavailing to provide the materials for war. In desperate need of everything, the South turned to consuming its accumulated wealth. Leads from window weights were taken to make bullets, cannons were cast from melted church bells, women's silk dresses made patchwork observation balloons, and less needed railroads lost their rails to lines that served an immediate need.

For private use as well as for public needs, the Southerner was forced into destructive makeshifts. Old clothes were patched, turned, and refurbished to appear again as "Sunday best." Coffee disappeared from tables to give place to chicory or parched corn, vegetable fat replaced tallow in candles, molasses was used for sweetening, and carpets were transformed into blankets. The spinning wheel and the hand loom worked heavily to supply needed replacement of clothes. Newspapers first limited themselves to single sheets, then appeared on wrapping paper and even on wall paper.

As supplies were exhausted, there was nothing to take their place. The blockade, increasingly effective as the war progressed, cut the Confederacy off from the world. The fall of New Orleans closed that port and the Mississippi River to imports. A fleet lay constantly off Charleston, and stone-filled vessels were sunk in the entrance to the harbor. The blockading squadron prevented access to the rivers of Virginia and to Pamlico and Albemarle Sounds in North Carolina. In Florida, the blockade was less effective, but the means of transportation into the upper South were so poor that the open coast was of little value. In fact, by 1863 access to the Confederacy was possible only through Wilmington, North Carolina, Mobile, and the Rio Grande River. The effectiveness of the blockade was such that normal steamers could not run in with cargoes. Specially built light-draught ships capable of high speeds alone dared take the risk. Goods from Europe were deposited at Nassau or Havana to await the trips of these daring vessels. Immediate necessities and high-value luxury goods were carried in by these ships —which were usually owned by Englishmen—and cotton was taken out. Large shipments were made to Matamoras, in Mexico, until the fall of Vicksburg severed the eastern from the western part of the Confederacy.

Such blockade running was unable to supply the government and was of little importance to the people. The government licensed blockade runners and required that part of the cargo of each ship should be of goods needed by the government and that government cotton be carried out. The North Carolina government made the same requirement of the ships which came to Wilmington. So great were the risks and so high the price of cotton that a vessel that could make a couple of trips before capture would show a good profit. But the very size of the profits indicated the effectiveness of the blockade. One government-owned vessel, the *Robert E. Lee,* made 30 trips between Wilmington and Nassau. North Carolina's account with the blockade runners brought $200,000 worth of drugs and surgical supplies in 1863. The Confederate government realized over £200,000 on cotton sales in England.

The poor results of all of these efforts to supply its needs indicates that the Confederacy starved to death. Both because of the scarcity of supplies and because of paper money, prices were high. Quoted in the fiat money of the Confederate treasury, the prices of commodities in common use ran to fabulous heights. Flour, which sold for $25 a barrel in the spring of 1863, sold for $1,000 in January, 1865. Potatoes ran as high as $100 a bushel, and sugar as high as $10 a pound. Reduced to a specie basis, these fantastic prices were but a little higher than the same commodities on the New York market; but there was neither gold nor silver in the Confederacy, while there was over a billion dollars in Treasury notes. The situation bore heavily upon the salaried classes of the cities, who were often faced with the specter of starvation. In the rural regions, especially where the armies of both sides did not raid, food existed in greater abundance than did hands for its harvest. It was not so much the lack of food as the failure of the entire distribution system that brought the Confederacy to collapse.

The most irritating result of the failure of the system of distribution was the widespread appearance of profiteering. Speculators in foodstuffs forced prices up. In March, 1863, Georgia's Bishop George F. Pierce declared that "restlessness and discontent" prevailed. "Extortion, pitiless extortion is making havoc in the land. . . . Avarice with full barns puts the bounties of Providence under bolts and bars, waiting with eager longings for higher prices." The "Jews of Richmond" were anathema to Confederates. Southern speculators, unlike their northern counterparts, did not emerge from the war with fortunes swollen by having fed on catastrophe. Their wealth was in Confederate paper and disappeared in the destruction to which they had so largely contributed.

In the midst of economic disorder, the women of the South suffered the most. At the beginning of the war, women banded themselves together in their communities to sew uniforms and make flags for the local companies. Soon they were cutting bandages and picking lint to dress wounds. The Confederate and the state governments attempted to organize the women for auxiliary war service and to bolster the morale of the men. Diaries and reminiscences of women who remained at home struggling to keep slaves at work and plantations in production abound in accounts of bitter hardship endured. To the daughter of the aristocracy, deprived of her accustomed luxuries, the war was indeed severe. To the wife of the poor farmer, working in the fields and an object of neighborhood charity, or fleeing at night from the ravages of war, the cause for which she suffered frequently did not seem to be worth the candle. While the more literate mistress of the plantation recorded her sufferings in a diary, the poorer woman sent pleas to her menfolk which often caused them to desert from the army.

3. Confederate Prisons

The complete inadequacy of the Confederacy's material resources and the failure of its transportation system was fully illustrated in the prisons, where hapless Union soldiers became the wards of an impoverished government. The first battle of Manassas brought some 50 officers and 1,000 men into Richmond as prisoners of war. No preparations had been made to care for the captives, who were bundled into abandoned tobacco warehouses in the city. Confederate military law required that prisoners should be issued the same rations and the same clothing as troops in the field. The prisoners, however, soon began to feel the effects of Confederate poverty. As the blockade became effective, sugar and coffee were taken from them and there was a steady deterioration in quality and decrease in quantity of their other rations. Clothing, lacking for the army, was never supplied to prisoners. Instead, clothes were taken from the prisoners at the time of their capture, and sometimes entire companies of Confederates were proudly garbed in Union blue while their victims shivered in discarded Confederate rags in ill-heated prisons. Once southern soldiers protested to Secretary Stanton against the "shoddy" uniforms sold to the Federal army by northern profiteers.

The suffering, mostly imaginary, of these prisoners in the Richmond warehouses led to demands on the northern government to begin a system of exchanges. Lincoln had adopted the theory that arrangements for exchanging prisoners would be an implied recognition of Confederate belligerency, but the increase of prisoners and of pressure forced a change of attitude. On July 22, 1862, a cartel for exchange was made between the two armies.

The cartel provided that prisoners captured should be released on parole and sent inside their own lines, where they were to perform no military duties until released by exchange. The system would avoid the expense of maintaining prison camps, and for a year prisoners were released on parole at the time of their capture. Difficulties, however, developed almost from the beginning. As the news of the cartel spread in the army, soldiers lost their dread of imprisonment and saw in the promise of a parole an opportunity to obtain a "little rest from soldiering." Surrenders in the field became common, and Secretary Stanton found his armies seriously handicapped. Moreover, the paroled soldiers, sent to army camps, refused to perform even garrison duty and insisted that the terms of their parole entitled them to be furloughed home until exchanged. Mutiny broke out at several northern camps, and the Federal officials concluded that imprisonment was preferable to a parole system. Minor administrative irregularities were magnified into major infractions of the cartel, and despite the best efforts of the Confederates, the northern War Department refused to exchange prisoners.

This abandonment of the cartel threw the prisoners back upon the Confederacy. Two prisons were established at Richmond: Libby Prison, an abandoned tobacco warehouse, was set aside for Federal officers, while enlisted men were confined on Belle Isle, in the James River. The immediate effect of this concentration of prisoners in Richmond was to increase prices and to cause a food shortage. Rations to the prisoners were cut, and the Confederate government was forced to permit the northern government to send supplies of food and clothing to the prisoners. Early in 1864, the shortage of supplies and the military danger of having so many prisoners, poorly guarded, in the capital led to the establishment of two new prisons at Macon and Andersonville, Georgia, where officers and men might be more safely confined.

The hardships which the prisoners underwent were magnified for propaganda purposes in the North. Newspapers carried atrocity stories to "fire the Northern heart" with hatred for the South and pictured prisoners as being deprived of food, clothing, and heat by the vindictive spirit of the rebels. The government gave all possible aid to the dissemination of such accounts and even published reports showing that the Confederates brutally starved prisoners and denied medical attention to the sick and wounded. A report of the Joint Committee on the Conduct of the War declared that the mistreatment of prisoners was the result of a "predetermined plan, originating somewhere in the rebel counsels, for destroying and disabling the soldiers of their enemy, who had honorably surrendered in the field." As a result of such propaganda, the northern press demanded that Confederate soldiers in northern prisons should be subjected to retaliatory treatment. The prison officials readily complied by reducing the rations in northern camps.

The establishment of Andersonville brought increased hardships to the Confederacy's prisoners. The prison consisted of a stockade of 16½ acres—later enlarged to 26—through which ran a stream of water. Pressure on Richmond led to prisoners being sent to the prison before barracks could be built. The prisoners were obliged to build huts or dig caves for their own shelter. Because they were unable to get supplies for cooking, the prison officials issued uncooked rations to their charges. Meat could not be obtained; and as the number of prisoners increased, meat rations disappeared and eventually only unbolted corn meal and sorghum were issued. During the summer of 1864, the number of prisoners—confined without shelter in 26 acres—increased to over 30,000. The stream through the camp could not carry off the refuse, and its banks soon became a fetid and disease-breeding swamp. Scurvy and diarrhea carried off thousands of the weakened men, and the hospital was inadequate to care for the sick.

No better evidence of the failure of the distributing system of the Confederacy can be found than the fact that these conditions existed in the midst of plenty. The shelterless prisoners were surrounded by a pine forest, and cabbage, which could not be carried out, was rotting in fields within sight of the stockade. The human failure was almost as great as the failure of the distributing system. Home guards did guard duty and occasionally shot a prisoner who ventured too close to the prison walls, but they were too few to regulate the conduct of their charges. Among the prisoners a gang of bounty jumpers robbed and murdered their fellows until a vigilance committee of the prisoners captured the "Raiders" and hanged six of them after trial by court martial. The officers of the prisons were inevitably drawn from those least efficient in field duty, but they struggled valiantly to obtain supplies. Their requisitions for food and clothing, and even for such things as nails and shovels, were ignored for the greater needs of the army in the field. Most efficient of the officers was Captain Henry Wirz, whom the prisoners, imbued with the belief that they were being deliberately starved, blamed for their misfortunes. At the close of the war, Wirz was given a farcial trial before a military commission and hanged for "conspiring" with Jefferson Davis to murder the prisoners in his charge. He was the victim of war psychosis: almost 13,000 graves at Andersonville mark the victims of Confederate economic collapse.

As Sherman marched through Georgia, the prisoners at Andersonville and Macon were moved to other prisons. Meanwhile, in Virginia, the versatile General Butler had turned his attention to the prisoners and, ignoring the cartel, had begun to exchange sick prisoners. When these were exhausted, the military officials continued to send prisoners in exchange. By the end of the war, most of the prisoners had been released.

4. Southern Morale

Equally important with the economic dislocations of the war were the psychological disturbances caused by the conflict. Although the war was caused by a clash of economic systems, the masses of people on either side would have been unwilling to suffer for the economic or political aggrandizement of either the masters of capital or the lords of the manor. In the decades before the war, the economic motives of New England industrialists and southern planters had been hidden behind a camouflage of moral arguments. The southern people had been taught through the years a hatred of the shrewd, scheming Yankee whose shady business dealings were surpassed in dishonesty by his hypocritical Puritanism. In contrast, the southern ideal had been that of the cavalier, a *beau ideal* of chivalry. While Northerners had been identifying themselves and their economic system with democracy, the Southerners had taken the aristocratic ideal as their own. In the North, the war became a crusade in behalf of democracy and freedom—ideals expressed by Lincoln's masterly epigram at the dedication of the cemetery at Gettysburg.

While the North was rationalizing the war in terms of the perpetuation of popular government, the South was justifying its actions in terms of constitutional rights, the protection of its chivalric civilization, and the preservation of its homes. General Butler became the type figure of Yankee brutality, and a southern crop of atrocity stories rivaled those concocted north of the Potomac. Northern soldiers marched to war singing, "As He died to make men holy, let us die to make men free," while the gray armies sang, "The despot's heel is on thy shore, Maryland, my Maryland." The Southerners were fighting for constitutional liberty against tyrannical invasion.

Aiding the morale of the Confederate armies and peoples was a religious revival which gave the war the note of a crusade. The leaders of the army were distinguished for piety. Robert E. Lee was the embodiment of the Christian ideal, and Stonewall Jackson prayed at all seasons and hesitated to march on Sundays. Generals gave full freedom to the ministers who frequented their camps, and prayer meetings were a normal preparation for battle. In the midst of the war, Jefferson Davis joined the Episcopal Church—thereby completing his evolution from an impoverished planter of Democratic and Baptist background into the ranks of the aristocracy. During the Atlanta campaign, General John B. Hood, who had lost a leg at Chickamauga, was baptized by the Bishop of Louisiana—General Leonidas Polk. Southerners were convinced that their cause had divine blessing.

Neither religion nor propaganda, however, could suffice to keep the South united in the face of military defeat and economic collapse. In the battle regions, families were forced to abandon their homes to become refugees, and in the mountain districts lived many who had always been opposed to the southern cause. Defeat and hardships contributed to the development of a discontent that found expression in secret societies opposed to the war. Three such societies, in separate regions, were organized with a paraphernalia of oaths, passwords, and grips; and these devoted their efforts to encouraging desertion from the armies, to aiding refugees to escape from the South, and to agitation for peace. The "Peace and Constitutional Society" flourished in Arkansas, the "Peace Society" centered in Alabama but spread over the middle

South, and the "Heroes of America" covered the Appalachian highlands. In other places, organized bands combined a desire for peace with a will to plunder and to harass loyal citizens. The societies surreptitiously participated in politics, electing "unknown" men to office. They gave information to the Federal armies and helped escaping prisoners, refugees, and even Negroes to reach the Union lines. Desertion spread in the armies, and the deserters, hiding in the hills, terrorized the countryside and defied arrest. Peace and Union sentiments replaced the initial enthusiasm for secession. In morale, as in economics and on the battlefield, the Confederate experiment eventually ended in failure.

The Last Days of the Confederacy

1. GRANT VERSUS LEE

MARCH 9, 1864, Ulysses S. Grant was commissioned lieutenant general and placed in command of all the Federal armies. The years of fumbling in Washington, trying out one commander after another, were over. Henceforth the Union forces had one commander and one plan of action. With the enormous resources in men and material of the North, and with the full confidence of the administration at his back, Grant faced the armies of a nation on the verge of collapse. That the war lasted another year was due to the determination of Jefferson Davis and the spirit of Robert E. Lee.

Grant's plan of campaign was not greatly different from that of his predecessors from McClellan to Meade. He would advance all of his armies simultaneously against the Confederates and concentrate upon the main objectives rather than scatter the armies over the various fields of war. In Virginia, the Army of the James, commanded by Butler, was in position to advance up the peninsula against Richmond; and the Army of the Potomac, commanded by Meade, faced Lee's Army of Northern Virginia across the Rapidan. At Chattanooga, Sherman commanded the western armies which faced Johnston, who had succeeded Bragg after Chattanooga. Johnston was in winter quarters at Dalton, Georgia. All of these armies, according to Grant's plan, were to move forward at the same time.

On May 4, the Army of the Potomac, accompanied by Grant, crossed the Rapidan and marched into the region known as the "Wilderness," where Lee was ready to give battle. His artillery worthless in the situation, his army broken by the wild terrain, Grant fought for two days without dislodging Lee. On May 7, Grant moved out of the Wilderness; but unlike all of his predecessors who had faced Lee, he did not withdraw across the river. Instead he moved to the right of Lee's position in an effort to outflank the Confederates. But Lee had the advantage of moving on an inside line, and on May 8, Grant found his opponent defending the road at Spotsylvania Court House. Again Grant attacked, but a week of throwing his superior forces against the undaunted Confederates brought no victory. Again Grant flanked and arrived at the North Anna, only to find Lee still across his path. This time the Federals flanked without attacking, and a series of such movements carried the armies to Cold Harbor. The Confederate position was within six miles of Richmond, and on June 2 Grant again gave battle. In the bloodiest half-hour of the war, Grant lost 7,000 men and was forced to give up the assault. His losses since crossing the Rapidan had been 55,000, while Lee's army of 60,000 had lost only 19,000 men. But the Union forces could refill their ranks, while Lee's loss was permanent.

Grant's campaign overland from Washington to Cold Harbor was sufficient to prove to Lincoln and the North that such a route to Richmond was impractical. With the lesson learned, Grant informed the government that he was going south of the Confederate capital to approach by the route which McClellan had been forced to abandon. At the same time that Grant had crossed the Rapidan, Butler had moved up the James River toward Richmond. However, Butler's army of the James had been "bottled up" at Bermuda Hundred. While an attack was launched against Petersburg, commanding the approach to Richmond, Grant moved his army across the river to take up position at City Point. The advance on Petersburg was delayed, and Lee hastened up to save the city. Grant thereupon settled down to siege operations, which, though slower, were sure eventually to exhaust the South. Throughout the following months the slow approach to Richmond went on.

Fully realizing the danger to the Confederate capital, Lee again attempted a diversion in the Valley. To repeat Jackson's feat of 1862, Jubal A. Early went with 17,000 men to clear the Valley and threaten Washington. Quickly winning a victory in the Valley, Early turned toward Washington, where once again panic reigned. But Early, arriving at the gates of the city, delayed for a night, and on the morrow troops from Grant's army drove him back into the Valley. There Early won victories at Kernstown and Winchester and began a raid which carried him to Chambersburg, Pennsylvania. Because it would not pay tribute, he burned the town and returned to the Valley.

Although these movements were dramatic, they lacked the power to disrupt Grant's determined purpose. Seriously frightened, Lincoln did not insist to Grant, as he had to McClellan, that troops be sent to defend Washington. In September, Grant sent General Philip H. Sheridan to drive Early from the Valley. At Winchester and Fishers Hill, Sheridan won decisive victories and then turned to destroying crops, burning barns, and spreading such devastation in Richmond's granary that "a crow flying over the country would need to carry his rations." Early returned to the attack, but Sheridan, riding from Martinsburg, came to Winchester in time to snatch victory from the Confederates. Thereafter Washington was safe from attack.

2. THE ATLANTA CAMPAIGN AND AFTER

While Grant moved against Lee in Virginia, Sherman was advancing against Johnston in Georgia. On May 4, 1864, the Federal general moved against Dalton, where he found the Confederates strongly placed. Instead of attacking, the Federal armies struck at Resaca, behind Dalton, threatening Johnston's connection with Atlanta. To protect his line, Johnston fell back, and Sherman again flanked. Each time that Johnston offered battle, Sherman pushed out his lines farther than the Confederates could reach; and each time Johnston fell back, yielding more territory. After a month of such operations, Sherman attacked at Kenesaw Mountain, but Johnston drove him back with considerable loss. Thereafter the flanking operations were resumed until July 9, when the invaders were within six miles of Atlanta.

Johnston's course was highly unpopular with the Confederate government and the people. From the first days of the Confederate army Davis had quarrelled with Johnston, and Bragg, whom Johnston had displaced in command of the army, was now Davis's principal military advisor. On July 17, Davis removed Johnston and gave the command to Hood, whose reputation as a fighter promised that he would defend Atlanta. Hood fought three battles in less than two weeks and lost all of them; but Atlanta, with its railroad lines and industries, was still in Confederate hands. For a month Sherman besieged the city, and on September 3 it fell before him.

In Atlanta, Sherman was far from secure. His lines of communication ran back to Chattanooga and from there to Nashville. Along that line, Hood's army and the daring cavalry of the brilliant Forrest threatened Sherman's scattered forces. Commanding at Nashville was George H. Thomas, upon whom Sherman depended to maintain his communications. Late in November, Hood approached and attacked Schofield at Franklin in Tennessee. In one of the most skillfully fought battles of the war, Schofield held off the Confederates and inflicted a loss of 6,000 men. Retiring on Nashville, Schofield joined Thomas in preparing for Hood's advance. As Hood gathered his forces, consternation seized the northern government. If Thomas should be defeated, the road into the North would be open and Sherman's army lost. Lincoln, Halleck, Stanton, and Grant urged Thomas to advance, but Thomas's actions seemed unnecessarily slow. Finally, however, on December 15, Thomas had completed every preparation and advanced on Hood. In a hard-fought battle, the Confederates were driven in disorder from the field. Hood's army was destroyed and scattered. Only Johnston in North Carolina was able to resist Sherman's onward march.

Before these battles were fought, Sherman had decided upon a daring enterprise. Realizing that much of his strength must be expended in guarding his long line of communications, he sought permission from Grant to strike out from Atlanta and live on the country until he could reach the seacoast and establish connections with the navy. Reluctantly Grant gave permission, and on November 15 Sherman burned Atlanta

Photo by U. S. Army Signal Corps

THE WATERFRONT AT SAVANNAH. Savannah was the objective of General William T. Sherman on his march through Georgia. On December 10, 1864, Sherman's troops began the siege of the port city, and on December 20 General William J. Hardee withdrew from the city and Sherman sent the news of its fall to President Lincoln as a Christmas present. The Confederacy was again cut in two.

and struck out across Georgia. He would, he said, pierce the hollow shell of the Confederacy.

Cutting a swath from 30 to 60 miles wide, Sherman began a march across the heart of Georgia to Savannah. For three weeks his government knew of his whereabouts only from southern papers, whose editors boasted that the daring move would result in the capture of Sherman and his army. The Federal troops, however, met no resistance. Hood was far away before Nashville, and the scattered cavalry and home guards could furnish no opposition to a victorious army. The soldiers plundered the countryside, raiding the storehouses of plantations and attracting a great concourse of Negroes, who followed the army secure in the knowledge that "de day ob jubilee" had come. On December 10, Sherman made contact with the naval vessels which had anxiously awaited his appearance and began a siege of Savannah. On December 20, General William J. Hardee withdrew from the city and Sherman sent the news of its fall to President Lincoln as a Christmas present. The Confederacy was again cut in two, and only Virginia and the Carolinas, surrounded by armies, were in touch with the Confederate government.

3. Conscription and Conflict

While determined Federal armies slowly constricted the Confederacy, the southern government in frenzied desperation made efforts to treat the symptoms of its fatal disease. Fundamentally, the lack of man power was the South's most serious problem, and the government's remedy was a more strict conscription. Early in 1864 Congress passed a new conscription act, making all men from 17 to 50 liable to service. However, the list of exemptions was large and gave renewed validity to the charge that the rich were escaping military duty. Physicians, editors, and preachers were exempt, and also the overseers of plantations having fifteen slaves. Moreover, civil employees of the states, whom the governors should certify to be "necessary for the proper administration of the state government," could not be drafted. The president might "detail" conscripts for essential nonmilitary services.

This law was badly drawn. In addition to laying the government open to criticism by the nature of the exemptions, the method of exemption seriously interfered with the act's purposes. The president was criticized for his "details," and governors took advantage of the provision enabling them to exempt civil servants by certifying that justices of the peace, clerks, and courthouse employees were necessary for state administration. Judges in the courts freely issued writs of *habeas corpus* to keep men from service, and lower courts decided that the conscription acts were unconstitutional. The entire system of conscription broke down and desertion increased until many regiments were reduced to skeleton organizations with more absentees than men present in the ranks.

In order to combat the declining morale, and thereby to increase the man power, Davis again asked congress for power to suspend the writ of *habeas corpus*. This time he reported on the activities of the peace societies. Fully aware of the danger, Congress gave the desired permission and empowered the president to arrest persons engaged in treasonable activities and to try them by military commissions. The act expired by limitation in the fall of the year and was not renewed. Like the conscription act, it came too late to change the situation.

With remedies to restore internal health proving ineffective, the Confederate government looked beyond the lines where the northern elections brought a flickering hope. Lincoln had been renominated by the Republicans, disguised as a "Union" party, but there was dissension in the party, and John C. Frémont had been nominated by "Radical Republicans." With a split in the ranks of the Republicans, the Democrats, influenced by western "copperheads," adopted a platform which declared the war a failure and nominated the popular General G. B. McClellan. Democrats promised peace, and Confederates looked forward to McClellan's victory. To aid the Democrats and to carry on a subversive propaganda, Davis sent Jacob Thompson and C. C. Clay to Canada. These agents made efforts to help the Democrats and sent hopeful reports back to Richmond. But once again Confederate hopes were dashed; Lincoln made adjustments with the Radicals, Sheridan raided the Valley, and Sherman took Atlanta to give the lie to the Democratic platform. In November, Lincoln was re-elected.

As hope failed, the malignant cancer of states' rights destroyed the remaining vitality of the Confederacy. With Sherman in Atlanta, Georgia's Governor Joseph E. Brown exercised his right to exempt men from conscription. In desperate need of men, Hood appealed to Davis for re-enforcements. Davis replied that he had made every effort to raise men, had called on militia and reserves and had revoked details, but was unable to obtain more troops. Brown had exempted justices of the peace and constables in the counties until he had held 8,000 men out of the Confederate armies. Moreover, Brown gave furloughs for 30 days to the Georgia soldiers in Hood's armies "to return to their homes and look for a time after important interests." The move was inspired by a desire to prevent these soldiers from being taken out of the state. At the same time, the governor threatened to recall the Georgia troops from the army in Virginia.

To prevent Brown's foolhardy actions, Davis left Richmond to attempt to restore harmony, visit Hood's army, and prepare future plans. In Augusta, Davis spoke of Beauregard as a man who would obey the president. Such remarks could do little to overcome the suspicion of despotism that Brown had raised. Yet Davis's appeal was not without effect. Howell Cobb joined him in addressing the people, and Brown was forced to agree with Beauregard on the use of the state's militia. The Georgia delegation in Richmond, although a majority of them were anti-Brown, joined in an appeal to the people to rise en masse against Sherman. "Burn all bridges and block up the roads in his route," urged the congressmen. "Assail the invader in front, flank, and rear, by night and day. Let him have no rest."

From Georgia, Davis went into Alabama to encourage the people. But Sherman's march brought an increase in disaffection; and when, early in 1865, he turned north to continue his destructive progress, it was South Carolina's turn to take up the cry of states' rights. In December, 1864, the South Carolina legislature passed a conscription act calling into the service of the state all males between sixteen and sixty. An accompanying "Exemption Act" defined classes who were not liable for Confederate conscription, and another act prevented the Confederacy from conscripting slave labor. "This legislation," declared General John S. Preston, "is an explicit declaration that this state does not intend to contribute another soldier or slave to the public defense."

In the opinion of the Charleston *Mercury* and the states'-rights groups in South Carolina, Davis had left the state defenseless. The newly inaugurated governor, Andrew G. Magrath, was intent upon pushing the war, but he would do it without aiding the Confederate government. As Sherman marched into his state, he proposed to Governor Vance that the two Carolinas should co-operate to fight on. Virginia, thought Magrath, would soon be lost, and the Virginia troops in Lee's army would refuse to serve outside of the state. Vance proposed two other remedies: he suggested that the governors should unite in demanding that Johnston be restored to command and that Lee should be made dictator of the Confederacy.

The latter proposal coincided with the desires of the anti-Davis majority of the Confederate Congress. In January, 1865, a group of congressmen proposed to Lee that he should take over the government. The general refused and the congressmen turned to other methods. Congress passed a bill creating the office of Commanding General. The Virginia legislature instructed Davis that Lee should be appointed to the new command. Moreover, Davis was less officially informed that he should make changes in his Cabinet. The Congress especially disliked Secretary of War James A. Seddon.

In the first days of his government, Davis had defied Congress when it attacked Secretary Benjamin. Strong in his constitutional beliefs, Davis could not yield the principle of control over his Cabinet. Now, however, he would sacrifice the constitution, his rights, and his power to obtain harmony. He agreed to Seddon's retirement, and on January 26, 1865, he signed the bill creating a commanding general. He immediately appointed Lee, but desperation could not move the general to sacrifice his principles. A firm believer in the subordination of military to civil authority, he accepted the office, saying, "I am indebted alone to the kindness of His Excellency, the President."

Not only was Davis willing to sacrifice his principles, but he was also ready to sacrifice the slave property of the South for independence. In his message to Congress, November 7, 1864, he suggested that slaves be purchased from their owners for labor service with the armies. The proposition brought down fire upon his head from constitutionalists and from those who feared that such a concentration of power in executive hands would produce despotism. Yet it was obvious that something must be done to get men, and the slaves were the last resource.

Virginia's governor, William Smith, recommended to his legislature that the state should arm the slaves and give them freedom. General Lee, surveying his depleted ranks, endorsed the plan. But the Virginia legislature was unwilling to emancipate slaves. Despite the opposition of Smith and Davis, the legislature provided for enlisting slaves without giving them their freedom. The Confederate Congress at the same time debated bills for Negro soldiers, and in March, 1865, passed an act empowering the president to accept slaves from owners and, if an insufficient number were offered, to call for 300,000 men "irrespective of color" from the states. Davis issued a general order announcing this law two weeks before Lee surrendered at Appomattox. The act specifically declared that the service of the Negroes should not alter their status as slaves. Several companies of Negroes, assigned to guard duty, were raised by Virginia; but this last desperate effort came too late to aid the dying Confederacy.

Paralleling his sacrifice of slavery to independence, Davis made another bid for foreign support. In November of 1864, Senator H. S. Foote had proposed that the Confederacy should sacrifice the Monroe Doctrine and join with Napoleon in return for recognition. The proposal died in committee, but it inspired Francis P. Blair of Missouri and Maryland with an idea for peace. To forestall such confederate action, Blair proposed to Lincoln that he should offer the South restoration, the abandonment of slavery, and a Mexican expedition of northern and southern armies under the command of President Davis. With Lincoln's permission, Blair visited Richmond, where he stirred up the peace party's hope but failed to inspire Davis. In the meantime, Davis proposed feeling out foreign sentiment on the abandonment of slavery. He appointed Duncan F. Kenner of Louisiana as a special agent to work with Mason and Slidell. Before Kenner arrived in England, Mason approached Lord Palmerston, who informed him gently but firmly that it was too late to regard the Confederacy as an independent power. Napoleon told Slidell that the question of slavery in the Confederacy had never been considered by France, and no change in southern policy could alter the fact that the Confederacy was defeated.

One other result came from these peace gestures. During the winter of 1864-1865 Vice-President Stephens again took up his opposition to the Confederate administration. Stephens accused Davis of hoping for the defeat of the northern peace party. Moreover, Stephens professed to believe that Lincoln was ready to make peace. After Blair's visit to Richmond, Davis appointed a commission, headed by Stephens, to confer with Lincoln on peace. The commissioners met Lincoln and Secretary Seward on board a steamer in Hampton Roads. Stephens proposed an armistice, while Lincoln offered peace only on terms of complete submission. When the commission returned with the news of their failure, Davis pointed out that only war was possible, and the peace movement was temporarily quieted. Peace, however, soon came on the battlefield.

4. APPOMATTOX

By the beginning of 1865 the Confederacy was reduced to a hollow shell. Internal dissension, diplomatic despair, and the failure to obtain re-enforcements could give but one answer. Military collapse followed quickly upon civil failure. On February 1, Sherman struck out from his base in Savannah to repeat in South Carolina his devastating march through Georgia. As his men crossed over into South Carolina, a new spirit possessed them. The newspapers of the state had boasted that its people would make a bolder resistance than had the Georgians. Sherman's men had read the threats and were eager to enter the state where secession and war had begun. As a result of this spirit, the restrictions on plundering, observed in Georgia, were ignored in South Carolina, and the men ranged far from the marching columns to bring fire and destruction to South Carolina's countryside. The army was composed of small farmers of the Middle West who seemed to react violently against the poor whites whom they found in the upcountry. Class hatred combined with the pent-up emotionalism of war psychosis to lay waste the land. Meantime, the Confederate and state forces could give but little opposition. Battles, which were no more than skirmishes, were fought, but did not delay the advancing army. At Columbia the city was burned, and Sherman did not disclaim credit for the fire.

In North Carolina, the vengeful mood of the army abated and there was less destruction and more discipline. Here Joseph E. Johnston gathered soldiers to make a stand. At Averysborough, on March 16, and at Bentonville on March 17, he was driven back. On March 23 Sherman halted his march at Goldsboro, where he waited for two weeks. Then he heard that Lee was falling back, and he advanced upon Raleigh, which Johnston abandoned, and on Greensboro. Near Durham, Johnston surrendered.

In Virginia, the campaign was delayed until after Sherman had moved. Early in March Sheridan came in from the Valley and joined Grant before Richmond. In the Confederate capital, Davis and Lee debated whether they should continue to defend Petersburg or fall back, abandoning Richmond to join Johnston in North Carolina. The political necessity of holding on to the capital persuaded the leaders to continue to fight in Virginia. One Confederate attack at Fort Steadman, on March 25, failed to break the Union lines; thereafter, the Southerners fought on the defensive. Sheridan pushed out to Five Forks, where he won a victory, and Grant, hearing the news, ordered an attack along his lines. Too weak to resist on all fronts, the Confederates were driven from Petersburg. With Petersburg gone, Richmond could not be defended, and the government ordered it abandoned. On April 3, Richmond was evacuated.

The end came quickly. Lee's army marched along the roads which converged at Amelia Court House, hoping to find rations there. But the train with the rations had gone on to Richmond, and the army, without food, pushed on toward Danville. The Union troops, pressing close, were ahead of them, and Lee turned toward Lynchburg. But again the Confederates were confronted by Federal troops. On the morning of April 9, the Confederate commander sent for General Grant.

The two commanders met at the house of Wilmer McLean at Appomattox. Grant was determined upon peace and reconciliation. He offered generous terms. The army was to be paroled to return to their homes, the men taking their horses, to remain until the war was over. Lee sadly signed the agreement, surrendering 28,000 officers and men.

The news of the surrender reached Johnston and Sherman in North Carolina. Immediately these generals sought a conference, and on April 18 they signed an agreement. This Sherman-Johnston convention was far more inclusive than the agreement that Grant made with Lee. It provided that the southern state legislatures should reassemble, and made other political arrangements. In Washington the terms were unacceptable, but Grant joined Sherman, and Johnston surrendered his army on the same terms as Lee had surrendered his. On May 4, a convention between Generals Canby and Richard Taylor surrendered the armies in the far South, while west of the Mississippi Kirby Smith surrendered his department on May 26. On the high seas, the cruiser *Shenandoah* fired the last shot on June 28, and on November 6, in Liverpool, hauled down the last Confederate flag.

Fleeing from the wreck of his government, Jefferson Davis made his way to Johnston's army, hoping that the war might go on. But Johnston's officers refused to continue a hopeless struggle. Davis left them to hasten toward Mexico. On May 10, in southern Georgia, he was captured and carried to Fortress Monroe. There, also, were Alexander Stephens and other high officials. The army, 174,000 war-weary soldiers, were making their way afoot to their wrecked homes.

The Problem of Reconstruction

1. THE PROSTRATE SOUTH

THE military aspects of the Civil War ended at Appomattox, but the conflict between the basic economic and social institutions of the North and the South, between the constitutional theories and the political practices of the sections, did not end when Lee's paroled soldiers returned to their homes. The basic differences remained, and much also remained for the Masters of Capital to do to make sure their victory over the Lords of the Manor. In the North, the victors faced the problems of retaining control of the national government and of effecting their economic penetration of the South. South of the Ohio and the Potomac, the ex-Confederates sought to adjust themselves to new conditions, to solve the social and economic problems which resulted from emancipation, to recreate a political society through which they might regain power in the nation, and to preserve a few remnants of their old way of life from the devastating onslaughts of "Yankee" ideas and ideals. Reconstruction, rather than the Civil War, destroyed the Old South.

The soldiers who returned from the war found widespread desolation at their homes. In the Shenandoah Valley, blackened chimneys stood sentinel over cold ash heaps that once were houses. Throughout the South, fences were down, weeds had overrun the fields, windows were broken, livestock had disappeared. The assessed valuation of property declined from 30 to 60 per cent in the decade after 1860. Charleston was "a city of ruins, of desolation, of vacant houses, of widowed women, of rotten wharves, of deserted warehouses, of weed-wild gardens, of

miles of grass-grown streets, of acres of pitiful and voiceful barrenness."
In Mobile, business was stagnant; and Atlanta's industrial sections were
in ashes.

More fundamental than the destruction of property and the paralysis of business was the disappearance of the South's basic economic
institution. Slavery had ended as the advancing Federal armies carried
news of the Emancipation Proclamation and the confiscation acts into
the Black Belt. Negroes, rejoicing in their freedom, had left their homes

Photo by U. S. Army Signal Corps

CHARLESTON IN 1865. The soldiers who returned from the war found widespread
desolation at their homes. Charleston was "a city of ruins, of desolation, of vacant
houses, of widowed women, of rotten wharves, of deserted warehouses, of weed-
wild gardens, of miles of grass-grown streets, of acres of pitiful and voiceful barrenness." Not until the middle of the twentieth century did Charleston regain her
place in the southern economy.

to wander into the cities or to become noisy and predatory camp followers about the garrisons. Over $1,000,000,000 worth of property, con-
stituting the largest single investment of the South, was thus permanently
lost. Moreover, the Negro was not only lost property—he was also lost
labor. In the cities and at the posts where they congregated, the Negroes
waited for the government which had set them free to care for them.
Planters' efforts to entice their former slaves back to labor for hire met
with no success.

Serious social problems were the immediate result of the disruption of the slave system. Slavery had served to discipline the labor force, but the first reaction of the Negro to emancipation was to acquire a gun, a dog, and frequently a new wife to accompany him on his wanderings. In the garrison towns he fell victim to the white man's diseases and vices. Mingled with some of the worst excesses of vice were the emotional disturbances of the camp meeting and the religious revival. Ne-

Photo by U. S. Army Signal Corps

ATLANTA's INDUSTRIAL SECTION IN 1865. The battle for Atlanta and the subsequent destruction of the city reduced much of the city to ashes. Sherman's Chief Engineer, in his official report, described the treatment of the city: "General Sherman directed me to destroy with engineer troops all railroads and property belonging thereto; all storehouses, machine shops, mills, factories, etc., within the lines of the enemy's defenses at Atlanta. The work of destruction was thoroughly done, under my personal supervision. . . . The designated buildings were first burned and the walls afterwards razed to the ground. . . ."

groes formed churches of their own, separating spiritually from their old masters. The zeal for equality led some to try learning to read, and a few even attempted Latin and Greek. But the little that could be done in educating them in a formal manner did not prevent their becoming victims of every salesman who offered hair straightener, skin bleaches, and even patriotically striped stakes with which to mark off the land which the government would soon distribute.

    In the midst of such excitement, manners and morals alike suffered in the Negro camps. Stealing from the whites—a minor offense in days of plenty when the culprit was one's own property—soon became an accepted means of subsistence. Under the tutelage of Yankees, the Negroes became impudent. Their impudence was but the ignorant assertion of a new-found equality, but nothing could have been more irritating to the Southerners. In a land where good manners had been an essential attribute of cultural achievement, bad manners were sins of great magnitude. Clashes between Negroes and the lower element of the whites became common. Among the better classes, the tendency to withdraw from their former kindly patronage of the Negro was marked. The old master class had not shared in the race prejudice that characterized the poor whites. Although the slaveowner had believed that the Negro was inferior, he had wished him well and had made such adjustments as were necessary to work with him in slavery. With the withdrawal of such a patriarchal cordiality, the prejudices of the poor whites became the dominant philosophy of the South. Perhaps this was the worst calamity of a "tragic era."

When the Confederate soldier returned to his home, he found that Federal treasury agents had been there before him. The close of the war opened a vast field for speculators, not the least of whom were officials sent out by the treasury department. The Federal government had restricted the trade in cotton during the war, and after peace came the restrictions remained to harass the Southerner. He was forbidden to use the great stores of cotton which had been accumulated during the war and which might have given him a basis on which to re-establish his credit. Government agents seized cotton that had been collected in warehouses under the Confederate tax-in-kind and cotton that was subject to claim by the Confederacy. In some places, ingenious agents collected delinquent Confederate taxes.

Cotton that was not so seized was subject to a 25 per cent tax, a shipping duty, and a revenue tax. The revenue tax alone, amounting to two or three cents a pound, produced $68,000,000—which more than covered the expenses of the government in "reconstructing" the South during the three years after Appomattox. The treasury agents, each presiding over a district, received a commission of 25 per cent on abandoned or confiscated property seized. The agents turned over $34,000,000 to the government on cotton alone. Much of the cotton was illegally seized, and for a generation cotton claims were presented to the treasury. In all, over 40,000 claimants were recompensed for cotton that had been wrongfully taken. In addition to cotton, the diligent and often dishonest agents seized horses, mules, tobacco, rice, and sugar. With movable property reduced to ashes or sequestered by the Federal government, and with no labor supply, the Southerner had only his land.

Conditions among the professions were as bad as those on the farms. Lawyers found the courts closed to them unless they could take oath that they had not willingly aided the Confederacy. Physicians had work but no remuneration. Schools were closed and teachers scattered. General Lee sought for employment and finally accepted the presidency of Washington College in Virginia, and many former Confederate officers turned to teaching. Engineers saw opportunities on every hand, but there was no capital to launch enterprises for their skill. Joseph E. Johnston became an insurance agent, and Beauregard took over the presidency of a bankrupt railroad and finally sold his name and prestige to the Louisiana State Lottery. Hundreds of officers thought of migrating to Mexico, Argentina, or Brazil, and some went. Unemployment was widespread, and high officers of the Confederate army were seen peddling homemade cakes about the Federal garrisons.

Like agriculture, commerce, and the professions, the South's public works and industry were destroyed. Canals, harbors, and wharves were useless and railroads were without ties, tracks, rolling stock, locomotives, or money. Railroads had been abandoned as their equipment was needed in vital lines, and no replacements had been made during four years. Bridges had been burned by retreating armies or by raiders. Sherman had destroyed 136 of the 281 miles of the Central Railroad of Georgia. Floods had washed out sections of the roadbeds of the Memphis and Little Rock Line. Depots had been burned everywhere. In industry, nothing was left. Iron works that had been developed during the war were torn out when it ended. Salt works had been destroyed by raiders. Cotton mills at Jackson and at Atlanta had been destroyed by Grant's and Sherman's armies. The banking capital of the South was gone.

2. The North and the Prostrate South

At the close of the war, the South was almost a *tabula rasa* upon which might be outlined a new society. Unfortunately, many people in the North saw opportunities for economic profit and political advancement in the defeated region. Hardly had the last musket been stacked when a horde of adventurers came into the southern states.

Long before the war ended, cotton speculators followed the advancing Federal armies to trade with the vanquished. At Vicksburg and Memphis they so harassed General Grant that he finally issued an order excluding "Jews as a class" from his department. In New Orleans, General Butler's civilian brother traded in cotton and did a thriving business in petty graft. Treasury agents took over abandoned plantations and worked them for the benefit of the government—and themselves. The Red River expedition was caused by, and failed because of, cotton speculators. Such activities whetted an appetite for profits; and when the war closed, northern businessmen looked to the South as a colony into which business might expand. "Sober, substantial men" everywhere, recorded Grant's aide-de-camp, were in favor of a lenient policy toward the South in order that business might penetrate the region. The New York *Commercial and Financial Chronicle* was sure that the Southerners would become loyal if they would "turn their energies to the pursuits of peace, and the accumulation of wealth." In order to encourage this transformation, the paper recorded that "Northern men, accustomed to business, have gone South" to give impetus to industrial development. Other newspapers took up the cry, advertising the South as a new land of opportunity and advising the Southerners to accept immigration and to welcome capital.

To the distressed planters, this northern migration appeared to offer salvation. Numbers offered their lands for sale, and many took in northern partners both because they needed capital and because they thought Negroes might work for northern men. Young officers from the Federal armies returned to the South to purchase plantations in order to extract a hasty profit from the soaring price of cotton. They, too, believed that the ex-slaves would work for Northerners. In North and South, companies of Northerners incorporated to develop the South's natural resources. The Tennessee Colonial, Agricultural, Mining and Manufacturing Company was chartered by one Tennessean and four New Yorkers, who raised $20,000 to engage in a variety of undertakings. General J. T. Wilder, who had commanded an Indiana regiment at Chickamauga, gathered what money he could from his neighbors at home and rushed back to east Tennessee to mine and manufacture iron. Plans ripened hurriedly to settle northern colonies in the South.

The number of those who went South for business reasons was augmented by migrants who were motivated by a missionary zeal. Northern groups with humanitarian impulses sent teachers into the South to educate the Negroes and the poorer whites. Their assumption that coracial education was possible was soon found to be an error, and few of the teachers remained. More permanent were the agents of northern churches who came South to take over southern church property. During the war, the Federal armies had occupied churches as garrisons, hospitals, and storehouses; at the end of the war, Secretary Stanton surrendered to bishops of the Methodist Episcopal Church "all houses of worship belonging to the Methodist Episcopal Church, South, in which a loyal preacher appointed by a loyal bishop does not officiate." The other churches that had divided during the slavery controversy obtained similar concessions from the War Department. "The true policy," declared one religious journal, "is to be upon the ground while society is in its chaotic state" and to organize churches that would free the South from "utter barbarism" by the "infusion of a purer, a liberty-loving Christianity." Army chaplains and volunteer missionaries co-operated with Unionist pastors in the South to restore the southern churches to northern communions. School property belonging to southern churches passed into the hands of northern religious educators, who attempted with varying success to carry South the northern gospel of business success and abolitionism.

While salesmen of hair-straighteners, would-be planters, idealistic teachers, grasping clergymen, and profit-seeking capitalists were ferreting out the opportunities for gain in the South, northern politicians were devising theories that would enable them to maintain their dominance in the government. The Negroes in the South, given the franchise, would vote the Republican ticket and thereby enable the party to remain in power in the nation. If the Republicans could hold a majority in Congress, the South might be remolded closer to the northern pattern, economic exploitation of the defeated region might be facilitated, and the tariff, internal improvements, and the banking system might be maintained.

In the beginning, only the more advanced politicians perceived the political necessity of preventing the old southern leaders from returning to power. Charles Sumner propounded a theory that the states, in attempting to secede, had committed suicide. They had ceased to be states and had become territories subject to "the exclusive jurisdiction of Congress." Sumner proposed that Congress should abolish slavery, grant full political and civil rights to Negroes, and provide for their education. Like Sumner, Thaddeus Stevens, representative from Pennsylvania, whose property had been destroyed by a Confederate raid, demanded that the North take vengeance on the South. Stevens advanced a "conquered province" theory which admitted that the South had seceded, but, having been defeated, was to be treated as conquered territory without regard to the restrictions of the Constitution. He proposed that the "proud nobility" be stripped of property and reduced to manual labor while new men should settle their estates. Old abolitionists and zealous Republicans soon subscribed to Sumner's and Stevens's views.

3. The New Nation

The problem of reorganizing the Southern system was complicated by the changes which the Civil War had wrought in the essential nature of the United States. Fundamentally, the war resulted in a new nation. Specifically, the nationalization had three substantial aspects. There were the constitutional changes that had destroyed the old rights of the states, the political changes that brought the overwhelming dominance of national political parties and personalities, and the economic nationalization which was marked by a national currency, a national bank system, and the creation and fostering of big business. These were substantial alterations in the system inherited from the Fathers. Each of them had their roots in the war itself.

Constitutionally, the change was marked by the adoption of amendments to the Constitution which created a new citizenship and asserted the supremacy of the national government over the life, liberty, and property of all the new citizens. The amendments were, however, only the formal symbols of already accomplished fact. Already during the war the Federal Government had asserted its power over the lives of the citizens of the states. It had established a national army, enforced a national draft over the objections of the states, and taxed the property and incomes of the people.

Politically the war resulted in a more complete dominance of party politics by national figures. The war-swollen patronage of the president, the use of the army in elections, the admission of pocket-borough states, and finally, the adoption of the Fifteenth Amendment placed unprecedented power in the hands of the officers of the national government. In 1860, sectional division in the Democratic Party ruined it as a national organization. At the same time, the Republican Party had only the most rudimentary national organization. Its strength was in the states, and in 1860 the state parties put Abraham Lincoln in the White House. In most of the northern states candidates for governor ran well ahead of Lincoln's electors. But by 1864, Lincoln had made the Republican Party into a national party, had won supremacy over the state organizations, and had made the governors dependent upon him for their elections. As they contemplated reconstruction, the Republicans sought means for retaining their power through the control of a newly created electorate in the South.

Closely integrated with the nationalization of politics was the nationalization of economic affairs. In the years before the Civil War, the states assumed responsibility for substantial areas of economic development and for the regulation of business. States licensed business, chartered corporations, subsidized turnpikes, canals, and railroads. *Laissez-faire* was the attitude of the Federal Government. States regulated the number of apprenticeships, chartered banks, subscribed to stock in railroads, and appointed members of the boards of directors with never a thought for the individual's free right to cultivate his own vineyard. But with the Civil War the Federal Government began to make inroads on the economic authority of the states. The national government issued bonds in unprecedented numbers and amounts. It issued a federal currency. It drove state bank notes out of existence and substituted its own national bank notes. It made state banking precarious and transformed state banks into members of a national banking system. It fostered industry with contracts and a protective tariff. It subsidized railroads with grants of land, money, and credit. Faced with the problems of reconstruction, the Federal Government set about to bring the "liberty and property" of all persons under the sheltering wing of the nation. The Congress prevented any southern state from capitalizing its war debt, as the Federal Government was capitalizing its war bonds, and using it as a basis for state credit.

Essentially, the Civil War was a war against the states—not only the states of the Southern Confederacy but of the loyal North as well. The war against the states brought alterations even in the verbal symbols of the American people. Abraham Lincoln began his administration by talking about the "Union"; by the end he talked only of the "Nation." His shift in vocabulary was indicative of the development of his own thought, and was symbolic of the substantive changes that had taken place under his administration. He had brought a nation into being, and men might no longer appeal to the constitutional rights of the states. Under the impact of war, fundamental human rights—freedom of assembly, of the press, freedom from arbitrary arrest, freedom from compulsory military service—rights which the states had earlier protected, had been seriously infringed. Moreover, in Maryland, Missouri, and Kentucky, and then Ohio and Pennsylvania, the Federal armies had interfered in elections to insure the election of loyal Republicans. The new nation came into being upon the wreckage both of states' rights and some of the ancient liberties of Americans.

In January, 1865, as the Southern Confederacy was tottering to a fall, Governor Austin Blair of Michigan summed up the situation. Blair was a fanatical abolitionist, and one of the fierce humanitarians who had demanded that slavery be destroyed and the South overrun. Now, retiring after four years as war governor, he told his legislature that the war's lessons had been useful. Once, he said, the "pernicious phrase 'Sovereign States' " had permeated the language and sapped loyalty to the national government. But now, he proclaimed, "there is and can be only one paramount national authority." The lesson, he said, was worth the cost. "Many a brave hero has bit the dust. . . . Many a household has been draped in mourning, and many a heart has broken," said the proud governor. "But who," he asked, "would take it back? That is precious which is bought with blood." Blair was right: the rhetoric of "states' rights" had disappeared and could no longer stir men to defend their substantive freedom from national aggression.

Out of the Civil War, too, had come other rhetorical changes which were to affect the course of reconstruction. The old states' rights dogmas had given way to a new vocabulary of humanitarianism. The doctrine of states' rights had been integrated with Jeffersonian concepts of democracy, honest and frugal husbandry, and of a God-endowed equality. The new rhetoric of humanitarians was integrated with national power. The government of the new nation would undertake humanitarian projects: the emancipation of the slaves, the education of freedmen, the extension of social and civil rights to minorities, even the civilizing of Indians. The national humanitarians, who had been given organization and voice during the war by the United States Sanitary Commission, the Christian Commission, the Freedmen's Aid Society, and many churches, advocated and implemented the total use of government power to effect "liberal" objectives. The new vocabulary was useful in the program which the national humanitarians had for the reconstruction of the South. The humanitarians excoriated slavery, proclaimed their own devotion to freedom, and demanded the unconditional subjugation of the southern states. A "free" South would mean better markets for Northern factories, a cheap labor supply for Northern capital, and the end of southern opposition to protective tariffs, a national banking system, and to railroads under federal protection. The destruction of states' rights, done under the name of humanitarianism, would bring an end to state regulation of industry.

The vocabulary was no longer the old words which the men of the trustee tradition had used, but the ideas were directly related to the older concepts. In Congress, the new trustee program of national humanitarians found its exponents among the radical group of the Republican Party. We will, said Congressman Owen Lovejoy of Illinois, "make a solitude and call it peace." The Senator from Oregon proposed to reduce the southern states "to the condition of territories and send from Massachusetts or Illinois governors to control them." And Michigan's Senator Zachariah Chandler, who had opposed compromise in 1861 because "without a little bloodletting this Union . . . will not be worth a rush," declared that "a rebel has sacrificed all his right. He has no right to life, liberty, or the pursuit of happiness." Thaddeus Stevens wanted the South "laid waste and made a desert" and "repeopled by a band of

freemen," while Senator Lyman Trumbull of Illinois announced unctu-
ously that "war means desolation, and they who have brought it on must
be made to feel all its horrors."

These radicals had no desire for an early peace, or a peace by
negotiation. They resolutely set their faces against Lincoln's moderate
plans for Reconstruction, and they shed only crocodile tears when John
Wilkes Booth's bullet removed Lincoln from the scene. The radicals
proposed to use the new rhetoric of humanitarianism to create and control a new southern electorate. The program would not restore the rights
of the states, and southern states were to be admitted into a new nation
—not into the old Federal Union.

4. Lincoln's Plan of Reconstruction

Unlike the radical politicians of his party, President Lincoln had
early moved to develop his own plan of reconstruction. Throughout the
war, Lincoln had carefully preserved the somewhat ridiculous little
Pierpont government in Virginia. After giving West Virginia permission
to become a state, Pierpont's Virginia was reduced to a few miles on
the south bank of the Potomac and the territory around Fortress Monroe
and Norfolk. Pierpont's capital was at Alexandria, where a legislature
of sixteen delegates and seven senators claimed jurisdiction over the
region within the Union lines. Although Pierpont occasionally embarrassed the military officials, Lincoln recognized and supported his government in hope it might prove a nucleus about which the state could
be reorganized.

A second step in Lincoln's policy was tried in Tennessee. As soon as
Nashville fell, the president appointed Andrew Johnson, the only
southern senator to refuse to abandon his seat, as military governor.
Johnson was instructed to establish courts, fill offices, and prepare the
way for a restoration of civil government. Johnson, however, faced difficulties in organizing discordant Unionist factions in Tennessee and
delayed calling for elections until he could be sure that the new government would be ardent supporters of the administration. Lincoln's Emancipation Proclamation produced consternation in the ranks of southern
moderates and Unionists, and drove many of them over to the secessionists. Johnson's arbitrary acts, and the increasing use of arbitrary power
by the national government offered little hope to old states' rights men
who were opposed to secession. Impatient with the delay, in September,
1863, Lincoln ordered Johnson to take steps to establish "a republican
form of state government." A convention assembled and provided for
choosing presidential electors for the 1864 election. In January, 1865,
another convention, chosen under the auspices of the military authorities,
amended the constitution by abolishing slavery, renounced the ordinance
of secession, and approved Johnson's acts. An election made "Parson"
Brownlow governor, and in April, just before Lee's surrender, he was
inaugurated.

Soon after establishing a military government in Tennessee, Lincoln appointed a military governor for Louisiana and instructed him to hold elections for Congress. The representatives elected were admitted, but the senators were not allowed to take their seats. In 1863, state elections were held under the state's constitution, and the governor, Michael Hahn, was also appointed military governor. In April, 1864, a constitutional convention drafted a new constitution abolishing slavery, and in October a civil government under the constitution was inaugurated.

As the Federal armies gained footholds in the other states, the president appointed more military governors. Only in Arkansas, however, were steps taken similar to those in Tennessee and Louisiana. In January, 1864, a convention met at Little Rock, repealed the ordinance of secession, repudiated the state's Confederate debt, and abolished slavery. A popular vote ratified the amendments and chose a civil government.

On December 8, 1863, while these military governments were preparing the way for civil establishments, Lincoln clarified his program in a "Proclamation of Amnesty and Reconstruction." With the exception of high civil and military officials of the Confederacy and those who had resigned Federal offices after taking an oath to uphold the Constitution, all Southerners might be restored to civil rights upon taking an oath of loyalty to the United States. When a number of citizens equal to 10 per cent of the state's vote in 1860 had taken the oath, they might establish a civil government by holding an election for state and local officials. Such a program was comparatively easy to carry out and bore promise of a rapid restoration of the southern states. It was well received in the North. In a letter to a Louisianian, the president had declared: "I shall do nothing in malice. What I deal with is too vast for malicious dealing." The majority of the northern people approved the sentiment.

But the radicals in Lincoln's party were not prepared to accept Lincoln's program. They perceived clearly that Lincoln, through the use of the army and the patronage, would easily be able to control an electorate made up of only ten per cent of the voters. The states would be, in effect, mere pocket-boroughs of the president. Lincoln's purpose was solely political, but the radicals in Congress were anxious that the restoration should take place in a manner that would serve their own economic and political ends. From the beginning of the war, an element in the Republican Party had been opposed to Lincoln. Old abolitionists for the most part, they had rejoiced in Frémont's emancipation proclamation and had cheered Butler's crude acts. Ensconced in the Committee on the Conduct of the War, they used the committee to harass generals in the field and to interfere with the president's control of the army. The committee had carefully fostered the worst expression of war psychosis and had broadcast atrocity stories of the massacre at Fort Pillow and of the Confederate prisons. Eager to punish the South, to destroy slavery, and to erect a new society on the ruins of the Confederacy, the radical leaders of Congress resented Lincoln's conciliatory attitude.

In the beginning, the strongest weapon in the radicals' hands was congressional jealousy of the executive. Lincoln had begun the war without consulting Congress and had steadily assumed powers that in peace would have belonged to the legislative branch. When Lincoln informed Congress of his Amnesty Proclamation, Thaddeus Stevens and Maryland's Henry Winter Davis proposed that a special committee be appointed to consider the treatment of the southern states. Davis became chairman of a special House committee, and Benjamin Wade, old abolitionist from Ohio's Western Reserve, took up the matter in the Senate. The procedure set forth in the radical Wade-Davis Bill was more elaborate than that of the Amnesty Proclamation. It provided that 50 per cent of the inhabitants should take an oath of loyalty before the state could resume civil government. Then the military governor should order an election for a convention which must amend the constitution to abolish slavery, repudiate the Confederate debt, and disfranchise all officials of state and Confederate governments and all military officers with a colonel's or higher rank.

This bill came to Lincoln in the last moments of Congress, and he gave it a pocket veto. Since an election was impending, however, Lincoln issued a proclamation explaining his act. He declared that he was unwilling to be committed to a single plan of reconstruction and was unwilling to see the free-state constitutions of Louisiana and Arkansas overthrown. He favored an amendment to the Federal Constitution abolishing slavery rather than separate action by the states. Should any state, however, prefer to follow the procedure of the Wade-Davis Bill, he would welcome it back into the Union.

Wade and Davis immediately answered in a manifesto declaring Lincoln's action to be a "studied outrage on the legislative authority of the people" and warning the president "that the authority of Congress is paramount and must be respected." For months past, the radicals had been looking for a candidate more malicious than Lincoln. Secretary Chase was first considered, but Lincoln defeated their move; then the radicals called a meeting in Cleveland, where they placed John C. Frémont in nomination. Throughout the summer, Frémont's candidacy threatened to take radical support from the Republican ticket, but in September Lincoln made bargains with the radicals and Frémont withdrew. In the election, the radicals supported Lincoln, who interpreted the result as an endorsement of his own plan of reconstruction.

But the radicals were unwilling to concede defeat, and in the congressional session of 1864-1865 they drew clearly the lines of opposition. The question came to the fore with the attempt of Louisiana's newly elected senators to take their seats. Senator Sumner led the opposition and threatened to block all appropriations unless a bill to recognize Louisiana's government was dropped. In the end, the administration's supporters withdrew, and the radicals had won their first victory. Lincoln's policy of peace yielded to the radical desire for vengeance.

Lincoln was pleased that Congress was not in session when Lee surrendered. As the war drew to an end, the president conferred with Grant and Sherman on his plans for the South. To Sherman, Lincoln intimated that he would prefer to have Jefferson Davis escape, and the general believed Lincoln wanted him to guarantee full civil rights to citizens and to recognize *de facto* the state governments already in session. When Richmond fell, Lincoln went to the Virginia capital, where he instructed the commander, General Godfrey Weitzel, to reassemble the Virginia legislature. Evidently the president was anxious to avoid the anarchy that might accompany an interregnum.

On April 11, Lincoln addressed a crowd who had called at the White House to rejoice at the news from Appomattox. He spoke of his program of reconstruction, reviewed the case of Louisiana, and declared that the theory of the status of the southern states was "a merely pernicious abstraction." "We all agree that the seceded States, so-called, are out of their proper practical relations with the Union, and that the sole object of the government, civil and military, in regard to those States, is to again get them into that proper practical relation. I believe it is not only possible, but in fact easier to do this without deciding, or even considering, whether these States have ever been out of the Union, than with it. Finding themselves safely at home, it would be utterly immaterial whether they had ever been abroad. Let us all join in doing the acts necessary to restoring the proper practical relations between these States and the Union, and each forever after innocently indulge his own opinion whether, in doing the acts, he brought the States from without the Union, or only gave them proper assistance, they never having been out of it."

For the next three days Lincoln discussed his plans with the Cabinet. On the night of April 14, the president attended the theater where he was shot by the actor John Wilkes Booth, a misguided and possibly deranged southern sympathizer. With his death the next day, the radicals gained a second victory for their policy of subjugation and vengeance.

5. Andrew Johnson's Plan of Reconstruction

Abraham Lincoln's successor had had a long and varied career before his accidental accession to the presidency. Born of poor parents in Raleigh, North Carolina, in 1808, Andrew Johnson had grown up in the South. But the South which Johnson knew was not the land of legend and the home of the cotton aristocrats. Heir to no acres where the fleecy staple could be grown, possessor of no slaves at the outset, Johnson had had to make his own living and had been bound out to a tailor. Escaping from his apprenticeship, he had made his way to Greeneville in east Tennessee, where he had opened a tailor shop. For some years Johnson had combined an interest in local politics with his tailoring business. Educating himself, he had become locally the champion of the artisan, the laborer, and the small farmer. With such a creed, he had risen successively through the offices of alderman and mayor of Greeneville, representative in the state legislature, state senator, congressman, governor, and United States Senator.

In national politics Johnson made himself conspicuous by his opposition to his fellow Southerners. Alone of the southern senators he was the representative of the small farming yeoman of his section. He was an adherent of the doctrines of states' rights after the best principles of Calhoun, but he rejected the leadership of Jefferson Davis. As a strict constructionist, Johnson could find no constitutional mandate for secession. Moreover, he believed that secession was a conspiracy of the cotton capitalists and the aristocrats. In Congress he had sponsored the Homestead Bill, anathema to the slaveholders' representatives, and had brought the wrath of his colleagues upon his head. Neither for himself nor for east Tennessee could Johnson perceive an attractive future in a Confederacy ruled by the squires for the benefit of cotton. When Tennessee seceded, Johnson retained his seat in the United States Senate. For the remainder of his term Johnson allied himself with the radicals and joined in their cries for vengeance against the South. He was a member of the radical Committee on the Conduct of the War, and was not least among them in urging harsh treatment for rebels. In 1864, Lincoln chose Johnson—a Southerner, a Democrat, and a radical—as a running mate in the "Union" party.

In personal qualities, Johnson was a man of rough intellectual vigor and of great physical and moral courage. His mind was strong if not great, drawing its strength from his deep knowledge of and devotion to the Constitution. In private, the president was a good-mannered, well-dressed gentleman; in public manner he was brusque. He had learned political oratory upon the Tennessee hustings, where the accepted technique was to batter one's opponents by personal attacks. Johnson's political experience had taught him to fight with verbal bludgeons. In the situation before him, Lincoln's witty rapier would have stood him in better stead. To great moral courage, a devotion to the Constitution, and a vigorous habit of speech the president added both obstinacy and indecision. The strange combination was to prove disastrous both for himself and for the South.

When Johnson was nominated for the vice-presidency, the radicals were delighted, and many of them were pleased when he became president. As soon as he was sworn in, they urged upon him their own policy of reconstruction. A radical caucus discussed Johnson's cabinet on the afternoon after Lincoln's death. Wade's Committee on the Conduct of the War called to assure the new president of their faith in him. "By the gods," exclaimed Wade, "there will be no trouble now in running the government."

Johnson had breathed many threats against the rebels during the war. Treason, he had proclaimed, should be made odious and traitors "punished and impoverished." Radicals urged that Lee be punished, and the Confederate commander appealed to Grant. The Union general came to the aid of his opponent, advised Lee to apply for pardon, and personally presented his case to the president. When Johnson asked when the southern generals could be punished, Grant replied that their paroles exempted them from civil processes. Lee was pardoned.

Yet Johnson, although yielding in this to moderation, gave way before rising radical sentiment and rejected the convention which Sherman made with Johnston. The news of this arrangement came while the body of Lincoln lay in state in the Capitol and before his murderer had been captured. In the excited state of northern feeling, Sherman's mild terms would have been unacceptable in the North. The Sherman-Johnston Convention had provided that the southern state legislatures should reassemble, and promised that they would be recognized by the president. Federal courts were to be re-established and soldiers and citizens were to be unmolested. In every respect this program was in accordance with Lincoln's program, but Lincoln's death had stirred up such bitterness in the North that Sherman's act seemed treasonable. Radicals capitalized upon Lincoln's murder, and in the Cabinet Secretary Stanton took the lead in urging the repudiation of the convention. Grant hurried to North Carolina to change the terms of the surrender, and northern newspapers denounced Sherman. Meanwhile, Johnson breathed vengeance, declaring that "traitors must take a back seat in the work of reconstruction."

But while Johnson was sympathetic with the radicals in their desire for the prosecution of the leading Southerners, he was actuated by different motives. The radicals' support came from industrial and financial centers, and the politicians were seeking to control the national government in behalf of the national banks, the protective tariff, and the railroads. To obtain this control, Negro suffrage was a necessity. To Johnson, on the other hand, the interests of industry, internal improvements, and finance made little appeal. He was concerned with the small farmers, the yeomen, and the poor whites of the South. To him, the downfall of the Confederacy offered opportunity to his own kind to control the South. Politically, Johnson would organize a party on the basis of the poorer whites rather than the Negro. It was upon the issue of Negro suffrage that Johnson split with the radicals.

As for Negro suffrage, Johnson had no objection to giving the ballot to the blacks, but he would have the states rather than the national government confer the suffrage. As a believer in states' rights, Johnson contended that the states had control over the suffrage. Johnson hoped that states would confer the vote upon Negroes who possessed sufficient property and intelligence to co-operate with the suppressed white classes of the South.

The first announcement of Johnson's program came in a Proclamation of Amnesty on May 29. In the preceding weeks Johnson had consulted the Cabinet and had formulated his proclamation only after having considered Lincoln's plans. Lincoln's proclamation was superseded by this plan. The major difference between the amnesty provisions of Lincoln's and Johnson's proclamations was the exclusion of holders of $20,000 worth of property from amnesty. This was a clear indication that Johnson expected to reconstruct the South through the poor whites and the yeoman farmers.

At the same time that his Amnesty Proclamation was announced, Johnson issued a proclamation for the reconstruction of North Carolina. For some weeks the president had been consulting the Unionist leaders of the state, and his program was based on their advice. Citing the constitutional requirement that each state have a republican form of government, and asserting that he was acting under his powers as commander-in-chief of the army, Johnson appointed W. W. Holden to be military governor of North Carolina. Holden had been the anti-Davis leader of the small farmers in the Confederacy. The provisional governor was instructed to administer an oath of allegiance and to call a convention, chosen by the loyal citizens of the state, which should make the necessary changes in the state constitution and prepare it to resume its normal relations with the other states of the Union. The state convention might set the requirements for the suffrage and for office-holding.

This plan, involving the calling of a state convention which might be expected to amend the constitution by repudiating the Confederate debt and granting limited Negro suffrage, was closer to the Wade-Davis Bill than to Lincoln's final plans. The radicals, however, had moved beyond the Wade-Davis Bill to the point where their leaders were insisting upon Negro suffrage. There was an immediate chorus of disapproval of Johnson's policy. "*Our* safety and the peace of the Country" declared one of them, "requires us to disenfranchise the Rebels and enfranchise the colored citizens in the revolted States." As Johnson issued more proclamations for the other southern states and appointed more governors, the radical opposition grew. Soon it was charging that the Johnson governors were appointing secessionists to office and discriminating against Union men. The radicals began to organize to control the coming Congress and to gather information to support their restrictive policy.

6. THE JOHNSONIAN GOVERNMENTS IN THE SOUTH

As the radicals began to criticize his acts, Johnson sent agents into the South to report on the sentiments of the southern people. Most notable of these agents were Carl Schurz and General Grant. Expected to make a report in favor of Johnson's policy, Schurz accepted money for articles from a radical newspaper, allowed Sumner's friends to pay the premium on his insurance policies, and returned from the South with a report that disloyal sentiments were prevalent and that Negro suffrage was necessary to protect the freedman. General Grant's report was of exactly opposite tenor and fully endorsed Johnson's lenient policy.

Meanwhile the provisional governors in the South assembled state conventions. Mississippi held the first convention. Governor William L. Sharkey had been a Whig and a leading Unionist in the 'fifties. In the elections, Unionists, many of them former Whigs, won seats in the convention. Members of the convention warned their colleagues that unless it followed Johnson's guidance, the state would be treated as a conquered province. The members annulled the ordinance of secession and declared that slavery should be abolished, but ignored Johnson's advice to grant a limited Negro suffrage. In Alabama a division developed between the Unionists of the northern section and representatives of the Black Belt. The old secessionist element delayed action on the debt and on abolishing slavery, although the north Alabamians won a final victory on these issues. The abandonment of the Negro in apportioning representation gave increased power to the small farmers of the northern section.

In South Carolina, Governor Benjamin F. Perry advised the convention that the "radical Republican party North are looking . . . to Negro suffrage. . . . They forget that this is a white man's government, and intended for white men only. . . . To extend universal suffrage to the freedmen in their present ignorant and degraded condition would be little less than folly and madness. It would be giving to the man of wealth and large landed possessions in the State a most undue influence in all elections on account of his power to vote at will his employees." The convention failed to grant Negro suffrage, but by ending the "three-fifths" representation of the Negroes, it turned control of the state over to the upcountry. Greater democracy in state administration came, with the popular election of the governor and presidential electors taking the place of elections by the legislature. In North Carolina a memorial from a Negro convention was ignored and the Confederate war debt was repudiated with bad grace.

In all of these states the Unionist element was in control and gave indications that a political party might be founded upon the former submerged white classes of the South. Yet the fact that these elements showed no inclination to grant Negro suffrage played into the hands of the northern radicals. South Carolina failed to repudiate her war debt, Mississippi organized a state militia, and none of the states gave evidence of humility. The radicals, who could look upon the rise of the southern yeomen and small farmers only with disapproval, redoubled their efforts to arouse northern sentiment against the South.

In the elections that followed, the Unionists won most of the offices and controlled the state legislatures. When the legislatures met in November, they ratified the Thirteenth Amendment abolishing slavery and showed their Unionism by electing senators who represented the old antisecessionist elements. Mississippi elected Governor Sharkey and the northern-born James L. Alcorn; Governor Perry and John L. Manning were selected by South Carolina; North Carolina elected Unionists. In Georgia, Alexander H. Stephens, just released from Fort Warren, advised the legislature to accept the situation with patience and make an honest effort at readjustment. Stephens and Hershel V. Johnson, the Douglas vice-presidential candidate in 1860, were elected to the Senate. By the time that Congress met in December, the southern states had governments, regularly elected and under the control of groups that had opposed secession and had fought against the government of the Confederacy. But the radicals were not interested in reconstructing the South for Andrew Johnson's small farmers, laborers, artisans, and poor whites.

Radical Reconstruction

1. Congress and Johnson

BY the time Congress met in December, 1865, the leading radicals agreed that Negro suffrage should be forced upon the South and that the control of reconstruction should be taken out of the president's hands. The majority of the northern people and of the Republican party were not in favor of the radical position, but quick action, close organization, and vituperative audacity brought a radical victory. A few days before Congress assembled, Thaddeus Stevens gathered his fellow radicals in a caucus, where they prepared to control the Republican party. In the Republican caucus the radicals committed the party to the policy of not admitting congressmen from the South. When the House of Representatives organized, the clerk, acting on instructions from the radicals, omitted the names of southern congressmen. Even Horace Maynard and other Tennesseans who had sat in the previous Congress were excluded. To the Democratic question, "If Tennessee is not in the Union . . . by what right does the President of the United States usurp a place in the White House?" the radicals gave no answer but proceeded to ignore the Johnson governments and to treat the southern states as outside the Union. A Joint Committee of Fifteen undertook to determine the conditions upon which the southern states would be entitled to representation in Congress.

Shortly after Congress reassembled, Secretary Seward announced that the Thirteenth Amendment, abolishing slavery, had been ratified by a sufficient number of states. The amendment had been adopted by the votes of the southern states, but the radicals ignored the inconsistency of accepting the highest sovereign act of a state at the same time that its representatives were excluded from Congress. In fact, since it made the three-fifths provision of the Constitution inoperative, the amendment had the strange effect of entitling the southern states to increased representation after the next census. This constituted an additional reason for imposing restrictions on the South.

As the successor of the Committee on the Conduct of the War, the Joint Committee took over the earlier committee's functions of disseminating propaganda against the South and fomenting dissension against the president. In both of these tasks the radical committee found conditions favorable to their purposes. Democrats, whose loyalty had been suspected during the war, endorsed Johnson's policy and embarrassed the moderate Republicans, who sought to defend the president against radical attacks. At the same time, the southern legislatures began to pass "Black Codes" which soon became valuable ammunition for the radical guns. These codes were efforts by the Southerners to solve the problems created by the South's disorganized labor force. Unfortunately, they were ineptly drawn and revealed the anti-Negro sentiments of the southern nonslaveholders as well as an almost criminal ignorance of northern psychology.

The southern codes were designed to regulate the activities of the Negroes upon a basis somewhere between slavery and complete equality with the whites. The old laws which had regulated the slaves were not applicable to the new situation; slavery had solved problems which now called for legislation. The family life of the Negro, his morals, and his personal conduct had been cared for by the system of slavery. They now needed legal definition. The Negroes' status in the courts had to be fixed, and care had to be provided for the old, the infirm, and the orphans.

By the codes that the legislatures drafted, Negroes were defined as those possessing one eighth or more of Negro blood, intermarriage of the races was prohibited, slave marriages were made valid, and the children of slaves were legitimatized. A Negro was permitted to testify in court where one party to a suit was of his own race. Some states provided schools for Negroes, but specified separation of the races in education. Mississippi invented the "Jim Crow" car. In several states, Negroes were required to obtain a license to carry arms, to preach, or to engage in trade. In Mississippi, a Negro might own land only in towns; in other states, only in the country. Apprenticeship laws were called into force to regulate Negroes, and Negro orphans were bound over to their former masters. All of the states passed strict vagrancy laws and provided that vagrants were to be hired out to the highest bidder to work out their fines, the former master being given a preference. South Carolina's laws instructed Negroes to rise early in the morning and retire at a reasonable hour.

As interpreted by the radicals, such laws proved that the Southerners were not accepting the results of the war but were attempting to re-establish the fact if not the name of slavery. If the Negro were to be saved from re-enslavement, the Federal Government would have to protect him against his former master. In order to accord the necessary protection, the radicals prepared to extend the powers and duration of the war-created Freedmen's Bureau.

The Bureau of Refugees, Freedmen, and Abandoned Lands had been an outgrowth of the experience of the Union armies in handling Negroes. Following upon Butler's declaration that Negroes were contraband, army officials put Negroes to work not only on fortifications but also on available abandoned lands. Benevolent societies whose agents followed the armies came under army regulations. The Treasury Department agents also made extensive use of the Negroes. In March, 1863, these agencies were consolidated in a bureau in the War Department. The Freedmen's Bureau was to control all matters relating to Negroes and refugees for one year after the war ended.

Since Johnson had declared the war at an end, the bureau would expire unless it were given a new lease on life. Senator Lyman Trumbull, of Illinois, introduced a bill to give the bureau power to act as a court to secure equal justice to the freedman. An agent of the bureau in each county would protect Negroes from injustice. The bureau would issue medical supplies and co-operate with private charitable agencies. Confiscated property might be allotted or sold to the freedmen. The Freedmen's Bureau would thus act as a substitute for the destroyed plantation system and make the Negroes "wards of the nation." Through it, they would be prepared to assume the obligations of citizenship under the auspices of the Republican party.

The bill passed Congress the first week in February, 1866. On February 19, Johnson returned it with a veto which pointed out that the bill made civil courts subordinate to military ones, and that no conditions justified this extension of military power. The bureau would permanently pauperize the freedmen by causing them to expect much from the government. The measure would antagonize the whites and keep alive war hatred between the sections.

Three days after the veto, Johnson's supporters assembled in a Washington theater to endorse the president's act. Carrying their resolutions, they went to the White House, where Johnson regaled his appreciative audience with denunciation of the radicals. Always a fiery speaker given to personal attacks, Johnson's oratorical techniques were those of recrimination and invective. Intoxicated by the cheers of the crowd, Johnson followed a temperate speech with intemperate remarks about his radical opponents, calling the names of Sumner, Stevens, and Wendell Phillips. Such expressions were unfortunate, for the next day radical newspapers charged that the president was drunk both when he made the speech and when he vetoed the Freedmen's Bureau Bill.

The radicals were unable to override the presidential veto in the Senate, but they succeeded in ousting one of New Jersey's senators and seating a radical in his place. This done, they waited for Johnson's veto of the Civil Rights Bill. This act was designed to "protect all persons of the United States in their civil rights, and to furnish the means of their vindication." The act provided that all persons born in the United States should have full rights in every state to make contracts, hold property, and enjoy such full protection of the laws "as is enjoyed by white citizens." Any person discriminating against Negroes under state laws should be tried in federal courts, whose decisions were to be enforced by the military. The law would give the two races in the South exactly equal status.

Johnson's friends urged him to accept this law, but the president refused to yield his constitutional scruples to the arguments of expediency. His veto message pointed out that the bill would give citizenship to Chinese on the Pacific Coast, that it would deny legislators their constitutional immunity from punishment, that it would make Negroes citizens of the United States without giving them state citizenship, and that the machinery for its execution was both inadequate and unconstitutional. The message made no impression on the radicals, who immediately put their strength to the test. For the first time in American history, Congress overrode an important veto.

Having proved their strength, the radicals announced their program in a report from the Joint Committee on Reconstruction. Stating that it had listened to testimony from many sources, the committee declared that the South deliberately purposed to oppress white Unionists and freedmen. The southern states had deliberately seceded from the Union and had waged war upon the United States until vanquished by arms. "These rebellious enemies were conquered by the people of the United States, acting through all the co-ordinate branches of the government, and not by the executive alone. The powers of conqueror are not so vested in the president that he can fix and regulate the terms and settlement and confer congressional representation on conquered rebels and traitors. . . . The question before Congress is, then, whether conquered enemies have the right, and shall be permitted at their own pleasure and on their own terms, to participate in making laws for their conquerors; whether conquered rebels may change their theater of operation from the battlefield, where they were defeated and overthrown, to the halls of Congress, and, through their representatives, seize upon the government which they fought to destroy. . . ." The radical committee proposed a Fourteenth Amendment to the Constitution which must be adopted by the southern states before representatives were admitted to Congress.

The Fourteenth Amendment began with a definition of citizenship. In contrast to the dictum of the Dred Scott decision, that federal citizenship depended upon state citizenship, the amendment declared that "all persons born or naturalized in the United States, and subject to the jurisdiction thereof, are citizens of the United States and of the State in which they reside." This wording had been especially designed by the committee, it was claimed later, to protect both Negroes and such "artificial persons" as corporations. The amendment provided that no state should abridge the privileges and immunities of United States citizens or deprive any person of life, liberty, or property without due process of law. States that deprived Negroes of the suffrage should suffer a proportionate reduction in their congressional representation. Ex-Confederates who had once taken an oath to support the Constitution should not hold federal office. Finally, the amendment asserted the validity of the national debt and repudiated that of the South. Thus the radicals prepared to accomplish their two purposes of giving political rights to the Negroes and economic security to big business. The amendment passed Congress on June 13 and went to the states.

With the passage, a month later, of a new Freedman's Bureau Bill, the radical program was complete. Before Congress adjourned, Tennessee's representatives were admitted to their seats. Under pressure from Governor Brownlow, the Tennessee legislature had ratified the Fourteenth Amendment. The Governor had invited carpetbaggers to Tennessee, had induced his legislature to disfranchise ex-Confederates, had resumed his ancient enmity to Andrew Johnson, and in other ways had shown his complete sympathy with the radical program. "Give my respects to the dead dog in the White House," telegraphed Brownlow to Congress as he sent tidings of the ratification. As a reward for such vituperative cooperation and as an example to the rest of the South, Congress readmitted Johnson's home state.

2. The Elections of 1866

With Johnson's state governments in operation and the radical program fully formulated, the issues were clear for the impending congressional elections. In the North, the radicals controlled the Republican machine. Johnson attempted to unite a party out of the heterogeneous elements of opposition. Copperheads, war Democrats, moderate Republicans, and the southern leaders opposed the radical program but could only be united with difficulty. Whatever hopes Johnson may have had of forming a people's party to meet the radical class party disappeared before political necessity. The Johnsonians were forced to try to unite discordant elements of the old parties.

The first effort to form a party to support the president was a call for a "National Union Convention" to meet in Philadelphia. With difficulty, Ohio's Clement L. Vallandigham was prevented from attending the convention, but Southerners came in numbers. The meeting opened with General Darius N. Couch of Massachusetts and Governor James L. Orr of South Carolina marching down the aisle together. Radical reporters immediately dubbed the meeting the "Arm in Arm Convention," while one editor was reminded of the entrance of the animals into the ark, "two by two, of clean beasts, and of beasts that are not clean, and of fowls, and of everything that creepeth upon the earth." The convention adopted resolutions declaring slavery at an end and asserting that southern whites could be trusted.

The radicals met this move by calling a meeting of the "Loyal Unionists of the South" at Philadelphia. "Parson" Brownlow led the southern delegates, whose number included many carpetbaggers and scalawags. The Convention endorsed the radicals and condemned Johnson for selecting secessionists rather than loyalists for southern offices. Two other conventions were held: the Johnsonians assembled a "Soldiers' and Sailors' Convention," in which both Confederates and Federals appeared, and the radicals countered with a similar meeting of Union veterans presided over by the violent Benjamin F. Butler.

Events played into the hands of the radicals. In April, a clash between Negro troops and police brought a race riot in Memphis in which forty-six Negroes were killed and four Negro churches and twelve schoolhouses burned. In July, a more serious riot in New Orleans resulted in the death of two hundred blacks and a dozen policemen. These incidents lent color to the radical claims that Negroes should be protected by the federal government. In September, the radical charges against Johnson received apparent confirmation when the president, in a "swing around the circle," visited various northern cities. Radicals heckled Johnson in his public appearances and tempted him again to vituperation. Their newspapers represented the president as drunk and incompetent to rule.

Against Johnson were an organized party, a large portion of the press, the industrial interests, and most of the churches of the North. The president himself had no party, and in many regions his supporters were forced to choose between radicals and Democrats with bad war records. The result was an overwhelming defeat for Johnson. The next Congress would contain 42 Republicans and 11 Democrats in the Senate and 143 Republicans and 49 Democrats in the House. The radicals had a two-thirds majority with which to override any presidential veto.

3. MILITARY GOVERNMENT FOR THE SOUTH

The radicals interpreted the elections of 1866 as a mandate to reconstruct the South after the congressional plan. "I was a conservative in the last session of this Congress," announced the sarcastic Stevens in high glee as Congress reassembled in December, 1866, "but I mean to be a radical henceforth." Filled with the same spirit, the other members prepared to force Negro suffrage on the southern states. Within an hour after the Senate reassembled, Sumner introduced a bill giving votes to Negroes in the District of Columbia. In a municipal election, the people of the District had just defeated this proposal by 7,137 to 36, but Sumner ignored their action and explained to the Senate, "as you once needed the muskets of the colored men, so you now need their votes." The bill passed, received Johnson's veto, and was immediately repassed over the veto. Congress also extended the suffrage to Negroes in the territories.

Negro suffrage was necessary to accomplish the full radical program. During the months since Congress adjourned, all of the southern states had rejected the Fourteenth Amendment. The states had acted upon Johnson's advice and had been unwilling to disfranchise the ex-Confederates. The best showing for the amendment was in North Carolina, where it received 10 of the 103 votes in the lower house of the legislature.

Since the states had refused to accept the amendment, Congress prepared to organize the southern governments. At the same time it determined to deprive the president of power to check the radical course. On March 2, 1867, in the last minutes of the session, it enacted three measures to accomplish these ends.

The first of the acts provided for military reconstruction of the South. Totally ignoring the existing governments, the act placed the ten states not represented in Congress in five military districts. Virginia constituted the first district; the Carolinas, the second; Georgia, Florida, and Alabama, the third; Mississippi and Arkansas, the fourth; and Louisiana and Texas, the fifth. Commanding each district was a brigadier or higher general, who had complete power over all civil officials. Upon him rested the responsibility for preparing the states under his command for readmission to the Union. In this process the military governor should register all citizens, white and black. Then he should order elections for a convention to adopt a new state constitution which must provide for Negro suffrage. This constitution would have to receive the approval of a majority of those registered and the further approval of Congress. Then, when a legislature, elected under the new constitution, should have ratified the Fourteenth Amendment, representatives and senators might be given seats if they could take the "ironclad oath."

The other two measures were specifically designed to limit Johnson's power for mischief. The first amended the Army Appropriation Act to provide that all orders from Johnson should pass through the hands of the general of the army. Some time before, the radicals had created the rank of general, to which Grant had been appointed. This move had been taken to prevent Johnson from using the army to support a *coup d'état.* Rumors had declared that the president planned to assemble his supporters and the southern representatives and recognize this body as the lawful Congress. With Grant indebted to the radicals and secretly advising them, he could prevent Johnson from ousting the radical Congress.

A second restriction on the president was the Tenure of Office Act. Johnson had attempted to dismiss radical officeholders, and had avoided the necessity for obtaining senatorial consent to his own appointees by making recess appointments. In order to protect radicals against dismissal, the Tenure of Office Act provided that the Senate must consent to the removal of any officer and that the president must report removals within twenty days of the convening of the Senate. Cabinet officers were to hold office during the term of the president who appointed them and for one month longer. This provision was inserted for the especial protection of Secretary Stanton, who acted as the radicals' spy in Johnson's Cabinet.

With these acts, the Thirty-Ninth Congress ended, but the radicals' fear that Johnson would use a recess to defeat their program caused them to pass a law assembling the fortieth Congress. A few minutes after the old Congress adjourned the new Congress convened with radicals taking the places of a number of Democrats and moderate Republicans. Conspicuous among the new members were Benjamin F. Butler, who came to the House from Massachusetts, and Senators Simon Cameron, Roscoe Conkling, and O. P. Morton, who added to the radical majority in the upper chamber. The session lasted until March 30, devoting its time to discussing a supplementary reconstruction act dealing with the manner of registering loyal voters and of holding elections in the South.

The administration of the reconstruction laws devolved upon President Johnson. Advised by his attorney-general that the acts were constitutional, Johnson appointed generals to command the five military districts. Stanton and Grant advised the president, and the generals selected were in sympathy with the acts they were to administer. Generals Schofield, Sickles, Pope, Ord, and Sheridan were chosen for the respective districts. Upon assuming their duties, the commanders found that the South was in good order. After the campaigns of 1866, northern newspapers had continued to inflame the popular mind with "southern outrages," but the radical leaders were well aware that the South was comparatively peaceful. The Civil Rights Act was in force, the Black Codes were inoperative, and the Freedmen's Bureau was caring for the Negroes. Military government was accordingly established with little friction.

The southern states, however, made efforts to block the establishment of military rule. Mississippi's governor sued for an injunction to prevent Johnson from executing the laws, and the governor of Georgia sought to enjoin Secretary Stanton. Johnson's attorney-general appeared before the Supreme Court to argue that the executive could not be sued; and the court, to avoid becoming involved in a political quarrel, upheld his contention.

The peaceful condition that the generals found in the South did not last long. Eight days after he assumed command over the Fifth Military District, General Sheridan removed the mayor and the attorney-general of New Orleans for their parts in the "massacre" of the preceding summer. Soon after, he removed the Board of Levee Commissioners and the governor of Louisiana. In Alabama, General Pope removed the mayor of Mobile, and in Virginia General Schofield excluded so many Confederates from the registration lists that even General Grant was moved to admonition. Before military rule was over, the generals had removed the governors of Georgia, Louisiana, Virginia, Mississippi, and Texas and thousands of local officials suspected of working against the reconstruction acts. In their places, the generals appointed "loyal" men, carpetbaggers from the north, and army officers. In the towns, they reorganized the police forces and soldiers patrolled the streets. Military officials supervised the courts, suspended laws, annulled court decrees, released prisoners, and instructed court officers how to select juries. The military authorities made law through army orders, announced stay laws, abolished the color line, levied and collected taxes, and made appropriations which the state treasurers were obliged to pay. They suppressed newspapers, licensed public meetings, dissolved the militia, and forbade parades.

4. Restoration of the Southern States

The first task before the major-generals in the South was the registration of the voting populace. They appointed registrars from the loyal or "radical" groups in each political subdivision. During the day, the registrars enrolled the Negroes on the poll books and at night they converted the new voters to Republicanism. The Union League, working hand in hand with the Freedmen's Bureau, aided in persuading the Negroes to cast Republican votes. Parallel with this registration of the blacks went the registrars' efforts to exclude Confederates from the voting lists. They scrutinized the war record of each white applicant, and rigidly applied the "iron-clad oath." By such methods they enrolled 703,000 Negroes and 627,000 whites.

In every state there was a radical majority of Negroes, scalawags, and carpetbaggers. The ex-Confederates and others who could not co-operate with the radicals formed "Conservative" parties but made little effort to contest the elections for the conventions. As a result, the well-organized radicals controlled all the conventions. Louisiana and South Carolina had Negro majorities.

The constitutions that these "black and tan" conventions adopted were adaptations of those of the northern states. Each new constitution proscribed Confederates. Many of the constitutions were beyond the needs of agricultural communities and opened broad avenues for later graft and corruption. In addition to drafting constitutions, the conventions also issued ordinances legalizing Negro marriages, forbidding segregation of the races in schools, and reorganizing the militia. Moreover, the conventions set a model of extravagance for later legislatures. The Florida convention issued $50,000 in scrip, the Mississippi convention cost over $250,000, and everywhere the members received exorbitant mileage allowances.

The conservatives who had been lethargic during the elections for the convention hastened to organize in hope of defeating these radical and proscriptive constitutions. In Georgia, where Joseph E. Brown had led the convention, the constitution was less obnoxious than in other states, and the conservatives accepted it. In Alabama, the whites conceived the idea of staying away from the polls and preventing a majority of the registered voters from approving the document. Congress, however, amended the Reconstruction Act and accepted Alabama's ratification. Arkansas also failed to muster a favorable majority of the registered voters, but its action came after the amendment. Louisiana and South Carolina were so overwhelmed by Negroes that the white conservatives made but feeble efforts, while in North Carolina and Florida the radicals had safe majorities. In Mississippi, the conservatives rallied sufficient strength to defeat the constitution. In Texas, the convention neglected to provide for an election, while in Virginia the military commander so thoroughly disapproved of the constitution that he refused to pay the expenses of an election.

At the same time that the voters accepted the new constitutions, they voted for state officers. Only in Georgia did the conservatives gain a foothold. The radicals, black and white, obtained seats in the legislatures and took over the local offices. Carpetbaggers received ten of the fourteen senate seats and furnished twenty of the South's thirty-five representatives. Of the seven newly elected governors, four were carpetbaggers. The lieutenant-governor of Louisiana, the secretary of state of South Carolina, and many of the state legislators were Negroes. By early June, most of the new governments were installed and the legislatures ratified the Fourteenth Amendment.

In Congress, the radicals smiled benign approval upon the fulfillment of their program. As a presidential election was approaching, the votes of the South were needed for the success of the Republican ticket. Late in June, 1868, the seven states that had ratified their constitutions were restored. Senators and representatives took their seats in the congressional chambers and the major-generals gave up their places to the radical governors. Only Virginia, Mississippi, and Texas were still out of the Union.

5. Impeachment of President Johnson

While the processes of reconstruction under radical auspices were under way in the South, the final scene in the dramatic struggle between president and Congress was enacted in Washington. From the beginning of the conflict, the radicals had talked of impeaching Johnson, and the judiciary committee of the House had worked all through the summer of 1867 seeking evidence of presidential misdeeds. The search was fruitless until Johnson played into radical hands by dismissing Secretary Stanton.

The secretary of war had long been a thorn in Johnson's side. As early as 1866 the president realized that Stanton was in full sympathy with the congressional radicals. The "Arm in Arm Convention" had privately recommended Stanton's dismissal. But Johnson's worst fault was indecision: his aggressiveness was more vocal than actual, and he delayed until August, 1867. Then, after the disloyal secretary had inflicted all possible damage on the administration, Johnson suspended him from office. In his place Johnson appointed General Grant to act as *ad interim* secretary of war. The change was of no benefit to Johnson, as Grant had long since gone over to the radicals.

When Congress met, the president reported his action to the Senate. Desirous of protecting their ally and of embarrassing Johnson, the Senate refused to concur in the dismissal. Immediately Grant surrendered the office to Stanton and reported his action to the president. A bitter quarrel between general and president ensued. Johnson alleged that Grant had promised to return the office to him, and the lie passed between the two high-placed antagonists. While this vituperative altercation was in progress, Johnson summarily dismissed Stanton and ordered General Lorenzo Thomas to take over the office. But Stanton refused to vacate his rooms, asserting his rights under the Tenure of Office Act.

Without hesitation, the House of Representatives voted to impeach the president for violating the Tenure of Office Act. Eleven articles of impeachment were drawn up and the case was presented to the Senate. But political considerations were uppermost in the minds of the senators, and they made little pretense of sitting on a court. The president's counsel were given little time to prepare their case, and the rules of evidence were adjusted to permit a vast amount of testimony that would not have been tolerated in a court of law.

Unfortunately for the radical cause, the partisanship displayed caused a public reaction in favor of the president. Opposition was also widespread to removing Johnson to make way for Senator Wade, next in the line of succession. Yet the radicals struggled valiantly to force a vote of guilty. Pressure was exerted on wavering senators. There were twelve Democrats in the Senate. Should they be joined by seven moderate Republicans, impeachment would fail. When the test came, exactly seven moderates voted with the Democrats, and the radicals failed—by one vote —in their effort to remove their enemy.

6. The Election of 1868

While the impeachment trial was going on, the presidential campaign of 1868 began. Before the country were the issues of financial policy and the reconstruction of the South. Republicans favored the radical reconstruction program, sound money, payment of the national debt in coin, and high tariffs. Democrats were less concerned about the national debt and were flirting with the "Ohio Idea" to pay off the war debt by an issue of greenbacks. Moreover, they endorsed the president's plans of reconstruction.

The Republican nominating convention wasted no time in naming General Grant as their candidate. The war-wrecked Democrats, however, groped blindly for both a platform and a suitable nominee. In the end, they adopted a platform favoring the "Ohio Idea" and nominated Horatio Seymour, a conservative New Yorker who repudiated the financial planks of the platform.

The outcome of the campaign was more a victory for sound finance than a popular approval of radical reconstruction. General Grant carried twenty-six states to Seymour's eight. Yet Grant's white vote was smaller than Seymour's; and had it not been for four hundred thousand Negroes, the Republican candidate would have been defeated. Thus the Negroes rewarded the party that had brought them the suffrage and saved the day for the bondholders and the industrialists.

CHAPTER 26

White Supremacy

1. THE LAGGARD STATES

THE election of 1868 fixed the radical Reconstruction policy upon the South at the same time that it assured the predominance of the Republican financial program for the nation. Under Grant, there would be no tampering with the currency and no legislation adverse to bankers, industrialists, and proponents of a high tariff. The South would not interfere with the radical control of the Federal Government, while, in the words of "Parson" Brownlow, "The election of Grant and Colfax means peace; it means that carpetbaggers are not to be molested . . . that capital, coming to us from abroad, whether of brains or hands, or money, is not to be spurned, proscribed, persecuted because it comes from north of a given line." Throughout the North there was a widespread expectation that the South would now become a suitable field for economic exploitation. Projects for building railroads, for developing mines, and for locating mills multiplied with the assurance that governmental policy would not be altered.

In order to hasten the completion of this field for northern exploitation, Grant proposed to Congress that the state constitutions be submitted to the electorate in Virginia, Mississippi, and Texas without the obnoxious clauses disfranchising Confederates. Since the elections were over, the necessity for these clauses was less pressing. Moreover, there was a growing impatience in the North to complete the work of Reconstruction. But the radicals determined to impose an additional penance upon these laggard states. Whereas they provided that the disfranchising clauses might be voted upon separately, they demanded that these states should approve the Fifteenth Amendment. This amendment would—its sponsors hoped—guarantee all citizens the right to vote and would insure the continuance of Negro suffrage and Republican ascendancy.

As soon as Grant made his recommendation to Congress, Virginia prepared for elections. Two parties emerged in the state: the one representing the radical elements nominated H. H. Wells, who had been acting as civil governor, and the other, adopting the name "Conservative," nominated a native Unionist, Gilbert C. Walker, for governor. Both parties set up claims to be Republican, and both appealed to the Washington leaders for recognition. As the Democrats were completely disorganized—although they supported Walker—and as the success of either faction would result in the completion of the Republican program, neither the president nor the party leaders interfered in the campaign. In the North it was generally believed that, as Horace Greeley put it, "Virginia, having had enough of Civil War and devastation, is about to subordinate political strife to industrial progress and material prosperity and thus advance to a future of power and wealth undreamed of in her past." In July, the elections gave the Conservative, Walker, a 20,000 majority. The Negro voters divided between the factions. In October, the Conservative legislature ratified the Fourteenth and Fifteenth Amendments, and on January 27, 1870, her senators and representatives having been seated, Virginia passed out of military rule.

Despite the success of the Republican program, the radical leaders took alarm at the Conservative victory in Virginia. Grant's secretary of the treasury, George S. Boutwell, a Massachusetts radical, advised against accepting the Virginia results and set himself to prevent a recurrence of such a misfortune in Mississippi. Here the people, objecting to the disfranchising clauses, had succeeded in defeating the radical constitution and had remained under military rule. Grant set November 30 as the date for the Mississippi election. Encouraged by the Virginia result, the Conservatives of Mississippi hit upon a visionary scheme to obtain President Grant's support by nominating his brother-in-law, Lewis Dent, for governor. The radicals nominated J. L. Alcorn, a native of Illinois who had been a Mississippi secessionist in 1861. Upon Boutwell's urging, Grant publicly repudiated Dent and threw his support to Alcorn. The election brought the adoption of the constitution and the defeat of Dent. The legislature approved the Fourteenth and Fifteenth Amendments, and in February Mississippi's congressmen were admitted. The two senators who came to represent the state were General Adelbert Ames of Massachusetts, who had been the military governor, and Hiram Revels, a Negro from Indiana.

In Texas the radicals nominated E. J. Davis while the Conservatives ran Andrew J. Hamilton. As in the other states, both factions asked for administration support, but the radical leaders in Washington prevailed upon Grant to remove federal office-holders who supported Hamilton. The radical legislature ratified the amendments, and the state was readmitted to the Union.

The radicals' fear of losing out in these last states was partly based upon their experience in Georgia. The 1867 election in Georgia had resulted in the choice of Rufus B. Bullock for governor and a legislature with a majority of whites. After approving the Fourteenth Amendment, this body decided that the new constitution, although it gave Negroes the suffrage, did not confer the right to hold office. Accordingly, the white members expelled their colored colleagues. When the electoral vote was counted, Benjamin F. Butler proposed that the state's vote should not be polled. The election result was announced without Georgia's ballots, and the radicals set themselves to punish the too-clever legislature. Georgia was remanded to military rule until the Negro legislators were restored and the Fifteenth Amendment ratified. On July 15, 1870, the state was held to have made sufficient amends to be restored to representation.

2. SOUTHERN SOCIETY

While the governments of the southern states were being recast on a radical model, profound changes were under way in southern society. In agriculture, in industry, and in the churches, the southern people made adjustments to new conditions.

Most far-reaching was the changed order in which the former slave found himself. The plantation system and slavery had taken care of the Negro of the Old South, but these institutions were destroyed. In their place, the black laborer found the Freedmen's Bureau and a number of philanthropic organizations designed to facilitate his assumption of the duties of citzenship. In each state the Freedmen's Bureau ended as the governments were released from military tutelage. Before it disappeared, however, it had made valiant efforts to rehabilitate the Negro.

The bureau had made an effort to encourage the Negroes to work the land. The abandoned and confiscated property held by the bureau was first parceled out among the freedmen; but, as Johnson's pardons were held to include a restoration of sequestered property, the amount of land in the bureau's hands steadily diminished. In the end, the bureau held lands which were worth nothing to their former owners and therefore could not benefit the Negroes. As its policy was doomed to failure, the bureau encouraged the Negroes to make contracts as agricultural tenants. As most planters were without money, a system of planting crops on shares grew up. The planters advanced credit at a store to carry the tenant through the year until the crop was marketed. Before the end of Reconstruction, many planters had become merchants as well as planters and were beginning to make their profits from extortionate mark-ups in the stores. Negro and poor white tenants tended constantly to fall deeper in debt to the planter-merchant.

In addition to taking care of the freedmen in agriculture, the Freedmen's Bureau made efforts to encourage Negro education. The Freedmen's Bureau Act authorized a commissioner of the bureau to lease school buildings when teachers were furnished by other organizations. The bureau expended over $1,330,680 in co-operation with the American Missionary Association and the American Freedmen's Union Association. These societies sent a number of teachers into the South. Negro normal schools were established to train teachers. Hampton Institute, Fisk University, and Howard University came into existence to furnish native leaders for the Negro race.

The whites of the South greatly resented the efforts of the bureau and of northern humanitarians. Doubtless the excessive zeal of some of the missionary teachers and bureau agents gave ample justification for the southern attitude. Such irritants came closer to the average southerner than did the corruption which characterized the state governments. The reaction of the people was to ostracize the Northerner who arrived in a southern community. The long pre-war tradition of suspecting "Yankees" was reconfirmed by the obnoxious conduct of some of the missionaries, and the better southern families excluded Northerners from their social circles. Perhaps no single factor was more effective in stirring up the resentment of the Northerners. Many of the carpetbaggers—who were mostly young men—wrote indignant letters to their northern congressmen urging more drastic legislation for the South. The southern suspicion of the Northerners remained as a permanent characteristic of a traditionally hospitable and gregarious people.

As the Negro was making progress under the guidance of his new-found friends, the white man of the South was faced with the necessity of reconstructing his whole economic and social system. Both religion and education felt changes as a result of the changed order. To the churches, the war brought devastation. During the conflict, church buildings were used by the federal armies, and at the end Secretary Stanton turned the confiscated property over to northern denominations, who placed army chaplains or Unionist ministers in the pulpits. Northern churches expected a reunion with their southern branches and also expected that the union would give control to the North. Only the Episcopal Church returned to the fold. Southern Methodists, Presbyterians, and Baptists retained their separate organizations. Northern Methodist bishops, especially Bishop Matthew Simpson, were anxious to extend their ecclesiastical jurisdiction. In east Tennessee and in Florida, the Northern Methodists managed to establish and maintain conferences among the Unionists and northern migrants, but their success was limited. The Methodist Episcopal Church, South, on the other hand, added a number of conferences from the border states.

Northern churchmen had somewhat greater success in attracting Negro communicants. Methodist bishops succeeded in separating the Negroes from the churches of their former masters. The Methodist Episcopal Church established a number of Negro congregations. The Negroes preferred, however, an organization of their own even though the Methodist General Conference permitted the ordination of Negro bishops. The African Methodist Episcopal Zion Church and the African Methodist Episcopal Church gained most of the Negro Methodists. In order to save what they could from the wreckage, the Southern Methodists sponsored the organization of the Colored Methodist Episcopal Church. Among the Baptists, separate congregations and associations were organized by the southern whites.

As was true of the churches, northern educators considered the southern school a fair field for missionary work. The alleged opposition of the southern aristocrats to free schools had been emphasized in northern war propaganda until it seemed a part of the victor's task to force public education upon the conquered section. Public schools in the South had been rudimentary before the war, and free education bore the taint of pauperism. The war had destroyed the colleges and killed or disabled the teachers. The colleges, most of them under denominational control, were opened to students by 1866-1867, and young men from the armies came in their poverty to the halls of learning. Trustees were burdened with the cares of administering institutions that had no money. General Lee's pay as president of Washington College was $1,500 a year and was often in arrears.

The Reconstruction constitutions set up elaborate school systems, and the radical legislatures made appropriations for the support of schools. Mixed schools were the exception, as neither whites nor blacks desired them. State superintendents were radicals, and the appropriations made for schools were frequently dissipated in corruption. Several states established state universities under radical auspices. Most of the school systems were too complicated for rural communities and met financial failure after the whites regained supremacy. Nevertheless, the educational systems of the South remained as the most socially desirable contribution of the radical state governments.

3. Carpetbag Government

The governments under the radical constitutions were composed largely of carpetbaggers and Negroes. The excesses of the radicals gradually alienated the native white unionists whom the Johnsonian program would have placed in control of the southern states. These men were forced to co-operate with the Democratic or the Conservative party. Carpetbag mismanagement and the radical program eventually brought a restoration of the older rulers against whom the Civil War had been fought. Carpetbaggers seized upon the more desirable political plums in the states, leaving lesser offices to the Negroes and giving little to the scalawags. In all the South, there were twelve carpetbag and eight scalawag governors, and in the congressional delegations men of northern birth outnumbered those who represented the southern loyalists. Negroes composed the majorities of several legislatures and held the balance of power in others.

The period between the adoption of the radical constitutions and the "redemption" of the states was characterized by gross corruption. In the nation, no state escaped misgovernment in this period. The municipal governments of New York, Philadelphia, Washington, and hundreds of smaller communities were controlled by plundering "rings" and dominated by "bosses" whose moral fiber was rotten. The national government itself was torn with scandals which ranged from a petty "salary grab" by congressmen to enormous plunderings of the internal revenues by a far-flung "Whiskey Ring." Both parties were involved in these public plunderings; and if most were laid at the door of the Republicans, it was largely because more of the members of that party were placed in positions where graft was possible. The situation that existed in the South was but one manifestation of a laxity in public morals which characterized the first days of the dominance of the masters of capital.

In the nation, the period was one of great interest in railroad construction and even greater interest in railroad financing. In the South, where war had brought destruction, there existed a great need for railroads. The constant urging of northern financial groups and of those who wished opportunity for investment in the South led to lavish grants to southern railroad projects. Railroad financing and legislative expenditures constituted the two main sources of corruption in the South. Many of the carpetbaggers were venal, while the Negroes who followed them were mostly ignorant and fell readily into schemes which brought them money, honors, and power. There had been nothing in slavery to prepare Negroes for the moral responsibilities of lawmakers.

The states with the smallest proportion of Negro population and legislators were the first to throw off radical rule. Virginia escaped with little disorder, while North Carolina had only a taste of the misfortunes that overtook her sister states. The first radical legislature of North Carolina had 38 Republicans and 12 Democrats in the Senate, and the Republicans outnumbered their opponents by two to one in the House. Railroads from Wilmington to the interior were badly needed, and the legislature adopted a plan of endorsing bonds for the benefit of new lines. Largely through reckless railroad financing, the debt of the state was increased from $16,000,000 to $40,000,000. The total assessed property in the state was $120,000,000, which was forced to bear a tax of over $1,000,000. The money was spent on the bribery of legislators, and few miles of railroad were constructed in the state.

In 1870, a revolt of the Conservatives succeeded in giving them control of the legislature despite the radicals' efforts to use the Negro militia to influence the election. The Democrats proceeded immediately to impeach Governor Holden for his misuse of the militia. Holden was found guilty, was replaced, and the state was "redeemed" for the Democrats.

South Carolina, with its large Negro population, had a history of corruption much longer than that of its northern neighbor. The radical Senate in 1868 numbered ten Negroes and fourteen white Republicans and seven Democrats. The House had a Negro majority. The governor, R. K. Scott, was a native of Ohio, and the speaker of the house, F. J. Moses, was a native white of notoriously low character. In 1872 Moses succeeded Scott in the governor's chair.

The radicals maintained themselves in South Carolina by use of the Negro militia. Fourteen regiments terrorized the wavering blacks and prevented whites from voting. In one electoral campaign, the militia cost the state $374,000. Frauds characterized the elections. Once in control, the radicals spent lavishly to build railroads. The state-owned stock in the Columbia and Greenville Railroad was lost through the mismanagement of the radical manager. The Blue Ridge Railroad had $2,000,000 of its scrip endorsed by the state and receivable for taxes.

Extensive graft occurred in connection with the refurnishings of the State House. Elaborate furnishings replaced—at exorbitant cost—the simple fixtures of a former day. Clocks costing $480, chandeliers costing $650, cuspidors at $8, and a mirror costing $750 were brought in. Members of the legislature whose rooms were used for committee rooms came into the possession of Brussels carpets, mirrors, and furniture. Even such things as women's lingerie and a metal casket, to say nothing of wines, groceries, and cigars, appeared as items of legislative expense.

Bribery developed into a high art in this Negro and carpetbagger government. Favors were procured from the legislature by bribery, and a congressman sold a West Point appointment. A census was taken in 1869 which cost $75,000, although a federal census costing $40,000 was taken the following year. The legislature reimbursed Speaker Moses for $1,000 which he lost in a horse race. A grandiose scheme for purchasing land for distribution to the Negroes resulted in the expenditure of almost $800,000, of which $225,000 was graft for the commission. In the end, the state came into possession of thousands of acres of worn-out and infertile land. The bonds of the state sank so low that $4 in bonds brought $1.20 on the New York market. Under the radical regime, the state debt increased from less than $6,000,000 to more than $25,000,000. The average legislative expense was $320,000 a season.

Georgia's story under the radical regime was similar to that of South Carolina. The legislature provided for an extensive railroad system and endorsed the bonds for over 30 railroads at rates of from $12,000 to $15,000 a mile. Most of the roads speedily went into bankruptcy, leaving the state debt increased by over $6,000,000. The state tax rate increased to two fifths of one per cent and the state debt to over $11,000,000. The manager of the state-owned railroad explained that he was able to "save" $30,000 out of his annual salary of $2,000 or $3,000 "by the exercise of the most rigid economy." The road, which had brought $25,000 a month into the treasury, was soon running at a deficit. Schools, too, were subject to excessive graft, and in 1870 the legislature took the school fund of $268,000 and the teachers were not paid.

Alabama was also a fertile field for railroad promoters. The legislature authorized the governor to endorse first mortgage bonds at the rate of $16,000 a mile upon the completion of each five-mile section. The governor made no effort to check up on the completion of the roads and issued bonds upon the certification of railroad officials who swore that sections were completed which had not been built.

Florida, too, had a railroad problem. The state enacted an internal improvement law administered by a board that was subservient to the railroad speculators. The legislature was largely composed of Negroes who received sealed envelopes each containing $1,000 for their votes.

Mississippi's constitution forbade state railroads, and so the state escaped some of the worst excesses of radical rule. However, an extensive scandal occurred in connection with improving the navigability of rivers. The cost of state printing increased from $8,000 a year before the war to $70,000. One year it reached $128,000. Although these increases in costs did not saddle the state with a large debt, the tax rate went as high as 14 mills on the dollar. Local governments were more graft-laden than was the state government.

In Arkansas and Texas, the story of the other states was repeated with little variation. The public debt increased in Arkansas through grants to railroads, although Governor Powell Clayton was among the better class of carpetbaggers. In Texas, the radical government found the state without debt and left it with one of $4,000,000, while the tax rate rose from 15 to 50 cents on $100.

By far the worst-governed state, with the possible exception of South Carolina, was Louisiana. In 1868 Henry C. Warmoth, a carpetbagger with a poor war record, was elected governor. Warmoth refrained from making claims of personal honesty but declared that he was not more dishonest than anyone else in politics. His eight years of public service netted him a fortune. Warmoth headed the radical party in the state, controlling elections through the appointment of a returning board which canvassed the returns. The municipal police and local constabulary were under the governor's control and were paid by the parishes.

The Louisiana Levee Company was established in 1870 and granted aid by the state. Railroads were aided by a legislative grant. Under Warmoth's railroad financing, the state debt increased from $6,-000,000 to nearly $50,000,000, amounting to 23 per cent of the total assessed value of property in the state.

State politics were in as bad a condition as finances. The collector of the port of New Orleans was James F. Casey, a brother-in-law of President Grant; the surveyor of the port was General Longstreet, turned radical. Between the "Customs House Gang"—headed by Casey and S. B. Packard, the federal marshal—and Warmoth, a feud broke out over the control of the state. Casey interpreted his position as that of official representative of the radicals and attempted to control Louisiana politics for the benefit of the national administration. Warmoth objected, with the result that each faction organized a legislature and appealed to Washington. Grant supported Casey, and Warmoth joined the Liberal Republicans in 1872. For four more years the state was under radical control and was the last state to be "redeemed" from Negro and carpetbagger misrule.

4. The White Man's Revolt

While this riot of Negro and carpetbagger corruption was under way, large numbers of southern whites were excluded from the polls and from holding office. Negroes and radicals controlled the ballot box, and the governors had command of a black militia which obeyed their orders. Through the militia, the Negro vote was purchased and coerced into support of the radicals. Frauds completed the work of insuring the dominance of the carpetbaggers. Yet, even when the radical star was in the ascendant, maturing signs of revolt portended the eventual dissolution of the scandalous system.

A large factor in the disintegration of the radical regime was the growing dissatisfaction of the Negroes with their new-found guardians. Although a fortunate few secured election to the legislature or to local offices, it was the carpetbaggers and the less worthy scalawags who took for themselves the better positions. Gradually, as the Negroes became more accustomed to exercising political rights, they began to question the proportionate division of the spoils. For the most part, the Negroes were inarticulate and leaderless, but their secret discontent caused them to take sides in the factional quarrels among Republicans. The masses of the Negroes, rapidly being forced to become sharecroppers, compared their return to virtual slavery with the roseate dreams that the carpetbaggers had promised to fulfill. The result was a loss of interest among the colored voters which made possible the Bourbon reaction.

At the same time that the Negroes were becoming lukewarm, the better elements of the native white loyalists were repelled by the rising tide of corruption. This element had been persuaded to remain quiet by the old proslavery argument and by the belief that the Negro was inferior to the white man. They had supported slavery and acquiesced in planter rule until the politicians of the aristocrats had precipitated secession. During the war, they had furnished the bulk of the deserters when they were forced into the Confederate army and had supported the peace societies and the revolt of the small farmer against the Confederacy. The Johnsonian program had promised to surrender the South to these small farmers, but the radical program had been based upon the votes of their ancient enemies, the Negroes. As did the Negroes, these loyalists found that the carpetbaggers held the offices and enriched themselves from the public treasury. Moreover, the rising tax rate affected small property-holders as well as large ones. The result was that these people accepted once again the old leadership.

The greatest factor, however, in the downfall of the radicals was the acquisition by the Conservatives of the techniques of revolution. The old planting groups, who had feared Negro rule because it was ignorant, would have preferred military government. The excesses of the radicals drove them to the point of desperation. The rising tax rate caused them to hold taxpayers' conventions to protest against expenditures, but the black taxmakers in the legislatures were not property-holders and had no sympathy with the plight of their former masters. In the beginning, the old leaders had hoped to control the Negro vote; but the Freedmen's Bureau and the Union League had defeated their dreams. In desperation, the planters turned to extra-legal means to secure a redemption of their states.

The agency that came to their hands was the Ku Klux Klan. Originally the Klan was formed in Pulaski, Tennessee, by a group of young men for their own amusement. Dressed in ghostly costumes, they frightened the superstitious Negroes of the community by appearing as the spirits of dead Confederates. As soon as the effects of this procedure were seen, the movement gained headway and men joined to obtain political and economic ends. The order spread until the entire South was included in the "Empire" presided over by General N. B. Forrest as "Grand Wizard." Each state was a "Realm," counties were "Provinces," senatorial districts were "Dominions," and the communities formed "Dens" of this mystic society whose officers were denominated "Grand Dragons," "Grand Titans," "Grand Giants," "Grand Cyclops," and "Hydras," "Furies," "Goblins," "Genii," and "Nighthawks."

The Ku Klux Klan was only the better known of a number of such organizations. Knights of the White Camelia, the White League, the White Line, the Pale Faces, and the Order of the White Rose were but a few of the names under which the disfranchised and overtaxed sought to regain control. Their methods were similar. In the beginning, they relied on the credulity of the Negroes to frighten them into subjection. When the Negroes penetrated the disguise, the Klan resorted to violence to gain their ends. Tarring and feathering, beatings, and even murder of obstreperous Negroes, unpopular scalawags, and offensive carpetbaggers became the rule. The Klan rode at midnight, visiting their wrath upon their hapless victims. At election time, the activities of the Klan increased, and as a result of early success the hooded men took courage and appeared more frequently. The terrorized Negroes were unable to identify their assailants, and the secrecy of the Klan's movements rendered official action impotent.

In desperation, the radicals in Congress passed enforcement acts to preserve their party in the South. In May, 1870, the first act was passed, ostensibly to carry out the provisions of the Fifteenth Amendment. The act made it a federal offense to wear masks on a public highway for purposes of intimidating any citizen from exercising the suffrage. The president was authorized to use the militia or the army to enforce any judicial process issued in pursuance of the act. The next year, a supplemental act was passed, but even this was found to be insufficient. In March, 1871, Grant asked for more power, and Congress, in the Ku Klux Act, authorized the president to intervene with military force in any locality, to declare martial law, and to suspend the writ of *habeas corpus*. President Grant used his power under this law only once. In October, 1871, he declared martial law in nine South Carolina counties. The federal marshals, however, made thousands of arrests.

After the passage of these laws, the Ku Klux movement declined, although not as a result of the legislation. The reason lay deeper in the social structure of the South. The Ku Klux Klan had its greatest strength in the old nonslaveholding regions. The mountains of North Carolina, the upcountries of South Carolina and Georgia, rather than the black belts, were the centers of the movement. As the Klansmen drew into their ranks the more violent elements of the community, moderate men withdrew. The leaders of the South who had originally supported the Klan denounced its excesses. In 1869, General Forrest ordered its dissolution, and its formal career ended. The depredations of masked men went on, however, giving the poorer whites renewed opportunity to wreak their vengeance upon their Negro neighbors. The Klan and the Union League together did much to drive a wedge between the lower classes of the whites and the Negroes. The division served once again to enable the old southern leaders to regain control. The Klan made possible the revival of the battle-cry of white supremacy which had been the mainstay of the planter aristocracy.

Partly as a result of the Ku Klux Klan and partly as a result of factional quarrels among the Republicans, the Conservatives won back their states. After the impeachment of Governor Holden, North Carolina remained in the "redeemed" column. In 1870, South Carolina Conservatives joined with discontented Republicans under the banner of reform. In 1872, two Republican factions struggled for control, and Franklin J. Moses became governor. Two years later, Democrats and reforming Republicans were barely defeated, but the victorious governor, D. H. Chamberlain, set about to reform his party. By 1876, Chamberlain was ready to lead a reform movement, but the Democratic strength had increased to the point where the Republicans were maintained only by election frauds and federal troops. In 1871, Georgia Democrats won the state elections and impeached Governor Rufus Bullock. Upon Bullock's resignation, a special election placed a Democrat in the governor's chair. The Democrats of Alabama gained control of the legislature in 1872, and although a Republican governor called and recognized a radical legislature, the administration refused to intervene, and the state passed into the Democratic ranks. Mississippi came to the verge of civil war before the whites regained control. In Vicksburg, white and black troops faced each other, and Grant sent General Sheridan to assume control. Sheridan called the leaders "banditti" in a dispatch to Grant—a particularly unfortunate remark because it inspired such a revulsion of feeling in the North that the administration could not support the radicals. In Arkansas, a factional quarrel known as the "Brooks-Baxter War" brought Democratic control in 1874, and a changed constitution insured a continuance of white supremacy. Texas went Democratic in 1874. By 1876 only South Carolina, Louisiana, and Florida were under Republican control.

5. THE NORTHERN REACTION

The restoration of white supremacy in the southern states would not have been possible without a reaction in northern sentiment. The radical politicians were interested in Reconstruction in order to control the black men's votes and thereby assure Republican majorities in Congress. The northern people, on the other hand, had only a humanitarian interest in the Negro and regarded the South primarily as a field for economic exploitation. As the full picture of southern conditions was unfolded, the people began to perceive the fundamental conflict between economic and political control of the conquered region. Horace Greeley and other northern publicists promised that the radical regimes would make possible southern industrial development. After the election of 1868, Greeley urged Northerners to plant colonies in the South and make investments in southern mines. To make possible this infiltration, Greeley advocated "universal amnesty" for the southern leaders.

Yet the southern states offered few inducements to migrating men and money. Competition with the free lands of the West and the continuance of disorders in the South prevented the expected development. Recognizing the evils which the radical policy had brought upon the South, moderate Republicans urged moderation and amnesty as a means of bringing the Southerners to accept a real economic reconstruction. Moderates pointed out that "capital and intelligence must lead" and advocated abandoning the Negroes and making an appeal to the "thinking and influential native Southerners"—the "intelligent, well-to-do, and controlling class." Horace Greeley soon championed this attitude in the New York *Tribune* and sent correspondents into the South who sent back reports of the high taxes and the corruption attending carpetbag rule. As the *Tribune's* correspondents described the melee in the South Carolina legislature, the moderates began to perceive the reasons for the Ku Klux Klan. In May, 1871, Greeley traveled through the South advocating the encouragement of industry and returned home to tell Northerners that the South was suffering from "decayed aristocracy and imported rascality." Both the Klan and the carpetbaggers should be removed.

The issue of the carpetbaggers appeared in the presidential campaign of 1872. In his four years in the White House, President Grant had antagonized many elements in the North. Assuming the office without previous political experience, Grant had a naïve concept of his position. He considered the presidency a proper reward for his military services. His constitutional concepts were but elementary. "The will of the people," said Grant before his election, "is the supreme law of the land." In accepting the Republican nomination, he had declared, with a pointed reference to Andrew Johnson, that he would have "no policy to enforce against the will of the people." In Grant's mind the president should interpret the wishes of Congress as the expression of the popular will. Such views soon made the president subservient to the radical majority. He supported the carpetbag governments of the South at the insistence of the congressional radicals. In 1870, the president, forgetting the principles which would make him subservient, wholeheartedly adopted an ill-advised scheme for the annexation of Santo Domingo. When Charles Sumner, Carl Schurz, and other leaders defeated a treaty of annexation, Grant declared war upon these senators, removed their patronage, and threw the full strength of the administration against them in their home states. As the election of 1872 approached, these dispossessed politicians combined with other opponents of the radical program —revenue reformers, free traders, and currency reformers—in a schismatic movement. Adopting the name "Liberal Republicans," this strange assortment of practical politicians and idealistic reformers held a national convention in Cincinnati where the confused delegates nominated Horace Greeley for president. The platform advocated universal amnesty and universal suffrage for the South and condemned the radicals. In desperation, the Democratic party endorsed the Liberal Republican platform and candidates. The Republicans renominated Grant.

Although the campaign was fought largely upon financial issues, Grant's victory in November was considered by the radicals as a popular endorsement of their southern program. The campaign, however, served to advertise the carpetbaggers of the South. Moderates, Liberals, and Democrats continued to deplore southern conditions until they persuaded northern businessmen that only a restoration of native white government would bring the peace necessary for economic penetration of the South. After the election, controversies between opposing factions in Arkansas and Louisiana gave renewed proof that the radical policy caused costly disorder. Moreover, it became evident that, as the Negroes were becoming restive under the carpetbaggers' rule, there was danger of a union of the blacks and the lower-class whites. One observer suggested that if the 6,000 illiterate adult males of Georgia were added to the Negroes, "so vast a mass of ignorance would be found that, if combined for any political purpose, it would sweep away all opposition the intelligent class might make. Many thoughtful men are apprehensive that the ignorant voters will, in the future, form a party by themselves as dangerous to the interests of society as the communists of France."

At the same time that the northern people were coming to condemn the misgovernment in the South, a series of scandals in the national government brought a realization that the radical program for the nation was leading to corruption. In rapid succession after the elections of 1872, the Crédit Mobilier scandal, the "Salary Grab" Act, the Shepherd Ring in Washington City, the collapse of Jay Cooke and Company, and the panic of 1873 passed before the eyes of the nation. Disgusted with the widespread corruption and overspeculation, the voters in 1874 elected a Democratic Congress. The incoming Democrats uprooted more scandals for political purposes, finding the Sanborn Contracts and the far-flung Whiskey Ring to present to the voters. By 1876, the country was ready to repudiate the radicals. The Republican convention made a bid for the return of the "Liberal Republicans" by nominating Rutherford B. Hayes, who had the respect of the party's reformers. The Democrats nominated Samuel J. Tilden, who had gained a reputation as a reformer by his fight against New York City's infamous Tweed Ring.

With the country already committed to a repudiation of the radicals, Tilden polled an overwhelming majority of the popular vote. But the carpetbag governments of three southern states enabled, the Republicans to wrest the presidency from the Democrats. On the night of the election, the Republican National Committee learned that the Democrats had not received the returns from Louisiana, Florida, and South Carolina. The Republicans had been willing to concede these states without a thought; but a hasty calculation showed that if the states were for Hayes, he would have 185 electoral votes to 184 for Tilden. Quickly the Republicans wired the southern leaders to "hold" their states, and the Republican National Committee brazenly claimed the election. Republican "visiting statesmen" hurried to the South bearing promises of preferment if Hayes were elected.

South Carolina's large Negro majority had undoubtedly carried that state for Hayes, but Louisiana was not so certain. Should even one electoral vote go to Tilden, he would be elected. The visiting Republican leaders supported the radical members of Louisiana's returning board in throwing out returns from the parishes until they had transformed a Tilden majority of almost 9,000 into a Hayes majority of over 3,000. Comparable methods in Florida turned a Democratic majority of 100 into a Republican victory of almost 100 votes.

The Democrats of the ravished states had no intention of permitting these frauds to go unchallenged. Amid threats of marching on Washington to inaugurate Tilden, Democratic legislatures prepared to give certificates of election to Democratic electors. When Congress assembled in December, 1876, there were two sets of electoral votes from Florida, Louisiana, and South Carolina. By agreement of the party leaders, these disputed votes were referred to an electoral commission of five senators, five representatives, and five justices of the Supreme Court. The political complexion of this commission was eight Republicans and seven Democrats. Voting strictly on party lines, the commission rejected the Tilden and accepted the Hayes votes. In each case the vote was eight to seven. As a result, Hayes received 185 votes and the presidency, to 184 votes for Tilden. On March 5, 1877, the Republican victor was inaugurated.

Meanwhile, in South Carolina and Louisiana, the Republican governors who had been counted in along with Hayes had been installed. In both states, the Democrats prepared to contest the inauguration by force of arms. But the governors appealed to Grant, who sent federal troops to their aid. Only through these troops were the governors retained. In this situation the southern leaders sought for an adjustment with the Republicans. Tilden's temporizing conduct during the electoral count had alienated many of his supporters, and there was less inclination to inaugurate him by force. On February 26, a number of southern leaders, including Senator John B. Gordon of Georgia, L. Q. C. Lamar, and Henry Watterson, met some of Hayes's personal friends at Wormley's Hotel in Washington. The Republicans promised that, in return for Democratic asquiescence in his inauguration, President Hayes would withdraw the troops from the South.

On that day Reconstruction ended. The Republicans deserted the Negro to the southern ruling class and abandoned whatever idealism had originally gone into the radical program. Henceforth, the South would be once again in the hands of the Bourbons; the Negro and the poor white would return to their economic and social, if not legal, status of ante-bellum days. On April 10, the federal troops left Columbia, and Governor Chamberlain followed them out of the city. On April 24,

New Orleans was freed from troops, and Hayes's bargain was fulfilled. The masters of capital were secure in the national government. The lords of the manor were in full sway over the South. The sectional controversy had ended in compromise and mutual political understanding. The Old South had ended: a New South had already appeared on the horizon.

Economic Development in the New South

1. Two Traditions

THE South that was returned to the native whites when President Hayes withdrew the federal troops was unable to return to the past it had known before the war. In half a generation, war and reconstruction had decimated the population, destroyed the greatest single type of property, and caused a tremendous social upheaval. As he regained control of his local governments, the white Southerner faced two alternatives: he might attempt to recreate the social, political, and economic structure of the Old South, or he might imitate the North in an effort to make the South like the rest of the nation. Nostalgia beckoned him to return to the old way of life; the "Yankee" virus of ambition and material progress urged him to create a "New South."

The demand for a New South modeled after the industrial and commercial North came mainly from those who had dissented from the plantation system of the ante-bellum South. Areas of small farmers and regions with industrial dreams had been restive under the regime of the planter aristocracy and some of them had come to the point of rebellion during the Confederacy. After Appomattox, such regions had gloried in their relief from subservience and had prepared for industrialization. Although people in these regions had become as bitter as any toward Negro and carpetbagger rule, they were unwilling to return to their earlier subjection to the planting areas.

In general, the reactions of two of the South's leaders may be taken as symbols of the conflict of ideals between Old and New. In the years after 1865, Robert E. Lee and Jefferson Davis took different courses.

Farm Security Administration, photo by Evans

THE LOST CAUSE: ANTE-BELLUM PLANTATION, VICKSBURG. With paint peeling off and standing in unkempt lawns, the gaunt, deserted mansions stood as mute evidence of the South's defeat. In *per capita* wealth, Mississippi dropped from fifth place among the states in 1860 to forty-fifth—and last—among the states in 1900.

In both cases their reactions involved a strange paradox. Jefferson Davis had been a Southern nationalist; Lee, sorrowfully drawing his sword at the call of his native state, typified the extreme states' rights position. Davis had risen to the cotton aristocracy of the Southwest; Lee was born to the manor. In the Pierce administration, Davis had desired railroads and commercial development for the South, while Lee had contented himself in the comparatively poorly paid profession of arms. Yet after the war Davis devoted himself to mourning the "Lost Cause"; while Lee, with never a backward glance, gave his efforts to building a new society. As a vigorous and verbose defender of the Old South, Davis made speeches excoriating the North, wrote histories of the Confederacy, and endeared himself to all whose sense of defeat had driven them into romanticism. As head of Washington College, Lee attempted to train the South's youth to face new problems. Eschewing the classical curriculum, President Lee established courses in journalism, agricultural chemistry, and engineering, and sought to impart a vocational and practical education. Rationalizing his own political failure, Davis became the South's last, though not its greatest, political philosopher, reasserting in books and speeches the legalistic and constitutional dogmas upon which the Confederacy had rested. In the Davis tradition, professional Southerners carried on the effort to "keep the niggers in their place" and to recreate the society of the old aristocracy; it resulted in the United Confederate Veterans and the United Daughters of the Confederacy, formed in 1894 to perpetuate the defeatist tradition and to glorify the social system of the Old South.

IN THE DAVIS TRADITION: A PLANTATION HOME AT JACKSON. Professional Southerners, romantic writers, and nostalgic veterans conjured up mental pictures of manor houses, of banjo-strumming Negroes, and of goateed squires of undreamed virtues who sipped mint juleps in an aura of lavender and old lace. The Davis tradition was responsible for the effort to recreate the society of the old aristocracy.

Following the pathway that Lee marked out but going far beyond the general's vision, the proponents of a "New South" abandoned the ideals of a rural society and stepped boldly forward toward industrialization. In the 'eighties, Henry W. Grady, editor of the Atlanta *Constitution,* gained fame as the prophet of the New South. "We have let economy take root and spread among us as rank as the crab grass which sprung from Sherman's cavalry camps, until we are ready to lay odds on the Georgia Yankee, as he manufactures relics of the battle-field in a one-story shanty and squeezes pure olive oil out of his cotton seed, against any downeaster that ever swapped nutmegs for flannel sausages in the Valley of Vermont." Grady himself was the product of the Georgia uplands, where cotton took poor root. His father had been a Whig, and the son resided in Atlanta, a city whose bellowing locomotives and smoking factories gave its chamber of commerce license to designate it "Queen City of the South." Grady dreamed of "a South the home of fifty millions of people; her cities vast hives of industry; . . . her streams vocal with whirring spindles." Louisville editor "Marse Henry" Watterson, echoing the spirit of the times, declared: "The South, having had its bellyfull of blood, has gotten a taste of money, and is too busy trying to make more of it to quarrel with anybody." The tradition of the pragmatic school has been responsible for the industrial system of the South—its textile mills, its railroads, its tourist camps and resorts, its mines and foundries, its public utilities, and its wage scales.

By the turn of the century a compromise between these two traditions had taken place. The ideals of the Old South were realized to a large extent in cotton, sugar, and rice; while the industrialization of the New South, largely in the mountain regions and the cities, and its newer agricultural interests, reflected the values of the imitators. There was, too, a tacit agreement on the division of laborers. The agricultural regions and the steel mills relied largely upon Negro labor, while the cotton mills employed whites from the hills or from the outnumbered "poor whites" of the black belts. The planters and the industrialists agreed in their attitudes toward labor and co-operated in politics to keep down the cost of government. The philosophy of the Old South, reminiscent of the proslavery argument, served to prevent proletarian revolt. Planter, politician, and industrialist sedulously played upon race prejudice to prevent united action among mill workers and plantation hands, and thus continued their dominance of the southern scene.

But however important they may have been in their own states, post-bellum Southern leaders were not independent. The most significant result of the war and reconstruction was the colonial status into which the South sank. Though they dominated their area, still they served as agents of Northern capitalists, working for wages, salaries, and commissions. They were managers rather than owners, and the profits from their enterprises flowed northward. And the enterprises they managed generally produced the raw materials or the natural resources for finishing in northern centers. Economic carpetbaggers, more subtle than those who followed Union armies into the South, exploited the resources of the region, penetrated its capital structure, and eventually came to dominate its economy from behind the scenes. In the light of that fact, Southern efforts to overcome poverty and the effects of the war seemed almost hopeless. The basic decisions were made outside the South.

2. THE NEW PLANTATION SYSTEM

Whatever dreams the forward-looking advocates of the "New South" may have had, the first task was the restoration of agriculture. Almost as soon as the Confederate soldiers came straggling home, planters began to reconstuct the plantation system, necessarily along new lines. Emancipation of the slaves had destroyed the labor system of the plantation, and now the planter needed a new method of getting Negroes to work. A few tried paying wages, but money in the hands of the Negroes dissipated the labor supply. Though the Freedmen's Bureau supported the wage system, too few planters could raise the cash for regular payments. The Bureau then advocated employment on contract but before the Bureau had ceased its operations the planters had generally resorted to the system of sharecropping.

Thus, in the years after 1865 the predominant characteristic of Southern agriculture was not slavery but the lien system, more prevalent than slavery had been, for it encompassed all races and all classes. Indeed, in keeping the region in poverty, it may have worked more economic evils upon the South than slavery had done. In order to raise credit for his crops the Southern landowner pledged his produce to a banker or factor who could finance him through the growing season. Merchants loaned freely to planters but exacted in return interest rates which sometimes ran from 40 to 100 per cent of the amount of the loan. Fortunate planters who could obtain wholesale credit usually became merchants themselves and let their lands out on shares to "croppers." Landless Negroes and poor whites became tenants of the merchant-planter, planted the crops which the owner specified, and frequently turned over their share of the crop as partial payment on the account at the store. In short, the seeker after credit mortgaged an unplanted crop to pay a loan of an indeterminate amount, at a rate of interest set by the lender. Under such conditions legal peonage soon replaced in practice the chattel slavery outlawed by constitutional amendments. The slave at least had been "capital goods," of ascertainable value, upon which credit could be obtained. With slavery gone, the South was dependent solely upon the land.

Nor were the laborers in the new system appreciably better off. The share of the crop that the tenant received depended upon the amount of capital that he brought to the enterprise. If the owner furnished seeds, animals, tools, and houses, and the tenant gave only his labor, the owner usually took three fourths of the crop. If the tenant furnished his own provisions, he received half the harvest. Later, when some tenants had acquired some property, both owner and tenant preferred the payment of a stated rent. But in any case, the owner required the tenant to purchase provisions and supplies from his store and determined the acreage which should be planted to cotton, the money-crop. Seldom was the "mark-up" at the store less than 50 per cent— it was frequently 100 per cent—and seldom was the tenant permitted to vary his crops to produce the foodstuffs which would free him from dependence on the merchant.

Within twenty-five years after the end of reconstruction, almost 70 per cent of the cotton farmers were tenants who were seldom able to break away from their economic bondage. "When one of these mortgages has been recorded against the southern farmer," Matthew B. Hammond said in 1897, "he has usually passed into a state of helpless peonage." In some states tenants were not permitted to move from the land if they owed money to the owner, thus becoming serfs. But the crop-lien system was also wasteful: it contained nothing to encourage frugality or abnormal exertion. As planters sometimes pointed out, the "cropper" labored only 51 days a year—the other 305 days he could loaf on the front porch of the "plantation" store. Shiftlessness was a common characteristic of white and black tenants. Furthermore, the constantly falling price of cotton prevented men from rising to a position of independence. Cotton prices declined from an average of twelve cents a pound during the 'seventies, to nine cents in the 'eighties, and seven cents during the 'nineties. In the next century the price varied from four to fourteen cents. Under such conditions tenants were unable to reduce their debts.

If the sharecropper was a victim of the crop-lien system, the merchant-planter was no less bound to the banker or factor who advanced his credit. Banks charged as high as 1.5 per cent interest per month. The exorbitant railroad rates supplemented the extortion of the bankers. An antiquated tax system, falling heaviest upon real property, impoverished the farmer. In truth, the old plantation system was re-established, with the store account replacing the overseer's whip, the sheriff performing the duties of the ante-bellum "patter-roller," and the exploitation of men still furnishing the source of profits. It was this state of affairs that provided fuel for Southern agrarian protests of the last two decades of the nineteenth century.

It was those conditions also that caused modification of the entire structure of Southern agriculture. The ante-bellum tendency toward consolidating holdings and expanding the size of plantations now reversed. In 1881, F. C. Morehead, president of the National Cotton Planters Association, estimated that fewer than one third of the Mississippi Valley cotton plantations were owned by those who had owned them in 1865. He reported that others were passing daily "into the hands of the commission merchants." Yet, hiding the facts of actual ownership, the figures from the censuses seemed to indicate that in the nine large cotton states of the southeast, the size of the average "farm" declined from 347 acres in 1860 to 156 acres in 1880. In the same time the number of farms increased from 449,936 to 1,110,294. But of these, almost one third were sharecropped. With this subdivision and reorganization of the old plantations, the economic self-sufficiency of the plantation disappeared. No longer was it possible for the planter to maintain spinners, weavers, blacksmiths, and shoemakers for the benefit of his hands. These services reappeared as enterprises in the villages, just as did the store supplying the goods which the plantation system had largely produced for itself. Yet even then the store came to dominate, and the doctor, the shoemaker, and the preacher were in debt to the merchant. This, too, contributed to making the store rather than the farm the central economic unit, but the new system was not greatly different from the old.

Despite the conditions under which it was produced, cotton remained the leading crop of the South and the principal export of the nation. The cotton area expanded westward with the opening of new fields in Texas and Oklahoma. In 1878, the year after federal troops left Southern capitals, the cotton crop reached the 1860 level. In the following year the South produced almost 5,500,000 bales, and a decade later had climbed to 8,500,000 bales. By 1894 production passed 10,000,000 bales, and in the next twenty years another 3,000,000 bales were added annually. By 1900, over 25,000,000 acres were planted to cotton.

But as the acreage and production increased, cotton prices declined. The 1880 crop of six and a half million bales brought 9.8¢ per pound, while the eleven million of 1898 sold for 5.7¢. Declining prices brought three effects: an expansion of acreage, especially in the virgin fields of Texas—from 1860 to 1880, more than seventeen million acres were added to the land cultivated in southern farms; intensive cultivation stimulated by the increased use of commercial fertilizers; and economies in costs of production. Thanks in part to lower prices of foods, tools, and wages, the cost of production declined from 8.32¢ a pound in 1876 to 5.29¢ in 1896. But with profits of less than a cent a pound, the cotton regions had little surplus for items of cultural improvement. The evils of poverty, land monopoly, absentee ownership, and the one-crop system, once blamed upon slavery, became more prevalent after emancipation than before, and not until the twentieth century, with its increasing urbanization and international crises, was there significant improvement.

3. Southern Agricultural Progress

Although cotton remained the greatest single crop of the New South, other staples continued to furnish a large portion of the revenues. The war almost destroyed the production of rice; abandonment of fields during the conflict resulted in destruction of dikes, and the fields were soon overgrown with weeds. As rice cultivation required more capital than cotton, planters were obliged to mortgage their lands. The disorganized labor situation furnished even more serious difficulties, for sharecropping was not so readily adapted to rice as to cotton. The difficulties led many rice planters to abandon the crop. In 1860 the Carolinas and Georgia produced 118 million bushels of rice; by 1900 the annual production barely exceeded one million bushels. But as rice culture declined in the old fields, it began again in southwestern Louisiana. There, Seaman Knapp, sometime professor of agriculture and president of Iowa State College, began a series of experiments and demonstrations. In 1886 he became head of a colonization project at Lake Charles, Louisiana, and attracted German and middle western farmers to the region. They demonstrated better farming methods and flooded creek bottoms to make rice fields. When drought threatened their water supply, they dug canals to tap larger rivers. By 1900 more than 500 miles of main canals existed in Acadia and neighboring parishes, and the Louisiana crop exceeded 10 million bushels. At the same time nearby counties in southeastern Texas, imitating the successful Louisiana experiment, produced nearly 8 million bushels.

Sugar production, largely confined to Louisiana, was almost totally destroyed by the war. The blockade forced growers to diversify in order to live on home produce and little seed cane was carried over. Peace brought a slow recovery. Because of the large investments required for land and mills, only large-scale production was profitable. Before the war sugar houses with a daily capacity of 200 tons could operate successfully, while by 1900 only those which could handle 1,500 to 2,000 tons remained in operation. The sugar planter solved many of his problems by adopting better machinery and increasing the sugar content of his cane through improved strains. After 1877 the Sugar Planters Association sponsored and popularized many new methods, while the sugar experiment station in New Orleans taught lessons in economy. Thanks to improved levees on the Mississippi, the area of sugar planting spread.

With heavy investments in land and mills and facing foreign competition, sugar producers clamored incessantly for a protective tariff. Fluctuations in the national tariff policy brought alternate prosperity and distress to the cane growers. Before 1890, a duty of 2½¢ a pound brought profits to producers but in that year Congress changed its policy, placed raw sugar on the free list, and paid a bounty of 1¾ to 2¢ a pound to the Louisiana producers. In 1894 that scheme was abandoned and imported sugar was taxed at 40 per cent of value. Since the world sugar price was low, foreign producers could still undersell the southern grower, however, and in 1897 domestic producers obtained a higher tariff. Reciprocity treaties with Cuba and the free admission of sugar from Puerto Rico and the Philippines continued the hardships under which the Louisiana producer labored. Meanwhile, the development of beet sugars in parts of the West reduced the profits of the sugar cane grower.

While cotton, rice, and sugar dominated the agricultural scene in the lower South, the principal money crop of the upper South was tobacco. Before the war the development of new grades of tobacco had brought a renewed prosperity to the tobacco regions. In the years after the war the crop spread to new areas and Kentucky took the lead over Virginia. By 1900 the annual value of the Kentucky crop was over $18,000,000. There, and in Tennessee, the dark, heavy varieties, notably burley, became the principal types. In other regions of the South different types of tobacco were grown: Virginia, the Carolinas, and East Tennessee grew a bright yellow grade especially valuable for fillers; Florida and Georgia produced the Sumatra and Cuban leaves used in cigar-manufacturing; North Carolina grew "flue-cured" tobacco for cigarettes.

The social system of the tobacco regions differed little from that of the ante-bellum period. Tobacco was never adapted to the plantation system of production and was generally a family crop grown on farms of ten acres or less. Small farmers engaged in diversified farming were the rule in the tobacco regions. And unlike the marketing of other staples, the marketing of tobacco remained in the hands of the producers. The credit system and sharecropping did not take deep root in the tobacco regions. The local warehouse remained the market place for tobacco; there the farmer brought his loose tobacco and it was graded and placed in piles. Buyers visited the warehouses, inspected the piles, and purchased either on their own account or for a manufacturer. Much of the tobacco crop was exported in bulk.

In addition to the rehabilitation of the staple crops the New South began a greater diversification of agriculture. Corn and wheat did not recover rapidly before the end of the century but new products brought far-reaching changes. Nuts, fruits, and vegetables carved new regions out of the South, reducing both the domain and the majesty of King Cotton. For the most part, these new regions were given over to small farms and did not succumb to the Cotton Kingdom's system of store credit and poverty-stricken tenancy.

Most important of these new agricultural interests was truck gardening, which before the turn of the century took over a considerable part of the Atlantic and Gulf coasts. The development of trucking was a natural outgrowth of the increasing industrialization of the nation. Northern cities with their demands for vegetables out of season furnished a market, while lower freight rates, speedy transportation, and refrigerator cars enabled the South to meet the demand. In 1885 Norfolk made its first rail shipment of vegetables to New York; before the close of the century the trucking business had grown to enormous proportions. The "Del-Mar-Va" district on the eastern shore of the Chesapeake produced potatoes, cabbage, asparagus, and spinach for nearby cities. Virginia's "Northern Neck" and western Maryland formed another truck area. A third area in southeastern Virginia and North Carolina, with its shipping center at Norfolk, added $4,000,000 worth of peanuts to the products shipped from other districts. Near Wilmington was an area which by 1900 was shipping 12 million quarts of strawberries to the North. The district between Charleston and Savannah added its wealth of small fruits and vegetables. Still further down the coast lay Florida, then only fifty-six hours from New York City; its producers shipped strawberries, peas, beans, tomatoes, and cucumbers.

The Gulf Coast also developed a truck-gardening interest. Improved rail connections to Chicago and the cities of the Middle West made possible the shipment of cabbages and potatoes from Mobile, strawberries and tomatoes from Mississippi, and peanuts and potatoes from western Tennessee. Before the century ended, Galveston, Jacksonville, Tyler, and Palestine in Texas were supplying fresh fruits and vegetables to St. Louis, Louisville, and Cincinnati. By 1900 truck gardening produced an annual income of nearly $80,000,000 for these new regions of the South.

Closely related to the fresh vegetable production was the development of fruit orchards in still other southern regions. The slopes of the Blue Ridge in Virginia gave up their oaks and pines to make room for apple trees. While waiting for the long growing apple trees to bear, impatient orchardists planted quicker-bearing peach trees between the rows. Soon the growers added grapes, pears, and plums. The Piedmont of North Carolina and the sand-hills country of South Carolina and Georgia proved readily adaptable to fruit growing. By 1900 Georgia had 100,000 acres planted to watermelons, and over seven million peach trees; Virginia and North Carolina had 4,500,000 apple trees, while promising beginnings of a wholly new agricultural interest had been laid in Louisiana, Texas, Arkansas, and Kentucky. Also, beginning in the 'eighties, Floridians began to grow oranges, and although at first suffering reverses as frosts killed the crops, were soon shipping out about a million boxes each year. In 1900, fruits added $14,000,000 to Southern incomes.

Southern agriculture adhered only in part to the traditions of the Old South. In the staple crop regions the Old South's economic and social system remained under the domination of the plantation, with only external changes. The regions of the newer agricultural pursuits, truck gardening and fruit growing, took their profits, their way of life, and eventually their modes of thought from the school of Robert E. Lee and Henry W. Grady.

4. The Industrialization of the South

While southern agriculturalists were making a significant effort to reproduce the social system and the economic arrangements of the Old South, the processes of industrialization began in the mountains and the urban regions. West Virginia, East Tennessee, and Kentucky, western North Carolina, and the hill country of Georgia and Alabama had never accepted the plantation system. Despite potential resources of iron and coal and water power, these regions along the spine of the Blue Ridge had succumbed to an agricultural regime and become the homes of small farmers. Yet Clay's American System had appealed to the residents of these regions, and they hoped for internal improvements, protective tariffs, and industrial development. So long as the slaveholders and the planting aristocracy dominated the South, the potential industrialists were handicapped. Industry did get a tiny toehold in the Old South but its advocates could not obtain from planters the requisite governmental assistance. But the Reconstruction period, when the old rulers were out of power, brought opportunities for the exploitation of natural resources and the growth of factories.

Before 1900 most of the southern factories were financed by local capital. The difficulties confronting agriculture caused many a former planter to turn his thoughts from farms to factories. The abolition of slavery forced accumulations of capital into other channels and throughout the South men harkened to the dreams of industrial wealth. The gospel of industrialism received the sanction of the pulpit and the blessings of the press. Every artificial stimulant was used to extract capital. Throughout the 'eighties, towns and cities began to vie with each other in building factories. Chambers of commerce, merchants' associations, and town councils offered to reward factories with tax exemptions, free factory sites, and full immunity from hampering regulations.

The prophets of industrialism argued that the establishment of mills near cotton fields would reduce the cost of transporting raw materials to distant factories and that southern power, whether from coal or water power, was cheaper than northern power. Suddenly, too, the Southern climate which, according to pre-war propaganda, was too hot for industrial workers or even for white laborers, now became an additional argument to entice industry. But the most impelling argument was the availability of cheap labor. Poor whites of the rural regions could tend spindles or give routine attention to machines. Such workers were overwhelmingly "Anglo-Saxon," conservative, and illiterate; they would appreciate the relief from agricultural poverty and would be suspicious of the labor organizer and the radical agitator. Long experience in the rule of slaves and the dominance of society had given the managerial class mastery over effective instruments of social control. The factories of the South were based upon the same principles of exploitation as had been the old plantation system. The profits came from low wages, long hours, and low standards of living.

Farm Security Administration, photo by Evans

COMPANY HOUSES AND STEEL MILLS, ENSLEY, ALABAMA. The southern mill villages resembled the ante-bellum plantations. The early southern industrialists formed companies, sold stock, and established their factories along the railroad lines near small towns. Since there was no concentrated labor supply readily available, the companies constructed cheap houses around the mills. The company took over responsibility for many aspects of community life, as had the plantation: it built the village church and paid the salary of the minister; it built the school, maintained the constable, and furnished what recreation facilities there were.

Even the mill villages resembled the ante-bellum plantations. The early southern industrialists formed companies, sold stock, and established their factories along the railroad lines near small towns. Cheap land and tax exemptions enabled them to begin with little more than credit and the promise of stock subscriptions. Since there was no concentrated labor supply readily available, the companies constructed cheap houses around the mills. Tenant farmers and mountain families came to dwell in the mill villages, to work long hours in the mill, and to spend their small wages in the company store. Yet the workers came gladly for there were compensations in the life of the mill towns. The company took over responsibility for many aspects of community life: it built the village church and paid the salary of the minister, who was expected to prevent labor unrest among his flock. The company built the school, selected the members of the school board, and paid the salaries of the teachers. It maintained the local constable, a deputy sheriff who was selected by the company. Later, when community houses and recreation facilities were demanded, the company furnished them and paid the directors' salaries. The worker's entire life centered in the mill and the mill owner's control over his labor force was as complete as that of the landowner over the share tenant in the new plantation system.

Under such a system of control the number of factories in the South grew rapidly. In 1880 southern states had 184 cotton mills, less than one fourth of the nation's total. Within the following twenty years each southern state multiplied its industrial capital from three to ten times; the industrial worker population more than doubled, and the capital invested increased from $250,000,000 to more than $1 billion. By

Photo by E. Bruce Thompson

THE AGRICULTURAL REGIONS RELIED LARGELY UPON NEGRO LABOR. With the crop-lien system and sharecropping replacing chattel slavery, the Negroes were seldom able to break away from the new bondage. Most of the freed Negroes lived in southern rural regions and were engaged in agriculture.

1900 there were 416 cotton mills in the South, or almost one half of the total. In all southern manufacturing the value of the product was $445,000,000 in 1880 and $1.4 billion in 1900.

Returns on investments in southern cotton mills were unusually high, and greatly exceeded those of northern mills. In 1882 the average return was 22 per cent, despite much bad management and some failures; profits of 30 to 75 per cent were not unknown. The reasons were not hard to find. Many of the southern mills utilized machinery of more recent technology than did those of the Northeast; the first American plant operated entirely by electricity was a southern plant. Such innovations gave southern mills an advantage, which with reduced transportation costs for raw materials, and cheap labor, yielded profits. Another factor was enthusiasm, engendered by such instruments as the Atlanta Cotton Exposition of 1881, at which North Carolina's Senator Z. B. Vance urged visitors "to see that we have renewed our youth at the fountain of industry and found the hills of gold in the energies of an imperishable race." Encouraged by remarks of that sort, Southerners doubled the number of their cotton spindles between 1880 and 1885, and converted even the buildings of the Atlanta Exposition into a cotton factory. Most of the increase came in the two Carolinas, with South Carolina—erstwhile home of the most vigorous opponents of industrialism—leading the South.

The high profits paid by southern factory capital made the regional industrial development a fertile field for outside investors. In the 1880's the capital was for the most part local but after the depression of 1893 northern capital began to move into southern mill centers. Southern mill promoters usually raised part of the stock locally by subscription and then offered stock in the enterprise to northern machinery suppliers and financiers. These often charged high rates of interest, demanded control of the mill, and took a large share of the profits. The pattern of colonialism was as clear in the factory South as in the plantation South.

The quarter century that followed Reconstruction also witnessed the beginnings of a large-scale exploitation of the South's natural resources. One of the region's richest assets was its forests. Over 60 per cent of the nation's timber wealth was in the southern states. The long leaf, the loblolly and the yellow pine, the cypress, red cedar and juniper, hemlock and balsam, white, red, and black oaks—in all over two dozen varieties of commercially useful timber—covered the South. Immediately after the Civil War, as part of the vindictive radical policy, the public lands in the South were closed to all but homesteaders, who could get 80 acres. Until 1867 only freedmen could make entry, but in that year the restriction was relaxed. By 1876, 40,000 original entries had been made in the five southern public-land states. But the return to home rule in that year brought an end to the homestead policy and a return to unrestricted entry. By 1888 large blocks of the most valuable timber and mineral lands in the South had passed into the hands of lumbermen and speculators, mostly nonresidents. When it was too late, Southerners discovered that men from the North and West controlled southern lumber and drained the profits from the rising lumber industry.

Typical of the new lumber barons of the South were Henry J. Lutcher and G. Bedell Moore, Pennsylvanians who moved their saw-mill operations to Orange, Texas. They called themselves "Lumber Kings of the World," and boasted in 1890 that none in the South cut as much timber as they. Daniel F. Sullivan, a native of England, also made a fortune in the southern forests. Beginning with the purchase of 250,000 acres of timberlands in Alabama and Florida, Sullivan soon became a "Gulf Coast Jay Gould in the timber business"; he won virtual control of the port of Pensacola through ownership of piers, railways, and lumber yards, and at his death in 1885 was working to gain control of Mobile lumber operations.

Farm Security Administration, photo by Shahn

COTTON PICKING IN PULASKI COUNTY, ARKANSAS. Many phases of cotton production, including the back-breaking task of picking or harvesting, resisted mechanization efforts. Long after most crops were sowed, cultivated, and harvested by machinery, cotton continued to be a hand operation. At harvest time, planters required great quantities of temporary labor, which, because it was necessary to get the crop in, had to be subsidized the rest of the year. As planters sometimes pointed out, the "croppers" labored only 51 days a year—the other 305 they could loaf on the front porch of the "plantation" store.

Most profits were made from the southern pine, quick growing and of an infinite variety of uses. Naval stores were still an important item in southern incomes: in 1900 the lower South received over $20,000,000 from turpentine alone. But much wood was taken for lumber. In 1895 the annual cut of pines exceeded seven billion board feet, and of cypress nearly five hundred million, while over three billion board feet of hardwood were taken out of the South. For the most part Southerners involved in the industry contented themselves with the sale of lumber but there was some southern fabrication of timber products. Cypress shingles were made in Mobile, New Orleans, and in Arkansas and North Carolina. In the 'nineties, furniture manufacturing began in North Carolina and by the turn of the century High Point was threatening to rival Grand Rapids as the furniture capital of the nation. The rapid exploitation of timber resources brought a growing demand for conservation practices, but these had to await the twentieth century, and some check on absentee owners, for fulfillment.

Less susceptible to quick exhaustion but more far-reaching in its social consequences was the development of the South's mining industries. The new needs of an industrial nation brought a rapid exploitation of the South's varied mineral wealth. Iron, coal, oil, granite, and phosphate abounded in the South and waited only for capital and enterprise. Both were soon forthcoming. Almost as soon as the war was over, iron mining and smelting began in East Tennessee. The rich iron and coal deposits of the entire Appalachian region, known before the war, were undeveloped until Yankee capital and southern management combined to work them. Farther south, in Alabama, large seams of hematite ores lay close to the surface. In 1870 a lone house stood near these ores at a site where the rails of the Louisville and Nashville railway line crossed those of the Alabama Great Southern Railroad. In 1871, at that spot, the city of Birmingham, ambitiously named, was incorporated, and furnaces appeared with almost magical rapidity. By 1900 the new city had $45,000,000 in assessed valuation of its property, nearly $7,500,000 invested in manufactures, and an income from its manufactured products of more than $12,500,000.

Birmingham's story of rapid growth based on profits from iron was duplicated in other parts of the South, though Alabama led the way. Within a decade after the founding of the city the state's iron production had increased tenfold; by 1890 the South was producing more pig iron than the whole country had produced before 1860. Between 1876 and 1900 southern pig iron production increased seventeen times compared to an eightfold growth for the nation. Here, too, outside capital exercised control over the southern industry. In 1889 Andrew Carnegie warned that "the South is Pennsylvania's most formidable industrial enemy," but northern financiers and railroad magnates determined the course of southern iron and steel. Indeed, it seemed that the Federal Brigadier was as prominent in the southern iron industry as was the Confederate Brigadier in Southern politics. Typical of New England industrialists who invested in Alabama coal mining were Daniel Pratt and Henry Fairchild DeBardeleben. Northern and English investors controlled furnaces and mines in Tennessee and Virginia, and the L & N, mostly owned by foreigners, directed traffic into its holdings in the mineral regions of Alabama.

Along with the mining of iron went the development of southern coal fields. Bituminous coal beds near Richmond, along the Dan River, and in the mountains of North Carolina and Kentucky, invited exploitation. In 1880 over six million tons of coal were taken from the South.

During the next twenty years West Virginia alone had an annual increase of one million tons; by 1900 the annual production of southern coal mines was nearly 50 million tons. The Pocahontas field in Virginia and West Virginia was conveniently near the industrial cities of the middle Atlantic and close to water transportation, making exploitation profitable. Next to West Virginia, Alabama and Kentucky ranked second and third in southern coal production.

The social consequences of coal mining were as far-reaching as were those of the cotton mill and the crop-lien system. Near the newly opened mines operators built towns for the miners of rude and unpainted shacks perched precariously on stilts against the sloping hills. The mining company owned the shacks and deducted rent from the miners' earnings; it also owned the commissary and paid the workers in scrip redeemable only at the company store. The workers, gathered from the neighboring hills, gave up the sturdy independence of mountaineers. Occasionally a catastrophe aroused social conscience and forced the establishment of safety devices in the mines. In 1890 West Virginia's legislature provided for two mining inspectors and in 1892 a state bureau of labor took over the inspection of mines. But social conscience was blind to other evils in the miners' lives. Following a wave of strikes in the 'eighties, West Virginia reorganized her militia to protect the mining companies, many of them owned by nonresidents, in their rights.

Just as new industries demanded coal for fuel and thus brought

Farm Security Administration, photo by Shahn

WEIGHING-IN COTTON, PULASKI COUNTY, ARKANSAS. As pickers were paid by the pound, at so much per hundred pounds, the weighing-in was an important time. Pickers often competed with each other for the honorary title of "best picker on the place."

COTTON GIN NEAR IRWINVILLE FARMS, GEORGIA. Though many plantations operated gins for their cotton, usually gins were independently operated. Cotton was removed from the mule-drawn wagons by suction pipes. On a busy day, several scores of wagons might line up beside the gin; while waiting their turn to unload, drivers slept on the cotton or passed along plantation gossip.

about the opening of southern coal fields, so new machines which needed oil for lubrication and factories and homes needing illumination caused widespread search for petroleum. By 1870 oil derricks had begun to compete with coal tipples in disfiguring West Virginia's hillsides. In the 'nineties the new state's oil production passed that of New York and Pennsylvania. Meanwhile, explorations had revealed other oil fields in Kentucky, Tennessee, Louisiana, Arkansas, and Texas, though it was not until 1901 that the major Texas discovery was made.

Each of the new industries of the New South brought social changes but none more than the development of phosphate mining. In South Carolina, Florida, Tennessee, and North Carolina were rich deposits, and in those and neighboring states the soil was already worn out. Before the war agricultural reformers had urged the use of fertilizers on the depleted fields of the Southeast, but their voices brought only empty echoes in a land with abundant virgin soil and a wasteful system of agriculture. The upheavals of the war, however, brought a new interest in improving the old fields. The proximity of the phosphate beds to the exhausted fields was almost providential intervention. In 1868 the Coosaw Mining Company, paying a dollar a ton royalty to the state for a monopoly, began working the deposits of South Carolina. Before its monopoly ended in 1893, the company had mined more than six million tons of phosphate. As the South Carolina production declined in the 'nineties, enormous new beds opened in Florida and Tennessee.

The impetus to search out and exploit southern mineral wealth produced other commodities. Pennsylvania capitalists developed copper mining along the boundary between Virginia and North Carolina and the Tennessee Copper Company erected a model smelting furnace at its Ducktown mines. Near Wytheville, Virginia, long-known lead mines began again to produce. In Georgia and North Carolina additional gold was discovered and in North Carolina and Texas, silver. Manganese in Georgia, Virginia, and Arkansas, ochre and asbestos in Georgia, and the mountain mineral springs added to the total of southern wealth. By 1900, too, the mineral clays of the South had given rise to a promising pottery industry. Granite from Georgia and marble from Tennessee competed with building stone from the old quarries of New England.

In most of its industrial development, however, the New South played only a minor role in the national situation. Impressive as were the

Farm Security Administration, photo by Post

COPPER-MINING AND SULPHURIC ACID PLANT, COPPER HILL, TENNESSEE. Far-reaching in its social consequences was the development of the South's mining industries. The new needs of an industrial nation brought a rapid exploitation of the South's varied mineral wealth. Copper from the seams near Ducktown, Tennessee, was used to assist the Confederate cause, but in the inspiration of the New South its output was increased.

figures of her manufactures and mines, they were relatively much less impressive than were the records of Yankee accomplishment. In tobacco manufacturing, however, the South led the nation. Before the war the revival of tobacco growing had stimulated the manufacture of chewing and smoking tobaccos and snuff. Immediately after the war Virginia, North Carolina, and Kentucky reopened factories. By 1880 Virginia had doubled both her capital and production over pre-war levels; Kentucky had passed her ante-bellum production, and Florida received unexpected benefits from tariffs which prompted many Havana cigarmakers to move their factories to Tampa.

Beginning about 1885 a series of developments changed the tobacco industry in the South. New techniques mechanized the process, from stemming the leaf to packaging. In that development, Southerners contributed practical innovations. The most important single invention was the cigarette rolling machine, introduced in 1880 by James A. Bonsack, a young Virginian. Other innovations in tobacco processing such as packing and labeling were also contributed by Southerners. The mechanical revolution was accompanied by a shift in taste to cigarettes, which enabled North Carolina to replace Virginia as the national leader and also presented both the temptation and the reward for centralization of control in the industry.

Southerners took the lead in the exploitation of the tobacco market and the elimination of competition in it. Men like Julian S. Carr, Richard J. Reynolds, James R. Day, and Washington Duke, operating in Durham, Reidsville, or Winston, in North Carolina, acted like other American businessmen of the Gilded Age. But they were not economic carpetbaggers from the North; they were native colonials who outmaneuvered the empire builders. Outstanding figures of the new tobacco industry were Washington Duke and his red-headed son James Buchanan ("Buck") Duke. A small farmer of the North Carolina hill country, Washington Duke left his children with relatives while he served a reluctant year in the Confederate army. At the close of the war he returned on foot with a half-dollar in his pocket and two blind mules as his reward. The Yankee army had swarmed past his hillside farm but surfeited with loot, had left a pile of leaf tobacco. His two sons—the other was named Benjamin— aided their father in pounding out this sole resource on the barn floor and packaging it under the ambitious label "Pro Bono Publico." Then, driving the blind mules, they set forth to sell their product.

Success attended them; they returned to purchase, pound, and package more tobacco. In 1872 they sold 125,000 pounds; in 1874 they built a factory in nearby Durham. By 1881 they began to cash in on the booming cigarette business and four years later they invaded New York with a branch factory. At the same time Bull Durham, a product packaged by Julian S. Carr's company, was selling five million pounds of smoking tobacco. Seeing the possibilities of centralization, "Buck" Duke set out to capture the industry. "If John D. Rockefeller can do what he is doing for oil," he said, "why should not I do it in tobacco?" In 1890 the leading manufacturers joined in the American Tobacco Company with

James B. Duke as president. For a decade the tobacco trust relentlessly pushed smaller companies to the wall and absorbed them. By 1900 the Dukes controlled the Continental Tobacco Company, monopolists of plug tobacco, the American Snuff Company, and the American Cigar Company. Through the United Cigar Stores they had a nationwide network of retail outlets. In 1911 the Supreme Court ordered the dissolution of the American Tobacco Company, but the dissolution was more apparent than real and the Dukes maintained their practical monopoly in the industry.

Southern railroad development paralleled the growth of mining and manufacturing. The war had done much to ruin the 10,000 miles of track which the South had possessed in 1860. By 1865 the embankments had washed away, the rails had warped and worn thin, the cuts and culverts had been choked with débris, and the rolling stock was almost useless—even on those few lines still operating. Needing full repairs, southern railroad companies found borrowing comparatively easy from the carpetbag governments and from northern financiers. In southern states east of the Mississippi, railroad mileage was doubled by 1880, while increases in the West amounted to more than triple the pre-war mileage. In 1882 the old southern dream of a transcontinental railroad linking the South with the Pacific coast was realized when the Southern Pacific was completed from New Orleans to San Francisco. Other rail construction went on within the region, with vast sums being invested by northern and foreign capitalists as well as local investors. In the 'eighties more than 180 new railroad companies opened operations in the Southeast, most of them to die of overexpansion, poor construction, or lack of traffic.

Over the struggling lines the shadow of consolidation fell. The panic of 1873 was the first serious blow, as it put southern railways into receivership, from which condition many never emerged as independent companies. In the 'seventies, twenty-five southern companies were in receivership, of which the influential Richmond and Danville acquired connections that carried it to Atlanta and eventually to the Mississippi at Greenville; Henry B. Plant got two lines, the nucleus of the Plant system; and the Louisville and Nashville obtained outlets to Birmingham, Mobile, and New Orleans. Other combinations were organized by William Mahone of Virginia and Henry S. McComb of Mississippi, a transplanted Yankee.

Throughout most of this process southern railroads were free from rate wars, for they were experimenting with one of the nation's first successful railway pooling arrangements. In 1875 twenty-five companies entered a pool to fix uniform rates and apportion profits. The Interstate Commerce Act of 1887 forced the pool out of existence, thus leading to a period of rate cuttings and further consolidation. Then, following the depression of 1893, southern railroads lost all semblance of independence. Insolvency forced rail managers to appeal to New York financiers. Drexel, Morgan and Company took over the Richmond and Danville, and with that as a nucleus, J. P. Morgan finally created the Southern Railroad. The Morgan interests also controlled the Mobile and Ohio, the Queen and Crescent, the Central of Georgia, and minor lines. In a "Pennsylvania

National Park Service

IN RICHMOND, THE RESULT WAS COMPROMISE. The older cities of the South experienced growing pains after the War. Richmond had been well on the way toward industrialization in the ante-bellum period, but there was no general agreement with the ideals of the New South. While Prophets of the New Order proclaimed the gospel of the smoking chimney, devotees of the Old bemoaned the passing of their way of life. The result was compromise.

Group" were the Chesapeake and Ohio, the Norfolk and Western, and the Baltimore and Ohio. A "Belmont Group" included the Louisville and Nashville and the Nashville, Chattanooga and St. Louis railroads. By 1900, only the Seaboard Air Line and the Plant Line, both extending into Florida, were independent of northern financial control.

Thus southern railroads joined national rail combinations. Beginning in 1886, they had widened their gauge to conform to the national standard. That change symbolized the developments taking place within the capital structure of southern railroads. The monopolistic practices of the roads provided fuel for Populistic appeals in the South, as elsewhere, and for years would supply the southern politician with his diatribes. "The highways are the property of great carrying corporations who command more men as their disciplined *employees* than the government's own standing army . . ." a Virginia minister proclaimed. "Each of these roads points virtually to New York. To that city, yes, to one corner of Wall Street in that city, centre all their debts, their loans, their revenues, their chief management."

5. Some Regional Changes

The total result of the reorganization of southern economies was that by 1900 a region had been created whose way of life was far different from that of the Old South. The Cotton Kingdom, its borders altered, showed fewer outward changes than did the other agricultural areas. The Appalachian highlands, transformed into a region of manufacturing, mining, and newer agricultural pursuits, retained but little of its older system. What was gone was the old planter tradition; the enlightened, conservative gentleman of the Old South, almost legendary, with time for intellectual and political interests, renowned for his manners and his recognition of fine social gradations. Now a new spirit pervaded the land: wherever the echoes of Henry Grady's philosophy resounded, men gave only lip service to the ideals of the Old South. The victory of the North was not confined to the battlefield and the forum but was seen in the glare of the blast furnaces, heard in the whirring spindles and the clacking rails, and breathed in the prayers of the preachers. "Next to the Grace of God, what Salisbury needs is a cotton mill," proclaimed an evangelist to his congregation. With a new economics blessed by an old theology, towns vied with one another to attract factories and to grow into cities. Boosters perched upon chambers of commerce to crow triumph over each new mine tipple, smoke stack, rail line, and loom.

In addition to the new factories, mines, and railroads, the New South witnessed the growth of cities. The cities of the Old South, with the exception of New Orleans, had been swollen villages, necessary but slightly incongruous in a rural society. The cities of the New South took no part of their spirit from their earlier days but strove to be like the urban areas of the North. Thus Atlanta proclaimed itself to be the "New York of the South," and Birmingham likened itself to Pittsburgh.

These two cities were the outstanding examples of the new Yankeefied spirit of the New South. In Atlanta only 300 houses remained standing after the fire that accompanied Sherman's occupation, but recovery went rapidly ahead. New businessmen arose and with energy and determination rebuilt the city. In 1877 they succeeded in capturing the state capital and they enticed many an industry. The city's rail connections were excellent and its enterprising capitalists ingenious. By 1880 Atlanta had an annual trade of forty million dollars, handled 100,000 bales of cotton a year, and was attracting attention by its "bustling, rustling, and whir." Young Woodrow Wilson, hanging out his shingle as a fledgling lawyer in 1882, explained that he selected Atlanta because it, "more than almost every other Southern city, offers all the advantages of business activity and enterprise." In 1881 under the stimulus of Editor Henry Grady and Hannibal I. Kimball, a carpetbagger from Maine who was notorious for his adroit public thievery, Atlanta held an International Cotton Exposition which quickly expanded to include a survey of all southern industry.

Atlanta experienced immediate benefits. Within six months of the exposition two million dollars were invested in Atlanta manufacturing enterprises and the gain was attributed to the fair. Shortly thereafter the Exposition Cotton Mills moved into the fair buildings; the Southern Agricultural Works, with a capital of $150,000, began to manufacture cultivators and cotton machinery; a new cottonseed oil mill, a cotton compress, and new fertilizer plants added to the city's growing wealth. In 1895 the Atlanta promoters repeated their exposition and boastfully waved statistics to prove their devotion to northern ideals. By 1900 their three hundred homes had grown to 20,000 and their population to 100,000. The city covered twelve square miles; its property assessment was $55,-000,000. It had ten railroad lines, $111,000,000 in bank clearings, and a wholesale trade of $45,000,000. Its cotton factories consumed 175,000 bales per annum. Its streets were wide, its buildings high, and its spirit had little in common with rural Georgia.

Even more than Atlanta, Birmingham was solely a product of the New South. In only a lesser degree was Chattanooga, whose population increased 125 per cent from 1880 to 1890. Farther up the Appalachian range Knoxville, fulfilling a dream which "Parson" Brownlow had held dear, turned to manufacturing and brought a swollen population to crowd its narrow streets. In West Virginia, Charleston, Huntington, Parkersburg, and Wheeling felt the impetus of new industries.

The older southern cities grew too, but they experienced more growing pains. In Richmond the inroads of industry were met with mixed feelings. While prophets of the New Order proclaimed the gospel of the smokestack, devotees of the Old bemoaned the passing of the genteel tradition, their way of life. The city should not be a "museum, kept intact under glass," the prophets said; but the older families strove to maintain the city's former charm. The result was compromise. The factories came, making articles of iron and wood, making cigarettes and even books. But the capitol preserved its classic simplicity, and monuments to the Confederate dead arose to remind men of their past.

Charleston too faced the problems of adjusting to the new winds of change, but it compromised less than did Virginia's metropolis. The old families remained along the Battery, their houses still turned resolutely away from the street. Beyond the shopping district magnolias grew and ladies danced at the St. Cecilia's Ball. Between 1870 and 1900 Charleston added but 852 to its population. But despite its hold upon the values of the Old, the city slowly yielded to the New. Cotton mills, rice mills, and fertilizer factories opened; late in the 'nineties the harbor was deepened for traffic of larger vessels. Upcountry, Columbia made her peace with the new order and soon began to count her cotton factories as almost equal to her memories. Savannah abandoned her horse cars and gas lights for electricity and between 1880 and 1900 saw her population almost double. Memphis grew as a cotton and lumber market while adding cotton mills. Nashville, Mobile, and Louisville shared in the general growth of southern cities. By 1900, of 140 cities in fourteen southern states from Maryland to Texas, eight had populations of over 50,000, and four boasted over 100,000 people. As they grew, cities began to dominate their surrounding areas. Urbanization changed the character of the southern way of life and made it more like that of the rest of the country.

As significant as urbanization in revealing the impact of the new spirit was the development of Florida. Before the war the state had been settled only in the interior and along the Gulf Coast. Its great areas of swamp lands and its white sanded shores had been inhabited only by scattered "Crackers" and Seminoles. Under a federal law of 1850 Florida had received title to her swamp lands and the legislature had set up a fund for internal improvements. The war stopped the drainage schemes and depleted the funds. Not until 1880, when Governor William D. Bloxham took office with a promise to drain the swamps, was any real progress made. To Hamilton Disston, a Philadelphia saw manufacturer, the governor offered alternate sections of all land Disston could recover from the region around Lake Okeechobee. In addition, the Philadelphian bought four million acres of swamp land for 25¢ an acre, and planned a huge colonization scheme. Many people, especially Englishmen, came to the swamp.

Meanwhile other forces were operating to create a boom in Florida. H. H. DeLand, a New York soda "king," purchased a tract in Volusia County from the state, laid out a city named for himself, and advertised for settlers. The settlers, many of them Swedes, planted orange groves under DeLand's guarantee of a ten per cent return on their investment. A killing frost in 1885, just as the trees began to produce, bankrupted the promoter, but the settlers persisted, grew oranges, and discovered additional profits in truck gardening. More successful were the beginnings of phosphate mining near Tampa, where the early rush to the newly discovered deposits resembled the more publicized gold rushes to the West.

Aiding in the development of Florida was Henry M. Flagler, Cleveland capitalist and Rockefeller's partner in Standard Oil. Visiting Florida in 1883, he was fascinated with its climate and natural beauty but disgusted with its hotels and railroads. Three years later he bought the first of the railroad lines which he built into the Florida East Coast Railroad. In 1892 he began new construction, pushing tracks down the Atlantic side of the peninsula. In two years he reached Palm Beach and in 1896 his tracks entered Miami. As he built the railroad, he also built hotels at St. Augustine, Ormond, Palm Beach, and Miami.

Thanks to such promoters, Florida grew prosperous. Railroads, hotels, and chambers of commerce combined to sing praises of its climate, its orange groves, and its tourist attractions. By 1900 Florida had 300,000 inhabitants. Its development was phenomenal: it was in tune with the spirit of the age. But that made Florida southern only in geography.

CHAPTER 28

Politics and Government in the New South, 1876-1900

1. NATIONAL POLITICS AND THE SOUTHERN QUESTION

THE South's accommodation to the new economic order gave pause to politicians of both South and North. Southern acceptance of northern values and ways of life, the adoption of Yankee business practices, and the growing economic interrelationships between the once hostile sections gave the "Southern issue" less potency as a political factor. From Appomattox to the disputed election of 1876 every national election found campaign orators vigorously waving the bloody shirt of the rebel menace. Condemnation of the South was the major theme of every Republican tirade and vote-seeking office-holders lost no opportunity to warn their constituents of Southern and Democratic conspiracies. If Democrats were elected to office, they said, the Southern wing of the party would dominate the nation. They would repudiate the national debt—or at least pay it in greenbacks—they would assume the Confederate debts and burden the taxpayers with pensions for Confederate soldiers. The economic consequences of the peace would all be lost.

Although their specific charges were absurd, the Republicans had reason to fear the Democrats. Emerging from the war under the stigma of having opposed the national effort, the northern Democrats sought new political issues. They seriously considered espousing the "Rag Baby" idea of paying off the nation's war bonds in greenbacks instead of gold.

They listened attentively when Clement L. Vallandigham, whom Lincoln had exiled from the North, proposed a "New Departure" which would abandon the Southern question and turn the spotlight upon economic issues. Perennially the Democrats questioned the tariff, pointed accusing fingers at the malfeasance of big business and at bribery and corruption in the national government. Republicans might well question whether the financial and industrial structure they had erected would be safe in Democratic hands.

But the Republican fears were groundless. Developments in Southern politics gave conservatives no cause for alarm. Democrats were as interested as were their Republican neighbors in railroads, factories, and mineral exploitation. In the South, as state after state was "redeemed" from Negro and carpetbag rule, "Bourbon" Democrats took control. Hard-headed businessmen, they harbored neither zeal nor economic heresy, but worked to create the New South. They welcomed capital investments and promoted industry and transportation. Their political and economic orientation was toward the East with its conservative philosophy, rather than to the agrarian West where Grangers sought controls over railroads and manufacturing corporations. Settlement of the disputed election of 1876, and the Compromise of 1877, which prevented continuation of civil strife, offered proof of the transformation of American politics and determined the course of the continuing reconstruction of the South.

After 1877 the Republican party was committed to sectional reconciliation. When southern congressmen accepted Hayes' inauguration, the hitherto violent *Harper's Weekly* admitted that the southern Democracy was "wonderfully like the best northern Republicanism," and the New York *Times,* voice of Republicanism, declared that "the consistency and decency of the Democratic Party in Congress are chiefly with the Southern members thereof." President Hayes reluctantly abandoned his plan to make General Joseph E. Johnston his secretary of war but he did add an ex-Confederate, Senator David M. Key of Tennessee, to his cabinet as postmaster general. As that portfolio bulged with the choicest patronage pickings, a Yankee politician, James N. Tyner, remained in the Post Office Department to supervise appointments in northern states. Old abolitionists, old-line Republicans, and opponents of Hayes' civil service reform program—men like Wendell Phillips, Roscoe Conkling, James G. Blaine, and Simon Cameron—were dissatisfied with the new peace policy. Under their urging, Republicans in the congressional campaign of 1878 and the presidential election of 1880 again brought out the bloody shirt. But this was a last-ditch stand. In local campaigns a faded blue uniform with an armless sleeve continued to be politically potent but the Republican party was learning to wear the new robes of peace. President Chester A. Arthur symbolized the change in his first annual message to Congress. In December, 1881, for the first time in forty years, a presidential message made no special reference to the South.

There was other evidence that sectional peace was the new order

of the day. Following Hayes' inauguration in March, 1877, federal occupation troops were withdrawn from the last southern states and for
the first time since 1865 southern whites were back in control. Federal
patronage was liberally distributed among southern Democrats: perhaps
one third of all southern appointments made in the first five months of
Hayes' administration went to southern members of the Democratic party.
The federal pork barrel also began to open to southern demands. Internal improvements paid from the national treasury, almost excluded from
the South since 1860, now began to appear in the region. River and harbor improvements, levees, and railroad construction were included in
the more than 300 bills for southern internal improvements introduced
into the new Congress in 1877. At long last the South got her railroad to
the Pacific. When in October, 1883, the Supreme Court declared unconstitutional the reconstruction era Civil Rights Act, the Negro was substantially abandoned to his former masters, and sectional discord seemed at
an end.

The first Democratic administration after the war gave Southerners
a new chance to show that they accepted the results of the conflict. In
the election of 1884, James G. Blaine's unsavory record made the Republican task difficult. Reform and integrity in public office, rather than the
South, were the issues, and voters preferred the record of Grover Cleveland. On the whole, southern influence on Cleveland was slight. Two
ex-Confederates, L. Q. C. Lamar of Mississippi and A. H. Garland of
Arkansas, became secretary of the interior and attorney general respectively, and Southerners occupied the embassies in Paris, Vienna, and
Madrid. Neither Cleveland nor the Southerners were radicals, and the
Democratic administration meant no change in the basic economic
structure of the nation. But Cleveland was a reformer, and "stalwart"
Republicans with no zeal for reform sought partisan ammunition from
his acts.

Cleveland's election, they plausibly alleged, had been possible
only because of the Solid South, where Democratic control was founded
upon corruption and violence. Moreover, in Republican eyes the President's patriotism was questionable. He vetoed over 200 requests for
private pensions for veterans, vetoed a general pension bill, and then
signed an order permitting the return of captured Confederate battleflags
to southern states. But Republican cries of "treason" rang hollow: honest
men of all parties approved Cleveland's vetoes and few were seriously
alarmed over the fading trophies of near-forgotten battles.

Cleveland's low-tariff message of 1887 gave the Republicans a
better issue and on it, in 1888, they elected Benjamin Harrison. Back in
power, Republicans sought a method of breaking the politically solid
South. In 1890 Massachusetts' Henry Cabot Lodge, spiritual descendant
of Charles Sumner, introduced a bill requiring congressional supervision
of elections in the states. The measure, immediately branded the "Force
Bill," alarmed the South and gained no popular support in the North.
The bill did not pass, thanks to a coalition of southern Democrats and
Western Silver Republicans, but its influence was greater than many a

legal enactment. Perhaps, indeed, Lodge was concerned with forcing the South to remain solidly Democratic. Southern Populists were growing in strength at the moment and the tradition which Lodge represented and the interests which he served had more to fear from agrarian populism than from the pro-industrial attitudes of the Southern Democrats. The Force Bill enabled politicians to appeal to the fear of federal interference in elections and out of that fear came, in time, a new crop of political demagogues who might use the issues of race to insure a united party in the South. The ultimate response of the Southerners gave assurance to the leaders of the new industrial nation.

2. THE BOURBON DEMOCRACY

The restoration of white supremacy in the southern states was accompanied by intimidation of Negroes and corruption at the ballot box. Those who profited from the expulsion of the carpetbaggers justified their tactics by blatant assertions that the South was "a white man's country" and that the "niggers must be put in their place." The lessons of reconstruction remained as permanent parts of Southern politics, and the groups who had obtained control held their position by appeals to race prejudice as well as by widespread corruption. The Negro question played the same part in southern politics that the bloody shirt did in northern vote-getting.

Although they claimed such a descent, the new southern politicians were not related to the old planter aristocracy. The men who led the way to home rule in the South called themselves "Conservatives" in opposition to "radical" Republicans. Politically they represented an alliance between southern Democrats and Whigs, who had been bitter rivals before the war. But a decade of bayonet rule had accomplished a unity the Old South had never known. It was an uneasy truce, with the followers of Henry Clay predominant over those of Andrew Jackson.

For these were the "Bourbons"—men who learned quickly from their Yankee teachers the advantages of plucking the fruits of a burgeoning and unashamed capitalism. For, though the name referred to those who had neither learned nor forgotten anything in the preceding decades, it did not fit the new leaders. To their opponents in the South they were known as "Bourbons" and compared to the French royal family "in their common hostility to popular government and democratic institutions." In 1882 William M. Lowe, alleging that he had been deprived of a seat in Congress by Democratic frauds, told the House of Representatives that "the southern Bourbon is an organized appetite. His idea of politics is patronage; his sole conception of party is an organization which acquires and distributes the offices. . . . The Bourbons indulge in practices that corrupt the fountain of politics."

Though they practiced political frauds, in economics they were conservatives. In general, they represented the rising businessmen, the merchant-planters, and the local industrialists. As interested as were their constituents in the industrial development of the section, they favored cheap government and low taxes and exempted new factories from regulation or taxation. With no desire to see an educated laboring class, they condemned public schools as "Yankee" institutions, gave only the most meager support to state universities, and adopted various devices to divert public funds from Negro education. From their political offices they managed the coal, iron, manufacturing, and railroad interests of the New South. Like their northern allies and financiers, they adhered to the Hamiltonian tradition. They joined in the fight for tariff increases and opposed organized labor and governmental regulation of business. However sensitive they might be on the race question, they were "safe" on economic matters. Indeed, their subservience to the Yankee angered such unreconstructed rebels as Georgia's Robert Toombs. "The South is ruled by as cowardly and venal a lot of place-hunting politicians as ever lived," he complained. "Like putrid bodies in the stream, they rise as they rot. . . . They lick the feet of Tammany corruptionists, and grovel in the dust before Northern money."

Despite Toombs' imprecations, leaders of the New South were joined in firm alliance with eastern conservatives. And, as he suggested, the course of southern politics was remarkably similar to that of the rest of the nation in the Gilded Age. Corruption at the polls was rife throughout the South. Despite the best efforts of the legislatures in gerrymandering the election districts, there were portions of every state where the Negroes would control local affairs unless the whites resorted to intimidation and corruption. State laws required separate boxes for each set of officers and judges threw out votes that were not placed in the proper receptacle. Shifting the location of the ballot boxes effectively disfranchised illiterate Negroes. Frequently voting districts cast more Democratic votes than they had registered voters. The appearance of armed men at the polls, apparently intoxicated, usually proved an effective deterrent to Negroes who wished to vote. But however distasteful, such practices were the order of the day in an America not far removed from rings, political bosses, and blatant corruption in high office. In imitating the seamy political conduct of the North, the South was but entering another phase of its becoming American.

Home rule was accomplished by making a farce of the democratic process, but it did not bring peace to southern politics. The temporary truce that united whites against carpetbag and Negro governments soon fell to pieces. The conflict between advocates of the two traditions—whether the post-war South would follow the lead of Jefferson Davis and "take its stand" for the Old South, or would look, with Robert E. Lee, to a New South—took political form. Division between southern whites was generally sectional within states, sometimes aligned along a North-South line, as in Alabama; sometimes East-West, as in Tennessee; or upcountry vs. low country, as in South Carolina. Though white organizations bore the party label "Democratic," the division was between planter-Democrats and industrialist-Whigs. Politically the New South thus continued the inner conflict of the Old; the white unity, born of desperation, was

deceptive. The "Solid South" was solidly Democratic, but that fact concealed divisions within the Democratic party as to which Democrats
should hold office. The "one-party" South contained warring factions
separated by issues perhaps even more basic than those that divided
political parties in the North.

The issues that divided southern Democrats were created by victory over carpetbag and Negro governments of reconstruction years, as
well as by the two traditions. In nearly every state there was a difference
of opinion over the settlement of the state debts incurred by the reconstruction governments; there were also widespread debates over state
aid to internal improvements. In each case, planter Democrats tended
to advocate repudiation of the debt and denial of government expenditures, while industrialist-financier oriented Democrats usually favored
sound credit and internal improvements. Small farmers and workers,
overlooked in the struggle, threatened revolt, which came in many states
by 1890.

In Virginia the redeemers organized as the "Conservative" party,
consisting of old Confederate Democrats, "True Republicans," old-
line Whigs, and some Negroes. The chief political issue was the state
debt, and it divided the "Solid" front of the Democratic party. By 1879
General William Mahone and H. H. Riddleberger had formed the Readjuster Party, dedicated to readjusting the state debt "on the basis of an
annual interest liability within the *certain* means of the State to pay."
In 1881 Readjuster William E. Cameron became governor, while Mahone
went to the Senate. The following year the Riddleberger Law, readjusting the state debt downward, became effective. Its purpose was to force
the state's creditors to share in the general depression. When the law
was upheld by the United States Supreme Court in 1883, conservatives
organized for battle against the Readjusters. General Mahone, now firmly
in command of the faction, had by now branched out, promising public
schools, repealing the poll tax requirement for voting, abolishing the
whipping post, and increasing corporate assessments for tax purposes.
Such Democratic radicalism stung the conservative Democratic wing into
action. With "Mahoneism" as the issue, in 1883 the Democratic machine
fashioned by John S. Barbour and Thomas S. Martin won control of the
state, which it held for the remainder of the century. It was not without
its factional struggle, however: in 1890 the legislature reduced the debt
to $19,000,000, bearing 2 per cent to 3 per cent interest, which marked
the defeat of the Funder, or "Debt-Payer" wing of the party.

In North Carolina the Democratic redeemers also suffered internal disagreements and saw the erection of a party machine controlled
by the eastern planter element. In 1876 Zebulon B. Vance, war governor
of the state, won an important gubernatorial election from Republican
candidate Thomas Settle, and the Conservatives were firmly in control.
But democratic principles suffered there as elsewhere after reconstruction.
In 1876 the legislature passed a county-government law which allowed
the assembly to appoint justices of the peace, who in turn selected county
commissioners. That arrangement provided white government in the

sixteen eastern Negro-belt counties and also established a Democratic machine which assumed control of western "white" counties. Chafing under such interference with their county governments and with their economic interests oriented northeastward, people in the Piedmont and mountain counties maintained their Republican connections. But there were also intraparty disagreements. Democrats debated the disposal of the state's holdings in railroad property—the Western North Carolina Railroad—acquired since 1835. Influenced by Governor Thomas J. Jarvis, who succeeded Vance in 1879, the legislature decided to sell the line and put the state out of the transportation business. The action reflected the spirit of the Conservatives, who became the allies and guardians of railroad and industrial interests and who championed laissez faire and antisocialistic attitudes. It was not strange that the state's farmers joined movements whose objective was reform.

South Carolina redeemers, rent by factional strife, were unable to establish an effective machine to control the state's politics. Wade Hampton, Confederate hero, led the way to home rule in 1876, when he won a heated election for governor. With the aid of Senator Matthew C. Butler, Hampton worked to establish a moderate solution to the Negro question. "The best friends of the colored men are the old slaveholders," he told Negro voters. He urged the Negroes to accept white leadership in return for recognition, protection, and certain civil rights. The Charleston *News and Courier* praised Hampton's efforts to ally Negroes with whites and boasted of a "long line of black faces peering out of red shirts" going to vote. Inadvertently that phrase provided Hampton's opponents with the label "Red Shirt Party" which they applied to Hampton and his followers. Many adamant white-supremacy South Carolinians would not accept Hampton's moderate road to reconciliation of the races based upon the old planter paternalism. General Martin W. Gary, who died in 1881, and later, Benjamin R. Tillman, capitalized upon the race question among "black belt" voters. Tillman's farm followers felt that they had driven out the carpetbaggers only to fall under the political control of Tidewater planters and new business interests, and they sometimes seemed more concerned with the "nigger" than with farmers.

Rejecting "fusion" with the Negroes, the Tillman faction defeated the Conservatives in 1890 with the aid of economic distress among farmers and the Eight-Box Law. The latter, adopted in 1882, required the voter to mark a separate ballot for each office and then to put the ballot into the appropriate box or have his vote invalidated. Frequent shifts of the boxes confused illiterate Negroes, but illiterate whites could get assistance from election officials. With white Democrats differing widely on important issues, white supremacy was the only issue which would keep them united.

Florida's booming economy determined the businesslike quality of its post-Reconstruction government. George F. Drew, a native of New Hampshire, was the governor who presided over the return to local control. He operated vast and successful lumbering and mercantile enterprises and had amassed a fortune since he settled in the state in 1865.

But though nominally a Democrat, Drew was not a Southerner by temperament. He had been a Unionist and had taken no part in the war. Thanks to Florida's alliance with industrial and commercial capitalists, however, Drew won the approval of influential citizens. William D. Bloxham, who succeeded Drew in office, enhanced Florida's economic growth by offering free land to visiting financiers. Indeed, he was so generous that he promised much more land than the state owned. The state made other inducements to outside capital: by 1886 it had followed other states in providing tax exemptions for new factories.

Like Florida, Georgia's native white government reflected the ideals of the New South rather than those of the Old. There the so-called "Bourbon Triumvirate" belied the name "Bourbon"; they were as progressive and forward-looking as any men in the country. The three, General John B. Gordon, Joseph E. Brown, and Alfred H. Colquitt, monopolized the state's three highest offices for the two decades following 1877. Gordon was the state's distinguished military hero and was lifetime commander of the United Confederate Veterans. But he was also connected with the New South business interests, particularly railroads, mining, manufacturing, and real estate. Brown, the state's war governor, became one of the leading industrialists of the New South, with considerable investments in railroads, mining, and industrials. Colquitt was the junior member of the association, and provided the link with Georgia's planters. Colquitt was one of the largest planters in the state but he also had successful investments in southern railroads, a fertilizer factory, and in coal mining. So closely allied with Yankee finance and business interests were the three that Georgia farmers, like those in South Carolina, smouldered into revolt under the leadership of Thomas E. Watson. Though they were unable to depose the triumvirate and their friends, the farmers gave the regular Democrats a real scare. For Watson, like Hampton, worked for political union with the Negro; while success was possible Watson befriended the Negroes but after 1892, when he was defeated by fraud and intimidation and by the Negro vote, he turned against the blacks. "The Negro question," he sadly declared, "is the invincible weapon of Bourbon Democracy in the South."

Alabama Democrats also faced the divisive issues of industrial growth and racial pressure. In 1874 native whites defeated the radicals and elected George S. Houston governor on a "white supremacy" and home-rule program. Houston was a lawyer with railroad connections; he served the economic interests of an Alabama dedicated to mining and manufacturing. Rufus W. Cobb succeeded Houston and continued the new political and economic program, but with less success in satisfying the urban groups whose interests collided with those of the agrarians. In 1885 the Birmingham *Chronicle* complained that the state government was in the hands of "old fogies," and added: "We want a Governor who knows that a smokestack in the mountains doesn't injure corn and cotton in the prairies." Edward A. O'Neal, who was governor from 1882 to 1886, also faced criticism for his support of railroad regulation and other reforms. Thomas Seay, who succeeded him, generally sided with the progressive faction, but managed to incur less unfavorable criticism than did his predecessors. Thus badly split, Alabama Democrats, like others, fell back upon the white-supremacy argument to reduce the threat of revolt.

Tennessee politics after redemption was marked by a similar cleavage within the supposedly united Democratic party. In the Volunteer State the division was between the cotton-planter area in the west whose spokesman was Senator Isham G. Harris, and the Whig-industrialist whose leader was Arthur S. Colyar, a Nashville publisher. Though for the most part the New South advocates held the reins of government, once, in 1882, the planters gained control by electing Alvin Hawkins to the governor's chair. They repudiated some of the state's bonds and established a railroad commission. Though this settlement did not last, Governor William B. Bates did manage to settle the debt issue and turned the party toward the economic development of the state.

In Kentucky a similar intraparty conflict developed and became so bitter that a governor was assassinated in a political struggle. There the issue was whether the state should extend assistance to the railroad interests—the Louisville and Nashville Railroad, which largely controlled the state government in the period—or whether, as advocated by agrarians, the state should regulate railroad activity. As agricultural prices fell in the 'eighties, special railway taxes and increasing freight rates led to the calling of a constitutional convention in 1890. After an extended struggle, the legislature in 1893 passed a law controlling railroads and explicitly defining the "extortion" of the railroads. Beginning in 1895, the Democratic offensive against both Republicans and the L & N was led by William Goebel, son of a German immigrant. The fight raged until 1899, when Goebel overcame the railroad opposition and captured the Democratic nomination in a move that split the party. After the vote, John Y. Brown, a friend of the railroads, was sworn in as governor, but the Assembly declared the vote fraudulent and gave the election to Goebel. On January 30, 1900, Goebel was shot as he approached the capitol in Frankfort, and he died on February 3. Though no one was ever convicted for the crime, people generally blamed the railroad officials. Goebel's assassination so shocked Kentuckians that a new railroad commission was empowered to control the railroads.

In Mississippi there was no bloodshed but there was deep-seated party faction. State politics from 1875 to 1900 was an almost ceaseless intraparty struggle for control of the single party; as elsewhere in the South, only an appeal to white supremacy would provide even superficial unity. Party division in Mississippi was not between planters and industrialists but between planters and poor farmers. Lacking coal, iron, and water power, Mississippi experienced only an embryonic industrial revolution in the period. Nonagricultural interests were centered in the railroads and in corporations exploiting the state's natural resources in lumber and oil. To serve these interests, Mississippi, like Georgia, had a triumvirate, composed of Lucius Q. C. Lamar, Edward C. Walthall, and James Z. George, all United States senators in the 'eighties. All three were corporation lawyers of the post-war generation. Lamar and Walthall represented railroad enterprise, while George enjoyed the largest corporate law practice in the state. During the period, only two men—John M. Stone and Robert Lowry—monopolized the governor's chair. They too were railroad lawyers, and like their colleagues elsewhere, resisted railroad regulation. They all sought financial and political alliance with Easterners, and thus alienated themselves from the farmers. Only seven of the seventeen Mississippi congressmen elected between 1876 and 1890 sympathized with farmer grievances. But the lower house of the state legislature was always dominated by agrarians, and the senate was not without its substantial minority. From these would come first the Populist and then the "Redneck" revolt which became important in the twentieth century.

Across the river in Arkansas the dominant Democratic forces also had confronted the problem of opposition from disgruntled agrarians. Native white government was re-established in 1874, after a bloody factional war, under Governor Augustus H. Garland. Though radicals were out, political differences continued to divide voters. Almost immediately following redemption, the small farmer element, organized politically as the Greenback Party and led by W. P. "Buck" Parks, challenged the conservatives. Though the regular Democrats maintained their hold upon the state's government, independent movements among farmers and small businessmen continued to harass the incumbents. Rufus K. Garland, brother of the redeemer governor, became the Greenback leader. He aspired to become the "Mahone of Arkansas" behind a coalition composed of those who disliked the conservative practice of catering to outsiders, and those who favored paper money. When such segments of the population were unable to achieve their aims through independent opposition parties, they formed farmers' organizations which became politically important in the Populist period.

In Louisiana the threat of agrarian revolt was buried under an astute party control which allied itself with conservatism and corruption. Many practices of the reconstruction era continued into the Democratic regime. Republican Governor Henry C. Warmoth, whose own political reputation could have been improved, expressed amazement at the lack of public morality he descried among Louisianans: "Everybody is demoralized down here," he charged. "Corruption is the fashion." Not only Warmoth but also many native state leaders followed the fashion. At the center of political power was the Louisiana State Lottery Company, whose managers reputedly had more political influence than the "Tweed ring in New York." The company pushed men into and out of office to protect its monopoly, and used the good name of Confederate hero Pierre G. T. Beauregard to enrich itself from the sale of tickets. Aided by lottery money, which went to friends of the company, Democrats ruled the state through the governor's unusually extensive appointive power. Not only did the chief executive appoint trustees of state institutions and other assistants, but he also named the governing bodies of each parish, which levied local taxes and wrote local ordinances; rural school boards, many judges, and all election registrars, who had power to admit or to exclude any individual from the voting lists. With a political stranglehold upon the state, conservative leaders befriended not only the lottery, but also outsiders who exploited the state's resources and controlled its economy. Small farmers in upstate Louisiana opposed the high-handed methods of the conservatives but they lacked the leadership other state agrarians enjoyed.

Texas "redeemers" differed little from the Democrats of other states. John H. Reagan, former Confederate Postmaster General, led an agrarian crusade from the beginning of the home-rule period. At the head of a farmer coalition, Reagan worked to free his state from its colonial status, and his weapon was regulation of railroads by state and federal governments. Despite the power of the railroad lobbyists, who bought legislators and officeholders, Texas farmers joined independent movements and in 1878 had won political victories on a Greenback-Labor ticket. When the independent movement declined in 1880, Texas protest to economic colonialism was channeled into farmers' organizations and the Populist crusade.

Thus in the years after the overthrow of the reconstruction governments, southern political activity displayed inner conflict rather than internal unity. And in every state one hotly debated issue arose—settlement of state debts incurred during the carpetbag era. In Virginia the question of state debts provided the basis for political activity; disagreements with West Virginia over the division of the state debt continued until 1919, when the two states reached a compromise settlement. West Virginia agreed to assume a debt of $14,500,000. Other states also had to face the problem of state debts. North Carolina's reconstruction debt amounted to over $13,000,000, and in 1879 the legislature repudiated all of it and funded the pre-war debt at less than 40 per cent. By compromising bonds issued before the war to aid railroads, the state succeeded in repudiating nearly 25 millions of indebtedness. South Carolina's total debt was never accurately estimated, for its carpetbag governments repudiated debts freely. In the end, the state had a debt of $7,000,000. Georgia repudiated over $9,000,000; Alabama's repudiation was over $13,000,000, while Florida's $4,000,000 was removed by the state supreme court without legislative action. Mississippi and Texas, both of which had pre-war records of debt repudiation, accepted their debts without attempting repudiation. Louisiana had nearly $50,000,000 in bonds which had been issued in aid of levees and railroads. The carpetbag regime attempted repudiation and refunding; after "redemption," a long struggle with bondholders in the courts resulted in a reduction to about $12,000,000. Arkansas repudiated about $13,000,000.

The total effect of these repudiations was to ruin the credit of the southern states—which they tended to regard as another evidence of outside attack upon the South. Northern and foreign bondholders formed associations to fight for repayment, but they were unable to collect. An exception was the state of South Dakota, which sued North Carolina in the United States Supreme Court and collected the difference between the face value and the refunded value of the southern state's bonds, but the Court refused to permit other states to become collection agencies for their citizens. Foreign bondholders constantly petitioned the State Department to take action against the southern states and the South's credit in Europe remained poor. For some time repudiation made northern capital hesitant about southern investments, but eventually the economy program of the Bourbons and the placidity of Southern labor conditions overcame their objections.

Southern "Bourbons," misnamed heirs of the legacy of unsuccessful war and reconstruction, welcomed northern capital into the New South and provided political institutions modeled after those of their northern allies. But despite their efforts at unity, political conflict continued to rage. The issues were local rather than national, and they reflected peculiar southern situations imposed by defeat, alien rule, and the ensuing debate about the nature of the New South. Political lines were not clearly drawn, but roughly divided between country and town, between planters and industrialists—or between planter and red-dirt farmer, and between friends of outside investors and southern chauvinists who preferred poverty to economic submission. All of these points of conflict emerged in the Populist campaigns of the 1890's.

3. SOUTHERN POPULISM AND PROGRESSIVISM

While southern businessmen and conservative politicians maintained an alliance with their counterparts in the East, the farmers of the South and West attempted to unite against their common enemy, colonial capitalism. In the South, carpetbag imperialists had seized control of government and economy and ruled through native white Democrats; in the West railroads exacted "all the traffic would bear" to oppress the farmers. Finding common ground in their agrarian complaints and railroad grievances, southern and western farmers joined forces to fight the last-ditch battle between agrarians and industrialists for the control of the national government. When they failed in 1896, American farmers accepted defeat; a century of internal agitation had come to an end and at last the results of the Civil War were indelibly inscribed into the national character.

The farmers, whether landowners or not, could point to very real grievances upon which to base their revolt. These classes suffered from the programs instigated by the new rulers of the South as well as from Republican control of the nation. In common with western farmers, the Southerners watched the panic of 1873 utterly disrupt land values so that for nearly thirty years lands would not sell. Cotton prices, moreover, went steadily down. As a result, banks would not take mortgages on lands, however excellent. Farmers seeking loans faced still another obstacle: the shortage of banks. Even in 1900 the southern banking system was inadequate to meet the needs of the region; there were fewer than

425 banks in the entire area and 123 counties in Georgia were entirely without banks. Then, in their debt-burdened condition, farmers demanded currency expansion which additional banks would have provided. In the thirty years after 1865 the amount of currency in circulation declined, while the population doubled. As a result, the constantly appreciating value of the dollar worked a hardship upon debtors. Also, rulers of the New South made a fetish of economy and refused to make appropriations from state funds for necessary services like roads and schools, all of which would serve the farmers. There was, then, real misery on southern farms in the 'eighties, which needed only leadership to break out in open revolt.

Throughout the South distressed farmers sought relief through the local Granges of the Patrons of Husbandry. By 1875 the South had over a thousand Granges. The Grangers did not form a separate party but expected to exert an influence upon individual politicians. Foresighted officeseekers espoused the Grange programs and promised to work for agrarian reforms. Martin Gary, Confederate brigadier and former secessionist, re-entered South Carolina politics with a program that combined white supremacy and farm relief. In Georgia Dr. William H. Felton, supported only by his politically acute wife and two small-town weekly newspapers, ran for Congress against Joseph E. Brown's Bourbon machine and won victories by attacks upon the "court-house rings" and the "developers of resources." In Kentucky a Granger-controlled legislature sent James B. Beck to the United States Senate. Elsewhere the Grangers made appreciable headway against the Bourbons. They did much to stimulate southern political activity, to educate illiterate farmers not only in reading and writing but also in new ways to farm, and to prepare the way for a greater farm revolt.

In 1875 an organization of farmers in Texas took the name of "Farmers' Alliance" and began to agitate against the land monopolists of the state. In 1880, after many vicissitudes, they formed the Grand State Alliance. The movement spread rapidly to other states. In Louisiana the Farmers' Union had obtained about 10,000 members when Dr. C. W. Macune, head of the Texas Alliance, proposed uniting the two groups in the National Farmers' Alliance and Co-operative Union of America. The Alliance proclaimed itself a business association, denied that it harbored political aspirations, and instead emphasized a "strong, solid, secret, and binding organization" to unite the "whole world of cotton raisers" for self-protection. At the same time another farmers' organization, the Agricultural Wheel, began in Arkansas and rolled over other states until it claimed 500,000 members. In 1889 the Wheel and the Alliance merged in the Farmers' and Laborers' Union of America and appealed for labor support. By 1890 the united body had over two million members. Paralleling this movement of the southern whites, the Colored Farmers' National Alliance and Co-operative Union aligned the Negro farmers with the general purposes and under the control of the organized white farmers.

In 1889 the Southern Alliance assembled in St. Louis in a joint meeting with the Northwest Alliance and the Knights of Labor. The three organizations failed to effect a national union, partly because northern farmers hesitated to enter an organization in which the more radical Southerners would be in a majority, in which secrecy was an important element, and from which Negroes were excluded; and partly because of divergent interests between the farmers of the two sections. Though the "makers of clothes were underfed" and the "makers of food were underclad," the producers found it difficult to work together.

Immediately after the St. Louis meeting the Southern Alliance began to expand its services to include the dissemination of scientific agricultural information, arrangements for co-operative marketing of produce, and establishment of state "exchanges" whereby the members could obtain credit. The Georgia Exchange saved farmers $200,000 in fertilizer alone. The Texas Alliance established an auspicious Exchange in Dallas to market cotton and grain and to purchase farm implements at a discount; an unwise credit system proved fatal to the scheme. In 1888 the Alliance won a victory over the trusts when, by united action, a price rise in jute bagging, used to wrap cotton bales, was defeated. All of these activities met opposition—even to the point of sabotage—from merchants, bankers, manufacturers, wholesalers; the railroads discriminated against participants. As a result, the co-operative features of the Alliance failed to accomplish permanent relief for the farmers' ills. With failure meeting their efforts in business, the Alliance men turned to politics.

Although northern farmers could see no hope in either of the major parties and wished to launch a third party, southern men preferred to work through the Democratic party. In South Carolina Ben Tillman, ex-Confederate, demanded the overthrow of the ruling factions within the party, and in North Carolina Colonel Leonidas L. Polk, later president of the Southern Alliance, launched a movement to force legislative reform. In these states the farmers scored successes. In 1888 Tillman's followers won a majority of the legislature and in North Carolina the farmers forced the election of an Alliance man as speaker of the House. In 1890 Tillman campaigned for the Democratic gubernatorial nomination against the low-country planters and businessmen, and the farmers won complete control of the party. In Georgia the Alliance, led by red-headed Thomas E. Watson, forced candidates to pledge support of farmers' demands. The Alliance also gained control of the party in Texas, Arkansas, and Tennessee. In all of the states, candidates of the farmers won control of the legislatures; they sent forty-four men to Congress, gained the support of several senators, and elected Governors Tillman in South Carolina, William J. Northen in Georgia, and James S. Hogg in Texas.

In their states the southern Alliance men showed less devotion to economy than had their predecessors. They made more appropriations for education, and South Carolina established an agricultural college in Calhoun's old home. Other states established railroad commissions to regulate rates and restricted the activities of banks, though they did nothing to relieve credit conditions. In South Carolina the state took over the control of liquor and created a state dispensary system designed to regulate liquor consumption. For the nation the Southern Alliance proposed a "subtreasury" plan which would enable farmers to create currency based upon produce in the same manner in which the National Banking system enabled bankers to circulate currency based upon government bonds. Under the subtreasury plan, farmers would deposit their crops in government warehouses (adjuncts of the United States Treasury, called "subtreasuries") and would receive certificates of deposit equal to a maximum of eighty per cent of the value of the produce. These certificates would circulate as legal tender, thus relieving the acute shortage of circulating medium. To the intense alarm of conservatives North and South, who controlled the money system, Tom Watson attempted to force Congress to discuss a measure to establish these subtreasuries.

As the elections of 1892 approached, the Farmers' Alliances of the northwestern states prepared to launch a third party. As Ignatius Donnelly, Minnesota farmer-politician, explained: "We propose to wipe the Mason and Dixon line out of our geography; to wipe the color line out of politics." Southerners, however, had captured the Democratic party in many states and were unwilling to desert the party which had secured white supremacy. Any division of the white vote between Democrats and Populists would create the danger of a return to Negro domination. Southern Alliance Democrats hoped to be able to commit the national party to agrarian principles, but the nominating convention in Chicago completely ignored the Southerners and renominated ex-President Grover Cleveland. When the leaders of the Alliance endorsed the Populist party, many Southerners deserted the Alliance to remain with the Democrats. But some Southerners organized Populist tickets, published Peoples' Party newspapers, and co-operated with the northwesterners. The Populists, who had nominated an ex-Confederate, Virginia's General James G. Field, for vice-president, made the mistake of sending ex-Union generals into the South to arouse enthusiasm for the third party movement.

In the elections the Populists, "Jeffersonian Democrats," and regular Democrats appealed to the Negroes to stay away from the polls. In every district in which there was a possibility that Alliance men might win, the ruling groups used the same tactics that had hitherto preserved the states from Negro control. In Lowndes County, Alabama, for example, the conservative candidate for governor received 2272 votes to 261 for his "Jeffersonian Democrat" opponent, but the final returns showed the vote to be 4995 to 361. Such methods throughout the Black Belt defeated the farmers' candidates. In addition to fraudulent returns, the Bourbons used intimidation, proscription, and actual violence to prevent the election of Alliance men. They shamelessly purchased Negro orators and Negro votes, provided entertainment for Negro voters, and even imported Negroes from adjoining states for use on election day. As a result, the South remained solidly Democratic, Cleveland carried the South, and conservatives replaced the farmers in control of most of its states.

By 1894 the "fusion" of Populists and Republicans had grown in strength throughout the South. Tillman, still at the head of the Democratic party in South Carolina, announced his candidacy for the United States Senate as an opponent of Cleveland. In Georgia, Tom Watson, defeated in 1892 by fraudulent Negro votes, sought to return to Congress on the Populist ticket. "Two years ago we were fed upon the ambrosia of Democratic expectations," Watson told the Georgia Populist convention; "today we are gnawing the cobs of Democratic reality." Similarly, in Alabama the bitter conflict between regular and "Jeffersonian" Democrats was repeated. But again the Bourbons resorted to fraud and force. Tillman won again in South Carolina. Watson was defeated in Georgia, but the Populists gained in the legislature. One Populist was elected to Congress from Alabama, but the Bourbons retained control of the state. The greatest victory for the farmer-dissenters came in North Carolina, where the Populists chose a United States Senator, four congressmen, a majority of the state senate, and a large number of the lower house. Republicans elected the other United States Senator, two congressmen, and, in alliance with the Populists, controlled the state assembly. Other Southern states sent Republican, Populist, or Alliance Democratic candidates to Congress.

Experience with Populism soon convinced many Southerners that a division of the Democratic vote meant Negro and Republican rule. The fusion government in North Carolina allowed Negroes to hold office, and riots resulted. The Democratic party offered itself as the only solution to the problem of maintaining white supremacy, and this by the methods of fraud, intimidation, and violence. Southern Alliance men, no longer daring to risk a third-party movement, determined to capture the national Democratic party. As the election of 1896 approached, Southerners endorsed proposals for the free coinage of silver and prepared to defeat the Cleveland element in the party. When the Democrats assembled at Chicago, Southerners cheered William Jennings Bryan. Only the diehard southern Populists were discontented. When the Populist party endorsed Bryan but nominated Tom Watson for the vice-presidency, southern farmers returned to the Democratic fold. Thus the conservatives, North and South, swallowed up their agrarian opponents, and Populism was all but forgotten. Its defeat was the real significance of the election of 1896. Populism was the mainstay of the agrarian revolt; with it gone, agrarian revolt was dead. The election of 1896 was the last aggressive stand of the American farmer against capitalist industry; his failure determined the character of the America of the twentieth century. Populist leaders were discouraged and broken. "No soldier of the Southern Confederacy carried away from Appomattox a heavier heart than I took with me into my enforced retirement," Watson declared. And he was right in comparing 1896 to Appomattox: far more than the surrender of Lee, the election of William McKinley marked the conclusion of the Civil War.

4. THE NEGRO IN POLITICS

The fundamental cause for the failure of Populism in the South was the fear that the Negro might be restored to control. The Populist attempt to unite the small farmers of both races into a solid organization of the oppressed against their oppressors frightened the conservatives. During the campaigns of 1888 to 1898, both Bourbons and Alliance men used Negro voters; and in North Carolina where the Populists had fused with Republicans, over one thousand Negroes held office. But the Bourbons, controlling the electoral machinery, made more effective use of the black man. They bought or intimidated the Negro, or fraudulently reported their votes. So long as they could control him, they had no objection to the Negro in politics.

But there were difficulties involved in the Negro vote. One of these was the ethical and economic cost of corrupt politics. "It is true we win these elections, but at heavy cost," reported a Louisiana Democratic newspaper, "and by the use of methods repugnant to our idea of political honesty and which must, in time, demoralize the people of Louisiana." An Alabama Democrat complained of the high cost of fraud: "We want to be relieved of purchasing the Negroes to carry elections. I want cheaper votes." Another difficulty was that the chief political struggle was not between whites and blacks but between competing white groups. Southern whites were divided—as in the post-reconstruction era—between the well-to-do and the "red-necks," and each side attempted to maneuver the Negro vote into its camp. It was not Negro control that the white farmers feared, but domination by Bourbons living in predominantly black counties. If the Negro were disqualified, it would reduce the voting strength of the Black Belts. White farmers therefore took the lead in demanding disfranchisement, not so much as a weapon against Negroes as against their white opponents.

The move to disfranchise the Negro in the South was the result of Henry Cabot Lodge's "Force Bill." In 1890 the bill to require federal supervision of national elections in the states passed the House of Representatives. Although it failed in the Senate, it served to remind Southerners that they were playing with fire in using Negroes in state and local elections. Supervised elections might result in Republican or Negro rule. Everywhere the Bourbons took warning and sought some more permanent means of easing the Negroes out of politics. If, in addition, they might disfranchise the discontented farmers, they might rule more securely.

Experiments with new electoral devices began in Mississippi in 1890. A new constitution prescribed a residence of two years in the state and one year in the voting district as a requirement for voting. In addition, the constitution required voters to pay a poll tax of two or three dollars eight months before the election. These provisions, bearing equally upon white and black, served effectively to disfranchise the poorer and more migratory members of both races. But in addition, the constitution provided the "understanding clause": the voter must be able to read a section of the constitution or be able to give a reasonable interpretation of a clause when read to him. Since the election officials were the judges of either the degree of literary skill or the reasonableness of the interpretation, they could exclude large numbers of Negroes from the polls. This program became known as the "Mississippi Plan."

In 1895 South Carolina amended her constitution after the Mississippi model, including the understanding clause. "Some people have said there is fraud in this understanding clause," Ben Tillman declared. "There is no particle of fraud or illegality in it. It is just simply showing partiality, perhaps, or discriminating. Ah, you grin." But because there was opposition to the clause, the South Carolina plan included a provision that illiterates who had paid taxes on $300 worth of property would be admitted to the suffrage. A list of crimes which disqualified voters contained those that were most common among Negroes, such as bigamy, adultery, wife-beating, and larceny.

In 1898 Louisiana changed her constitution by adding residence requirements, literacy tests, and poll taxes as prerequisites for voting. Since an honest administration of these provisions would disfranchise many whites, the constitution provided that any persons, or the sons or grandsons of any person, who was eligible to vote in any state on January 1, 1867, could be placed upon a permanent registration roll. In 1900 North Carolina adopted similar devices, and the next year Alabama and Virginia followed. In 1908 Georgia amended her constitution, and in 1910 the new state of Oklahoma, joining the Union and the Solid South at the same time, drafted a constitution that contained a "grandfather clause" which would have permanently permitted illiterate whites to vote, while permanently disfranchising illiterate Negroes. In 1915 the United States Supreme Court declared the Oklahoma provisions unconstitutional.

Ostensibly designed to prevent Negroes from voting while paying lip service to the Fourteenth and Fifteenth Amendments to the United States Constitution, these new constitutional changes in southern states effectively disfranchised white voters. In 1910 the Atlanta *Constitution,* a vigorous opponent of its state's action, declared that "this new registration law was deliberately devised to disfranchise the country vote— the farmers of Georgia . . ."; and the president of the Alabama constitutional convention admitted that "the true philosophy of the movement was to establish restricted suffrage, and to place the power of government in the hands of the intelligent and virtuous." Mississippi's constitution of 1890 not only disfranchised the Negroes, but also put a majority of the state's white population under the control of a minority in the Black Belt counties. So loud was the outcry that the constitutional convention decided not to submit the document to the electorate for ratification. Instead, the convention merely declared the new constitution the law of the land. That course of action was followed by all the southern states except Alabama. There the white counties rejected the new constitution, while Black Belt counties adopted it by majorities sometimes greater than the total white voting population. But the new constitutional changes produced the results their framers intended—drastic reductions in southern electorates. In Mississippi an electorate of over 250,000 was reduced to less than 77,000, and other states witnessed similar results. Voting in the South was regarded as a privilege, and an oligarchy of the "right people" ruled the region.

The exclusion of Negroes from political activity resulted in further discriminations in social and economic life. Segregation, or legal separation of the races, became the pattern of Southern society. By legislation, states and cities prohibited Negroes from residing in certain districts, and deprived them of equal accommodations on common carriers. Such laws were known as "Jim Crow" laws, from a derogatory euphemism for the Negro. Beginning in 1887 in Florida, separate coach laws spread over the South, and soon legal separation for waiting rooms, street cars, courts, schools, hotels, theater entrances, and hospitals appeared. The new Negro codes regulated race relations more completely than the Black Codes of reconstruction days had ever contemplated. Even the Supreme Court co-operated in the universal abandonment of the Negro. In 1896, in *Plessy v. Ferguson,* the Court admitted that legislation was "powerless to eradicate racial instincts" and laid the foundations of the "separate but equal" doctrine for the justification of legal segregation. Two years later, in *Williams v. Mississippi,* the Court accepted the Mississippi Plan for legal disfranchisement of the Negro.

As in the high court, in local tribunals the administration of justice bore heavily upon the unprotected Negro. Economic pressure and a lack of educational facilities drove the blacks to commit many petty crimes. White judges, many of the politicians with unreasoning devotion to "white supremacy," dealt harshly with Negro culprits brought before them. For long there was a common belief that the justice meted to the Negro differed from that given the white man. Although the names of Negroes were included on lists of eligibles for jury duty, such names were never drawn for panels and Negroes were tried before juries of their white "peers." Many unfortunate Negroes, accused of crimes against the whites, were not brought to trial at all but were lynched—another name for mob attack upon a single person or small group of persons assumed guilty and immediately executed. Such popular justice reached a peak during the disfranchisement proceedings of the 'nineties. In that decade lynchings averaged 187 per year, while a decade later the average had dropped to 92. Though many Southerners deeply regretted the conduct of their more unruly neighbors, lynchings continued into the twentieth century. That illustrated the difficulty southern Populists faced in attempting to unite the races on a common political platform.

The Populist movement resulted not only in Negro disfranchisement but in the complete domination of the Democratic party in the South. The futility of casting opposition votes and the foregone conclusion that the Democrats would win the elections led voters to remain at home on election days. But vestiges of the farmers' revolt remained and the rural population could be aroused to support candidates who made the right appeals. Thus the Democratic party witnessed frequent internal struggles between the heirs of the Populists and the allies of the Bourbons. Representatives of the "wool hat boys," the "red-necks," and generally the poorer classes of the southern population arose to campaign for the Democratic nomination against politicians who represented the merchant-planters, the bankers, and the industrialists.

In politics as in economics, the generation of struggle resulted in the victory of the New South. By 1900 the white farmer and the Negro had been effectively disfranchised and the Bourbons were in control. Toward the close of the century several events symbolized the victory. First, the defeat of Bryan in 1896 had indicated that farmers everywhere were waging a losing fight against industry. In that year, it was freely asserted, the southern Bourbons "voted for Bryan and prayed for McKinley." Evidently their prayers were answered, and the new administration, beginning amid returning prosperity, gave new assurances to business. The Spanish-American War brought new evidence that the rupture of the nation in the Civil War had been welded together in the industrial fires. Fitzhugh Lee and "Fighting Joe" Wheeler, veterans of the Confederacy, became major generals, and sons of Confederate veterans wore the blue uniform of the United States. To the imperialism that followed the war the South gave hearty assent.

The Culture of a Colony

1. The South Surrenders

AS the economic and political conflict continued between advocates of
the Old and New South, it was also waged in the realm of culture:
religion, education, journalism, and literature. And in those aspects of
southern life the struggle was more significant than elsewhere. While the
South had never professed to be a geographic entity, Southerners had
boasted of its civilization and its way of life. Fifteen years of defeat,
poverty, and frustration had threatened the old order. The tone of Southern life was lower after 1876 than it had been before 1860, for the planting
gentry who had set the Old South's standards were broken and scattered.
New men, worshiping strange gods, became bellwethers for southern
fashions. The squirearchy had paid allegiance—albeit at times hypocritically
—to a philosophy which contained essential values and which made the
South a distinctive civilization. Admirers of those values did not surrender
easily to the imitators who would make the South a cultural appendage of
the North.

The struggle for a separate civilization had been waged even
before the war. In 1834 in the first issue of the *Southern Literary
Messenger*, the editor had demanded, "Are we to be doomed forever to
a kind of vassalage to our northern neighbors?" He proposed that
Southerners "buckle on our armor and assert our mental independence."
In the New South, with the issue drawn between the two traditions of
Davis and the diehard rebels and Lee and the collaborators, cultural
independence was all the more important. And as in economics and in
politics, the New triumphed over the Old. In the last quarter of the
century the South was a cultural colony drawing its intellectual and
literary values from the victorious East. "The South, under defeat, lost

her philosophy," an English visitor observed. Yankee ways of living had their inevitable effect upon southern culture. Young men growing up during the discouraging days of reconstruction began to adopt the standards of the businessmen and politicians of the North and to deny the principles for which their fathers had fought. "I rejoice in the failure of the Confederacy," said young Woodrow Wilson in 1880. "Even the damnable cruelty and folly of reconstruction were to be preferred to help-less independence." Methodist Bishop Atticus G. Haygood of Georgia criticized the croakers and groaners who had misled the South. "Above all things," he said, "we need to have done with the solid South." North Carolina novelist Walter Hines Page, tired of the adoration by older men of the "mythic beauties of a mythic past," cynically remarked in 1881 that "what North Carolina most needs is a few first-class funerals." Politicians began to take up the cry. Ex-Confederate General and Georgia Senator Benjamin H. Hill declared that Southerners should not waste time and effort in "defense of theories and systems, however valued in their day, which have been swept down by the moving avalanche of actual events. We can live neither in nor by the defeated past."

Against such heresy the advocates of the Old South stood aghast. Jefferson Davis, his popularity enhanced by a stupid Northern policy that martyrized him, never surrendered to the siren song of progress. In speeches, magazine articles, and letters, he declared that the cause of the Confederacy was the cause of constitutional liberty. The publication in 1881 of his *Rise and Fall of the Southern Confederacy* was the last important Southern work of constitutional interpretation. "Until I can be convinced that we were rebels, traitors, and warring against the compact of our Fathers," he declaimed, "it will not be possible for me to join the throng who hurrah for the pillagers and house burners who invaded our homes." Many confirmed ex-Confederates agreed with their president. Among them, General Jubal A. Early never furled the flag of his re-sistance. "If ever I repudiate, disown, or apologize for the cause for which Lee fought, and Jackson died, may the lightning of Heaven blast me," he said in 1889, and added that "the Confederate who has deserted since the war is infinitely worse than one who deserted during the war." Among the other intransigent Rebels were Robert Toombs of Georgia, who regretted only the deaths and the defeat; Alfred T. Bledsoe, editor of the *Southern Review* at Baltimore; the Reverend Robert L. Dabney, Pres-byterian minister and professor at Union Theological Seminary in Virginia; and Dr. Benjamin M. Palmer, Presbyterian leader of Louisiana. Dr. Dabney, fearing that "the Yankees have killed that which made the South the South," advocated emigration. "Then let the Yankees keep the blighted soil, with the miserable free negroes, and despotize as they please." He did not emigrate, but neither did he bow the knee to the conqueror. His *Defense of Virginia* was the last serious apology for slavery. Bledsoe and Palmer agreed with the fiery Virginia theologian on the righteousness of the Old South's theories and philosophy.

But the voices of the unrepentant and the unreconstructed were puny indeed amid the clamor of "Yankeeism." Henry W. Grady and Daniel

A. Tompkins were but the better known among the New South's industrial spokesmen. Everywhere there was insistent demand for more imitation of the North and its victorious ways. In 1877 Louisville editor Henry Watterson remarked that the "ambition of the South is to out-Yankee the Yankee." Four years later even Mississippians joined the parade; a Vicksburg editor said that "we are in favor of the South, from the Potomac to the Rio Grande, being thoroughly and permanently Yankeeized." Mark Twain sensed the character of the New South: "Brisk men, energetic of movement and speech; the dollar their god, how to get it their religion." Ministers of Christian denominations, perhaps feeling the competition, also remarked the new values of the South. A North Carolina minister in an open letter to his colleagues in 1887 warned that "the standard of character erected by the blatant portion of the New South—that portion that reviles the Old South—is the *brazen* standard of money making."

Against progress, industrialism, and wealth the defenders of the agrarian ways of the Old South fought a hopeless action. Southerners eagerly dethroned the old idols, denied the faith of their fathers, and gloried in their colonial status. By 1889 an observer could declare that "society becomes yearly more and more alike North and South." By the end of the century it had become clear that the surrender at Appomattox was not the defeat of the Old South but that the cultural surrender which followed it did make southern independence a Lost Cause.

2. THE SOUTHERN CHURCHES

If there were sustained resistance to northern domination over Southern standards, it came from the southern churches. Their independent existence was directly threatened by the wave of Yankeeism. Southern churchmen, many of them Confederate military veterans, continued the struggle from behind their pulpits. In the last quarter of the nineteenth century, the centers of southern sentiment were the religious organizations of the South. Their primary efforts were directed toward maintaining their ecclesiastical independence, and they made use of affronted southern pride and the legend of the Lost Cause. The Davis tradition therefore met congenial reception in religious congregations. The challenge of social reform did not.

In the colonial and revolutionary period southern popular churches had been agencies of social reform. Methodists, Baptists, and Presbyterians of the frontier and the back country had waged incessant war upon the Established Church. In the early national period these same churches had fostered democracy, denounced aristocratic controls, and often excoriated slavery. But the beginnings of the antislavery crusade had brought about a change. As members of the popular sects rose in economic and social position, the churches tended to become more conservative. The disestablishment of the Episcopal Church was quickly followed by the practical establishment of the other churches. Each of them came to have a vested interest in the maintenance of the established order. They became supporters of slavery, their ministers accepted the Biblical arguments for the peculiar institution, and they withdrew from communion with the churches of the North.

In the post-war period the churches continued to give spiritual sanction to the existing social order. The Bourbon in politics was paralleled by the Bourbon in the church: a conservative social philosophy engendered adherence to an orthodox theology. With the degradation of southern leaders following the defeat, the Protestant ministry gained stature among southern masses and kept them under control. When the churches dealt with social matters at all, their voices sang the song of the New South. An evangelist might preach Salisbury's need for a cotton mill, but no evangelist advocated improved conditions in the mill villages. Southern churches steadfastly resisted the "social gospel" which was gaining ground in the North. They ignored the social problems of the Negro, the sharecropper, and the mill worker. Church papers often became strong defenders of the trusts.

Instead of dealing with social problems, southern churches confined themselves to preaching the need for individual redemption. The search for personal salvation directed attention from the crying need for social reform. The church devoted more time to snatching "brands from the burning" than they did to putting out the fire. Sin was a personal matter and the exorcising of personal sins occupied the churchmen's major attention.

Though southern churches were generally orthodox, each denomination had its special brand of revealed truth. Methodist, Baptist, Presbyterian, and Episcopal churches agreed on ignoring social problems but differed violently with each other on the means of individual salvation. Baptists insisted upon immersion, Presbyterians upon the Westminster Confession, Methodists upon a special doctrine of holiness and sanctification, and Episcopalians relied upon apostolic succession. All believed in the Virgin Birth, in the plenary verbal inspiration of the Scriptures, in immortality, and in the physical existence of Heaven and Hell—doctrines which came to be known as the Fundamentals. Each, however, taught the exclusiveness of its own doctrines.

Religion in the New South was predominantly Christian. There were a few Jewish congregations in each state, chiefly in the urban centers, and some disorganized Unitarians, but no other non-Christian faiths. In addition, southerners were overwhelmingly Protestant. The eight southern states east of the Mississippi comprised the most completely Protestant area in the Western Hemisphere. Roman Catholic congregations numbered only a small fraction of the total churches. With the exception of Kentucky, where Protestants totaled 80 per cent of the church membership, in southern states east of the Mississippi over 96 per cent were Protestant. Louisiana was the only southern state in which Protestants were in a minority. In 1870, for example, Georgia had 1,369 Baptist, 134 Presbyterian, and 1,248 Methodist churches, but only 14 Roman Catholic communions. Only Kentucky, Louisiana, and Maryland could count over 100 Roman Catholic churches.

Among all churches in the South, growth after the Civil War was phenomenal. From 1870 to 1906 the census showed that Southern Baptists increased the number of their congregations five hundred per cent from just over 8,000 to almost 40,000; Methodists jumped from 10,000 to 32,000 churches; Presbyterians grew from 2,500 to 5,700 groups; and Episcopalians increased from nearly 800 to almost 2,000 churches.

Along with revivalistic increases in membership, southern ecclesiastical development in the period was colored by a continuing struggle for denominational independence of Yankee encroachments. Sectional schism had first appeared in the evangelical denominations, and it hung on longer there than elsewhere. Southerners could not prevent northern control of their state governments and of their economic resources, but they waged holy war to keep their churches independent. Yankee prelates attempted to extend their ecclesiastical domain over the South as a means of political and moral control. "A united church extending from the Lakes to the Gulf will be the strongest bond of a restored nationality," ran one northern Methodist editorial, and another proclaimed that "a subjugate people have no . . . right to apply their peculiar moral ideas." Sometimes northern clerics seized southern churches and their property by force. Northern missionaries regarded the South as "a far more important . . . theater of Christian benevolent operations than all foreign nations put together," and pressed southward to establish schools, churches, and religious journals. Such imperialistic efforts succeeded only in confirming the southern bodies in their separation. Until they too went down in the general surrender, southern churches resisted northern invasion. Once again an outside attack had hardened southern sentiment into divergent nationalism.

Presbyterians, who had split along sectional lines in 1861, remained divided despite earnest efforts of Yankee reconcilers like Henry J. Van Dyke of Brooklyn. Opposition to northern requests for a "fraternal friendship" was led by Dr. Benjamin M. Palmer and Dr. Robert L. Dabney, who feared it would lead to reunion of the denomination. In 1870 at the General Assembly in Louisville, Dabney spoke eloquently against fusion. He could not, he said, "forgive these people, who have invaded our country, burned our cities, destroyed our homes, slain our young men, and spread desolation and ruin over our land!" Largely through the efforts of Dabney and Palmer, the fusion attempt failed.

In other Protestant denominations, sectional patriotism also became religious duty. Along with the Presbyterians, Baptists and Methodists had divided before the war, proclaiming that slavery was the fundamental reason for their action. After emancipation they found other justification for remaining independent. Southern Baptists in associational meetings voted unanimously for continued division, listing new grievances. They complained that the northern Baptist Home Mission society had received permission from the national government to seize Southern Baptist property. Southern Methodists also asserted their determination to maintain a separate existence. Bishops of the South declared that "whatever cause had been lost, that of Southern Methodism survived." Up to 1900 only the Episcopal Church among major denominations had successfully reunited after a wartime separation.

Northern clerical carpetbaggers hardened determination among southern whites, but among Negroes they quickly took control. Missionaries turned their attentions to the freedmen and established schools and colleges for Negroes in the South. Until 1880 northern churchmen provided about the only education the freedmen received. Seeing the great inroads the Yankees were making among the Negroes, Southern churchmen tried to establish separate organizations they could control, but with little success. Negroes rushed to join northern denominations. Southern Methodists, for example, claiming 208,000 Negro members in 1860, could count only 49,000 six years later. Northern Methodist bishops like Matthew Simpson, Davis W. Clark, and Gilbert Haven regarded proselyting in the South as an essential element in the reconstruction. As their religious as well as their political mentors, freedmen seemed to prefer northern churchmen to their former masters. As spiritual disfranchisement did not seem feasible, segregated churches appeared, with the Negro churches oriented northward.

By 1900 southern churches were separated from their northern brethren, and also from their colored southern brethren. The dual segregation tended to intensify the conservatism of southern religious leaders and to justify their defense of the established order. But southern religion also suffered from the poverty and the educational difficulties that beset the entire region. This, coupled with the fear of outside control —born of a real threat during and after reconstruction—created a closed mind which rejected the prevailing theological trends of the day. Ecumenicism, higher criticism of the Bible, and Darwinism, which affected theological conclusions elsewhere, were largely ignored in the South if for no other reason than that they prevailed in Yankeedom. A new mental blockade was thrown around the South by its religionists. Southern preachers catered to the ignorance and prejudices of their flocks and any new interpretation of revealed truth was labeled "Modernism" and thereby condemned. Several professors in southern denominational colleges, notably Alexander Winchell of Vanderbilt, James Woodrow of South Carolina Presbyterian Seminary, and Crawford H. Toy of the Southern Baptist Theological Seminary, lost their positions for espousing the views of Darwin and Lyell, which seemed to conflict with the Fundamentals.

Southern sectionalism, which had begun as a defense of constitutional liberties and human rights, now found its final resting place among strange bedfellows—the southern churches. The South, once a land of broad intellectual liberalism, became the home of an alien Puritanism and, strangely, was ridiculed for its piety by New England critics. States and communities passed "blue laws," and the region was widely known as the "Bible Belt." Southern churches, speaking for the common man, exerted a powerful influence for Southernism.

3. EDUCATION IN THE SOUTH

While southern churches were closing their doors to the winds of new social and theological thought, southern education was at its lowest ebb. The poor state of southern schools had its inevitable result in all aspects of southern life. The ante-bellum South, inspired by the Jacksonian democratic awakening, had adopted the idea of free public education. By 1829 every southern state except South Carolina had a state educational system, with county boards or supervisors. Rural conditions, plus the planter tradition that every man should educate his own children, kept the systems from developing, but the idea was there. Indeed, southern schools in general were in better condition in 1860 than at any time before 1900. Reconstruction regimes in southern states talked about public education but did little except to put the public schools into new state constitutions and to make provisions for Negro education.

Public schools did not prosper in the reconstruction era. Finance and administration were beset by inadequate legislation passed hastily by ill-informed carpetbag governments. Fraud and misappropriation of schools funds characterized reconstruction education. In the 1870's over $1,500,000 in school appropriations was diverted to other purposes in Virginia, and other states had similar experience. Because of shortages in funds, public schools temporarily closed in 1872 in Georgia and in South Carolina, and the following year in Alabama. Public education also suffered from racial conflict. In 1873 and 1874, when the Civil Rights bill was under discussion in Congress, many southern whites advocated dismantling the state schools. As one Virginia county expressed it, "should the civil rights bill, or any bill providing for mixed schools, be passed by Congress, the white people of the county will, with one voice, say, 'Away, away with the public school system.'" Southern schools were also forced to bear the burden of poorly qualified supervisors and teachers, as well as low wages. "We have been working with dull tools in order to save the cost of a grindstone," said Henry Ruffner, superintendent of education in Virginia. Furthermore, there was the almost hopeless task of educating the freedmen, who were illiterate. These factors weakened southern education throughout the period, and public schools fought for their own existence.

When "redeemers" resumed control of southern states, education presented one of their more pressing challenges. Until 1900, however, education failed to develop as its supporters hoped, and the most important cause was general poverty and a resulting scarcity of taxable property. The Bourbons were not hostile to education and did all they could in the face of debt and depression. In 1880 Mississippi, where the assessed valuation of taxable property was $110,628,129, appropriated $830,704 for education, at the rate of 7½ mills; New York, with $2,651,-940,000 in property, appropriated $10,412,378 for education, at the rate of 4 mills. Thirteen southern states had less taxable wealth between them than did New York alone; the thirteen expended a total of $7,132,651 on education, or over $3 million less than did New York. And still they did more with what they had than the Empire State did. In 1884 Jabez L. M. Curry, the South's leading educational statesman, cited a mass of statistics on taxable wealth and educational appropriations in the South, and concluded, "What the South has done for free education is marvelous."

WASHINGTON AND LEE UNIVERSITY. In 1865, following the surrender at Appomattox, Robert E. Lee became president of Washington College in Virginia. There he turned his back upon the Lost Cause and looked to a New South. Eschewing the classical curriculum, President Lee established courses in journalism, revived engineering, and sought to impart a vocational and practical education. The college, which added the Confederate General's name to its own, thus marked the way to the New South and also to the South's educational renaissance.

But it was a pitifully feeble effort. In 1880 the average annual expenditure for each enrolled pupil ranged from 87¢ in North Carolina to $5.56 in Delaware, with only five states spending $2 or more. Of northern states, only three spent less than $5 per child. These facts were reflected in the extremely high illiteracy rates in the South. In 1889, 37 per cent of adult southerners were illiterate, and in eight Southern states the rate of adult illiteracy was over 40 per cent. Most of these were freedmen; 75 per cent of southern Negroes were illiterate. One observer reported that the balance of power in all southern states was held by illiterates unable to read a ballot.

In the crisis, philanthropic agencies offered assistance to the cause of southern education. The first of a number of wealthy men to aid the South was George Peabody, a London banker born in Massachusetts. In 1867 Peabody placed $2,100,000 in the hands of trustees to be used for "the promotion and encouragement of intellectual, moral, or industrial education among the young of the more destitute portion" of the southern states. "This I give to the suffering South," he said, "for the good of the country." Dr. Barnas Sears, President of Brown University, became the general agent of the trustees. Sears traveled over the South, attempting to arouse the people to the need for schools. To the trustees, the agent reported in favor of aiding public rather than private schools, of supporting normal schools, and of assisting in forming associations of teachers. Thanks to the activities of the Peabody trustees, a new desire for schools sprang up in the South. With this development, the trustees devoted their funds almost exclusively to teacher-training. The George Peabody College for Teachers was established at Nashville and became the leading normal school of the South. In the thirty years between 1867 and 1897 the trustees distributed nearly $2,000,000 in the southern states.

In 1881, upon the death of Dr. Sears, the trustees chose Dr. J. L. M. Curry as general agent. Curry was a native of Alabama, a member of the United States and Confederate Congresses, a Baptist minister, and a professor in the University of Richmond. His rare combination of qualities enabled him to obtain a hearing throughout the South. Until his death in 1903, Curry did more than any other single man to further education "from the Potomac to the Rio Grande."

Another important educational philanthropy was the fund established by John F. Slater of Norwich, Connecticut, in 1882, for the education of Negroes. Under the direction of Georgia Methodist Bishop A. G. Haygood, Slater funds went to 35 southern schools and colleges for freedmen, especially those emphasizing manual and vocational training. Northern churches, particularly Congregationalists and northern Methodists, also worked to raise educational standards among the Negroes. In 1889 the Atlanta *Constitution* reported that "more money has been spent by Northern men for collegiate education for negroes in Atlanta alone than any six Southern states have given to collegiate education for white boys. The Northern Methodist Church alone is spending more money in the South for higher education than all the Southern States combined give to their colleges."

But the problem was too big for private philanthropy alone. In the 1880's there was strong sentiment for national government aid to education, which would have been of particular assistance to the South. The most persistent effort to tap the national treasury to improve the schools was the Blair Bill, submitted by New Hampshire Republican Senator Henry W. Blair. The first Blair Bill, introduced in December, 1881, provided for the appropriation of $105,000,000 from the national government, to be distributed over a ten-year period, on the basis of illiteracy. There were four Blair education bills in the decade, differing on details of administration and the amount appropriated. Only one bill passed in the Senate, and none of them ever came up for a vote in the House.

With the most illiterates, the South would have received at least two thirds of the proposed assistance. Southern educators almost solidly approved Blair's scheme, but politicians and editors were divided. Most support in the South came from the "redeemer" or Bourbon group, who were dedicated to industrial development and alliance with the East; opposition generally arose among the agrarian-minded who emphasized the traditional Democratic virtues of states' rights and low taxes. Some opposed the "useless, impractical, mischievous, and dishonest attempt to teach literary arts to all negroes," to use the words of the Reverend Robert L. Dabney of Virginia. Other Old South spokesmen objected to Blair's plan because they feared—with reason—that it would mean federal control of education. Congress needed to supervise education in the South, said Republican Albion W. Tourgée in an article published in the *North American Review* in 1881, because textbooks prescribed by Southern authorities "openly and ably defend the right of secession, and extol the Confederacy and its leaders. . . ." National aid to education, with Congressional supervision, was necessary, Tourgée concluded, because it would destroy the "sentiment in which the doctrine of State rights is grounded." But a main reason for southern opposition to the Blair bills was the hostility aroused by the patronizing attitude of the Yankees.

After 1890 the Blair plan was no longer a political issue, but Southern education was in as dire a plight as ever. Southerners were left to solve the problem by themselves and finance their education out of their poverty. As a result, there was little improvement in southern schools before 1900. In rural areas, by far the more important parts of the South, there were practically no public schools, but the towns made a start toward establishing school systems. Richmond, Norfolk, Charleston, Atlanta, Mobile, Nashville, and Memphis, among others, had free schools supported by local taxation, and they varied in quality from excellent to poor. In the absence of a uniform public school system, private schools were organized by teachers who lived on the tuition fees, or by groups of individuals who co-operated to support a school.

Before 1900 many southern church groups operated elementary and secondary schools, intended both as educational institutions for their children and missionary activities for their denominations. At the end of the century, Baptists were operating over seventy academies in North Carolina alone, and other denominations worked to meet educational needs of their people. Often they hindered public education; they could not compete with free schooling provided by the state, so they opposed state educational aid, particularly on the high school and college levels. They rationalized their action with the contention that education was a religious matter that should be left to the churches. In 1896 a North Carolina Baptist group declared that "the future civilization of America depends . . . on the extent to which distinctively Christian education shall be encouraged. The State has no more right to supply it on Wednesday in a college, male or female, than it has to provide it in a church on Sunday."

If the education for southern whites was a haphazard thing about which there was more debate than action, the education of Negroes was even more so. Until 1865, state laws had forbidden teaching slaves to read and write; there were violations, but very few. As a result, practically all freedmen were illiterate. The Freedmen's Bureau and the reconstruction governments had begun the work of educating them, but it was an arduous task. After 1876, many of the "redeemers" advocated Negro

DR. W. E. B. DuBois. The most persistent critic of Booker T. Washington and the "Atlanta Compromise" was William E. Burghardt DuBois. Born in Massachusetts of free Negro ancestry, DuBois was well educated at Fisk University in Nashville, at Harvard University where he received the Ph.D. degree, and at the University of Berlin. In 1896 he accepted a position at Atlanta University, where he began the scientific sociological study of the Negro in the South. In novels, journalistic writings, historical studies, and sociological researches, Dr. DuBois pointed out the burden of discrimination under which the Negro labored.

education as a means of social control. J. L. M. Curry, agent of the Peabody Fund; Gustavus J. Orr, Georgia superintendent of education; Henry Ruffner, Virginia superintendent; and Bishop A. G. Haygood of the Slater Fund, were leaders who favored education for the Negroes.

But as with the education of the whites, the chief barrier to Negro schooling was poverty. "I see in the South millions of unlettered children; I see in the South, wasted and desolated by war, an inability to educate them," said Mississippi Senator James Z. George in 1884. "I see on the part of the propertied classes of the South a willingness to help them; but . . . there is in many of the states . . . an inability to meet the demand." But there were other obstacles to Negro education. Southern whites were generally opposed to the idea of Negro schools and often took the position that the Negro was uneducable. Poorer whites were bitterly opposed to the Negro education when their own schools were deficient. Expressing a common view of his poor-white supporters, James K. Vardaman of Mississippi said, "What the North is sending South is not money but dynamite; this education is ruining our Negroes. They're demanding equality." Finally, though many Negroes welcomed education as a means of removing the stigma of slavery, many others were indifferent and content to remain illiterate.

With the aid of Peabody and Slater philanthropies, northern church activities, and meager state aid, Negro primary schools were slowly established. But the founding of institutes or "colleges" was widespread. By the end of the century there were more than 65 colleges for Negroes in the South. Among the more outstanding were Howard College in Washington, established in 1867 by the Congregational Church and the Federal Government; Virginia State College (1882); Hampton College in Virginia (1868); Judson C. Smith in Charlotte (1867); Paine College in Augusta (1883); Atlanta University (1865); Fisk University, Nashville (1865); Dillard College, New Orleans (1869); LeMoyne, in Memphis (1870); and Tuskegee Normal and Industrial Institute, in Alabama (1881). The work of these and other Negro colleges was hampered because so few Negroes were prepared for higher education.

There was, therefore, a debate over the course Negro education should take. In 1895 Booker T. Washington, president of Tuskegee Institute, addressed the Atlanta Exposition. There he propounded the thesis that the Negroes should acquire something to recognize before they demanded recognition. Washington proclaimed his love for the South and his desire to remain there; he proposed to adapt his Negro followers to their environment instead of trying to change it. Working largely through education the Washington cohorts sought to reconcile differences with the whites, to give Negro youth a vocational education along craft lines, and to forget political disfranchisement and social ostracism. Washington's objective was to teach his people ways in which they could be useful. "I would say, 'Cast down your bucket where you are,'" he said. "Cast it down in agriculture, mechanics, in commerce, in domestic service, and in the professions."

Washington's most persistent opponent was Dr. William E. Burghardt DuBois, born in Massachusetts of free Negro ancestry. DuBois was well educated at Fisk University in Nashville, Harvard University where he received the Ph.D. degree, and at the University of Berlin. In 1896 he accepted a position at Atlanta University, where he began the scientific sociological study of the Negro in the South. In novels, journalistic writings, historical studies, and sociological researches, Dr. DuBois pointed out the burden of discrimination under which the Negro labored. He objected to the "Atlanta Compromise" of the Tuskegee group and also to Washington's narrow educational program with its limited material objectives. If liberal studies were beneficial to the whites, DuBois wanted them for the Negroes too. "If we make money the object of man-training, we shall develop money-makers but not necessarily men," he said. He also denounced what he saw as Washington's supine acceptance of an inferior position and demanded civil equality with the whites. Southern whites therefore found Washington's philosophy more comfortable than that of DuBois, and supported without hesitation Washington's Tuskegee

Institute and other schools designed to adapt the Negro to a subordinate status. As New South whites debated the two traditions of intransigeance and imitation, so Negroes engaged in a similar disagreement; and as the Lee tradition of adapting to an inferior status in the nation triumphed among the whites, they fostered the conservative Washington in his efforts to get Negroes to accept an inferior status in the South. But, unlike the Davis tradition among southern whites, the DuBois school did not die in the nineteenth century.

Despite the continuation of discrimination and race prejudice, the Negro made remarkable progress after reconstruction. The primary need of the emancipated Negro was for schools, and the New South undertook to provide them. In practice, Negro schools received a smaller proportion of school funds than did white schools. Negro teachers received less than did white teachers and were generally more deficient in training and ability. Owing partly to the poor schools, Negroes generally took little interest in education.

Higher education for southern whites did not involve a basic debate, as among Negroes, but it was in a low state in the period before 1900. War and reconstruction saw a decline in college equipment and property, and the complete annihilation of endowment funds. When colleges reopened after the war they barely managed to remain open. Before the war the South had established more denominational colleges than it could support, and they declined in the general weakness of southern education. Few new colleges for white students opened in the period. Vanderbilt University and the George Peabody Normal College were founded in Nashville in 1875; Johns Hopkins, founded in 1867 in Baltimore, made a conscious effort to develop a graduate program based on the German model, and drew students from the South.

The state universities shared in the educational decline. In 1884 Alabama's entire appropriation for the university was only $24,000, and ten years later North Carolina appropriated only $74,000 for higher education. In 1900 Harvard University received more revenue than did all Southern colleges combined. Southern efforts to increase appropriations to higher education met opposition from the advocates of church-related colleges who feared public competition. North Carolina churchmen who operated denominational academies and colleges agreed with the Baptists of that state in declaring that "the appropriation of the taxes of the people to higher education does, in our opinion, hinder rather than help the educational interests of the State."

But the real reason for the deficient educational system of the South lay, not in bickering between church and state, but in extreme poverty. Southerners faced the unpleasant dilemma of being too poor to afford the debilitating effects of great public ignorance and of being too poor to do anything about it. By 1900 the amounts expended for each school-age child in the South had declined a bit from 1889, now ranging from 50¢ in Alabama and North Carolina to $1.46 in Florida and Texas. That paid for a school term that averaged almost a third shorter than the national average, and paid abysmal teacher salaries. North Carolina and Alabama paid teachers only $24 per month, while Florida was the highest in the South at $34. In 1900 no southern state had a compulsory attendance law, so that only 60 per cent of school-age children were enrolled at all, and on the average only 40 per cent were present. Rural schoolhouses in the South averaged only $100 each in value, which did not encourage attendance. Only 10 per cent of the pupils completed the fifth grade and only one in 70 reached the eighth grade. Again the results were evident in the statistics of adult illiteracy, which ranged from 30 per cent to 45 per cent of the total adult population, a rate three times as high as the national average. "It is a misnomer to say that we have a system of public schools," said the South Carolina superintendent of education in 1900.

But there were signs of an educational awakening in the South, made possible by the economic revival of the 1890's. In the decade there was an increase of almost 50 per cent in taxable property in the South, which produced more revenue. In all southern states there were increased appropriations for education, and some special education taxes were approved. Other factors enhanced the movement for better schools: literacy tests for voters placed a premium upon elementary education and improved roads made possible consolidated rural schools.

Southern educational leaders also influenced the advance. In 1898 there began a series of annual conferences at Capon Springs, West Virginia, which soon became the Conference for Education in the South. At the early meetings, leadership was assumed by such men as Dr. Curry of the Peabody Fund; J. A. Quarles, A. K. Nelson, and Harry St. George Tucker, of Washington and Lee University; Ormand Stone, A. H. Tuttle, and Charles W. Kent of the University of Virginia; Protestant Episcopal Bishops Thomas U. Dudley of Kentucky and Cleland K. Nelson of Georgia and Moravian Bishop Howard E. Rondthaler of North Carolina; and Presidents C. E. Menserve of Shaw University, Edwin A. Alderman of Tulane, and William L. Wilson of Washington and Lee. In 1901 the Conference for Education in the South established the Southern Education Board and authorized it to carry on a campaign of propaganda and to conduct a Bureau of Information and Advice on Legislation and School Organization. The Board was authorized to receive and to disburse funds. The next year the General Education Board was established as a further result of the Capon Springs conferences. The Southern Education Board devoted its efforts to encouraging legislation and taxation for schools, although it also administered funds. John D. Rockefeller and others made large contributions to its work.

Philanthropic assistance to southern education, much of which had as part of its purpose the destruction of distinctively southern attitudes, gave evidence of the colonial status of southern life. Poverty-ridden and disorganized, the South was a fertile field for northern cultural imperialism. More than any other aspect of southern backwardness, the educational system was important. A sound school system had to precede the improvement of other areas and culture. Many southern peculiarities which other Americans ridiculed, such as demagogic politics and fundamentalistic religion, could be traced to weaknesses in southern education. By 1900 southern leaders were beginning to attack the bases of that weakness and were making noticeable improvements.

4. LITERATURE AND THE NEW SOUTH

As northern educational assistance testified to southern colonialism, so northern support of southern writing caused authors to conform more and more to national standards. From the close of the Civil War, southern letters reflected fully the changing forces in the South. Without publishers and without local patronage, the South was reduced to the status of a cultural colony, its writers forced to seek the favors of alien publishers, editors, and readers. The section lacked literary centers, had few enlightened and objective critics, and not enough wealth and leisure to support a literary community. But the South did not lack aspiring authors, many of them women who turned out gushy pap designed to glorify the plantation and to romanticize slavery. The successful writers, however, were those who learned either to avoid controversial materials and to portray localism rather than sectionalism, or to accept northern interpretations of secession and emancipation. In the realm of literature even as much as in politics and business, the New South demonstrated its subservient status in the nation.

Authorship was a more important occupation in the New South than in the Old. Ante-bellum Southerners had never been strongest in the creating of belles-lettres. Polemics and essays, oratory and argument, and constitutional exposition and the social sciences had filled a more important place in southern literature. Thomas Jefferson, John Marshall, Spencer Roane, John Taylor, Thomas R. Dew, John C. Calhoun, and George Fitzhugh had fitted the southern taste more than had Poe, or Simms, or Timrod. William L. Yancey had boasted of the literarily mute South: "Our poetry is our lives," he had said; "our fiction will come when truth has ceased to satisfy us; as for our history we have made about all that glorified the United States." But after Appomattox, truth was distasteful and many Southerners sought refuge in romanticized defenses of the Lost Cause. "Overthrown in our efforts to establish a political nationality by *force of arms*," Paul Hamilton Hayne said in 1866, "we may yet establish an intellectual dynasty more glorious and permanent by *force of thought*."

But like the military efforts of Lee and Stuart and Beauregard, the Southern literary effort was doomed to failure. Soon even Hayne recognized it: "The few scholars, writers, thinkers, of which my own unfortunate section can boast, are being drawn daily more closely towards their Northern brethren—brethren now in reality and not in name alone." Reconciliation was the major theme of the new generation of southern writers, and by the late 1870's the northern reading public had discovered the charm of a no longer belligerent South. By tacitly accepting the northern view of the war, southern writers could write for a national audience. Irwin Russell, Sherwood Bonner, Joel Chandler Harris, Mary Noailles Murfree, James Lane Allen, Kate Chopin, Grace King, and Thomas Nelson Page used "local color" and dialect to gain northern readers and support. If by 1900 the northern conception of southern life was a warped collection of images drawn from Foster's songs, "Uncle Tom" and minstrel shows, "Ole Virginny," and Uncle Remus, southern writers were responsible.

After the war "local color" dominated the American literary scene. "The everyday existence of the plain people is the stuff of which literature is made," explained a contemporary critic. Such work required little formal training; a keen eye for local details and an astute ear for dialectal nuances made an acceptable author. Provincial peculiarities abounded in the South, from the proud Creoles of Louisiana to the rustic crackers of Georgia, the individualistic mountaineer, and the various types of Negro character. It would have been "a miracle of stupidity," said W. P. Trent, "if, in the . . . heyday of provincial literature the New South had missed [its] golden opportunity." The New South did not, and as a result, southern themes dominated American literature in the period. Judge Albion W. Tourgée, a stubbornly unreconstructed radical, complained in 1888 that American literature was "not only Southern in type, but" he thought, "distinctly Confederate in sympathy." A foreigner who knew America only by her fiction, he said, "would undoubtedly conclude that the South was the seat of intellectual empire in America, and the African the chief romantic element of our population."

In the beginning, Confederate literature was indeed the objective of many southern writers. Soon after Appomattox enterprising editors began literary magazines for the cultivation of a sectional literature. *Scott's Monthly* (December 1865-December 1869), founded by Atlanta minister W. J. Scott; *The Land We Love* (1866-1869), with an omnivorous subtitle, "A New Monthly Magazine Devoted to Literature, Military History, and Agriculture," was edited by ex-Confederate General Daniel H. Hill in Charlotte, North Carolina; *The Southern Review* (1867-1879), edited by West Point graduate Albert Taylor Bledsoe in Baltimore, and in 1871 became the official organ of the Southern Methodist Church; *Southern Magazine* (begun in 1866 as the Richmond *Eclectic,* it became the *Southern* in 1871 and lasted until 1875), founded by Moses D. Hoge and William Hand Browne; all contributed to the development of a distinctly southern literature. The best known southern magazine in the 'eighties was the *Southern Bivouac* (1882-1887), devoted to the Lost Cause in poems, stories, and articles.

All of these journals were short-lived, for as southern authors learned to adapt to northern literary prejudices, national magazines which offered more money accepted their work. The few Southerners who could afford the luxury of a literary magazine usually preferred the better-printed, better-edited northern product, or enjoyed the distinction of receiving an English magazine. In 1868 General D. H. Hill made a survey of what magazines Southerners were buying; in one city northern journals outsold southern competition by eight to one, and in another it was 240 to one. "The truth is," a southern observer lamented, "our people do not care for home-wares. They prefer the foreign product." More important was the fact that there was little demand for magazines other than farm journals and religious periodicals.

In the effort to produce a literature justifying the Confederate cause, southern writers labored in poverty and obscurity. William Gilmore Simms (1806-1870) survived the conflict but lost his house, his wife, and two children during the war years. Although critical of southern tastes, he continued to write. Hoping to raise again the banner of southern literature, he founded *The Nineteenth Century* as a journal for southern thought. But the South gave no patronage, and Simms wrote bad stories and poor poetry for second-rate northern journals. His last futile work was to edit a volume of *War Poetry of the South*. Paul Hamilton Hayne (1830-1886) left Charleston after the war, moved to a wretched shack in Georgia's pine barrens, and spent the last twenty years of his life turning out hackwork poems. In the better ones he glorified the southern landscape with delicacy and feeling. He never became reconciled to the new order in the Southland. "Great God!" he exclaimed. "It makes my blood boil in my veins when I think of the South flinging away the priceless jewels of which no force can deprive her: her individuality, her Southern character, her Southern honor. . . ." But the South he cherished did not honor him or buy his poems. His native city Charleston, he said bitterly, had "with tremendous effort,—succeeded in ordering just 15 copies (!!) of my volume!" Hayne did not surrender to the commercial impulse, however. In a poem entitled "South Carolina to the States of the North," he protested the injustices of enforced reconstruction. Hayne's poems have not remained favorites, but he was a representative Southern poet of his time, although almost alone among those who refused to accept the new order. Henry Timrod (1828-1867) survived the war broken in health and spirit and spent a year in "beggary, starvation, death, grief, utter want of hope" before he died.

Less unhappy than these Charleston poets but no less devoted to the Confederate cause was Virginia's novelist, John Esten Cooke (1830-1886). A prolific writer, he continued his output even while serving as an officer in Lee's army. After the war he combined farming in his native Shenandoah Valley with an unremitting literary industry. His theme was the historic glory of the Old Dominion and the greatness of the Confederacy. A romancer of the cavalier tradition, he abstained from comment on the forces of social change that surrounded him. The only exception to his escapist detachment was in the *Heir of Gaymount* (1870), in which he advocated intensive farming for the New South. He was the first important writer to treat the Civil War in fiction; his best-known works were *Surry of Eagle's Nest* (1866), *Mohun* (1869), and *Hilt to Hilt* (1869).

Sidney Lanier (1842-1881) turned his back upon the adoration of the Lost Cause and became a thoroughly nationalized poet. He criticized the South for its provincialism: ". . . the habit of regarding our literature as *Southern* literature, our poetry as *Southern* poetry, our pictures as

Southern pictures. . . . For, the basis of it is hate, and Art will have nothing to do with hate." Lanier expressed contempt for the sentimental novels southern women were writing and urged his countrymen to recognize and accept the new currents of thought in the South. "Our people have failed to perceive the deeper movements underrunning the time," he told his brother in 1870; "They lie wholly off, out of the stream of thought, and whirl their poor old dead leaves of recollections round and round, in a piteous eddy that has all the wear and tear of motion without any of the rewards of progress." He was the South's—and perhaps the nation's—greatest lyric poet, but he suffered the fate of other southern writers. In 1875 he joked to a northern friend that "with us of the younger generation in the South since the War, pretty much the whole of life has been merely not dying!" Lanier lived, played the flute in a Baltimore symphony orchestra, delivered scholarly lectures on literary criticism at Johns Hopkins University, and wrote "potboiling" boys' books and philosophical essays on music. His greatest works were poems describing the marshes of his native Georgia, "The Marshes of Glynn," and "Song of the Chattahoochie." A novel, *Tiger-Lilies* (1867), a romantic, immature work, described Lanier's experiences as a soldier and a prisoner of war. In a poem, "Corn," published in 1875, he condemned the old cotton aristocracy of the South and praised the small farmer who grew corn; and in an essay on the New South he espoused the current dogmas of progress.

With his appreciation for national culture, Lanier marked a transition in southern letters. After him, southern writers gave increasing voice to the philosophy of the New South and avoided subjects and themes that might offend northern readers. At first this took the form of "local-color" writings. The new nationalism that emerged from the Civil War demanded that local divergences be brought into harmony with the national scene. Local-color artists in the South essayed the literary task of presenting special character types to fit into the American tradition. Augustus B. Longstreet had long since exploited the literary possibilities of rural Georgia. In his tradition came Richard Malcolm Johnston (1822-1898), a Georgia-born lawyer and teacher with a gift for story-telling. His *Dukesborough Tales* (1871 and 1874) bore the nostalgic dedication, "To the Memories of the Old Times: the Grim and Rude, but Hearty Old Times in Georgia." Johnston published over eighty short stories, two novels, *Old Mark Langston* (1883), and *Widow Guthrie* (1893), and two novelettes. His tales were character studies rather than short stories, abounding in humor and with little sectional bitterness.

Two other important southern writers used the traditions of their localities as bases for their tales. Joel Chandler Harris (1848-1908) filled a column in the Atlanta *Constitution* with stories he remembered from his childhood. Beginning in 1880 with *Uncle Remus: His Songs and His Sayings,* Harris published six volumes of folktales from the plantation world of the Old South. In Uncle Remus he created one of the few great characters in American fiction. The Uncle Remus tales sold widely,

added local color to the national picture and their stories gave veracity even to serious works. The Confederate soldier and his suffering wife merged imperceptibly into the "Colonel" and "Ole Missus."

Historical writing reflected the changing South almost as well as belles-lettres. As northern capital moved into the South and southern writers pealed the wedding bells for the Yankee lad and the Dixie maid, the writers of history turned to the theme of reconciliation. Amid the national symphony of clattering shuttles, whistling locomotives, and changing northern cash registers, only the Republican politician sounded an inharmonious note. Strangely enough, those who had once led the music were out of tune. Force Bills and querulous inquisitions into southern elections were in ill accord with the prevailing mood. In 1890, as devotees of the bloody shirt supported Senator Lodge's Force Bill, southern members of Congress combined in a work of historical exposition. *Why the Solid South* was a review, state by state, of the bloody history of reconstruction. Polemics, rather than history, the book came at a time when public patience with the excesses of Big Business and its alliance with the Republicans was strained. A wide audience read the book, and writers of history accepted its conclusions.

In the 1890's, scholarly historians began questioning the Republican version of the Civil War and reconstruction periods. In 1891 James Ford Rhodes, a Cleveland manufacturer, published the first of his five-volume *History of the United States from the Compromise of 1850,* and won immediate fame for his fair-mindedness. Within a few years Professor William A. Dunning had begun to attract young Southerners to his seminar at Columbia University. In 1898 Dunning published a volume of *Essays on the Civil War and Reconstruction,* and in the first years of the new century such students as Walter L. Fleming, James W. Garner, Mildred Thompson, Charles W. Ramsdell, and J. G. de R. Hamilton presented studies of the reconstruction period in Alabama, Mississippi, South Carolina, Georgia, Texas, and North Carolina as dissertations for the Ph.D. degree. Others of Dunning's students studied other phases of southern history, and in other universities historical seminars studied anew the South's story in the Civil War and reconstruction.

These studies furnished a badly needed revision of the accepted picture. Radical Republican writings had painted the Confederacy and the post-war South in morality of black and white. The Democrats, secessionists, and Bourbons were black, the Negroes and the high-minded missionaries of northern civilization were pure white. The monographs of the newer scholars reversed the colors. Republicans, Negroes, Carpetbaggers, and Scalawags were black, while Democratic Southerners were—at least relatively—white. The new doctrine won ready acceptance. The wedding bells of reconciliation echoed clear in the bright morning of the rising nation. The young doctors of philosophy, mostly Southerners, went to southern colleges and universities to participate in the renaissance of southern education and to build a New South.

As scholars, politicians, and military heroes wrote for the South, so southern orators spoke for it. There had been many prominent orators in the Old South, for oratory blossomed in the South as literature flowered in New England. The fine art of public speaking lived through the war and voices of the Old South were raised again in counsel and exhortation, singing the songs of the New South—of conformity and adaptation. Georgia war governor Joseph E. Brown set the new mood in 1880 when he urged his hearers to "unite and move forward harmoniously in the new era as citizens of the new South for the promotion of the good of the whole country." Ultimately even the most reluctant of southern orators took that stand and admitted defeat. Their impassioned perorations had led the South to secession and war; now they led their people to accept the new state of affairs.

Southern oratory, minstrelsy, argumentation, and fiction worked together to render the southern tradition innocuous to a new nation. William Malone Baskerville, a southern literary critic, declared that the new southern literary effort had as its objective the conversion of the northern disbeliever: "The South is leading a new invasion against the North," he said. Writers of the New South did succeed where ante-bellum southern apologists had failed: they persuaded northern readers to accept a more favorable picture of the South and its life than that presented by abolitionists. In doing so, they denied or standardized southern values, farcically oversentimentalized southern life, and in the end did more harm to southern distinctiveness than did abolitionist attacks. A few, like Paul Hamilton Hayne, recognized the significance of southern literary acceptance. "The South that we knew is dead, beyond chance of resurrection," he mourned. "And the South to be, will prove the bastard offspring of Yankee thrift upon Southern necessity, a mere Monster, fat it may be, and puffed up with vanity, and greed, shining with a rank material oiliness,—but no more like the grand old South, of chivalrous and majestic memory. . . ." In letters, more than in other aspects of southern life, the South was a colony in an imperial nation.

5. SOUTHERN DISTINCTIVES

In 1876 the South was a distinct section in the nation, conscious of the threats against its way of life. By 1900 the feeling of southernism was vanishing, and the South was being readmitted to the nation, but in a subservient status. In all major culture areas southerners surrendered, but in everyday life they clung to their distinctive ways. Poor roads and a rural society contributed to the maintenance of provincial differences, and a generic poverty did the rest. Southerners refused to order their diet to fit the national norm; southern towns and villages stubbornly repudiated the efforts of macadamizers to exorcise the mud and dust of their streets; and in other aspects of life Southerners successfully opposed the nationalizing trend.

Southern food continued to harass the national nutritional experts. Southerners, unaware of the virtues of vitamins and a balanced diet, thrived on the traditional "white diet" of their fathers. Hog and hominy, rice, corn meal, black-eye and "field" peas dominated their tables. When they prepared string beans, collards, mustard greens, or "turnip sallet," they boiled the vegetable with a generous chunk of fatback which deposited a thick layer of grease over the concoction. The favorite holiday fare of the rural South was "country ham with red-eye gravy," and hot biscuits; or a young chicken, disjointed into succulent drumsticks, thighs, breasts, "pulley-bone," and wings, back, and neck, rolled in flour and fried slowly in deep fat. Sweet potatoes, candied with butter and sugar or baked into a pie; okra boiled into a slimy gumbo or rolled in corn meal and fried crisp; fresh pig skins cut into thin strips and fried into tasty tidbits known as "cracklin's"; chitterlings, souse, brains and eggs, ramp and poke "sallet": the Southern table was alike the delight of its adherents and the bane of dieticians.

Likewise to the horror of public health authorities, Southerners who lived in towns and cities remained rural in their living standards. In 1881 the president of the Louisiana State Board of Health diagnosed New Orleans' ills. "The gutters of the 472 miles of dirt streets are in foul condition, being at various points choked up with garbage, filth and mud, and consequently may be regarded simply as receptacles for putrid matters and stagnant waters," he said. "The street crossings are in like manner more or less obstructed with filth and black stinking mud." In 1888 the United States Commissioner of Labor scored Richmond for the "bad drainage of the city, bad drinking water, and unsanitary homes." All over the South sewage was primitive and sanitation was ignored with rural abandon. Open wells were the usual source of drinking water. As a result, Southerners were visited by epidemics of typhoid. Malaria, tuberculosis, hookworm, pellagra, and, until 1905, yellow fever, were also prevalent in the South. But despite the real need, before 1900 there were practically no organized public health services. There were no county health agencies and only the Mississippi and Florida State Boards of Health expended as much for their services as one cent per person in 1900.

At the turn of the century the southern road system left much to be desired. Main Street of the average county seat in the deep South was likely to be completely at the mercy of the elements, with mud a foot deep in the rainy season. Across country there were almost no all-weather roads so that travel was extremely difficult except by rail. Streams were traversed at fords or on dubious log bridges. Though there were some permanent roads built in the Upper South in the years before the Great War, most Southerners had to await more prosperous conditions—mainly more automobiles—to "get out of the mud."

People who lived in such splendid isolation continued to live as their fathers had lived. In the cabins of tenant farmers an observer in 1890 found a "shackling bed, tricked out in gaudy patchwork, a few defunct 'split-bottom' chairs, a rickety table, and a jumble of battered crockery." Sunbonnets and wool hats adorned the heads of rural Southerners, who were garbed in cheap cottons or woolens. Seasons were "hog-killin'," "cotton-choppin'," and "'tween crops," and the day was regulated by the sun rather than by the clock. Entertainment centered around the rural church, with "all-day singing with dinner on the grounds," a favorite. For country dancing, violins (known as fiddles), banjos, and guitars were pressed into service by untrained but energetic musicians.

The "hill-billy" music they made was a genuine American product bearing little resemblance to the artificial compositions of better-trained musicians. The Negro spiritual, another purely domestic southern music, was also the creation of the traditional, rural South. The voluminous catalog of spirituals which poured from the souls of black folk was introduced to a national audience by the Fisk Jubilee Singers, a fund-raising organization from Nashville's Fisk University. The spiritual told of the Negro's toil and exposure, with its outlook strained through the white man's religion:

> "Dere's no rain to wet you,
> Dere's no sun to burn you,
> Oh, push along, believer,
> I want to go home."

They sang also of mother and child:

> "Yonder's my ole mudder,
> Been waggin' at de hill so long;
> 'Bout time she cross over,
> Git home bime-by."

In a plaintive minor key, the spirituals were an expression of a great hope in a fair future in another world where men would judge men by their yearnings rather than by their skins. They contained a simple, natural beauty which even the musical technicians in their arrangements could not conceal.

For all his woes, however, the Negro was not the only oppressed Southerner, and not all of life was pleasant. Much of the industrial expansion in the South was built upon the backs and fingers of women and children who had to find work to augment the low wages paid their men. Increases in percentages of women and children in the labor force were greater than for men. In the decade after 1885 in certain Alabama industries, the male laborers increased 31 per cent, while the number of women increased 75 per cent, girls under 18, 158 per cent, and teen-aged boys, 81 per cent. In Kentucky in the same period, the male industrial population increased by only 3 per cent, while women increased 70 per cent, girls by 65 per cent and boys 76 per cent. Of the total number of male children between the ages of 10 and 14 employed in the nation in 1890, over half were in the impoverished South (256,502 of a total of 400,586); of 202,427 girls in the same age group nationally employed, southern states had 130,546.

By 1900 the situation had become even worse as child labor became the normal procedure in southern textile mills and children dominated the labor force. In 1900 thirty per cent of southern spindle operators were under 16, and over half of those were between 13 and 16.

An age limit of 14 would have closed every cotton mill in North Carolina, according to a past president of the American Cotton Manufacturers' Association, because before 1900 seventy-five per cent of the spinners were under that age. Another Association president estimated that only 30 per cent of the mill workers were over 21 years of age. Between 1880 and 1900 child labor (under 16) increased 600 per cent in southern mills. And yet in none of the important textile states in the South was there a child labor law. In 1887 Alabama passed legislation limiting to eight hours a child's working day but that was repealed at the request of a New England company that began building a factory in the state in 1895. "Eastern capital may now be invited South without having the disadvantage of the restriction in the hours of labor of women and children," exulted a repeal advocate.

There were almost no southern labor organizations to speak for the workers. In January 1898, Eugene V. Debs, the Social Democrat, found but one trades organization in Georgia and said that "the few who are still organized dare not say their soul is their own." But later that year Prince W. Greene organized a local union and struck in protest to wage cuts at a Columbus, Georgia, mill. When his local applied for admission in the American Federation of Labor, the national organization assigned them to the National Union of Textile Workers. It had so few members that the Southerners were able to elect Greene its national president. There were other strikes at southern mills in 1899 and 1900; in Augusta mill operators broke a strike by a lockout, as did Caesar Cone in his mills near Greensboro. By 1900 Samuel Gompers, president of the American Federation of Labor, had plans for union invasion and child labor legislation in the South. The twentieth century would likely witness a revolution in southern factory labor organization.

The absence of social legislation or of labor organization was the result of many factors, including ignorance and poverty and resulting conservatism. Also, it may have been partly because women were still excluded from the suffrage.

The Old South had not been in sympathy with the philosophy of feminism and it was not until after the Civil War that the women's movement reached the South. Even then the suffragettes met ridicule: "God forbid that the day will come when we will see women turned loose upon the nation, a set of raving, tearing politicians, standing elbow to elbow with the rabble and the toughs; unsexing themselves to the detriment of the home and of all social and domestic relations," a Texas editor said in 1894. But despite the opposition, defenders of feminism held their congresses, made their speeches and conducted their parades. "The ballot means to women the same as it means to men," an Equal Rights official declaimed. "It is a weapon, a power, a force whereby we may realize the highest form of self-government." In a decade in which the Negro was disfranchised, southern women embarrassed their men with their ardent demands for enfranchisement, and before 1900 they won no approval for their cause.

Though women were excluded from the ballot, one—Julia Tutwiler of Alabama—made permanent changes in the iniquitous convict-lease system which prevailed in southern penal institutions. In the Old South much of the crime was punished on the plantation without the state's participation, but most of the southern states had penitentiaries. The war left them destroyed and helpless to meet the problem posed by emancipation, which almost doubled the crime rate. Freedmen, away from the restraints of the overseer and on the verge of starvation, found it easy to turn to petty theft. With no money to build new jails and penitentiaries or to subsist prisoners, the states leased convicts to private industry which needed labor for railroad construction, mining, or plantation maintenance. In the Lower South, especially in Mississippi, Alabama, and Georgia, the leases were for long terms and the states gave the lessors absolute control over the convicts, and there conditions were most corrupt. In 1871 Georgia leased all her convicts to three penitentiary companies for twenty years. The state got the same amount of money regardless of the number of convicts, so the companies wanted as many penal offenders as they could get and took as little care of their charges as they could get away with. There was no segregation of race or sex in the prison camps and illegitimacy flourished. Children of all ages were caught up in the toils of the system; some only eight years old were sentenced to the chain gang.

These conditions led to a demand for reform in the system. Robert Alston, William H. Felton, and Tom Watson criticized it in Georgia and forced modifications. In 1881 a law provided that to keep down brutality the state should have an overseer who could visit the prison camps unannounced; ten years later the state ordered racial segregation in the camps, and in 1893 an attempt was made to separate the young from the "hardened" criminals. Developments in Georgia were typical of those in other southern states. Leasing ended in 1890 in Mississippi by a provision of the state's constitution of that year and the state bought farms to work the convicts, under direction of the state agricultural college at Starkville. Julia Tutwiler was the leader of reform in Alabama; she attacked the system as a new slavery which had all the evil and none of the good of the old chattel system. Not until the twentieth century, however, did her state stop convict leases.

Every effort of the reformers met determined opposition of vested interests within the ranks of "redeemer" politicians. Use of convict labor at seven to eight cents a day provided the basis for many fortunes in the New South. John H. Bankhead, state warden of Alabama, grew rich in a short time with the leasing system, as did Senators Joseph E. Brown and John B. Gordon of Georgia, and Colonel Arthur S. Colyar, Democratic leader in Tennessee. The "penitentiary ring" was as unscrupulous and as corrupt as were the radicals and carpetbaggers during reconstruction, and manipulated state legislatures as cynically.

Though Southerners were able to maintain a distinctive way of life in the realm of the unimportant, in other ways they acted and talked like their northern neighbors. In education, religion, literature, and labor exploitation and the amassing of wealth based upon it, they were well on their way toward complete imitation of national norms by 1900. Sixteen years earlier the editors of *Harper's Weekly* had declared that the "South has become a part of the modern world," and that "there is no longer a North or a South in business or in society." By the end of the century it had become true except in the artifacts of everyday life. But imitation illustrated that the South was a cultural colony in an imperial nation.

Economic Nationalization
of the South, 1900-1932

1. INDUSTRIAL GROWTH

BY the beginning of the twentieth century the forces of the New South almost achieved their victory over the traditions of the plantation. The farmer and the Negro had been put in their minor places and the South given over to the northern way of life. Henceforth the South would develop its industries, build its schools and cities, and regulate its life in imitation of the North.

Industry had taken firm root in the New South. For the most part the factories, the mines, and the railroads had grown up locally, were originally financed by local capital, and were controlled by southern men. Even when northern entrepreneurs—economic carpetbaggers—came into the South to develop industries, they came as individuals and made more or less strenuous exertions to adjust themselves to the local communities. To a considerable extent the industrialization of the South from Appomattox to the Spanish-American War was but the continuation and stimulation of forces which had been present in the ante-bellum South. The war had released these forces from the restraining hand of cotton capitalism and had given them free rein.

But such a situation was not to last. Soon the New South's industry was caught in the dragnet of Yankee finance. Hardly had industry become established in the South when northern capital began to come to its aid, extend credit for expansion, and eventually take over control. The panic of 1893 gave New York financiers control of the South's railroads. The coal and oil of West Virginia quickly fell into the hands of still other groups of capitalists. The American Tobacco Company, beginning in North Carolina, migrated to New York and consolidated the industry. Thereafter southern tobacco was held in the grasp of a nation-wide trust. In 1907 President Roosevelt, ignoring antitrust legislation, consented to the acquisition of the Tennessee Coal and Iron and Railroad Company by United States Steel.

The process of nationalization transformed every aspect of southern life as southern businessmen became agents, retainers or commission merchants, but rarely principals. The enterprises they directed became increasingly composed of branch industrial plants, branch banks, chain stores, captive mines, and local outlets for national firms. Locally owned power companies became adjuncts of national power companies with headquarters in New York. National newspaper chains owned southern journals and dictated their editorial policies. The chain store pushed the local merchant onto the back streets. Insurance companies foreclosed their mortgages on farms and plantations. Chambers of commerce hailed the process and sent agents scurrying over the land to entice new businesses to locate in their towns. Cities and states vied with each other in offering tax exemptions and special favors for new industries. Politicians translated the statistics of the South's dependence into the oratory of progress.

The greatest extent of dependence was in northern control of southern railways. Following the panic of 1893 J. Pierpont Morgan had reorganized several defunct lines into the Southern Railway, and soon it controlled 7,500 miles of rail. Morgan now dominated rail transportation into southern coal fields, the iron industry from east Tennessee to Birmingham, and the region of cotton textiles and tobacco, lumber, and Florida citrus. The Southern system pointed the way to further "reorganization" in the South. In May, 1902, the Atlantic Coast Line assumed control of the rail empire of Henry B. Plant, and now laid claim to 1,676 miles of track through that system; in the same year the A. C. L. bought into the Louisville and Nashville. These negotiations increased the line's trackage to more than 10,000 miles, from Norfolk and Tampa to New Orleans and Louisville. Except for insignificant local lines, the southern roads were effectively centralized under outside control. But they were managed by Southerners. Morgan chose Samuel Spencer, a Confederate veteran, to preside over the Southern Railroad. "Born and reared in the South, and identified by my life's work with Southern interests, I feel that I have a right to speak to you as one of your own people," Spencer said in 1906.

Henry M. Flagler, the Yankee railroad builder who constructed lines down Florida's east coast, continued his efforts into the new century. By 1912 he had gone beyond Miami to Key West. Alongside his rails he built resort hotels, sold lands, and encouraged production of goods to be shipped over his line.

Safely under the control of northern financial interests, southern rail construction rapidly extended the railroad net in the twentieth century. In 1900 the South had about one fourth of the rail mileage of the country (54,926 out of 193,346 miles). Under the impact of a world war and an ensuing prosperity decade, the South built one half of the country's additional rail mileage. By 1910 the South had 32.4 per cent of the total mileage, and had regained the relative position in railroads which she had held in 1860. In 1930 the South had about one third of the total rail mileage (82,000 out of 249,000 miles), one third of the land area and one third of the population. It was as well supplied as was the country at large.

Twentieth-century southern railroads were almost completely dominated by a few large companies owned by outside capital. Lines like the Illinois Central, the Southern Pacific, the Missouri, Kansas, and Texas, the Rock Island, and the "Frisco" were owned by northern and western financiers. Usually these lines extended their control in the South by purchase of short lines built by southern enterprise. In the eastern area, along the Chesapeake Bay, the important roads were the Norfolk and Western, which tapped the rich Pocahontas coal fields of western Virginia; the Baltimore and Ohio, which operated a main line from Baltimore to New York and also hauled coal from the Maryland fields around Cumberland; and the Chesapeake and Ohio, which served the West Virginia coal area. South of these lines the Atlantic Coast Line and the Seaboard Air Line operated between the Potomac and the Florida Gulf Coast ports. The southern piedmont rail traffic was dominated by the Southern Railway system, with a main line from Washington to Atlanta, curving through the piedmont region and thence to Birmingham, Chattanooga, Memphis, and New Orleans. In the central area, the Louisville and Nashville and the Illinois Central connected the Gulf South with the Ohio River and the Great Lakes region. West of the Mississippi the Southern Pacific, the Missouri-Kansas-Texas, known from its initials as the "Katy," and the "Frisco" lines branched out from New Orleans and the Gulf, northward and westward.

Further examples of northern control of southern enterprise were provided by the iron and steel industry. The panic of 1893 brought reorganization and centralization which put outside interests more firmly in control than before. One southern firm which withstood the panic was the Tennessee Coal, Iron and Railroad Company, which dominated the Alabama industry. Using newer open-hearth methods of refining iron ore, the Ensley mills supplied a national market. But another depression proved too much for the Tennessee Company. In 1907 the Harriman Company sent to Ensley for 150,000 tons of rails. That was disturbing to Pennsylvania steel operators and their Wall Street financiers. Therefore, in the fall of 1907 the United States Steel Corporation, under the astute guidance of J. P. Morgan, purchased the Tennessee Company for a fraction of its value.

As the sale was contrary to the anti-trust legislation, President Roosevelt was persuaded to announce that it was merely an unselfish action to halt the further spread of the panic then influencing business. Birmingham's leaders outdid themselves in welcoming the steel trust.

The city's newspapers optimistically predicted that the merger would "make the Birmingham District the largest steel manufacturing center in the universe."

Farm Security Administration, photo by Lange

A WHITE SHARECROPPER FAMILY IN GEORGIA. Within twenty-five years after the end of Reconstruction, almost seventy per cent of the cotton farmers were tenants, who were seldom able to break away from their economic bondage. In some states, tenants were not permitted to move from the land if they owed money to the owner, thus becoming serfs. The share of the crop that the tenant received depended upon the amount of capital that he brought to the enterprise.

But the rosy future did not appear immediately. Now under outside control, though with a Southerner, George G. Crawford of Georgia, as president of the Tennessee subsidiary, the southern mills were prevented from fully developing their resources. The South's relative share of the nation's pig iron production decreased after the merger, from 14 per cent of the total in 1900 to only 11 per cent in 1930. In actual tonnage, southern pig iron production increased, however, from 1,965,000 tons in 1900 to 4,480,000 tons in 1930. Moreover, the southern producers were unable to turn out the fine finished products on which the greatest profits could be made. Instead, they had to content themselves with pig iron and such relatively simple fabrication as sheet and bar iron, water and sewer pipe, rails, structural steel, bolts and rivets, and wire. After World War I, iron pipe manufacturing absorbed much of the iron output and the South led the world in its production.

The war economy aided southern steel and pig iron manufacturers, and furnaces and rolling mills multiplied in Alabama, Tennessee, and

West Virginia. Outside the Birmingham area, however, they could be made profitable only when prices were high. After the war the furnaces in other southern fields had to shut down. In 1917 there were 47 blast furnaces in Alabama, 19 in Virginia, 16 in Tennessee, 7 in Kentucky, and others in Georgia and Texas. By 1930 these had been reduced to 24 in Alabama and 6 in Tennessee.

The Birmingham area had an unusual advantage in iron production. Nowhere else in the world were the essential raw materials so easily combined within a few miles of each other. But the Steel Trust imposed an artificial burden upon the Alabama industry: the "Pittsburgh Plus" pricing system. Under that arrangement buyers paid the Pittsburgh price for steel, plus freight charges to the purchaser's city, even if the steel were actually refined only a few miles away. Southern steel users were thus unable to capitalize on locally produced Birmingham steel and to avoid unnecessary freight rates. In 1924, as a result of legal action brought by midwestern steel fabricators, a new system of multiple-basing-points was adopted by which cities other than Pittsburgh were used in calculation of freight charges to be added to steel prices. This gave some relief, but southern iron and steel furnaces continued to follow the national pattern.

Only in cotton manufacturing could the South claim leadership in the fabrication of raw materials into finished products. Shortly after the turn of the century, New England cotton mills began a southern migration. Many of them established branches in the South, and a few moved bodily. By 1925 the number of active spindles in the South exceeded those of New England and in 1930 had many more, or 18,586,000 to 11,351,000 in New England. At the same time southern weavers had passed their northern competitors, with 344,966 looms to 268,404 in the northeast. By 1930 the southern textile producers were able to dominate output; North Carolina produced about 20 per cent of the nation's cotton goods (Massachusetts was down to 18.7 per cent), South Carolina nearly 15 per cent, and Georgia 12 per cent. North Carolina was thus the first southern state to surpass in production of cotton goods a northern state. Kannapolis had the largest towel mills in the world, Durham had the largest hosiery mills in the world; Greensboro's Cone Mills were the nation's largest denim producers; Roanoke Rapids boasted the country's damask mills; and Winston-Salem unblushingly claimed the nation's largest men's underwear mills. The state led the nation in the amount of raw materials consumed annually and in the number of textile mills—in 1928 there were 579 mills with a combined spindleage of 6,388,160, and by 1930 twenty-six new mills had been constructed.

Southern cotton-goods producers were able to utilize nearby sources of raw materials and thus to beat competition. In 1929 the four leading southern cotton-manufacturing states produced 4,260,000 bales of raw cotton, and in the following year they consumed 4,219,000 bales. They were assisted by the fact that most of their market was a local one, and again freight charges were saved. Southern mill workers were native-born, docile, and quick to learn. Also they were willing to work long hours. In 1928 the work hours per week averaged 55 in Alabama, 56 in Georgia, 50 in Massachusetts, 56 in North Carolina, 53 in Rhode Island, and 55 in South Carolina.

Farm Security Administration, photo by Marion Post Wolcott

NEGRO SHARECROPPERS IN GEORGIA, MOVING FROM ONE MAN'S FARM TO ANOTHER. Pursuing the hope that "next year will be better on another farm," Negro tenants moved from one shack to another.

Southern mills were usually located outside the cities and around them the owners constructed villages for their workers. Some attention was given to comfort and sanitation. In 1929 Alabama passed a law that gave cotton-mill communities until 1931 to establish a piped system of sewage for every home, but other textile states left such regulation to the paternalistic spirit of the mill owners. Some villages had community centers, some provided a nurse or other medical care, and southern mills spent large sums for education, libraries, or churches.

Because of the local raw material supply, the local market, and the contented labor supply, southern mills produced fine fabrics at from 14 to 18 per cent cheaper than the New England mills. "Frankly, we are up against it," said an official of the Fall River Cotton Manufacturers' Association of Massachusetts. "We can operate only at a loss, and if we are to remain in business there is but one thing we can do, follow the general move to the South, to the Carolinas. . . . To compete with southern mills and New England labor conditions is impossible; even the attempt is suicide."

Aiding in the development of industry was the development of electric power. The Southern Power Company, beginning its operations shortly after the turn of the century, inaugurated an era of electrification. Important utility companies such as the Alabama Power Company, the Tennessee Electric Power Company, and the Carolina Power and Light Company, served over 2,000,000 consumers. The greatest potential source of hydroelectric power was in the Muscle Shoals of the Tennessee River. From the vicinity of Chattanooga to Florence, Alabama, the Tennessee was unfit for navigation. The forty miles from Decatur to Florence consisted of a series of rapids to which the name "Muscle Shoals" had been applied. Long regarded as a source of power, the river remained undeveloped until the first World War. The need for nitrates for explosives led the United States government to construct two nitrate plants and to build one dam. A second dam, called Wilson Dam, was only partially completed at the close of the war.

Most of the 18,000,000 kilowatt hours of electricity which the South produced in 1929 was generated from coal, oil, or gas, rather than by water power. However, hydroelectric power was making headway and needed only the stimulus of the Tennessee Valley Authority to make it eventually the leading source of power. Electric power brought both dispersal and diversity to industry. Smaller mills could tap new local supplies of cheap labor.

Stimulated further by electric power, other industries grew rapidly. Rayon, a man-made fiber chemically produced from the cellulose in wood chips or cotton linters, was made in the South. Of the 29 rayon plants in the United States in 1929, 14 were in the South, under control of a British firm, the American Viscose Company, and of American Du Pont interests. The southern plants were located in Virginia, Tennessee, Georgia, Maryland, Delaware, West Virginia, and North Carolina.

Tobacco manufacture was also controlled from outside the South. In 1911 a Supreme Court ruling ordered the American Tobacco Company to be broken down into smaller units. The trust was divided into sixteen "successor companies," the most important of which were R. J. Reynolds Tobacco Company, P. Lorillard Company, Liggett and Myers Tobacco Company, and the American Tobacco Company. An important result was the appearance of the distinctive brands of blended cigarettes in packages of twenty. In 1912 Chesterfields appeared, followed in 1913 by Camels and in 1916 by Lucky Strike.

Reynolds quickly dominated the expanding cigarette market by promoting Camels. By 1923 the brand had captured 45 per cent of the total sales and maintained at least one third of the market. To meet growing demands, more efficient rolling and packaging machines were invented and the entire cigarette-making process became highly mechanized. By 1929 the industry, centered in Virginia and North Carolina, was producing 122 billion cigarettes annually. In that year 61 per cent of the nation's output was made in North Carolina, and more than 120 million pounds of manufactured tobacco for the domestic market. Because of the excise taxes on tobacco products, the Tar Heel state in 1928 paid more taxes into the federal treasury than any other state except New York. Tobacco manufacture was also profitable to the producers: in the same

Farm Security Administration, photo by Post

NEGRO TENANT'S HOME BESIDE THE MISSISSIPPI LEVEE IN LOUISIANA. Rural southerners continued to live as their fathers had lived. In the cabins of tenant farmers, an observer in 1890 found a "shackling bed, tricked out in gaudy patchwork, a few defunct 'split-bottom' chairs, a rickety table, and a jumble of battered crockery." Sanitation was primitive, and in the hot months the occupants generally moved bedding to the porch, and the doors disappeared.

year Reynolds' net profits for the year were probably more than the value of the plants.

Though chemical production was an innovation in the new century, the New South quickly became a part of the industry. Texas and Louisiana produced all of the domestic sulphur, from mines or wells along the Gulf Coast. At Muscle Shoals, near Sheffield, Alabama, there were plants equipped to manufacture ammonium nitrate and cyanamide, artificial fertilizers. Nitrocellulose, from which smokeless gunpowder, celluloid, photographic film, paints and plastics may be made, was also produced on the Tennessee River. Commercial acetylene gas was manufactured in North Carolina. At Tuskegee Institute in Alabama the great Negro chemist Dr. George Washington Carver discovered more than 300 useful products from the lowly peanut and a hundred by-products of the sweet potato. In the 1920's, helium gas from Texas fields became an important commodity. A rare, non-inflammable gas, helium was eminently suited to dirigibles. Natural gas of the flammable variety was widely used in home heating and cooking. In 1931 a pipeline was completed from Texas to Chicago and the Midwest, making possible the exportation of that valuable resource.

The South exported other types of power to the rest of the country in the first third of the century. Southern coalfields continued to yield fuel for the nation's furnaces. By 1929 the southern production was about 40 per cent of the national total, with West Virginia leading the way with 138,500,000 tons. Coal mining in the South increased fourfold in the period, gaining from 54,510,000 tons in 1900 to 202,092,000 tons in 1930. Most of the coal came from West Virginia, Kentucky, Alabama, and Virginia.

Petroleum from the Southwest lubricated the nation's wheels and propelled its internal combustion engines. With the discovery of oil in East Texas in 1901 the American oil industry experienced a revolution. At Spindletop, near Beaumont, a "gusher" well was tapped which caused a major oil rush to the new field. When average daily production of the eastern oil wells was two barrels, the Spindletop well produced nearly 110,000 barrels per day. Special trains carried prospectors from Pennsylvania and other eastern oil centers, and by the end of the year over 500 wells had pierced the oil dome within an area of five square miles. In the second year after the discovery the Spindletop area produced 17.5 million barrels (42 gallons to a barrel) of oil. In 1897 Oklahoma had produced its first thousand barrels; ten years later its output was over 43 million barrels. In 1902 Louisiana wells produced 549,000 barrels and two years later yielded nearly three million. In 1910 Oklahoma produced 52,000,000 barrels, Texas 8,899,000, and Louisiana 6,841,000. New discoveries were made in the next decade. In 1926 prospectors made a strike in the Texas panhandle about fifty miles from Amarillo, and in 1929 a new field was opened in northeastern Texas in Van Zandt County.

Oil discoveries stimulated the construction of refineries and investments in oil transportation. In 1930 there were more than 150 oil refineries in the South, of which 83 were in Texas, Oklahoma had 45, Louisiana 13, and Arkansas 10. The largest Texas refineries were along the Gulf Coast on navigable channels. Crude and refined oil were pumped through an extensive network of pipelines, boosted by pumping stations. In 1930 there were about 37,000 miles of oil pipeline in the Southwest and to midwest refinery points.

Lumber and timber products were also important in the southern economy. Exploiting the southern forests faster than they could be replaced, lumbermen continually increased the rate of cutting. In 1900 southern forests supplied nearly 32 per cent of the timber cut in the United States; by 1930 the percentage had increased to 47 per cent. Among southern states, Mississippi, Louisiana, and Alabama were the largest suppliers of lumber, each cutting over two billion board feet in 1929. Texas, Arkansas, Georgia, North and South Carolina, and Florida yielded over a billion board feet each in the same year. In the southern pine belt some of the world's largest sawmills, fed by timber brought from great distances by motor truck and rail, worked incessantly to reduce the forests to building materials.

The increased cutting caused alarm that southern forests were being depleted, and conservationists worked to save them. Since 1910 there had been fears that the long-leafed pine was being exterminated, and in the 1920's other native trees seemed doomed to extinction. In 1921 the United States Forest Service reported that lumbermen were taking southern timber about four times faster than it could be replaced. With predictions that the forests were being wastefully exploited, the conservation movement gained adherents. Southern states established forestry departments and passed laws encouraging tree plantings, and in 1932 the Federal Government began the reforestation of poor lands.

Although more than forty per cent of the nation's lumber was cut in southern forests, most of it was shipped outside the South to be finished. Northern fabricators bought lumber from the Gulf south, and sold it back as furniture, farm implements, or millwork. But by 1932 there were 143 furniture factories in North Carolina, and the state ranked fifth in the value of furniture it manufactured annually. For many years the southern producers had to display their wares at furniture expositions in the north but a huge Southern Furniture Exposition Building was erected at High Point where semiannual fairs attracted national purchasers. In 1927 North Carolina and Virginia, the only southern states where wooden furniture construction was an important industry, manufactured household goods worth $78,953,000.

The southern naval stores industry continued to contribute to northern incomes. Research extended the uses of turpentine, tar, pitch, and rosin to include the manufacture of paints and varnishes, soap and disinfectants, oilcloth, linoleum, and roofing materials. About 1900, forestry researchers also discovered new methods of procuring the gum without damage to the tree. The new method, developed by Chemist C. H. Herty of the Bureau of Forestry in the years 1901-1905, was called the cup method. Requiring a smaller wound, Herty's system also captured more of the resin. Within twenty years the new method had added more than ten million dollars to the annual value of the turpentine industry. Another innovation appeared in the same period: the distilling of turpentine from pine stumps, old logs, and mill refuse. In 1929 the southern pine forests yielded 31,321,000 gallons of turpentine from living trees and 4,619,000 gallons from wood.

Paper fabrication was another local use for southern timber. In 1906 the United States Forest Service began researches into possible uses for pulpwood and out of these studies came the sulphate process of making paper pulp from the southern pine. At first the pine pulp was suitable only for "kraft" paper, a brown wrapping and sacking material, but that was an important commercial product. Shortly after the introduction of the sulphate process, in 1909, comsumption of yellow pine increased, and by 1926, 685,000 cords went into pulp. Often sawmill operators built paper mills near their plants and made use of sawdust and bark siding that previously had been burned.

Building materials other than lumber were also made from wood pulp. "Celotex," an insulating wallboard, was manufactured from cane sugar waste in Louisiana. Bagasse, the residue of cane pulp from which the juice had been extracted, was treated and pressed into thick sheets. "Masonite," another manufactured building material, was made in a plant near Laurel, Mississippi, from wood fiber. It was more compact and more finely worked than was "celotex."

As befitted a colony, the South's greatest economic activity was the exploitation and exportation of her natural resources. By 1932 southern mineral deposits were supplying national needs. The southern states produced more than one third of the United States' output, or a total of $1.8 billion. Petroleum and coal contributed most of that, but other materials of less monetary value were equally as important to industrial processes. Phosphate rock was produced in Florida, Tennessee, and South Carolina; after 1903, Florida led all the states in its supply. In 1930, southern output was just under four million tons, valued at almost $14 million. Alabama, Tennessee, and Texas produced cement from native limestone, but made only seven per cent of the national product. Granite came from quarries in the piedmont and in Texas, and marble from Georgia and Tennessee.

A much more important southern mineral resource was bauxite, from which aluminum was refined. The entire American source of bauxite came from Arkansas, Georgia, Alabama, and Tennessee, with Arkansas the largest producer. The deposits in north Georgia were worked from 1889, and two years later operations began in Arkansas. By 1900, shipments from the Ozarks were significant. In 1929, 331,000 tons of the ore were mined in the southern mountains. The bauxite was chemically reduced to alumina, or aluminum oxide. In 1932 the largest plant for that process was at East St. Louis, Illinois. Aluminum was produced from the oxide at Maryville, Tennessee, but most of it was made elsewhere because of the immense power requirements. Almost all the mine operations and refining plants for American aluminum were owned or controlled by Aluminum Corporation of America, a Pittsburgh firm.

Farm Security Administration, photo by Vachon

NEGRO HOUSING IN NORTH MEMPHIS, TENNESSEE. When Negroes moved to town, their plantation background, added to the ever-present poverty and ignorance, produced slum conditions. Even into the twentieth century, Negro sections in many southern cities lacked paved streets, sewers, street lighting, and water piped into houses.

Distillation of grain spirits into whiskey was a distinctively southern enterprise. In Louisville, Frankfort, and Lexington, Kentucky, and in Tennessee mountain villages, distillers turned out products which sold all over the country. Prohibition, in effect in the United States under the eighteenth Amendment from 1917 till 1933, put the distillers temporarily out of business and opened the market to the bootleggers. Though most of the larger stills discovered by Volstead Act officials were in larger cities, sternly independent mountaineers in inaccessible coves turned out an unaged distillate known locally as "white lightnin'," "white mule," or "tiger blood."

In nearly all of these industries except moonshining, however, ownership and control rested in northern hands. Pittsburgh interests controlled southern iron, steel, and aluminum. Branches of Goodyear and Goodrich made tires and fabrics in the South. Eastman Kodak, the Corning Glass Works, the American Painting Company, and the Commonwealth and Southern had branches or subsidies in the southern states. For the most part, management rested in southern hands. Superintendents and foremen were drawn from the locality. To the tasks of management they brought ability to handle the local laborers. They participated in local politics and made sure that government was friendly to industry. They set the tone for the chambers of commerce. They joined the Kiwanis. And they were loudest in their praises of the New South.

2. Capital and Labor in Southern Industry

The social system of the New South was foreign in origin and, at best, was a transplanting and an imitation. Reorientation about the factory, the store, and the mine involved new and difficult adjustments. Nowhere were difficulties of adjustment more clear than in the relations of capital and labor. Throughout the South the poor whites furnished the labor supply for cotton mills, coal mines, and tobacco factories. After as before the war, immigrants shunned the South. By 1920, the foreign-born residents of the South were but a negligible portion of the total population. Texas, with many Mexicans, led the South in this respect with 7.8 per cent, while North Carolina had but three tenths of one per cent of foreigners. With the exception of a few who came to the coal mines, the majority of the Europeans remained near the seacoast. Native-born Southerners worked the mills.

The principal argument for the establishment of industry in the South was labor's docility. Southern industrialists took pride in the fact that their laborers were content to work longer hours for lower pay than were the factory workers of the North. For decades the workers themselves were content, welcoming the comparatively simple tasks of the cotton mills as a relief from the impoverished drudgery of the tenant farms. Enjoying to the fullest the opportunity for contacts with their fellows, finding emotional outlets in the revivals at the company-supported church, and living in houses superior to the shacks of the rural regions, the mill workers felt no particular class consciousness and gave no heed to the labor movement that blossomed elsewhere in the United States.

Only in the tobacco factories and as unskilled labor in the iron and lumber industries were the Negroes admitted to southern industry. There was no place in the mill villages for the blacks. The poor whites who had jobs in the new factories considered their employment but another proof of the intellectual and biological superiority to the "sons of Ham." In the few cases where Negro labor was tried, it proved unsuccessful. The same difficulties that had faced the planter in his search for an overseer—that of finding white foremen who could supervise Negro workers—faced the factory owners. For reasons of the master's control, it was considered impossible for the two races to work side by side. The result was that the Negroes were relegated to agriculture, to personal service, or to employment as artisans in the towns.

Yet the presence of the Negro workers served to keep the white workers docile. The higher wage of the white man enabled him to feel and assert his superiority, while the fact that the Negro could displace him served to keep him out of the hands of radical agitators. Labor unions in the South were almost exclusively confined to the whites but their activities were crippled by the constant threat of the unorganized and lower-paid Negroes.

The white workers in the mill villages remained content, or at least passive, until industry had obtained a good foothold in the South. The low wages and long hours of the southern operatives, however, constituted a problem for organized labor in other portions of the country. When northern mill owners moved their mills to the South, the northern working population was stranded. Only a few of the more highly skilled northern workers followed their mills to the South. Early in the migration the International Union of Textile Workers, with the approval of the American Federation of Labor, began to form unions in the South. After a merger with the United Textile Workers of America, unionization went forward rapidly. From 1903 to 1918 the union sent down organizers who formed new locals each year.

To the general surprise of those who had counted upon the docility of southern labor, the organizers had little difficulty in obtaining members. Women as well as men joined the organization. The organizers were not faced with language barriers as they were in the North, and a few speeches in the village hall were sufficient to form a local. The real problem, however, was to hold the members. Employers opposed the unions and took advantage of slack seasons to discharge members. Left to themselves the unions died off rapidly.

Some locals, however, revealed a determined unionism. Strikes at Atlanta in 1914, at Anderson, South Carolina, in 1916, and at Columbus, Georgia, in 1918, were especially bitter, but the mill owners had the support of the troops, the newspapers, and the general public. As a result, the movement collapsed with complete victory for the employers.

With a more rapid movement of textile mills to the South after the first World War, the United Textile Workers determined to make a new drive in the South. In eight months of 1919, 67 new locals came into action. Forty-three of these were in North Carolina where there were 40,000 paid-up members; South Carolina accounted for an additional 5,000 new unionists. As soon as the unions were formed, they demanded a shorter day and a shorter week. Strikes were numerous. At Charlotte, Concord, and Kannapolis, North Carolina, and at Rock Hill and Granite-ville in South Carolina, the unions won a part of their demands. In 1920 the work of organization slackened, but 37 new locals were formed. A general business depression gave the mill owners an excuse for closing plants or for reducing wages. In 1921 when lower wages were announced, 9,000 workers at Charlotte, Concord, Kannapolis, Huntersville, and Rock Hill made a desperate last stand. The strike lasted for weeks and the laborers were defeated. Reductions came and the failure of the strikes caused a decline in membership until barely 2,000 southern laborers remained in the organization.

For a half-dozen years peace reigned on the southern industrial front and the southern mill owners began once again to congratulate themselves on their docile labor. But beneath the surface the workers were still dissatisfied. In 1927 and 1928 southern unions began once more to organize and to agitate. The adoption of the "stretch-out," by which one weaver cared for as many as one hundred looms, caused widespread discontent. In October 1928 labor delegates from six southern states met at Chattanooga to prepare for action.

On March 13, 1929, the 3,500 employees of the American Glanzatoff Rayon Company at Elizabethton, Tennessee, struck for higher wages. Two thousand other employees of the Bemberg Company joined them. The companies appealed for troops and the Tennessee National Guard arrived on the scene. The guardsmen were sworn in as special deputies and acted under the nominal direction of the company-selected sheriff. The district court forbade picketing and picketers were arrested en masse. A mob attacked the strikers and drove northern organizers out of town. With violence threatening, unions and employers accepted government arbitration.

A second textile strike occurred the following month at Gastonia, North Carolina. Here the communist National Textile Workers Union organized the employees of the Loray Mill, controlled by Rhode Island capital. The workers demanded an eight-hour day and a five-day week with a minimum wage of $20. With the assistance of the National Guard, the company evicted strikers from the company-owned houses. The workers established a tent colony and a mob destroyed their headquarters. When police attempted to invade the tent colony, there was shooting and the chief of police was killed. One hundred strikers were subpoenaed, and eleven men and three women faced charges of murder. Seven were found guilty of second-degree murder and received sentences of from five to twenty years. On the other hand, members of a gang who mobbed and murdered the workers escaped indictment until the governor in-terfered. A farcical trial resulted in their acquittal.

Other strikes occurred at Marion, North Carolina, at several points in South Carolina, and at Danville, Virginia. In each case the same phenomena of National Guardsmen and company-inspired mobs, court injunctions, and widespread popular disapproval characterized the outbreaks.

Photo by E. Bruce Thompson

A STORE IN MISSISSIPPI. This store is typical of thousands of small retail outlets, catering to a rural trade, with its metal roof shading benches for idlers, and peeling handbills posted at random.

These disorders were succeeded in 1931 and 1932 by outbreaks in the coal fields of southeastern Kentucky. In Knox, Harlan, and Bell counties the coal miners earned a weekly average of $52.50 per family. When deductions were made for the company-supplied houses, medical care, fuel, and mining supplies, the average family of five received a total of $36.75 for a week's work. Frequently this was paid in brass checks that the company store accepted. The mines near Harlan belonged to the Peabody Coal Company, the Mellon interests of Pittsburgh, the United States Steel Corporation, and the International Harvester Company. Early in 1931 wage cuts led to dissatisfaction and the United Mine Workers began to organize the discontented workers. The strike began in April. The governor sent the National Guard, and the IWW and the Communist International Labor Defense appeared on the scene. Wide publicity caused radical writers, professional men, and college students to attempt to assist the strikers. Guardsmen met the visitors at the county line and refused them permission to enter. The mine owners appealed to the provincialism of the people and stirred them to resentment against outside interference. The organizer, the secretary, and five members of the

Harlan union were tried for participation in riots and were sentenced to life imprisonment.

These strikes were sufficient indication that southern labor had passed beyond its earlier docility. At the same time they indicated the difficulties in the way of achieving success for the workers. The government officials were almost invariably in sympathy with the companies and were willing to use the militia to suppress the laborers. Moreover, the "red" specter seemed to have an especial power to terrify southern communities. Newspapers and the public were hostile to the workers. By 1932 the South had become a land of red baiters, and the American Legion, the National Guard, and the chambers of commerce united in condemning the "communism" which had sought to invade a once happy land.

3. THE PLIGHT OF AGRICULTURE

During these decades when the philosophy of the New South dominated the southern regions, men slowly learned that multiplying spindles and mounting slag piles did not necessarily imply higher standards of living or bring greater success in the perennial pursuit of happiness. The combination of northern finance, southern management, and exploited labor brought conflicts, distress, and bloodshed. The economic nationalization of the South merely added the problems of the industrial nation to those already present in the agricultural South.

The preoccupation of prophets and pundits with progress could not entirely blind them to the plight of agriculture. Despite industrial growth and the expansion of southern cities, Southerners remained an agricultural people. In 1930 the South had 65 per cent of its population in rural areas, while the nation as a whole had 44 per cent on the land. Fifty per cent of the farm population of the United States lived in the South. Yet the southern farmer had the lowest income, per farm and per capita, in the United States. He produced 96 per cent of the nation's cotton and sweet potatoes, 87 per cent of its tobacco, and 84 per cent of its rice, but he received only 37 per cent of the total crop value of the country. Southern agricultural progress lagged far behind its industry's.

Not all sections of southern agriculture were equally distressed, nor was the decline steady over the years. Times of booms alternated with times of depressions, and some crops showed relatively steady progress. Among those crops were the fruits, nuts, and vegetables grown along the coastal plain, which found a ready market in northern cities. From 1927 to 1931 the orchards of "apple-lachia" yielded a yearly average of 35,510,000 bushels, and the southern peach crop averaged nineteen million bushels. In 1933 Florida orchards produced over eighteen million boxes of oranges and nearly eleven million boxes of grapefruit. Texas, coming late into production in the lower Rio Grande valley, produced 1,130,000 boxes of grapefruit in 1933. The truck gardens of the Chesapeake region produced corn, peanuts, strawberries, potatoes, tomatoes, peas, watermelons, and cantaloupes, and other truck areas shipped cabbage, celery, and onions. Although adverse weather might produce temporary decline, the first three decades of the twentieth century witnessed a steady progress and a growing prosperity in these areas.

Farm Security Administration, photo by Marion Post

The Sectional Controversy Had Ended in Compromise.

The tobacco area in the upper South was also adapted to diversified farming and could profit from its proximity to northern markets. For some time, however, diversification was delayed and tobacco remained the principal money crop. So long as the market was open, tobacco growers were prosperous. Just after the Civil War, Kentucky farmers began to grow burley tobacco and to enjoy a new wealth. The rise of the American Tobacco Company, however, soon brought distress to the growers. The trust, in suspected collusion with agents of English companies, controlled the markets and forced down prices. In Kentucky 85 of the state's 119 counties were economically dependent upon tobacco. Operating on close margins, the farmers quickly felt the pinch of the trust's activities. As early as 1901 Kentucky farmers talked of acreage restrictions to increase prices. The following year the American Society of Equity was organized as a farmers' "union." Kentucky tobacco growers joined the Society and co-operated in restricting crops, and in 1905 combined against selling at low prices. Failing to secure results, they threatened to "strike"—they would stop growing tobacco. Members agreed to deliver unsold 1906 tobacco and the entire 1907 crop to warehouses and hold it until the price rose to 15 cents a pound. Unless their demands were met, they pledged not to grow tobacco in 1908. The farmers also resorted to night-riding to force co-operation from other farmers. On December 7, 1907, five hundred masked riders burned $200,000 worth of property in Hopkinsville. In the "Black Patch War" which followed, night-riders destroyed crops, burned warehouses, and spread terror through the country before the state government used troops to suppress them.

The "Great Tobacco Strike" was a success in 1908. The Trust did not accede to farmer demands so Equity members refused to grow the leaf. The crop that year was only 18 per cent of normal, and the result was victory for the farmers. It was a short-lived victory, however, for the 1909 crop was a large one following the good price year, and in the following year the Supreme Court ordered the dissolution of the Trust. But the trouble led to a new organization of tobacco marketing—the loose-leaf sales houses—which restored prosperity.

During the first World War tobacco prices boomed. Kentucky's crop in 1919-1920 sold for $80,000,000. But overexpansion and collapse followed in quick succession. The next year prices dropped to less than one per cent of the 1920 average. The farmers closed the auction rooms and immediately set about to form a co-operative marketing association. With financial backing from Kentucky banks and the Federal Government, the Burley Association began to bring order and rising prices to the tobacco industry. In other tobacco areas similar experiences produced a like evolution.

The tobacco areas, however, profited as much from diversification as from controlling their market. The region's adaptability to corn and forage stimulated stock farming and cattle raising. Kentucky's bluegrass region produced sheep, dairy and beef cattle, and hogs, in addition to the blooded horses that gave it fame. Along the slopes of Virginia's Blue Ridge the apple trees supplanted the tobacco crop. In southwestern Virginia vegetables for local canning factories made a new crop. Tobacco remained the leading crop over most of its old domain but its cultivation did not exclude that of other crops. The whole social system based on tobacco planting was readily adaptable to other types of agricultural production.

Most of the South's agricultural population as well as its farm area was devoted to cotton. Here the plight of agriculture was greatest, and here the problems were most insoluble. The "Cotton Kingdom" extended from eastern North Carolina to central Texas. It produced about 60 per cent of the world's supply of cotton and about one half of the southern crop was sold abroad. Its price was fixed in the world market and the conditions that prevailed in the cotton region were partly attributable to the fact that southern cotton competed with the products of exploited labor throughout the world.

During the first decade of the twentieth century, conditions in the Cotton Kingdom showed steady improvement. The number of tenants declined, and the crop-lien system became less onerous in its burdens. But about 1910 a series of disasters came to the cotton planters. First the boll weevil began its ravages, working steadily from the Mississippi Delta to the Atlantic Coastal Plain. In its train came disaster, modified only in a limited degree by diversified farming. One enthusiastic Alabama town erected a monument to the boll weevil because it had forced the farmer to turn to new crops. But the reformation was slight. Within a few years the worst ravages had passed and the cotton planters had learned to cope with the pest. Like flame-stunned moths they returned to cotton.

Then new cotton areas in Oklahoma, Texas, and even California increased the production and decreased the pride. Next, the first World War made cotton prices fluctuate violently. The price first went down to less than ten cents a pound, then quickly rose to forty cents; finally, in 1921 it suddenly dropped again to less than ten cents a pound. For the next decade King Cotton was sick. During the prosperous 'twenties, with prices of all commodities rising, the cotton producers were unable to share in the general prosperity.

The uncertainties of life in the Cotton Kingdom brought an increase in tenancy. From 1910 to 1930 farms operated by tenants in ten cotton-producing states increased from 55.1 per cent to 61.8 per cent. Moreover, in those years, white tenancy increased enormously. Small farmers sank from the owning to the renting class, and from there quickly dropped to being sharecroppers or wage laborers. A tendency to break up large individually-owned plantations into smaller holdings was paralleled by a tendency for corporations to acquire larger acreage. In those two decades the amount of mortgage debt in seven cotton states almost quadrupled. Foreclosures frequently broke up the larger estates into smaller units, but they resulted also in bringing many scattered holdings into the hands of banks and insurance companies.

The credit system involved both owners and tenants. Long-term debts of planters, secured by land, buildings, animals, and machinery, covered almost 50 per cent of the assessed value of plantations in the cotton states. Short-term debts of landlords, mostly from banks, were secured by hypothecating crops. Practically all tenants had short-term debts for subsistence advances from merchants. In 1930 these averaged $12.80 per family per month, ran for about seven months, and consumed more than 10 per cent of the sharecroppers' annual income in interest charges.

Under such a system, the income of both landlord and tenant was low and precarious. On 645 typical plantations, scattered over seven states, the gross cash income in 1934 was but slightly over $5,000; and the net income—including the value of home-consumed products—was $2,500. On these same plantations the sharecroppers annually averaged $312 per family or $71 per capita, the renters had $354 per family, while a family of wage laborers earned $180. These figures were higher than the average for the preceding years.

Tenants received, in addition to their share of the crop, house rent and firewood. The houses were the poorest in the nation. The typical tenant's home was an unpainted wooden shack of two, three, or four rooms. It was seldom screened, and never had other than primitive sanitation. It sat in a bare, unkempt yard, devoid of flowers or other decorations—except a broken-down car which doubled as a hen-roost. About the house the tenant might have a few chickens, some hogs, and a garden. Perhaps one third of his income went to the store for flour, lard, salt pork, kerosene, and patent medicines. Few tenants had cows, and fewer used any dairy products. The lack of adequate housing and sanitation made him susceptible to pneumonia, typhoid fever, malaria, and tuberculosis. The lack of a balanced diet brought pellagra and digestive disorders.

Farm Security Administration, photo by Shahn

FAMILY OF A REHABILITATION CLIENT IN ARKANSAS.

Conditions in the Cotton Kingdom did not encourage stability. Discontent, however, took the form of physical mobility rather than social revolt. Tenants moved from farm to farm seeking always for better land or better landlords. White tenants shifted from the farms to the mill towns and back again to the farms. Negroes, with less welcome in the towns, were relatively more stable than whites.

The system produced deterioration of both land and men. The low income level of the cotton regions prevented an adequate school system. Large families and frequent migration increased the school problems, but the southern states had but a small appropriation for each child. Since children were useful in the cotton fields, the school terms were usually adjusted to the cotton crop. Moreover, the necessity of maintaining separate schools for two races lowered the educational facilities for both. In some areas, consolidated schools for whites raised standards, but the Negroes received only the little schooling that a one-room schoolhouse and a poorly trained teacher could give. Salaries for teachers, both white and Negro, were lower in the cotton regions than in any other part of the nation. Negro teachers were paid less than their white counterparts. Southern racial segregation was based upon the myth of "separate but equal"; the patent inequality in the separate educational systems would lead to later federal intervention.

Neglect of the land, next to the neglect of man, was the most serious fault of the Cotton Kingdom. The tenant system "mined" the land and within a few years made necessary increasing applications of fertilizer. Moreover, lack of adequate care and foresight contributed to intensify the problem of erosion. The sloping surface of the land, the torrential rains, and the removal of the forest covering brought about a soil loss estimated at $75,000,000 a year. By 1925 one South Carolina county had lost over 90,000 acres of productive land, and a soil expert estimated that 60 per cent of the Piedmont regions had lost from four to eighteen inches of soil. Early attention to the problem of erosion would have saved this natural resource, but despite warnings and examples the subjects of King Cotton gave no heed to the advice. The tenant system, exploiting man and land alike, had no place for better methods of agriculture.

Economically, by 1932 the South was still in a colonial status. Her industry was controlled by outside interests; only nine of some two hundred important corporations had their headquarters in the South. Even those businesses which were managed from the South had to depend upon outside financial backing. Southern farm lands declined in value; many acres passed out of southern control into the hands of mortgage holders and insurance companies. But in the Southwest the petroleum and chemical industries were threatening to establish a center of capital without northern control. As the blight of depression fell upon the land after 1929, the economic conflict between the sections went on unabated.

The South in Politics, 1900-1932

1. THE POLITICS OF WHITE SUPREMACY

THE twentieth century marked the return of the South to a position of political responsibility in the nation. Its leadership was not, however, as great as before the Civil War. In the first half of the century no Southerner living in the South was elected to the presidency. Southerners were able to influence national policy through control of executive cabinet posts and congressional committees. In the Progressive Movement, in Woodrow Wilson's "New Freedom," in the first World War, and in the decade of "normalcy" which followed, Southerners provided constructive political leadership.

Throughout most of the South a one-party system prevailed. Memories of the Civil War and the lessons of reconstruction made Southerners eschew the Republican party. But because it was "solid," the South was able to play a dominant role in Democratic affairs. The two-thirds rule in Democratic nominating conventions gave the southern wing a veto on presidential candidates. After the dissipation of the Populist menace and the disfranchisement of the Negro, there was no serious danger that the Solid South would be broken, and before 1928 it was not.

The certainty that the Democrats would win elections led voters to remain at home on election days. In 1920 the eleven ex-Confederate states, with a population of over 25,000,000, cast but 2,609,000 votes for president. Eleven northern states with equal electoral votes and almost the same population cast 8,472,000 votes. Only 8.5 per cent of South Carolina's voting population went to the polls, although a contest of local issues took 44.6 per cent of North Carolina's voters to the ballot boxes. The average for the South was 2.5 per cent, while the comparable northern states polled over 10 per cent of the total eligible population. Indiana and Georgia, almost equal in population, polled 74.1 and 10.9 respectively. In the congressional elections of 1922 the northern states drew almost one half of the legal voters to the polls while but one tenth of the qualified Southerners cast ballots.

Although the Democrats effectively prevented the Republican party from obtaining a foothold in the South, southern Republicans played an important part in the Republican party. In the mountain regions of Virginia, North Carolina, Kentucky, and Tennessee, districts customarily returned Republicans to Congress; but in the rest of the South the active Republicans were largely limited to those who were willing to sacrifice social standing for the fleshpots of federal office. Postmasters and other federal officers formed the nucleus of the proscribed party and went through the futile motions of holding conventions, nominating candidates, and making half-hearted campaigns.

In the national party the South was a "rotten borough" whose delegates to the national Republican conventions could always be counted as loyal supporters of the president who had appointed them to office. In 1908 the Pennsylvania delegates to the national convention pointed out that the entire South had cast but 254,461 Republican votes in the preceding presidential election. Yet in 1908 there were 216 southern delegates, comprising more than one fifth of the convention membership. The Southerners had as many votes as the normally Republican states of California, Illinois, Indiana, Iowa, Michigan, Maine, and Ohio. Alabama's delegation was equal to that of Massachusetts. In 1912 the southern delegates forced the nomination of Taft and were largely responsible for the split of the party. In 1916 the southern delegation was reduced and the new apportionment carried over to the convention of 1920. In 1924, however, the convention raised the number of southern delegates.

The northern Negro vote was an important factor in national political affairs and influenced the Federal Government's treatment of southern blacks. Theodore Roosevelt, who became president in 1901, discomfited southern whites and delighted Negroes by inviting Booker T. Washington to dine at the White House. "The least we can say now," a Richmond editor growled, "is that we deplore the President's taste, and we distrust his wisdom." Southerners were further outraged when the president appointed a Negro Republican, William D. Crum, to the Collectorship of the Port of Charleston. When local whites demanded the resignation of the Negro postmistress at Indianola, Mississippi, Roosevelt closed the post office rather than comply. These deeds enhanced Roosevelt's popularity among Negroes, but many of them changed their opinion after the Brownsville affair. In 1906 Negro troops at the Texas post were dishonorably discharged without a trial following a shooting in the town.

These developments emphasized the fact that the Negro was the unifying factor in southern politics and a mighty force on the national scene. Since the disfranchisement of the Negro, southern voters were agreed upon the necessity of keeping him "in his place" and of maintaining white supremacy. Southern racism often spilled over to include hatred for anything "foreign": Roman Catholics, Jews, aliens with strange names. Politicians in the South played upon these earthy prejudices and expressed in colorful, pithy language the fears and hatreds of their unlettered constituents. But aside from the universal acceptance of white supremacy, southern politicians of the twentieth century differed but slightly from the national norm. They learned to build "machines," they stood by the "people" against their enemies, and they defined the enemies as corporations, public utilities, outside interests, or just vaguely as the "special interests."

At the turn of the century southern politics continued the course set by the Populist conflict and the subsequent united white front. There was but one party, but within its confines candidates for public office exhibited greater divergence and more bitterness than did contenders in states with competing parties.

The outstanding characteristic of southern politics in the new century was the development of the "demagogue." An ancient political figure, he was not unique to the South. He was the natural result of Negro disfranchisement and the Jim Crow laws, and the ignorance and provincialism that prevailed among southern whites. With the black expelled from politics, political divisions occurred only within white ranks. The older conservative leaders were drawn from the well-to-do groups representing the interests of the "New South": mill owners and managers, the professional classes, and other urban groups. These fashioned new "machines" to insure success at the polls—Thomas S. Martin in Virginia, Furnifold M. Simmons in North Carolina, and Edward H. Crump in Tennessee were typical—and played upon Negro phobia to sway the masses.

Ambitious newcomers who sought a public career often had to rebel against the machine. It was dangerous to buck the hierarchy, so the new men needed all the support they could get. They turned to the people, the rural tenants and the poor whites in mill villages and farm towns. They became demagogues. In their appeals to the masses they attacked the rich, the bankers and the railroad magnates, Wall Street, and other popular whipping boys. They presented themselves as defenders of the "poor, hard-working, God-fearing farmer." Generally the well-to-do worked against them, held their noses when mentioning them, and recounted anecdotes of their alleged ignorance and crudity in an effort to discredit them.

Such attacks, especially those that came from without the South, served only to solidify their popular support. The demagogues' chief appeal was that they "belonged," that they were "just one of the boys." They paraded their prejudices, their tobacco juice, their homey quirks, and their humble background. Eugene Talmadge of Georgia declared that he did not care to carry a single county with a streetcar. Huey P. Long of Louisiana did not mind admitting that he lacked the polish of higher education. But, he said, "I do not have to color what comes into my mind and into my heart. I say it unvarnished." Jeff Davis, beloved of the residents of the Arkansas hills, was described as a "carrot-headed, red-faced, loud-mouthed, strong-limbed, ox-driving mountaineer lawyer, and a friend of the fellow who brews forty-rod bug-juice back in the mountains."

Typical of the demagogic tirades against the Negro were those of Mississippi's James K. Vardaman. Forty years of experience, he said, had proved that the Negro was congenitally unsuited for the same educational program provided for the white. He urged the state legislature "to put a stop to the worse than wasting a half million dollars annually —money taken from the toiling white men and women of Mississippi— and devoted to the vain purpose of trying to make something of the Negro which the Great Architect . . . failed to provide for in the original plan of creation."

Vardaman capitalized upon the poor white's disgust with the local aristocracy. Dressed in pure white, immaculately overdressed, with his long black locks falling down to his shoulders, and mounted upon an ox-drawn lumberwagon, Vardaman campaigned against both the aristocrats and the Negroes. "He stood for the poor white against the 'nigger' —those were his qualifications as a statesman," said the son of his most unremitting enemy, William A. Percy. "He was such a splendid ham actor," Percy continued, "his inability to reason was so contagious, it was so impossible to determine where his idealism ended and his demagoguery began."

Vardaman served a term as governor from 1904 to 1908, an administration featured by regulation of railroads, lumber companies, and other big business firms. Railroads, factories, telegraph and telephone companies, he said, should be taxed according to their "real value . . . just as the farmer's home is taxed." He demanded reforms in the tax structure and in the state penitentiary, the abolition of the "school book trust" of the American Book Company, and a reduction of the legal rate of interest. While he was governor the state established a school textbook commission which broke the monopoly of the "trust," and passed laws regulating insurance companies, railroads, utilities, banks, manufacturers, and trusts.

Vardaman's successor in the esteem of Mississippi "rednecks" was Theodore G. Bilbo, a one-time theological student. Bilbo served as governor from 1916 to 1920 and from 1926 to 1932, advocating the cause of the poor whites against the corporations. "People of Mississippi," he said, "the fight between the classes and the masses, between the corporate influences and the people is on, and it will be a fight to the finish." As chief executive he improved public education and state services (hospitals and eleemosynary institutions) for the state's poor. The basis of his popularity, however, was his association with the little people of the state. "He was one of them and he had risen from obscurity to the fame of glittering infamy," said William A. Percy; "it was as if they themselves had crashed the headlines."

Cole L. Blease followed Ben Tillman in South Carolina as Bilbo followed Vardaman in Mississippi. Blease also made his appeal to the disinherited whites—the mill hands and the tenant farmers. He praised lynchers and promised to "wipe the inferior race from the face of the earth." Such talk concealed the fact that, unlike most demagogues in the South, he accomplished very little for the people who put him into office. He was governor of South Carolina from 1911 to 1915, and in 1924 was elected to the Senate.

HUEY P. LONG. Perhaps the ablest of the "demagogues" was Huey P. Long of Louisiana. Rising to the office of governor in 1928 and to the Senate in 1930, Long ruled his state with an iron hand. He sponsored a system of good roads, befriended the public school system and the Louisiana State University, and launched violent attacks upon corporate wealth. He advocated a "Share the Wealth" program to confiscate great fortunes and distribute them throughout the population. This would, Long promised, provide every family with a home, a car, and $2,500 annual income. The "Kingfish" did not mind admitting that he lacked the polish of higher education. But, he said, "I do not have to color what comes into my mind and heart. I say it unvarnished."

Others of the southern demagogues were James E. Ferguson of Texas, "Alfalfa Bill" Murray of Oklahoma, and J. Thomas Heflin of Alabama. Jim Ferguson was the darling of the Lone Star State's dispossessed masses and anathema to the wealthy vested interests. His enemies worked every trick in an effort to forestall his corporation regulation and "trust-busting" schemes. In 1917 the state legislature found him guilty of malpractice, removed him from the governor's office, and declared that he could never again serve as an official in Texas. Only momentarily stumped, Ferguson adopted a highly original gambit: he offered his wife Miriam as a candidate. "Ma" Ferguson was elected Texas governor in 1924 and in 1932 and carried on her husband's program. In Alabama Tom Heflin championed the second Ku Klux Klan and vociferously berated the Vatican. Appealing for the votes of Protestant and alien-distrusting Alabamians, Heflin pretended that there was a Jesuit plot to poison him and carefully inspected his food.

Last of the demagogues and perhaps the ablest among them was Huey P. Long of Louisiana. Rising to the office of governor in 1928 and to the Senate in 1930, Long ruled his state with an iron hand. His political machine proved highly efficient in procuring funds, and the governor assumed dictatorial power over the legislature. He sponsored a system of good roads, befriended the public school system and the Louisiana State University, and launched violent attacks upon corporate wealth. Master of the arts of Southern demagogic oratory, Long did not attack the "nigger," but he repealed the poll tax which disfranchised the poorer whites.

After a pyrotechnic governorship, Long transferred his talents to the United States Senate in 1930, where he soon gained national attention by his violent speeches, rude conduct, and intemperate attacks upon the administration of Franklin D. Roosevelt. To the alarm of conservatives everywhere, Long advocated a "Share the Wealth" program to confiscate great fortunes and distribute them throughout the population. This would provide every family with a home, a car, and $2,500 annual income, Long promised. At a time of national depression Long's theme song, "Every Man a King," gained widespread adherence. Still retaining his dictatorial power in Louisiana, the "Kingfish" was apparently on the eve of launching himself as a presidential candidate when in 1935 he was assassinated in the state house in Baton Rouge.

In the main, the social program of these demagogues reflected the old Populist opposition. Once in office, however, they generally voted with the Bourbons and attacked faraway enemies. They were noisy and they enlivened the southern political scene with the garish colors of a rude, ribald humor. But there were genuine progressives in the South and they made changes that were farther reaching and more significant than the colorful aberrations of the demagogues.

2. THE SOUTHERN PROGRESSIVES

Beside the demagogues, their constructive statesmanship often overshadowed by the colorful excesses of the hatemongers, there were southern politicians who were among the nation's ablest. Their work amply illustrated the fact that not all politics in the South turned on a program of silence toward pertinent issues or appeals to prejudices. Indeed, some of the men who gained national reputations for their atti-

tudes toward the Negro were in the forefront of the progressive movement. Those politicians who appealed to the masses did so in the name
of the "people" against their economic and social oppressors. By 1898
the Southerners had definitely discarded the Populist party but the cause
of the common man and the small farmer did not disappear so easily
from southern politics. Under the impact of the farmer revolt, the victorious conservatives adopted reforms in state governments that made
them pioneers in the progressive movement which soon dominated the
national scene.

The populist agitation had produced a widespread demand for
economic and social reforms. Gradually rising farm prices after 1896
moderated these demands, and then leadership in southern liberal movements passed to urban groups: progressive editors, politicians, and businessmen. The southern progressives were moderate Democrats, neither
Populists nor Bourbons. But their objectives were similar to those of the
Populists; they favored popular education, greater democratic control
of government, and an end to the economic policy of laissez-faire.

In proportion to its population the South had more leaders committed to such a progressive program than any other section of the
country. Nearly every state could claim at least one. In Virginia there
were Carter Glass, Andrew Jackson Montague, and William A. Jones; in
North Carolina, Charles B. Aycock, Robert B. Glenn, Josephus Daniels,
Claude and William Kitchin, and Walter Clark; in Georgia, Hoke Smith
and Thomas W. Hardwick; in Florida, Frank L. Mayer and Napoleon
B. Broward; in Alabama, Braxton B. Comer; in Mississippi, James K.
Vardaman and Theodore G. Bilbo; in Tennessee, Austin Peay and Edward H. Crump; in Kentucky, Ollie M. James and John C. W. Beckham;
in Louisiana, John M. Parker; in Texas, Dan Moody, James S. Hogg,
Charles A. Culberson, and Robert L. Henry; in Arkansas, Jeff Davis; and
in Oklahoma, which became a state in 1907, Robert L. Owen and Thomas
P. Gore.

These men were progressives because they accepted the idea that
government should be "given back to the people," and then under more
democratic control its power should be used to curb the excesses of
"big business," especially the railroads. But the race agitation of the
previous decade had hardened southern color lines. Southern progressive
democracy therefore was exclusively for the white man. This fact tended
to conceal the effective work southern progressives did in other matters.

Typical of these men was Austin Peay of Tennessee. Entering
state politics in 1900, he served first in the legislature and then as chairman of the state Democratic Committee. In 1922 he became governor
and held the office for six years. Attacking the political machine that
ruled the state, he supported administrative reforms, tax reforms, and
educational improvement. He reduced the number of state departments
and boards from sixty-four to eight; he reorganized the highway department and built an efficient highway system. He supported the state
university, secured an eight-month term for all schools, and raised

teachers' standards and salaries. He obtained the establishment of the Great Smoky Mountains National Park. Such leaders did much to offset the bad repute that demagogues and machine politicians had brought upon the South.

Both Populism and the philosophy of the New South forced a gradual broadening of the functions of government. The effort to keep abreast of the North produced improvements in highways, multiplication of schools and extension of their terms, and modernized systems for caring for the poor, the insane, and the criminal. New and statewide care of public health began. Everywhere states strove to pull themselves out of the mud and to send their children to school. Thus, during the 'twenties Tennessee increased her paved highways from less than 500 to more than 5,000 miles and instituted eight-month school terms in eighty-two of her ninety-five counties. Departments and commissioners of agriculture and the extension divisions of state universities sent out county agents and home demonstrators to teach better methods of farming and to improve domestic life. Public health agencies sought to eradicate hookworm and to decrease malaria. State hospitals for the care and cure of tubercular patients increased.

But the southern progressives did more than attempt to keep abreast of the North. In many matters most closely associated with the progressive movement southern leaders led the way. They pioneered in railroad legislation. Virginia took the first step in 1877, immediately after the "redeemers" resumed control, and established a railroad commission like that in Massachusetts. Until 1901 it was only a supervisory body, but in that year it became a corporation commission with complete administrative, legislative, and judicial authority over railroads and other corporations. In the following year South Carolina established a similar commission. Georgia, however, was with California the first state in the nation to regulate rates effectively (1879). Eventually nearly all southern states copied the Georgia system. In 1907 under the leadership of Governor Hoke Smith, the Railroad Commission's powers were broadly extended to include the regulation of all public utilities. It even had power to control stock issues to prevent watering and fraud.

Other states also adopted commissions with regulatory authority over railroads and utility corporations: Mississippi (1886), Texas (1891), Tennessee and Florida (1897), Louisiana (1898), Arkansas and North Carolina (1899), Kentucky (1900), and Alabama (1907).

Thus by 1907 every southern state had a railroad commission which reduced and regulated rates and attempted to control and abolish discriminations against small shippers. Southern leaders also exerted significant influence on the national movement for railroad regulation. John H. Reagan of Texas was called the father of the Interstate Commerce Commission Act of 1887, and in 1906 Ben Tillman handled the floor fight for the Hepburn rate regulation bill in the Senate.

The southern progressives also reformed party machinery and the electoral process in their states by adopting the direct primary for party nominations. Every county in South Carolina used the direct primary before 1890, and in 1896 it was employed by the state Democratic party. The direct party primary was adopted in 1897 in Arkansas, Georgia in 1898, Florida and Tennessee in 1901, Alabama and Mississippi in 1902, Kentucky and Texas in 1905, Louisiana in 1906, Oklahoma in 1907, Virginia in 1913, and North Carolina in 1915. The direct primary in America began in the South and most southern states were using it before Wisconsin adopted it in 1903.

Every southern state also took steps to reform the electoral process and make fraud more difficult. Seven states prohibited the candidate from making appointments prior to the election; Arkansas and Texas made it illegal for a candidate to transport voters to the polls; Arkansas, Alabama, Louisiana, and Missouri declared it unlawful to solicit campaign funds from a candidate. By 1920 ten states had made it illegal to offer a bribe to a voter and every southern state had outlawed voter intimidation. Other states had laws on the books to provide secret ballots, to limit campaign expenditures, and to prevent illegal registration of voters and fraudulent voting. Progressives in no other section did more to make the democratic electoral process more effective.

Progressives in southern states also acted to allow voters to determine their preferences for national officials. Although the Constitution provided for the election of senators by state legislatures, by the time the Seventeenth Amendment went into effect (May 13, 1913), senatorial candidates in every southern state were selected by a primary election. The presidential preference primary, usually considered part of the Wisconsin Idea, was also adopted in the South: in Florida, Georgia, and Mississippi in 1912, and in Texas in 1913. The democratic devices of initiative, referendum, and recall were not popular in the South, but were included in the Oklahoma Constitution of 1907, and in Arkansas in 1909.

Southern progressives also pioneered in reforms of municipal government. The commission form of city government originated in Galveston, Texas, in 1900, following a great hurricane and devastating flood. By 1914 it had spread to most of the large cities in the South: Birmingham, Mobile, Montgomery, Shreveport, New Orleans, Wilmington, Oklahoma City, El Paso, Columbia, Chattanooga, Knoxville, Memphis, Dallas, San Antonio, Fort Worth, Houston, Austin, and many smaller cities. By 1907 the plan was widely adopted in Texas, but it got into the political science textbooks as the "Des Moines Plan" after that city adopted it in 1907.

Similarly the South lost credit for instituting the city manager form of municipal government. The country's first city manager was in Staunton, Virginia, in 1908, and in 1911 the plan was introduced at Sumter, South Carolina. But it was widely imitated over the country as the "Dayton Idea" after the Ohio city belatedly installed a manager in 1914.

Southern progressives thus instigated reforms which became the pattern of state and national action. There were weaknesses in the southern program: there was little interest in curing the ills of farm tenancy or in alleviating the plight of the Negro. Otherwise the Southerners resembled midwestern progressives. They engaged in "trust-bustin' "; they established commissions to regulate banks, insurance companies, as well as public utilities and railroads; and they wrote unfair practices acts, safety and inspection laws for mines and factories, pure food and drug laws, penitentiary reforms, and other humanitarian legislation. They were, of course, far removed from the nationalist Progressives who stemmed from the East. Social reformers of the nationalist tradition were latter-day representatives of the older "trustees" whose doctrine of stewardship had led them to impose improvements on the land. The Populist-Progressives of the West and South, trying to use government for reforms, were always conscious of the democratic base of government. They insisted on expanding the areas of democratic control at the same time that they imposed new functions on the government. Southerners had little in common with such nationalist Progressives as Theodore Roosevelt and the Bull Moose faction.

These reform programs were directed by an assemblage of Progressive governors in southern states such as Napoleon B. Broward of Florida; William Goebel of Kentucky, who was assassinated in a struggle over taxation and regulation of corporations and railroads; Charles B. Aycock of North Carolina, whose main interest was public education; James K. Vardaman of Mississippi, Braxton B. Comer of Alabama, Hoke Smith of Georgia, and the colorful Jeff Davis of Arkansas.

Only Kentucky experienced assassination but opposition was strong in all states, coming chiefly from railroads and other vested interests. The symbol of railroad power was the federal court injunction halting regulatory action of the state railroad commission. In such cases, southern states'-righters often rebelled. In North Carolina in 1907 a state court ignored a federal court order and temporarily created a sharp clash between federal and state authority. The impasse ended when the railroad surrendered and compromised the issue (a maximum passenger rate of two and a quarter cents per mile) with the state commission.

In Florida and Texas insurance companies were also under attack. In 1907 the Robertson Law in Texas required every insurance company doing business in the state to invest in Texas at least 75 per cent of the legal reserve required by its home state. Jeff Davis, as attorney-general of Arkansas, alarmed conservatives everywhere with his war on insurance companies; he brought 126 suits against fire insurance companies alone. Texas also attacked oil companies in a struggle against monopoly that continued throughout the period.

In general the southern progressives were the well-to-do, those who had something to ship over the rails, something to insure, or the resources to speculate in oil properties. They reflected the ambitions of their leaders—Comer the mill owner, Broward the jack-of-all-trades, Smith the publisher—and marked a new struggle for southern independence against the ancient alien enemy. When their constituents sent them to Congress they carried the fight to the national capital with progressive legislation which made up the backbone of the Wilsonian New Freedom.

3. The South and the Nation

The first decade of the new century saw the return of Southerners to national leadership. In 1912, for the first time since 1860, a Southerner living in the South was an active candidate for the Democratic party's presidential nomination. Oscar W. Underwood, born in Kentucky in 1862 but living in Birmingham, had the support of conservative Southerners—those who disliked the "excessive" centralization and liberalism of Woodrow Wilson's program. But the "New Freedom" accepted the traditional assumptions of free enterprise and economic individualism and promised governmental assistance to remove obstacles to the operation of a free market.

A more extreme political liberalism was that of Theodore Roosevelt and the Progressive party, which advocated active governmental participation in economic affairs. Taft, the regular Republican candidate, made only minor efforts to sway southern voters. A victory for any of the other three candidates would be a victory for the South. Roosevelt made a serious effort to win southern votes, and spoke in southern cities. In New Orleans he said, "I came here not to ask you to follow me, but to ask you to join me. . . . I want you to take your share in steering the wheels of the nation."

But Roosevelt's southern excursion stumbled over the rock of Negro participation. He wanted black support in the North and white support in the South, and he could not have both. A "Lily-White" Progressive party organized in the South and refused to admit Negroes to its membership or conventions. In Georgia, Florida, Alabama, and Mississippi, rival white and Negro Progressive groups named delegates to the national convention and claimed the blessings of Roosevelt. Forced to decide between the conflicting elements, he tried to compromise; he would seat both delegations from the four states but give the state's vote to the whites. That solution did not suit either faction nor either section. Northern liberals decried Roosevelt's "cavalier treatment of the southern Negro," while southern newspapers castigated the Progressives as the "black" party for seating Negroes.

As a result, Roosevelt failed in his efforts to crack the Solid South. Led by Wilson, the Democrats won their first presidential election in twenty years and brought about a major shift in American political geography as Southerners assumed control of the national government. Wilson was born in Staunton, Virginia, in 1856, and grew up in Georgia and in North Carolina. He attended the University of Virginia's law school, and always considered himself a Virginian. After practicing law in Atlanta, Wilson entered Johns Hopkins University's graduate school, where he received the doctorate in political science. He taught in several colleges before going to his alma mater, Princeton University, where he became president in 1902. In 1910 Wilson became governor of New Jersey and attracted national attention as a liberal reformer in that eastern den of political thieves. But before he could cleanse the stables he received the Democratic nomination in 1912.

President Wilson, himself a Southerner, appointed Southerners to his cabinet. In the eight years of his administration Carter Glass of Virginia, David F. Houston of Missouri, J. C. McReynolds of Tennessee, Thomas W. Gregory of Texas, Albert S. Burleson of Texas, Josephus Daniels of North Carolina, John B. Payne of Virginia, and Joshua W. Alexander of Missouri served as heads of executive departments.

Democrats also controlled both houses of Congress. Thanks to long tenure, Southerners were chairmen of all the important committees. In the Senate Hoke Smith of Georgia headed the Committee on Education and Labor; Furnifold M. Simmons of North Carolina, Finance; Augustus O. Bacon of Georgia, Foreign Relations; Charles A. Culberson of Texas, Judiciary; Joseph F. Johnston of Alabama, Military Affairs; Benjamin R. Tillman of South Carolina, Naval Affairs; John H. Bankhead of Alabama, Post Offices and Post Roads; Lee S. Overman of North Carolina, Rules; and Thomas S. Martin of Virginia, Appropriations.

In the House of Representatives, Champ Clark of Missouri was Speaker, and the influential committees were headed by Southerners. The Ways and Means Committee, of which Oscar W. Underwood of Alabama was chairman, served as the steering committee. Other southern chairmen were Asbury F. Lever of South Carolina, Agriculture; Carter Glass of Virginia, Banking and Currency; Dudley M. Hughes of Georgia, Education; Henry D. Flood of Virginia, Foreign Affairs; William C. Adamson of Georgia, Interstate and Foreign Commerce; Henry D. Clayton of Alabama, Judiciary; James Hay of Virginia, Military Affairs; Lemuel P. Padgett of Tennessee, Naval Affairs; John A. Moon of Tennessee, Post Offices and Post Roads; and Robert L. Henry of Texas, Rules.

These men with their southern colleagues wrote the major legislation which made up the "New Freedom." Underwood wrote the tariff which bore his name, revising the rates downward, putting sugar and wool on the free list and generally following Populist demands of twenty years earlier. Cordell Hull, a former mountain judge from Tennessee and now sitting in the House, wrote the tariff bill's chief innovation, the income tax provision. Proclaimed constitutional by the Sixteenth Amendment on February 25, 1913, the income tax, at least in its inception, was an agrarian weapon against wage-earning industrial workers and was another Populist plank.

The second significant act of the Progressive New Freedom was the Glass-Owens banking reform, usually referred to as the Federal Reserve Act. Carter Glass of the House Committee on Banking and Currency wrote the basic law to decentralize monetary control by establishing twelve regional banks, and to provide a more flexible currency. This too was a Populist demand, but the Federal Reserve was far from the Populist idea. It did conform to southern conservative ideas, however.

"The regional reserve banks," Underwood explained, "will in the end secure to all the people all the advantages that state control would vouchsafe for them." Glass, a small, redheaded man with the habit of speaking through the left side of his mouth, received credit for the banking law. "You are, more than any single man, entitled to the credit for this real victory in the cause of the people of this country," Secretary of the Treasury William G. McAdoo told him.

The third main plank in the New Freedom's platform was a new antitrust act. Representative Henry D. Clayton of Alabama prepared five bills establishing an interstate trade commission, prohibiting interlocking directorates, defining unlawful business practices, and amending the Sherman Anti-Trust Act to prevent unfair competition. The Clayton bills passed the House on June 5, 1914, and with the aid of Senator Charles A. Culberson of Texas, passed the Senate on September 2. In the House, the Clayton Anti-Trust Law had the support of John C. Floyd of Arkansas and Charles C. Carlin of Virginia, and on the vote there was no southern Democratic opposition. With the passage of trust regulatory legislation, the southern congressional leaders had redeemed Wilson's campaign promises. Congressman Tom Heflin of Alabama exulted: "Labor is employed, wages are good, the earth has yielded abundantly, and the Democratic Party is in control, God reigns, and all is well with the Republic."

Southern congressmen also contributed to the divinely ordained well-being of the Republic with the development of a new foreign policy whose chief ingredient was a rejection of earlier and more militant attitudes. Virginia's William A. Jones, chairman of the House Committee on Insular Affairs, proposed a bill to grant independence to the Philippine Islands. In similar spirit, many southern lawmakers objected to American expansionist and interventionist schemes. Augustus O. Bacon of Georgia, chairman of the Senate Committee on Foreign Affairs, led a fight against armed intervention in Mexico after the Villa forays. Southerners also opposed the administration's efforts to prepare militarily for the European war, which began in 1914. Claude Kitchin of North Carolina, who assumed leadership in the House when Underwood entered the Senate, and Mississippi's James K. Vardaman joined the "little group of willful men" in opposing the preparedness program.

The growing militant spirit affected the South as much as the rest of the country, but Southern congressmen remained unmoved. James Hay of Virginia, chairman of the House Committee on Military Affairs, used his influence against military expansion. On March 6, 1916, however, he joined other Democrats in passing the National Defense Bill, which established a Regular Army of 143,000 and a National Guard of 400,000. And another southern leader, Thomas S. Martin of Virginia, chairman of the Senate Appropriations Committee, strenuously objected to expending funds for war purposes, but he yielded to the pressure of public opinion. "I am opposed," he said, "but I am under duress. If I oppose Wilson, his claquers in Virginia all cry out, 'Tom Martin is a reactionary,' and hound me." Martin said that it was a "bitter pill" to be held up by the man in the White House.

Thus unwillingly did southern Progressive congressmen go to war. Despite the determined opposition of many of them, the southern delegation in Congress voted with their colleagues for war. James K. Vardaman of Mississippi was one of six senators who voted Nay, and House Majority Leader Claude Kitchin of North Carolina surprised the country by voting against his party's administration. But though only four southern congressmen voted against the war resolution, the South was by no means united on the issue. "I am from a State that does not want war," Representative J. Willard Ragsdale of South Carolina told the House, and other Dixie delegates introduced letters and petitions from their constituents that revealed the strong peace sentiment in the South. Perhaps the continuing hope of sectional reconciliation stirred in American breasts as it did in that of Congressman Fred Talbott of Maryland. "The old Confederate will join the old Union soldier," he promised; "the sons of the old Confederates and the sons of the old Union veterans will all join together, and we will have a great big United States victory as the outcome of this war."

But the vote to intervene in the European conflict did not bring to an end the southern criticism of administration militarism. The Army's determination to adopt universal conscription rather than rely on the traditional voluntary force drew fire from Southerners. Mississippi's Thomas U. Sisson said, "I see more danger to America in establishing the conscription system than I do from any German invasion or any German army." In the Senate his fellow Mississippian Vardaman wanted to know why the conscription of men was not accompanied by a draft of wealth. Kenneth D. McKellar of Tennessee also stood out against the mounting war hysteria.

Two incidents in McKellar's state illustrated the war's impact upon the South, herself defeated and humiliated only a half-century earlier. In the mind and conscience of a simple East Tennessee mountaineer who became an American legend as Sergeant Alvin C. York, a struggle went on about the moral problems of the war. And at the other end of the state, in Memphis, citizens prepared to go to war lest a "Judas state" named Germany "trample upon and fling to the winds the rules of international law," but paused long enough to burn alive a half-witted Negro for an unproven crime.

Meanwhile, throughout the South the war effort affected more and more people. The Army erected camps for its mushrooming National Army in the moderate climate of southern states, all of them named for historic figures, and many chosen to balance southern and northern heroes. In Maryland there was Camp Meade; in Virginia, Camp Lee; Camp Greene in North Carolina; Camps Wadsworth, Jackson, and Sevier in South Carolina; Gordon, Hancock, and Wheeler in Georgia; Taylor in Kentucky; McClellan and Sheridan in Alabama; Shelby in Mississippi; Pike in Arkansas; Beauregard in Louisiana; Doniphan in

Oklahoma; and Bowie, MacArthur, Logan, and Travis in Texas. Newport News served as a major port of embarkation; 288,000 troops departed through the port facilities there.

Southerners bore their share of the war in other ways. Sons and grandsons of men who had stood at Gettysburg or had seen the Wilderness mingled their blood with that of descendants of Union veterans at far-away places whose names they could not pronounce: Château-Thierry, Saint-Mihiel, and villages in the Argonne forest. Back in Washington, Claude Kitchin, who had stood almost alone in opposing entry into the war, now incurred the anger of Americans for his efforts to pay for the war by taxation. Bitterly he denounced the war profiteers: "They are willing to fight this war out if somebody else will do the fighting. They are willing to pay for the war if somebody else will do the paying." Business interests and the press, which objected to Kitchin's plan for increased postal rates, became so irate at the North Carolinian that they tried to make him and his financial program the central issue in the elections of 1918. To depose Kitchin as House leader, they reiterated, Republicans must control the Congress. With Republican attacks upon President Wilson and other aspects of southern political idealism and progressivism that had influenced government since 1913, the Democrats lost the midterm elections. Such papers as the New York *World* blamed the defeat upon the party's "Southern sectional leaders."

In the peacemaking and the formulation of the League of Nations, leaders from the South played their traditional role as balance-wheels against the extremists. Though their efforts were pitifully weak, the Southerners did what they could to prevent a harsh settlement that would only breed future wars. Memories of the reconstruction acts and the collapse of the southern economy impelled them to seek moderation for the vindictive demands of the Allies. Southerners in Congress worked against the conservative reaction similar to that that followed the Civil War. One of its manifestations was an effort to relieve the rich of the war tax burden and fasten it upon the poor and on future generations.

There were other signs of the reversal of pre-war tendencies. A revival of the Ku Klux Klan attracted national attention, though aside from a few demagogic southern leaders, the second Klan had slight following in the South. In the early 1920's the center of Klan strength was in Indiana. It resisted the internationalism implicit in the League of Nations and also the supposed threat of Bolshevism in America—the "Red Scare." In that fear the Klan was joined by super-patriotic national organizations. Finally, the "Roaring 'Twenties" was a business man's paradise, dominated by such moguls as the Mellons, the Garys, the Fricks, the Insulls, and their political representatives, Warren G. Harding, Calvin Coolidge, and Herbert Hoover.

The pressure toward conformity was almost irresistible, but some Americans refused to compromise. Efforts of the military to use the war sentiment for a universal military training and service scheme met southern opposition. Senator Kenneth D. McKellar of Tennessee said: "If it is a bad thing for Germany to have universal military training now—and we say so in our treaty–how does it happen that it is a good thing for free America to have it now?" Southern Democrats joined other members of their party in defeating Wilson's military policy in 1920. Claude Kitchin continued his efforts to tax the war profiteers: "They should not be relieved of taxes as long as there is a single disabled soldier, or a single widow or orphan of a dead soldier in need." Southerners also resisted other aspects of national fiscal policy of the 'twenties: the tariff, foreign loans in lieu of foreign purchases, and a short-sighted farm program.

After the war Southerners slipped apathetically into the attitude of "normalcy" which characterized the country. Aside from the critics of the *status quo,* most of whom served in Washington, southern politicians were not interested in upsetting the one-party system. As had been true earlier, such conflict as politics afforded usually occurred within the party and that between the "machine" candidate and an ambitious "maverick" or independent. The new economic forces entering the South found the one-party machine system useful for their purposes, so as a rule few changes were made.

The pattern of southern politics in the "normalcy" decade was the machine. In Virginia it took its instructions from Harry F. Byrd, Winchester apple-grower, who became governor in 1926 and who ruled economically and efficiently. North Carolina's politics were dominated by Furnifold M. Simmons, who served as Senator from 1900 to 1930. Simmons' hegemony was threatened in 1920 by O. Max Gardner of Shelby; so promising was the newcomer that in 1928 he became governor with machine support. In that year Simmons bolted the Democratic party to support Hoover, an action that spelled his dethronement in 1930 by Josiah W. Bailey, a Baptist editor, who won Simmons' senate seat. Throughout the period Tar Heel Republicans were a strong threat to the dominant Democrats; in 1928 they carried the state for Hoover and took 33 per cent of the state's vote for their gubernatorial candidate. South Carolina, its political action hampered by the presence of the Negro, was overshadowed by Coleman L. Blease, who was elected to the senate in 1924.

In Georgia, Eugene Talmadge took over control of the senate and inherited Tom Watson's Populistic following and many of his talking points. Snapping his bright red galluses and condemning the enemies of the farmers, Talmadge ran for the office of Commissioner of Agriculture in 1926 and later served as governor. The Neill Primary Act of 1917 established the county unit system which simplified rural control of state politics; it gave each county twice as many unit votes as it had members in the state House of Representatives. So long as rural counties remained united, they had an advantage in choosing state officials. The Neill Act was intended to save the state from the pernicious influences of Atlanta and other urban centers. In Alabama, the Bibb Graves machine controlled internal politics; Graves was governor from 1927 to 1931.

Tennessee was the scene of a spirited political battle in the 1920's between Memphis boss Edward H. Crump and other Democratic politicians. Crump, born in nearby Holly Springs, Mississippi, in 1875, sought his fortune in the Bluff City metropolis at the age of seventeen. By 1900 he was successful in business and entered local politics as a reformer pledged to exorcise Memphis's dens of iniquity. In ten years he had assumed control of the city and county and by 1920 was ready to reach out for control of the state. The anti-organization leader was Austin Peay, governor from 1922 to 1928. In 1932 the Crump candidate, Hill McAllister, was elected governor, and the Memphis politician had won his fight. The hills of East Tennessee harbored a hard core of Republicans, however, and consistently returned Carroll Reece to Congress.

Similar intraparty conflict, with slight but determined Republican opposition, took place in other southern states. In Mississippi the division was between hill folk and the delta planters, with the cause of the "red-necks" of the hills ably pleaded by Theodore Bilbo. "In the minds of the newly powerful hill people of Mississippi," an observer reported, "the large corporations and 'trusts' became confused with their old masters, the delta folk." In 1923 Bilbo lost the governorship to Henry Whitfield, president of Mississippi State College for Women, but "The Man" won a close race in 1927 and re-established himself. Texas politicians—the Fergusons, "Pa" and "Ma," and a naturalized Yankee songwriter and flour merchant, W. Lee O'Daniel—won office by sparring noisily with the corporations. Louisiana was engaged in the exciting pastime of making every man a king under the inspired leadership of the ambitious "Kingfish," Huey P. Long.

In 1928 came the only exception to solid Democratic control of southern states in presidential elections. In that year the national party nominated the "Happy Warrior," Al Smith, who was a Roman Catholic, a champion of unrestricted sale of alcoholic beverages (a position Southerners labeled "wet"), and a resident of New York, which Southerners believed the source of all the evils of urbanism. Smith was thus an affront to all the southern niceties. In contrast Republicans offered Herbert Hoover, a "dry," a Protestant of the Quaker persuasion, and uncluttered with urban connections. Though it was a fearsome plunge, many Southerners overcame the Solid South presentiment at the name Republican— a holdover from reconstruction. Five ex-Confederate states—Florida, North Carolina, Virginia, Tennessee, and Texas—gave their electoral votes to a Republican candidate, and a shift of 7,100 votes would have put Alabama into Hoover's column. Generally, counties with high Negro populations remained unwaveringly Democratic; while counties with small Negro populations were willing to bolt the traditional party. Only in Arkansas did most of the "white counties" vote Democratic; there probably the determining factor was the fact that Arkansas' Senator Joseph T. Robinson was Democratic candidate for the vice-presidency.

Following the rebellion of 1928, Southerners returned to the Democratic fold, and economic factors after 1929 led them to vote along with their fellow countrymen for the Democratic presidential nominee in 1932, though he was also a New Yorker and a "wet." But the 1928 election had served notice upon the country that there was a limit to the South's docile acceptance of the Democratic candidate regardless of his background.

Thus in the first third of the twentieth century, southern influence in national affairs had increased dramatically. Southern congressmen and state leaders played a significant part in the Progressive movement, belying the stereotype of the reactionary southern politician. Furthermore, the broad spirit of national interest which characterized their work contrasted sharply with the provincial caricature usually drawn of southern leaders. Even the "demagogues" made good on many of their campaign promises, worked to awaken the political interest of southern rural masses, and joined the national fight against unregulated laissez-faire business interests. On these matters the South was playing its traditional role in American history: it was directing the nation down the path of moderate yet democratic reform. By 1932 it was clear that the South was well on the way out of its position of political subservience in the nation.

Southern Society and Culture, 1900-1932

1. THE SOUTHERN PEOPLE

IN politics and in business affairs the first third of the twentieth century witnessed the faltering return of the South toward a position of independence and leadership. At the same time, developments in southern life and culture indicated that many of the major differences between the South and the nation were being erased. But the process of nationalization was not yet complete. Southern variations from the national norm still existed in the areas of literature, philosophy and religion, education, and society. These provided the South with its distinctive civilization and the nation with its most interesting provincial culture, its most placid labor force, and some of its most pressing social problems.

Nowhere was the South more distinctive than in the nature of its people. In character they ranged from the allegedly effete Virginia Tidewater gentleman and the fiercely independent southern mountaineer through the Negroes of various shades and social levels, to the cosmopolite of the New Orleans French Quarter and to the Texas oil millionaire investing in hotels and universities. So diverse were the southern people that, strictly speaking, there existed no such category. Still, several generalizations were possible. Southerners were more rural than was the nation at large, more dependent upon farming, more illiterate, poorer in this world's goods, more willing to migrate to town or out of the section to seek the greener pasture, and more fertile than the rest of the country. Indeed, the South furnished the population pool out of which the nation drew its labor supply.

The southern people were increasing faster than the national average. In 1900 there were 24,523,527 Southerners, and by 1930 they had grown to a total of 37,857,633, for a gain of 54 per cent. Population in the Southeast was also becoming relatively "whiter." The white population increased from 11,212,000 in 1900 to 17,746,000 in 1930, or 58 per cent, while Negroes increased from 6,851,000 to 7,784,000, or only 13.6 per cent. But Negroes were still a large minority in the South, and still largely concentrated in the South. In 1930 nearly one third of the southern population was black. Only Kentucky, Tennessee, Texas, and West Virginia had fewer than 25 per cent Negroes; Mississippi's population was half Negro, and Alabama, Georgia, Louisiana, and South Carolina were more than one-third Negro. And in 1930 nearly three fourths of the nation's Negroes lived in the South.

Another characteristic of the southern population in the first third of the century was its mobility. Southern people were on the move. There was a marked migration across the Potomac and the Ohio rivers to northern urban centers. By 1920 over 2,375,000 whites and almost 400,000 Negroes had moved out of the region. In the 1920's the upheavals of the World War, the continuing agricultural depression, the harsh tenancy regulations, and the boll-weevil epidemic contributed to the Great Migration. In the decade, over a million southern whites and about 615,000 Negroes emigrated. Thus the Southeast, with its unusually high birth rate (20 per thousand people) replenished the population of the nation.

The movement of Southerners provided more than people, however; it also brought new problems. Perhaps the most significant contribution of the South to the nation has been the problem of the Negro minority, whether as slaves on southern plantations or as slum-dwellers in northern cities. The migration of Negroes northward was so great as to suggest the possibility that northern crusaders demanded the abolition of slavery to bring the underground railroad above ground and make industrial exploitation of the Negroes possible. At any rate, the Negroes were moving north, taking rural mores to the tenements and making cement plantations of their neighborhoods.

Most of them left homes in the Deep South states of Mississippi, Alabama, Georgia, and South Carolina, and most of them went to a few industrial cities—to Chicago, St. Louis, Cleveland, Detroit, New York, and Philadelphia. The Negro population of Michigan increased 182 per cent, and both Wisconsin and New York showed gains of over 100 per cent. Where they went the Negroes made cities within cities, not assimilating themselves into the population but settling where there were other Negroes. They provided most of their own commercial and professional needs and their own entertainment. In Chicago, for example, where the Negro population increased from 109,458 to 233,903 in the 'twenties, the "Black Belt" extended almost eight miles southward from the Loop. In that area Negroes completely displaced all other elements of the population.

The migration of Southerners north introduced Northerners to racial tensions as well as to "jazz" music; it also affected life in the

South. For along with the down-and-out went many of the South's leaders. Southerners were unsuccessful in holding their talented professional people, many of whom succumbed to more munificent offers from northern universities, hospitals, and research centers. From 1899 to 1936 the South lost an estimated 13,355 distinguished persons of leadership and ability; percentagewise that was nearly three times as high as the total emigration. The South was producing—and in most cases, training—leaders for the nation, especially for the Midwest and the Far West. The tendency was for the talented notables to find positions outside the South, leaving a higher percentage of mediocrity behind.

Southerners were not only moving north. They also moved from farms to towns and cities. The South was rapidly becoming urbanized; in the 1920's all southern states except Georgia and Virginia increased their urban populations by 25 per cent or more. Farms of the Southeast showed a net loss of nearly three millions of people, and the heaviest losses were in Kentucky, Georgia, and South Carolina. These movements affected southern urban population; by 1930 the Southeast had thirteen cities larger than 100,000. So rapid was the shift to urbanization that it resulted in unplanned communities with poor streets and rudimentary sanitation facilities. Southern towns were still aggregations of rural folk living by rural folkways—urban communities only by census definition.

Despite the rapid shift to the towns, the southern people remained largely a rural population in 1930. In that year Florida was the only southern state with more than half its population living in urban areas. For the South as a whole the pattern of country life remained. In 1930 the population density per square mile ranged from 65 in North Carolina and Kentucky to 22 in Texas. Most Southerners continued to live on farms; most southern income was still from farm commodities; and the South was a land of farmers and small farms. Almost 38 per cent of the nation's farms were in southern states; Mississippi alone had more farms than did the entire Far West. Southern farms had the lowest average acreage in the nation, at 71 acres. Mississippi's average farm was smallest in 1930, with only 53 acres. For the whole Southeast, 80 per cent of the farms were under 100 acres, and only one per cent were over 500 acres.

These economic facts of southern life had their inevitable effects upon southern standards of living. In 1930 the South had the lowest per capita wealth in the nation ($1,498 compared to $3,665 for the Northwest), the fewest number of large incomes (only seven of more than a million dollars annually, compared to 513 in the Northeast), and the lowest average farm income—only Florida and Texas averaged over $1,500 per year per farm. This meant poor schools and roads, low health standards, and few comforts of life. The South in 1930 was still a poverty-stricken area.

Because of ignorance and poverty, southerners suffered from diseases peculiar to their region. Hookworm, caused by lack of sanitation and cleanliness, was pandemic in rural areas, and malaria debilitated its hundreds of thousands. The dreaded yellow fever struck chronically until 1905. Pellagra, a diet-deficiency disease, was especially widespread in the winters when people ate "hog and hominy." Tuberculosis and syphilis, while not peculiar to the South, still attacked southerners. Mississippi, Alabama, and Georgia suffered the nation's highest incidence of syphilis. Other diseases that sapped southern energies were typhoid, smallpox, and diphtheria.

But the picture was not all black. Southerners were making improvements faster than were Americans in other regions. They were so far behind that their amazing material progress before 1930 was not clearly obvious. In nearly every category of measurement Southerners made greater gains than did the nation as a whole. From 1900 to 1930 the South had a larger ratio of wealth increase; a larger rate of increase in basic industrial development; a larger increase in the value of manufacturing added to products; a larger increase in roads, water power, public utilities, and public education. By giant strides the South was catching up with the promise of American life.

2. THE NEGRO IN THE SOUTH

No single section of the southern population was farther from the ideal American life than the Negro. Only recently removed from chattel slavery, remanded to an economic and political servitude but slightly different, and relegated by law to a subservient and inferior position, Negroes were at the bottom of an extremely poor social order. Changes were under way, however, which promised to make the Negro a more nearly equal member of the southern community.

Always the Negro was more a problem than a person. Actively and passively he continued to play a part in southern politics as well as national affairs. The presence of the enfranchised Negro had given the Bourbons an excuse to resort to corruption in order to obtain and hold control over state and local governments. The threat of Negro dominance prevented the Populist movement from releasing the Bourbon yoke. Yet although the Negro was disfranchised by new constitutions, he played even an active part in local elections. In cities such as Memphis he continued to vote, and his vote—always controlled by whites—determined many a contest between Democratic factions. Even when he did not vote, his very presence gave oratorical ammunition to Bourbon-allied demagogues. "Cotton Tom" Heflin of Alabama, Coleman L. Blease of South Carolina, James K. Vardaman of Mississippi, and Jeff Davis of Arkansas based their phenomenal political careers on "cussing the nigger."

In industry, too, the Negro played a passive but potent part. White laborers did not welcome the Negro as a fellow worker and the Negro did not adapt himself readily to industrial routine. Yet the presence of the black man who might be called into the mill kept wages low. Industrial carpetbaggers who invested in southern communities accepted local social restrictions to avoid difficulties; as outsiders, they were already on the defensive socially. Prejudice—sedulously cultivated by the dominant groups—excluded the Negro from the textile mills as it did from the voting booths. The Negro was relegated to agriculture, to personal service, or to employment as an artisan in the towns.

The plantation system produced more Negro artisans than did the era of freedom. The necessity of producing goods on the plantation had led to the training of Negro blacksmiths, carpenters, cabinetmakers, and weavers. The post-war years opened up few opportunities for Negroes to follow the trades. White competition shoved them from their vocations. The willingness of the Negro to work for low wages depressed the wages of whites as well. In general, there was a considerable wage differential between the races for the same types of work. In 1900 it was estimated that Negro carpenters were willing to work for 75 cents to $1.25 a day, while white carpenters required $1.50 or more a day. Contractors frequently employed gangs composed of a few white workers to do the more precise tasks and a larger number of Negroes to perform the more laborious and rougher work.

From the close of the Civil War, the proportion of Negroes in the southern population steadily declined. In 1860 the Negro population was 4,441,930, and in 1930 it was 11,891,143. In the earlier year, only a few hundred thousand had lived outside the South; but in 1930, 21 per cent, or 2,529,566 lived in the North and West. The total population of the South in 1930 was 39,619,000, while in 1860 it had been 12,180,077. In 1860 the Negroes had constituted 34.2 per cent of the southern population; in 1930 they were 23.7 per cent. Part of the relative decline in the Negro population was due to poor sanitary conditions, great infant mortality, and the peculiar susceptibility of the Negro to tuberculosis; part was due to an increased migration to the North.

As with the total southern population, a considerable shift of Negroes from rural to urban regions within the South had taken place. Whereas there had been few Negroes living in cities in 1860, the urban Negro population in 1930 was nearly 3,000,000. In 1860 the Negroes had been almost exclusively plantation laborers; in 1930, but 4,500,000 southern Negroes were engaged in agriculture. In that year almost 80 per cent of the Negro farmers were tenants. The average Negro-operated farm had but 42.6 acres. After 1870 the average farm and the total number of Negro farmers underwent a steady decrease. At the same time, the value of Negro agricultural holdings decreased.

In the cities, the Negroes engaged largely in personal services. They became carpenters, shoemakers, garage mechanics, teamsters, drivers of taxicabs, janitors, and domestics. Professional men—lawyers, ministers, doctors, and dentists—practiced in the Negro districts; and grocers, dairymen, furniture dealers, and theater owners catered to their own people. Restaurants, hotels, and barber and beauty shops were managed by Negroes for the patronage of one or the other race. The number of Negro professionals in the Southeast was the lowest, in relation to population, in the entire country, but was increasing in the 1920's.

Intangible lines of cleavage marked the race line in many of these vocations. White and black laborers worked side by side on even the most menial tasks; carpenters, stonemasons, painters, and mechanics worked

Farm Security Administration, photo by Shahn

NEGRO HOUSING IN NATCHEZ, MISSISSIPPI.

together. Negro and white women performed many of the same tasks, yet Negro men and white women never worked together. White people patronized restaurants and hotels operated by Negroes but seldom bought from Negro stores and never availed themselves of the services of Negro lawyers or ministers. Negro nurses, but never a Negro physician, might care for white patients. The dividing lines, incomprehensible to an outsider, were thoroughly understood by Southerners of both races. Wherever the Negro appeared in a subordinate capacity, he was welcomed; when he appeared as equal or superior, he was anathema. White men might boss mixed gangs of roadworkers but Negro foremen could exercise authority only over their own race. Negro nursemaids might accompany their employers in waiting rooms and on Pullmans, but the lone Negro traveler was consigned to the "Jim Crow" car.

Comparatively few southern Negroes showed resentment against occupying such subordinate positions. The ever-present danger of race riots and lynch law (an average of 154 mob deaths in 1899 and an average of 31 in 1929) served to prevent any attempt to force social recognition. To the sensitive, educated, and ambitious Negroes, however, the constant denial of equality was particularly oppressive. Many of them left the South, hoping to find acceptance in places where there was less prejudice. Scholars and educators, however, were largely forced to earn their livelihood in academic circles, and there were few Negro schools outside of the South. Writers and artists were occasionally able to make a place for themselves in white society. An unknown number of Negroes of light skin "passed" into the white race, but these were condemned by the better class of Negroes and lived in constant fear of being discovered.

Two different schools of thought developed among the Negroes as they contemplated the social, political, and economic discriminations to which they were subjected. One group of Negroes clung to the philosophy of Booker T. Washington and the "Atlanta Compromise," which held that the Negroes should improve their position by fitting themselves into the prevailing southern caste system. Washington's desire for accommodation was intended to allay white fears of aggressive Negro demands and to bargain for security and education in return for racial peace. Until his death in 1915 Washington served in an unofficial capacity as ambassador to white politicians and philanthropists, and he won substantial gains for his people.

The other school of Negro thought was that of William E. Burghardt DuBois, who charged that the Atlanta Compromise surrendered the Negro's humanity and equality as an American citizen for material gains of questionable value. DuBois began his attack upon Washington's philosophy in 1903 with the publication of his most famous book, *The Souls of Black Folk*. He condemned Washington's apparent acceptance of the southern social caste system, his submission to judicial and political injustices to Negroes, and his willingness to reduce Negro education to the level of vocational training. In 1905 DuBois appealed to all Negroes who rejected the Washington program (which he said produced "Uncle Toms" and "white man's niggers") to meet in conference and plan a more aggressive program. In June, 1905, at Niagara Falls, Canada, a group of men organized the "Niagara Movement" to obtain for the Negro "every single right that belongs to a freeborn American, political, civil and social."

The Niagara Movement, which grew into the National Association for the Advancement of Colored People, was the first organized Negro protest to the conditions of an unequal freedom. Its chief accomplishments were in making vocal Negro discontent. In 1906 the Niagara group marched barefoot to Harpers Ferry, the scene of the John Brown raid, and called for a new assault upon Southern society. "In the past year the work of the Negro hater has flourished in the land," they announced. "Never before in the modern age has a great and civilized folk threatened to adopt so cowardly a creed in the treatment of its fellow-citizens, born and bred on its soil." The next year the DuBois group met in Boston and at old Faneuil Hall attempted to invoke the old spirit of abolitionism. The Niagara Movement reached its climax on Lincoln's Birthday, 1909, when Oswald Garrison Villard, grandson of William Lloyd Garrison, appealed "to all believers in democracy to join in a National conference for the discussion of present evils, the voicing of protests, and the renewal of the struggle for civil and political liberty."

In 1910 DuBois and Villard, with a group of notables including Jane Addams, William Dean Howells, and John Dewey, organized the National Association for the Advancement of Colored People. It inherited the program but not the methods of the Niagara Movement. Using civil suits, publicity, and organized protest, the NAACP worked to end legal segregation, to obtain equal education, the complete political emancipation of the Negro, and the enforcement of the Fourteenth and Fifteenth Amendments. DuBois left Atlanta to become editor of the new organization's magazine, *The Crisis*, which by 1918 circulated over 100,000 copies each month.

The NAACP quickly became the voice of Negro protest, and DuBois became its brain. Negroes were leaving the farm and were moving north. For those who moved, Washington's philosophy no longer had meaning; they listened gladly to DuBois' more uncompromising demands. Negro leaders, following DuBois' leadership, promised support for the war of 1917, but demanded Negro officers, an end to lynching, the vote for Negroes, universal and free public education, abolition of segregation, and civil rights for Negroes. By 1921 there were more than 400 branches of the NAACP in the United States, working together to provide security to Negro life and property, civil and political equality, and better job opportunities.

Negro hopes, elevated by the promises of a war to make the world safe for democracy, were dashed in the "Red Summer" of 1919. DuBois spoke the mind of returning Negro soldiers when he proclaimed: "*We return. We return from fighting. We return fighting.* Make way for Democracy! We saved it in France, and by the Great Jehovah, we will save it in the USA or know the reason why." Negro soldiers soon learned that the Statue of Liberty still gazed toward France, and that the reason why was the new Ku Klux Klan. At the end of the war the Klan emerged with a plan for "uniting native-born white Christians for concerted action in the preservation of American institutions and the supremacy of the white race." At one public meeting in the land seized from the redskins, one Klansman said: "We would not rob the colored population of their right, but we demand that they respect the rights of the white race in whose country they are permitted to reside."

The Kluxers used violence to teach Negroes to respect the rights of white Americans. In the first post-war year more than 70 Negroes were lynched, some of them still in their military uniforms. Fourteen Negroes were publicly burned, of whom eleven were burned alive. In the last half of 1919 there were at least 25 race riots in American urban centers—notably in Washington, Chicago, Omaha, Knoxville, Longview, Texas, and Elaine, Arkansas. Other outbreaks of mob violence occurred throughout the 'twenties, but none were as serious as those of 1919. Sadly, Negro leaders had to agree with the Chicago editor who said that "The 'German Hun' is beaten but the world is made no safer for Democracy."

The national scope of the post-war rioting indicated that the race problem was no longer the exclusive property of the South. And the Negro's efforts to win a place in American life for himself, whether by co-operation, advocated by Washington, or by protest, represented by DuBois and the NAACP, revealed his pathetic desire for accommodation. While immigrants from other lands sought to keep alive their native language and culture and resisted every effort to melt them into the American pot, Negroes unashamedly begged to become Americans. No African language newspaper reported news from home to American Negroes; no African foods, folksongs, or fashions influenced American life. Negroes had no desire to be hyphenated Americans; they wanted accommodation in the American pattern, and completely. If their dress was gaudy or if they equated a car with success, they were mirroring what they understood to be the American way.

Although the Negroes strove diligently to be amalgamated into the national norm, they made no inconsiderable contributions to American culture. American music was enriched by the voices of Roland Hayes and Paul Robeson, while the Fisk Jubilee Singers popularized the "spirituals." The attempt to accredit "jazz" music to the Afro-American failed, but Negro orchestras did much to spread that American contribution to musical art. The stage also gave opportunity to talented blacks, and in 1933 the Pulitzer Prize in drama went to Marc Connelly's *The Green Pastures*, which had an all-Negro cast. In art the work of Henry O. Tanner, the painter of Biblical characters, and Meta Vaux Warwick, the sculptor, rivaled the best work of whites.

In the field of scholarship Negroes also made contributions. Tuskegee's Dr. George Carver took leading rank as an industrial scientist as he developed many useful products from the lowly peanut and the yellow yam, and extracted dyestuffs from Alabama's red clay. Dr. Daniel Williams performed the first successful operation on the human heart. In history W. E. B. DuBois made outstanding contributions and Dr. Carter

G. Woodson founded the Association for the Study of Negro Life and History, which in 1916 began publication of the scholarly *Journal of Negro History*. In 1931 the Bureau of Educational Research of Howard University began publication of the *Journal of Negro Education*, edited by Charles H. Thompson.

DR. CARTER G. WOODSON. A pioneer Negro scholar, Dr. Woodson was born in Virginia in 1875. He was educated at Berea College, the University of Chicago, and Harvard University, where he received the Ph.D. degree in 1912. He was the author of a dozen books on Negro history and life, was the Executive Director of the Association for the Study of Negro Life and History, and was founder and for many years the editor of the scholarly *Journal of Negro History*.

Negro leaders formed various organizations to encourage the development of their race. The National Association of Negro Business Men attempted to assert the Negro's importance in commerce and to act as a chamber of commerce for colored business interests. The NAACP did conspicuous work in uncovering cases of discrimination and injustice and gave such publicity to the lynching records of the southern states that it shamed white men into co-operating with the Negroes.

As the Negro made progress, the intelligent whites began to understand that the Negro was essentially the problem of the nation. With this understanding there came an increasing tendency toward interracial co-operation. Negroes and whites sat on boards and commissions to consult over their common problems. The Commission on Interracial Co-operation sponsored many such efforts, while churches,

YMCA's, and labor unions, each after its own kind, worked to promote harmony and sympathetic understanding between the two races in the South.

3. Religion and the South's Problems

The one area in which the Negro had no necessity for accommodation or obsequious Uncle Tomism was religion. His churches were American, Protestant, evangelical, and above suspicion. But the Negro sent no missionaries to the whites. There was no Negro evangelist in the tradition of Dwight L. Moody, Billy Sunday, or Gypsy Smith; there was no Negro equivalent of Niebuhr defining the nature of God. In religion the Negro could have exercised a moral superiority that would have made the blatant prejudices of the Ku Klux and the claims of white supremacy ridiculous. But the Negroes abdicated religious leadership to the dominant and unmeek whites.

Negroes did organize their own churches and took pride in their independence. In 1915 the principal denominations of Negro Christians were of the evangelical type—Baptists and Methodists in particular. Negro Baptists numbered about 2,750,000 members, and the African Methodist Episcopal Church claimed over 500,000. In addition, Negroes organized new Christian denominations, often with attractive titles and based upon miraculous revelations from God. In 1895 in Arkansas C. P. Jones and C. H. Mason established the Church of God in Christ and in the following year in Oklahoma William S. Crowdy founded the Church of God and Saints of Christ, which taught that Negroes were descended from the ten lost tribes of Israel. Another Negro religious organization was the Church of God, Holiness, established in Atlanta in 1914 by the Reverend K. H. Burress. In 1926 Alabama reported thirteen churches of the Apostolic Overcoming Holy Church of God, and Texas had 54 Churches of the Living God, "The Pillar and Ground of Truth."

Southern whites, especially the poor and illiterate, also sought spiritual satisfaction from primitive sects called "Holy Rollers." In 1896 Bishop C. P. Jones separated from the Mason group and organized the Church of Christ (Holiness) USA at Selma, Alabama, and in 1898 in Anderson, S. C., millennialist leaders from ten states founded the Pentecostal Holiness Church. The most important of the Holiness groups was the Church of God, founded in 1907 in Bradley County, Tennessee. In 1922 a segment of the Church of God, led by A. J. Tomlinson, seceded from the parent body and established an annual assembly at Cleveland, Tennessee. The Church of God maintained the doctrine of "sanctification as a second definite experience subsequent to regeneration" and presented as evidence of sanctification speaking in tongues "as the Spirit gives utterance."

The millennialist sects were ultraconservative in their theology but even the more traditional denominations were in the forefront of Fundamentalism. In 1910, at a national gathering, the five doctrines of Fundamentalism were defined as the virgin birth of Jesus, the physical resurrection of Christ, inerrancy of scriptures, the substitutionary view of the Atonement, and the imminent physical second coming of Christ. The southern Protestant church heartily assented to the Fundamentals and fulminated against the Modernists who questioned any of them.

In general, the southern churches were Protestant and orthodox, regardless of the names the members adopted for themselves. "Scratch any sectarian skin and the same orthodox blood flows," reported Edwin McNeill Poteat, Jr., in 1934. Newer denominations and those which sounded "modern" did not appeal to Southerners. In 1934 only seven per cent of the nation's Unitarian churches were in the South and only 13 per cent of the Christian Scientist churches. Roman Catholics were also in a minority; only in Louisiana did they number more than one third of the church membership in 1926.

All churches in the South showed marked increases in membership in the twenty years after 1906, with the greatest growth in the Southwest. In that part of the South west of the Mississippi church membership increased by 28.4 per cent; along the Atlantic seaboard the gain was 23.3 per cent, and in the four states of Kentucky, Tennessee, Alabama, and Mississippi, churches added 16 per cent of new members. Numbers of churches revealed similar growth. Texas, fifth in estimated population in 1926, was first in the nation in number of churches; Georgia, estimated to be eleventh in total population, was third in number of churches. North Carolina and Alabama, fourteenth and sixteenth in total population, were fifth and sixth in churches.

In southern churches old-fashioned shouting sermons were the rule. Hell was a literal place, the "eternal abode of the damned," according to the definition given by one evangelical denomination. There were exact and unyielding definitions of sin, too, usually encompassing the more obvious of humanity's less acceptable pleasures. To save the sinner from eternal damnation, preachers exhorted their flocks to repent, to be "convicted of sin," and to kneel at the "mourner's bench" for prayer. There were periodic "revivals," or "protracted meetings," with visiting evangelists, loud repetitions of Moody and Sankey hymns, and a community interest which often disrupted secular activities. In the rural South the "shouting Methodist" was not yet extinct.

Fundamentalism in the South often also expressed itself in the halls of legislation. "Blue laws," once typical of Calvinistic New England, now came to the South to make illegal what the censors defined as immoral. In all southern states except Louisiana and Oklahoma there were laws prohibiting Sunday movies and nearly all states undertook to regulate commercial activities on the Sabbath. In the 1920's there was also a movement to prohibit by law the teaching of evolution in the schools. As one observer put it, "The South may be living in the twentieth century, but it has skipped the nineteenth." The apparent conflict between science and religion had been met and resolved in Europe and in the North a half-century before it reached the South.

Farm Security Administration, photo by Vachon

COUNTRY CHURCH IN VIRGINIA.

As accrediting associations forced higher standards on denominational colleges, and as young Southerners studied in universities outside their section, the churches began to learn that the theories of science did not conform to the Fundamental interpretations of the Bible. Rather than surrender traditional views of Genesis, Southerners came to oppose science. "The rationalists of the past century succeeded in mowing down the world with their attacks upon the Bible, their sneering disbelief in the supernatural and their open effort to discount the history of the Bible narratives," a North Carolina Baptist group declared. "The battle is on in the schools between a materialistic and a spiritual interpretation of life."

The climax of the anti-science movement came in May, 1925, when a high school biology teacher, John T. Scopes, was arrested on charges that he "did unlawfully, wilfully teach in the public schools of Rhea County, Tennessee . . . certain theory and theories that deny the story of the Divine Creation of man as taught in the Bible, and did teach instead that man has descended from a lower order of animals." In a celebrated trial in Dayton, Tennessee, William Jennings Bryan of Nebraska, long an advocate of anti-evolution laws, engaged in verbal clashes with Chicago's avowed agnostic, Clarence Darrow, who defended Scopes. The jury upheld Genesis, found Scopes guilty, and he was fined $100. In January, 1927, the Supreme Court of Tennessee upheld the anti-evolution law, though it reversed the decision against Scopes. Bryan's death five days after the Scopes trial ended removed one of the law's most articulate champions and public ridicule soon caused most of the states quietly to repeal or to ignore the restrictive statutes.

The Scopes trial was not without repercussion in the South, however. Chancellor James H. Kirkland of Vanderbilt said that "the answer to the episode at Dayton is the building of new laboratories . . . for the teaching of science. The remedy for narrow sectarianism and a belligerent fundamentalism is the establishment on this campus of a School of Religion, illustrating in its methods and its organization the strength of a common faith and the glory of universal worship." But Fundamentalists maintained their position against all learned heresies. A Bible College established in Tennessee in the wake of the Scopes trial required its faculty to subscribe to the principle that the "origin of man was by fiat of God in the act of creation as related in the Book of Genesis." A South Carolina Bible College, also founded in the 1920's, explained that its science course would mention "important theories of modern science, and the proper attitude of Christians toward those which affect one's belief in divine revelation is explained." And the dictum of William Louis Poteat, Professor of Biology and President of Wake Forest College in North Carolina, that he could be a scientist and a Christian too, scandalized the faithful. The episode provided, as well, ammunition to Northern economic rivals and professional liberals who could thereafter point to the Scopes trial as convincing evidence of the South's decadence.

Paralleling the religious crusade against science was the fight against strong drink. Drunkenness was an individual sin and thus came within the list of things the churches could denounce with comfort. Under the influence of the Anti-Saloon League and the Woman's Christian Temperance Union the churches organized temperance societies and gave their support only to political candidates who proclaimed themselves "bone-dry." Local option on the sale of beverage alcohol spread until the arid regions coincided with the "Bible Belt." The fact that intemperance was most common among poorer whites and Negroes made prohibition a safe crusade. Rural southerners, who controlled their states, demanded and got laws outlawing liquor. Alabama had a fantastic law forbidding possession or sale of any liquid which "tastes like, foams like, smells like, or looks like beer," whether alcoholic or not, and even outlawed possession of glassware shaped like a beer bottle or a whisky flask. Georgia prohibited alcoholic beverages and also "liquor, beverages or drinks made in imitation of or as a substitute for beer, ale, wine or whiskey or other alcoholic or spirited vinous or malt liquors."

Under the influence of the "thou shalt not" philosophy of ethics that prevailed in the South in the 1920's, most southern states were legally "dry" before the Eighteenth Amendment was added to the United States Constitution on January 29, 1919. Methodist Bishop James Cannon, Jr., of Virginia was an outstanding leader of the prohibition forces. After the 18th Amendment, the South supported prohibition, at least until it became identified with Hoover, the Republican Party, and the Depression. No matter how "wet" a politician might drink, the southern churches forced him to vote "dry." Many Southerners themselves happily laughed off the inconsistencies of demanding legal prohibition and enjoying the glass. Mississippians, as Will Rogers said, will vote dry "so long as the voters can stagger to the polls." And a Mississippi judge insisted upon "the right to drink my whiskey without the stigma of legality."

Churches also gave tacit approval to the aims, if not the methods, of the revived Ku Klux Klan. Nowhere was the division between denominational leaders—editors of religious journals and state and regional officers—and southern church membership greater than upon the Klan issue. It was a preacher, Thomas Dixon, who wrote *The Leopard's Spots* and *The Clansman,* which glorified the old Klan and stimulated race hatred. Based on these books, a motion picture, *The Birth of a Nation,* inspired the evangelist William J. Simmons to revive the old organization. Appealing to prejudice against Negroes, Jews, and Catholics, the Klan made headway in the South and spread over the entire nation. In other parts of the country it served to glorify a cheap "Americanism" in conflict with foreign "isms"; in the South, where Jews, Catholics, and foreigners were few, it was an agency in perpetuating race hatred. Though practically all denominational papers denounced the Klan and state and regional associations of southern Christians adopted resolutions against it, its southern membership was largely drawn from the evangelical denominations, and many of its officers were Protestant ministers. Eventually the hoodlumism of the Klan was supplemented by criminal acts and a disgusted public snatched the concealing robes from the Klansmen; but the movement lingered on in fitful if impotent existence in the south.

The churches' intolerant stand on prohibition, "blue laws," and the objective search for truth in the academic world, and the activity of their members in the Klan, marked the high point of their reactionary careers. The collapse of these movements produced some changes. Here and there, throughout the 1920's, ministers raised their voices against an orthodoxy that was a cloak for reaction and oppression. Even in the denominational colleges teachers and students began to consider problems of race and class relations. YMCA's brought white and Negro youths together for conferences. Fundamentalism still controlled the churches, but as the depression gave new emphasis to the South's economic situation, many turned to the church with a demand that it transfer its attentions to other problems. None would deny the influence of the churches in southern life. William Archer, an Englishman who toured the South in 1910, reported that "the South is by a long way the most simply and sincerely religious country that I was ever in."

4. THE MARCH OF EDUCATION

That much of southern religion retained its intolerance and exhibitionism may have been at least partly the result of the southern educational system. In 1900 the section contained more adult illiterates than any other part of the nation and its schools were the country's poorest. "In the southern states," said University of Tennessee President Charles W. Dabney in 1901, "in schoolhouses costing an average of $276 each, under teachers receiving an average salary of $25 a month, we are giving the children in actual attendance five cents' worth of education a day for eighty-seven days only in the year." Illiteracy figures reflected that parsimony. In 1900 nearly twelve per cent of native white Southerners were illiterate compared to 4.6 in the nation.

But even as Dabney spoke, changes were under way that transformed southern education. Between 1900 and 1932, in every category of measurement, the South's rate of improvement was relatively higher than that for the country as a whole. In *total* value of school property the southern increase was over twice as much as the national, and in the value per unit schoolhouse, the South increased by three times the country's gain. Average salaries of teachers in the South increased fifty per cent over the national rate; and in expenditure per pupil the South also showed substantial improvement.

Most of these gains were made possible by increased wealth in the region, making possible higher taxes for education, but they also owed much to a few leaders and philanthropists who worked for better schooling in the South. Dabney himself established the Bureau of Investigation and Information at Knoxville to provide materials for education campaigns. In North Carolina, Charles B. Aycock, the "Education Governor," made school opportunities for all children his major campaign platform; other Tar Heel educational leaders were Charles D. McIver, Edwin A. Alderman, and Walter Hines Page. Edgar Gardner Murphy took up the fight in Alabama. These men, with northern philanthropists Robert C. Ogden, John D. Rockefeller, Jr., and George Foster Peabody, organized the Conference for Southern Education which in

1901 established the Southern Education Board. Peabody provided about $40,000 to subsidize the Board's early operation.

In 1903 the movement gained momentum when Congress incorporated the General Education Board, which at first would "devote itself to studying and aiding to promote the educational needs of the people of our Southern States." Between 1902 and 1909 the General Board received $53,000,000 from the Rockefellers. With its funds it offered to pay the salary of an inspector of high schools in each southern state. By 1910 all southern states had accepted the offer and the Board had expended over $240,000 on the program. The inspectors, who also taught secondary education in the state university, raised the standards of southern preparatory schools.

New legislation also assisted the schools. Bond issues for high schools and compulsory attendance laws served to further the educational effort. In 1906 Virginia, and in 1907 North Carolina appropriated $50,000 each to establish a system of secondary schools. In 1908 Kentucky enacted the County School Administration Law to provide for rural high schools. By 1918 all southern states had adopted a compulsory attendance law which required attendance at school of children within stipulated age limits. These laws restricted child labor in mills and factories and therefore served a double function. Beginning in Tennessee in 1905, states enacted compulsory school attendance laws: North Carolina in 1907; Virginia in 1908; Arkansas in 1909; Louisiana in 1910; South Carolina, Texas, Florida, and Alabama in 1915; Georgia in 1916; and Mississippi in 1918. Yet before 1932 the laws were not adequately enforced in any southern state. As a result, in 1930 only 81.5 per cent of school-age children were enrolled and only 76.1 per cent of those were in average daily attendance. And in the same year, the South continued in the nation's lowest bracket in the number of illiterates over ten years of age. South Carolina, with 14.9 per cent, had the highest rate, but her sister states crowded the bottom. Much still remained to be done before the South would solve her educational problems.

Negro education in the South paralleled that for whites, but on a much lower level. From almost nothing in the nineteenth century, tremendous improvements had taken place. Negroes had risen from nearly four-fifths illiteracy to less than one-fifth, and from almost no schools and no pupils, to number nearly 2,000,000 pupils and 40,000 teachers. But still Negro educational achievement was only about half that of the whites. Negro illiteracy continued to be more prevalent than for whites; in Mississippi it was ten times higher, and in Alabama and South Carolina it was five times higher. Teacher salaries were generally lower for Negroes than for whites—in Mississippi Negroes received only 30 per cent of the salary paid whites for similar positions. The school term averaged 49 days less per year for Negroes than for whites, and the amount expended for each Negro child of school age was only about one forth as much as the expenditure for each white. Discriminations in other matters such as school consolidations and public transportation, or specialized courses like laboratory science, were even more evident.

Farm Security Administration, photo by Post

SATURDAY AFTERNOON IN A MISSISSIPPI TOWN.

The segregated school system in the South was not so great a financial burden as it appeared to be, for the schools provided for whites and for Negroes were manifestly unequal, and were becoming more so each year. In South Carolina, for example, in 1900 the white child received for education about $5.75 for every dollar expended for each Negro child, and by 1915 the ratio had become $12.37 to each dollar spent on the Negro child's education. It was such developments that gave northern crusaders an excuse to ignore the racial settlement of 1877 and to intervene in the southern race problem.

The first crusaders were northern philanthropists who contributed to the cause of Negro education. In addition to the philanthropies of the Southern and the General Education boards, the Rosenwald Fund sought to help the Negro. Established by Julius Rosenwald of Chicago, head of Sears, Roebuck and Company, the Fund assisted in the construction of more than 5,000 Negro school buildings in fifteen states. The Fund also contributed approximately $600,000 to finance eleven county library demonstrations in seven states, and donated books to Negro schools— in many instances the only books the Negro students had. In 1905 Miss Anna T. Jeanes, the Quaker daughter of a Philadelphia merchant, established the Jeanes Fund of $1,200,000 for the Assistance of Negro Rural Schools in the South, which provided visiting teachers for extension work and industrial education in rural schools. In 1910 the Phelps-Stokes Fund, provided by the will of Mrs. Carolina Phelps-Stokes, began to make direct appropriations to schools to improve their condition and service and served as a clearinghouse for specialized studies of Negro educational problems. The philanthropists made great contributions to southern education, but they did little to remove discriminations toward Negroes and their schools. They may even have contributed to the uneven distribution of the tax money, for whites felt that if the Funds were going to educate the Negroes, then the state's money should go to the white schools.

What was true of Negro elementary and secondary schools was also true of higher education. Neglected by the states, most colleges and universities were privately supported. Every southern state had a Negro agricultural and mechanical college, but most Negro students were in private schools, largely because of the poor equipment furnished by the state. In 1913 there were 96 Negro institutions offering college courses, but only a very few of them had enough equipment and faculty to be called a college. In 1932 nearly 28,000 Negro students were enrolled in colleges in the South, and in that year received about 1,250 degrees. The best of the Negro colleges, Fisk in Nashville and Howard in Washington, D.C., strengthened their curricula and faculties in the 1920's, and mergers of the Negro colleges in Atlanta and in New Orleans greatly facilitated their work.

Negro professional education also greatly improved. Earlier, Negroes had to leave the South to receive training for the professions— and many continued to do so—but by 1932 it was available on a limited basis. Medical and dental instruction was offered at Howard University and at Meharry Medical College in Nashville. In 1931 these two schools graduated 108 physicians, 23 dentists, and 25 pharmacists, and were still unable to meet the demand.

Increasingly, Negro leaders were being drawn from the alumni of the southern colleges. This had its effect upon Negro leadership in the South, which was passing from the older group, typified by the un-educated preacher, to the new Negro: the educated preacher, teacher, lawyer, and business man. After another World War, fought for the "Four Freedoms," it would be difficult for the South to maintain a dual educational system that contained manifest inequities. But with depression reducing the tax revenues, there was in the 'thirties little talk of equalizing the separate school systems.

Not all of the southern colleges for whites, however, were of the highest standards. The state universities of Virginia, North Carolina, Louisiana, and Texas ranked with the best in the nation, and some of the private universities such as Vanderbilt and Duke ranked high. Generally the physical equipment was poorer than in the North and the better members of their poorer-paid teaching staffs were frequently at-tracted to northern schools. The example of Vanderbilt and the forma-tion in 1895 of the Southern Association of Colleges and Secondary Schools did much to raise standards and to give promise that higher education in the South would soon approach the national level.

By 1930 serious obstacles to southern education were still in existence. Despite industrialization, the South was still poor and con-tinued to object to high taxes. Inadequate and antiquated tax systems prevented the fullest support of education. The sparsely populated rural regions were still unable to maintain schools within the reach of all, although the motor bus and good roads were diminishing the importance of such factors. More serious was the prevalence of objections to public education on religious grounds. To many the public schools were god-less places in which the children would be weaned away from the faith of their ancestors. The Scopes trial illustrated those feelings. Less dra-matic pressures frequently forced university and college professors to refrain from comment on sociological, political, religious, or economic questions. Freedom of speech was frequently prohibited, and some southern colleges and universities were indicted by the Association of American University Professors for ignoring the profession's standards of tenure and of academic freedom.

5. Literature of the Early Twentieth Century

The pressures under which teachers worked did not prevent southern writers from painting the South in the harsh light of realism, but they did subject the writers to a sharp division over methods and materials. The earlier disagreement over the nature of the New South continued into the twentieth century. The South was torn between the philosophies of Jefferson Davis and Henry W. Grady, and the struggle was intensified as more rapid change took place. Industrialism spread into the southern Piedmont as far as Birmingham, bringing material progress; the first World War, with its moral impact upon the South, drove a wedge between the Old and the New. As Dean Donald Davidson of Vanderbilt University remembered the early years of the century, "Industrial commercialism was rampant. In no section were its activities more blatant than in the South, where old and historic communities were crawling on their bellies to persuade some petty manufacturer of pants or socks to take up his tax-exempt residence in their midst."

Those who were disgusted at such conduct feared that in its eagerness to "belong to the age" the South was denying its faith and betraying its way of life. In the period of transition, southern writers tried to express the rootless feelings of a people who rejected the values of the past but were uneasy with the dollars-and-cents standards of the day. It was the judgment of the present by the accusing finger of the past that gave meaning to southern letters in the new century. Not everyone appreciated the efforts of the regional writers at social criticism. H. L. Mencken, in a celebrated essay, "The Sahara of the Bozart," first published in 1917, characterized the South as "almost as sterile, artistically, intellectually, culturally, as the Sahara Desert. There are single acres in Europe," he continued, "that house more first-rate men than all the states south of the Potomac." But Mencken's exaggeration did not fit the facts, for the desert South was blossoming like the rose. A new generation was arising that had no memory of the Civil War and was able to see the past in better perspective. Thus writers could continue the defense of the South while realistically probing its shortcomings, and while maintaining a profound skepticism for "progress" based solely upon material criteria. It was a conflict between what the people of the South were and what they were being urged to become.

Apostles of the New South and its "progress" poked fun at the defenders of the Old. O. Henry (William Sydney Porter), born in Greensboro, North Carolina, and brought up in Texas, but more at home on the streets of New York, revealed his anti-romantic sentiment in such stories as "A Municipal Report" and "A Blackjack Bargainer." James Branch Cabell, in *The Rivet in Grandfather's Neck* (1915), depicted Virginia ladies and gentlemen as hypocrites; but it was the attempted suppression of his *Jurgen* in 1919 for alleged obscenity that made him the darling of the younger group. Ellen Glasgow, in *The Battleground* (1902), began a series of novels describing the rise of the middle class as the dominant force in southern life. "What the South needs," she said, "is blood and irony." With her *Barren Ground* (1925), Miss Glasgow turned to realism to provide it.

Other southern writers busily perpetuated the legendary South in romanticized historical novels. F. Hopkinson Smith, in *Colonel Carter of Cartersville* (1891), and *The Fortunes of Oliver Horn* (1902) described the life of the well-to-do South of the past. James Lane Allen, viewing history through Bluegrass spectacles, hit the bestseller list with *The Choir Invisible* (1897) and *The Sword of Youth* (1914), and penned a host of other works idealizing Kentucky's colorful history. Another Kentuckian, John Fox, Jr., appealed to the nation's tear-ducts with the lachrymose *Little Shepherd of Kingdom Come* (1903) and *The Trail of the Lonesome Pine* (1908), the last a story of the coming of the railroad to Big Stone Gap, Virginia, largely autobiographical. Thomas Dixon, Jr., of North Carolina, evoked sectional and racial bitterness in his lurid novels of Reconstruction, *The Leopard's Spots* (1902), *The Clansman* (1905), and *The Traitor* (1907). Mary Johnston won a national audience for her sentimentalized novels of the Old South, *To Have and To Hold* (1900), *Lewis Rand* (1908), *The Long Roll* (1911), and *Cease Firing* (1912). *Cease Firing*, with its somber overtones of defeat and struggle against impossible odds, was distasteful to the romantics but was probably the most nearly accurate picture of the war. Winston Churchill, born in St. Louis, chose a fictitious southern family, the Carvels, as the subjects of his stories about the Revolution and the Civil War: *Richard Carvel* (1899), *The Crisis* (1901), and *The Crossing* (1904). Roark Bradford once again presented the simple and childlike Negro in *Ol' Man Adam an' His Chillun* (1928), which became the basis of Marc Connelly's play *The Green Pastures* (1930). Elizabeth Madox Roberts wrote of the poor whites, finding them quaint philosophers rather than social dregs. Stark Young returned to the old plantation in *So Red the Rose* (1934) to portray the "Colonel" and the "Ole Missus" on the verandah in the best manner of John Esten Cooke.

But some southern writers turned a realistic eye on the contemporary scene. In *Queed* (1911), Henry Sydnor Harrison set his main character against a southern city rocked by problems of race. In *V. V.'s Eyes* (1913) he described conditions in the tobacco factories. Corra Harris wrote compelling descriptions of the drab life in southern parsonages. In a widely read trilogy, *The Forge* (1931), *The Store* (1932), and *Unfinished Cathedral* (1934), Thomas S. Stribling painted the degeneration of once-proud Southern families. Du Bose Heyward and Julia Peterkin, in South Carolina, wrote of the Negro as a primitive creature, while Paul Green and Howard Odum saw him in terms of his struggles against racial discriminations, not as an Uncle Remus or an Uncle Tom. Other writers turned to the mill villages, the sharecroppers' cabins, and the barren mountains for their material. Thomas Wolfe, born in Asheville, wrote at great length of his own personal alienation from the world. Though he wrote about Asheville and about people he knew there, and about his own family, his novels were not really about the South. In *Look Homeward, Angel, the Story of a Buried Life* (1929) and in its sequel, *Of Time and the River: a Legend of Man's Hunger in His Youth* (1935) he told in wordy, episodic fashion of his inner struggle with the standards of his time.

With the work of William Faulkner and Erskine Caldwell came the "ultrarealists" who described the seamy side of Southern life. Faulkner, a native Mississippian, portrayed the impact upon life and morals of the changes taking place and of the psychological failure of Southerners to find meaning in life. In *The Sound and the Fury* (1929) Faulkner de-

scribed the degradation of an old southern family, and in *Sartoris* (1929)
he continued that theme. The Sartorises and Compsons, descendants of
the old families, became increasingly incapable of understanding their
world; from the red-clay hills arose the Snopeses, without principle or
honor, to seize control. And the image of the glorious past, like an accusing finger, made the present odious; it turned Sartorises and Compsons
into Snopeses in all but name. *As I Lay Dying* (1930) was a tale told in
quiet horror of a man journeying through storms with the putrifying
corpse of his wife to take her to the grave she requested. In *Sanctuary*
(1931) he described the flower of Southern womanhood defiled, mocked,
and corrupted, but really happy in depravity. With shocking sex-symbols
—brutal rapes, illegitimacies, miscegenation, and prostitution—and telling
his stories through the confused thought processes of his characters, often
mentally deficient, Faulkner developed his view of the debasement of
the southern tradition. "I've seed de first en de last," said the Negro
cook Dilsey, in *The Sound and the Fury*; "I seed de beginnin', en now
I sees de endin'."

If Faulkner's South was ravished and tortured, he saw it as
tragedy; the South of Erskine Caldwell was unrelievedly bestial, ribald,
and shallow. In his novel, *Tobacco Road* (1932), which was translated
into a long-run Broadway play, Caldwell attracted a national audience by
his seriocomic portrayal of the filthy and obscene life of a poor-white
Georgia family. In *God's Little Acre* (1933), he varied his theme but
little and raised the tone of his view of rural Georgia not at all. If the
Caldwell and Faulkner characters were recognizably southern, they were
not typical. "One may admit that the Southern States have more than an
equal share of degeneracy and deterioration," said Ellen Glasgow; "but
the multitude of half-wits, and whole idiots, and nymphomaniacs, and
paranoics, and rakehells in general, that populate the modern literary
South could flourish nowhere but in the weird pages of melodrama. . . .
It may be magnificent, indeed, but it is not realism, and it is not pecul-
iarly Southern."

Southern writers had attached themselves firmly to the national
pattern, though there was little unity or agreement among them. Misty
romanticism and raw realism blossomed side by side. There was no resolving the differences between the two schools, though their very divergence reflected the conflicts in southern life. Other branches of letters
gave adherence to one or the other philosophy. For the most part the
poet sided with the traditionalists rather than with the critics. Early in
the 1920's there was a resurgence of southern poetry, led by John Gould
Fletcher, Allen Tate, Robert Penn Warren, and John Crowe Ransom.
The Poetry Society of South Carolina offered encouragement to aspiring
versifiers and the "Fugitive Group" at Nashville—so named because of
its support of *The Fugitive*, a literary magazine published at Nashville
from 1922 to 1925—numbered an impressive array of talented poets. In
these years, too, other "little magazines" essayed the almost needless task
of stimulating and reviving Southern literary art: *The Double Dealer*
(New Orleans, 1921-1926), *The Reviewer* (Richmond and Chapel Hill,

1921-1925), and *The Southwest Review* (Dallas, 1924). The goal set by *The Double Dealer* and announced in its first issue, was perhaps typical of them all: "*The Double Dealer* . . . wishes to be known as the re-builder, the driver of the first pile into the mud of this artistic stagnation which has been our portion since the Civil War." These transitory reviews gave opportunities to able new writers who, once "discovered," went on to write for national magazines or for such more stable journals as the *Sewanee Review, The South Atlantic Quarterly,* or the *Virginia Quarterly Review.*

The conflict between literary modernists and fundamentalists also found expression in biography, history, and social science. In biography John Donald Wade wrote the life of August Baldwin Longstreet, Allen Tate wrote on Jefferson Davis, Andrew N. Lytle on Bedford Forrest, and Robert Penn Warren on John Brown. These works, able and brilliant, stemmed from the traditionalist school and celebrated anew the glories of the Old South. So too did Hamilton J. Eckenrode, whose *Jefferson Davis* asserted that the Confederacy was fighting the last battle of Nordic civilization. Gerald Johnson's journalistic account of Andrew Jackson, *Epic in Homespun,* and Douglas Southall Freeman's monumental biography of Robert E. Lee, sprang from the same school of thought. But at the same time "progressives" were examining other characters from the southern past. George Fort Milton and Robert W. Winston wrote new biographies of Andrew Johnson—their choice of subject matter rather than their treatment carrying implications of their attitude. Broadus Mitchell turned to *William Gregg: Factory Master of the Old South* in explicit defense of an industrial, progressive South.

In history there was new activity with the formation of active historical societies and state departments of archives and history, with professional curators of public records. At the beginning of the century the South had many state historical organizations which were generally of social rather than scholarly appeal. The Southern Historical Society had its headquarters in Richmond but its membership was declining; the Southern History Association had an office in Washington, directed by Colyar Meriwether and Stephen B. Weeks, and about 300 members. State historical societies of varying vitality existed in Maryland, Virginia, North Carolina, South Carolina, Georgia, Alabama, Mississippi, Louisiana, Texas, Arkansas, Tennessee, and Kentucky. Some of these groups published historical journals. State agencies for the collection of historical materials were also forming in the period. Alabama had a Department of Archives and History with Thomas M. Owen as its director; Mississippi employed Dunbar Rowland in a similar capacity; Texas' archives were cared for by E. W. Winkler; South Carolina's Historical Commission by A. S. Salley; and North Carolina placed Robert D. W. Connor in charge of its public papers. In 1934 when the National Archives opened in Washington, Connor became its first Archivist. The new historical activity was paralleled by sound analyses of the South's past. F. B. Simkins and R. B. Woody re-examined *South Carolina During Reconstruction* and Simkins studied the *Tillman Movement in South Carolina* from the viewpoint of the Progressives, while such scholars as Ulrich B. Phillips, Walter L. Fleming, William E. Dodd, and Frank L. Owsley clung to the traditionalist side.

It was in the area of the social sciences that these divergent attitudes toward the South's problems found formulation. North Carolina and Vanderbilt universities came, respectively, to be recognized as the centers of progressivism and traditionalism. Beginning about 1919, a series of studies centering largely at the University of North Carolina examined conditions in Southern industry, described living conditions among tenant farmers and industrial workers, and surveyed the implications of the South's economic system. Claudius Murchison, Peter Molyneux, Broadus Mitchell, George S. Mitchell, Charles S. Johnson, Rupert Vance, Howard Odum, and many others contributed studies which eventually resulted in plans for a nationwide program of regional development. Social scientists in the South met for the joint purposes of discussing the South's natural and human resources and of devising schemes for the control of industry and agriculture for the common benefit.

An opposite point of view found expression among a group of "Young Confederates" whose capital was at Vanderbilt University. Donald Davidson, John Crowe Ransom, Allen Tate, John Donald Wade, an' others of this group had been poets, writers of fiction, and teachers of literature before they developed into social scientists. As members of the "Fugitive" group of poets they recoiled from the crassness of an enveloping industrialism. To the study of southern problems they brought the training and the insight of literary criticism. In *I'll Take My Stand*, twelve of these "Young Confederates" set forth their fundamental grievances against industrialism and "progress" and the philosophy of the New South. Like the sociologists and economists of Chapel Hill, they quarreled with the New South. The difference lay in the techniques of their criticism and in their solutions. The Young Confederates found a classical model for social organization in the Old South, and their solution proposed the abandonment of industry, a retreat from urbanization, and a return to the virtues of an agrarian society.

Neither the regionalists nor the fugitives were in a position to take action. Neither had control of powerful political or social institutions. Only by indirect means could either group implement social change. Yet while politicians evaded responsibility and the preachers sought to divert men's eyes from social sores, southern writers were facing honestly the problems of southern life. From Appomattox to the New Deal, southern literature was a better reflection of the changing South than the "Solid South" of the politicians.

Oratory continued to hold its place in the southern tradition. "The Southerner will follow a good speaker whether he be a labor leader, or a revivalist, or a lyncher," an observer commented. Perhaps the most influential spokesmen for the South were still the politicians, however; the "demagogues" won and held their followings among the southern masses by the power of their speech. Huey Long was especially noted for his rhetorical abilities, and James K. Vardaman, Theodore G. Bilbo, and

Eugene Talmadge were known as verbal spellbinders. Labor leaders like
Fred Erwin Beal (who organized the Gastonia strike of 1929), were also
men of the spoken word. The revivalists were by professional necessity
accustomed to convince their hearers by forceful and colorful invective.
Southerners, with a long record of oratory, continued to admire and to
respond to oral appeals.

The speakers, as well as the writers, pointed up the fact of the
divided South. Perhaps the poet Allen Tate approached the crux of the
South's dilemma in his "Ode to the Confederate Dead." Tate described
a young Southerner standing by a cemetery looking at the gravestones
of the Civil War dead. Musing, he compared their certainty about their
world and its values with the lack of faith of the modern South. The
Rebels knew why they fought, why they died, and what they believed;
the moderns, cut off from the world, could believe in nothing and had to
create a subjective reality within themselves in order to withstand the
harsh and alien world that had moved in upon them. He imagined the
death of the soldiers:

> Now that the salt of their blood
> Stiffens the saltier oblivion of the sea,
> Seals the malignant purity of the flood,
> What shall we who count our days and bow
> Our heads with a commemorial woe
> In the ribboned coats of grim felicity;
> What shall we say of the bones, unclean,
> Whose verdurous anonymity will grow?
> The ragged arms, the ragged heads and eyes
> Lost in those acres of the insane green?

And in conclusion he departed, uncertain about which were the living
and which the dead:

> Leave now
> The shut gate and the decomposing wall:
> The gentle serpent, green in the mulberry bush,
> Riots with his tongue through the hush—
> Sentinel of the grave who counts us all!*

* Allen Tate, *Poems, 1922-1947*. (New York: Scribner's, 1948.)

The New Deal and the New South

1. THE GREAT DEPRESSION

SOUTHERN writers, following the evolution of the New South with skillful pens, were constantly aware of the problems with which the section had to deal. But literature only reflected conditions—it could not implement change. Southern churches, adhering to a rigid theology and the Bourbon philosophy of the New South, took on an obscurantist attitude and made no effort to solve the myriad problems of Southern life. State and local governments, though they instituted reforms, continued to carry out the demands of the dominant groups. Meanwhile, the problems of capital and labor, of landlord and tenant, of white man and black, went from bad to worse. Long before the market collapse of 1929 and the ensuing depression, the South had been approaching economic disaster. The outlines of the Great Depression were already familiar to Southerners.

For a decade after the first World War the United States enjoyed prosperity. Old industries received a new stimulation and new industries sprang quickly into full growth. Radio, motion pictures, automobiles and accessories, chemical industries, paper and printing, lumber and building materials attracted capital and technological skills and increased the human enjoyment of consumer goods. But while old and new industries were enjoying a boom, older and perhaps more fundamental elements in American economic life were not sharing equally in the new prosperity. The overcapitalized and debt-burdened railroads, meeting new forms of competition from automobiles, trucks, motor buses, and even airplanes, were unable to run at a profit or to improve their services. The American merchant marine and shipping interests declined steadily despite constant government subsidies. Moreover, and more important for the South, American agriculture slumped and failed to respond to panaceas prescribed by distraught politicians.

Southern agriculture suffered both from the peculiar socio-economic system of the South and from the general situation in the nation. As a colony of northern financial interests, the Cotton Kingdom had long paid an exorbitant tribute to its northern conquerors. During the first World War, European and American demands for cotton had raised prices and induced an increased production. Under the stimulation of war, planters increased their mortgages. From 1917 to 1919 the average price of cotton exceeded 27 cents a pound, and in 1919 it reached 35 cents. In that year the total value of the cotton crop was two billion dollars, establishing a record not equaled until 1948. After the war boom, cotton prices fell off sharply; in 1920 the average price dropped from 35 cents to 16 cents a pound. In 1921, because of the boll weevil and the declining price, planters reduced their cotton acreage from 36 to 30 million acres and cut production from twelve and a half million to 8 million bales. These conditions made mortgage payments and interest charges difficult to meet. Tenant farmers ceased to rise into the owning classes and an increasing number of sharecroppers became wage laborers. Real estate values in the Cotton Kingdom and also in the rice, sugar, and tobacco areas fell sharply.

The primary element in the southern agricultural depression was the declining market. Prior to the first World War American industrial expansion was largely financed by foreign capital. To meet interest charges on the borrowed money the United States exported cotton and tobacco from the South and wheat and beef from the Middle West. But after 1920 the United States became a creditor nation, exporting capital to other countries. The bulk of American overseas investments was in such agricultural areas as Latin America and the Far East. These lands could best meet their debt charges by sending their agricultural products to the United States. Thus Cuba and Mexico grew tobacco, and Brazil, Mexico, China, Egypt, India, and Russia grew cotton. The foreign markets for southern cotton decreased.

Moreover, at the same time, the domestic market suffered. Style changes made less demand upon the cotton fields, for new chemical fabrics like rayon were growing in popularity. As a result of the drop in demand there were great surpluses of cotton. At the end of the 1931 season the world carry-over amounted to over 18 million bales, of which 72 per cent was American. Cotton suffered, and the Cotton Kingdom became more poverty-stricken.

The solutions of the problem of agriculture were simple, but not easy to accomplish. There was disagreement over methods of easing agriculture's ills. Agriculture might be abandoned as a national interest. The farmers might be moved to the cities and given jobs in factories, and the foodstuffs and raw materials of the nation might be imported from the "backward" areas of the earth. This was the internationalist solution, more appealing to industrialists and bankers than to farmers and cotton planters. Another suggestion was a nationalist one and proposed the abandonment of foreign trade. A balanced economy, producing only for domestic needs, might save the farmer and the South. To this end, both the regionalists of Chapel Hill and the Young Confederates of Nashville seemed to look. But such a solution, even if it met with approval from the masters of capital, would entail drastic social reforms, economic adjustments, and national planning on an unprecedented scale.

As a practical solution, of course, either alternative was impossible. Yet any measure that fell between these suggested solutions was but a palliative. Throughout the 1920's the industry-dominated government wrestled with agriculture's problems. The Capper-Volstead Co-operative act of 1922 sought to encourage agricultural co-operatives. The Federal Intermediate Credit Act of 1923 provided easier credit for farm co-operatives. The McNary-Haugen bill, which was before Congress in varying forms from 1924 to 1928 and was vetoed by President Calvin Coolidge in 1927 and in 1928, was an effort to separate the domestic market from the export market. Under the plan an agricultural export corporation, with capital furnished by the government and directed by a Federal Farm Board, would purchase surpluses and sell them abroad for whatever they would bring. Losses from the "dumping" would be repaid by an equalization fee assessed on all domestic sales. In the same period Congress debated an "export debenture" plan to provide bounties to exporters of farm products in the form of debentures, which would be receivable for the payment of import duties. Finally, in 1929 the Agricultural Marketing Act created a Federal Farm Board which might use a revolving fund of $500,000,000 to establish and subsidize agricultural co-operatives. Stabilization corporations, with funds supplied by the board, might handle, control, and market the surpluses.

The system did not work. The Federal Farm Board loaned to cotton co-operatives, for cotton held off the market, at sixteen cents a pound. This did not stop prices from falling, and a Cotton Stabilization Corporation, with board funds, purchased over a million and a quarter bales—the entire carry-over of 1929-1930. Still prices fell, and the next year the corporation again purchased the entire carry-over. With over three million bales on its hands—which it attempted to market abroad—the corporation lost $150,000,000. The price of cotton fell to 5.7 cents, which was except for 1894 the lowest price since the Civil War. Comparable experiences attended the board's efforts in tobacco and wheat. American agriculture in general, and southern agriculture in particular, continued in the doldrums and contributed no little part to the eventual collapse in 1929 and the resulting general depression.

Preceding the general depression and contributing to it was the Florida boom and its deflation. In 1923 and 1924 a combination of real estate promoters, railroads, bus lines, and local chambers of commerce began to advertise Florida as the winter home of the nation. A speculative craze spread over the peninsula. From Pensacola to St. Petersburg, from

Jacksonville to Key West, orange groves and sand flats, swamp lands and city lots mounted to fabulous prices. Rococo hotels and flimsy houses sprang up like magic. Miami and St. Petersburg reached out toward each other across the Everglades. Yankee tourists, Florida crackers, get-rich-quick promoters, butchers, bakers, and Seminole Indians scrambled over one another in a rush to multiply the profits. Suddenly a hurricane swept the peninsula, wrecking the jimcrack buildings, upturning the crazy streets, and blowing the paper profits out to sea. In its wake the speculators departed, prices fell, and shoemakers who had been million-aires searched the wreckage for their lasts.

Had the boom been confined to Florida, its collapse would not have been so serious to the rest of the South. But the mania in Florida had spread to other states. It extended along the Gulf Coast to Mobile, to Biloxi, to St. Charles, and to New Orleans; it followed the seaboard to Savannah and Charleston. It reached inland to Atlanta, to Chattanooga, to Asheville. Land values spiraled, then cracked. And with them went business houses, factories, and corporations. During the 'twenties, 71 per cent of the banks of Florida failed; in South Carolina, 49 per cent, and in North Carolina 20 per cent went into bankruptcy.

The depression of the 'thirties quickly revealed that the South's industry was as unsound as its agriculture. With the exception of tobacco manufacturing, which was well integrated, mechanized, and controlled, southern industries were disorganized. The coal and iron mining com-panies were competing with one another and there was no union among the textile factories. All were marginal producers in the national economic scene. All depended upon low wages and long hours to maintain a profit. As a result, when collapse came northern capital withdrew its support. Northern companies closed their southern branches. Since the southern factories had never built up the purchasing power of their own laboring forces, they could not resort to production for the domestic market.

The situation in the cotton industry revealed the worst defects of southern industry. King Cotton was sick—sick from internal disorders. Innumerable small factories existed, each devoted to some small part in the manufacture of cotton goods. The spinning mills made yarn to sell to the weaving mills, which made cloth. Converting plants "finished" the "gray goods" that came from the weavers and sold them in turn to the garment manufacturers. These goods went, in turn, to the jobber and the retailer. At each step in the progress from cotton patch to garment shop, commission merchants handled the goods and extracted a profit. It was small wonder that the Negro tenant woman who hoed the cotton plants could ill afford a cotton smock, or that the toiler in the mill could not buy the products of his handiwork.

Not only was southern industry disorganized; it was also inade-quate. Despite the pundits of the New South, despite the open-handed lures of the chambers of commerce, southern industry was not diversi-fied. Its power resources were relatively undeveloped, and it produced no electrical appliances. Its highways had grown from mud roads to boulevards, yet it manufactured no automobiles, few tires, and fewer accessories. Its sands and its clays were valuable, but it had no glass industry and few potteries. It had iron mines and foundries, yet it made few machines and no precision tools. It grew sugar and drilled oil wells; it raised vegetables and cattle. Yet it had no packing industry, no widespread canning industry, and almost no refineries. Southern industry for the most part was still concerned with bulky, crude products. It had neither been integrated into the national pattern nor become self-sufficient in the section.

The depression brought more disorders and additional hardships. Beginning with the stock market crash of October 24, 1929, the economic crisis soon spread to all areas of the country. Though the South had long known poverty, the depression had profound repercussions in the region. Ninety per cent of the market for southern lumber disappeared. Farm lands fell under the sheriff's hammer for tax delinquency. Wages declined and unemployment increased. Labor troubles, already mounting in intensity, also increased. Labor unions penetrated the South, Communists moved in to organize discontent, and the lines formed for new warfare between capital and labor.

It would have been a departure from American traditions not to have blamed these conditions upon the government. In 1928 President Herbert Hoover had received more support in the South than had any Republican candidate since reconstruction, but he quickly became the symbol of depression. By 1932 the Solid South was solidly back in the Democratic column and was casting its united vote for Franklin D. Roosevelt, who promised a New Deal for all classes and sections in the nation. "This Nation," Roosevelt told a farm audience in Topeka, "cannot endure if it is half 'boom' and half 'broke.'"

2. New Deal Policies and Agencies

Advocates of a new crusade to force the South into the national image made use of Franklin Roosevelt's new "house divided" speech, as well as the grinding poverty of "shoeless southerners." But the economic philosophy of the New Deal was completely capitalistic and its welfare state a buttress to the sanctity of property. Throughout the campaign of 1932 and often during the development of the New Deal, opponents of the new president raised the cry of "socialism." Yet the first action of the new administration gave the lie to the charge. Franklin D. Roosevelt took office in the blackest days of the Great Depression. On every hand were bank failures and ominous clouds of portending doom. Roosevelt immediately ordered the banks closed and on March 9 sent Congress an Emergency Banking Bill. The new law permitted sound banks to reopen and furnished them currency to cover their assets. The President's failure to nationalize the banks and assume direct control over the nation's credit structure—a move which, at the moment, would have had wide approval—was proof that the New Deal was no socialistic revolution.

Instead as the New Deal unfolded its program, it became evident that the administration would use the government to aid capitalism. It elaborated a plan of recovery that would work for the benefit of big business at the same time that it brought about better relations between capital and labor. Laborers would be assured employment and a living wage; farmers would be given a subsidy. The needy would receive care. To accomplish these things a succession of new laws set up a host of new governmental agencies. To facilitate the work, the administration spent lavishly, raising the national debt to figures that lost all meaning in their astronomical magnitude. The New Deal put men to work on a variety of projects—the Civil Works Administration, the Federal Emergency Recovery Administration, the Public Works Administration, and the Works Progress Administration. The PWA and the WPA built new buildings, made roads, surveyed parks and historical records, and erected airports, bridges, and monuments. The South shared the largess with the rest of the nation, getting new courthouses, new post offices, new schoolhouses, and new payrolls. A Federal Housing Administration aided in the construction of new homes; a Civilian Conservation Corps surveyed park and picnic areas, planted trees and drained swamps; and a Federal Deposit Insurance Corporation guaranteed bank deposits. The government assumed new functions and new responsibilities in the crisis, but did not disturb the basic outlines of the capitalistic system.

Several aspects of the New Deal were of especial concern to the South. The incoming administration lost no time in tackling the problems of agriculture. The Agricultural Adjustment Act of May 12, 1933, proposed to maintain the price levels (or an equivalent purchasing power) of the years before the first World War, and to regulate farm production. Acreage allocations were given farmers for basic commodities and wholesale plowing-under and slaughter of animals ensued. The reduction in production was intended to increase prices of wheat, cotton, corn, tobacco, and rice by removing surpluses from the market. Direct payments were made to farmers in return for reduced acreage. It was a program of planned scarcity at public expense, and in operation the scheme proved to be unsound. Southern farmers reduced their acreage, cashed their government checks, and applied more fertilizer to the remaining fields. In 1934 the failure was recognized by the Cotton and Tobacco Control Acts which allotted quotas of production to states. Each county and each planter received a quota, supplemented with tax-exempt certificates and enforced by a prohibitive tax upon any surplus production. Then, by further legislation, the government lent money on warehouse receipts.

Not even those restrictions prevented farmers from increasing production. By 1936, after three years of the AAA, cotton crops had increased tremendously. In that year, when the Supreme Court held that the AAA was an unconstitutional exercise of power, the New Deal took refuge in a Soil Conservation and Domestic Allotment Act. Under the guise of soil conservation and improvement, the act gave a direct subsidy to agriculture and directly controlled the production and prices of agricultural commodities. Still production increased. In 1937 the cotton crop totaled nearly 19 million bales, the highest on record, increasing world cotton carry-over to over 22 million bales. Clearly the problem of surplus production had not been solved. The following year a more stringent control law passed the Congress—the Agricultural Adjustment Act of 1938. It prescribed a system of acreage allotments, plus marketing quotas with heavy penalties for excess production and various pay-ments to the farmer for reduced acreage, soil conservation, and crop storage loans. The new AAA reduced the cotton yield to 12 million bales, but the huge carry-over precluded any increase in price. The net result was that returns from cotton were less than 40 per cent of the average in the 1920's, and only slightly above the 1931 level. After five years the New Deal had made no improvement in the plight of King Cotton. In 1939 American cotton was "dumped" on the international market; but it was the war which began in September of that year that brought southern agriculture out of its slump.

Another aspect of rural depression was the lack of credit facilities, and President Roosevelt sought to remedy the problem. "I tell you frankly that it is a new and untrod path," he explained to Congress, "but I tell you with equal frankness that an unprecedented condition calls for the trial of new means to rescue agriculture." Congress responded with the Federal Farm Mortgage Corporation, established in 1933, to loan money on agricultural lands at low interest rates. To make loans for the produc-tion and marketing of farm commodities, the Farm Credit Act of 1933 created two new credit institutions to operate along with the Federal Reserve Banks—twelve Production Credit Corporations, and twelve Banks for Co-operatives. These agencies were combined into the Farm Credit Administration. In the next year the Frazier-Lemke Farm Mortgage Act provided a five-year moratorium to protect farmers from foreclosures. In 1935 the Supreme Court declared the Frazier-Lemke Act to be uncon-stitutional. Finally, the government attempted to solve other problems of rural finance by the Farm Security Administration Act of 1937. Under this, the program of loans continued, augmented by information on agri-cultural methods and efforts at co-operative living. In 1938 at Lake Dick, Arkansas, a co-operative village began operating the first of a series of co-operative farms. In all, the agency established 164 such experimental communities.

Elaborate and complicated though these experiments were, they brought but slight change in the southern agricultural scene. The gov-ernment's program was designed to benefit landlords rather than tenants. In the early days when immediate and direct relief was prof-fered, landlords and merchants shifted tenants and laborers from the store accounts to the relief rolls. Tenant farmers reduced their acreage in accordance with AAA requirements, while landlords collected the benefit payments. After a time, cotton prices rose and relief lists declined, while direct complaints to Washington resulted in more care that "bene-fit" payments should benefit the rightful payees.

The New Deal's program of rehabilitation made greater progress in the South than in other sections. In fact, the publicity value of the South was great, and politicians did not neglect the vote-getting appeal that lay in tearful portrayals of the sharecroppers' condition—or the opportunity it offered to attract attention away from their own social and economic maladjustments. Once more the South was being used as Americans had used it before; it was "the issue" in national politics. To dramatize it, photographers came with cameras to peer into the lined faces of the lowly; Mrs. Eleanor Roosevelt visited and inspected the croppers' shacks; Secretary of Labor Frances Perkins made an unfortunate remark about Southerners being without shoes; and eventually even the president himself was moved to add his voice. In 1938 in the report of a National Emergency Council, Roosevelt declared that "It is my conviction that the South presents right now the nation's No. 1 economic problem—the nation's problem, not merely the South's. For we have an economic unbalance in the nation as a whole, due to this very condition of the South."

Southern spokesmen quickly answered the President. They pointed out that great relief sums had gone to industrial states such as Pennsylvania and New York, and that such areas were more nearly the nation's economic problems than was the South. But their best argument, contained within the N.E.C. report itself, was that any economic unbalance in the South was the result of absentee ownership of the section's resources. "The public utilities in the South are almost completely controlled by outside interests," the report admitted. "All the major railroad systems are owned and controlled elsewhere. Most of the great electric holding company systems, whose operating companies furnish the light, heat, and power for Southern homes and industries, are directed, managed, and owned by outside interests. Likewise the transmission and distribution of natural gas . . . is almost completely in the hands of remote financial institutions. The richest deposits of the iron ore, coal, and limestone that form the basis for the steel industry in Birmingham are owned or controlled outside of the region." Such information, long the common knowledge of Southerners who knew their region, gained stature and circulation by publication in a supposedly neutral government document.

Southern protests to the President's pronouncement did not end the new crusade against the "backward" South, which intensified in the following twenty years. But such public notice of the plight of the rural poor in the South inspired efforts to furnish tenants with greater opportunities. The Bankhead-Jones Farm Tenant Act offered government-guaranteed loans to tenants and sharecroppers who wanted to buy farms, and relief agencies furnished work stock to tenants of the lower tenure status. Various efforts at rehabilitation resulted in giving some tenants an opportunity to own their lands, while educational programs bore some promise of bringing a greater diversification and a better balance to southern agriculture.

The industrial aspects of the New Deal bore no more promise of a fundamental settlement of southern problems than did the agricultural program. In industry, as in agriculture, the New Deal sought to maintain old price levels and to protect the capitalist system. It also furnished aid to organized labor. The National Industrial Recovery Act of June 16, 1933, established a board that was to administer codes of fair competition drawn up by trade and industrial associations. Each code should contain a recognition of union labor and provide for collective bargaining. The cotton textile industry, already organized by the Cotton Textile Institute, was the first industry to adopt a code and to receive the Blue Eagle, symbol of co-operation. Other industries rapidly followed, and the South soon had an integration of industries and a formal recognition of labor hitherto beyond the reformer's dreams.

In operation NIRA quickly proved to be no reform measure. The Act took effect at the beginning of a promising business rise and there was some feeling that its operation had hindered rather than helped recovery. Industry momentarily revived, but it became apparent that the system fostered monopolies and reversed the victories that the American people had won in their long battle against the trusts. In practice, NIRA provided self-regulation of business; it meant that the parties immediately affected wrote the rules by which they would operate, and would then call in government to enforce the rules. The trade associations and the United States Chamber of Commerce supported NIRA to stabilize economic conditions—a position their critics described as restoring high profits. Small businesses were easier victims of their larger competitors. Eventually, in May, 1935, the Supreme Court declared the act unconstitutional.

Meanwhile, the New Deal's attempt to regulate prices and wages brought no help to southern employers. The codes of fair competition established by the National Recovery Administration provided for a wage differential between northern and southern labor. But as the proposed wage-scale for the South was considerably higher than the prevailing rates, the southern industrialists were among the first to denounce the NRA. Failure to comply with the codes soon led to more labor discontent. Southern employers attempted to force workers into company unions and refused to recognize locals affiliated with the American Federation of Labor. Partly to obtain union recognition and partly to obtain the hours and wages proposed in the New Deal program, southern textile workers went on strike in 1934. Strikes were especially violent in Georgia, where Governor Eugene Talmadge, completely out of sympathy with the national administration, treated the strikers as revolutionaries. At Atlanta and Rossville the strikers were placed in concentration camps.

Late in 1934 the Southern States Industrial Council, composed of representatives of leading southern industries, met in Chattanooga to protest against the New Deal. A Nashville editor addressed the assemblage on the possibilities yet confronting southern industry. The South, he asserted, "stands at the threshold of a new era in which it will see its raw materials made into a greater variety of new products than ever before." Other speakers reiterated the same idea, pointing especially to the possibility of using southern pine as pulp for newsprint, while the entire council was agreed that governmental competition would prevent opportunities for the exploitation of new resources. In order to facilitate new industrial development, the council proposed a "subnormal" code of wages for southern labor and suggested that $9.50 for men, $8.00 for women, and $6.00 for children per week would compensate the South for the "handicaps occasioned by distance . . . and inferior workmen." The entire object of union labor, asserted one orator, is to "force high rates of wages, short hours." These elements, he declared, "tend to the destruction of any industry dominated by it."

The council formally adopted a report which declared that the "South is confronted by particular problems, the most imminent of which is to preserve and protect our industrial opportunities. . . . Our larger industrial development must first be made possible by removing the manifest obstacles which restrain it." Specifically, the council demanded wage differentials that would protect southern industry against northern competition and insisted upon "keeping southern labor free" from disturbance by "the professional activities of outside agitators."

The decision of the Supreme Court invalidating the NIRA enabled the southern industrialists to restore the wage levels that would enable them to compete with the northern producers. In the next year the employers of labor showed even greater vigilance in promoting a "red scare" in the industrial regions. By 1936 the class lines in the South were clearly drawn and southern labor had definitely ceased to be docile. For two years, marked in the nation by a new economic "recession," southern industrial struggles continued. To the president's repeated suggestions for reform legislation southern congressmen gave steady opposition. Over their protest, however, the Congress enacted, June 13, 1939, a Wages and Hours Act which established minimum wages and maximum hours for industries producing goods for interstate or foreign commerce. Southern interests vigorously protested that freight differentials made it impossible for them to compete in the national market and that this entitled them to a lower wage scale. Because of their opposition to these and other aspects of his reform program, President Roosevelt attempted to "purge" Senator Walter George of Georgia, and several other southern Democratic congressmen. Resentment at this interference as much as sympathy with the recalcitrant attitude of the legislators caused the voters to return them to Congress.

Armed with the new law, however, the unions made new advances in the South. The split in the ranks of organized labor acted as a stimulus rather than a deterrent to unionization. John L. Lewis's Committee for Industrial Organization challenged the American Federation of Labor, and both groups made gains in the South. Conflicts between them added to the troubles of the harassed southern industrialists but showed them as well that southern workers were able to organize and demand their rights. Only the Negroes remained unorganized, and to the majority of southern industrialists it must have seemed that the New Deal's reform program had prevented a full enjoyment of the recovery measures.

3. THE TENNESSEE VALLEY AUTHORITY

Neither in its measures for relief nor its measures for recovery was the New Deal especially successful in the South. Bourbon Democratic politicians, alert enough for the spoils of office and the new patronage, watched suspiciously as "Brain Trusters" gained control of the government and attempted to combine reform with recovery. Welcome though recovery might have been, they did not wish to purchase it at the price of altering the South's delicate social structure.

One New Deal program in the South did threaten the established order—the Tennessee Valley Authority, the greatest experiment in social and economic reform attempted by the new administration. For fifteen years after World War I, the Wilson Dam and two nitrate plants that the government had constructed on the Tennessee River lay idle. From Tennessee came insistent demands that these unproductive properties be put to work, and from practical businessmen and impractical theorists came various projects and proposals. The most publicized—if not the most sound—proposition came from Henry Ford, who wished to take over the nitrate plants to produce cheap fertilizer. Senator George Norris thought such a grant would be "the greatest gift ever bestowed upon mortal man since salvation was made free to the human race." Norris wanted to use the dam and plants in a much broader way, to benefit more people. The Republicans, who controlled the nation, however, hesitated either to release the properties or to develop them under government auspices. Presidents Coolidge and Hoover vetoed Norris's bills to utilize Tennessee River waters. But the New Deal was less sensitive to the wishes of private enterprise, and in May, 1933, President Roosevelt signed into law the third Norris bill and created the Tennessee Valley Authority to operate and develop the properties.

At the head of the TVA were three directors—President A. E. Morgan of Antioch College, chairman; President Harcourt A. Morgan of the University of Tennessee, and David E. Lilienthal, State Utility Commissioner of Wisconsin. These directors were authorized to build dams, power plants, and transmission lines for power; to develop and market fertilizers; to engage in projects for flood control; and to sponsor social improvement in the seven states that touched the Tennessee River's valley. Ostensibly, the flood control and navigation aspects of the project were the more important; actually, the power production program was uppermost in the mind of the Authority's sponsors and directors. They intended the TVA to generate and sell power to individuals, corporations, municipalities, and co-operatives. As they saw it, its costs and its rates were to become a "yardstick" by which the charges of private utilities could be measured. To encourage wider use of electricity, especially in rural regions, the Electric Home and Farm Authority, a credit agency which was practically a subsidiary of the TVA, began operation in the valley.

The navigation and flood control aspects of the TVA involved both the construction of dams on the publicly owned waterways and the co-operation of private land owners in adjacent farming regions. The directors immediately made plans for an elaborate and unified system of dams on the river and its principal tributaries. The Wilson Dam, already constructed, submerged Muscle Shoals in its sixteen mile reservoir. In 1936 the Authority completed Norris Dam, on the Clinch River twenty-five miles above Knoxville, and Wheeler Dam, at the head of the Wilson reservoir, which formed a lake 74 miles long. Below Wilson was the Pickwick Landing Dam, while above Wheeler was the Guntersville Dam. Seven miles above Chattanooga was the Chickamauga Dam, and above the Chickamauga reservoir lay the Watts Bar Dam. On a tributary of the Tennessee was the Hiwassee Dam. In 1939, by purchase of the Tennessee Electric Power Company's facilities, the TVA acquired five major dams and power plants. The unified operation of these dams and reservoirs reduced the danger of destructive floods; maintained a nine-foot channel for navigation stretching 650 miles and making Knoxville in the mountains a river port; balanced seasonal fluctuation in the river, and incidentally, supplied vast quantities of hydroelectric power.

Tennessee Valley Authority

SITE OF TVA's HIWASSEE DAM ON THE TENNESSEE RIVER.

Flood control involved more than the mere construction of dams. To control the source of the run-off, the TVA had to gain the co-operation of landowners in projects of improved land management and agricultural practices. On model farms TVA technicians demonstrated ways to halt soil erosion and to rebuild wornout and eroded land with fertilizers and lime; farmers learned how to construct and maintain lakes and ponds to hold back the water. To this aspect of the work President H. A. Morgan gave his attention and succeeded in teaching farmers better methods of retaining moisture in the soil and of more profitable farming by diversification.

The flood-control portions of the TVA's task were simple as compared with its power program. Connected with the various dams were hydroelectric plants with a capacity of well over a million horsepower. The law authorized the sale of this power to existing companies, newly created co-operatives, and municipally-owned distributing systems. Early in 1934 Tupelo, Mississippi, with a publicly owned system, became TVA's first customer, and later in the same year the first rural electric co-operative began operating in Alcorn County, Mississippi. As the use of TVA power spread, it brought unaccustomed competition to the private power companies which already served parts of the region. Attack from these companies, supported by New South Bourbons and all opponents of "socialism," was immediate and unremitting. The opposition charged that the government's intention was to encourage public ownership and to destroy private business. If flood control and improved river navigation were the purposes of the TVA, they declared, the dams were too large and too expensive. Moreover, they charged that the TVA's rates for power were too low. Too much of the cost of producing power was charged to flood control, and the "yardstick" thus was marked to measure the private utilities' rates adversely. Carrying their charges to the courts, the opponents lost. In 1936 the Supreme Court found that the dams were "reasonably adapted" to the constitutional purposes of flood control and that the sale of surplus power was a legitimate "incidental" activity. In addition, the Court upheld the right of the TVA to create markets for its power, and of the PWA to loan money to cities to purchase municipal distributing systems.

Soon Knoxville, Nashville, Memphis, and Chattanooga were purchasing power from the TVA and distributing it through their own municipally owned systems. More than half a hundred smaller communities did likewise, and dozens of rural co-operatives, created by the TVA, used the power. In 1939 after a bitter court fight the TVA acquired the properties of the Tennessee Electric Power Company. In the midst of the controversy the chairman of the board of directors, Dr. A. E. Morgan, brought charges against his fellow directors. At an unprecedented hearing before President Roosevelt Dr. Morgan refused to produce evidence to support his charges. He was removed from office and former Senator James P. Pope was appointed to the board. A Joint Congressional Investigating Committee failed to sustain the exchairman's charges and reported favorably on TVA's policies, program, and rate structure.

The conflict brought bankruptcy to George Fort Milton, liberal editor of the Chattanooga News, whose ardent support of the TVA cost him his newspaper. It gave momentary prominence to Wendell Willkie, New York utility executive of the Commonwealth and Southern combine, whose fight against the TVA made him acceptable to the Republican party as their 1940 candidate for the presidency. Willkie was fond of saying that "the Tennessee River flows through seven states and drains the nation," and he alleged that the "yardstick" for utility rates provided by TVA was "rubber from the first inch to the last." But the decisions of the Roosevelt-dominated Supreme Court, and the failure of the Republicans in 1940, insured the continuance of the New Deal's most far-reaching and most successful experiment.

Tennessee Valley Authority

THE HIWASSEE DAM. This dam, 1,287 feet long and 307 feet above the bed of the river, was a part of the first group of dams on the Tennessee River built under the TVA program.

With the United States becoming the "arsenal of democracy," it was advantageous that TVA's resources were not hampered in 1940. On July 31, 1940, the first emergency program under the national defense program authorized Watts Bar Steam Plant and Cherokee Dam on the Holston River, the third of the primary tributaries of the Tennessee to be controlled. A year later TVA was empowered to construct four additional dams in the Hiwassee watershed. Douglas Dam on the French Broad River, and Fontana Dam on the Little Tennessee, were also built during the war as the defense program expanded. TVA played a vital role in the nation's war effort. It produced ammonium nitrate for explosives, phosphorus for incendiary and smoke bombs, concentrated phosphate fertilizers for victory gardens, dicalcium phosphate for cattle feed, calcium carbide for synthetic rubber production, as well as maps of over a half-million square miles of enemy territory prepared from aerial photographs. The navigation on the Tennessee, made possible by TVA dams, linked the river to the inland waterway network. Military vehicles were assembled in the Valley and shipped out by barge; ocean-going ships were built on ways in Decatur, Alabama, and floated down-river to the Gulf. At the same town the Alabama Flour Mills manufactured flour from wheat brought by barge by way of the Mississippi and the Missouri, from the midwestern granary. A firm in Chattanooga was engaged in similar activity.

The TVA by-products and river navigation were important, but it was electric power that made the greatest contribution to the military program. When the President declared a national emergency the system enlarged its capacity and produced unprecedented quantities of hydro-electric power. The largest user was the Federal Government itself. The Oak Ridge installation of the "Manhattan Project," which produced the atomic bomb, was placed near Knoxville because of the availability of great amounts of electricity. Aluminum plants in East Tennessee required large supplies of power, as did other plants working on war contracts. An indication of the expansion and vital contribution of the TVA to the war was its output. In 1939 the system generated less than two billion kilowatt hours of power; in 1945 its production totaled nearly twelve billion kwh.

4. THE SOUTH AND THE NEW DEAL'S FOREIGN POLICY

Although southern politicians might look skeptically at the TVA and the relief agencies of the New Deal in the 1930's, they gave enthusiastic support to the foreign policy of the Roosevelt administration. The prosperity of the South's agriculture and much of its industry was dependent on foreign markets. Much of the products of the South were shipped abroad. The developments of foreign outlets for southern products was imperative.

The Republican tariff policy of the 'twenties had proved disastrous to the South. In 1922 the Fordney-McCumber Tariff benefited industry but depressed agriculture. The Smoot-Hawley Tariff of 1930 raised the tariff walls still higher. These acts curtailed foreign trade and cut off the foreign market for southern commodities. The Coolidge and Hoover administrations seemed more concerned with industrialists than with farmers. To aid in selling industrial products abroad, they encouraged foreign loans. These loans could only be repaid with goods, but the Republicans were unwilling to permit foreign goods to flood the American market. The United States bought tea, coffee, silk, rubber, manganese, and tin from Latin America and the Orient. The American loans were made to Europe. Perhaps, Republicans believed, the payments from Europe might come—by a process of triangulation—from these imports. In the meantime, Coolidge and Hoover would support agriculture by having the government buy the surplus. The system led to disaster.

Southern critics of the Republican policy condemned as fallacies sacrificing agriculture to industry and supporting foreign trade by money loans. With southern interests in mind, they proposed lowering the tariffs, stopping the export of capital, and negotiating trade agreements. If the South lost its foreign markets, the entire southern system, they contended, would collapse, and far-reaching social adjustments would ensue. These fears caused Southerners to watch the new administration's foreign policy with concern.

In the beginning the New Deal's foreign policy vacillated between nationalism and internationalism. In its relief measures and its agricultural program it seemed to be following the basic principles of the Republicans. It would subsidize agriculture and restrict agricultural production to the needs of the domestic market. Moreover, in 1933 the administration's refusal to co-operate with the gold nations in stabilizing currency broke up the World Conference and committed the country to economic nationalism. The policy might operate as a temporary relief but it did not solve any problems. And the development of foreign sources of cotton, the increasing use of foreign-grown silk, and the general shutting off of foreign markets left the South with serious problems. Despite the New Deal's agricultural panaceas, the cotton surplus remained.

Yet the South was not without a potent voice in the national policy-making councils. Southern senators and congressmen, by virtue of extended service, became chairmen of important congressional committees in the general Democratic victory. There were also Southerners in the executive departments; South Carolina's Daniel C. Roper was Secretary of Commerce; Virginia's Claude A. Swanson was Secretary of the Navy; Marvin McIntire and Stephen Early, secretaries to the president, came from Kentucky and Virginia. Southerners were ministers or ambassadors to Bolivia, Brazil, China, Ecuador, Egypt, Guatemala, Honduras, Mexico, Rumania, and Uruguay. The most powerful influence in the New Deal's foreign policy-making was the Secretary of State, Cordell Hull of Tennessee.

Long experience in watching American foreign affairs and trade policies from the Senate had enabled Secretary Hull to become a persuasive critic of the Republican program. He had opposed the high tariffs and the resultant subsidies to foreign customers. He entered the State Department with a program of his own that promised benefits to both southern agriculture and American commerce. He would write reciprocal trade agreements with foreign nations, thus reducing tariff barriers. Beginning in 1934 the Secretary negotiated trade agreements with various Latin American countries by which they reduced duties on such American exports as automobiles, machinery, and cotton textiles in return for American reductions on their exports. Within two years American sales to these countries increased over 40 per cent.

The reciprocal trade pacts, too, proved but a temporary palliative. The trade agreements opened markets for industry but jeopardized agriculture. For unless Argentina could sell the United States her wheat and beef she could not buy American automobiles. An expanding American capitalism was still confronted with the problem of American agriculture. If farmers were sacrificed, American industry might continue to dominate the world's markets. Secretary Hull's popularity with financiers and industrialists grew as farmers and planters became suspicious. Meanwhile Brazil, Egypt, China, and India grew more cotton and Japan paid for scrap iron and oil with silk.

In the meantime, developments on the European continent intensified the difficulties. In 1933 Adolf Hitler and the National Socialist Party came into power in Germany, pledged to renounce the Versailles Treaty of 1919. The Nazis began a vigorous policy of rebuilding both the economic and the military strength of the country. They revived German industry—partly by crushing organized labor and partly by driving out the owners—and directed it to producing goods for a powerful nation. They recaptured, by methods more effective than ethical, the industrial regions of Central Europe which had belonged to the German and Austrian empires before 1914. In foreign trade the Nazis resorted to a system of barter arrangements. They traded the goods of German industries for the raw materials and agricultural products of South America, Asia, and Africa. With an economic system unified under a totalitarian regime they were able to undersell American competitors in these markets. Moreover, an elaborate system of political agents, economic missionaries, and propagandists spread the philosophy of the Nazis in the lands where they traded. Barter and propaganda together boded ill for Secretary Hull's trade agreements and for American trade generally.

President Roosevelt, who took office two months after the Hitlerite *coup* in Germany, watched with suspicion the Nazi political and economic system. His "Good Neighbor" policy in Latin America, aided by the trade agreements, furnished sharp competition for the expanding Nazis. He gave active support to France and England in their efforts to prevent Europe's smaller countries from falling under Hitler's sway. He demanded and got increasing support for the American navy. He denounced the aggressors and in 1937 declared that they should be "quarantined." In 1939, after England and France declared war on Germany over the second partition of Poland, Roosevelt prepared to give them material aid. He promised to make the United States the "arsenal of democracy."

As the President's policy of unarmed intervention unfolded, opposition came from all parts of the United States except the militant South. In the nation pacifists were joined by die-hard Republicans who hated Roosevelt and by Communists who loved Russia. Americans who preferred domestic social reform to foreign adventure were joined by those who feared that a war economy would hasten socialism and domestic upheaval. As the President moved from the repeal of the Johnson Debt Default Act, to the repeal of the Embargo Act, to the Lend-Lease Act, the "isolationists" charged that he was "preparing to lead the country into a vast program of armament as a means of spending money to avert another depression—houses for the dogs of war rather than the mutts of peace" and to "shift the psychological reactions of the nation to the patriotic motif in order to distract attention from the disintegrating domestic situation." Eventually they charged that each "measure short of war" was but another step into the world conflict. Senator Burton K. Wheeler, who had long opposed the New Deal's foreign policy, said that Lend-Lease was the administration's new farm policy and would mean "ploughing under every fourth American boy."

In general, Southerners who may have opposed the New Deal's

requirement for ploughing under every fourth row of cotton did not appreciate Wheeler's sarcasm. Full support for the administration's foreign policy came from the South. Efforts of "America First" to turn public opinion away from the war in Europe came to complete failure, but there were occasional dissenting votes cast in letters to southern newspapers. "When the land of the Ku Klux Klan, chattel slavery, Judge Lynch and the poll tax starts whooping it up for the four freedoms," a disgruntled Alabamian wrote the Birmingham *News*, "that alone ought to be enough to make it suspicious to the minds of all thinking men everywhere." And Erskine Caldwell, the Georgia novelist, declared that the southern interventionist attitude was but another sign of the South's ignorance. But those were exceptional; the majority of Southerners supported the administration's militant foreign policy.

Most southern congressmen gave full-throated approval to each step. Senator Claude Pepper of Florida was generally recognized as the administration's spokesman on foreign policy, and he raised his voice continuously in favor of stopping the "aggressor" nations of Europe by armed intervention. Gallup polls and other surveys of public opinion showed consistently that the New Deal foreign policy received a higher percentage of popular support in the South than in any other section. In 1941, extension of the Burke-Wadsworth peacetime draft passed the House by only one vote, but the delegations from Alabama, Georgia, Louisiana, Mississippi, North Carolina, Texas, and Virginia were all solidly in favor of it. Only one opposing vote came from each of four other southern states: South Carolina, Arkansas, Kentucky, and Florida; and only two Tennessee Representatives voted Nay. Without the almost solid bloc of southern votes, neither the draft extension nor the revision of the Neutrality Act would have passed the Congress. When in December, 1941, the Japanese precipitated war by an air raid on Hawaii and the Philippines, the Southerners were psychologically ready and enthusiastic for the conflict.

The Political Return of the South

1. THE NEW CRUSADE

THE war that began in 1941 marked the emergence of the United States into a position of world leadership and the South, as part of the nation, played an important part in it. In the armed services overseas Southerners joined their compatriots in waging war against the European and Asian enemies of American influence. At home southern industry and agriculture changed during the conflict. Governmental expenditures contributed to material growth in the South—a development which had been under way since Reconstruction—and war-born prosperity accelerated the South's escape from a century-old colonialism. The war, moreover, wrought fundamental changes in southern life. The suddenly increased demand for labor intensified the migration of rural Southerners to other sections of the country and to urban areas within the South. These economic and social changes, significant in themselves, exerted important influence upon political affairs in a rejuvenated South. Southern politicians were, in general, more like those of the rest of the nation and resembled less the colorful, often erratic officials of the first third of the century. But without the excitement—and even charm—of the "demagogues," the South continued to play its traditional role in American political life. Many of the issues that divided the national parties were Southern in origin and, with proper agitation, served to divert attention from pressing problems in other parts of the country. The global war for the "four freedoms" became a new crusade against the South and its way of life.

Even before the Pearl Harbor attack, discrimination against the Negroes, widely regarded as solely a southern phenomenon, threatened the mobilization program. When Jim Crow restrictions limited Negro job opportunities, Negro leaders planned a march on Washington. To forestall such an event, on June 25, 1941, President Roosevelt issued Executive Order 8802 enunciating a policy "to encourage full participation in the national defense program by all citizens of the United States, regardless of race, creed, color, or national origin . . . ." To enforce the order the President appointed a Committee on Fair Employment Practices. Despite these efforts, racial discrimination continued in war plants all over the country. But Southerners who objected to FEPC drew the heaviest fire from New Deal Democrats.

Southerners also complained that their section was not fairly treated in the allocation of war plants. The South got camps, ordnance depots, explosives factories, and shell-loading plants built at government expense; but of those plants which were readily convertible to peacetime uses—heavy machinery, assembly plants or electrical equipment facilities —few appeared in the South. It was true that a larger percentage of military installations were located in the South. With about a quarter of the land area the region received 30.1 per cent of the federal money expended for camps and bases. The favorable climate and wide ranges of open land influenced the selection of southern sites for training camps and air fields. As in 1917, many of them bore the names of Civil War heroes. The names of Gordon, Jackson, Lee, Bragg, Beauregard, Hood, Shelby, A. P. Hill, Van Dorn, Polk, and Pickett were in the news again as designations for army cantonments. The South also received 15.4 per cent of the government money spent on ship construction and repair, and 11.6 per cent of the ordnance plant money.

But the war also brought new industries to the South, industries that made a permanent addition to its economy. Aluminum reduction plants appeared in East Tennessee and ship construction began along the southern coast at Portsmouth, Wilmington, Charleston, Mobile, Pascagoula, and New Orleans, and even on the Tennessee River at Decatur, Alabama. Birmingham iron and steel mills prospered as never before. Baton Rouge got huge oil refineries and a synthetic rubber factory and Texans began to refine tin and to assemble aircraft and expanded their production of petroleum and chemicals. Much more significant was the installation at Oak Ridge, near Knoxville, which produced the atomic bomb and put the South ahead of the nation in the power source of the future.

The economic magic of war found expression in wartime politics in the South. As southern economy gained strength and independence, the region became the target of national critics, and commentators in the South found more to criticize in the New Deal. With the coming of the war the Republicans gained steadily upon their opponents. The elections of 1942 reduced the Democratic majorities in Congress and in 1943 Kentuckians chose a Republican as their governor. Southern opponents of Franklin Roosevelt and the New Deal blamed the administration for the wartime bureaucracy and the expansion of the national debt, the Civil Rights program for Negroes, and for the ill effects of agricultural experiments upon southern farmers. Still, in 1944 the President continued to advocate programs that antagonized Southerners. In that year his announced platform was the ratifying of a "Second Bill of Rights" to equalize opportunity for all citizens, and to insure a lasting peace. Vice-President Henry A. Wallace further irritated Southerners by proclaiming that "the new democracy, the democracy of the common man, includes not only the Bill of Rights but also economic democracy." Wallace called for continued government relief and reform expenditures after the war. Wallace also led the administration's fight against segregation and demanded that "the poll tax must go!"

Such talk increased southern determination to force changes in the Democratic Party in 1944. Though Roosevelt easily won the nomination for a fourth term, the convention passed over Wallace and named Senator Harry S. Truman of Missouri as the vice-presidential candidate. This change was generally regarded as a compromise with southern Democrats, but many Southerners remained dissatisfied with the party. In Texas the disaffection reached the point of rebellion; a group calling itself the "Texas Regulars" bolted the Democratic Party and formed an independent organization. An unusually heavy Republican vote in the South indicated that there was widespread resentment in the section. The popular vote was the closest it had been since 1916.

Harry Truman proved to be as inimical to Southern prerogatives as had Henry Wallace. On April 12, 1945, at the death of Roosevelt, Truman succeeded to the presidency. He soon announced a domestic program which antagonized Southerners. On September 6, 1945, in a message to Congress, Truman defined the "Fair Deal": public housing, a fair employment practices law; more TVA's on the Missouri and Arkansas rivers; a higher minimum wage law, and an extended social security program. The announcement frightened the free enterprise rugged individualist wings of both major parties and many southern Democrats and northern Republicans allied to fight a common enemy. Southern politicians struck back with filibuster defeats of administration measures—the Fair Employment Practices bill of 1945 and laws against lynching and poll taxes. In the national elections of 1946 the Republicans won control of both houses of Congress for the first time in sixteen years.

Southerners felt themselves to be on the defensive in a series of attacks by outside critics upon race relations in the South. In 1946 the Supreme Court removed the legal support for the South's cherished "separate but equal" doctrine governing segregation of the races. In *Morgan v. Virginia* the Court denied the State's authority to impose segregation upon interstate carriers, a decision which reversed the 1896 *Plessy v. Ferguson* decision. Southerners were further angered in October, 1947, when Truman appointed a fifteen-man committee on Civil Rights with General Electric executive Charles Edward Wilson as its chairman. The committee's report, entitled *To Secure These Rights*, proposed a sweeping civil rights program. Calling for a "new charter of human freedom," the committee specified congressional legislation outlawing poll taxes, "white" primaries, and other state restrictions upon the franchise; strengthening the Civil Rights section of the Justice Department and extending its jurisdiction over electoral irregularities; a federal anti-lynching law and a Fair Employment Practices Act; an end to segregation of housing in cities; and a recommendation that federal grants-in-aid to states be conditioned upon the abolition of racial segregation. In February, 1948, Truman requested Congress to implement the Civil Rights program with legislation. When it did not, he had his campaign issue for that year.

To Southern leaders like Carter Glass and Harry Byrd of Virginia, James F. Byrnes and J. Strom Thurmond of South Carolina, Walter F. George of Georgia, and W. Lee O'Daniel of Texas, the Roosevelt-Truman domestic program was a declaration of war against the South. It seemed to be based upon the fear of southern economic independence and justified by the contentions of the Swedish sociologist Gunnar Myrdal in *An American Dilemma* (1944), a critical analysis of American racial arrangements. Making use of the time-honored Southern weapon of states' rights, Southerners fought back. In 1946 at his inaugural as Virginia's governor, William M. Tuck declared that "if this policy of expansion of Federal activities into state fields continues it will result in the virtual abolition of the states." A year later an Alabamian, Charles Wallace Collins, provided the blueprint for a southern rebellion in *Whither Solid South?* (1947). Spokesmen for the South defined states' rights as the only guarantee against "a kind of Kremlin in Washington"; they said that FEPC had been "hatched in the brains of Communists" and that Civil Rights laws were the "demands of the parlor pinks and subversives." The program was a new crusade aimed only at the South, asserted Mississippi's Senator James Eastland. "This proves that organized mongrel minorities control the government," he said. "I'm going to fight it to the last ditch. They're not going to Harlemize the country."

While most Southerners appeared to be concerned over the racial equality inherent in Truman's program, there was an economic aspect to the new crusade. Wealthy natural gas and oil promoters in the Southwest objected to the president's determination to regulate their activity, and private electric power interests chafed under the TVA competition and the threat of new government power projects. Changed economic conditions in the South made it the target of national regulatory bodies. In 1947 the Supreme Court handed down two decisions concerning the question of sovereignty for regulation purposes. First, it awarded control over the Tidelands oil wells—those located on the continental shelf far out under the Gulf or off the California coast—to the Federal Government. The tidelands case promptly entered national politics as the oil corporations pushed for congressional action to insure state regulation. They charged that the court action was an invasion of state sovereignty and they condemned Truman and the Fair Dealers for supporting the Court. As a result, much oil money and leadership went into the states'-rights wing of the Democratic party. Another Supreme Court case in

1947 further infuriated the southwestern drillers. It declared that "independent" natural gas producers—those not affiliated with a petroleum corporation—were subject to control by the Federal Power Commission because gas entered interstate commerce.

2. The Revolt of 1948

Southern dissatisfaction with the Democratic party was thus based upon fear of Negro equality established by a new abolition crusade, and the action of President Truman and the Supreme Court against racial discrimination and the economic interests of the South. Southerners regarded Republicans as but little better than the Democrats: the GOP had advocated a fair employment practices program in 1944, and New York, whose governor was a leading candidate, had such a law. But in 1948 dissident Southerners had somewhere else to go. In an effort to preserve the vanishing political influence of the South, Southerners bolted the national party and formed a separate political organization dedicated to states' rights.

Their plan of action was a modern interpretation of John C. Calhoun's political teachings of a century earlier. If the South nominated an independent candidate who could carry the electoral votes of the eleven ex-Confederate states, it would hold the balance of power, especially if the election were as close as that of 1944. The House of Representatives would then have power to select a president, with each state having one vote. There, reasoned South Carolina Governor J. Strom Thurmond, it would be impossible for any candidate to win without the southern votes. It would give the South a veto over the candidate at worst, and the right to name him at best. With the threat of filibuster hanging over their heads, Republicans would probably accept a southern Democrat rather than a "progressive" northern Republican; and Democrats would prefer any Democrat to a Republican. Thus, according to the states'-rights plan, the southern party could control the presidency.

The southern leaders had a good chance of success, for 1948—the first presidential election after the war—was a confused race. The Republicans, confident of victory, nominated New York's Governor Thomas E. Dewey. Henry A. Wallace, ousted by the Democrats in 1944 and unhappy at the seeming rejection of pre-war social gains, offered himself as a presidential candidate on a hastily manufactured "Progressive" ticket. Norman Thomas, the perennial Socialist candidate, also appealed to those voters who preferred continued government planning; there was also the usual quota of splinter parties. At the Democratic convention in Philadelphia, the southern wing found itself unable to obtain any part of its pre-convention demands. The two-thirds rule for the selection of the candidate, repealed in 1936, was not restored; a civil rights plank was included in the platform; and the states'-rights Southerners were unable to block the nomination of Harry Truman or to control the vice-presidency, which went to Kentucky Senator Alben W. Barkley. Before the convention Alabama's delegation had declared that "if . . . the national party attempts to nullify the Constitution of our state and to crucify the South, the Democratic party of Alabama owes it no allegiance." So, singing "Dixie," thirty-five Southern delegates, mostly from Alabama and Mississippi, walked out of the convention. Two days later, on July 17 at Birmingham, they organized the States' Rights party, popularly known as "Dixiecrats."

The new party proclaimed itself the "true" heir of Jefferson and Jackson. Since 1933, they said, the Federal Government had steadily assumed functions and powers constitutionally reserved to the states. "A long chain of abuses and usurpations of power by unfaithful leaders who are alien to the Democratic parties of the states here represented has become intolerable to those who believe in the preservation of constitutional government and individual liberty in America," the Birmingham convention declared. A group of southern governors at Birmingham agreed that "a vast majority of the Democrats of the South are determined to restore the Democratic party to the principles of Jefferson and Jackson and will resort to whatever means are necessary to accomplish this end." And Mississippi's Governor Fielding Wright announced that "this is not a bolt. This is not a fourth party. I say to you that we are the true Democrats of the Southland and these United States." The States' Rights party selected South Carolina Governor J. Strom Thurmond as presidential candidate and Wright as his running mate. Thurmond was the son of a farmer who had supported Ben Tillman; as governor of South Carolina he had sponsored progressive reforms designed to improve living conditions in rural areas. Fielding Wright was a native Mississippi lawyer of Vicksburg, whose clients had included several oil companies.

The platform was a mixture of statesmanship and petulance. Much of it was a diatribe against the Philadelphia platform of the Democratic party. As the statement of a protest party it was primarily a negative listing of what it opposed. The party cited the Tenth Amendment and the states' rights plank adopted in the first Democratic platform in 1840 (which concerned slavery and which contributed to the defeat of the party in that year). It deplored the "gradual but certain growth of a totalitarian state by domination and control of a politically minded Supreme Court." Southern remonstrances had received only contempt, it said; "the latest response to our entreaties was a Democratic convention in Philadelphia rigged to embarrass and humiliate the South." The States' Righters avowed their determination to save the Constitution from invasion and destruction, and to oppose the "totalitarian, centralized, bureaucratic government and the police state" of the Republican and Democratic platforms.

Specifically the party recorded its opposition to FEPC, to the elimination of segregation and to the Democratic program of civil rights, termed "Social equality by Federal fiat." The platform closed with an appeal to all "who are opposed to totalitarianism at home and abroad" to join in "ignominiously defeating" Truman and Dewey and the police

J. Strom Thurmond. A native of Edgefield, South Carolina, Thurmond was the States' Rights candidate for the presidency in 1948. He served in the State Senate, as Circuit Judge, military officer, Governor, and Senator from his state. He was recommended as candidate for President by the Conference of States' Rights Democrats at Birmingham on July 17, 1948, and was nominated at a convention in Houston on August 11. "This is no sectional or regional matter," he told the Houston gathering. "No citizen of any state is safe, if any political party is allowed to go unchallenged when it undertakes to barter away this sacred constitutional right [of state sovereignty] for political advantage."

state in America. In summary, the issues raised by the party, as its apologists saw them, were "stateism versus private enterprise, the further rise of Federal power in time of peace over the individual person" and the view that the "classification of man into races belongs to mythology because men of all races have been found to be equally capable in every respect and in a democracy such as ours they should be merged without distinction."

Though most States' Rights voters were interested in the white-supremacy appeal, the party made an effort to win over representatives of new economic interests in the South. Many of its leaders were drawn from those classes, for while southern politicians accepted the tenets of the Dixiecrat platform in theory, in practice they looked the other way. With the exception of those in South Carolina, Alabama, and Mississippi, the experienced political leaders remained faithful to the Democratic party. That left the Dixiecrats to face the electorate with amateurs—younger businessmen, advertising agents, corporation executives, and lawyers. Among the States' Rights leaders were representatives of the National Association of Manufacturers, lawyers from the South Carolina Power Company and the South Carolina Cotton Manufacturers' Association; the head of the New Orleans telephone company, the director of the Mississippi Delta Cotton Council, a Houston oil millionaire, and several oil corporation lawyers.

The leadership of the new party thus reflected changes in the Southern economy. In October, 1948, in an address at Houston, Governor Thurmond pointed this out. "We are going forward in the South," he said. "We are bringing in new industries, developing our ports and harbors, increasing our public facilities . . . without dictation from Washington." In general the party received the support of investors and managers who preferred the existing free enterprise economic system to the Fair Deal alternative, which seemed to be state capitalism and centralized control. The motivation of Dixiecrats was economic and political, for the civil rights program endangered the privileged status of planters, landlords, bankers, and those manufacturers whose profits depended upon cheap labor. To win the votes of the masses, these economic interests were translated into states' rights on the racist level. Once again, as in the 1880's, the Bourbons held the poorer whites in line by threats of Negro equality. Belying the ancient phrase about the French ruling house, the white tenants in the South had learned nothing, while the Bourbons had forgotten nothing.

The Dixiecrat candidates failed in their attempt to throw the election into the House of Representatives and they failed because they were unable to win the Southern electoral votes. The party carried only four states—South Carolina, Alabama, Mississippi, and Louisana—and received the vote of one Tennessee elector, for a total of 38 electoral votes and 1,168,000 popular votes. But President Truman won the Southern states of Virginia, West Virginia, Kentucky, Tennessee, Georgia, Florida, Arkansas, Texas, and Oklahoma. Even in the four Dixiecrat states the victory was not one-sided. There the traditional cleavage between planters and farmers continued. The greatest States' Rights strength lay in the "black" counties in which a few planters and tenants voted for a large Negro population and in urban areas where businessmen supported the planters. In many of the "white" counties there were Democratic majorities. The revolt of 1948 was based upon new wealth in the South. The new managerial classes moved easily into the Bourbon camp and took up the fight against the farmer-demagogue coalition. But there would be no new Civil War, for these were not new Confederates.

For all their talk of states' rights and white supremacy, the Dixiecrats demonstrated that the South was American and that reconstruction had ended. The TVA and southwestern oil and the multitude of southern economic interests changing the character of many southern regions provided both the reason for the revolt and the object for which it existed. Half a century after American politics had adjusted to the demands of northern economic pressures, Southerners demanded similar favors for their distinctive interests. Basically they were imitators rather than rebels. They represented a new group bidding for dominance in the new regions and though they spoke with tongues of the squires, they adhered to the traditions of the trustees.

3. NATIONAL POLITICS IN THE 'FIFTIES

In the period following 1948 national politicians continued to woo southern support. President Truman attempted to hold the loyalty of southern Democrats by appointing their leaders to high office in his administration. During the eight years he was in office he named James F. Byrnes of South Carolina and George C. Marshall of Virginia to head the State Department; Fred M. Vinson of Kentucky and John W. Snyder of Missouri to the Treasury; Kenneth Royall of North Carolina to the War Department; Louis Johnson of West Virginia and George C. Marshall to the newly-established Department of Defense; Tom Clark of Texas to the Attorney-General's office; and Robert Hannegan of Missouri to the Post Office Department. The president appointed Wilson Wyatt, mayor of Louisville, as his post-war "Housing Expediter." Despite Truman's efforts, Southerners in Congress holding important committee assignments were able to block much of his Fair Deal program. Because of southern opposition to the Roosevelt-Truman domestic policies, the ex-Confederate states assisted in ratifying the Twenty-Second Amendment to the Constitution in 1951. It limited the tenure of the Chief Executive to a maximum of ten years.

Issues raised by the South influenced the elections of the 1950's. In the campaign of 1952 the Democrats prevented another southern bolt—though the platform contained a firm civil rights plank—by making concessions to the South. One of these was the nomination of Senator John Sparkman of Alabama as the vice-presidential candidate. Better than anything else Sparkman illustrated the cleavage in the South between Dixiecrats and Democrats. Aside from the fact that he had won high political office in a southern state, Sparkman was everything that the Dixiecrats were not. He was the son of a tenant farmer, one of a family of eleven children who had worked his way up by ability, ambition, and hard work. Sparkman knew first hand the plight of the southern poor whites and the part played by the New and Fair Deals to improve their lot. Other concessions to southern sentiment were made by the Democratic presidential nominee Governor Adlai E. Stevenson of Illinois. Stevenson made an effort to placate the Southerners without surrendering the party's civil rights plank or his own views on tidelands oil regulation.

In a campaign speech in Richmond in September, 1952, Stevenson traced the historical background of the South's problems. After the Civil War, he said, the South became a colony of the North. "The victor's settlement permitted the South to keep its charm, its mockingbirds, and its beaten biscuits. For himself the victor retained only the money and the power." Like his Illinois compatriot of ninety years earlier, he admitted his inability to solve the racial problems of the South. Stevenson rejected the view that the South was a prison in which half the population were prisoners and the other half were wardens. He also declared himself opposed to "unjustifiable" anti-Negroism in one place and anti-Southernism in another.

Stevenson's efforts at sectional peace left many Southerners unimpressed. They seemed to prefer his opponent, Republican candidate Dwight D. Eisenhower. A native of Texas and a West Pointer who had spent his entire life in the Army, Eisenhower was immensely popular as a war hero. He endeared himself to States' Righters in the South with an apparent mixture of Jeffersonian and Hamiltonian principles. He voiced a view of government more Jeffersonian than that of the Jeffersonian Democrats. Eisenhower said he wanted government "smaller rather than bigger," and was interested in "finding things it can stop doing instead of seeking new things for it to do." At the same time the ex-Dixiecrats responded to the Hamiltonian "partnership" he proposed between government and business. During the campaign he promised Texans that he favored state control of tidelands oil. The Republican platform also appealed to dissident Southerners. It charged that the Democrats favored "national socialism," and that they had wrecked free enterprise by excessive government interference in business. On the touchy matter of civil rights the Republicans essayed a compromise. To appease sensitive Southerners they declared it the "primary responsibility of each State to order and control its own domestic institutions." To win the northern Negro vote the party pledged federal legislation to eliminate lynching, to abolish the poll tax as a prerequisite to voting, and segregation in the District of Columbia. It also promised some sort of federal fair employment practices law.

The election of 1952 contained important innovations for the South. It was the first election since 1860 in which the major candidates made a campaign in the section. Another innovation was the emergence of a vigorous southern Republican party, a fact that led many observers to declare the Solid South at an end and to predict the return of two-party politics. More important in the election, however, were the numerous "Democrats for Eisenhower" clubs which sought to salve southern consciences for the "crime" of voting Republican. The 1952 election also marked the return of the Negro to the electorate. In 1948 only about twelve per cent of voting-age Negroes in the South were registered to vote but by 1952 over one fourth of the eligibles were registered. This amounted to approximately 1,200,000 in the country. In the South, Texas had the largest Negro electorate, with 175,000; Georgia had 145,000; Florida registered 120,913, North Carolina around 100,000, and Tennessee over 85,000. The most dramatic increase was in Louisiana where only 1,672 Negroes registered in 1948 and four years later there were 108,724.

When the votes were counted Stevenson and the Democrats had carried only nine states and they were all in the South. For all the talk of "liberal Democrats" and southern rebellion against the party, the Solid South remained solid. With 27,300,000 popular votes, Stevenson received the 39 electoral votes the Dixiecrats had coveted in 1948. The Republicans carried 39 states with 33,900,000 popular votes and received 442 electoral votes. But the victory was largely that of Eisenhower, for the party barely controlled the Congress. The Republican margin in the Senate was only one vote, and in the House it was only ten. The new cabinet was made up of businessmen—eight millionaires and a plumber, ran the gibe. Only Houston editor Mrs. Oveta Culp Hobby, Secretary of the newly established Department of Health, Education, and Welfare, was from the South. Business and government were so closely intermingled in the new administration that defeated candidate Stevenson joked that the New Deal had been replaced by the Big Deal. But the narrow Republican hold over Congress meant government by coalition with southern Democrats.

The election of 1956 was a repetition of 1952. The major candidates were the same and there was a similar tone to the platforms and campaign appeals. The "Ikecrats" appeared again in southern states and the Republicans fared better in the South than ever before. Eisenhower carried Florida, Kentucky, Louisiana, Tennessee, Texas, Virginia, and West Virginia in the South—five of them traditionally Democratic, and one, Louisiana, in the Deep South. In the South as a whole Eisenhower won a plurality of the popular votes but his opponents carried seven states—six southern and the border state of Missouri. There were two States' Rights candidates in the race: T. Coleman Andrews, who received 155,894 votes, and Harry F. Byrd, who got 134,157. One Alabama elector, instead of voting for Stevenson, cast his ballot for Judge Walter B. Jones of Montgomery. Though the Republicans swept the presidential election, their opponents continued to control the Congress.

The southern electorate continued its practice of returning veteran lawmakers to Washington for term after term. As a result, when Democrats organized the Congress, Southerners controlled many of the important committees in both houses. Indeed, in the mid 1950's Texans determined action in Congress—Lyndon B. Johnson was Senate Majority Leader and Sam Rayburn was Speaker of the House. Four representatives from Arkansas held chairmanships of major congressional committees. Many northern Democrats objected to southern political power in the Congress. In 1958 former New York Senator Herbert H. Lehman criticized his southern colleagues. As a result of the congressional seniority system, he said that the South had "all the advantages" in lawmaking, a situation which he held was "utterly unrepresentative of the country." Lehman complained that representatives from New York, Pennsylvania, Illinois, and California, "the four largest states in the Union with more than a fourth of the total population of the nation, have no chairmanships whatever in the Senate and together have only two chairmanships of relatively minor committees in the House."

4. RACE AND THE COURT

The Negro played a central role in the national political activity. His treatment by southern states and the Federal Government was a major issue dividing parties and even became a factor in the international "Cold War." The Negro had always been one of the main problems in American history. Whether as slave, freedman, tenant, illiterate, diseased, or disfranchised, he provided the rallying force for political organizations, humanitarian reformers, and social philosophers. He was the most popular object of humanitarian concern and the subject of a new abolitionist crusade directed against the South. In the contemporary South the Negro continued to wield unusual influence upon public affairs and he began to play a more active part in them. Perhaps the most significant change in southern political and social arrangements was the emergence of the New Negro.

The depression of the 1930's brought a change in Negro leadership. For more than thirty years W. E. B. DuBois had voiced the aspirations of America's black minority and he bitterly opposed any settlement that resembled segregation. But the economic crisis, in which Negroes suffered out of proportion to their numbers, demanded something new. DuBois suggested voluntary segregation into a Negro co-operative economy within the American economy. That idea, suggesting that the Negro was a separate community within the citizen body, was anathema to Negroes, and they ended his association with the National Association for the Advancement of Colored People. Leadership passed to new men —Carter G. Woodson, Walter White, Thurgood Marshall, Ralph Bunche. These men used the federal court system to further their program of complete legal equality by 1963—the centennial of emancipation.

The new leadership got assistance from diverse quarters. The NAACP provided legal aid and widespread publicity for the new crusade. Organizations to abolish segregation in the South kept congressional hoppers full of resolutions demanding civil rights legislation. The national Democratic party took up the issue, reflecting the shift of Negro population into a commanding position in key northern congressional districts. Most important was the support of the Supreme Court, which found constitutional basis for outlawing racial segregation. The integration of the Negro into the white citizen body—the last step in the Americanization of the South—aroused some Southerners to "massive resistance," but most of them indicated a willingness to grant the Negro his civil dues.

The intensified campaign against the racial status quo in the South began during the war against the German Nazis. It seemed incongruous to many Americans to send segregated armies against a people regarded as dangerous because of their racist theories. Caught in an ideological dilemma, the Federal Government issued civil rights decrees and fair employment orders to which southern "die-hards" objected. But the war emphasized the tendencies that were making racial ill-will a national problem. As in World War I, the war accelerated Negro migration to urban centers of the North. There they began to move into previously all-white neighborhoods. As a result there were serious riots. In June, 1943, in Detroit 25 Negroes were killed in a riot so serious that federal troops were called in to restore order. There was other race violence in Boston, New York, and Los Angeles.

Following the global struggle, the conflict with the Communist world for the allegiance of Asians and Africans brought legal segregation again into the headlines. An American Secretary of State declared that segregation embarrassed the United States in foreign affairs. "The segregation of school children on a racial basis is one of the practices in the United States which has been singled out for hostile comment in the United Nations and elsewhere," he said. "Other peoples cannot understand how such a practice can exist in a country which professes to be a staunch supporter of freedom, justice, and democracy." Such views resulted in a strange anomaly: the "Cold War" with Communism motivated attacks upon Southern race relations—conduct which Southern politicians declared was "communist inspired."

But Negro leaders spurned Communism and its methods for attaining their objectives. They used constitutional guarantees and the judicial system to plead their cause. Gradually the lawyers for the Negroes got the Supreme Court to qualify and then to dismantle the elaborate legal wall of segregation. In a continuing stream of decisions it revised and then reversed altogether its "separate but equal" dictum of the nineteenth century. The judicial basis for legal separation was the decision in *Plessy v. Ferguson* (1896), which sustained a Louisiana statute requiring a separate railway coach for Negroes, and cited school segregation in support of its action. In a strong dissent from the *Plessy* decision Justice John M. Harlan foresaw the Court's later shift. "In respect to civil rights, common to all citizens," he said, "the Constitution of the United States does not, I think, permit any public authority to know the race of those entitled to be protected in the enjoyment of these rights." But the Court's majority opinion permitted separate public facilities, provided they were equal in quality.

The direct judicial application of that view to public education came in 1927 with *Gong Lum v. Rice*. The Court decided that Mississippi authorities could compel a Chinese-American child to attend a colored school without depriving him of equal right. But the Court made it clear that it expected "facilities for education equal to that offered to all," and in subsequent decisions reiterated that requirement. For schools to be separate, the Court held, they must be equal. Before 1950 in most of the South they were noticeably not that.

Meanwhile the Court acted in other areas of racial discrimination. In 1941 it delivered two significant decisions. In the *Classic* case it denied a Louisiana white primary law: the Court declared that primary elections were not the exclusive property of the party. In *Mitchell v. United States* the Court ordered that a Negro who bought first-class accommodations for rail travel must receive them even if they were only available in a section reserved for whites. In 1944 in *Smith v. Allwright,* the Court declared that a political party was an agent of the State when it held a primary election and therefore such elections came under the Fifteenth Amendment. That decision marked the end of the "white primary," long the refuge of white supremacy at the polls. Two years later the Court acted against another cherished southern practice. In *Morgan v. Virginia* (1946) it decided that states could not require Negroes to ride apart from other passengers on buses engaged in interstate commerce.

There was also further action against state efforts to maintain the white primary despite the Court's decisions. In 1947 a Federal District judge in South Carolina, J. Waties Waring, struck down an attempt by that state to evade the spirit of the *Classic* decision by making the Democratic party a private club. "Private clubs and business organizations do not vote and elect a President of the United States . . . ; and under the law of our land, all citizens are entitled to a voice in such elections," Waring said. "It is time for South Carolina to rejoin the Union. It is time to fall in step with the other states and to adopt the American way of conducting elections. . . . It is important that once and for all," he concluded, "the members of this Party be made to understand—and that is the purpose of this opinion—that they will be required to obey and carry out the orders of this court, not only in the technical respects but in the true spirit and meaning of the same."

In 1948 other bastions of segregation fell. One of these was the national defense establishment. On July 26 in an executive order, President Truman declared that "there shall be equality of treatment and opportunity for all persons in the armed services without regard to race, color, religion, or national origin." By 1953 the services had ended segregation; soldiers marched in integrated columns down Main Streets in southern towns, lived together in cantonments and aboard ship, and ate together in mess halls and wardrooms. Another wall of segregation was the state university in the South. In *McLaurin v. Oklahoma State Regents* the Supreme Court extended its *Gong Lum* decision. If professional training of equal quality was not available in Negro state schools, the Court said, a colored applicant must be accepted in the professional school established for whites. Paying the tuition for Negroes to attend schools outside the state did not provide equal facilities. A Texas case, *Sweatt v. Painter,* also held that professional schools must be equal or the Negro applicant must be accepted by the state university for whites. And in the general destruction of segregation, property restrictions went the way of other discriminations. In *Shelly v. Kraemer,* the Court decided that property owners who entered into "gentlemen's agreements" to restrict the race of buyers or dwellers could not enforce them at law.

In a 1950 extension of the professional school cases, the Court would not agree to placing Negro professional students in a screened-off portion of the classroom or to special one-student classes. "Such restrictions impair and inhibit his ability to study, engage in discussions and exchange views with other students, and, in general, to learn his profession." The Court declared that there was a constitutional distinction "between restrictions imposed by the State which prohibits the intellectual commingling of students, and the refusal of individuals to commingle where the state presents no such bar." The problem, said the Court, was the effort of the state to deprive the Negro the "opportunity to secure acceptance by his fellow students on his own merits." Students in the South commended the Court for its action. At the University of Mississippi they petitioned for Negro graduate students, arguing that "the pigment of a man's skin should not make any difference." In 1950 the University of Texas student newspaper declared: "All over the South the new change is being accepted with good grace. Nowhere has there been a suggestion that race relations have been injured, rather to the contrary." By 1952 Negroes were admitted to state universities on the graduate level in ten southern states—Virginia, West Virginia, North Carolina, Maryland, Missouri, Arkansas, Louisiana, Kentucky, Texas, and Oklahoma.

In the integration of public transportation facilities there were other court actions. In *Henderson v. United States* (1950) the Court outlawed the railroad practice of forcing Negroes to eat in a screened-off section of the dining car. In 1953 in *Chance v. Atlantic Coast Line Railroad* the Court went all the way and removed the legal basis for segregated cars in interstate commerce. It was a significant decision. With the main contention of *Plessy v. Ferguson* thus denied, it was only a matter of time until judicial logic required the denial of its subsidiary remarks about the public schools.

After 1945, feeling the pressures upon them, the southern states made a heroic effort to equalize their segregated public schools. North and South Carolina both provided equal pay for teachers regardless of race in an effort to improve Negro education. In 1951 the thirteen Southern states spent nearly four times as much on education as in 1939 and over eight times as much for new buildings, mostly in Negro sections. In his inaugural address as governor of South Carolina in 1951 James F. Byrnes said, "It is our duty to provide for the races substantial equality in school facilities. . . . If we demand respect for states' rights, we must discharge state responsibilities. A primary responsibility of a state is the education of its children." In Georgia lawmakers already feared the coming of integrated schools. In February, 1951, the legislature allocated $50,000,000 to education, with the proviso that a school for whites would lose its share of the fund if it admitted Negro pupils, either voluntarily or upon court order.

Southern states spent great sums in an effort to equalize their schools and thus maintain racial separation, but the Court was not satisfied. By 1952 five cases had reached the Court, from South Carolina, Virginia, Delaware, Kansas, and Washington, D.C., aimed at segregation itself. It heard arguments in 1952, then asked for more information. On May 17, 1954, it handed down a unanimous decision in favor of the Negro plaintiffs. Based upon sociological and psychological theories, the Court held that "segregation of children in public schools solely on the basis of race, even though the physical facilities and other 'tangible' factors may be equal, deprives the children of the minority group of equal educational opportunities."

> To separate them from others of similar age and qualifications solely because of their race generates a feeling of inferiority as to their status in the community that may affect their hearts and minds in a way unlikely ever to be undone. . . . We conclude that in the field of public education the doctrine of "separate but equal" has no place. Separate educational facilities are inherently unequal. Therefore, we hold that the plaintiffs and others similarly situated for whom the actions have been brought are, by reason of the segregation complained of, deprived of the equal protection of the laws guaranteed by the Fourteenth Amendment. This disposition makes unnecessary any discussion whether such segregation also violates the Due Process Clause of the Fourteenth Amendment.

The Court allowed time for the attorneys to present further briefs suggesting ways to "implement" the decision. On May 31, 1955, it ordered compliance, directing lower courts to prepare "such orders and decrees consistent with this opinion as are necessary and proper to admit to public schools on a racially nondiscriminatory basis with all deliberate speed the parties to these cases." Chief Justice Earl Warren added the admonition "that the vitality of these constitutional principles cannot be allowed to yield simply because of disagreement with them." Three years after the original arguments on the school cases racial segregation of the public schools was declared unconstitutional.

The national leadership had a whole year to prepare plans to direct the change in southern life patterns, but it took no action. Into the vacuum moved southern die-hards. The first reaction to the Court's action came in Mississippi. In July, 1954, in Indianola, opponents formed a White Citizens' Council to preserve segregation. Many Southerners expected federal district judges to overrule the Court. Lieutenant-Governor Ernest Vandiver of Georgia said, "Thank God, we've got good Federal judges." But the federal judges, even those with southern educations and backgrounds, found for the Negro plaintiffs rather than for the white defenders. By 1956 nineteen antisegregation decisions had been delivered by federal courts in the South. Thus encouraged, Negro leaders appealed to the courts in new cases all over the region. In 1955 alone, 170 school districts in seventeen states were affected.

As the NAACP expanded its assault upon the citadels of segregated schools, the White Citizens' Councils also spread across the South. They waged economic war upon those who signed petitions for school cases in their districts. The signers sometimes lost their jobs and found their credit cut off at stores and banks. Politicians also took up the cause of segregation. Senator Harry F. Byrd of Virginia called for "massive resistance" to the court action. Using language reminiscent of an earlier resistance to outside interference in southern affairs, in January, 1956, the governors of Mississippi, South Carolina, Georgia, and Virginia met in Richmond to write a new Virginia Resolution. They reiterated the doctrine of interposition of state authority to protect people from federal encroachments. In March of the same year 96 congressmen from eleven southern states, in a "Southern Manifesto," pledged themselves to use all legal means to reverse the decision. They considered the action an "abuse of judicial power . . . contrary to established law and the Constitution," and a general encroachment on the constitutional rights reserved to the states. Alabama's legislature took a page out of South Carolina's earlier skirmish with Andrew Jackson and declared the Supreme Court decision "null, void, and of no effect" within the state. Mississippi created a State Sovereignty Commission "to prohibit . . . compliance with the integration decisions."

Southern lawmakers plotted legal subterfuges to circumvent the integration order. The common practice was to decentralize the school administrations and to require separate cases in many districts. States also provided Pupil Placement laws permitting county and city Boards of Education to assign pupils to public schools. As North Carolina's "Pearsall Plan" explained it: "to provide for the orderly and efficient administration of the public schools, and provide for the effective instruction, health, safety, and general welfare of the pupils." Florida's pupil placement law used identical language to state its purposes. Another plan, adopted in some form in Virginia, North Carolina, Georgia, and Mississippi, provided that if the courts ordered public schools integrated, they might be turned over to private managers, with funds directly from the state government or to parents to be paid for tuition. Since the court cited sociological and psychological theories in its decision, some southern states, as Georgia, authorized local school boards to use similar criteria for assigning pupils to schools. "The decision tortured the Constitution," said Alabama editor John Temple Graves; "the South will torture the decision."

The court decision and the resulting furor of resistance measures produced several significant results. It separated the border states from the Deep South. Not one representative from Kentucky or Oklahoma signed the "Southern Manifesto," and in the border states schools were gradually integrating. It also reduced the number of southern moderates who tried to steer a middle course between the "immediatists" of the NAACP and the "massive resisters" of the Ku Klux and the White Citizens' Councils. Two North Carolina congressmen who refused to sign the Manifesto lost their seats to avowed segregationists, and Governor Jim Folsom of Alabama lost to a rabid segregationist in a race for Democratic national committee post. Other moderates became outspoken enemies of the court and its decision, as did Florida's Governor LeRoy Collins and Arkansas' Governor Orval Faubus.

For a short time the South had reached a constitutional impasse. The Court had defined its position and many people, respectable and in high office, had determined to resist it. In September, 1957, when Governor Faubus called out the state's National Guard to prevent threatened disorder by forcibly keeping Negroes out of Little Rock's Central High School, President Eisenhower "federalized" the Arkansas guardsmen and ordered United States Army paratroopers on duty to enforce the Arkansas court order. Citizens joked that they lived in "occupied Arkansas," but the impasse had been broken by federal bayonets. In May, 1958, the troops were withdrawn. The Army announced that it had cost $3,693,000 to keep eight Negro children in the Little Rock High School. (Nine had entered the school in the fall, but one withdrew during the year.)

In the fall Faubus closed the Little Rock high schools rather than comply with the Federal Court order to admit Negro pupils. A hastily prepared election approved his program of leasing the school property to a private corporation. In a special convocation the Supreme Court declared that action to be an unconstitutional "evasion," leaving the matter far from settled. Harassed school officials began televising high school courses. In May, 1959, a recall election intended to rid the school board of moderates resulted in a surprising upset defeat for Faubus and the segregationists. A Federal court order in June set aside a state school-closing law, and Little Rock school authorities prepared to re-open the schools in the fall.

Integration of the public schools took place in other parts of the border South without violence and without federal intervention. In September, 1957, pupils were integrated in 740 of the 9,004 southern school districts, with the most nearly integrated school systems in the border section. Maryland, West Virginia, Kentucky, Missouri, and Oklahoma led the South in the percentage of integrated pupils. One fifth or more of the Negro students in these states attended integrated schools. The bloc of states to the south, excluding Virginia, had begun token integration; in North Carolina, Tennessee, Arkansas, and Texas, fewer than one per cent of Negro children were integrated. In the Deep South and in Virginia, the schools remained completely segregated, but there were cracks in the color curtain.

In Virginia, "massive resistance" received a setback from Federal Judge Albert V. Bryan, who ordered that school authorities in Alexandria could "no longer refuse admittance" to Negro children. In May, 1958, there were suits pending in Alexandria, Charlottesville, and in Prince Edward County. Nevertheless, in May, 1958, on the fourth anniversary of the Supreme Court decision, *Southern School News*, an information agency, reported that seven southern states—Alabama, Florida, Georgia, Louisiana, Mississippi, South Carolina, and Virginia—continued to maintain complete segregation. Federal court orders to admit Negro pupils to previously all-white schools in Virginia in the fall of 1958 brought a school-closing law into effect there. Governor J. Lindsay Almond, Jr., ordered schools closed in Front Royal, Charlottesville, and Norfolk. In June, 1959, in Prince Edward County, county supervisors abandoned public schools entirely rather than submit to integration.

In the meantime another attack upon the South had been blunted by southern congressmen. The Civil Rights Act of 1957, the first legislation on the subject since reconstruction days, brought sectional jealousies into the open. The law created a Federal Civil Rights Commission with subpoena powers, established a Civil Rights Section in the Department of Justice, and authorized federal prosecutors to obtain federal court injunctions against "actual or threatened interference with the right to vote." To get the bill past the Senate (where civil rights debate postponed action on a $600,000,000 public power program for the Niagara Falls area), it was weakened by the addition of jury trials for criminal contempt cases in civil rights matters.

Many northern leaders condemned the Senate for its action. United Auto Workers President Walter P. Reuther called the "Senate's persistent refusal to enact civil rights legislation the longest sitdown strike in history." When the Senate vote on the weakened measure was announced, Vice-President Richard M. Nixon said: "This is one of the saddest days in the history of the Senate because it was a vote against the right to vote." President Eisenhower declared that the Senate amendments rendered "largely ineffective the aim of the measure to protect the voting rights of Negroes in the South." Despite his dislike for it, the president on September 9, 1957, signed the bill into law.

The following spring the Civil Rights Commission was appointed by the president. Gordon M. Tiffany of New Hampshire became the staff director and in March, 1958, the Senate confirmed the Commission's six members. The Southern members, all Democrats, were former Governors John S. Battle of Virginia and Doyle E. Carlton of Florida, and Robert G. Storey, Dean of the Southern Methodist University Law School. By May, 1958, the Commission was ready to go to work inquiring into complaints that voting rights had been denied on the basis of race or creed.

Even without the assistance of the Supreme Court and the Civil Rights Commission, Negroes were winning a place for themselves in a white world. Talented colored Americans, given opportunity to prove themselves, led their fellow citizens in many important endeavors. John Hope Franklin and Benjamin Quarles were typical of a new generation of Negro historians; Charles S. Johnson contributed to the sociology of race. Ralph Bunche won international acclaim as a peacemaker. Richard Wright and Langston Hughes made significant contributions to American letters. Negroes also played a leading part in the entertainment and sports worlds. For many years Joe Louis held the world's heavyweight boxing championship, and in the 1950's other Negroes reached pugilistic fame. In baseball, the superior playing of Jackie Robinson showed managers and owners what they were missing. As a result, many major league teams included Negro players.

Negroes also excelled in the musical world. On January 7, 1955, contralto Marian Anderson made operatic history at the Metropolitan with her debut in Verdi's *A Masked Ball*. In more popular music, Negroes set the entertainment standards for Americans. W. C. Handy of Memphis composed "blues" which seemed to express the isolation and rejection that many people felt. Negro performers appealed to the American ear, from the haunting spirituals of Mahalia Jackson to the more popular styles of such musicians as Ella Fitzgerald, Nat "King" Cole, Count Basie, and Louis "Satchmo" Armstrong. The Negro's contribution to other areas of show business was typified by actor Eddie "Rochester" Anderson, dancer Bill Robinson, singer Paul Robeson, character actress Hattie McDaniel, and playwright Lorraine Hansberry, author of A *Raisin in the Sun* (1959).

5. SOUTHERN POLITICS

In the years after 1940, as the Negro won increasing acceptance in the nation, he continued to provide the focal point for southern politics. There were real issues confronting the electorates, but personality appeals and race relations tended to obscure them. Local politics followed its traditional pattern. Schism continued between the "black belts" and other parts of the states. The local division took its coloring from events in the national Democratic party. The national party adopted the northern Negro and "liberal," and abandoned its alliance with southern Democrats in the "black belts." The Bourbon element, traditionally Democratic, sought a new alignment with national politicians. That effort had repercussions in local affairs. Anti-administration Southerners paraded under a variety of banners: "Regulars," Dixiecrats, States' Righters, or "Democrats for [the Republican nominee]."

The uncertain political arrangements meant that "black-belt" politicians were once again engaged in the old trick of uniting all southern whites against "outside intervention." As before, it took racial form. Southern leaders might fulminate against the Court or the Civil Rights Law, but without those evidences of "invasion," real political revolution might have hit the South. As they had done so many times before, the humanitarian reformers, however sincere, played into the hands of southern political leaders. The agitators simplified the task of maintaining traditional racial and economic arrangements. Without the resolutions of the American Civil Liberties Union, the Americans for Democratic Action, or a Supreme Court decision to hold up to southern masses as examples of outside interference, the voters might have had a chance to consider their own interests.

Southern voting restrictions marked the success of whites in the black belt counties to unite against the Negro. Poll taxes remained a prerequisite to voting in the Deep South until the 1950's. Everywhere the one-party system of primaries and legal restrictions upon the franchise reduced the size of the southern electorate. The average number of voters continued to be smaller than in the country as a whole. Less than one third of adult Southerners voted in gubernatorial elections; in Virginia it was twelve per cent. In 1948 the only states with fewer than 30 per cent of adults voting were all in the South. After 1950 many legal restraints on Negro voting were removed, so that in 1952 there were drastic increases in the size of the colored electorate.

These voting changes affected the course of politics in the South. The Eisenhower-Stevenson campaign of 1952 recorded a major shift in Negro political orientation. Because the Democratic party had abandoned southern whites and many of them consequently supported the Republican candidate, southern Negroes voted Democratic in great numbers, breaking a Republican habit of seventy-five years. It was largely the colored vote which kept the Deep South solidly Democratic. Dixiecrats —the Bourbon element—rather than southern Republicans, were the allies of the national Republican party because they were more likely to control local politics. This reversal of political alignment by which southern whites voted Republican while southern Negroes cast Democratic ballots reflected fundamental changes in southern life. Basically the political issues continued to follow time-worn patterns concerning the nature of the South. In general, those who could best prosper by a continuation of the established political, social (meaning racial), and economic arrangements joined the Dixiecrats or voted Republican; those whose inclinations were toward changes found surprising acceptance in Democratic ranks.

In most of the South black-belt leaders managed to control the state congressional delegations. Within the states, however, there was little general agreement on public issues. Factions tended to form along regional lines according to the ratio of whites to Negroes. In areas predominantly white, including the hills, political conduct varied from the accepted pattern. Out of the southern highlands arose perennial rebellion against the planters of the black belts and the manufacturers, bankers, and shippers of the New South. Leaders of the "red-necks" of the hills successfully challenged the Bourbon machines. In Alabama, Hugo Black and James E. "Kissin' Jim" Folsom; in Louisiana, the Long family; in Mississippi, Theodore G. Bilbo, Paul B. Johnson, John C. Stennis and John E. Rankin; in Tennessee, Estes Kefauver; in Virginia, John Flannagan Jr.; in Georgia, the Talmadges; in South Carolina, Olin D. Johnston; and in Arkansas, Orval Faubus all drew their strength from counties predominantly white. Such men adhered to the Democratic party, regarding it as the national equivalent of their local factions. Other factors which affected southern politics were the rejuvenation of agrarian liberalism by its acceptance by urban leaders, and the race question, brought home by the Truman civil rights policies and by Supreme Court decisions.

These tendencies appeared in local politics in southern states. In Virginia the Byrd machine easily maintained control. Rebellion appeared in the mountains, with John W. Flannagan, Jr., winning a congressional seat. The machine generally controlled the state, however. Because the economy-minded Byrd stood squarely against the free-spending New Deal, the national Democratic party assisted men such as Moss Plunkett or Martin Hutchinson, who opposed the organization. Anti-machine votes came mainly from the Tidewater cities, the suburbs of Washington, and the mountain counties. In 1945 William M. Tuck succeeded Governor Colgate W. Darden, Jr. Four years later John S. Battle won the gubernatorial election and was succeeded by Thomas B. Stanley and J. Lindsay Almond, Jr. From his Senate seat Harry F. Byrd continued to speak for Virginia and the South. "I believe that in the past 25 years we have done more to destroy the rights of states, and for that matter, individuals, than in all our previous history," he said in 1958.

It was a quarter-century "of profligate public spending and unbelievable waste," he went on; "of piling up new debts and increasing taxes, of cheapening our dollar, of continuing to destroy states rights and of concentrating greater and greater power in Washington." Thus Byrd stated the position of much of the white South. "And, of course," he concluded, "the political segregation decision of 1954 was the high crime of the federal judiciary."

In North Carolina the organization was known as the "Shelby Dynasty," for the friends and relations of O. Max Gardner of Shelby in Cleveland County. In 1932 J. C. B. Ehringhaus was Gardner's gubernatorial candidate and four years later the "Boss's" brother-in-law, Clyde R. Hoey, inhabited the governor's mansion in Raleigh. In the following decade the anti-organization faction became stronger, though Hoey became Senator in 1944 as R. Gregg Cherry became Governor. In 1948 W. Kerr Scott won the gubernatorial election on a "Go Forward" program which frightened the more cautious corporation-centered machine. The next year the legislature authorized a $200,000,000 secondary road bond issue and $25,000,000 for school expansion. Within four years the state had built over fourteen thousand miles of highways and eight thousand new classrooms and had added a third of a billion dollars worth of improvements to state institutions. Such activity the opposition termed "reckless spending," and they came out fighting. In 1950 Raleigh attorney Willis Smith defeated University President Frank P. Graham for the Senate in an election dominated by states' rights and the Truman civil and economic program. Race was a factor in North Carolina politics for the first time since the white supremacy campaign of 1900. Two years later the cautious, businesslike element was firmly in control as William B. Umstead won the governor's chair. In 1954 Scott went to the Senate, Samuel L. Ervin, Jr., of the State Supreme Court was appointed to fill the Senate seat of the late Clyde R. Hoey, and Lieutenant Governor Luther H. Hodges succeeded to the governorship upon the death of Umstead. In 1956 Hodges won a term of his own as governor.

As in Virginia, the court order to end school segregation had political effect among Tar Heels. In 1956 three congressmen—Thurmond Chatham, Charles B. Deane, and F. E. Carlyle—lost their seats, in part because they had refused to sign the "Southern Manifesto" pledging massive resistance to the integration decision. By 1958, however, the Manifesto issue was no longer important.

In South Carolina the Negro issue tended to obscure other issues. With 39 per cent of the population colored, the whites banded together to maintain control. There were divisions, however, between the interests of the Coastal Plain and those of the industrial Piedmont. Politically the state separated at the fall line. Burnet R. Maybank and "Cotton Ed" Smith represented the Tidewater and Olin D. Johnston the hills. Smith was a colorful orator who fought the New Deal and defended white supremacy and southern womanhood. Johnston and Strom Thurmond inherited the Tillman-Blease following but on the issues of states' rights and segregation there was little debate. In 1946 Thurmond became governor and two years later he was the Dixiecrat nominee for president, a movement that split South Carolina politics. In 1950 James F. Byrnes succeeded Thurmond, who lost a Senatorial election to Johnston. The Eisenhower-Stevenson campaign also divided South Carolina Democrats; Byrnes announced that he intended to vote for "Ike." Hostility growing out of the 1952 election continued two years later at the death of Senator Maybank. Governor George B. Timmerman appointed a Stevenson man, Edgar A. Brown, to fill the vacancy, but the Dixiecrat element arose in protest and in an unprecedented write-in vote succeeded in electing Thurmond.

Georgia's internal politics after 1940 accurately reflected the division of interests in the contemporary South. The forces working to make the South like America collided head on with economic and social interests which depended upon continuation of the established order. The internal cleavage was between rural and urban counties as well as between black belt and hills. The spokesman for rural Georgia was Eugene Talmadge, his son Herman, and their friends. The Talmadge strength in Georgia counties was directly related to the proportion of Negroes in the population, and was greater below the fall line than above. City dwellers generally rejected the Talmadge demagoguery, but Georgia's peculiar county-unit system offset their often greater numerical strength. The county-unit vote worked to the advantage of rural areas. Each county had a unit vote of from one to six units; however greater the population, no county could cast more than six times the vote of the one of least population. Eight counties with the most inhabitants, 1,227,160 in 1950, cast 48 of the 410 unit votes. The 116 counties of least population (1,207,249 in 1950) controlled 232 unit votes, nearly five times as many. Thirty-five other counties, totaling 1,010,169 people, cast 130 votes.

Since 1950 the situation was also affected by drastic shifts in population from rural to urban areas. By 1958 an estimated 42 per cent of the population lived in eight counties with only 12 per cent of the unit votes. Despite the shift there was no change in the apportionment. As a result, Georgia politicians could successfully ignore the interests of urban areas. Rural counties, more illiterate and race sensitive, responded to demagoguery and white supremacy appeals. Rural counties also received much more school and road funds than did the urban communities, which paid most of the taxes.

Such sore points contributed to rural-urban cleavages in Georgia politics. Governor Ellis Arnall spoke for urban industrial interests in 1944 when he worked to end sectional freight-rate discrimination and to grant citizenship rights to Negroes. The constitution of 1945 repealed the poll tax as a prerequisite to voting, which frightened the white supremacists. The next year Eugene Talmadge ran for governor against James V. Carmichael, who advocated "making the Negro a citizen." The two differed on the issue of suddenly enfranchising the Negro or of continuing disfranchisement by other means. Carmichael won the popular vote 314,421 to 305,777, but Talmadge had more county unit-votes, 242 to 148. Before he was inaugurated, Talmadge died, and the new con-

stitution was not clear on the succession. Herman Talmadge was cam-
paigning for election by the Assembly, which voted for him. Lieutenant
Governor-elect Melvin E. Thompson was the choice of Georgia courts;
and some thought that incumbent Arnall should hold the office until
replaced in a special election. Thompson took office after some hilarious
shenanigans, but the Assembly refused to concede defeat. When the
new governor vetoed a primary election bill, the state legislators adjourned without making necessary appropriations.

The dispute colored Georgia politics for years. In 1948 Herman
Talmadge took his case to the people and was triumphantly vindicated,
winning 130 of the 159 counties and ousting Thompson. The following
year he called a special legislative session to increase taxes on corporations and to levy new excises to pay appropriations to public schools
and rural roads. Racial integration was also an issue in Georgia. In 1954
the Assembly authorized state and municipal governments to grant funds
to citizens for educational purposes in an effort to circumvent the
Supreme Court decision. In the same year Lieutenant Governor S. Marvin
Griffin succeeded Talmadge.

Under the leadership of Spessard Holland, Millard Caldwell,
Fuller Warren, Daniel T. McCarthy, and LeRoy Collins, Florida increased its population and its material prosperity. Immigration from the
North and an urban population contributed to its Republican minority.
The great distances within the state lines prevented the development of
closely knit factions or a consistent sectional division. There were continuous interest-groups, however. The mechanized truck and citrus farms,
the tourist business, and the real estate and industrial interests pre-deter-
mined that Florida's politics would be more business-oriented than in
more rural southern states.

In Alabama politics demonstrated the conflict between black
belt and the rest of the state. In 1946 James E. Folsom challenged the
black-belt politicians with a program of care for the aged, school improvements, and roads. "Big Jim" carried almost all of the state except
the counties with more than 45 per cent Negro population. In the same
year another hill-man, John Sparkman, won a Senate seat. In 1950 black-
belt control was threatened again with a plan to reapportion representation in the state Senate, to grant by constitutional amendment one senator
for each of the 67 counties instead of only 35 senators for the entire
state. The voters rejected the proposed amendment in 1951. In another
tilt between friends and enemies of Folsom, administration forces in the
state legislature voted down expanded voting restrictions on Negroes.
In the conflict Gordon Persons was governor but in 1954 Folsom won another term on a "Y'all come" campaign. He vetoed racial segregation
bills and urged moderation of race tension: "Hate," he said in his inaugural in 1955, "can destroy any man or any society, but by working
together we can accomplish any desired goal."

In Tennessee, political campaigns were often the extended shadow
of Edward H. Crump, who tried to rule the state from Memphis. His
machine represented the established order in the state and drew its

strength from the West Tennessee lowlands and the East Tennessee Republican counties. Until 1948, with James N. McCord as governor, the organization had little difficulty in maintaining control. In that year opponents of Crump, supported by business and professional groups, backed Estes Kefauver for the Senate and Gordon Browning for governor. Mr. Crump fought back in his traditionally colorful manner. "I have said before . . . that in the art galleries of Paris there are twenty-seven pictures of Judas Iscariot—none look alike but all resemble Gordon Browning," he said in a newspaper advertisement; "that neither his head, heart nor hand can be trusted; that he would milk his neighbor's cow through a crack in the fence; that of the two hundred and six bones in his body there isn't one that is genuine; that his heart has beaten over two billion times without a single sincere beat." Crump called Kefauver a raccoon, who would deceive people as to his real intent. Kefauver began wearing a coonskin cap, which became his political trademark: he was not Crump's coon, he announced. Despite Crump's invective, his opponents won office. They brought change with them. In 1949 the legislature abolished the poll tax as a requirement for voting in primary elections.

Kentucky was also drawing away from the South. Politically it was an exception in the South—it experienced genuine two-party politics by name and not just by faction. In the elections of 1943 a Republican, Simeon S. Willis, won the governor's office by nearly 9,000 votes. At the same time Republicans captured all other state offices except that of Secretary of State, which remained Democratic by the slim margin of 114 votes. In 1946 Republican John S. Cooper was elected to the Senate and the party won three congressional elections. In the following year the trend was reversed when Earle C. Clements, a Democrat, won the gubernatorial race. In 1950 Clements went to the Senate and Lieutenant Governor Lawrence W. Wetherby became governor until 1956, when A. B. "Happy" Chandler succeeded him.

In Mississippi, as in South Carolina, the Negro was the focal point of local politics. Keeping him "in his place" despite "meddling" by outsiders was the central theme of campaigns. Generally the winning candidate was the most adept at defending white supremacy. On most other issues the internal division was between the Delta—a flat, rich region along the Mississippi River north of Vicksburg—and the hills. Because Mississippi was legally dry (but with an inconsistent tax on unlawful sales of beverage alcohol) there were also alliances between law-enforcement officers and bootleggers. The immigration of industry and the rapid expansion of oil fields created a new cleavage between Old and New. The Bourbon element, typified by the Delta planters, managed to wield an influence far beyond their numbers by means of voting restrictions and the Negro scare. In 1940 the census enumerated 2,121,000 people in the state; in the 1948 election only 192,190 voters participated. As in the other Old South states, there was a close correlation between the party vote and the proportion of Negroes in the population. Delta counties, with 70 to 90 per cent Negro population, voted for those candidates likely to maintain the established social and economic order. In 1946, when Governor Thomas L. Bailey died, Lieutenant Governor Fielding Wright became the first Delta governor in years. Two years later Wright defeated the hill-candidate Paul B. Johnson, Jr., for a term of his own. In 1952 the veteran Mississippi politician Hugh White became governor, and four years later the crusading J. P. Coleman followed him. John C. Stennis and John E. Rankin represented the interests of the eastern hills, while James O. Eastland was a Delta planter.

Arkansas politics reflected the divergent nature of the state itself. In the south and east it was a southern state, with Delta plantations and a high ratio of Negroes; in the west it resembled the southwest oil and mineral regions; in the northwest it was a mountain state. In J. W. Fulbright, Brooks Hays, and John L. McClellan, who went to Congress in 1942, the state had chosen efficient representatives. Homer M. Atkins, Ben T. Laney, Sidney S. McMath, and Francis Cherry guided the state's post-war growth. In 1954 Orval Faubus, born in the Ozarks, won the state's highest office over his Republican opponent, Pratt Remmell, by 188,518 to 114,673—the largest vote ever cast in Arkansas for a Republican. In the same year the Supreme Court decision ending segregation found a co-operative Arkansas, until 1957. Faubus in his second term brought Little Rock into world notice by calling out state troops to keep order by forcibly excluding nine Negro children. In the clash which followed between federal and state authority, Army regulars were flown in to enforce federal court orders.

In Louisiana, as in Tennessee, a single man influenced the course of events. The assassination of Huey P. Long in 1935 did not end his control over the state. For a decade pro- and anti-Long forces continued to battle for the plums of political power. One Long follower, Mayor Robert S. Maestri of New Orleans, remained in office until 1946. Others were defeated in 1940 with the victory of the self-styled "reform" wing of the Democratic party in the state, which in 1942 instituted a civil service system, and made other changes. In 1948, however, the Long machine returned to power. Earl K. Long, a brother of Huey, was governor, and Russell B. Long, Huey's son, was senator. The victory marked a return to the Long program. The civil service regulations were scrapped; public welfare programs were expanded, appropriations for education increased, laws restricting organized labor were relaxed, and conservation laws tightened to reduce waste and theft of natural resources.

In 1952 the anti-Long "reform" group backed Robert F. Kennon, who won the gubernatorial race. Kennon restored the civil service program, reduced excise taxes, and made administrative changes to simplify state government. The new governor joined the "Democrats for Eisenhower" movement of 1952. Tidelands oil and government regulation of private enterprise were significant in Louisiana's Republican vote in 1956.

Texas, like Louisiana, had independent wealth and resources which made her people sensitive to actions of the national government. Much of the wealth was from the extractive enterprises—mining, oil-well drill-ing, and prospecting—in which there was an element of risk and in which legislation such as depletion allowances and severance taxes and public regulatory action influenced success or failure. These conditions tended to affect Texas thinking on the relations between government and busi-ness. In the Lone Star state, therefore, political activity concerned not sectional conflict but more fundamental questions of economics. In brief, it was a question of being for the New Deal or against the New Deal, for the national administration or against it.

In the 1940's generally, the successful local politicians condemned the Roosevelt-Truman administration. Governor R. Coke Stevenson and Senator W. Lee "Pappy" O'Daniel waged war on the New Deal and in 1944 took the field against Roosevelt's fourth term campaign. An anti-administration ticket offered uninstructed electors to voters who called themselves the "Texas Regular Democrats." They polled 135,479 votes, and the Republican candidate Dewey got 191,425, for a total of over 326,000 anti-Roosevelt votes. The Democrat electors pledged to Roose-velt got 821,605 ballots, however, largely because of the war issue.

The intra-party conflict continued in Texas after the war. In 1946 Beauford Jester defeated Homer P. Rainey for governor. Rainey had been removed as president of the University of Texas for "liberalism" and alleged economic "radicalism." In 1948, however, Lyndon B. John-son won over Coke Stevenson on a pro-administration campaign for the Senate. Johnson's majority was only 87 votes out of a total of 988,295 cast—probably America's closest vote in a major election. The next year, upon the death of Jester, Lieutenant Governor Allan Shivers succeeded to the governor's office. In 1952 Shivers defeated the pro-administration candidate Ralph Yarborough and then supported Eisenhower because he promised state regulation of tidelands oil. In 1956 attorney general Price Daniel, who also opposed the national Democratic policies, became governor. By that time a change was likely as public reputations had been tarnished by scandals in insurance and in misuse of public funds, especially a state bond issue of $100,000,000 to help war veterans buy farm lands.

Texas' growing pains illustrated the political dilemma of the contemporary South. Drastic changes altered the face of the South, while its philosophy still emphasized old values. Southerners were con-vinced that they differed from "Yankees" in their interpretation of the good life. White supremacy and states' rights were the mottoes by which Southerners described the older values, but at stake was the southern way of life. It was challenged, not so much by New Dealers or northern humanitarians, but by the material changes of the mid-twen-tieth century. Adjustments to the new age of rapid communication and plentiful power created problems, but they were not insurmountable. The faith of Southerners was well stated by an editorial in the Nashville *Tennesseean* on the day following the Supreme Court decision on school segregation. "It is not going to bring overnight revolution, but the South is and has been for years a land of change," it said. "Its people—of both races—have learned to live with change. They can learn to live with this one. Given a reasonable amount of time and understanding, they will." Southern roots were too deep for the new changes to bowl them over. With growing economic strength and cultural integrity, the Southern future looked bright indeed.

The South Moves Toward Economic Independence

1. Industrial Boom

THE political changes in the contemporary South reflected important and far-reaching economic developments in the region. In material prosperity the South was rapidly catching up with the rest of the country. After 1940, in most economic measurements, there was a marked reduction in the differences between the South and the nation. Henry W. Grady's dream of seventy-five years earlier of a southern industry "mounting to a splendor that should dazzle and illumine the world" was becoming a reality. The New Deal, the war, and the post-war international aid programs stimulated southern economic activity. Industrial employment almost doubled, while manufacturing payrolls increased more than five times. Significantly, much of the new industrial growth was in enterprise unknown or unimportant before 1940. Also, an increasing percentage of the new investments was local capital. As the South became the "Nation's Number One Economic Opportunity," it was at the same time breaking out of its colonial status, with its own capital, to assume economic direction and economic power over its own resources. The process of nationalization was complete, for it had achieved an equality so long denied.

After 1929 the growth of southern industry was continuous. In that year the South had about one sixth of the nation's manufacturing plants, employed one in seven of the industrial workers, and received one tenth of the wages. The depression decade of the 1930's marked a decline in southern economy, but not so great as that of the nation as a whole. In general, southern industry produced nondurable goods—food, tobacco, and textiles. In the depression these did not suffer so severely nor recover so rapidly as did the more durable goods industries. By 1939 the southern economy had practically regained its position of a decade earlier.

The South made significant contributions to war production, though in the preparedness period the section did not receive its share of the expenditures. Prior to July 1, 1941, the South got defense contracts worth $70 per capita, while the national average was $128 per capita. But as the war approached, Southerners played an important part in it. Southern shipyards expanded as the United States Maritime Commission constructed new shipways for building merchant vessels. The Norfolk Navy Yard and the Newport News Shipbuilding and Drydock Company constructed battleships, aircraft carriers, cruisers, and escort vessels for the battle fleet. Nashville, Memphis, and Dallas had aircraft assemblies, and nearly every state had munitions plants or shell-loading and storage installations. By 1944, there was marked increase in war plant construction and production in the South, with a decrease in peacetime pursuits such as textiles and furniture. War increases in metals, chemicals, and machinery brought boom conditions to Texas and the Southwest.

Because its labor force was more easily assimilable, the end of the war brought the South fewer demobilization problems than other sections faced. As a result the post-war expansion began quicker. By 1948 the South had received 35 per cent of the $1,900,000,000 post-war investment in new plants and buildings, and the industrial labor force had increased by 50 per cent. Much of the growth consisted of the immigration of branch plants. Most large southern production—in tobacco, petroleum refineries, rayon, paper, and pulpwood—was owned by outside interests. That was true also of railroads and public utilities. Normally, the successful local enterprise became nationally owned through the sale of stocks, and then moved its headquarters to the marts of trade in the Northeast. But throughout the South and especially in the Southwest, local ownership and control became more common.

Southerners continued to attract outside investors. Using the motto of the Southern Railway ("Look Ahead—Look South"), every state established an industrial development board or commission. These agencies advertised for branch plants, using the appeals of climate, recreation, and the presence of water, power, natural resources, and labor. Some states offered special inducements: money subsidies; free sites, buildings, or cheap leases; tax exemptions or special rates; or the provision of free utilities. Such bonuses were usually not successful. "A request by an industry for gratuitous aid is generally a danger signal," concluded the Tennessee State Planning Commission, "for sound enterprises do not seek outright gifts." Still, tax exemptions were offered by eight states in the South: Alabama, Arkansas, Kentucky, Louisiana, Mississippi, Oklahoma, South Carolina, and Tennessee. In addition, Florida, Georgia, and Virginia experimented with such inducements but dropped the plan.

The most important effort to attract industry was Mississippi's "Balance Agriculture with Industry" plan. It was the brain-child of Hugh White, president of White Lumber Company of Columbia, and later governor of the state. In 1929 his town seemed dead but White determined to revive it. He decided to import new industries and with several citizens on a committee, went to work. In 1932 they made a contract with a shirt and pajama factory to provide it with building and a five-year tax exemption. On its part, the company agreed to employ 500 local workers and promised that within ten years its total payroll would equal a million dollars. This requirement was met in only four years. Following the first successful venture, other industries came to Columbia. In 1935 White was elected governor on a "B.A.W.I." platform, and his program was enacted. Though it was not as dramatically successful as it had been in Columbia, still in 1938 the value of industrial production exceeded agricultural production for the first time in the state's history. The state legislature authorized communities, under certain conditions, to enter into contracts with industry and to provide buildings and tax exemptions. By 1940, almost a million dollars in bonds had helped to establish twelve plants. A shipyard at Pascagoula, a subsidiary of the Ingalls Shipbuilding Company of Birmingham, hired more workers than all the others combined. The war hurt the program and prevented the success its proponents expected. After the war, oil brought boom to Mississippi, and new industries entered the state.

New southern industries differed slightly, if at all, from the national norm. By 1950 the north-south wage differential was disappearing as large corporations such as Ford and Western Electric eliminated it. Despite the large southern labor force, the low degree of urbanization, and an overcrowded agriculture, pay differences disappeared. But at the same time output per man-hour increased. In some industries output was 25 per cent higher in the South. The value added by manufacture remained lower in the South but it was rising rapidly. In the eight years before 1947 it increased 244 per cent, while the national increase was 198 per cent.

In the decade after 1950 the rate discrimination of southern freight on the railroads was substantially removed. In the late 1930's, when the South was defined as the nation's "number one economic problem," adverse freight rates were in part to blame. As presidential advisor Harry Hopkins said in Memphis in 1938: "The freight rate structure was planned to clinch the industrial supremacy of the North and East." To work for revision, a Southern Governors' Conference was organized at Warm Springs, Georgia, in 1934—though it was not called that until 1939. The governors agitated in the press and appealed to the Interstate Commerce Commission for a review of the rate structure, which was then based upon the costs of an earlier period of commercial activity. Southern rates were 37 per cent higher than were those for "official" or eastern territory. After a ten-year fight, the governors finally won a political victory in an economic argument. In 1943 Governor Ellis Arnall of Georgia said that "nothing but cold-blooded politics, waged with relentless unity, would rescue the South from its accepted role as a disfavored tom cat, prowling the political and economic backyards of a nation addicted to sectional snobbery." In 1947 the ICC yielded to pressure and ordered revisions, and in May the Supreme Court upheld the changes. The fight so unified the southern governors that the organization they had formed outlived the purpose for which they formed it.

The freight-rate decision, along with other factors in the post-war years, stimulated the growth of southern industries. One of the oldest, textiles, was now almost completely dominated by the South. By 1950, 85 per cent of the nation's spindle-hours were operated in southern mills, and they consumed more than 87 per cent of the cotton which went into cloth. The war, with price controls, brought about a significant change; the no-risk profits enticed manufacturers into finishing, converting, and marketing textiles. In the competition the small finishing plants in the South had to gain control of weaving processes or sell out, and most of them sold. Considerable control thus passed to large corporations centered in New York and Philadelphia. But some southern companies were able to remain independent; others reached out to control northern activities. The Burlington Mills Corporation, a North Carolina firm, operated 82 plants in several states, including New Jersey and Pennsylvania, and in at least eight foreign countries. The Cone Mills, also a Tar Heel enterprise, had 18 plants, and produced the world's largest supply of denim cloth for the popular "jeans."

Textiles were important in the Carolinas, Georgia, Tennessee, and Alabama. Spinning and weaving were declining in relative importance in the South, however, as other enterprises expanded. By 1950 workers in textiles had declined from one third to 27 per cent of all industrial workers. Newer fabrics and fibers were increasing. Rayon, a chemically created fabric, was primarily a southern industry; by 1947 the South produced 60 per cent of the nation's supply. Virginia, with six plants, led the nation; Tennessee was second; and Georgia, North Carolina, and South Carolina also produced the material. Since the war the manufacture of nylon hosiery and the new synthetic fibers has risen rapidly. Celanese, orlon, and dacron were produced in the South, while woolen production increased. Connected with the textile industry were other enterprises: factories producing textile machinery, dye works, transportation, and box plants.

Another important southern industry was food processing, which had expanded over the entire region. Where vegetables were grown, canning factories and frozen-food processors operated. Much of Florida's citrus production left the state as frozen concentrate. Seafood processing was an important element in southern prosperity. Oysters from the Chesapeake, shrimp, shellfish, and a variety of food fish from the Atlantic and the Gulf, and frogs from Louisiana's bayou country added to southern incomes. About half of the southern industry's receipts was from menhaden, a fish which was not eaten but was processed for oil to be used in chemicals and fertilizers. The largest crabmeat packing plant in the

South was in North Carolina, while Louisiana ranked first in shrimp production. Other foods were oleomargarine, meat and dairy products, and nuts and oils. Oleomargarine production in the South increased during the war, with Texas and Georgia in the lead. The spread was made of cottonseed and peanut oils, with soybean oil a later addition. After the war discriminatory federal legislation on oleo was repealed, which aided the industry. Nut processing contributed to southern payrolls; pecans brought increasing amounts, and peanuts went into a large variety of products. The nation's largest peanut-butter factory was at Enterprise, Alabama. Canned milk, butter, and cheese production marked the increase in dairy cattle; meat-packing plants, preparing beef, pork, ham, sausage, franks, and canned and loaf meats illustrated the growing importance of livestock. Many other southern products appeared on the nation's dining tables: salt, red pepper sauce, hydrogenated and liquid shortenings, mayonnaise and salad dressings, fruit, jams and jellies, tomato catsup, pickles, wheat and soya flour and cornmeal, and bottled soft drinks and beer.

Other southern industries were closely connected with farms and forests. Tobacco continued to be important, with southern plants producing 95 per cent of the nation's cigarettes, 32 per cent of the cigars, and over 60 per cent of manufactured tobacco in other forms. A high degree of automation made possible an almost incredible cigarette output. In furniture manufacturing, the South had over one quarter of the workers and was taking over the leadership in wooden furniture. Lumber, pulpwood and wood products were increasingly prosperous. Georgia had the home office of the world's largest plywood producer. Southern pine forests contributed a host of subsidiary products such as adhesives, plastics, linoleum, paint, soap, disinfectant, and shoe polish. Hundreds of chemical products were derived from resinous stumps. Paper products of all kinds, from newsprint to waxed milk cartons, emerged from forest products. The Union Bag Company of Savannah was the world's largest producer of kraft type bags and containers. The southern chemical industry, which discovered such by-products, was the fastest growing enterprise in the region. It included plastics and synthetics—such as rubber and fibers—and fertilizers, insecticides, and other materials for southern farms.

Perhaps the basic reason for southern industrial expansion after the war was the phenomenal increase in supplies of electric power. The most important power project in the South was the Tennessee Valley Authority, a New Deal agency. After the war, with its usefulness fully demonstrated, TVA continued to expand and to prevent floods. In 1946, 1947, 1948, 1950, and 1954, the dams prevented what would have been among the largest floods in history. In 1949 the TVA completed Watauga Dam and a year later the South Holston Dam; in 1953 and 1954 the Boone and Fort Patrick Henry dams were completed, all four on the Holston River. Also in 1949, with hydro-electric sites all utilized and no foreseeable limit to demand for power, the TVA began construction of the first of its series of new steam plants. Though its power and flood

Photo Courtesy TVA

ELECTRICITY CHANGES THE SOUTHERN SCENE. In 1930 only three per cent of the nation's farms had electricity, and in the rural South the percentage was probably lower. But by 1950 more than 90 per cent of farms had electric service to lighten work as well as the evening hours.

control programs had been proved, this growth was not without critics. A second round of charges and investigations took place when President Harry Truman named David E. Lilienthal to the Atomic Energy Commission and promoted Gordon R. Clapp to the chairmanship of the TVA Board of Directors. After long and heated hearings, the Senate confirmed both men.

Despite the charges of its critics, the TVA paid its own way. The Government Corporations Appropriation Bill of 1948 required TVA to repay to the Treasury, within forty years, the public investments it had received, estimated at $348,239,240. By 1957 it was well ahead of its repayment schedule, having paid over a quarter of a billion dollars, of which $186,500,000 was for investment reduction. Moreover, the TVA paid five per cent of its gross sales of power to states and counties in which it operated, in lieu of taxes. In some counties it was the largest single source of public revenue. In 1956 TVA's gross power revenues totaled $221,600,000, and its net revenue was $53,900,000 for a return of 3.9 per cent on its capital investment. It generated a total of 57.5 billion kilowatt hours of power, using 34 major dams, seven modern and four older steam plants of considerable size, and other smaller hydro and steam plants, and carried over nearly 11,000 miles of high-voltage transmission lines.

The ample supply of cheap electrical power and the reclamation and flood-control programs of the TVA brought about a major revolution in the region. In 1933 fewer than three per cent of the farms had electricity but in 1956 more than 93 per cent of them did. Appliance sales boomed as farmers put electricity to work for their families, with ranges, refrigerators, washers, heating units, and such farm implements as automatic milkers and milk coolers. The large lakes created by the TVA dams made the Valley a playground, and thousands of tourists flocked to the "beaches in the mountains." They bought sporting goods—fishing tackle, camping and picnic equipment, and outboard motors and boats. And as living standards increased, so did the number and quality of schools, libraries, hospitals and clinics, and roads.

Photo Courtesy TVA

TVA DAMS CREATE COMMERCIAL ARTERIES. By raising the level of the Tennessee River, the TVA system of dams maintained a nine-foot channel for navigation stretching 650 miles and made Knoxville in the mountains a river port. In this picture, twenty-four barges—three acres of freight—are moved upstream by a towboat.

By far the greatest change brought about by the TVA, however, was the industrial boom that followed the electrical transmission lines. Heavy chemical processing industries requiring cheap power, water, and low-cost transportation of bulky raw materials, established plants in the Valley, and hundreds of more ordinary industries and consumer service companies accompanied them. Construction and expansion of plants brought unprecedented activity in all areas of the economy. Near the mouth of the Tennessee River at Calvert City, Kentucky, there was a hydrofluoric acid plant, and others producing ferro alloys, acetylene, and plastics, as well as other chemicals. At New Johnsonville, Tennessee, there was a titanium reduction plant; at Muscle Shoals there were electro-metallurgical, aluminum, die-casting, caustic soda, and chlorine plants. At Decatur, Alabama, there were copper tube, chemical fiber, and air conditioning equipment factories. At other points on the river were plants producing industrial abrasives, titanium sponge, nuclear power equip-ment, military ordnance, newsprint and unbleached sulphate paper; there were also grain elevators, flour mills, bulk terminals for gasoline and oil, brick and tile kilns, and mines. All this contributed to the new economic strength of the South and financed its challenge to northern and eastern capitalists. For, though much of the Tennessee Valley industry was con-trolled by absentee owners, an increasing portion of it was the result of local capital and management.

Another major source of potential power was atomic energy. In addi-tion to the Oak Ridge installation, the Atomic Energy Commission con-structed a nuclear plant at Aiken, South Carolina, at an expense of over one and a half billion dollars—twice as costly as the entire Panama Canal. There was another atomic energy installation at Paducah, Kentucky (whose power requirements precipitated the Dixon-Yates contract for constructing an electric steam plant to supply Memphis and to relieve TVA). These plants brought enormous payrolls and construction prosperity to the South and gave the section an advantage in the fuel of the future. Uranium, the raw material of atomic energy, was controlled in large measure by southwestern interests.

Until nuclear energy became a viable alternative, petroleum was the most important source of energy and fuel in the country. The south-western states of Texas, Oklahoma, Arkansas, Louisiana, and Mississippi were the most productive suppliers of petroleum and its products. Oil for fuel displaced coal as the principal source, and natural gas approached coal in importance. Together oil and gas supplied two thirds of the energy consumed in the United States. Pipelines carried southwestern gas to northern consumers; the most important such line was the "Big Inch," a 24-inch pipeline from Longview, Texas, to Linden, New Jersey, com-pleted in 1943. The presence of natural gas at eight cents a thousand cubic feet (the same amount sold for $2.42 in New York City) made the Gulf South a profitable industrial site. For example, a chemical plant at Seadrift, Texas, used twice as much gas as the whole state of Connecticut.

Besides the immigration of industries using gas as a fuel, there was an increase in plants using gas as a raw material. These were known as the petrochemical industries. Using natural gas or waste gases from oil refining operations, petrochemical plants from Brownsville, Texas, to New Orleans turned out a wide variety of products ranging from medicines to raincoats. Texas had more than 70 petrochemical plants with 85 per cent of the nation's production. Literally thousands of prod-ucts and by-products used petrochemicals in their processing. Examples of the varied products of petrochemical processes were synthetic rubber,

ELECTRICITY BRINGS HEAVY INDUSTRY TO THE SOUTH. Since the completion of the Tennessee River navigation channel, a number of large industries have located along the river. Most of these were industries requiring great quantities of water, electric power, or cheap transportation for bulky goods. Shipbuilders and chemical industries were among the new Tennessee Valley enterprises. This picture shows a flour mill in Alabama.

lube-oil additives, anti-freeze, lacquer and drug solvents, inks, paints, paint driers, fungicides, cosmetics, detergents, rust preventatives, roofing materials, waterproofings, paving asphalt, and saponification agents. One of the more important of the petrochemicals was carbon black, used in rubber, inks, phonograph records and similar compounds. Another was liquefied petroleum gas (LPG), stored under pressure to keep it in a compact liquid state until used. It was widely used as a household fuel in areas not served with natural gas. Petroleum thus opened a new source for organic chemicals with almost infinite uses. The growth of petrochemicals was fantastic. In 1925 the total came to 16,100,000,000 pounds, and by 1956 it was more than doubled, to 35,000,000,000 pounds. Industry engineers predicted that in the next decade 50 per cent of the total chemical output of the nation would come from petroleum products. The capital investment in petrochemicals increased from $350,000,000 in 1940 to over $4,000,000,000 in 1956.

Much of the petrochemical industry was financed by local capital and managed by southwestern oil men. Thus, with abundant water power

Photo courtesy U. S. Atomic Energy Commission

ATOMIC ENERGY IN THE SOUTH. The American Museum of Atomic Energy at Oak Ridge, Tennessee, symbolizes the coming of the atomic age. Because the Manhattan Project for the construction of the atomic bomb required vast quantities of electricity, its major installation was in the Tennessee Valley, near Knoxville. In addition to the Oak Ridge installation, the U. S. Atomic Energy Commission constructed a nuclear plant at Aiken, S. C., at an expense of over one and a half billion dollars— twice as costly as the entire Panama Canal. These plants, with another at Paducah, Kentucky, brought enormous payrolls and construction prosperity to the South, and gave the section an advantage in the fuel of the future.

for electricity, the beginnings of an atomic power supply and the nation's leading source of petroleum, natural gas, and petrochemicals, the South had the opportunity to shake off its economic subservience to the masters of coal, the displaced power king. Texas was the primary source of petroleum, pumping over a billion barrels of crude oil, more than 42 per cent

Photo Courtesy Standard Oil Co. (N.J.)

TIDELANDS OIL OPERATION. In their search for new sources of petroleum, geologists and oil engineers have moved out on the continental shelf in the Gulf of Mexico. Jurisdictional conflicts between the states involved—chiefly Louisiana, Texas, and California—and the federal government were contributing factors to the Dixiecrat revolt of 1948.

of the national supply, and nearly five trillion cubic feet of natural gas, or 51.2 per cent of the total. Louisiana pumped more than 256,000,000 barrels of oil in 1953 and 1,293,644,000 cubic feet of natural gas. Arkansas contributed 29,681,000 barrels of oil in the same year and 41,510,000 cubic feet of gas. Mississippi was a latecomer in oil but its discovery had profound consequences for the economy of the Magnolia State. The first strike was at Yazoo City in 1939, and in 1945, at Heidelberg, in the "piney woods," a major oil rush began. Thereafter in southeastern Mississippi, the unpleasant smell of oil wells drowned out the scent of magnolias.

Other mineral products were also important in the South. West Virginia and Kentucky led southern production of coal, with Virginia, Alabama, and Tennessee also mining the fuel. Alabama was first in the production of pig iron, while Texas and Georgia yielded some iron ore. Cement was produced in Texas, Alabama, and Tennessee. Aluminum was smelted in East Tennessee and Northern Alabama. Other important minerals were clays, stone, sand, and gravel in nearly all states; bauxite in Arkansas; phosphate rock, zircon, ilmenite and rutile from Florida; salt and sulphur from Louisiana and Texas; feldspar, mica, talc, and tungsten from North Carolina; phosphate rock and zinc from Tennessee; gypsum, helium, and lime from Texas; and lead, lime, and zinc from Virginia.

Southern industry was closely associated with natural resources and farm products. But by 1950 a shift was under way. Auto assembly lines, factories producing machinery and electrical goods, and similar plants requiring highly developed skills began to appear in the South. The presence of aircraft factories in Texas, electronics installations in the Carolinas, an electric bulb plant in Alabama, and a lock factory in Mississippi was evidence that southern industry had come of age.

The developing southern economy raised living standards of Southerners and increased their share of the national wealth. In 1929 Southerners received 15 per cent of the nation's income payments to individuals and by 1950 they received 19.7 per cent. In current dollars, that meant an increase from $12,400,000,000 to $42,800,000,000, an increase of 245 per cent, compared with an increase of 149 per cent for the nation. Southern banking assets increased tremendously, from 8.9 per cent of the national total in 1930 to 14.6 per cent in 1950. Southerners produced 24.2 per cent of the automobiles. Government payments to Southerners doubled in the twenty-year period, most of it in forms unused in 1930: relief and public welfare, social security payments, and military and veterans' benefits. Trade and services in southern communities employed one third of the labor force and received about one fourth of the total income, as commercial services gradually replaced household servants. Since 1940, as a result of those changes, the South grew richer but more dependent upon government finance. The growth of industry in the South and the decline in the importance of agriculture as a means of income almost exactly paralleled national development in the 1870's. In that respect the South approached the national norm.

Tourism was a growing industry. The South had nearly half of the nation's coastline, including nearly all that was suitable for winter resorts. The southern mountains provided the most spectacular scenery in eastern America, and they were close to population centers. In winter tourists visited the sandhills of Carolina, the beaches of Florida and the Gulf Coast, the hot springs of Arkansas, or the fruit orchards of the Rio Grande Valley. In summer the beaches of Virginia and the Carolinas, the mountains, with the highest peaks east of the Rockies, and the caverns of Virginia and Kentucky appealed to visitors. There was deep-sea fishing off the coast of the Carolinas and Florida and in the Gulf; and fresh-water fishing in the inland streams and lakes. In southern forests the hunter stalked quail, deer, bear, wild boars, and many other animals. Historical sites also attracted tourists: Williamburg, Charleston, Atlanta, and New

Orleans had local charm for sale. The southern battlefields were increasingly popular. In addition there were uniquely southern attractions: outdoor inspirational dramas celebrating historical events. Typical of these productions were *The Lost Colony*, at Manteo; *Unto These Hills*, at Cherokee; and *The Common Glory*, at Williamsburg.

2. THE CRISIS OF AGRICULTURE

In the years after 1940 southern industry achieved significant stature, but in the same period agriculture declined sharply in importance. The war changed many of the conditions which had characterized Southern agriculture in the earlier decade. It accelerated long-term trends in population movement, mechanization, and changes in land use. Farm prices rose sharply under the impact of war demand. The average price for cotton increased 72 per cent in 1942, from 9.9 cents to 17 cents; by 1945 it had reached 22.5 cents. Still, farm incomes were low. In South Atlantic states income per farm averaged $1,497 and in South Central states it was $1,479, compared with an average of $1,704 for the North Atlantic region and $4,027 for the West.

The war changed uses of southern farmlands. As labor was short, poor submarginal lands lay idle. By 1945 at least one fifth of the land was unused. Much of it was later turned into pasture. The presence of Army installations and war industries increased the local markets for fresh eggs and dairy products, fruits, vegetables, and fresh meats. In addition, the war brought large demands for cottonseed and soybean oils and livestock feeds. In Georgia, Alabama, Texas, North Carolina, and Virginia, farmers almost doubled their acreages of peanuts. In the grasslands of Alabama and Mississippi there was a major shift to a livestock grazing economy. In the Yazoo and Mississippi deltas, planters continued to concentrate on cotton, though many added soybeans and oats. Farther west, cotton became the most profitable crop, though in the Texas Panhandle winter wheat occasionally replaced the fiber.

In the post-war period cotton was dethroned in the Southeast. "Cotton is moving west, cattle are moving east, Negroes are moving north, and Yankees are moving south," ran the popular saying. In 1946 cotton prices increased 45 per cent and agricultural authorities feared that southern farmers would plow up the new crops and glut the market with the staple. But stiff competition from man-made fibers challenged King Cotton's domain. In 1937 rayon production had totaled 8 per cent of cotton's; by 1950 it had reached 29 per cent of cotton's. The most serious competition of rayon was in automobile tires; by 1950 more than two thirds of the tire market had been captured by rayon fibers. Other synthetics such as nylon, Orlon, and Dacron also displaced cotton, especially in ladies' garments. Another change was the use of paper shipping bags rather than cotton bags.

This contributed to the decline of agriculture. Net income from farming dropped by more than one third. In 1930, 42 per cent of all gainfully employed Southerners were in agriculture; by 1950 only 22 per cent of them were on farms. In more than half the counties of the Southeast the average farm family received less than $1,000 per year. President Eisenhower called these counties "pockets of rural poverty." Certain areas such as the North Carolina Piedmont and the Central Basin of Tennessee fared well; others, like the upper coastal plains of South Carolina, Georgia, and Alabama did less well. In general, when farmers prospered it was near a developing urban center. In 1930 only twenty counties in the South, in Virginia, Florida, and Kentucky, enjoyed standards of living equal to the national average. By 1950, however, as urbanization increased, there were 100 such counties and they were found in all states except Arkansas and South Carolina. Southern agricultural prosperity was thus tied to urban-industrial development.

Cotton, the mainstay of southern farm economy, had lost its pre-eminence. In 1929 cotton provided 46 per cent of all cash farm receipts but by 1950 it had declined to 25 per cent. In the same period acreage devoted to cotton culture was down over 52 per cent. In the ten years prior to 1957, average yearly production was 13,669,000 bales; in 1957 the crop was only 10,964,000 bales. The 1957 combined lint and cottonseed value was down 23 per cent from the year before. Significantly, in 1957 the first and second states in cotton production were Texas and California, while older cotton states such as Alabama, Georgia, and the Carolinas were farther down the list.

Cotton was not the only crop that suffered in the agricultural changes. Corn production was down almost 20 per cent, and tobacco by over 26 per cent. Much of this reduction was the result of national agricultural policies. But other crops moved in to take the place of the older mainstays. From 1929 to 1950 peanuts were increased over 208 per cent; soybeans, 851 per cent; citrus fruits, 550 per cent; rice, 95 per cent; wheat, 66 per cent; hay, 42 per cent; and truck crops, 34 per cent. There were also increases in the number and quality of livestock. Beef cattle, milk cows, sheep, hogs, and chickens increased by substantial amounts. More important, nondescript animals were replaced by purebred Black Angus, Holstein, and Hereford breeds, which meant increases in milk and meat. "Brahma" cattle, a cross between an Indian import and native cows, became common.

An important development in the Southeast was the growth of broiler (or "fryer") chicken production. In 1936 a poor cotton crop and a devastating tornado forced a Georgia farmer, Jesse D. Jewell, to seek new means of livelihood. His only asset was a supply of chickenfeed. He decided to lend feed and baby chicks to his neighbors on a share-cropping plan and to guarantee to sell the birds when they got large enough. The project did well. During the war, with other meats rationed or unavailable, people turned to poultry. Jewell prospered along with his farmer-partners. He delivered chicks to farmers and in ten weeks collected the grown broilers for processing and freezing. By 1955 Jewell's firm shipped over 30,000 frozen broilers a day. Other men followed Jewell's lead; broiler production in Georgia was up 162 per cent. In South Carolina, the number of chickens increased from 9,440,000 in 1940 to 22,553,000 in 1952, and turkeys had increased tenfold. In North Carolina and Tennessee poultry was also an important cash crop.

Other commodities contributed to farm income in the South. Rice made a comeback after an earlier depression. Texas, Louisiana, Arkansas, and Mississippi were the leading rice states. Grains for food and fodder were widely grown, with wheat, oats, barley, and rye the most important. In the Southwest, sorghum grain was a valuable fodder crop. Fruits—apples, peaches, pears, and grapes—brought handsome profits to orchardists in the Carolinas, Virginia, Tennessee, Texas, and Georgia. Pecans were harvested in most southern states. Sugar cane grew in Louisiana and Florida and citrus fruits in Florida, Louisiana, and Texas. In 1955 Florida shipped 91,000,000 boxes of oranges, 38,000,000 of grapefruit, and 4,600,000 of tangerines. Texas produced 1,800,000 boxes of oranges and 2,800,000 of grapefruit, while Louisiana shipped 215,000 boxes of oranges.

Tobacco was an important cash crop in the southeastern states and varied from the burley and flue-cured bright tobaccos of the East to the piquant black perique of Louisiana. Consumption of flue-cured tobacco—the chief ingredient of cigarettes—increased in 1957 after a lung-cancer scare turned smokers to filter-tip brands. In each state there were specialty crops such as tung in Mississippi, pimento peppers in Georgia, and red-hot peppers in Mississippi and Louisiana. Every state grew potatoes and sweet potatoes. Truck crops—tomatoes, beans, cabbages, other green vegetables, cucumbers, squash, asparagus, artichokes and cauliflower—increased with the population and the standard of living.

In large measure the changes in southern agriculture were made possible by rapid increases in farm mechanization. From 1940 to 1950 the increase in tractors was almost 250 per cent, considerably more than twice the national rate. In South Carolina the increase was 467 per cent, the largest of any state. The increase in power tools paralleled the shift away from cotton, with its demand for hand labor, to livestock and other crops adapted to mechanized cultivation and harvesting. It also meant a trend toward larger units to make mechanization profitable. Beginning in the late 1930's, the first successful cotton-picker made cotton mechanization practicable. The development of the Rust brothers in Memphis, the machine was constructed on a farm tractor and picked the fiber with moving spindles. The crop was now sown by mechanical seeders, weeded by flame-throwers, sprayed for boll weevils and other pests with new insecticides from low-flying aircraft, and could be harvested by machine. The picker caught on slowly, since it collected leaves and trash along with the cotton. Defoliants were developed to remove the cotton leaves before the pickers moved among the plants. In the Southwest and in the Yazoo-Mississippi Delta a new revolution in the cotton economy was under way. With cotton declining in importance, the development came too late to displace enough farm laborers to create a major problem.

While mechanization moved on rapidly, southern farmers became increasingly dependent upon government. The South changed from the nation's number one economic problem to a stepchild of the Federal

Government, dependent upon its economic policies for continued prosperity. It created an embarrassing situation in which government was an economic necessity, but it was evil when it moved into social areas. Government action maintained farm prices by purchasing basic commodities when their prices fell below stipulated levels. The Department of Agriculture issued acreage allocations permitting the holder to grow and sell certain regulated commodities at guaranteed profits.

New federal farm bills improved the farmer's situation. The Agriculture Act of 1948 reduced price supports of some crops to 60 per cent of parity, while redefining parity. It now meant the average price received for the commodity during the previous ten years—a time when prices were held artificially high by parity payments and planned purchases. One observer commented that "control programs that tend to raise prices are introduced; prices rise; then the new prices are made into a new base for the calculation of support prices." The law was amended by the Agriculture Act of 1949 which went into effect in January, 1950. It provided that when surpluses existed, growers of the surplus commodities could make adjustments by voting acreage allotments and marketing quotas. The law did not impose marketing quotas but made possible quotas imposed by farmers themselves by voting in a referendum requiring a two-thirds majority. It declared that the parity price of a basic commodity under the new method "shall not be less than its parity price computed in the manner used prior to the enactment of the Agriculture Act of 1949." The law included farm wages among prices paid by farmers in computing parity, which raised prices considerably.

Even more valuable to southern farmers were acreage allocations permitting cultivation and sale of specified commodities. The allocations changed hands with the sale of farm lands and contributed to increases in the price of farms. However valuable the land, it was of little use without a crop allocation. It was a man-made valuation, created by the Department of Agriculture. It made a "vested interest" in the continuation of government controls by giving growers a monopoly of production enforced by federal agencies. The marketing quotas could be ended only by a vote of more than one third of the farmers concerned, in a referendum open only to growers. It was not likely that they would vote to dismantle a program which enriched them so much. Another agricultural program with far-reaching consequences for the South was the soil-bank plan which went into effect in 1956. The Federal Government paid farmers to turn land producing surplus crops into pastures or woodlands. Like a new enclosure movement, the program closed marginal lands and drastically depopulated many rural regions.

Government action also increased the number of owner-operated farms. Financial assistance made ownership easier, while the new agricultural regulation including farm wages in the calculation of prices encouraged hired help rather than the use of tenants. As a result, the number of tenant-operated farms in the South was lower than at any time since 1890. In 1930, 42.5 per cent of southern farms were operated by owners; fifteen years later the figure had risen to 57.8 per cent and was increasing rapidly. By 1950 sharecropping had virtually ended for whites but still continued for colored farmers. After 1940 the number of farms operated on shares declined 36 per cent; the number of white tenants fell by 27 per cent, but of Negroes only 9.6 per cent. Tenants shared the improved living conditions in the rural South and the peonage conditions of the first half-century after emancipation had almost disappeared.

Farmers in general were better off and particular farmers were well off indeed, but few of them were wealthy. Pockets of rural poverty contributed to the South's low economic standings. The average per capita income in the South in 1950 was only $1,045, compared to the national average of $1,436. Alabama, Arkansas, Georgia, Kentucky, Mississippi, North Carolina, South Carolina, and Tennessee had per capita incomes of less than $1,000. Farm poverty contributed to the depressed conditions. Only Florida, Maryland, and Texas were higher in cash income from farms (average per farm) than the national average of $5,191. The average cash income per farm in Alabama was only $1,547; in Arkansas, $2,666; South Carolina, $1,812; Mississippi, $1,773; and Georgia, $2,381. But government action, better roads, electricity, a constantly increasing population, and a steady migration to urban areas enhanced the economic potential of the rural South. Agriculture was in transition toward a more diversified and more stable position.

Economically the South was making giant strides toward independence. In doing so many Southerners accepted the scale of values of the rest of the country. Perhaps no change was more significant than that made in Charleston. "Too poor to paint and too proud to whitewash" since 1865, the old city continued its leisurely, sedate life, with more than 600 clubs and associations like the philosophical Piping and Marching Society of Lower Chalmers Street and the ancient, retiring St. Cecilia's Society. But north of Broad Street a bustling economic community sprang up. After 1945 Charleston added over a hundred diverse industries and her port was thirteenth in the nation in commerce. Industrial payrolls increased twelve times, from $3 million to $36 million, and bank clearings from $163,000,000 in 1945 to $405,000,000 in 1956. The Cooper-Santee water development promised ten billion gallons of water a day— a great inducement to manufacturers. The Gulf Oil Company bought 3,000 acres for a refinery, and the city fathers confidently anticipated the arrival of petrochemicals and other lucrative industries. Defenders of the old charm of Charleston chafed at the materialism of the New, and bitterly protested the destruction of stately buildings for such utilitarian purposes as parking lots and shopping centers. But the victory of the New in Charleston, the symbol of the Old, was typical of the South at mid-century.

CHAPTER 36

Cultural Distinctives in the Contemporary South

1. THE PEOPLE OF THE SOUTH

IN the years after 1940, great changes swept over the South. As it became richer, more urbanized, and increasingly dependent upon industry and commerce, it took giant strides toward integration into the nation. Southerners co-operated in national projects, readily accepted the values and the behavior-patterns of Americans everywhere, and in practice seemed ready to discard an outmoded separatism. But in theory, Southerners still held to the creed that there was a distinctive—and superior—civilization below the Potomac. To prove it, many of them waved miniature Confederate battleflags at football games, took pleasure in condemning Yankees and the Federal Government, and made jokes about saving their Confederate money.

Such conduct had the air of a college prank about it, but there was a germ of purpose in the reiterated rebel yell. Though the differences which separated the South from the nation were rapidly disappearing in all significant areas, there remained cultural distinctives which identified the section. The writing of Southern authors continued to dominate literature in America; southern musicians called the tune on the national stage; southern evangelists called men back to worship an ancient God; southern food and drink delighted the palates of gourmets everywhere. Moreover, there was an educational improvement which promised

591

to make the South equal to national norms. Despite the social change which accompanied a mushrooming economy and which made the South more and more American, traditional southern culture had not altogether disappeared.

At the heart of the social upheaval in the South were changes in the pattern of population. The depression of the 1930's reduced the outward migration of people. For the only decade in the century, the South had a higher percentage of population gain than did the rest of the country. But the war that began in 1941 reversed the trend. To 1945 there was an unusually high rate of exodus, with approximately 2,500,000 people leaving the South. The loss was greater in rural areas. In the same period, farm population declined by more than 3,000,000 people. Though some of the migrants returned to the farm after the war, the net agricultural loss for the war decade was over one fifth of the total.

Correspondingly, there was an increase in southern urban population. In 1930 only one third of Southerners resided in towns; by 1950 almost half did. Another quarter of the population was classed as "rural non-farm," so almost three fourths of all Southerners were urban or worked in urban conditions—a fact of great significance in understanding the change in Southern attitudes. As the urban population grew, there was an increase in the number of southern cities. Of American cities of over 100,000 population, thirty-two, or one third of them, were in the census South. Most of the South's large metropolitan areas were in the southwest. Houston, New Orleans, Dallas, Atlanta, Louisville, San Antonio, Memphis, and Fort Worth were among the first forty American cities in 1950, and each of them contained more than 300,000 people.

Emigration to other sections of the country continued, and continued to be greater among Negroes than whites. These changes made the South proportionally "whiter" than before. In the twenty years after 1930, for every Negro increase the white population increased tenfold; in the decade after 1940 the whites increased proportionally thirty times faster than did Negroes. In the rest of the country the Negro population more than doubled. But in southern states the Negro remained an important factor, ranging from 45 per cent in Mississippi, 39 per cent in South Carolina, and 32 per cent in Alabama and Louisiana, 12 per cent in Texas, and 7 per cent in Kentucky.

In the 1950's the population continued its earlier trends. It increased because of the unusually high birth rate, but emigration reduced the rate of growth. Between 1950 and 1955 three states, Alabama, Arkansas, and Mississippi, had a net population loss, while in other south central states the population increased at a rate slower than the national average. In some rural areas the exodus was so great that it adversely affected southern life. "For those who remain, the population out-movements may undermine local institutions," a University of Tennessee report observed. "Merchants lose customers, schools lose their pupils, churches their congregations, families their solidarity, and real estate its value." Many of those who sought more promising positions in the North and West were in the productive 20 to 35 year age group. Reversing the earlier trend, in the 1950's the majority of the migrants were white—sometimes as high as 60 per cent.

At the same time there was a significant influx of managers and highly-skilled workers into the South, pulled by the migration of industry. Families from New England lived beside those from the Midwest in Mississippi; people from Ohio and Minnesota drilled for oil in Texas. Many of them admired the charm of the South. One transplanted Yankee manager in Charleston caught the spirit of the city when he noted that "there's so much to do here, fishing, the beaches, it's a shame you have to work at all." The interregional migrations promised a new sectional understanding as well as a new national culture.

2. Improvements in Education

A primary demand of the newcomers as well as of native Southerners was for educational betterment. Many observers blamed the South's ills, from its recurring outbreaks of violence to its industrial backwardness, on educational deficiencies. Certainly there was room for improvement. The South continued to lag behind the rest of the country in educational achievements. With a higher proportion of children than the national average and a lower number of adult wage-earning taxpayers, the South remained relatively poor in education. Illiteracy among southern adults continued higher than the national rate and southern schools were generally poorer and less well attended. Teachers' salaries were among the nation's lowest, a fact which contributed to the emigration of teachers to other sections. With the national average $2,639 in 1950, Arkansas paid its teachers an average of only $1,545, and Mississippi $1,256. Only Maryland and Florida paid teachers a salary higher than the national average. Southern teachers could expect a higher pupil load than the national rate and less specialized equipment. School libraries were usually poorly stocked.

Yet, with growing southern prosperity, improvement came. Southern leaders recognized the handicaps under which their children labored. In the years after 1940 southern states made great changes in their educational systems. Spurred on by federal court action demanding equality of educational opportunities for all children, legislatures appropriated increased amounts for school construction and operation. The South ranked low in educational achievements but it ranked among the highest in educational effort. Southerners continued to expend a larger percentage of their total personal income on education than the average of the rest of the country. Since 1937 all southern states had improved their relative standings in percentage of personal income expended for education. For income of all sorts, every southern state paid a higher percentage than the national average.

Such efforts produced results. Teachers' salaries were increased; professional administrative staffs planned and supervised the school systems; and modern plants replaced the antiquated, often dangerous buildings of a generation earlier. Better roads made consolidation feasible, and the one- or two-room schoolhouses were fast disappearing. States provided textbooks for all pupils, and school boards supplied improved teaching aids in greater quantities. State teachers' colleges, while changing their names to "State Colleges," expanded their curricula and turned out thousands of certified teachers. The future looked bright for southern education.

The improvements were noteworthy, but they were unevenly spread over the South. There was unfortunately a differential between the schools in urban and those in rural areas. With higher tax valuations to draw upon, school boards in cities and urbanized counties could offer salary supplements and more acceptable teaching conditions. In some mountain areas, particularly in Kentucky, Tennessee, and Arkansas, educational standards continued to be low. Thousands of children were unable to attend winter sessions and there were many substandard buildings and poorly prepared teachers. There was also a difference in educational achievement among southern states. What was true for Florida and North Carolina was not true for Arkansas or Mississippi. In addition, a distinction continued between schools for whites and those for Negroes, despite the fact that much of the increased educational expenditures went to improve schools for colored pupils and to augment Negro teacher salaries.

Pressure from the federal courts, the fear of national legislation on education, and the vision of southern educational statesmen led to improvement in Negro education. In many southern school districts Negro schools were more modern and were better equipped than were those for white pupils. In North and South Carolina teacher pay schedules were equalized. School officials established Negro high schools in those counties which had none, and provided better transportation, libraries, and science laboratories for Negro pupils. But because most southern Negroes continued to dwell in rural districts, in general their schools fell below local white standards and their teachers labored under heavier loads, with less remuneration.

Nevertheless, many Negro educators did not favor school integration. As one observer commented, "Negroes have vested interests in separate schools, vested interests imperiled by proposed changes." For professional reasons, teachers feared that integration would deprive them of positions for which they had trained themselves at considerable expense. In the nonsegregated schools in other parts of the country Negro teachers and administrators were not employed in proportion to their numbers. There was some suspicion that integration of southern schools was a vicious attempt to take Negro education out of Negro hands. Other Negro teachers declared that the best interests of both races would best be served in separate schools where social status would remain unchallenged. In addition, there was concerted white resistance to the change. For these reasons, the Supreme Court decision of May 17, 1954, declaring racially segregated schools to be inherently unequal, only slowly affected education in the Deep South. By rigid laws and constitutional amendments, southern lawmakers sought to circumvent the Court's decision.

The improvements in public school equipment and educational achievement for whites and Negroes were matched by the steady advancement of southern colleges and universities. After 1945, with veterans' programs causing a tremendous increase in the number of students, higher education boomed. State universities expanded their staffs, strengthened their curricula, and launched building programs designed to replace temporary structures and to meet serious classroom shortages. Great universities such as the state universities of North Carolina, Kentucky, Georgia, Louisiana, and Texas, and independent institutions like Duke, Vanderbilt, Peabody, Emory, Tulane, and Rice, emerged in the South.

Southern graduate and technical education was greatly improved. Medical and dental schools were established in those states which had none, sometimes with financial assistance from the Federal Government. Law schools, in which the South had been traditionally strong, continued their careful work. Sound graduate programs in the larger universities produced candidates for southern college faculties. Technical training, in which the South had lagged behind the rest of the country, was given new impetus by the postwar boom. Virginia Polytechnic, North Carolina State College, Clemson, Georgia Technical, Alabama Polytechnic, the University of Tennessee, and technological schools in Louisiana and Texas offered engineering courses the equal of any in the country.

Because not all states could afford to offer all technical courses, in 1947 a regional educational system was established. Ten years earlier O. J. Hagen, President of the Association of Governing Boards of State Universities and Allied Institutions, projected such a plan. "Each institution," he said, "would devote its energies to doing a few things well, but for the region as a whole, all things would be done well." In October, 1947, the Southern Governors' Conference met in Asheville and authorized a central planning board for a regional university system to provide "either within the several states or without . . . adequate facilities for higher education for both whites and Negroes." The governors proposed to unite the educational and political leadership of the South into a single body based upon a compact ratified by state legislatures. Thirteen states approved the plan and a Board of Control for Southern Regional Education was established in 1948. The governor of each member state, with three persons appointed by each governor, served on the board. John E. Ivey, Jr., first director of the Board, explained the purpose of the regional system: "Since no institution can build a graduate program of top strength in all fields, each major university or graduate school can contribute to the whole region by specializing in selected fields and making such programs available to out-of-state students." The program was especially effective in providing courses which were expensive to operate and for which there was slight demand, such as forestry or veterinary medicine.

Immediately there was criticism that the plan was a ruse to circumvent court orders requiring that racially separated schools must be equal. If a southern state did not offer equal facilities in a particular field such as nursing or library science, ran the charge, it could escape its responsibility by sending the applicant to another state where the course was available in a segregated institution. But the Board of Control remained neutral on the subject of segregation. When a Maryland girl objected to the decision that she obtain nursing training at Meharry Medical School in Nashville, the Board would not support the state. "It is not the purpose of the board," it said, "that the regional compact and the contracts for services thereunder shall serve any state as a legal defense for avoiding responsibilities established under the existing state and Federal laws and court decisions."

The case disproved charges of discrimination against the Board of Control but it illustrated the continuing poverty of Negro higher education in the South. Except for graduate students and those in specialized courses, Negroes were excluded from colleges for whites. As a result, almost all the Negro colleges in America were located in the South. Of the 114 Negro colleges in the South in 1950, nearly half were unable to meet minimum accrediting standards of the regional associations. Before Negroes were admitted to state university graduate schools, no southern state offered Negroes a graduate program leading to the doctorate. Two medical schools in the South produced 80 per cent of the Negro physicians and dentists. In 1950, in the entire South, only $10,500,000 was spent on Negro higher education, an amount only two thirds as great as the budget for Louisiana State University.

But with the 1954 Supreme Court decision, southern lawmakers increased appropriations to Negro colleges. Physical plants were improved and expanded, salary schedules were increased, and there was a general advance in educational standards. Graduate schools, sometimes of a makeshift variety, were established for Negroes, as were law and medical schools. A survey of Negro law, medical, and graduate schools revealed that conditions still did not equal the facilities provided for white students. But significant improvements were being made. Segregation barriers gave way slowly, but even as they did, higher education for Negroes measured great improvements.

3. Religion in the Contemporary South

As education improved, and as the South became more prosperous and more urbanized, its religion continued to exert a strong influence. Southerners attended churches in greater numbers and with greater regularity than did the inhabitants of other sections. Out of a total population of some 34,000,000, in 1936 the census counted over 12,500,000 church members in twelve southern states. Most of these belonged to local organizations of the evangelical Protestant sects—Methodists, Baptists, Presbyterians, Disciples of Christ, Nazarenes, Lutherans of the

Missouri Synod, the Church of God, and a host of smaller denominations. In the District of Columbia and in seven southern states, Negro Baptists had more churches; in five southern states the Southern Baptist Convention churches were most numerous. The Roman Catholic Church led in number of local units, though not always in membership, in Maryland, Kentucky, Louisiana, Florida, and Texas.

In the number of churches, seven southern states were among the first eleven American states. On the average, however, they had fewer members than those in other sections. In the cities, southern churches averaged fewer than 300 members, while in rural areas they were even smaller. They were active organizations, though. The southern churches ranked high in Sunday School attendance, in per capita donations, and in rate of growth. But the southern churches did not measure up to national averages in valuation of church property.

There were several significant developments in southern religion. One of these was the religious imperialism of southern churchmen. The Southern Baptists were perhaps the most active in this regard. They organized churches northward to Chicago, where they announced their presence by holding one of their annual conventions. They also moved into the West and staked out their claims by operating a theological seminary in California. A North Carolina Baptist association declared in 1929: "If the Baptists are to dominate the South and the South is to dominate America, and America is to dominate the world, then we must redouble our efforts to strengthen and encourage the teaching of the Christian religion as the Baptists understand it." In the light of the national expansion of the Southern Baptist Convention, there were plans to change its name.

In a similar manner, other southern churches set out to evangelize the country. The Churches of God, with headquarters in Cleveland, Tennessee, and Salem, Virginia, claimed local congregations in northern states. Another example of southern religious imperialism was Billy Graham, a North Carolina revivalist who had presided over a Minnesota Bible college. From New York's Madison Square Garden and San Francisco's Cow Palace to London's Harringay Arena and in Sydney, Australia, Graham preached an evangelical gospel that had long been the trademark of southern tent revivalists.

Another significant development in southern religion was its growing tendency to adapt its theology to the national norms. A generation earlier, such modernistic ideas as the Darwinian theory, the higher criticism of the Scriptures, or the ecumenical movement, were largely unknown or unacceptable among southern churchmen. But increasingly the movements that modified dogmas in the nineteenth century seeped into southern religion. Theology professors openly discussed critical interpretations of the Bible and here and there a daring minister initiated his flock into the new learning. Perhaps there was no more significant evidence of religion's changes in the South than the reluctant incorporation of geology departments in the denominational colleges.

Another new emphasis was the churches' stand upon social and economic matters, including the race problem. In 1957 the Southern Presbyterian Church's Council on Christian Relations declared that "the Christian faith has never countenanced racial discrimination," and exhorted Presbyterians to work for an "honest and durable adjustment" to the new situation. There was opposition to the proposal. The Presbytery of Central Mississippi requested that the report be defeated and the Council be dissolved because it "keeps our church stirred up in a most distressing manner." The Presbytery of Tuscaloosa, Alabama, called the report an "unwarranted interference with what we believe to be the spiritual convictions of a large majority of the membership of our church." The Mississippi and Alabama Presbyterians were unsuccessful in their attacks upon the Council.

Other southern denominations also recognized the problem. Methodist Bishop William J. King of New Orleans declared that "the two most compelling social problems facing the people called Christians are war and race. For us in America and some other parts of the world the racial problem is our most difficult one. We must face this problem frankly and in the spirit of Jesus Christ," he said. "The prophet rather than the traditionalist must lead." And an Emory University professor warned southern churchmen that "a new socio-economic order is emerging in the South, and if the church does not address itself to the problems and needs of men caught up in this transition, it will be justly passed by as irrelevant or condemned as reactionary."

While southern whites considered social injustices in their midst, the Negro churches assumed a new importance in southern life. They were able to employ better trained ministers, to construct more durable edifices, and to exert a wholesome influence on their communities. Theologically the Negro churches were orthodox, and in general Negroes continued to favor the traditional Protestant denominations. In the years following 1940, however, the Roman Catholics appealed for colored communicants by offering parochial schools often superior to public schools provided for colored children, as well as integrated worship.

Illustrative of the significant place of Negro churches in the South and of their new pastoral leadership, was the Mongomery bus boycott led by the Reverend Martin Luther King, Jr. Son of an Atlanta Baptist minister, King attended Morehouse College and Crozer Theological Seminary and received the Ph.D. from Boston University. In 1954 he returned to his native South and accepted a pastorate in Montgomery. The next year he became head of the Montgomery Improvement Association, a group protesting segregation on city buses. He won national attention and sympathy with his program of passive resistance. "This is a spiritual movement," he told Montgomery Negroes. "Violence will defeat our purpose. Violence is not only impractical but immoral." When white hoodlums bombed his house and fired shotguns at Negroes, King continued to exhort his people not to hate. With Negro churches providing meeting places and guidance, the boycott was successful. To many observers the Montgomery story, if emulated elsewhere, seemed to offer hope that changes could be made without violence or ill-will.

Religious education for whites also offered possibilities for solving southern problems. Religiously centered institutions of higher learning expanded and prospered along with their state-financed sister schools. The denominational colleges sought to cushion the shock of modern knowledge by providing a religious basis for it. But as they received handsome endowments and became economically independent of the sects that had founded them, they tended to lose their religious fervor. Aside from compulsory chapel attendance and a required course in religion, many of the church colleges were indistinguishable from the secular institutions.

That development gave rise to the "Bible institutes," designed to return religious education to the faith of the fathers. Finding their distinctives in denominational doctrines or in a stubbornly independent New Testament "old landmarkism," numerous institutes reinforced the religious assumptions of their students. Rigidly segregated and firmly supporting the new economic masters of the South—who financed many of them—they adhered to a traditional orthodoxy. Eschewing concern with the liberal sins of social and economic injustices, they thundered against "worldliness": the social dance, the theater, the demon rum, and the "female sins"—low-cut dresses, bobbed hair, cosmetics, and women preachers. Many offered courses in Bible science, "angel-ology," and soul-winning. They laid greater stress on theology than on scholarship and their advocates harried the accredited denominational colleges for their attempts at scholarly objectivity. While some southern churchmen were ready to confront the section's problems, others continued to create them.

4. Culture in the South

The churches were not alone in their inner conflict. Every aspect of southern life reflected its growing pains. Talented Southerners dominated the field of popular music with performers like Mississippi's Elvis Presley and Tennessee's Roy Acuff and Ernie Ford. At the same time symphony orchestras performed in southern cities and the Louisville Symphony made musical history with its Commissioning Project to record contemporary music. Southerners composed little serious music but their folk-tunes formed the basis of Aaron Copland's *Appalachian Spring,* and the South provided the background for George Gershwin's folk opera, *Porgy and Bess.*

A similar division existed in southern cookery. There was a long tradition of good eating in the South, but there were striking dietary differences among Southerners. The "white diet" among rural folk (grits, cornbread, sowbelly, and hominy) competed with gourmet foods at fine restaurants like Antoine's in New Orleans. Southerners consumed great quantities of ham, hot biscuits, and "greens," and savored such delicacies as barbecued beef and pork, fried fish and chicken, and hushpuppies. For the old-timers there were chitterlings, ramp (an odorous variety of wild onion), or burgoo (a stew of assorted wild animals such as rabbits and squirrels, cooked with vegetables).

Each part of the South had its distinctive food. In the Florida keys, lime pie delighted hungry visitors. In other regions pecan pies, potato pies, and pralines tempted appetites. Citrus fruit from Florida and the Rio Grande provided necessary vitamins for the American breakfast table, while Coca-Cola was a southern contribution to the world's diet. Oysters from the Chesapeake and from the Gulf went into menus all over the South. In Louisiana, Creole cookery with shrimp dishes and gumbos were the local delicacies. In Texas there was a strong Mexican influence on cooking.

Certain alcoholic beverages were also traditional in the South. Bourbon and branch water was a widespread favorite and there was a heavy *sub rosa* traffic in homemade potions, locally labeled white mule or mountain dew. In Kentucky the mint julep was a trademark of the bluegrass region. Also famous were the militia punches, the especial pride of historic military units. The most cherished of these was the Chatham Artillery punch, a carefully guarded recipe owned by the Savannah militia. It was a delicate blending of rum, brandy, rye whisky, catawba wine, champagne, and tea, in the proper proportions.

Over their well-stocked tables literate Southerners could discuss the flowering of southern letters. The most significant writing in America was southern, either in origin or in subject matter, and the most outstanding group of writers lived in the South. In general they dealt with two major subjects. First was the impact of change upon the South. They sensed the transition through which the South was moving and the consequent values by which Southerners had once lived. Their work was often symbolic, illustrating the degradation of the aristocratic element they had known. In 1941, William Alexander Percy of Mississippi mourned that "the old Southern way of life in which I had been reared existed no more and its values were ignored or derided." Southern writers set themselves to catalog the inexorable disappearance of the traditional civilization. Another group of writers catered to a national audience by describing the primitive and more earthy aspects of the South. In their pages a century later the abolitionist view of the South as a barbarous region was accepted.

The South's most outstanding writer was William Faulkner, though he was perhaps least known among Southerners. He continued the epic story of the South's spiritual suicide he had begun in his earlier work. In *Wild Palms* (1939) he included two separate stories, symbolically related; in *The Hamlet* (1940) he returned to Snopeses, the degraded people from the canebrakes who overran the aristocratic South of the past. *Intruder in the Dust* (1948) was the story of a near-lynching in Mississippi; *Knight's Gambit* (1949) was a collection of short stories, often told in mystic symbolism. *Requiem for a Nun* (1951) completed the sordid allegory of *Sanctuary*. *A Fable* (1954) was a symbolic reference to Easter and a plea for pacifism. In his work Faulkner made use of disgusting incidents to point up the conflict within modern man and the deliberate destruction of the South's traditional civilization.

Faulkner went largely unread in the South and many of those who read him disliked his work because of the bad light in which he appeared to put the region. "He is a propagandist of degradation," said the editor of a Jackson newspaper, "and properly belongs to the privy school of literature." But Faulkner's writing was acclaimed elsewhere. He won numerous literary awards in America and in 1950 received the Nobel Prize for Literature. In his acceptance speech, made in Stockholm, he condemned that modern writing which had neither heart nor compassion. Many authors, he said, wrote "not of love but of lust, of defeats in which nobody loses anything of value, of victories without hope, and worst of all without pity or compassion." That, he went on, was writing "not of the heart but of the glands." Faulkner saw the writer's task as a lofty one: "It is his privilege to help man endure by lifting his heart, by reminding him of the courage and honor and hope and pride and compassion and pity and sacrifice which have been the glory of his past."

Robert Penn Warren was another celebrated southern author. His *Night Rider* (1939) was a novel of the tobacco wars in Kentucky. *At Heaven's Gate* (1943) was a confused description of a southern community, while *All the King's Men* (1946) told of the rise and fall of a southern politician resembling Huey P. Long. It received the Pulitzer Prize in 1947, and in the following year was produced as a play on Broadway. *World Enough and Time* (1950) was a dark tale of Kentucky in the 1820's, and *Brother to Dragons* (1953), a lengthy poem dealing with Jeffersonian America. *Band of Angels* (1955) dealt with miscegenation in the Old South.

Among the more effective writers in the contemporary South was a group of women. Eudora Welty specialized in short stories, mostly laid in her native Mississippi. *A Curtain of Green* (1941) was her first collection, followed a year later by *The Robber Bridegroom*, a fantasy about the daughter of a Mississippi planter. *Delta Wedding* (1946) was her first attempt at a full-length novel, but with *The Golden Apples* (1949) she returned to the more familiar medium of the short story. One of her best tales was *The Ponder Heart* (1954), an engaging description of an unusual character. Another collection of stories, *The Bride of Innisfallen*, came in 1955. Some of her stories, among them "A Worn Path," "The Wide Net," and "Livvie Is Black," won O. Henry Memorial Short Story awards.

Many other distaff novelists published successful books about the South. Monumental in length and in its effect in perpetuating the stereotype of the Old South and its destruction was Margaret Mitchell's *Gone With The Wind* (1936). The novel set a record by selling more than a million copies in its first year, and for its excellence the author received the Pulitzer Prize in 1937. Two years later it reached an even larger audience as a motion picture. With a vixenish heroine, a charming scoundrel hero, grinning Negroes, and the traditionally broad verandas and smiling fields, the book recreated for a new generation the romantic view of the South. In 1941 Ellen Glasgow won the Pulitzer Prize for *In This Our Life,* a tale of decayed aristocrats in a southern town. Her autobiographical *The Woman Within* appeared in 1955. Carolyn Gordon told a tale of early Kentucky in *Green Centuries* (1941). Elizabeth Madox Roberts published a volume of poetry, *Song in the Meadow,* in 1940, and six stories of simple Kentucky folk, *Not by Strange Gods,* a year later. Willa Cather returned to her native Virginia for materials for her *Sapphira and the Slave Girl* (1940). Inglis Fletcher recounted lusty tales of early Carolina in a series of historical novels; and Rebecca Yancey William, in *The Vanishing Virginian* (1940), recalled delightful anecdotes of her father. Josephine Pinckney in *Hilton Head* (1941) and *Three O'Clock Dinner* (1945) wrote historical novels of old South Carolina. Other important books on southern life came from the pens of Marjorie Kennan Rawlings, Lella Warren, Elizabeth Pickett Chevalier, Rachel Field, Frances O. Gaither, Adria Locke Langley, Frances Parkinson Keyes, Elizabeth Spencer, Anne G. Winslow, Harriet L. Arnow, Shirley Ann Grau, Frances Gray Patton, Carson McCullers, and Flannery O'Connor. No other section could boast so extensive a roster of important women writers.

Though outnumbered by their feminine colleagues, male writers also contributed to southern literature. In *Sea Island Lady* (1939), Francis Griswold told a romantic story of a northern woman in Civil War South Carolina. James Street wrote a multi-volume history of the imaginary Dabney family in a series of novels beginning with *Tap Roots* (1942). Jesse Stuart described his native Kentucky hills with nostalgic stories like *Taps for Private Tussie* (1943) and semi-autobiographical accounts of hill-folk like *The Thread That Runs So True* (1949). Erskine Caldwell continued his appeals to the sensational with such works as *Georgia Boy* (1943), *Tragic Ground* (1944), and *The Sure Hand of God* (1947). In *Other Voices, Other Rooms* (1948) Truman Capote told an unusual tale of the South. Arthur Gordon recounted the macabre details of a Georgia lynching in *Reprisal* (1950). Shelby Foote, in novels such as *Shiloh* (1952), vividly described Civil War conflict, while James Agee employed poetic prose in *The Morning Watch* (1951) and *A Death in the Family* (1957), the last a posthumous novel. *The View from Pompey's Head* (1955) of Hamilton Basso was an attempt to explain the South in terms of Shintoism; in *The Light Infantry Ball* (1959) the author continued his fictional treatment of southern distinctives.

The problem of race relations in the South attracted the attention of a growing number of writers. Lillian Smith, in *Strange Fruit* (1944) and *Killers of the Dream* (1949) dealt with race friction in the modern South. Richard Wright's *Black Boy* (1945) told of a Negro's growing up in the South. Worth T. Hedden wrote an award winning book on race relations in *The Other Room* (1948), as did Bucklin Moon in *Without Magnolias* (1949). Ray Sprigle, in *In the Land of Jim Crow* (1949), and Carl T. Rowan, in *South of Freedom* (1952), wrote journalistic reports on segregation. More scholarly accounts were Gunnar Myrdal's two-volume *The*

American Dilemma: The Negro Problem and Modern Democracy (1944), E. Franklin Frazier's *The Negro in the United States* (1949), John H. Franklin's *From Slavery to Freedom* (1946), and C. Vann Woodward's *The Strange Career of Jim Crow* (1955). Other important books about the Negro were written by Fannie Cook, Jefferson Young, Hubert Creekmore, and J. C. Furnas.

Poetry also flourished in the South. In 1939 John Gould Fletcher won a Pulitzer Prize for his collected poems. In 1941 he published *South Star*, a poem about Arkansas, and in 1946, *Burning Mountain.* John Crowe Ransom published his *Selected Poems* in 1945, and in the same year a new Negro poet, Gwendolyn Brooks, appeared with *A Street in Bronzeville.* Allan Tate edited *A Southern Vanguard* in 1947 and published *Poems, 1922-1947* the following year. Arna Bontemps and Langston Hughes edited an anthology, *The Poetry of the Negro, 1746-1949* (1949). Randall Jarrell, who in 1956 became poetry consultant to the Library of Congress, published many volumes, including his *Selected Poems* (1955).

In drama, Tennessee Williams thrice won the New York Drama Critics Award for the best play of the year—in 1945 for *The Glass Menagerie*, in 1948 for *A Streetcar Named Desire*, and in 1955 for *Cat On a Hot Tin Roof.* Like other authors who catered to a national audience, Williams described a profane, perverted South.

Several notable autobiographies appeared in the period. Josephus Daniels wrote *A Tar Heel Editor* (1939 and 1941) describing the South and the nation as they appeared from his office window. Mississippian William Alexander Percy penned a sensitive account of the changing South he had lived through in *Lanterns on the Levee* (1941).

Biographies of leading Southerners were popular among scholars. Oliver P. Chitwood wrote on John Tyler; Douglas S. Freeman on Lee and Washington; Hudson Strode on Jefferson Davis; Robert D. Meade on Judah P. Benjamin and Patrick Henry; Raymond B. Nixon on Henry W. Grady; Charles M. Wiltse on Calhoun; Francis B. Simkins on Ben Tillman; and Dewey W. Grantham on Hoke Smith; Dumas Malone and Nathan Schachner on Thomas Jefferson; and Arthur S. Link on Wilson. There were also new biographies of Civil War generals. John P. Dyer studied "Fightin' Joe" Wheeler; Robert S. Henry wrote on Nathan B. Forrest; Joseph H. Parks on Edmund Kirby Smith; and T. Harry Williams on Beauregard. The Southern Biography Series, published by the Louisiana State University Press, contained important contributions to an understanding of the men who made the South.

Other scholarly studies added to the region's knowledge of its past and present. Rupert B. Vance, in *All These People: The Nation's Human Resources in the South* (1945) presented a sociological and demographic description of the southern population. V. O. Key, Jr., and others, published *Southern Politics in State and Nation* (1948), a political scientist's view of one-party politics in the South. Jay B. Hubbell surveyed *The South in American Literature, 1607-1900* (1954), while Calvin B. Hoover and B. U. Ratchford thoroughly reported on the *Economic Resources and Policies of the South* (1951). Scholarly journals provided publication media for the findings of students. *Social Forces* and the *Southern Economic Journal* won national recognition in their fields, while *The Journal of Southern History* established itself as a basic quarterly of American history. University presses published books on state and regional topics. A multi-volumed *History of the South* synthesized the South's past in thorough fashion. Sponsored by the Louisiana State University Press and the Littlefield Fund for Southern History of the University of Texas, the first of ten volumes appeared in 1947. State historical and literary societies flourished, with many of them presenting awards to local writers as incentives to scholarship and literature. Intellectually the South had moved out of the desert; it was becoming the literary and scholarly oasis of American thought.

5. THE SOUTHERN HERITAGE

As Southerners studied their past they found much in which they could take pride. No American region had produced more of the national ideals than had the South. Indeed, in the original eighteenth century definition of the word, none was more *American*. Southerners were proud of being ladies and gentlemen and of living the genteel life. Geography and climate combined to strengthen and keep vigorous the ancient traditions of the squire and the yeoman. The planter was more than an entrepreneur engaged in providing subsistence for himself and family. Patterning his life after the English squires, he educated his sons in the best of the classical education and accepted the obligation to take his place in civic affairs. But he did not govern his fellow men; he represented them. In general, Southerners were personally independent and took a lively interest in politics. The courthouse yard was the political science classroom of the masses and the politician's stump was the means of discussing significant issues. Southern precincts sent men of character and ability to represent them in state and national capitals.

These men and their constituents remained loyal to the Revolutionary ideals of federalism and individual freedom. The South thus served as the norm by which changes in the rest of the country might be measured. And changes came. The Jeffersonian economic war with Great Britain in the early nineteenth century drove New England commercial capital into manufacturing. Industrial prosperity demanded favors from a more highly centralized government. Southerners whose fathers had largely created the central government now found its power used against them.

To oppose northern interests, southern leaders attempted to unite the masses. Abolitionist propaganda, plus the use of violence to suppress nonconformists, made the task easier. Indeed, without outside attacks there would have been no southern unity. The southern leaders seeking to manage their own affairs through their states took refuge in the theories of states' rights—which men of all sections had utilized at one time or another; emphasized the federal nature of the American government, and pointed to the Tenth Amendment to justify opposition to federal "encroachments." But the rural nature of the South was against them; "King Numbers" favored the enemy. When enough Southerners concluded that they could no longer live as they pleased in the Union, they attempted to establish an independent nation. Its failure was the result of many factors, an important one of which was the prior failure of southern leaders to unify the South.

Another aspect of the South's defeat was the lack of material resources. Though there was a budding industry in the South in 1860, still 90 per cent of the manufactured items, and especially the heavy industry, were in the North. Had Southerners admired statistics or been constrained by material things, there would likely have been no secession. They were interested in a principle, and convinced themselves that things were unimportant or could be obtained easily.

Again, the South lacked a crusading, moralistic zeal. Confederates fought for their homes and they battled valiantly. But northern soldiers felt themselves crusaders for Truth and Righteousness. No more significant distinction between the contenders existed than that in the songs they sang as they prepared for battle. Rebels sang about the tyrant heel on holy soil and how they wished they were in Dixie where they would take their stand. But the blue-clad troops sang a marching anthem of the glory of God's Truth marching on:

> "In the beauty of the lilies Christ was born across the sea,
> With a glory in his bosom that transfigures you and me;
> As He died to make men holy, let us die to make men free;
> While God is marching on."

Southerners were religious people but they lacked the harsh Cromwellian assurance that they were serving as God's Anointed in invading enemy country. They were at an ideological disadvantage in the struggle.

These factors pointed up the major elements in the southern heritage. The South was the last stronghold of the American traditions of the squire and the yeoman. It was the home of a local patriotism which made Southerners proud of their states to which they gave prior allegiance. The plantation society at its best emphasized the virtues and vices of the English squirearchy. The movement for southern unity, assisted by a defensive mechanism against criticism and attacks by outsiders, was a main theme in southern history. Southern statesmen had penned the Declaration of Independence and had played major roles in determining other American issues. And the humiliation of defeat contributed not only to the continuation of a southern nationalism but also to southern attitudes toward other humbled people in the world.

But another ingredient in the southern heritage was determined optimism. Having to dig out of the slough of defeat and despair and rebuild their homes and businesses with no capital, no banking institutions, and no governmental co-operation made heroes of the least of them. Though it meant a long century of poverty and near-peonage, these worst of problems were not insoluble. The new civilization that grew upon the ashes of the old was not the same as the old. A more comfortable way of life appeared.

In 1860, on the occasion of South Carolina's secession, Robert Barnwell Rhett predicted that the historian of 2000 A.D. would write glowingly of the Southern Confederacy. "And extending their empire across this continent to the Pacific, and down through Mexico to the other side of the Gulf, and over the isles of the sea," Rhett envisioned, "they established an empire and wrought out a civilization that has never been equaled or surpassed—a civilization teeming with orators, poets, philosophers, statesmen and historians equal to those of Greece and Rome." But the Confederacy Rhett praised lasted less than five years, and the empire Americans established over the islands of the sea was not Southern. By their own bootstraps, however, Southerners did work out a civilization, a set of cultural distinctives that gave color and flavor to American life. Having done that, no problem would be too great for them to solve. The future of the South in the American nation was bright.

Index